# Tracing Value Change in the International Legal Order

# Tracing Value Change in the International Legal Order

*Perspectives from Legal and Political Science*

*Edited by*
HEIKE KRIEGER
ANDREA LIESE

OXFORD
UNIVERSITY PRESS

OXFORD
UNIVERSITY PRESS

Great Clarendon Street, Oxford, OX2 6DP,
United Kingdom

Oxford University Press is a department of the University of Oxford.
It furthers the University's objective of excellence in research, scholarship,
and education by publishing worldwide. Oxford is a registered trade mark of
Oxford University Press in the UK and in certain other countries



First Edition published in 2023



Published in the United States of America by Oxford University Press
198 Madison Avenue, New York, NY 10016, United States of America

British Library Cataloguing in Publication Data
Data available

Library of Congress Control Number: 2023936358

ISBN 978–0–19–285583–1

DOI: 10.1093/oso/9780192855831.001.0001

Printed and bound in the UK by
Clays Ltd, Elcograf S.p.A.

# Acknowledgements

On 24 February 2022, the Russian Federation invaded Ukraine. Both the manifest act of aggression and the events that followed are symptomatic of the current state of the international legal order. While the blatant disregard for peace as one of the foundational values of the international order sends yet another shock wave through the international system, some reactions of the international community give hope for its robustness. The reactivation of the Uniting-for-Peace Resolution by the Security Council for the first time since 1982, the adoption of UN GA Res ES-11/1 with 141 votes in favour, 5 against, and 34 abstentions, and the support for UN GA Res 76/262, which establishes a 'standing mandate for a General Assembly debate when a veto is cast in the Security Council', send a strong signal of the willingness to make the UN system work. Firm reactions by the ICJ, the ICC and its member states, and the European Court of Human Rights confirm that the international community is determined to uphold the international rule of law. Ukraine relies resolutely on international law and on legal procedures to counter Russian aggression. However, condemnation of the invasion is not unequivocal. States such as China, India, and South Africa have provided no legal response in line with the Articles on State Responsibility and still maintain close ties with the Russian Federation. At the time of writing, the ongoing conflict is increasingly testing both the willingness of states and the effectiveness of legal responses to end blatant violations of international law. The overall picture remains ambiguous.

Our book represents an endeavour to assess the ambiguous state of the current international legal order. We assume that if foundational values of the international order change, despite attempts to embed them in law, such a change will exert a relevant and lasting effect on the international legal system as a whole. To assess this hypothesis, the book systematically evaluates and analyses normative changes in international law and explores drivers and mechanisms through interdisciplinary exchange between scholars of international law and international relations.

The seeds of this book were planted when we began collaborating in the Berlin Potsdam Research Group (*Kolleg-Forschungsgruppe,* KFG) on 'The International Rule of Law – Rise or Decline?' funded by the German Research Foundation (DFG) starting in 2015. In the following year, in 2016, several events raised concerns that the international legal order might be declining. The United Kingdom's European Union membership referendum had taken place; Burundi, the Gambia, and South Africa had announced their withdrawals from the Rome Statute of the ICC; and Donald Trump, whose campaign had declared NATO as obsolete and had emphasized opposition to multilateral treaties such as the Paris Agreement and a renegotiation of trade agreements, had won the United States presidential election. The interdisciplinary research group has since examined the role of international law in a changing global order and aimed to assess the 'type' of international law that we may see emerging under current conditions. The research group has offered an inspiring setting for this book and enabled us to invite renowned scholars of international law and international relations to discuss, from an interdisciplinary perspective, how international law and its underlying values are changing. The first KFG workshop on 'Decline or Transformation? Norm Change and Values in International Law' in Berlin set the stage and initiated the dialogue between lawyers and political scientists. Its results are now published in this book.

We are grateful to many who helped us with the overall development of the book. In addition to the contributors of this book, we thank those who participated as discussants, experts, or rapporteurs at the above mentioned workshop: Björnstjern Baade, Helmut Breitmeier, Dana Burchardt, Fan Yuwen, Christopher McCrudden, André de Hoogh, Markus Jachtenfuchs, Balingene Kahombo, Georg Nolte, Vera Rusinova, Shirley Scott, Peter-Tobias Stoll, Nina Tannenwald, Andreas Zimmermann, Velimir Zivkovic, and Michael Zürn. Simon Blätgen and Martin Hinrichs participated in our initial discussions on how to conceive such an interdisciplinary project. Together with Eva Ritte, they prepared and organized the authors' workshop diligently and enthusiastically.

The book itself profited from extensive support, for which we are grateful. The anonymous reviewers of Oxford University Press provided excellent and valuable feedback that greatly helped us to improve the book's composition and refine the overall argument. We thank the KFG members, particularly Andrew Hurrell and Nina Reiners, for their valuable comments on our framework. Thanks are also due to all the people involved in different stages of the editing process, in particular Leonie Blankenstein, Deborah Anne Bowen, and Christina Jugel, as well as Aurelio Corneo, Laura Kraft, Toritseju Nanna, Louisa Reutter, Alena Rogge, and Sophie Schuberth. Nathanael van der Beek managed the final editing process meticulously. We would also like to thank Merel Alston, Jack McNichol, and Rebecca Lewis at Oxford University Press for their advice and for shepherding the book along.

The direction in which international law is currently moving is far from clear. Yet, as international relations and international law scholars, we share the conviction that the international legal order matters. We hope our book provides a missing piece of the puzzle explaining why this is the case.

Heike Krieger and Andrea Liese
Berlin and Potsdam, July 2022

# Contents

# List of Abbreviations

| | |
|---|---|
| ACHR | American Convention on Human Rights (adopted 22 November 1969, entered into force 18 July 1978) 1144 UNTS 123 |
| AEOI | Atomic Energy Organization of Iran |
| AP | Additional Protocol |
| APHIS | United States Department of Agriculture's Animal and Plant Health Inspection Service |
| Art | article |
| AU | African Union |
| Banjul Charter | African Charter on Human and Peoples' Rights (adopted 27 June 1981, entered into force 21 October 1986) 1520 UNTS 217 |
| BCH | Biosafety Clearing-House |
| Beijing Platform for Action | Beijing Declaration and Platform for Action \| Beijing+5 Political Declaration |
| Belém do Pará Convention | Inter-American Convention for the Prevention, Punishment and Elimination of Violence against Women (adopted 9 June 1994, entered into force 5 March 1995) |
| Brundtland Report | Report of the World Commission on Environment and Development (4 August 1987) UN Doc A/42/427 |
| C-Fam | Center for Family and Human Rights |
| Cairo Programme of Action | Programme of Action of the International Conference on Population and Development |
| Cartagena Protocol | Cartagena Protocol on Biosafety to the Convention on Biological Diversity (adopted 29 January 2000, entered into force 11 September 2003) 2226 UNTS 208 |
| CAT | United Nations Convention against Torture, Cruel, Inhumane, and other Degrading Treatment and Punishment (adopted 10 December 1984, entered into force 26 June 1987) 1456 UNTS 85 |
| CBD | Convention on Biological Diversity (adopted 5 June 1992, entered into force 29 December 1993) 1760 UNTS 79 |
| CBDR | common but differentiated responsibilities |
| CCPR | Human Rights Committee |
| CEDAW | United Nations Convention on the Elimination of Discrimination against Women (adopted 18 December 1979, entered into force 3 September 1981) 1249 UNTS 13 |
| CEDAW Committee | Committee for the Elimination of All Forms of Discrimination against Women |
| CEE | Central and Eastern European |
| CESCR | Committee on Economic, Social and Cultural Rights |

| | |
|---|---|
| CIL | Customary International Law |
| CIRI | David Cingranelli and David Richard's Human Rights Data Project |
| CoE | Council of Europe |
| CSA | Comprehensive Safeguards Agreement |
| ECHR | European Convention on Human Rights (adopted 4 November 1950, entered into force 3 September 1953) 213 UNTS 221 |
| ECOSOC | United Nations Economic and Social Council |
| ECtHR | European Court of Human Rights |
| eg | exempli gratia/for example |
| EU | European Union |
| FAO | United Nations Food and Agriculture Organization |
| FPA | Foreign Policy Analysis |
| FWCW | Fourth World Conference on Women |
| GATT | 1947 General Agreement on Tariffs and Trade (adopted 30 October 1947, entered into force 1 January 1948) 55 UNTS 187 |
| General Act | General Act for the Pacific Settlement of International Disputes of 1928 |
| GM | genetically modified |
| GMOs | genetically modified organisms |
| GoFF | Group of Friends of the Family |
| GREVIO | Group of experts on action against violence against women and domestic violence |
| IACtHR | Inter-American Court of Human Rights |
| IAEA | International Atomic Energy Agency |
| ibid | ibidem/in the same place |
| ICC | International Criminal Court |
| ICCPR | International Covenant on Civil and Political Rights (adopted 16 December 1966, entered into force 23 March 1976) 999 UNTS 171 |
| ICESCR | International Covenant on Economic, Social and Cultural Rights (adopted 16 December 1966, entered into force 3 January 1976) 993 UNTS 3 |
| ICJ | International Court of Justice |
| ICJ Statute | Statute of the International Court of Justice (adopted 26 June 1945, entered into force 24 October 1945) UKTS 67 (1946) |
| ICPD | International Conference on Population and Development |
| ICRC | International Committee of the Red Cross |
| ICTY | International Criminal Tribunal for the Former Yugoslavia |
| ie | id est/that is |
| IFIs | International Financial Institutions |
| IHL | International Humanitarian Law |
| ILA | International Law Association |
| ILC | United Nations International Law Commission |
| IOs | International Organizations |
| IR | International Relations |

| | |
|---|---|
| ISA | International Studies Association |
| ISIL | Islamic State of Iraq and the Levant |
| ISIS | Islamic State of Iraq and Syria |
| Istanbul Convention | Council of Europe Convention on Preventing Violence against Women and Domestic Violence (adopted 11 May 2011, entered into force 1 August 2014) CETS 210 |
| JCPoA | Joint Comprehensive Plan of Action |
| LMOs | living modified organisms |
| LMS | Like-Minded States |
| MDGs | millennium development goals |
| NAM | non-aligned movement |
| NATO | North Atlantic Treaty Organization |
| NGOs | non-governmental organizations |
| NHRIs | National Human Rights Institutions |
| NNWS | Non-Nuclear Weapon States |
| NPT | Treaty on the Non-Proliferation of Nuclear Weapons (adopted 1 July 1968, entered into force 5 March 1970) 729 UNTS 161 |
| NWS | Nuclear Weapon States |
| OEA | Organización de los Estados Americanos |
| OECD | Organisation for Economic Co-operation and Development |
| OHCHR | Office of the High Commissioner for Human Rights |
| OIC | Organisation for Islamic Cooperation |
| OPCAT | Optional Protocol to the Convention against Torture and Other Cruel, Inhuman or Degrading Treatment or Punishment (adopted 18 December 2002, entered into force 22 June 2006) 2375 UNTS 237 |
| PiS | Law and Justice Party |
| PSI | Proliferation Security Initiative |
| PTC | ICC Pre-Trial Chamber |
| PTS | Political Terror Scale |
| R2P | responsibility to protect |
| RIDL | Release of Insects Carrying a Dominant Lethal |
| Russia | Russian Federation |
| RwP | principle of responsibility while protecting |
| SDGs | sustainable development goals |
| SGBV | sexual and gender-based violence |
| SIT | sterile insect technique |
| SNSC | Supreme National Security Council |
| SOFA | Status of Forces Agreements |
| SPS | World Trade Organization Agreement on the Application of Sanitary and Phytosanitary Measures, Annex 1A to the Marrakesh Agreement Establishing the World Trade Organization (adopted 15 April 1994, entered into force 1 January 1995) 1867 UNTS 493 |
| SRHR | sexual and reproductive health and rights |
| TFEU | Treaty of the Functioning of the European Union |

| | |
|---|---|
| TPNW | Treaty on the Prohibition of Nuclear Weapons (adopted 7 July 2017, entered into force 22 January 2021) UN Doc A/CONF.229/2017/8 |
| Treaty Bodies | human rights treaty monitoring bodies |
| TWAIL | Third World Approach to International Law |
| UDHR | Universal Declaration of Human Rights (adopted 10 December 1948) UNGA Res 217 A(III) |
| UK | United Kingdom |
| UN | United Nations |
| UNAEC | United Nations Atomic Energy Commission |
| UNCED | United Nations Conference on the Environment and Development |
| UNCLOS | United Nations Convention on the Law of the Sea (adopted 10 December 1982, entered into force 16 November 1994) 1833 UNTS 399 |
| UNFCCC | United Nations Framework Convention on Climate Change (adopted 20 January 1994) UN Doc A/RES/48/189 |
| UNGA | United Nations General Assembly |
| UNSC | United Nations Security Council |
| UNTS | United Nations Treaty Series |
| UPR | Universal Periodic Review |
| US | United States |
| VCLT | Vienna Convention on the Law of Treaties (adopted 23 May 1969, entered into force 27 January 1980) 1155 UNTS 331 |
| WHO | World Health Organization |
| WMD | weapons of mass destruction |
| WTO | World Trade Organization |

# List of Contributors

**Adam Bower** is Senior Lecturer in the School of International Relations at the University of St Andrews, United Kingdom.

**Srinivas Burra** is Associate Professor at the Faculty of Legal Studies South Asian University, New Delhi, India.

**Malcolm Jorgensen** is Senior Research Fellow at the Max Planck Institute for Comparative Public Law and International Law, Heidelberg, Germany.

**Thomas Kleinlein** is Professor of Public Law, Public International Law, European Union Law, and Comparative Law at the Friedrich Schiller University Jena, Germany.

**Heike Krieger** is Professor of International and Public Law at the Freie Universität Berlin, Germany.

**Lea Barbara Kuhlmann** is Doctoral Researcher at the Chair of International and Public Law at the Freie Universität Berlin, Germany.

**Max Lesch** is Postdoctoral Researcher at the Peace Research Institute Frankfurt, Germany.

**Andrea Liese** is Professor of International Relations at the University of Potsdam, Germany.

**Theresa Reinold** is Junior Professor of Global and Transnational Cooperation Research at the University of Duisburg-Essen, Germany.

**Conny Roggeband** is Associate Professor in Public Policy and Governance at the Department of Political Science at University of Amsterdam, The Netherlands.

**Wayne Sandholtz** holds the John A. McCone Chair in International Relations and is Professor of International Relations and Law at the University of Southern California, Los Angeles, USA.

**Sandra Schwindenhammer** is Assistant Professor of International Relations at the Justus Liebig University Giessen, Germany.

**Mirko Sossai** is Associate Professor of International Law at the Department of Law at the Roma Tre University, Italy.

**Dominik Steiger** is Professor of Public International Law, European Law and Public Law at Technische Universität Dresden, Germany.

**Peter-Tobias Stoll** holds the Jean Monnet Chair for European Union and Global Sustainable Development through Law and is Professor of Public Law and Public International Law at the University of Göttingen, Germany.

**Alexandros Tokhi** is a postdoctoral Research Fellow at the Institute of Political Science at the Goethe University in Frankfurt am Main, Germany.

**Erika de Wet** is Professor of International Law and is Head of the Institute of International Law and International Relations at the University of Graz, Austria.

**Antje Wiener** is Professor of Political Science, especially Global Governance at the University of Hamburg, Germany.

**Lisbeth Zimmermann** is Professor of International Institutions and Peace Processes at the Goethe University Frankfurt, Germany.

# 1
# Introduction
## Value Change in the International Legal Order

*Heike Krieger and Andrea Liese*

### 1. A Metamorphosis of International Law?

Can a metamorphosis of international law be identified while it is still underway? Law is always navigating the tension between preserving the status quo and adapting to new exigencies. In certain periods, change seems to accelerate. Over recent years, concerns have been raised in various academic disciplines that the international order and with it international law are undergoing a transformation, if not a crisis of historic proportions.[1] Fundamental and intersecting challenges have emerged, affecting elements of international law that were added or strengthened after the end of the Cold War. Indications of change are manifold, but their interpretation remains difficult. Was the United Kingdom's withdrawal from the European Union a unique case, or does it signal a general trend toward renationalization and away from international institutions? Is the continuing Russian annexation of Crimea and the military attack on Ukraine a symptom of a global power shift that calls established legal rules and their underlying values into question, or is it merely another expression of great-power ignorance of international legal standards? Could international condemnation of these attacks strengthen international law?[2]

Normative evaluations of change depend on the yardstick and reference point being used. Current challenges to the international legal order, which appear to have escalated into a crisis, follow a long period of perceived rise of international law. In the politics of the 1990s, there was renewed interest in a 'move to law' in international relations (IR).[3] The increasing number of international treaties, the proliferation of international courts and tribunals, the rising authority and expanding scope of activities of international organizations, the increasing human rights orientation and growing engagement of civil society with international law were seen as expressions of these developments. There was a perception, particularly in the Global North, that

[1] Jutta Brunnée, 'Multilateralism in Crisis' (2018) 112 Proceedings of the ASIL Annual Meeting 335; Mette Eilstrup-Sangiovanni and Stephanie C Hofmann, 'Of the Contemporary Global Order, Crisis, and Change' (2020) 27 Journal of European Public Policy 1077; Trine Flockhart, 'Is this the End? Resilience, Ontological Security, and the Crisis of the Liberal International Order' (2020) 41 Contemporary Security Policy 215; Heike Krieger and Georg Nolte, 'The International Rule of Law – Rise or Decline? Points of Departure' in Heike Krieger, Georg Nolte, and Andreas Zimmermann (eds), *The International Rule of Law – Rise or Decline? Approaching Current Foundational Challenges* (OUP 2019) 3.

[2] UNGA Res ES-11/1 (18 March 2022) UN Doc A/RES/ES-11/1.

[3] Judith Goldstein and others, 'Introduction: Legalization and World Politics' (2000) 54 International Organization 385.

Heike Krieger and Andrea Liese, *Introduction* In: *Tracing Value Change in the International Legal Order.*
Edited by: Heike Krieger and Andrea Liese, Oxford University Press. 
DOI: 10.1093/oso/9780192855831.003.0001

fundamental normative contestations within the international order were decreasing as major multilateral agreements were concluded. These seemed to indicate a normative consensus over 'common values' of an international community.[4] The United Nations 2005 World Summit Outcome confirmed this perception by stating: 'We reaffirm that our common fundamental values, including freedom, equality, solidarity, tolerance, respect for all human rights, respect for nature and shared responsibility, are essential to international relations.'[5]

We treat these fundamental common values as a reference point. We assume in this book that if these values change, despite attempts to embed them in law, such a change will exert a relevant and lasting effect on the international legal system as a whole.

To assess the effects of the current crisis, the book systematically evaluates and analyses normative changes in international law and explores their drivers and mechanisms through interdisciplinary exchange between scholars of international law and IR. First, it addresses the question of whether we are witnessing a period of fundamental transformation or metamorphosis (*Verwandlung*) of international law with potentially irreversible effects, yet another period of norm change *within* international law (*Wandel*),[6] or a period of turbulence and ambivalence that will ultimately leave the value orientation of international law unaffected. A metamorphosis would require that more is changing than a single legal norm or a specific international institution. 'Change implies that some things change but other things remain the same [ … ]. Metamorphosis implies a much more radical transformation in which the old certainties of modern societies are falling away and something quite new is emerging.'[7] In other words, we are interested in whether the observed change is occurring *within* the given system of legal norms or whether this is a fundamental change of the system itself.[8] Accordingly, the case studies in this book focus on changes in political and legal discourse and social and legal practices and assess whether these changes affect the underlying values and/or the social and legal validity of the respective norms. By examining these findings together, we are able to distinguish value change from metamorphosis.

Second, by contrasting the various attempts of a diverse set of actors—including states, non-state actors, international organizations, and courts—to induce or prevent value change and metamorphosis, the book also contributes to a better and more nuanced understanding of the conditions under which international legal values are upheld. It also identifies the mechanisms that ensure robust international norms.

[4] See eg Dino Kritsiotis, 'Imagining the International Community' (2002) 13 European Journal of International Law 961; Bruno Simma and Andreas Paulus, 'The "International Community": Facing the Challenge of Globalization' (1998) 9 European Journal of International Law 266, 272. For a list of pertinent values see p. 6 below.

[5] UNGA Res 60/1 (24 October 2005) UN Doc A/RES/60/1 para 4.

[6] Martti Koskenniemi, *International Law and the Far Right* (Asser Press 2019) 34, 36 distinguishes between revolution and adaption.

[7] Ulrich Beck, *The Metamorphosis of the World: How Climate Change is Transforming our Concept of the World* (Polity 2016) 4.

[8] Cf Michael Zürn, *A Theory of Global Governance: Authority, Legitimacy, and Contestation* (OUP 2018) 107; for a similar standard in assessing the fate of the global order Eilstrup-Sangiovanni and Hofmann (n 1) 1078.

This introduction lays the groundwork for our undertaking. In Section 2, we discuss the benefits of interdisciplinary exchange for assessing the trajectory of value change in the international legal order. We present basic concepts from the respective disciplinary perspectives in Section 3. In Sections 4 and 5, we elaborate on our research question and explain our research design, and in Section 6, we conclude by summarizing the aims and key contributions of the individual conceptual and empirical chapters.

## 2. The Benefits of Interdisciplinary Collaboration

The study of change in international law has increasingly become an interdisciplinary endeavour.[9] Interdisciplinary perspectives are beneficial and in some cases necessary to assess the overall trajectory of change. For international lawyers who use traditional legal methods of norm identification, norm interpretation, and norm application, it is difficult to grasp the long-term effects of change in the political and legal discourse and social and legal practices.[10] A strictly positivist analysis of the Trump administration's approach to international law, for instance, risks stopping short by stating that the politics of withdrawal are in line with consent-based international law and that 'an arrogant tone and a rude, narcissistic chief executive' do not matter 'as long as there are no language or behavioral rules in place in international law'.[11]

The perspectives of political science and IR add to this analysis by assessing how discursive attacks and non-compliance affect the validity and robustness of norms, documenting observed trends, explaining the causes, and specifying mechanisms of both change and robustness in norms and their underlying values. When empirically studying norm development, IR usually takes a broader frame: it considers both legal and non-legal norms as well as their interplay. A primary goal of research on international norms is to theorize how norms come into existence, change, cease to exist, or persist in times of crisis.[12] Thus, in an interdisciplinary analysis, IR norm research helps to understand how norms are affected by broader socio-political developments, even when their legal status remains unchanged.

[9] See eg Tanja E Aalberts and Ingo Venzke, 'Moving Beyond Interdisciplinary Turf Wars: Towards an Understanding of International Law as Practice' in Jean d'Aspremont and others (eds), *International Law as a Profession* (OUP 2017); Nico Krisch and Ezgi Yildiz (eds), *The Many Paths of Change in International Law* (OUP forthcoming); Kyle Rapp, 'Justifying Force: International Law, Foreign Policy Decision-Making, and the Use of Force' (2022) 28 European Journal of International Relations 337 ; Nina Reiners, *Transnational Lawmaking Coalitions for Human Rights* (CUP 2021).

[10] Cf Georg Nolte, 'Treaties and their Practice – Symptoms of their Rise or Decline' (2017) 392 Recueil des Cours de l'Academie de Droit International 205, 222–30.

[11] Oliver Dörr, 'Völkerrechtliche Grenzen des Populismus? Der amerikanische Präsident und das geltende Völkerrecht' (2018) 73 JuristenZeitung 224, 231: 'Neu ist der großspurige Ton und der ungehobelte Narziss an der Spitze der Exekutive – aber solange das Völkerrecht keine Sprach- oder Benimmregeln kennt, [gehört das nicht zu unserem Thema.]'; English translation in the text is by the authors.

[12] See eg Martha Finnemore and Kathryn Sikkink, 'International Norm Dynamics and Political Change' (1998) 52 International Organization 887; Nicole Deitelhoff and Lisbeth Zimmermann, 'Norms under Challenge: Unpacking the Dynamics of Norm Robustness' (2019) 4 Journal of Global Security Studies 2; Wayne Sandholtz and Kendall W Stiles, *International Norms and Cycles of Change* (OUP 2009).

While incorporating this perspective, we do not reject the idea of law's relative autonomy from politics.[13] Instead, we assume that this autonomy fosters the persistence of certain values despite critical contestations. In order to understand how law's autonomy works, the perspective of international lawyers is decisive in explaining how legal norms can be interpreted and changed and what purposes they fulfill within a legal system, thus providing a reference point against which we can evaluate current developments. To understand whether and how a legal norm has changed, it is crucial to evaluate secondary legal rules on law-making and law-breaking. The decentralized character of international law poses particular challenges in cases where there are no clear findings of courts or other bodies providing authoritative interpretations.

Against this background, we bring scholars of international law and IR together to evaluate the impact of current attacks on the international legal order because of their shared interest in how the drivers, mechanisms, and processes of change—internal and external to the law—interact. Both disciplines share the assumption that law stabilizes norms by shielding them from specific challenges. Whereas scholars of international relations investigate the broad range of conditions under which this assumption holds, legal scholars argue that the legal structures and practices of legal or legally relevant institutions and actors protect values.

## 3. Definitions

To facilitate interdisciplinary dialogue, it is important to define a few basic concepts, even if they may seem to require no explanation from the respective disciplinary perspectives. Whereas definitions of some concepts such as compliance and law overlap between the two disciplines, the concepts of norms, values, contestation, and norm and value change require clarification from each disciplinary standpoint.

### 3.1 Norms and Values

In line with a generally accepted definition in IR, we understand norms as 'collective expectations about proper behavior for a given identity'.[14] This definition emphasizes a collective, that is, intersubjective expectation about the appropriateness of actors' behaviour. Norms can therefore be characterized by 'their prescriptive (or evaluative) quality of "oughtness"'.[15] Norms may relate to the international community, specific regional communities, or other imagined communities (eg, an alliance or the community of liberal/Western states). In our view, the interdisciplinary connection can be made to community interests, as 'it is precisely the prescriptive (or evaluative) quality

[13] Cf Jan Klabbers, 'The Relative Autonomy of International Law or the Forgotten Politics of Interdisciplinarity' in Robert Beck (ed), *Law and Disciplinarity* (Palgrave McMillan 2013) 34.

[14] Ronald L Jepperson, Alexander Wendt, and Peter J Katzenstein, 'Norms, Identity, and Culture in National Security' in Peter J Katzenstein (ed), *The Culture of National Security: Norms and Identity in World Politics* (Columbia University Press 1996) 54.

[15] Finnemore and Sikkink (n 12) 891.

of "oughtness" that sets norms apart from other kinds of rules. [ ... ] We only know what is appropriate by reference to the judgements of a community or a society'.[16]

Typically norms either prohibit or constrain 'bad' behaviour, or they permit or legitimate 'good' behaviour. This does not imply that actors comply with all norms all of the time and in all situations. Instances of non-compliance alone do not undermine a norm's validity, as long as peers or authorities disapprove or the non-compliance remains the exception. When non-compliant states explain how a norm does not apply in a particular case or argue that it must be weighed against alternative norms, they affirm its general normative validity.[17] As an intersubjective expectation, a norm may change and its meaning may be contested.[18] We share the interest of this line of IR research in examining whether the value protected by a legal norm is changing.[19]

Values—as moral principles or shared ideas of a desirable 'good' or an avoidable 'bad'—are a core component of norms.[20] They represent the 'ideational portion of the norm'.[21] Several legal norms may refer to the same value, and several values may underlie individual norms or complexes of norms. For instance, equality as a value underpins legal norms against unequal treatment and racial or religious discrimination, as well as norms surrounding freedom from discrimination at work and women's rights.

Norms may be legal (embodied in treaty law, customary law, or general legal principles) or social (embodied in non-legally binding declarations and social expectations). Many, but not all, international norms find expression in legal norms. Traditionally, legal norms are based on the sources of international law as laid down in Article 38 of the Statute of the International Court of Justice (ICJ Statute)[22] and interpreted according to Articles 31 and 32 of the Vienna Convention on the Law of Treaties (VCLT).[23] According to Article 38 of the ICJ Statute, legal norms may be derived from different sources and may have different qualities: we can distinguish between treaty law, customary international law (CIL), and general principles of law. Legal acts such as resolutions of international organizations or other legally relevant practices that derive their legally binding effect from the pertinent treaty regime may reflect CIL or

[16] ibid.

[17] See Nicole Deitelhoff and Lisbeth Zimmermann, 'Things We Lost in the Fire: How Different Types of Contestation Affect the Robustness of International Norms' (2020) 22 International Studies Review 51; Thomas Risse, '"Let's Argue!": Communicative Action in World Politics' (2000) 54 International Organization 1.

[18] Antje Wiener, *A Theory of Contestation* (Springer 2014); Antje Wiener, 'Enacting Meaning-in-Use: Qualitative Research on Norms and International Relations' (2009) 35 Review of International Studies 175, 179.

[19] Norm change is, of course, possible without a change in values, for example, when merely the behavioural prescriptions change or when the norm is applied to a new problem.

[20] See also Carla Winston, 'Norm Structure, Diffusion, and Evolution: A Conceptual Approach' (2018) 24 European Journal of International Relations 638, 639–42; Michelle Jurkovich, 'What Isn't a Norm? Redefining the Conceptual Boundaries of "Norms" in the Human Rights Literature' (2020) 22 International Studies Review 693, 694–97.

[21] Carla Winston, 'Words Count: Discourse and the Quantitative Analysis of International Norms' (2020) 19 Journal of Human Rights 138, 138.

[22] Statute of the International Court of Justice (adopted 26 June 1945, entered into force 24 October 1945) 15 UNCIO 355.

[23] Vienna Convention on the Law of Treaties (adopted 23 May 1969, entered into force 27 January 1980) 1155 UNTS 331.

may be considered as subsequent (or other) practice according to Article 31(3)(b) and Article 32 VCLT. Based on Articles 53 and 64 VCLT and CIL, some legal norms are endowed with the specific legal character of *ius cogens*. Such a peremptory norm of international law permits no derogation, and it can be modified only by a subsequent norm of general international law with the same character. A treaty that conflicts with such a norm is void.

While values are traditionally based on ethics, philosophy, morals, or religion, the idea that basic ethical principles or shared foundational interests should be formulated in legal terms has informed the development of international law.[24] The idea that international law endorses certain foundational values is essential for international legal discourse.[25] In legal practice, this idea has been expressed, for instance, by the International Court of Justice in the 1951 Advisory Opinion on the Genocide Convention, whose object is 'to confirm and endorse the most elementary principles of morality'.[26] In 2016, the proposal of a draft conclusion on *ius cogens* defining peremptory norms as norms that 'protect the fundamental values of the international community' triggered a sweeping critical debate in the International Law Commission (ILC).[27] Nevertheless, this draft demonstrated the persistence of a value orientation irrespective of its philosophical or theoretical grounding in natural law,[28] sociology, or communicative theories. We therefore define legal values or legally protected values as normative conceptions of certain interests or goods that are protected by international law. They reflect a shared understanding of the international community and claim to be enduring.[29] In international law, legally protected values include peace and international security, human dignity, human life and bodily integrity, gender equality, the environment and natural resources, sustainable development, and accountability for serious human rights violations.[30] In our book, we do not aim to enter into a broader normative debate on the extent to which (international) law should reflect moral and ethical demands.[31] Instead, we are interested in the more empirical endeavour of tracing value change in legal norms.

[24] Jochen Bernsdorff and Ingo Venzke, 'Ethos, Ethics, and Morality in International Relations' in Rüdiger Wolfrum (ed), *Max Planck Encyclopedia of Public International Law* (OUP 2011) para 2.

[25] eg Martti Koskenniemi, 'A History of International Law Histories' in Anne Peters and Bardo Fassbender (eds), *The Oxford Handbook of the History of International Law* (OUP 2012) 943 starts his account with Ernest Nys, *Les origines du droit international* (Castaignes Bruxelles 1894) 404–05, who saw international law as a motor for realizing the universal value of humanity; Louis Henkin, *International Law: Politics and Values* (Nijhoff 1995); Emmanuelle Jouanette, 'Universalism and Imperialism' (2007) 18 European Journal of International Law 379, 385; Andreas Paulus, *Die Internationale Gemeinschaft im Völkerrecht* (Beck 2001); Santiago Villalpando, 'The Legal Dimension of the International Community' (2010) 21 European Journal of International Law 387; Otto Spijkers, *The United Nations, the Evolution of Global Values and International Law* (Intersentia 2011). For criticism, see Section 4.3.

[26] *Reservations to the Convention on the Prevention and Punishment of the Crime of Genocide* (Advisory Opinion) [1951] ICJ Rep 15, 23.

[27] International Law Commission (ILC), 'Report of the International Law Commission. Sixty-eighth session' (2 May–10 June and 4 July–12 August 2016) UN Doc A/71/10, 300, 303 para. 126.

[28] For an argument in favour of natural law, see Mary Ellen O'Connell, *The Art of Law in the International Community* (CUP 2019).

[29] Otto Spijkers, 'Global Values in the UN Charter' (2012) 59 Netherlands International Law Review 361, 363.

[30] For a list see Mehrdad Payandeh, *Internationales Gemeinschaftsrecht* (Springer Verlag 2010) 100–24.

[31] For a starting point of the debate in the twentieth century: Herbert LA Hart, 'Positivism and the Separation of Law and Morals' (1958) 71 Harvard Law Review 593; for a view that morals cannot be

## 3.2 Contestation and Change

An important driver of norm change is contestation. In the first wave of IR norm scholarship, established and internalized norms were understood to be robust and even habitually complied with,[32] whereas the subsequent wave of research took issue with the view of 'norms as things' with fixed content[33] for failing to account for the dynamics of norm change. In IR constructivist norm research, there is now widespread consensus that the intersubjective nature of norms implies that their meaning is not fixed but open for interpretation. Norms are not stable, but contested and dynamic.[34] The behaviours and actions that norms prescribe may, however, change over time: 'The regulative and constitutive implications of norms but also their normative and prescriptive content differ depending on time, place, or social context.'[35] In addition, imprecise treaty language and overlapping or colliding norms invite contestation.[36] Accordingly, Sandholtz argues that 'all normative structures generate disputes'[37] and Wiener holds that norms 'are contested by default'.[38] Wiener, whose argument on the contested nature of norms and theory of contestation has inspired much of the debate, argues that contestation is a social practice of objecting to norms, that is, challenging either the meaning or the meaning-in-use of norms.[39]

IR norm research has introduced several 'ideal types' of contestation. In this book, Wiener distinguishes between reactive and proactive types of contestation, while Sandholtz distinguishes between discursive and behavioural forms of contestation. Additional typologies have been developed by other scholars. For example, Welsh distinguishes between procedural contestation and substantive contestation,[40] with the former referring to the process of norm development and the related question of who should develop a norm, and the latter referring to the content of the norm. Deitelhoff

understood independently of the law: Tony Honoré, 'The Dependence of Morality on Law' (1993) 13 Oxford Journal of Legal Studies 1.

32 Finnemore and Sikkink (n 12).

33 Mona L Krook and Jacqui True, 'Rethinking the Life Cycles of International Norms: The United Nations and the Global Promotion of Gender Equality' (2012) 18 European Journal of International Relations 103.

34 Antje Wiener, 'The Dual Quality of Norms and Governance beyond the State: Sociological and Normative Approaches to Interaction' (2007) 10 Critical Review of International Social and Political Philosophy 47; Antje Wiener, *The Invisible Constitution of Politics. Contested Norms and International Encounters* (CUP 2008); Jeffrey S Lantis and Carmen Wunderlich, 'Reevaluating Constructivist Norm Theory: A Three-Dimensional Norms Research Program' (2022) 24 International Studies Review < https://doi.org/10.1093/isr/viab059> accessed 5 March 2022; Caroline Fehl and Elvira Rosert, 'It's Complicated: A Conceptual Framework for Studying Relations and Interactions between International Norms' (2020) PRIF Working Paper No 49 <www.hsfk.de/fileadmin/HSFK/hsfk_publikationen/PRIF_WP_49.pdf> accessed 5 March 2022; Sandholtz and Stiles (n 12).

35 Holger Niemann and Henrik Schillinger, 'Contestation "All the Way Down"? The Grammar of Contestation in Norm Research' (2017) 43 Review of International Studies 29, 29–30.

36 Sassan Gholiagha, Anna Holzscheiter, and Andrea Liese, 'Activating Norm Collisions: Interface Conflicts in International Drug Control' (2020) 9 Global Constitutionalism 290.

37 Wayne Sandholtz, 'Dynamics of International Norm Change: Rules against Wartime Plunder' (2008) 14 European Journal of International Relations 101, 105.

38 Wiener, 'Enacting Meaning-in-use' (n 18) 179.

39 Wiener, *A Theory of Contestation* (n 18).

40 Jennifer M Welsh, 'Norm Contestation and the Responsibility to Protect' (2013) 5 Global Responsibility to Protect 365.

and Zimmermann developed a typology that is often referenced in IR.[41] They distinguish between applicatory contestation, which refers to the frequently expressed disapproval of the application of a norm to a specific situation, from validity contestation, which targets a norm's validity and, thus, the core of its meaning.

The various ideal types are typically used to explain different outcomes, that is, they are linked to the strengthening or weakening of a norm. Whereas contestation can be seen as an opportunity to enhance the social legitimacy of a norm through dialogue among a diverse set of actors,[42] many scholars are concerned that it opens the floodgates to norm decay. Deitelhoff and Zimmermann have hypothesized that validity contestation weakens a norm, whereas applicatory contestation strengthens a norm. Yet permanent applicatory contestations are also likely to weaken a norm when actors fail to 'achieve renewed consensus or compromise on a norm's meaning and application'.[43]

The concept of contestation is not a legal one, but it is used in the legal literature to describe a social practice. From a doctrinal perspective on international law, not every social practice directly affects the legal validity or legal content of a value underlying a norm because a legal norm can only be formed, terminated, or modified through a legal act by a competent actor—usually a state. This act must furthermore be accompanied by an intention to create, change, or end a legal norm (*opinio iuris*) and must be part of a legal agreement. Identifying whether a particular social practice qualifies as a legal act requires an act of interpretation to discern the state's legal conviction. Thereby, law distinguishes between forms of contestation, which are legally relevant, and discursive critique, which remains outside the legal sphere and is therefore—doctrinally speaking—irrelevant. Moreover, from a positivist perspective, the legal validity of a rule can decouple from its social validity. A formal legal act is required for a norm to cease to be legally binding. Even *desuetudo*—'the rejection of a rule through subsequent non-enforcement or non-compliance'[44]—requires an explicit or 'tacit agreement to terminate or modify' a rule of international law.[45] The formality of laws thus makes it more difficult for lawyers to grasp the relevance of changes in the social validity of norms and their underlying values.

The same applies to the idea of norm erosion. Due to the binary structure of law (in force versus not in force), such processes are more difficult to conceptualize. From a doctrinal legal perspective, norm erosion—as a form of change—may consist of various legally relevant phenomena that reduce the legal effects of a rule or a principle, thereby also signaling a shift in the prioritization of values. For example, while states are entitled to lawfully withdraw from treaties, any withdrawal reduces the sphere of application of a multilateral treaty. Likewise, interpretative changes may erode legal

[41] Deitelhoff and Zimmermann, 'Things we Lost in the Fire' (n 17).

[42] Antje Wiener, Chapter 2 in this book.

[43] Deitelhoff and Zimmermann, 'Things we Lost in the Fire' (n 17) 8. See also Anette Stimmer, 'Beyond Internalization: Alternative Endings of the Norm Life Cycle' (2019) 63 International Studies Quarterly 270, 270, and 272. Stimmer further argues that applicatory contestation may have different results depending on whether actors agree or disagree on a norm's frame and claim.

[44] Jan Wouters and Sten Verhoeven, 'Desuetudo' in Rüdiger Wolfrum (ed), *Max Planck Encyclopedia of Public International Law* (OUP 2011) para 1.

[45] ibid, paras 10, 15, 17.

rules. A restrictive reading of the constitutive elements of a prohibition as well as an extensive reading of its exceptions may reduce the scope of a prohibition and thus also its legal effects. Moreover, some interpretative disputes may stretch the limits of *lege artis* interpretation, particularly in view of the object and purpose of a given norm. While such phenomena do not terminate the legal validity of a rule, they may affect the rule's scope and effect and thereby represent an erosion of the rule's objective.

Many of the current challenges to international law find expression in forms of contestation. This book therefore pays close attention to the various types and forms of contestation and their outcomes. Again, the research in IR offers conceptual guidance. It has studied how norms change when actors diffuse, adapt, translate, localize, resist, or contest norms,[46] and has examined various outcomes: at the extreme, these include norm erosion,[47] norm decay,[48] and norm replacement.[49] However, and given that a norm rarely disappears entirely, the focus is often on the degrees to which a norm has been weakened, has remained 'robust' or 'resilient', or has even been strengthened. For our goal of identifying value change, it seems central to focus on the changing content and the changing strength of a norm.

Recalling the elements of norms introduced above, the content of a norm can change with regard to the value that underlies it, the behaviour it prescribes, and the situation or problem to which it applies. Although all are relevant, we are mainly interested in value change. Changes in norm strength are of particular interest to those who argue that contestation may weaken or strengthen a norm. Again, recalling the definition presented above of a norm as a collective expectation about appropriate behaviour, one may conceptualize and measure norm strength as 'the extent of collective expectations related to a principled idea'.[50] One way to operationalize norm strength is to look at the degree of institutionalization or legalization, that is, the extent to which a norm is codified in international law and the proportion of states that have ratified or otherwise formally endorsed the norm.[51] Another way is to look at the norm's shared acceptance and intersubjective meaning in political or societal discourse, that is, the degree to which states but also international organizations expect an actor to behave in a certain way in a given situation and thus to uphold a shared moral principle or value.[52] To conceptually distinguish this form of intersubjective expectation from expectations stemming from a process of institutionalization or legalization, we refer to the latter as social validity.

[46] For example, Amitav Acharya, 'How Ideas Spread: Whose Norms Matter? Norm Localization and Institutional Change in Asian Regionalism' (2004) 58 International Organization 239; Sandholtz, 'Dynamics of International Norm Change' (n 37).

[47] Elvira Rosert and Sonja Schirmbeck, 'Zur Erosion internationaler Normen. Folterverbot und nukleares Tabu in der Diskussion' (2007) 14 Zeitschrift für internationale Beziehungen 253.

[48] Diana Panke and Ulrich Petersohn, 'Why International Norms Disappear Sometimes' (2012) 18 European Journal of International Relations 719; Ryder McKeown, 'Norm Regress: US Revisionism and the Slow Death of the Torture Norm' (2009) 23 International Relations 5.

[49] Wayne Sandholtz, Chapter 3 in this book.

[50] Michal Ben-Josef Hirsch and Jennifer Dixon, 'Conceptualizing and Assessing Norm Strength in International Relations' (2021) 27 European Journal of International Relations 521, 524.

[51] ibid 526.

[52] See related notions ibid 525, but also Deitelhoff and Zimmermann 'Norms under Challenge' (n 12) 7.

Combining the dimensions of norm content and norm strength, we arrive at three types of value change. First, the value protected by a legal norm, that is, its substantive content, may change. Second, the institutionalization of the value, that is, the degree to which it is legally protected, may change.[53] Third, the social validity of the norm and its underlying value, that is, an accepted non-legal standard of appropriateness, may change.

## 4. Conceptual Framework: Assessing International Law's Trajectory Through Value Change

To assess whether we are currently observing a metamorphosis of international law, a period of norm change *within* international law, or simply a period of turbulence and ambivalence, we propose a conceptual framework that focuses on change in the value orientation of international law (see Section 4.1). We posit that a value orientation is a decisive foundational feature of international law (see Section 4.2) not least because of law's function of 'locking in' values against future policy choices (see Section 4.3). We argue further that it is precisely the value orientation of international law that is at the core of current contestations (see Section 4.4).

### 4.1. Value Change as an Indication of a Metamorphosis

A variety of methodological approaches appear potentially useful to evaluate a metamorphosis of the international legal order. All of these approaches seek to systemically approximate relevant elements of change and capture their impact on the direction in which international law is moving.

One way to conceive of a genuine metamorphosis of international law is to identify essential characteristics of international law and assess whether they are changing. These characteristics include the binding character of the law and its binarity, formalism, and ability to steer behaviour. Such an understanding of metamorphosis requires, in particular, that the secondary rules of international law are being affected. Technological changes may be a case in point since they may challenge legally established understandings of agency and responsibility, as is the case with autonomous weapons. They may also affect our understanding of durability and thus stability in view of their 'speed of change and rate of scaling', as is the case with artificial intelligence.[54] Moreover, challenges such as climate change, that can be characterized as 'wicked problems', may affect law's essential characteristics. The term 'wicked problems' refers to 'complex, intractable, open-ended, or unpredictable' problems that cannot be solved optimally.[55] Such challenges require high flexibility and adaptability

[53] See Sandholtz and Stiles (n 12) 7, 18: The norm can become more authoritative, more formal, more specific and/or more legalized; cf Sandholtz and Stiles (n 12) 18.

[54] Benedict Kingsbury, 'Infrastructure and InfraReg: On Rousing the International Law "Wizards of Is"' (2019) 8 Cambridge Journal of International Law 172, 185–86.

[55] John Alford and Brian W Head, 'Wicked and Less Wicked Problems: A Typology and a Contingency Framework' (2017) 36 Policy and Society 397; Horst WJ Rittel and Melvin M Webber, 'Dilemmas in a General Theory of Planning' (1973) 4 Policy Sciences 155.

and may, in the view of some scholars, prompt a turn toward informality.[56] Other scholars have discussed whether the impact of non-state actors and cosmopolitan claims[57] on the law-making process signal 'the end of international law' and a turn toward global law.[58]

While these are significant developments in themselves, we suggest that a metamorphosis in the sense of a foundational paradigm shift would also occur if the values protected by international law changed either in substance or in legal or social validity. This would include shifts in the prioritization of these values, and the extreme case in which the idea of legally protecting such values itself is dismissed. The criticism may be raised that by this yardstick, more than one foundational element of the international (legal) order would have to be transformed for metamorphosis as a fundamental systemic change to occur.[59] It could even be argued that metamorphosis would require every foundational element of the order to be transformed.

Indeed, we consider it highly likely that change in one foundational element will be accompanied by the transformation of other elements. The establishment of the individual's subjectivity under international law after 1945, for instance, went hand in hand with an expansion of legally protected individual rights—that is, values—and the creation of new institutions including regional human rights courts. Still, we focus on assessing change in the value orientation of international law for three reasons. First, many have claimed that the value orientation of international law is at the centre of the international legal order that has developed since 1945 and even more so since the end of the Cold War (see Section 4.2). Second, in structural terms, value change affects a foundational objective of legalization: states deliberately use law's function to 'lock in'[60] certain values and behavioural prescriptions against future policy choices (see Section 4.3). Third, it may be assumed that it is precisely the value orientation of international law that is at the core of current contestations stemming from shifting identities, changing power constellations, and the various deficiencies of attempts by the United States and the West more generally to imprint their values upon the international order (see Section 4.4).

## 4.2. The Relevance of International Law's Value Orientation

One of the defining features of the international legal order that was carved out in 1945 and has further been shaped since 1990 is the idea that it protects common

[56] Jutta Brunnée, 'The Rule of International (Environmental) Law and Complex Problems' in Heike Krieger, Georg Nolte, and Andreas Zimmermann (eds), *The International Rule of Law – Rise or Decline?* (OUP 2019) 213–214.

[57] See eg Mattias Kumm, 'The Cosmopolitan Turn in Constitutionalism' (2013) 20 Indiana Journal of Global Legal Studies 605; for a moderating approach Eirik Bjorge, 'Legal Cosmopolitanism in International Law' (2020) 9 Global Constitutionalism 552.

[58] See eg, ESIL 2021, Concluding Panel of the 16th ESIL Conference (Stockholm) <https://esil2021.se/conference-programme/> accessed 5 March 2022.

[59] For an institutional perspective: Samantha Besson, *Reconstruire l'ordre institutionel international* (Fayard 2021).

[60] Andrew Moravcsik, 'The Origins of Human Rights Regimes: Democratic Delegation in Postwar Europe' (2000) 54 International Organization 217.

values. When Friedmann characterized what we term the 'metamorphosis of the international legal order' from a law of coordination to a law of cooperation in his 1964 book on the changing structure of international law, the role of values (common interests) constituted an important argument:

> Unlike the traditional law of nations, which is predicated upon the assumption of conflicts of national interest, which it seeks to stabilise and regulate, co-operative international law requires a community of interests [ … ]. The challenge posed by the changes in the structure of the international society of our time does not mean the abolition of self-interest in international relations; it does, however, radically affect the dimensions and objectives of self-interest. Such new developments as the international financial and welfare agencies, or the developing European communities, are a tentative expression of new world-wide interests in security, survival and co-operation for the preservation and development of vital needs and resources of mankind [...]. International law [ … ] is today overwhelmingly an agent of progress and evolution.[61]

Since Friedmann, the reliance on an expanding value orientation of international law has been used as a strategy 'for constructing progress narratives of international law'. This has become one of the dominant narratives in academic discourses, relying on the assumption that the 'value-oriented international law is "better" law than a morally (seemingly) neutral law', and that it 'gains plausibility against the background of the experiences with a value-neutral understanding of law in the World War II era'.[62]

Since the end of the Cold War, international lawyers have been developing theoretical frameworks to describe a move towards a stronger value-based international order. The most far-reaching analysis and prediction—historically contingent upon the (over-)optimistic atmosphere of the 1990s, particularly in the West—was the idea of a 'constitutionalization' of international law.[63] Drawing on earlier research on the 'international community'[64] and its constitutionalization,[65] proponents of this idea argued that the 'value poverty' of classical bilateralist international law had been overcome through an orientation toward the common values of a legally constituted international community, as enshrined in concepts of 'community interests', 'community values', or 'global goods'.[66] Rather than undergoing a simple process of juridification, these values had to exhibit a 'specific quality as foundational norms'.[67] Thus, some

[61] Wolfgang Friedmann, *The Changing Structure of International Law* (Columbia University Press 1964) 57–58.

[62] Tilmann Altwicker and Oliver Diggelmann, 'How is Progress Constructed in International Legal Scholarship?' (2014) 25 European Journal of International Law 425, 432, 434.

[63] See eg, Jan Klabbers, Anne Peters, and Geir Ulfstein (eds), *The Constitutionalization of International Law* (OUP 2009).

[64] René-Jean Dupuy, *La Communauté internationale entre le mythe et l'histoire* (Economica 1986); Hermann Mosler, *The International Society as a Legal Community* (Sijthoff & Noordhoff 1980).

[65] Alfred Verdross, *Die Verfassung der Völkerrechtsgemeinschaft* (Julius Springer 1926).

[66] Bruno Simma, 'From Bilateralism to Community Interest in International Law' (1994) 250 Recueil des Cours de l'Academie de Droit International 217; Thomas M Franck, *Fairness in International Law and Institutions* (OUP 1998).

[67] Stefan Kadelbach and Thomas Kleinlein, 'Überstaatliches Verfassungsrecht. Zur Konstitutionalisierung im Völkerrecht' (2006) 44 Archiv des Völkerrechts 235, 253; English translation in the text is by the authors;

authors underscored the evolution of hierarchies in international law based on norms of *ius cogens* and obligations *erga omnes*.[68] The hierarchization of norms allowed these scholars to conceive of international law as a relatively autonomous body of law vis-à-vis the state, reflecting a prioritization of certain values over others. Consequently, in their view, the authority of international institutions was strengthened, and values such as human rights and the rule of law were protected by these institutions, further limiting states' sovereignty.

Such readings of the value orientation and progress narrative were never uncontested.[69] Other scholars have underscored the abusive intentions that a reference to values in international law might entail.[70] Some have argued that states actually 'use international law to entrench normatively undesirable outcomes'.[71] Others have criticized the inherent claim that values represent a context-independent 'objective truth'.[72] The most radical perspectives come from critical legal studies emphasizing the postcolonial constellation and the continuing imperialism within the international legal order. Third-world approaches to international law (TWAIL) by neo-Marxist and postcolonial scholars and other voices from critical legal studies[73] highlighted the negative effects of post-Cold War legal developments early on. These approaches 'strived to show that some of the discipline's core concepts and arguments not only incorporate Western ideas about the world but also support the material interests of imperialist centers'.[74] In particular, *Anghie* stresses that the post-Cold War period of US American hegemony replicated colonial and imperialist patterns. He thus reveals how democratic states have instrumentalized a value orientation to claim superiority,[75] for example, through practices of interventionism.[76] TWAIL approaches lay

see also Heike Krieger, 'Verfassung im Völkerrecht – Konstitutionelle Elemente jenseits des Staates?' (2016) 75 Veröffentlichungen der Vereinigung der Deutschen Staatsrechtslehrer 439, 445.

[68] Erika de Wet and Jure Vidmar, *Hierarchy in International Law: The Place of Human Rights* (OUP 2012); Christian Tomuschat, 'Obligations Arising for States Without or Against Their Will' (1993) 241 Recueil des Cours de l'Academie de Droit International 195, 307; Thomas Kleinlein, *Konstitutionalisierung im Völkerrecht* (Springer 2012) 21.

[69] Bernsdorff and Venzke (n 24), paras 4–12.

[70] ibid, paras 5–8 trace the 'scepticism' back to Kelsen and Schmitt.

[71] Jack L Goldsmith and Eric A Posner, *The Limits of International Law* (OUP 2005) 4; for a focus on instrumental uses of international law see also Ian Hurd, *How to Do Things with International Law* (Princeton University Press 2017).

[72] Jean d'Aspremont, 'The Foundations of the International Legal Order' (2009) 18 Finnish Yearbook of International Law 219, 221.

[73] Martti Koskenniemi, 'International Law in Europe' (2005) 16 European Journal of International Law 113, 121–22.

[74] Ntina Tzouvala, 'The Spectre of Eurocentrism in International Legal History' (2020) 31 Yale Journal of Law and the Humanities 413, at 415, 418–19, 421; see also: Búzás Zoltan, 'Racism and Antiracism in the Liberal International Order' (2021) 75 International Organization 440.

[75] Anthony Anghie, 'Rethinking Sovereignty in International Law' (2009) 5 Annual Review of Law and Social Science 291, 303; Anthony Anghie, *Imperialism, Sovereignty and the Making of International Law* (CUP 2005).

[76] Rose Parfitt, *The Process of International Legal Reproduction* (CUP 2019); see also Sara Kendall, 'Cartographies of the Present: "Contingent Sovereignty" and Territorial Integrity' (2016) 47 Netherlands Yearbook of International Law 83, 100; Anne Orford, *International Authority and the Responsibility to Protect* (CUP 2011). For a mainstream criticism of human rights-based interventionism: Ingrid Wuerth, 'International Law in the Post-Human Rights Era' (2017) 96 Texas Law Review 279, 281ff.

bare the extent to which hegemonic interests are reflected in and imprinted upon the structures and, in particular, the value-orientation of international law. Similarly, IR scholars have emphasized that the international (legal) order was strongly shaped by US leadership after the Second World War[77] and further dominated by liberal democracies after the Cold War.[78]

While scholars who subscribe to a progress narrative in international law and those who criticize the imposition of values could hardly be further apart in their positions, both agree on the relevance of international law's value orientation. Hence, there are good grounds to argue for value change as a reference point for a potential metamorphosis of international law.

### 4.3. International Law's Function of Locking in Values

A number of structural factors also speak in favour of assessing change against the reference point of international law's value orientation. The protection of common values by international legal instruments signals their fundamental relevance. Such instruments show that governments (and other actors) have not only reached an agreement but are using international organizations and international law to effectively enforce their policy and value preferences at a particular point in time.[79] They deliberately use law's function of 'locking in'[80] certain values and related behavioural prescriptions, that is, norms, against future policy choices. The accelerated processes of legalization in the 1990s resulted in a number of common values being enshrined in legal agreements. Mechanisms of legal obligation and enforcement are designed to limit and sometimes even prevent change. This is true especially for *ius cogens* norms that are specifically designed to protect the underlying values from change. *Ius cogens* norms express the prioritization of some values over others. The concern with what is at stake when values change despite their legalization is shared by research in the social sciences as well. In social science disciplines, societal change is regarded as a core element of modernity, which is defined by a permanent sense and process of development but does not necessarily touch on foundational concepts or certainties. Only when these certainties begin breaking down is fundamental transformation considered to take place.[81] Consequently, from a social science perspective, fundamental transformation occurs when the certainties guaranteed by foundational values begin to change.

[77] G John Ikenberry, 'The End of Liberal International Order?' (2018) 94 International Affairs 7; Alexander Cooley and Daniel Nexon, *Exit from hegemony: The unraveling of the American global order* (OUP 2020).

[78] Tanja Börzel and Michael Zürn, 'Contestations of the Liberal International Order: From Liberal Multilateralism to Postnational Liberalism' (2021) 75 International Organization 282.

[79] Kenneth W Abbott and Duncan Snidal, 'Law, Legalization, and Politics: An Agenda for the Next Generation of IL/IR Scholars' in Jeffrey L Dunoff and Mark A Pollack (eds), *Interdisciplinary Perspectives on International Law and International Relations: The State of the Art* (CUP 2013) 35.

[80] Andrew Moravcsik, 'The Origins of Human Rights Regimes: Democratic Delegation in Postwar Europe' (2000) 54 International Organization 217.

[81] Beck (n 7).

### 4.4. Current Challenges for the Value Orientation of International Law

Evidence that certainties are disappearing may be inferred from a review of current academic discourses. As noted above, research on contestation and its consequences has increased substantially in recent years. A common thread of this research is the sense that the depth and scope of current contestations go beyond regular norm change in international law. No single cause has been identified for these developments. We focus on current challenges that address the value orientation of international law: shifting identities and a spread of populism and autocratic regimes, changing power constellations, transnational crises or shocks, but also technological change.

Shifting identities are observable in many regions of the world that have turned away from global multilateralism to emphasize regional or national identities. As a consequence of globalization, there are increasing numbers of actors whose political, cultural, and historical identities impact international law. The diffusion of power, agency, and political consciousness among states and diverse non-state actors has multiplied the diverging claims and interpretations.[82] Several countries have challenged norms that were long considered robust. Domestic power shifts and democratic backsliding—for example, in several Eastern European countries—have shaken value-based legal norms such as women's rights and freedom of the press. In these cases, autocratic, populist, and/or nationalist movements have openly contested the substance of norms and instead stressed alternative norms including national sovereignty. China and Russia as well as the US under the Trump administration have pushed national sovereignty as a central value of the international order and have even challenged the modern understanding of sovereignty as limited, divided, and accountable in favour of conceptions of 'extralegal and organic sovereignty'.[83] A similar backlash has emerged in other Western countries where populist and nationalist policies are challenging the authority of international (legal) institutions. Even international institutions that the US had long supported, such as the World Trade Organization (WTO), have come under attack.[84]

Changing power constellations have accelerated these developments. The shift from a unipolar to a multipolar world order has opened up new spaces for states and other actors to openly contest international law. Not only China and Russia but also states and social and political movements from both the Global South and the Global North are proposing different views of how the international legal order should be developed and (re-)conceptualized.[85] Some of these actors favour a shift to regional institutions

[82] Andrew Hurrell, 'Cultural Diversity within Global International Society' in Andrew Phillips and Christian Reus-Smit (eds), *Culture and Order in World Politics* (CUP 2020) 118.

[83] Roland Paris, 'The Right to Dominate: How Old Ideas About Sovereignty Pose New Challenges for World Order' (2020) 74 International Organization 453, 454.

[84] M P Ram Mohan and Vishakha Raj, 'Appellate Body Crisis at the World Trade Organization: View from India' (2021) 55 Journal of World Trade 829.

[85] From the vast literature see Anthea Roberts, *Is International Law International?* (OUP 2017) 279; from the vast IR literature see Hanns W Maull (ed), *The Rise and Decline of the Post-Cold War International Order* (OUP 2018).

or a turn to bilateral or non-binding agreements, for example, in the context of China's Belt and Road Initiative.[86] Others are expressing their long-held scepticism about what they conceive as 'Western' norms or (the Western application of) legal instruments. Among the norms under attack by various actors are human rights in general and women's rights in particular. International institutions have been accused of racism—Gambia, for example, made this accusation against the International Criminal Court. Japan's withdrawal from the International Whaling Commission or past announcements by African countries of their withdrawal from the Rome Statute[87] have challenged the view that international law established since the end of the Cold War could be permanent. Instead these moves suggest that some states are seeking to lower their level of commitment to international legal values.

Transnational crises and shocks such as the global refugee crisis, the international financial crisis, and above all the security threats stemming from non-state actors have led to a reformulation of national interests and have been accompanied by criticisms of the existing normative order. In this context, some states have voiced concerns that legal frameworks are either ineffective or unfair in creating unequal distributive effects. Others have argued that norms limit their options to an extent that jeopardizes effective problem-solving, for instance, in crime prevention. Consequently, some states have tried to expand their range of action, if necessary by challenging norms that limit the responses they deem legitimate and necessary. Examples include the post-9/11 attempts to expand the right to self-defence against non-state actors and to circumvent the prohibition against torture and ill-treatment.[88] Other states view these developments as signaling the failure of a Western value-based order and have criticized Western states for a policy of double standards.[89] In this sense, many of today's challenges are framed as resistance against developments in the post-Cold War era. Contesting states seek to reverse a trend in which, in their view, the US and the West more generally have imposed their liberal values on the international order and thus asserted their normative superiority.[90] Western military interventionism and pro-democratic regime change have led to a loss of Western credibility in the wake of the 1999 Kosovo intervention, the 2003 US/UK intervention in Iraq, and the disastrous

[86] Alejandro Rodiles, 'Infrastructural Developmentalism and its Many Types of Global Law: A Comparison between the UN Sustainable Development Goals and China's Belt & Road Initiative' (2022) 10 London Review of International Law 367.

[87] Rome Statute of the International Criminal Court (adopted 17 July 1998, entered into force 1 July 2002) 2187 UNTS 90.

[88] Andrea Liese, 'Exceptional Necessity: How Liberal Democracies Contest the Prohibition of Torture and Ill-Treatment when Countering Terrorism' (2009) 5 Journal of International Law and International Relations 17.

[89] Joint Statement of the Russian Federation and the People's Republic of China on the International Relations Entering a New Era and the Global Sustainable Development from 2022 <http://en.kremlin.ru/supplement/5770> accessed 8 March 2022; the Declaration of the People's Republic of China and the Russian Federation on the Promotion of International Law from 2016 <https://www.fmprc.gov.cn/mfa_eng/wjdt_665385/2649_665393/201608/t20160801_679466.html> accessed 8 March 2022; Iran, Russia Issue Declaration on Promotion of International Law from 2020 <https://en.mfa.ir/portal/newsview/599243/iran-russia-issue-declaration-on-promotion-of-intl-law> accessed 8 March 2022.

[90] Christoph Daase and Nicole Deitelhoff, 'Wenn die Geltung schwindet – Die Krise der liberalen Weltordnung und die Herrschaftsproblematik internationaler Politik' in Rainer Forst and Klaus Günther (eds), *Normative Ordnungen* (Suhrkamp Verlag 2021) 177, 180, 184.

ending of the Afghanistan intervention in 2021. The same holds true for how Europe is dealing with refugees crossing the Mediterranean and Asia Minor.

From a different perspective, the rise of new technologies may intensify the pressure for change in the international legal order. New technological developments have always tended to either challenge or promote legal norms. Yet the emergence of nanotechnology, synthetic biotechnology, artificial intelligence, and cyberspace,[91] as well as digital currency raises the question of whether these technologies accelerate norm change and thus lead to value change.

## 5. Research Design for the Evaluation of Metamorphosis in International Law through Value Change

All of the contributions in this book faced the challenge of how to assess and evaluate changes that may be driven by the developments described above. We argue that to understand value change, three elements must be examined: the value protected by a legal norm, its legal validity, and its social validity. All three elements may change as a result of a process of contestation, and a change in one element may affect the other elements. A metamorphosis may occur when more than one element and more than one of international law's foundational values are affected.

- First, a legally protected value might change (*substantial value change*).
- Second, the institutionalization of a value, that is, the degree to which it is legally protected, may change (*change in the legal status of a value*).
- Third, legally protected values might not change in the formal sense, but might lose their social validity and, thus, lose their power to structure actors' behaviour (*social validity decline*).

Our framework for assessing value change lends itself primarily to examining changes in a specific value that is protected by a specific norm. However, for a broader picture, it is equally important to assess the relationships between different values and the legal norms that protect them. Thus, we assume that change in the three elements described above might also manifest itself in shifts in the prioritization of values within the international legal order. Such substantive shifts in value prioritization may also indicate a metamorphosis of the international legal order.

To enable us to examine the state of metamorphosis, the norms analysed in the empirical chapters were chosen to represent the concept of a value-based international law—either as it emerged after the Second World War or as it was shaped further after the Cold War. Moreover, the choice of norms enables us to better understand the conditions under which change occurs and the mechanisms that lead to either the metamorphosis or robustness of international law. A variety of actors have recently contested one or the other of these norms. These actors come from a wide spectrum, including major powers, states from the Global North and the Global South,

[91] Dana Burchardt and Maria Varaki (eds), 'The Impact of Digitalisation on International Law' 24 (2023) German Law Journal (forthcoming).

democracies, and autocracies. By comparing the individual contributions, we can thus probe whether the effects of contestation depend on the power position of the contesting actor. In addition, the chosen norms encompass different stages of *legalization* and *institutionalization*. Finally, they vary in terms of their age or maturity, that is, the *duration* of validity. In the following section, we briefly outline how this variation addresses core assumptions of the literature on norm robustness.

The effects of contestation are likely to depend on the degrees of legalization and institutionalization of a norm. IR scholars assume that legalized norms are more robust than non-legalized ones because they come with a higher degree of obligation, necessitating justification when not complied with and potentially alarming norm defenders, and because non-compliance can more often be monitored and sanctioned.[92] Likewise, highly institutionalized norms, that is, norms that are incorporated into the policies of international organizations, are less prone to change because the institutional embeddedness provides norm defenders with discursive and political resources.[93]

It is also crucial to consider the 'age' of a norm, that is, the duration of its existence. Younger treaty norms are likely to be less contested and show few if any changes simply because they mirror recent state consensus and more recent commitments. Older norms, whether derived from practice or treaty law, are more likely to come under pressure when global power structures, state preferences, societal expectations, or the underlying problems change. In order to delineate change and metamorphosis, it is important not only to examine processes of erosion but also to analyse the fate of more recently established legal norms.

Inspired by constructivist IR norm research, we sought to focus on the idea that disputed norms change in recursive cycles as a result of the interplay between rules and behaviour, or more precisely, between expectations, actions, arguments over the meaning of the norm and its range of application, and rule change.[94] We aimed to compare different forms of actors' engagement with norms, such as contestation in discourse[95] or non-compliance in practice.[96] We asked whether the consequences of these engagements were similar or whether they varied across different norm cycles and issue areas. Changing values and the idea of their legal protection are not the only possible indications of metamorphosis in international law. The values that a legal system aims to protect are embedded in its structures and institutions. Deep value contestations put pressure on institutions to develop new practices in order to remain capable of acting. This pressure will inevitably affect legal structures as well.[97] We

[92] See Panke and Petersohn, 'Why International Norms Disappear Sometimes' (n 48).

[93] Sandholtz, Chapter 3 in this book.

[94] Terence C Halliday, 'Recursivity of Global Normmaking: A Sociolegal Agenda' (2009) 5 Annual Review of Law and Social Science 263; Sandholtz, 'Dynamics of International Norm Change' (n 37); Sandholtz and Stiles (n 12); Wiener, 'The Dual Quality of Norms' (n 34).

[95] Deitelhoff and Zimmermann, 'Things we Lost in the Fire' (n 17); Wiener, *A Theory of Contestation* (n 18).

[96] See Michael J Glennon, 'How International Rules Die' (2005) 93 Georgetown Law Journal 939; Diana Panke and Ulrich Petersohn, 'Norm Challenges and Norm Death: The Inexplicable?' (2016) 51 Cooperation and Conflict 3.

[97] See Heike Krieger, 'Populist Governments and International Law' (2019) 30 European Journal of International Law 971.

therefore considered it important to be precise about the specific object of contestation so that in answering these questions, we would be able to infer broader dynamics of change or metamorphosis in the international legal order.

## 6. Structure and Contributions of This Book

In order to systematically assess value change, the book combines theoretical and methodological frameworks with individual case studies. Chapters 2 to 5 provide a set of conceptualizations and tools to assess and analyse value change. United by the argument that change is continuous and a defining feature of international norms and international law, the four conceptual chapters can be read as highly complementary. They also agree that it is challenging to determine how fundamental value change occurs. Each offers specific concepts, frames, and tools that inspire and guide the adjacent case studies. Chapters 2 and 3 address norm change from an IR perspective. Here, international law forms a sub-category of norms. In Chapter 2, Antje Wiener addresses value decline and norm change as interconnected phenomena and offers a conceptual framework to understand and explain practice-based norm change from the perspective of an IR scholar. Her chapter presents analytical tools to locate and evaluate contestations and to analyse norm change. This includes distinguishing between reactive contestations consisting solely of objection and proactive contestations that involve critically engaging with a norm's values. In Chapter 3, Wayne Sandholtz explores processes of change and decline in international legal norms. He proposes to pay more attention to disputes, which reveal actors' beliefs regarding the validity of a norm, when assessing norm change and norm robustness. Furthermore, he reflects on and identifies sources of resilience that are built into international norms. Chapters 4 and 5 deal with legal perspectives on value change. Thomas Kleinlein focuses on the distinction between formal and informal modes of legal change by examining doctrinal categories that define methods to manage change in international law. He highlights the relevance of informal change through legal interpretations in face of high hurdles for formal treaty-making. In Chapter 5, Erika de Wet focuses on peremptory norms of international law (*ius cogens*), which establish a norm hierarchy in international law to safeguard foundational values of the international community. She criticizes that both states and courts are reluctant to attribute legal consequences to norms with a *ius cogens* character so that it remains doubtful whether these norms offer a shield against erosion of norms or their underlying values.

Chapters 6 to 17 trace and analyse value change in the international legal order, focusing on foundational norms of the post-1945 order or on norms representing the rise of the international legal order post-1990. The case studies cover:

- the prohibition of torture and the protection of women's rights as two core human rights norms protecting fundamental values such as physical integrity and gender equality;
- the prohibition on the use of force as well as the non-proliferation of nuclear weapons as two core norms related to international peace and security;

- sustainability norms and accountability for core international crimes as two norms that were institutionalized mainly after the Cold War. The latter cases focus on the International Criminal Court and also represent 'the golden age of international courts' that may have reached its peak.[98]

The challenges to each norm, the reactions by norm defenders, and the current validity and strength of each norm are the focus of two chapters each, one by an IR scholar and one by an international lawyer. While the chapters review, draw on, and extend their core discipline's views and, consequently, have different disciplinary emphases, they all take the position of the other discipline or an interdisciplinary perspective into account.

The chapters by *Lesch and Zimmermann* and by *Steiger* scrutinize whether the prohibition of torture has been eroded by torture practices, official reinterpretations or discursive contestations in the context of counterterrorism policies in certain states. In Chapter 6, Max Lesch and Lisbeth Zimmermann study the long-term effects of the reinterpretations, discursive contestations and norm violations by Israel and the US from the 1990s to 2010. They propose to assess the strength of the norm surrounding the prohibition of torture in the dimensions of behaviour and discourse. Their analysis finds no indication of a change in the strength of the international torture prohibition. Neither the value's legal status nor its substance have changed. The complementary Chapter 7 by Dominik Steiger examines whether US behavioural and discursive contestations against the anti-torture norm have influenced the legal position of other actors and thus eroded the prohibition of torture. Using a different method than Lesch and Zimmermann, he still comes to a similar conclusion.

The chapters by Theresa Reinold (Chapter 8) and Srinivas Burra (Chapter 9) analyse whether the value underlying the legal norm of not using force and the related right to self-defence have changed through legal interpretations based on pertinent practices of states. Focusing on the international military campaign against the Islamic State, in Chapter 8, Reinold traces recent changes in the right to self-defence. She argues that in this case, the emergence of dissonance within a legal system—or in the system's relationship with its political environment—drove change. The complementary Chapter 9 by Burra engages with the legal controversies around the right to self-defence against non-state actors in the territory of another state. From a Third World perspective, he assesses changes in the norm and its underlying value: While the wording of the UN-Charta has remained in place, norm promoters that advocate interpretative changes strongly influence the discourse.

The chapters by Adam Bower (Chapter 10) and Malcolm Jorgensen (Chapter 11) evaluate the impact of different contestations raised against one of the younger norms and their underlying value examined in this book, namely the norms of legal accountability and anti-impunity and their institutionalization via the International Criminal Court (ICC). In Chapter 10, Bower studies the effects of contestation of the ICC's authority He argues that the meaning and limits of the anti-impunity norm were always contested and states invoked competing norms to restrict the Court's authority.. Still,

[98] See Sandholtz, Chapter 3 in this book.

the observable attacks on the legitimacy of the Court have not resulted in a substantial value change or a decline in the norm's loss of legal status but rather a narrowing of the scope of its application. In Chapter 11, Jorgensen refers to the same tensions, but shifts the focus to US contestations against ICC jurisdiction over nationals of non-parties, i.e. over US personnel in the Afghanistan investigation. In that case, foreign policy beliefs of the US have operated as a major driver of change in the accountability value.

The chapters by Alexandros Tokhi (Chapter 12) and Mirko Sossai (Chapter 13) assess change in the foundational value of international peace and security by scrutinizing the nuclear non-proliferation and nuclear non-use norms. In Chapter 12, Tokhi focuses on authoritarian states' behavioral contestation of and nonadherence to the Treaty on the Non-Proliferation of Nuclear Weapons (NPT)'s nonproliferation norm. He studies the Iranian nuclear crisis to understand why some autocracies respect the norm whereas others violate it and to identify how norm defenders could better address NPT violations. In Chapter 13, Sossai highlights the tension between national interests and values of the international community as an important driver of value change in the nuclear weapons regime. The failure of the nuclear-weapons states to comply with their disarmament obligations prompted a recalibration of the regime's value orientation as demonstrated by the conclusion of the Treaty on the Prohibition of Nuclear Weapons which aspires to protect the value of humanity. This turn was accompanied by a forum shift from the NPT regime to the General Assembly.

The chapters by Conny Roggeband (Chapter 14) and Lea Barbara Kuhlmann (Chapter 15) assess whether gender equality norms—which had been expanded and strengthened in the 1990s—have changed due to opposition to treaty law and countermobilization. In Chapter 14, Roggeband traces changes in legal norms promoting gender equality at the international and national levels. These norms face severe countermobilization, which is enabled by democratic backsliding, a diminishing civic space and access to UN for a. While she finds that the legal status of women's norms has not yet declined, legally protected values are losing their validity in several countries. The complementary Chapter 15 by Kuhlmann casts doubt on the findings that countermobilization dynamics have necessarily affected women's rights. According to Kuhlmann contestations of women's rights have persisted since these rights were first placed on the international agenda but accompanied by numerous (impermissible) reservations and interpretative declarations to the pertinent treaties. Still, she attributes the robustness of women rights and their underlying values to the entrechment of reproductive rights in human rights law and the practices of the UN human rights treaty bodies.

The chapters by Sandra Schwindenhammer (Chapter 16) and Peter-Tobias Stoll (Chapter 17) address sustainability norms—a collection of connected but distinct legal norms that protect the same value of sustainable development. Developed after the Rio Conference of 1992, they have driven further international treatymaking and norm development in related sectors, including trade. They can thus be seen as contributing to the rise of international law in the 1990s. In Chapter 16, Schwindenhammer analyses changes in the value-based legal norms of food security, sustainability, biodiversity, and human health. The validity of these sustainability norms is challenged by regime complexity and technology innovation. Her case study of genetically modified insect technology shows that no central international organization has been able to settle norm collisions. In addition, technological innovation is empowering new (private) norm entrepreneurs, leading to further norm contestation. In Chapter 17, Stoll discusses a related case, the international regulation on trade in genetically modified organisms (GMOs), to examine how the values of sustainable development and the principle of precaution became legally protected and how they have since impacted the course of further legal developments, including WTO dispute settlement. He doubts that 'the value of precaution as initially established by the Rio Conference still stands'.

On the basis of the case studies included in this book, the concluding Chapter 18 infers the broader dynamics of change or metamorphosis in the international legal order and discusses the robustness of certain norms of international law.

# PART I
# CONCEPTUALIZING CHANGE AND RESILIENCE OF (LEGAL) NORMS

# 2
# Norm(ative) Change in International Relations
## A Conceptual Framework

*Antje Wiener*

## 1. Introduction

Current contestations of norms of the "liberal international order" (Lake, Martin and Risse 2021) stand in notable contrast with the appreciation of norms during earlier rise of the UN order of international law in the post-cold war period. This prompts us '"to question certain widely held assumptions about" international law's general development, be they *generally held (factual) expectations* and *(normative) aspirations*'.[1,2] Against this backdrop, the editors of this book have invited scholars from international law and international relations (IR) to assess value change in the international legal order.[3]

To address the intrinsically linked themes of norm change and normative change (*hereafter*: norm(ative) change), this chapter details a bi-focal approach to norms. To that end, it reflects and takes account of the complex and often under-appreciated interrelation between *fact-based* and *value-based* conceptions of norms. The approach is developed from the perspective of IR theory and especially norm contestation research that straddles the boundaries of law and politics. It is argued that, so far, IR scholarship has largely kept the interrelation between fact-based and value-based inquiries of norm change apart.[4] This separation has left a research gap which presents the ongoing and topical challenge of addressing both, the *normativity* of norms in addition to the—by now well-researched—*normalcy* of norms. Of these two tiers, each serves as an indicator for norm(ative) change: normalcy refers to fact-based

[1] Research for this chapter has been conducted in the context of the Cluster of Excellence 'CLICCS – Climate, Climatic Change, and Society', especially B2, at the Center for Earth System Research and Sustainability (CEN) of Universität Hamburg, Germany funded by the German Research Foundation / Deutsche Forschungsgemeinschaft (DFG) Project Number: 390683824. I am grateful for this support. For research assistance I thank Deborah Kirchgässner and Paula Bäurich.

[2] Heike Krieger and Georg Nolte, 'The International Rule of Law – Rise or Decline? – Points of Departure', KFG Working Paper Series No 1, 5; emphasis added AW.

[3] Heike Krieger and Andrea Liese, Chapter 1 in this book.

[4] Toni Erskine, 'Normative International Relations Theory' in Tim Dunne, Milja Kurki, and Steve Smith (eds), *International Relations Theory: Discipline and Diversity* (OUP 2013); Jonathan Havercroft, 'Social Constructivism and International Ethics' in Brent J Steele and Eric A Heinze (eds), *Routledge Handbook on Ethics in International Relations* (Routledge 2018). For an update including both perspectives, see especially Phil Orchard and Antje Wiener (eds), *Contesting the World: Norm Research in Theory and Practice* (Cambridge University Press forthcoming).

Antje Wiener, *Norm(ative) Change in International Relations* In: *Tracing Value Change in the International Legal Order*. Edited by: Heike Krieger and Andrea Liese, Oxford University Press. © Antje Wiener 2023.
DOI: 10.1093/oso/9780192855831.003.0002

change, and in turn normativity indicates value-based change. As Jonathan Havercroft has shown, the predominant interest in the latter has generated a perception of 'cryptonormativity' that derives the 'goodness' of liberal norms from behaviour rather than from values.[5]

To reverse this bracketing of a value-based perspective on norms, this chapter sketches a conceptual framework that centres on practice-based norm(ative) change. Building on theories of contestation and interactive international law, it argues that a turn towards practices of contestation and validation enables us to assess degrees of 'sustainable normativity'[6] that reflects the state of legitimacy in global order.[7] Following the *quod omnes tangit* principle (what touches all must be approved by all)[8] the framework centres on the questions 'whose practices count?' (observation) and 'whose practices ought to count?' (evaluation).[9] To establish the state of sustainable normativity, empirical research begins from observing global norm contestations, to then follow them to local sites in order to evaluate affected stakeholders' access to norm contestation and validation in light of the normative opportunity structures that set the conditions for norm(ative) change locally. It then engages selected stakeholder groups' respective discursive interventions in a global multilogue to identify norm(ative) change.

The remainder of the chapter is organized in three sections. The next Section 2 presents three axioms underlying the conceptual framework to study norm(ative) change. They are visualized by a triangular operation to analyse norm(ative) change in relation with practices and norms.[10] Section 3 recalls three key interests that have guided IR norms research after the return to norms in the late 1980s. They include, first, allocating change in and through practice; second, identifying behavioural change with reference to norm-following; and third, identifying norm(ative) change with reference to discursive practice. Section 4, the *final* section of the chapter, presents the two analytical tools of the conceptual frame, namely, the norm typology and the cycle-grid model. It also indicates how to apply these tools with reference to illustrative case scenarios. The conclusion recalls the key elements of the conceptual framework for research on norm(ative) change in IR in light of the challenge of establishing sustainable normativity in the global order.

## 2. Three Axioms for Studying Norm(ative) Change

This book's theme is topical, for it sheds light on the general question of how to frame research on normative change and which methods to apply. *How do we, as students of*

[5] Havercroft (n 4) 116; Jason Ralph, 'Norms, Normativity and Pragmatist Justification. Advancing the 'third move' in Norm Studies', in: Orchard and Wiener, *Contesting the World* (FN 4).

[6] Antje Wiener, *Contestation and Constitution of Norms in Global International Relations* (CUP 2018)chapter 3.

[7] Here, the Theory of Contestation refers to the 'legitimacy gap' in global governance, for example, Antje Wiener, *A Theory of Contestation* (Springer Verlag 2014) chapter 3.

[8] David Owen and James Tully, 'Redistribution and Recognition: Two Approaches' in Anthony Simon Laden and David Owen (eds), *Multiculturalism and Political Theory* (CUP 2007).

[9] Wiener, *Contestation and Constitution* (n 6) 1.

[10] See Figure 2.1.

*international law and IR, answer this question about normative change?* This chapter approaches the question from the perspective of an IR scholar. It offers a conceptual framework to understand and explain norm-change and normative change (hereafter: norm(ative) change). In doing so, it engages an 'international relations perspective', which, as the editors stress, 'is well suited to examine if, how and why values embodied in international norms are changing'.[11] The key objective lies in offering a conceptual frame that takes into account the societal context (such as especially socio-cultural background knowledge) and the political rules of engagement (such as the normative opportunity structure) which constitute the environment in which norm(ative) change takes place through practice.[12]

Three axioms inform the conceptual frame. First, norms lie *in* the practice and therefore all practices are normative.[13] Second, given that what touches all must be approved by all (*quod omnes tangit*), analysing norm(ative) change must acknowledge both fact-based (whose practices count) and value-based (whose practices ought to count) drivers of norm(ative) change.[14] And, third, following the theories of contestation[15] and, relatedly, interactive international law[16] the leading normative claim holds that 'only a contested norm can ever be a good norm'.[17] Against this backdrop, this chapter addresses value decline and norm transformation as interconnected phenomena that are part of a larger historical process of global norm(ative) change. In a nutshell, it proposes a bi-focal approach to norms that conceptualizes the fact-based and value-based dimensions of norms as inter-related, and details a conceptual framework to study norm(ative) change.

The general argument begins from the observation that despite the widely shared constructivist understanding that norms and their meanings are context-dependent,[18] norms research has predominantly addressed the effect of norms on behavioural change, and especially the behaviour of states.[19] Essentially, therefore, we know more about the practice of norm-following and strategies to enhance or enforce compliance, than about norm-generation as a bottom-up process that centres on relations between people, including individuals.[20] The former demonstrates whether a

[11] Krieger and Liese (n 3) 5–6.

[12] Martha Finnemore and Stephen J Toope, 'Alternatives to "Legalization": Richer Views of Law and Politics' (2001) 55 International Organization 743; Emanuel Adler, *World Ordering: A Social Theory of Cognitive Evolution* (CUP 2019).

[13] Adler (n 12).

[14] Owen and Tully (n 8).

[15] Wiener, *A Theory of Contestation* (n 7).

[16] Jutta Brunnée and Stephen J Toope, *Legitimacy and Legality in International Law* (CUP 2010).

[17] Antje Wiener, 'The Concept of Contestation of Norms – An Interview' in Michael Reder and others (eds), *Yearbook on Practical Philosophy in a Global Perspective* (YPPGP-JPPGP) (4th edn, Karl Alber Publishing 2020).

[18] Friedrich Kratochwil, 'The Force of Prescription' (1984) 38 International Organization 685; Mona L Krook and Jacqui True, (2012) 'Rethinking the Life Cycles of International Norms: The United Nations and the Global Promotion of Gender Equality' (2012) 18 European Journal of International Relations 103; Antje Wiener, 'The Dual Quality of Norms and Governance beyond the State: Sociological and Normative Approaches to "Interaction"' (2007) 10 Critical Review of International Social and Political Philosophy 47.

[19] Peter J Katzenstein (ed), *The Culture of National Security. Norms and Identity in World Politics* (Columbia University Press 1996); Martha Finnemore and Kathryn Sikkink, 'International Norm Dynamics and Political Change' (1998) 52 International Organization 887.

[20] Sassan Gholiagha, *The Humanisation of Global Politics: International Criminal Law, the Responsibility to Protect, and Drones* (CUP 2022); Maren Hofius and others, 'Den Schleier lichten? Kritische

'powerful' or 'robust' norm matters to state actors.[21] The latter asks whose practices count, and whose practices ought to count in order to achieve legitimacy of governance norms, thereby raising normative questions that move norms research beyond facts and towards values.[22] By doing so, this approach ultimately seeks to establish whether a normative order is based on equal access to contestation for its constituent agents, identifying access to contestation as the condition for sustainable normativity based on ethical and legal terms.[23]

With regard to the legitimacy and legality of the international legal order, a bi-focal approach that is able to capture both fact-based and value-based triggers of norm(ative) change is therefore key. Regarding effects on the international legal order, it is proposed to examine norm-generative practices of contestation in order to identify norm(ative) change and establish how it affects the modicum of 'sustainable normativity, i.e. a widely-shared perception of legality or justice that corresponds with a given social environment' required for maintaining the legitimacy of the international legal order.[24] To document the point, this chapter turns to the practices that are—actually—carried out (ie 'the doing') vis-à-vis a norm that works in and/or emerges from a given context such as a socially constituted and politically regulated order. It is argued that by studying norm-generative practices rather than norm-following practices, it becomes possible to identify pathways to participation via 'organizing principles' at the meso-scale of global order.

With a view to undertaking the empirical research steps that lead to sites of contestation and facilitate the database to carry out normative evaluation, it is important to note that while interrelated, research on 'norm' change and research on 'normative' change have been largely addressed by distinct methodological and conceptual frames. To take account of norm(ative) change that includes both as interrelated, this chapter recalls the key features of the 'bi-focal' approach which connects ethical principles with social practices.[25] It is argued that in order to establish the effect that norm contestations have on change of the global order, it is necessary to overcome the bi-furcated perspective that either addresses 'norms as social facts' or 'as ethical values'.[26] To that end, the chapter recalls the 'bi-focal'—empirical and normative—approach which 'postulates that both the legitimation of norms and the generation of norms

Normenforschung, Freiheit und Gleichberechtigung im Kontext des "Arabischen Frühlings"' (2014) 21 Zeitschrift für Internationale Beziehungen 85.

[21] Thomas Risse, Steve C Ropp, and Kathryn Sikkink (eds), *The Power of Human Rights: International Norms and Domestic Change* (CUP 1999); Nicole Deitelhoff and Lisbeth Zimmermann, 'Norms under Challenge: Unpacking the Dynamics of Norm Robustness' (2019) 4 Journal of Global Security Studies 2.

[22] Wiener, *A Theory of Contestation* (n 7); Wiener, *Contestation and Constitution* (n 6).

[23] Brunnée and Toope (n 16); James Tully, 'The Unfreedom of the Moderns in Comparison to their Ideals of Constitutional Democracy' (2002) 65 The Modern Law Review 204; Wiener, *Contestation and Constitution* (n 6).

[24] Wiener, *Contestation and Constitution* (n 6) 38; citing Kratochwil (n 18); Owen and Tully (n 8); Rainer Forst, 'The Justification of Human Rights and the Basic Right to Justification: A Reflexive Approach' (2010) 120 Ethics 711; Brunnée and Toope (n 16).

[25] Havercroft (n 4); Wiener, *A Theory of Contestation* (n 7); Eglantine Staunton and Jason Ralph, 'The Responsibility to Protect Norm Cluster and the Challenge of Atrocity Prevention: An Analysis of the European Union's Strategy in Myanmar' (2020) 26 European Journal of International Relations 660.

[26] Havercroft (n 4) 116.

come about not via compliance, but via contestation'.[27] According to this approach, which draws on James Tully's public philosophy, conflict is a form of justice.[28]

Against this backdrop and following the theory of contestation, the focus lies on the distinct practices of 'reactive and proactive contestation'. This practice-based framework to study norm(ative) change aims to map scenarios of stakeholder engagement at local sites. It therefore assesses the legitimacy of the international order through case-based research of norm(ative) change that also facilitate perspectival claims on long-term conditions that are indicated by degrees of sustainable normativity. Conceptually speaking, this framework zooms in on the conditions that facilitate access to practices of contestation as the drivers of norm(ative) change. To establish the conditions of affected stakeholders' access to these practices, the conceptual framework allows for zooming in on local contestations that are conditioned by local 'normative opportunity structures' on the one hand, and then zooming out onto the global stage to explore potential pathways for staging global multilogues including a majority of affected stakeholders to explore 'themes of tension' and 'global issues' that are reflected by the global 'normative structure of meaning-in-use', on the other.[29] Norm(ative) change in a global context is thus assessed with reference to two analytically distinct—local and global—normative structures.

The framework centres on two methodological tools. The *first* is the norm typology that makes norm research viable for interdisciplinary research by distinguishing types of norms according to their moral reach and the expected degree of contestedness. The *second* is the cycle-grid model which facilitates a three-by-three table and the overlaying cycle that enable allocating the respective practices of contestation and types of validation.[30] The argument is developed against the background of the *three main axioms* of norms research which hold that first, norms have a dual quality: they are socially constructed and structuring; second, norms lie in the practice; and third, normative meaning is always contested.[31] Following the interconnected concepts of 'norm(ative) change', 'norms', and 'practice', respectively, the triangle situates early constructivist research on behaviour vis-à-vis norms (point B), with research on norm-change based on discursive practices (point C) on the one hand, and practice-based concepts of norm(ative) change (point A).

The triangle highlights the challenge of that arises for research that seeks to analyse 'norm(ative)' change that takes account of both norms as social facts and norms as ethical values (compare point A at the top of the triangle). To that end, it presents

[27] ibid 122, citing Wiener, *A Theory of Contestation* (n 7).

[28] James Tully, *Public Philosophy in a New Key*, vol 1 (CUP 2008); James Tully, *Public Philosophy in a New Key*, vol 2 (CUP 2008); Tully, 'The unfreedom' (n 23); James Tully, 'Recognition and Dialogue: The Emergence of a New Field' (2004) 7 Critical Review of International Social and Political Philosophy 84.

[29] Wiener, *Contestation and Constitution* (n 6) chapter 8.

[30] Antje Wiener, *The Invisible Constitution of Politics: Contested Norms and International Encounters* (CUP 2008) 66; Wiener, *Contestation and Constitution* (n 6); Figure 2.1 and Table 3.1 respectively, Wiener, 'The Concept of Contestation of Norms' (n 17).

[31] Antje Wiener, 'Contested Compliance: Interventions on the Normative Structure of World Politics' (2004) 10 European Journal of International Relations 189; Wiener, 'The dual quality' (n 18); Uwe Puetter and Antje Wiener, 'Introduction: Contested Norms in International Relations' (2009) 5 Journal of International Law and International Relations 1 (Special Issue); Krook and True (n 18); Clara Winston, 'Norm Structure, Diffusion, and Evolution: A Conceptual Approach' (2017) 24 European Journal of International Relations 638.

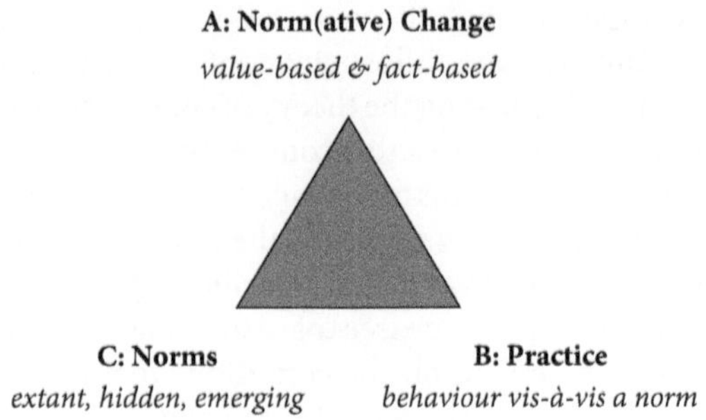


**Figure 1.** Triangle

norms and practices as necessarily related on the base line (compare points B and C of the triangle). Thus, it becomes possible to address change which is indicated with reference to a *norm* itself (does a formerly hidden norm emerge, does an extant norm change, is a new norm constituted?) as well as change that is revealed with reference to the underlying *normative value* of a norm (degrees of legality, legitimacy, or acceptance). While the concepts at points B (practice) and C (norms) of the triangle represent the core elements that have been addressed by constructivist norms research over the past two decades, the norm(ative) practice concept at point A highlights the persistent and ongoing challenge of tackling values in relation with norms which norms researchers have often commented upon.[32] Following the practice-based perspective on norm(ative) change at point A of the triangle, the following section recalls the main constructivist arguments with regard to points B and C of the triangle.

## 3. Indicators of 'Change': Extant Constructivist Norms Research

With the research object of analysing 'norm(ative)' change in IR in view, this section first identifies leading research questions that have been identified by the well-known constructivist literature on norms in IR by scholars working at the interface of IR theory and international law. Second, it turns to the argument about 'degrees of sustainable normativity' global society and how to identify them with the help of a conceptual framework and specific research tools. Throughout, this chapter uses the term 'norm(ative)' rather than 'norm' or 'normative' because neither change takes place in isolation. Norm change is identified with reference to local normative opportunity structure, in turn normative change is identified with reference to global normative structure of meaning-in-use.[33] Through the method of zooming in on local sites of

[32] Compare Finnemore and Sikkink (n 19) 891; Katzenstein (n 19) 5; yet barely managed to master Mervyn Frost, 'A Turn not Taken: Ethics in IR at the Millennium' (1998) 24 Review of International Studies 119; Havercroft (n 4).

[33] Jennifer Milliken, 'The Study of Discourse in International Relations: A Critique of Research and Methods' (1999) 5 European Journal of International Relations 225; Antje Wiener, 'Enacting

contestation and then zooming out towards staging global multilogues, norm(ative) change, norms, and practices are analytically connected.[34] It follows that change is indicated both with reference to a specific norm and with reference to the underlying normative value of a norm. Both are revealed through practice vis-à-vis the norm, this practice is brought to the fore by 'norm-violations'[35] and or 'contested compliance'[36] with an extant norm.

## 3.1 Allocating Change Within and Through Practice

Constructivist norm research has predominantly been interested in addressing the 'dynamics' of 'change' in relation with norms.[37] Notably, when probed for the indicator for 'change', most researchers would not focus to substantial change of *a* given norm but would instead analyse changing patterns of—state—agents' *behaviour* with regard to a given norm. That is, when 'norms returned' to IR with the critical regimes literature[38] in the late 1980s,[39] constructivist scholarship considered changing state behaviour as a key indicator to demonstrate the important impact of norms. As 'social facts' norms were considered as a key indicator of behaviour next to material facts.[40] At the time, and throughout much of the following decade, change was therefore identified with reference to behaviour, and norms, by contrast, were considered as stable structures that had a powerful effect: they were perceived as structuring state behaviour which, in turn, had a stabilizing effect on the power (or, legitimacy) of international law and order.

This allocation of the indicator for change has paved the development of norms research for two decades, and it matters for today's questions with regard to norm(ative) change. Today, as the editors emphasize, studying norm change and normative change is no longer a mere matter of studying behaviour, nor should it be. While studying norm change based on the concept of norms as social facts has by now been well-researched, value-based normative change still remains under-researched. The current challenge therefore lies in the task of addressing norm(ative) change along the two substantively and qualitatively different dimensions of change, namely, studying norms as both social facts *and* as ethical values.[41] Leading questions are therefore twofold. *First*, with regard to norm change, researchers ask whether a formerly hidden norm emerges, an extant norm changes, or whether a new norm is constituted. For

Meaning-in-Use: Qualitative Research on Norms and International Relations' (2009) 35 Review of International Studies 175.

[34] Compare Figure 2.1.

[35] Carmen Wunderlich, *Rogue States as Norm Entrepreneurs* (Springer Verlag 2020).

[36] Wiener, 'Contested compliance' (n 31).

[37] Finnemore and Sikkink (n 19); Deitelhoff and Zimmermann (n 21); Anette Stimmer and Lea Wisken, 'The Dynamics of Dissent: When Actions are Louder than Words' (2019) 95 International Affairs 515.

[38] Friedrich Kratochwil and John Gerard Ruggie, 'International Organization: A State of the Art on an Art of the State' (1986) 40 International Organization 753.

[39] Finnemore and Sikkink (n 19) 890.

[40] Katzenstein (n 19); Finnemore and Sikkink (n 19); John Gerard Ruggie, *Constructing the World Polity: Essays on International Institutionalization* (Routledge 1998).

[41] Havercroft (n 4).

example, with regard to the prohibition of sexualized violence during wartime as a codified fundamental norm of international law (= extant *type 1* norm), the 'culture of impunity' was a formerly hidden norm that emerged through contestations (= emergent formerly hidden *type 2* norm), and the acceptance of 'women's meaningful participation' emerged through behavioural practice (= new *type 3* norm)?[42]

In turn, *second*, in order to identify change with regard to underlying normative values researchers raise questions about changing degrees of legality, legitimacy, or acceptance of a norm.[43] This involves, for example, whether normative opportunity structures are strengthened through the growing acceptance of 'norm bundles' such as the Women, Peace and Security strategy.[44] The conceptual framework presented in this chapter addresses these dimensions and links them based on a 'bi-focal' approach to research on norm(ative) change.[45] Section 3.2 and Section 3.3 address the two dimensions in their turn. And the following Section 4 then turns to the conceptual framework (ie the bi-focal approach) and its two central tools (ie the norm typology and the cycle-grid model) that are offered as a vantage point to study degrees of sustainable normativity.

### 3.2 Behavioural Change: Norm-Following

With the 'return to norms' in IR theory in the 1990s,[46] social constructivists forged a new research programme which centred on 'norm-following'. As Finnemore and Sikkink emphasize when explaining emergence, cascade, internalization as the three stages of the norm 'life-cycle', 'we argue that the primary mechanism for promoting norm cascades is *an active process of international socialization intended to induce norm breakers to become norm followers*'.[47] Constructivists were well aware of the normative environment that set the conditions for compliance with good norms such as for example women's rights, the abolition of slavery, or human rights. That is, 'new norms never enter a normative vacuum but instead emerge in a highly contested normative space where they must compete with other norms and perceptions of interest'.[48]

At the time, the focus on compliant behaviour did reveal large patterns of change in so far as it triggered a paradigmatic shift in how to think about the importance of 'the social' as the fabric that did in fact matter for the constitution of international

[42] Jacqui True and Antje Wiener, 'Everyone Wants (a) Peace: The Dynamics of Rhetoric and Practice on "Women, Peace and Security"' (2019) 95 International Affairs 553, 558 (Table 1); Wiener, *Contestation and Constitution* (n 6) 181 (Table 7.1).

[43] Brunnée and Toope (n 16).

[44] True and Wiener (n 42) 553.

[45] Havercroft (n 4) 116.

[46] As Finnemore and Sikkink argued: 'The "turn" away from norms and normative concerns began with the behavioral revolution and its enthusiasm for measurement.' Finnemore and Sikkink (n 19) 889.

[47] Finnemore and Sikkink (n 19) 902; emphasis added by author.

[48] 'In the case of women's suffrage and later women's rights, norm entrepreneurs encountered alternative norms about women's interests and the appropriate role for women. In other words, new norms never enter a normative vacuum but instead emerge in a highly contested normative space where they must compete with other norms and perceptions of interest. This normative contestation has important implications for our understandings of the ways in which a "logic of appropriateness" relates to norms.' Finnemore and Sikkink (n 19) 897.

orders, borders, and identities, and equally the question whether or not the norms of this order were implemented. This was acknowledged by international lawyers and IR theorists alike.[49] And, social constructivist norms research has identified significant behavioural change with reference to norms that was expressed as 'international norm dynamics and political change'. This research followed a core research interest 'in the role norms play in political change'.[50]

With a 'return to norms' in IR theory in the 1990s[51] social constructivists forged a new research programme which centred on 'norm-following'. What constructivist norms research does very well is to explain norm compliance with reference to behaviour. Behavioural change was explained with reference to organization sociology and there especially March and Olson's rediscovery of institutions and their impact on habit, appropriateness, and social recognition that were observed in given social communities.[52] In this regard, social recognition documents the appropriateness of a norm in a given normative environment. However, to demonstrate that a norm is followed merely documents behaviour vis-à-vis a norm. It does not reveal anything about the substantive quality of a norm. As Toni Erskine notes, 'somebody needs to defend evaluative criteria (however grounded) for moral judgment if there is any hope of the happy marriage between the ethical and the empirical in IR'.[53]

## 3.3 Norm-Change: Discursive Contestation

As long as research brackets norm-generative practices, this substantive quality of normative change therefore remains unknown. To bring this normative quality that end, it must be de-bracketed. Research on contestation has begun to address the task of analytical de-bracketing with varying degrees of success. Effectively, constructivist research that sought to unpack practices of dissent proposed various types of contestation that distinguished discursive from behavioural contestation. For example, Stimmer and Wisken 'differentiate between contestation by means of discourse, which we call "discursive contestation", and contestation by means of actions that affect implementation, which we call "behavioural contestation"'.[54] While both types of contestation define behaviour vis-à-vis a given norm, it is important to note the latent long-term effect that lies buried by the concept of behavioural contestation. In other words, as long as it remains unspecified by discursive contestation, behavioural contestation is likely to generate a lasting unknown threat of a future normative backlash: as long as the underlying normative values that motivate behavioural contestation remain analytically bracketed, important information with regard to

[49] Compare Finnemore and Toope (n 12).
[50] Finnemore and Sikkink (n 19) 888.
[51] As Finnemore and Sikkink argued: 'The "turn" away from norms and normative concerns began with the behavioral revolution and its enthusiasm for measurement.' Finnemore and Sikkink (n 19) 889.
[52] James G March and Johan P Olson, *Rediscovering Institutions: The Organizational Basis of Politics* (Free Press 1989).
[53] Toni Erskine, 'Whose Progress, Which Morals? Constructivism, Normative IR Theory and the Limits and Possibilities of Studying Ethics in World Politics' (2012) 4 International Theory 449, 458–59; in critical appreciation of Richard Price (ed), *Moral Limit and Possibility in World Politics* (CUP 2008).
[54] Stimmer and Wisken (n 37) 516.

identifying policy options to counter norm-breaching, such as for example pathways to participation[55] remains unaccounted for. The following picks up from these distinct practices of norm validation to address the task of de-bracketing norm(ative) change.

In retrospect, it is notable that rather than focusing on practices of contestation and their effect on normative change, social constructivist empirical research prioritized studying compliance with norms as indicated by norm-following and while finding the norm-generative effects of contestation observed by lawyers 'instructive'[56] largely left research on contestation and therewith details of the variety of norm-generative practices to international lawyers. This separation between norm-following and norm-generative behaviour meant that norm-generation was predominantly studied as a formal rather than a socio-cultural process. They criticize social constructivists for being unable to study norm-generative effects, as 'they struggle to explain the emergence and constitution of norms themselves'.[57] This has become a main point of critique of the 'practice turners'[58] who suggest studying the shared knowledge about interconnected elements of the larger practice instead.[59]

The practice-based and relational concept of norm(ative) change that is visualized by the triangle[60] seeks to re-incorporate cultural knowledge. In addition to the international law literature on norm-generative practice as constitutive for the legal validity of a norm, this reference to everyday experience, cultural capability, and background knowledge[61] accounts for norm-generative practices that are constitutive for cultural validity of a norm. Together, social recognition, formal validation, and cultural validation represent practice-based accounts to answer the question of 'whose practices count' in the larger constitutive process of normative order. To recall this norm-generative process, it is important to study discursive practices rather than behavioural practices. For non-discursive behaviour such as social recognition or behavioural contestation merely reflects the workings of a norm that is perceived *as a social fact*. It cannot reveal information about the meanings an agent associates with a norm, that is, the workings of a norm as an ethical value. It follows that to devise the ethical value of a norm from its observed power as a social fact would imply working with the principle of 'cryptonormativism'. As Jonathan Havercroft observed, the 'focus on demonstrating that norms exist and shape the behaviors of states necessarily brackets the international ethics question of whether or not a norm is "good" or "bad," "just" or "unjust"'. And as a consequence of this methodological bracketing of the 'normative' dimension of norms, 'a kind of cryptonormativism has crept into constructivist research'. That is, 'constructivist scholars often assume or imply that a given

[55] See eg the Women Peace and Security (WPS) 'norm bundle', True and Wiener (n 42).

[56] Finnemore and Sikkink (n 19) 915.

[57] Christian Bueger and Frank Gadinger, 'The Play of International Practice' (2015) 59 International Studies Quarterly 449.

[58] Maren Hofius, '"Theory of the Gap": Addressing the Relationship between Practice and Theory' (2020) 9 Global Constitutionalism 169.

[59] Bueger and Gadinger (n 57) 4; citing Andreas Reckwitz, 'Toward a Theory of Social Practices: A Development in Culturalist Theorizing' (2002) 5 European Journal of Social Theory 243, 250.

[60] See Figure 2.1.

[61] Etienne Wenger, *Communities of Practice: Learning, Meaning, and Identity* (CUP 1998).

norm (such as norms prohibiting weapons use, norms against torture, or norms promoting human rights) is good without fully elaborating the reasons for it'.[62]

To address the editors' question about the type of norm(ative) change the crisis of international law implies, requires studying practices of discursive contestation that disclose why and how norms are objected by whom and under which wider normative conditions. The only way of tapping into the meanings that a plurality of affected stakeholders ascribes to a norm's meanings therefore lies in the empirical analysis of discursive contestation. While this has been done quite comprehensively by constructivist norms research over the past two decades, most research has centred on discursive contestation as practiced within given formalized settings.[63] Yet, these formalized settings are exclusively accessible to a selection of privileged agents such as state representatives, bureaucrats and/or diplomats. This implies that the empirically collected 'repertoire' generated through the collection of discursive contestations leaves the majority of affected stakeholders to one side. Rather than taking account of the *quod omnes tangit* principle as a condition of sustainable normativity, these contestatory practices remain exclusive.

Focusing on elite-based discursive contestation is therefore more likely to work inside political communities with formal membership with a functioning liberal representational scheme that relies on a strict separation of internal and external norms (and obligations) is maintained,[64] and which therefore is more capable of keeping latent behavioural contestation in check. In a globalized setting with plural forms of political representation that reflect complex economic, social, and cultural inter-relations the meanings that are associated with norms even though they may be shared in principle become more diverse. Consider for example the general acceptance of fundamental norms (*type 1* norms) such as human rights, democracy and the rule of law which are characterized by an expectation of a low degree of (proactive) contestation, but which will become more contested when it comes to detailed implementation with regard to the specific organizing principles (*type 2* norms) and standardized procedures (*type 3* norms) that are required for their implementation.[65] To understand norm(ative) change and to build on that insight in order to establish and maintain sustainable normativity in global society, therefore requires a conceptual frame that facilitates tapping into the discursive contestatory practices of the plurality of global agents. The following turns to the details of this conceptual frame.

## 4. Norm(ative) Change and Sustainable Normativity

This section details the conceptual framework to study norm(ative) change. It is known as the 'bi-focal' approach because it links the two pillars of norms studies, that

[62] Havercroft (n 4) 117.

[63] Compare especially the literature following Jürgen Habermas, *Moral Consciousness and Communicative Action* (MIT Press 1995) and Klaus Günther, *The Sense of Appropriateness: Application Discourses in Morality and Law* (SUNY 1993); eg Deitelhoff and Zimmermann (n 21).

[64] Beate Jahn, 'Liberal Internationalism: Historical Trajectory and Current Prospects' (2018) 94 International Affairs 43.

[65] Compare Table 2.1.

is, norms as social facts and norms as ethical values. In the following, this section details the elements and concepts of this framework and illustrates their application as it evolves. The framework centres on the norm typology and the cycle-grid model. Both facilitate an interdisciplinary perspective on norm(ative) change that frames norms research as an activity that 'follows the conflict'[66] in order to establish the basis for sustained normativity. The research framework is structured by three ethical principles, each of which initiates distinct research activities.

First, the principle of *contestedness* (P1) reflects diversity and distinct individual background experience which imply that a norm's meanings are always contested when addressed by those affected by it. Therefore, norm contestation is central to establishing mutually shared recognition at local sites where global norms stand to be implemented. The principle of contestedness indicates the first research activity of identifying contestations through sensitizing reading and zooming in on local sites of conflict.

Second, the principle of *quod omnes tangit* (P2) implies the ground rule of what touches all must be approved by all. Therefore, it matters to establish whose practices count in local norm contestations, and relatedly, raise the question of whose practices ought to count in order to improve access to contestation as a condition for sustainable normativity. The *quod omnes tangit* principle leads to the second research activity of mapping local sites of norm contestation.

And third, the principle of *sustainable normativity* (P3) represents a situation where local access to practices of norm contestation and types of norm validation are balanced. It serves as an indicator for assessing the probability of conflict as a consequence of a tip of the balance, when affected stakeholders' access to proactive contestation is threatened. The principle of sustainable normativity enables the third and fourth research activities of identifying norm-change and evaluating normative change, respectively.

The conceptual framework details four research steps: *first*, sensitizing reading identifies and defines a contested norm according to the norm typology; *second*, zooming in on the site of contestation with reference to the cycle-grid; *third*, identifying conditions of access to contestation for affected stakeholders; and *fourth* evaluating norm change with reference to the local normative opportunity structure, as well as normative change with reference to the global normative structure of meaning-in-use.[67] The following summarizes this conceptual framework and illustrates its application with reference to the two methodological tools—norm typology and cycle-grid model—and points of illustration through case scenarios.[68]

[66] George E Marcus, 'Ethnography in/of the World System: The Emergence of Multi-Sited Ethnography' (1995) 24 Annual Review of Anthropology 95, 110.

[67] Wiener, *Contestation and Constitution* (n 6) especially chapter 8.

[68] The framework is developed and illustrated in considerably more detail in its book-length version which details three illustrative case scenarios based on the norms of fundamental rights, the prohibition of torture and the prohibition of sexualized violence against women and girls during wartime; see Wiener, *Contestation and Constitution* (n 6); and for a summary of the framework and research results see ibid 222 (Table 8.1).

## 4.1 Norm Typology

The bi-focal approach seeks to tackle the challenge of de-bracketing norm-generative practices. Taking account of the constructivist axiom that 'while stable at times, in principle, the meaning of norms is always contested'.[69] The primary research step consists in sensitizing reading where the principle of 'contestedness' is conceived as a 'sensitising concept'.[70] Subsequent research 'follows the conflict'[71] about norms to the sites of contestation, establishes the conditions of participation in the conflict for all affected stakeholders, and evaluates norm(ative) change. While contestation lies in the nature of socially constituted entities like norms, the efforts to capture the work of norms have often fallen hostage to the conundrum of multidisciplinarity.[72] To avoid interdisciplinary misunderstandings[73] and enable more focused efforts to study shared research issues based on a terminology that allows for more rigorous transdisciplinary research collaboration,[74] the norm typology helps clarifying the terminology, especially with regard to the definition of types of *norms* as well as the types of *practices* that are brought to bear in relation to them.

Underlying are three assumptions that are devised from qualitative methodologies in the social sciences: *first*, the relation between practice and norms is a necessary condition in order to understand norm(ative) change as indicated by the triangle;[75] *second*, norms come in different types that can be generally distinguished with reference to these indicators: on the one hand, the degree of objection to a norm (observable as practices of contestation) and on the other hand, the moral or ethical reach of a norm (devised from ethical theories). Together the respective degree of contestation and moral reach of a norm represent the analytical relation between norms as social facts and as ethical values.[76] This relational display underlies the distinction of three norm types. Against this background, the typology provides a methodological

[69] Wiener, 'Contested compliance' (n 31); Wiener, 'The dual quality' (n 18); Krook and True (n 18); Winston (n 31).

[70] Herbert Blumer, 'What is Wrong with Social Theory?' (1954) 18 American Sociological Review 3, 7; cited in Glenn A Bowen, 'Grounded Theory and Sensitizing Concepts' (2006) 5 International Journal of Qualitative Methods 1, 2.

[71] Marcus (n 66).

[72] For a philosophical and more general take on disciplinary distinctions including the social sciences and life sciences, note these three definitions: '*Multidisciplinarity* draws on knowledge from different disciplines but stays within the boundaries of those fields. *Interdisciplinarity* analyses, synthesizes, and harmonizes links between disciplines into a coordinated and coherent whole. *Transdisciplinarity* integrates the natural, social and health sciences in a humanities context, and in doing so transcends each of their traditional boundaries' citing Bernard CK Choi and Anita WP Pak, 'Multidisciplinarity, Interdisciplinarity and Transdisciplinarity in Health Research, Services, Education and Policy: 1. Definitions, Objectives, and Evidence of Effectiveness' (2006) 29 Clinical and Investigative Medicine 351, 359, in David Alvargonzález, 'Multidisciplinarity, Interdisciplinarity, Transdisciplinarity, and the Sciences' (2011) 25 International Studies in the Philosophy of Science 387, 388.

[73] The following definition of interdisciplinary applies here: 'interdisciplinarity refers to an activity that exists among existing disciplines or in a reciprocal relationship between them'. Notably, 'interdisciplinarity would not negate the independence of each discipline' Alvargonzález (n 72) 388.

[74] The following definition of transdisciplinarity applies: transdisciplinarity 'concerns transcending the disciplines, going across and through the different disciplines, and beyond each individual discipline', ibid 388.

[75] Compare Figure 2.1.

[76] Havercroft (n 4).

**Table 2.1** Norm Typology

| **Climate Governance** | |
|---|---|
| **Type 1 – Macro: Fundamental principles**<br>*Example: Climate justice, Protection of Humankind (UNCLOS)* | **Moral reach:** (high)<br>**Contestation:**<br>Reactive (low)<br>Proactive (high) |
| **Type 2 — Meso: Organizing principles**<br>*Examples: Common But Differentiated Responsibility (CBDR), Responsibility to Protect (R2P), Deep Decarbonization* | **Moral reach:** (moderate)<br>**Contestation:**<br>Reactive (moderate)<br>Proactive (medium-high) |
| **Type 3 – Micro: Standards**<br>*Example: CO2 emission standards, temperature increase between 1.5 and 2%, fishing quotas* | **Moral reach:** (low)<br>**Contestation:**<br>Reactive (high)<br>Proactive (low) |

reference for research that seeks to establish two things: first, *why* a given norm is considered as more or less prone to contestation; and second, *where* at the distinct scales of order the norm is 'at work'.[77]

Table 2.1 illustrates the distinct norm types with reference to global climate governance where fundamental norms (*type 1*) include protecting human kind[78] and climate justice; organizing principles (*type 2*) include the principle of Common but Differentiated Responsibility;[79] and the standards (*type 3*) of CO2 emission goals and limits of temperature increase, for example. Each norm type entails a distinct degree of moral reach and institutional detail, respectively, which implies that distinct inputs of contestation. For example, the need for proactive contestation is especially high with fundamental norms (*type 1*) which are defined based on *values* leave details of norm implementation to be negotiated amongst stakeholders, on the top of the range, and reactive contestation where standards (*type 3*) represent institutional or legal facts, that stakeholders may object to, rather than critically engage with, on the other. The most important and politically relevant norms are organizing principles (*type 2*) which represent a hybrid quality, insofar as they are derived from values, while leaving a relatively broad and flexible margin for negotiation with reference to procedures and institutions. It is here, at the meso-scale of any order (local, regional, national, global) where the two fact- and value-based dimensions of norms are present. It is here, where issue-related value-based policy strategies are generated through practice.

Together with the cycle-grid model[80] which will be presented further in this chapter, this typology allows for assessing and addressing the sustainable normativity in global society. The types of norms include three types of norms: fundamental norms (*type 1*),

[77] Wiener, *Contestation and Constitution* (n 6) 62.

[78] Convention on the Law of the Sea (adopted 10 December 1982, entered into force 16 November 1994) 1833 UNTS 399 (UNCLOS).

[79] United Nations Framework Convention on Climate Change (adopted 20 January 1994) UN Doc A/RES/48/189 (UNFCCC).

[80] Compare Figure 2.2.

organizing principles (*type 2*), and standardized procedures and rules (*type 3*). As the following will detail, most theories have an established terminology of referring to *type 1* and *type 3* norms, even when not using these typological distinctions. What most theories lack is the concept of *type 2* norms, yet, as I have argued elsewhere, it is usually the *type 2* norm which indicates room for compromise and space for progress with regard to building novel pathways for international policy strategies. It is argued that *type 2* norms represent a central role in the norm-generative process. This is due to the balance between reactive and proactive contestation at the meso-scale of political order. The following first details the typology and then offers illustrative examples before the norm-generative effect of the distinct practices of discursive contestation will be addressed in the concluding section on sustainable normativity.

Fundamental norms entail the broadest possible moral or ethical reach and the lowest degree of contestation as *type 1* norms. These norms include human rights, democracy, sovereignty, the rule of law, torture prohibition, sustainable fishery, the right to fish, and so on. They are located the macro-scale of global order. In the language of international law *type 1* norms are also referred to as peremptory norms, *grundnorms*, or principles.[81] At the opposite end of the typology's spectrum we find standardized or regulations with a very limited moral or ethical reach, yet with a high probability of contestation. These are classified as *type 3* norms. Lawyers also refer to these norms as 'rules'.[82] *Type 3* norms provide the details for implementing *type 1* norms. They are located at the micro-scale of global order and contested on local sites. Alexy summarizes the relation concisely when noting that:

> (R)ules are norms that require something definitively. They are definitive commands. [ ... ] If a rule is valid and applicable, it is definitively required that exactly what it demands be done. If this is done, the rule is complied with; if this is not done, the rule is not complied with. By contrast, principles are norms requiring that something be realized to the greatest extent possible, given the factual and legal possibilities at hand. Thus, principles are optimization requirements.[83]

What has been addressed in less concise terms are 'organizing principles' or *type 2* norms that are located at the meso-scale 'in-between' *type 1* fundamental norms and *type 3* standardized rules. These *type 2* norms play a central role for norm-generative purposes, for they emerge directly from practices through 'doing' politics or policy-making. Examples of these *type 2* norms range from the well-known principles of common but differentiated responsibility (CBDR), the responsibility to protect (R2P) and, relatedly, the less prominent principle of responsibility while protecting (RwP) or the *Solange* principle of European Union politics.[84] They are hence shared by groups of

[81] Compare Erika de Wet, Chapter 5 in this book; Anne-Marie Slaughter, 'Disaggregated Sovereignty: Towards the Public Accountability of Global Government Networks' (2004) 39 Government and Opposition 159; Robert Alexy, 'The Dual Nature of Law' (2010) 23 Ratio Juris 167.

[82] Alexy, 'The Dual Nature of Law' (n 81).

[83] ibid; Robert Alexy, 'The Construction of Constitutional Rights' (2012) 91 Revue française de droit constitutionnel 465, 466.

[84] Compare the prototypes listed in Table 2.1.

policy-makers or politically engaging affected stakeholders. As such, this type of norm comes closest to being generated through discursive practices of contestation (as opposed to mere reiterated interactive behaviour). This norm-generative effect of discursive contestation at the meso-scale is significant with regard to assessing sustainable normativity. The effect remains to be established by the four research stages (ie sensitizing reading, mapping contestation, evaluating access to contestation, identifying norm(ative) change). The following will elaborate on the details of this evaluation with reference to the three practices of norm validation (as the cycle-grid model demonstrates in more detail below).[85]

To summarize, the recourse to a norm 'typology' is carried with reference to interdisciplinary sources drawing on sociological methodology, on constructivist norms research, as well as on public philosophy.[86] It offers three main conceptual reference points for research that seeks to study norm(ative) change. *First*, it offers a conceptual framework that speaks to the state-of-the-art literature in both IR theory and international law. This interdisciplinary context seeks to prevent cross-disciplinary misinterpretations and provide a background for forging more rigorous transdisciplinary research on norm(ative) change. *Second*, by linking types of norms through distinct practices of contestation (ie reactive and proactive) at the macro-, meso-, and micro-scales of global order, it becomes possible to account for and evaluate the norm-generative effect of discursive practice with reference to norms as social facts and norms as ethical values. And *third*, the typology allows for assessing norm change with regard to stages of norm change with regard to categories of emergent, extant, and hidden norms.[87] When applying the typology to study norm(ative) change, case studies will undertake empirical research that identifies types of norms, practices of contestation and norm change with reference to selected situations of conflict where the principle of 'contestedness' is brought to the fore by contested encounters.

[85] The distinction between rules and principles requires establishing the weight of one principle over another when opposing principles are at play. To that end, Alexy proposes a focus on 'balancing'. As he explains, '(R)ules aside, the legal possibilities are determined essentially by opposing principles. For this reason, principles, each taken alone, always comprise merely *prima facie* requirements. The determination of the appropriate degree of satisfaction of one principle relative to the requirements of other principles is brought about by means of balancing. Thus, *balancing is the specific form of application of principles*.' Alexy, 'Constitutional Rights' (n 83) 466; emphasis added by author.

[86] The norm typology has been developed through interdisciplinary conversations over the past two decades. It was kicked off by recurring critical encounters in academia and beyond that centred on diverging interpretations of the citizenship norm: while some defined citizenship according to the standardized rules and regulations that followed from the status, others regarded it as a fundamental norm with a significant role in the process of state-building. By distinguishing the two norms according to their respective moral reach and expected degree of contestation where the former ranks as a *type 3* norm and the latter as a *type 1* norm, it became possible to consider the findings of the respective empirical research as complementary rather than competitive, and thus make sense of the 'workings' of these respective norm-types. The current chapter summarizes the typology drawing on earlier publications of the typology (see Wiener, *The Invisible Constitution of Politics* (n 30); Wiener, *A Theory of Contestation* (n 7); Wiener, *Contestation and Constitution* (n 6)).

[87] Wiener, *Contestation and Constitution* (n 6).

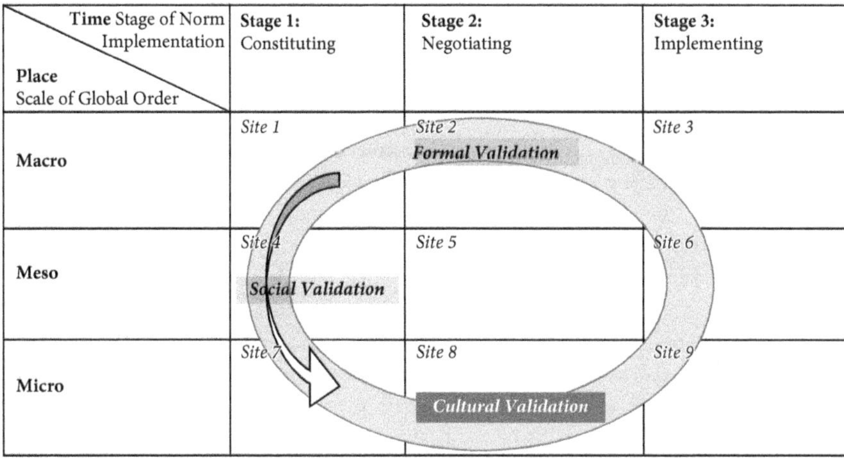


**Figure 2.** Cycle Grid Model
*Source:* Wiener, *Contestation and Constitution* (n 6) 44

## 4.2 The Cycle-Grid Model

To evaluate the effect of the norm(ative) change that is generated through practices of contestation, the cycle-grid model represents a selection of nine ideal-typical local sites on the grid where types of norms, involved stakeholders and local normative opportunity structures are accounted for through local mapping on site.[88] The following details the application of the cycle-grid model.

The grid offers a frame to present the interconnectedness of local contestations with global normative change.

> By establishing a connection between interaction on the ground and contested norms in the global normative structure of meaning-in-use through engagement, the practices of norm validation and contestation are brought to bear through mapping and evaluating the utterances of distinct affected stakeholders. This connection is generated by turning directly to the 'field of interaction in which the conflict arises'.[89]

Against this background, the next steps include identifying practices of contestation: are they merely reactive (ie revealing objection to a norm or its violation) or are they proactive (ie revealing proper access to critical engagement with normative substance)? As well as evaluating access to the three practices of norm validation (ie formal, social, and cultural) that ought to be available to affected stakeholders in the best-case scenario in accordance with the *quod omnes tangit* principle. 'To situate agency on the ground through these practices', the model 'differentiate(s) three practices of norm validation (formal, social and cultural validation) and two types

[88] Compare Figure 2.2.
[89] Wiener, *Contestation and Constitution* (n 6) 30.

of contestation (reactive and pro-active)'.[90] In this regard, praxiography suggests the method of 'zooming in on a distinct practice, a crisis situation, or an object'[91]. The method is helpful for examining practices of norm validation on site.

The model reflects the bi-focal approach with reference to the distinction of nine sites that allow for allocating and zooming in on local sites of contestation (on the grid) and, in addition, for evaluation of the conditions of access to contestation that constrain or enable affected stakeholders' participation in norm-generative practice on these sites (on the cycle). The three practices of norm validation (formal, social, and cultural) demonstrate the range of options. In the best-case scenario, the most powerful stakeholders will have access to all three practices of norm validation and therefore achieve the highest degree of legitimacy, therewith sustaining the legality of a norm. By contrast, in the expected everyday scenario affected stakeholders will be expected to enjoy access to contestation that is constrained according to societal, political, geographic, or economic conditions on site. This bi-focal approach thus expands social constructivist research that centred on norm-following behaviour[92] insofar as it adds three practices of norm validation that have been developed from the '"political approach" to norm conflict that begins with a conflict instead of with a norm, and then turns to "struggles over recognition" about a norm'.[93]

While earlier constructivist research stressed constitutive over evaluative norms and hence established an analytical preference for the normalcy of norms,[94] the resulting emphasis on constitutive practices leaves room to add a normative dimension that seeks to appreciate the norm-generative effect of all practices of validation, that is, formal validation, social recognition (aka habitual validation), and cultural validation. The cycle model is designed to take account of both contingent and principled conditions that influence norm implementation. *Three research assumptions* follow for allocating practices of reactive and proactive norm contestation empirically. First, given the indication of breaches with extant fundamental norms through objection by affected stakeholders, reactive contestation is expected to occur on Sites 3, 6, and 9 (ie the macro-, meso-, and micro-scales at the implementing stage). Second, pending on the involved stakeholders and the local conditions for critical engagement with these breaches, proactive contestation is most likely to take place at Sites 2, 5, and 8 (ie the macro-, meso-, and micro-scales at the negotiating stage). And third, depending on the affected stakeholder's position vis-à- vis formal government institutions, both reactive and proactive contestation may take place at Sites 1, 4, and 7 (ie the macro-, meso-, and micro-scales at the constituting scale). Notably, the ascription of the distinct scales of global order depends on the contestation repertoire within the wider global context. For example, the allocation of, say, state representatives engaging in contestatory practices depends on their position vis-à-vis a given norm conflict. That

[90] ibid.

[91] Bueger and Gadinger (n 57) 9; Maren Hofius, 'Community at the Border or the Boundaries of Community? The Case of EU Field Diplomats' (2016) 42 Review of International Studies 939, 942.

[92] As shown in Section 1.

[93] Wiener, *Contestation and Constitution* (n 6) 38; Owen and Tully (n 8) 267.

[94] Katzenstein (n 19).

is, in case scenarios that examine globally constituted norms, state representatives are located on Site 7.[95]

To summarize, by allocating contestations to sites, empirical research establishes where distinct groups of stakeholders engage. Given the importance of dialogue for achieving shared positions (such as organizing principles) or pathways for policy-making to counter breaches of norms, stakeholders would need to engage on the same site. This stands to be examined empirically.[96] The cycle-grid model advances an 'agency-centred vantage point' that emphasizes the question of 'access'. That is, who among the affected stakeholders has the opportunity, if not the right, to partake in this interaction? In most cases of conflict about extant fundamental norms in IR, access to norm validation and contestation remains clearly restricted (ie favouring state representatives operating through international organizations). And the access opportunities become even more exclusive with court proceedings. The exploratory approach circumvents these restrictions by putting affected stakeholders into a dialogue, even though they have—most likely—not been in a real-time conversation.[97] Drawing on the principles of mutual recognition and mutual elucidation that are central to Tully's public philosophy,[98] the link is performed by academic intervention when zooming out of a local conflict. That is, following the conflict allows for zooming in on a conflict site, mapping the details and evaluating access to then intervene by establishing a series of inter-textual encounters. The intention is to 'give affected stakeholders a "virtual voice" in the global multilogue':[99]

> Following from the exercise of allocating stakeholders and compiling contestation repertoires, the next research endeavour identifies the conditions of access to norm validation. This assessment of access to practices of norm validation is undertaken to in order to evaluate the cultural underpinnings of the norm-change that is generated through these contestations. The evaluation is facilitated by the spatio-temporal allocation of practices of norm validation at each site, and by taking spatio-temporal stages of governance and socio-cultural layers of society into account. Notably, the cycle metaphor is used to indicate conditions of unequal access to norm validation. The three practices are *on* the revolving cycle, and the arrow indicates the condition that, in principle, each practice ought to be accessible for all stakeholders at all times. This is not the case in practice, however because contingent normative opportunity structures apply. To document that, research examines which practice is accessible to whom. This is achieved through the method of zooming in on sites of contestation. At each site affected stakeholders encounter themselves in a contingent context that enables or constraints distinct options of access to three practices of norm validation.[100]

[95] This is the case in the torture prohibition case scenario, Wiener, *Contestation and Constitution* (n 6) chapter 6.

[96] Wiener, *Contestation and Constitution* (n 6) 43–44; emphasis added.

[97] ibid 30.

[98] See especially James Tully, 'Deparochializing Political Theory and Beyond: A Dialogue Approach to Comparative Thought' (2016) 1 Journal of World Philosophies 1; James Tully, 'Reciprocal Elucidation' in Dimitrios Karmis and Jocelyn Maclure (eds), *Civic Freedom in an Age of Diversity: The Public Philosophy of James Tully* (McGill-Queens University Press) (2023).

[99] Wiener, *Contestation and Constitution* (n 6) 4.

[100] ibid 44–45.

## 5. Conclusion

In order to address the question 'Whose practice counts?' in global norm conflicts, the cycle-grid model offers a framework to illustrate a conflict that usually centres on an extant *type 1* norm. This is achieved through the method of sensitizing reading as the first of four steps to analyse norm(ative) change. The second step then follows the conflict to locate it on one of the nine ideal-typical sites on the cycle-grid model[101] to identify affected stakeholders. To address the question 'Whose practices ought to count?', stakeholders' access to the practices of contestation (ie reactive = objection only, or proactive = critical engagement with the norm's substantive values) and the three types of norm validation (formal, social, cultural) is assessed and evaluated against the *quod omnes tangit* principle and the local normative opportunity structure which defines the local conditions of participation.[102] It is therefore key to understanding the conditions of sustainable normativity in a given case. Typically, research will seek to group affected stakeholders according to their claims regarding a given norm conflict. And it will then organize interventions in a series of settings according to the time and place of these interventions. To analyse norm(ative) change it is helpful to study practices of contestation prior to and following a point in time when a significant change with regard to the quality of a norm has been accomplished. For example, with regard to global climate governance, such moments are represented in 1995 with the Kyoto Protocol, with regard to the prohibition of sexual violence the moment is represented by Resolution 1325 that established Women, Peace and Security policy in 2000, and so on.

By reconstructing the reactive and proactive contestations about the breaches with a given norm, it becomes possible to demonstrate how extant norms are contested, how hidden norms come to the fore, or, how new norms emerge. Of key interest with regard to the goal of achieving sustainable normativity, that is, a balance between access to reactive contestation allowing stakeholders to voice objection on the one hand, and proactive contestation enabling stakeholders to critically engage with a norm's substance on the other, are emerging organizing principles (*type 2* norms) and/or pathways towards them. The cycle-grid model's distinction among three practices of norm validation helps bringing a second—previously hidden—*type 2* norm to the fore.

The purpose of applying a bi-focal approach to study the norm(ative) effect of a norm conflict lies in establishing whether a change of the normative opportunity structure merely contributed to *institutional change within the normative opportunity structure*, or, whether the contestations (ie the practice repertoire of a given conflict) might potentially have a *wider transformative effect on the global normative structure of meaning-in-use*. Two research assumptions guide the analysis. First, in a sub-unit of global society (ie as demonstrated by practices on site) the degree of sustainable normativity is expected to rise with balanced access to reactive and proactive contestation on behalf of affected stakeholders. Second, and relatedly, when this balance is threatened and reactive contestation prevails, the potential for political conflict beyond a sub-unit grows (ie as demonstrated by practices on $n + 1$ sites). To examine the effect

[101] See Figure 2.2.
[102] Compare also Brunnée and Toope (n 16).

of both practices of contestation over the two periods (ie settings 1 and 2 in a given case scenario), the empirical research zooms in on the contestations and maps these within a global multilogue. Against this background, multiple and distinct contributions within a conflict that is mapped over time, are reconstructed with reference to specific utterances and then evaluated with regard to novel norms and global normative change. This reconstruction of contestations that form part of a global norm conflict follows the step of sensitizing reading. It shows how access to the two types of contestation (ie reactive or proactive) and the three practices of norm validation (ie formal, social, and cultural) in reflection of the normative opportunity structure on site, works on normative change in global society.

The cycle-grid model offers the framework for identifying norm validation at local sites. Sensitizing reading—applying the principle of contestedness (P1)—indicates instances where the sexual violence norm is breached. The conceptual framework features an agency-centred approach that begins from the practice to explore its effect on norm change. It facilitates studying contestation repertoires for a given norm conflict and evaluating affected stakeholders' opportunities to generate norm appropriation through access to norm validation as the platform for proactive contestation. In a chosen case scenario the run-up to a 'landmark' moment in the trajectory was indicated by *re*active contestation, and the follow-up brought *pro*active contestations to the fore as the driver for normative change and, more generally normative change, as it were. The potential for norm appropriation is probed against the principle of sustainable normativity (P3) and the potential for proactive contestation is probed against the *quod omnes tangit* principle (P2). The sensitizing reading is guided by the principle of contestedness (P1), seeking to locate local contestations according to stages of norm implementation and scales of global order. The cycle-grid model thus serves as a frame to allocate practices of contestation on the *grid* and, relatedly, determine the conditions for specific stakeholders' proactive contestation based on the *cycle*'s three practices of norm validation. As such the cycle-grid model seeks to move beyond a research operationalization from the starting point of a choice between a pre-defined 'bottom-up' or 'top-down' perspective. Instead, it allows researchers to take into account the impact of crisscrossing normative orders which do not develop along state-centred organizational patterns, and shed light on crisscrossing stakeholder practices that engage with these orders.

To summarize, the bi-focal approach facilitates a frame to demonstrate how practices of contestation and norm validation change the meaning-in-use throughout the process of norm implementation.[103] According to this frame, empirical research is based on a principled evaluation of norm(ative) change. That is, in addition to observable norm change, the moral reach of this change is evaluated by taking the *quod omnes tangit* principle (P2) and the *sustainable normativity* principle (P3) into account when studying norm(ative) change in global society. To account for crisis effects

[103] For the latter, see also Laura Shepherd's insightful article on NGOs and the UNSC as the two main sites of 'authority' for the construction of meaning in the UN policy process; see Laura J Shepherd, 'Power and Authority in the Production of United Nations Security Council Resolution 1325' (2008) 52 International Studies Quarterly 383, 384, quoting Dvora Yanow, *How Does a Policy Mean? Interpreting Policy and Organizational Actions* (Georgetown University Press 1996).

of international law, the illustrative case that was summarized in Section 4, followed a global conflict to the local sites where affected stakeholders engaged in contestations about breaches of the norm. The underlying ethical goal consists in countering injustice, the empirical study asks whether the negotiation and implementation of the sexual violence prohibition norm has generated organizing principles that facilitate novel pathways of participation (ie measures or policies that enhance access for affected stakeholders).[104]

Following the cycle-grid model, the best possible outcome of proactive contestation consists in emergent *type 2* norms that enhance access to norm validation for affected stakeholders. These organizing principles are key indicators of norm(ative) change. When taking into account that, by definition, *type 2* norms are key to establishing and maintaining a *modicum* of normative sustainability (ie medium moral reach and degree of contestation), they point towards pathways for enhanced participation (ie 'entry points' bringing stakeholders into policy-making and/or politics). Given contingent environments in each global conflict scenario, outcomes are expected to differ. For example, proactive contestation may either generate more than one *type 2* norm, or shed light on other previously hidden norms. If the latter is the case, the sensitizing reading of available primary and secondary sources will add to the literature on both empirical and normative accounts, as it were.

Notably, the bifocal approach emphasizes the local-global co-constitution of norm(ative) change. For each norm conflict represents global proportions insofar as it comes to the fore through objections to the perceived situation of injustice from the perspective of affected stakeholders at a variety of locations. When presented as a process spanning an arc from the constitution of an extant norm through contestations of norm breaches to the re-constitution of the global normative structure of meaning-in-use, these trajectories reveal critical engagements that bring cultural background capabilities to bear. The trajectories are contingent. They span norm contestations which are shaped by a variety of contingencies which the cycle-grid model allows to locate (grids) and evaluate (cycle).

[104] The pathways reflects what is called 'entry points' for addressing impacts on Sexual and Gender Based Violence (SGBV); see <www.unhcr.org/sexual-and-gender-based-violence.html> and recurrence of conflict, for example, at present through International Financial Institutions (IFIs) in the policy debate.

# 3

# Is Winter Coming?

## Norm Challenges and Norm Resilience

*Wayne Sandholtz*

### 1. Introduction

International norms display a paradoxical duality in that they are always in a state of both stability and change. Stability is necessary in order for norms to play their role of shaping behaviour and expectations, but change is also necessary, as rules must adapt to the endless variety of experience and to the changing needs of those who live under them. Change is usually incremental and piecemeal when it occurs in forums and processes that are familiar, like negotiation or litigation. But change is unsettling when it is rapid or far-reaching. Current challenges to a variety of basic regional and international norms lead us to wonder if fundamental rules that have organized relations among states are being weakened or even abandoned. Perhaps, even the values underlying the current systems of international norms and law are in question.

Norms are coming under stress both from non-compliance and from challenges to their underlying validity. Indeed, some of the foundational norms of the post-war order—free trade, the prohibition of the use of force, the sanctity of basic human-dignity rights—have recently been called into question. A brief overview outlines the breadth of the challenges; the lists below are illustrative, not exhaustive.

#### 1.1 The Use of Force

Commentators have seen military interventions as evidence of the erosion of the prohibition on the threat or use of force codified in Article 2(4) United Nations (UN) Charter:

- North Atlantic Treaty Organization (NATO) bombing campaign in Kosovo, 1999;
- United States (US) invasion of Iraq, 2003;
- NATO bombing in Libya, 2011;
- Russian annexation of Crimea, 2014;
- Russian invasion of Ukraine, 2022.

Wayne Sandholtz, *Is Winter Coming?* In: *Tracing Value Change in the International Legal Order.* Edited by: Heike Krieger and Andrea Liese, Oxford University Press.  DOI: 10.1093/oso/9780192855831.003.0003

## 1.2 Free Trade

A series of events have called into question the future of multilateral trade regimes:

- The British vote to exit the European Union, 2016;
- Trump's rejection of the Trans-Pacific Partnership, 2017;
- US blockade on World Trade Organization (WTO) Appellate Body appointments, 2017–19,[1] raising fears that the Trump administration's goal was 'to blow up the entire legal framework governing world trade'.[2]

## 1.3 Investor–State Dispute Settlement

The system for resolving disputes between foreign investors and host governments has in recent years become one of 'the most controversial issue[s] in global governance'.[3] Three Latin American countries have withdrawn from the International Centre for Settlement of Investment Disputes Convention and others have threatened to join them.

## 1.4 Political Rights

A turn away from basic norms of democracy and democratic institutions:

- Russia: state control of media, suppression of political opposition, political control of courts;
- Hungary: state restrictions on free expression and press freedoms, political control of courts;
- Poland: increasing state control of media, curbs on political gatherings, political control of courts;
- Turkey: crackdown on political dissent, attacks and restrictions on independent media, political control of courts;
- Venezuela: repression of dissent and political opposition, attacks against journalists, political control of courts.

[1] Eduardo Porter, 'Trump's trade endgame could be the undoing of global rules' *The New York Times* (New York City, 31 October 2017).

[2] See Gregory Shaffer, Manfred Elsig, and Mark A Pollack, 'Trump is fighting an open war on trade. His stealth war on trade may be even more important' *The Washington Post* (Washington, D.C., 27 September 2017); Porter (n 1).

[3] Krzysztof J Pelc, 'What explains the low success rate of investor-state disputes?' (2017) 71 International Organization 559, 559.

## 1.5 Press Freedom

Freedom of the press is under assault around the globe, with rising state control of news media and imprisonment and assassination of journalists:

- Freedom House reports that 'Global press freedom declined to its lowest point in 13 years in 2016 amid unprecedented threats to journalists and media outlets in major democracies and new moves by authoritarian states to control the media, including beyond their borders';[4]
- Major declines in press freedom in Russia, Turkey, Poland, Hungary, Bolivia, Venezuela, Burundi, and Democratic Republic of Congo;
- Explicit threats to press freedom by former US president Trump.

## 1.6 Core Physical Integrity Rights

Serious violations of fundamental physical integrity rights raise concern for the future of the human rights regime:

- US torture in the 'war on terror';
- Large-scale extra-judicial killings in the Philippines;
- Ethnic cleansing of the Rohingya in Myanmar.

## 1.7 Backlash Against International Courts

The golden age of international courts may have peaked, with various international tribunals facing rising resistance or backlash:[5]

- The US blockades the WTO's Appellate Body;
- Burundi and the Philippines withdraw from the International Criminal Court and others threaten to follow suit;
- The European Court of Human Rights ejects Russia and faces backlash from the United Kingdom;
- Venezuela withdraws from the Inter-American Court of Human Rights, the Dominican Republic takes steps in that direction, and other states resist the Court's rulings.

Challenges to international legal norms, the institutions that support them, and perhaps even to the underlying values naturally raise concerns about the direction

[4] Michael J Abramowitz, 'Freedom of the Press 2017: Press Freedom's Dark Horizon' (2017) <https://freedomhouse.org/report/freedom-press/freedom-press-2017> accessed 19 November 2021.

[5] Wayne Sandholtz, Yining Bei, and Kayla Caldwell, 'Backlash and International Human Rights Courts' in Alison Brysk and Michael Stohl (eds), *Contracting Human Rights: Crisis, Accountability, and Opportunity* (Edward Elgar 2018).

of change in international norms and law and about a possible serious retrenchment. Assessing change in underlying values is daunting because these are rooted in world-cultural forces that shift slowly and over periods of decades, if not centuries. Equally important, if current challenges to international norms and law indicate a shift in values, the values being emphasized in the current challenges are also part of the broader world normative structures. That is, the threats to international norms in trade, democracy, and rights generally prioritize sovereignty and state prerogatives. And sovereignty norms are still one of the foundations of the modern international system. If current challenges to international norms represent in part a reassertion of sovereignty, they portend not the emergence of new values but a re-emphasis on values that have been central to international law all along. This is not to argue that a renewed emphasis on sovereignty values would not be destabilizing or threaten the prosperity and basic rights of millions of people. Indeed, the revival of some forms of sovereignty assertions (à la 1930s) would be highly dangerous and potentially destructive.

In this chapter, I explore processes of change and decline in international norms, of which I consider international law a sub-category. Recent developments place at risk some of the gains made under the current order. High-profile instances of non-compliance, and explicit efforts to undermine the validity of core norms, have raised the prospect of a tidal change in fundamental international institutions. But I urge caution in reaching that conclusion too quickly, emphasizing the following points:

1. Norm contestation and non-compliance fluctuate over time, and norm change is continuous. It is difficult at any given moment to determine the trajectory of norm change.
2. International norms have built-in sources of resiliency.

The next section briefly reviews how political science and international relations (IR) have tended to make norm compliance central to the assessment of norm strength, sometimes with the misleading assumption that widespread non-compliance with a norm signals its decay or death. A more useful approach to norm robustness places equal or, at times, greater emphasis on discursive support for (or opposition to) international norms.[6] The third section argues that disputes are crucial to assessing norm strength because actors' beliefs regarding the validity of norms are revealed in those disputes. A discussion of dispute dynamics leads to the argument that norms do not really die, but rather are replaced or modified through disputation. A final section posits three sources of international norm resilience: embeddedness in larger normative structures; domestic incorporation; and institutionalization in law. A brief conclusion outlines some of the challenges ahead.

## 2. The Compliance Trap

When political scientists and scholars of IR became aware again of norms and law in the 1980s, it was probably inevitable that compliance would become a central focus.

[6] For an analysis of discursive practice and normative change, see Antje Wiener, Chapter 2 in this book.

After all, political science has been dominated by behaviourism since the 1960s. Positive political science requires measuring behaviour and explaining it with empirically falsifiable theories. When it came to norms and law, the seemingly obvious choice of phenomena to study was the behaviour of those who are supposed to be subject to norms. Norm compliance is behaviour, it is observable, and it is therefore—in principle—measurable. By following this path, IR and international law scholars have produced insightful empirical research that sheds light on how and why international norms affect behaviour, for which actors, and under what circumstances.[7] But, as this section argues, the assumption that compliance is the key to norm robustness (or decline) leads into a cul-de-sac.

Research on international norms has moved through important stages. Norm scholars first had to show that norms matter, in that they shape interests and conduct. Norm research moved to address the puzzle of how new norms emerge and diffuse. Attention then turned to how norms change over time. Of course, throughout this growth of norm research, there should never have been a presumption that norms could develop in only one direction: emerging, diffusing, being implemented, and finally taken for granted.[8] Nevertheless, when events (as discussed above) seemed to throw important cosmopolitan liberal norms into question (torture, disappearance, free trade), analysts had few tools for understanding how even 'good' norms might weaken, decline, or die. The growing interest in norm robustness and norm decline was a healthy response. Much of the scholarly conversation regarding norm decline and death, however, has revolved around the question of compliance. Unfortunately, the presumed link between non-compliance and norm decline has led to some theoretical dead-ends and clouded some of the core issues—the compliance trap.

The theoretical dead end is the notion that once non-compliance with a norm becomes rampant, the norm ceases to exist.[9] That position is flawed because (among other reasons) it mistakenly assumes that widespread norm violations directly reflect the social status of the underlying norm, that is, the degree to which actors continue to believe that the norm expresses a shared standard of acceptable behaviour. If many actors violate a norm, in other words, it must not be a norm. But actors routinely violate norms that they, and society more broadly, continue to accept as valid.

Moreover, as Kratochwil and Ruggie pointed out, norms are valid counterfactually. That is, the existence of norms cannot be disproven by the observation that they are

[7] Empirical research on international norm compliance is too large to summarize briefly, but representative works include Emilie M Hafner-Burton and Kiyoteru Tsutsui, 'Justice Lost! The Failure of International Human Rights Law To Matter Where Needed Most' (2007) 44 Journal of Peace Research 407; Oona A Hathaway, 'Do Human Rights Treaties Make a Difference?' (2002) 111 Yale Law Journal 1935; Judith Kelley, 'Who Keeps International Commitments and Why? The International Criminal Court and Bilateral Nonsurrender Agreements' (2007) 101 The American Political Science Review 573; Todd Landman, *Protecting Human Rights: A Comparative Study* (Georgetown University Press 2005); Eric Neumayer, 'Do International Human Rights Treaties Improve Respect for Human Rights?' (2005) 49 Journal of Conflict Resolution 925; Wayne Sandholtz, 'Treaties, Constitutions, Courts, and Human Rights' (2012) 11 Journal of Human Rights 17; Beth A Simmons, *Mobilizing for Human Rights: International Law in Domestic Politics* (CUP 2009); Jana von Stein, 'Do Treaties Constrain or Screen? Selection Bias and Treaty Compliance' (2005) 44 The American Political Science Review 611.

[8] Thomas Risse, Stephen C Ropp, and Kathryn Sikkink (eds), *The Persistent Power of Human Rights: From Commitment to Compliance* (CUP 2013).

[9] Michael Glennon, 'How International Rules Die' (2005) 93 Georgetown Law Journal 52.

violated.[10] Violations, even when widespread, do not speak for themselves.[11] All norms are hedged about with qualifications and permissible exceptions. Every rule is encircled by a penumbra of uncertainty, a zone in which its meaning for a specific case is unclear or indeterminate. And many rules bump against other norms that apply, or could apply, to the same act. Many acts, therefore, cannot straightforwardly be classified as norm violations.

Consequently, there must be a second dimension—in addition to the behavioural one—by which to assess whether norms are gaining in strength or declining. Thus, Zimmermann and Deitelhoff note that any assessment of norm robustness (and therefore of changes in norm strength) must take into account both behavioural and discursive dimensions. The latter involves norm 'validity' or the extent to which 'a norm enjoys widespread acceptance of its claims by norm addressees'.[12] Price offers a useful set of questions that the norm researcher should ask when evaluating the status of a potential customary norm. The logic of the questions makes them applicable beyond the subject matter for which Price applies them, namely, customary law and the prohibition of anti-personnel landmines. The analyst should search out evidence of state practice (behaviour) and evidence of how states understand the norms and their violation.[13] Research on norm decline recognizes this key insight. Norms decline when behavioural non-compliance is combined with discursive practices that either fail to defend the existing norm or accept an alternative rule.[14] Panke and Petersohn, for example, argue that if norm violations increase and other actors do not condemn the violations, the norm is weakening.[15] Similarly, McKeown argues that when norm violators offer justifications for their behaviour and other actors accept the justification, the norm may be on a path toward extinction.[16]

I argue that the international law approach for evaluating customary international law (CIL) offers a general model for assessing change in the strength of international norms. The point is not to determine whether or not a particular norm constitutes a norm of CIL. International law scholars contest how CIL should be determined and question the role it should play in international law, even whether it remains a useful category. The point is that both practice and understanding, revealed through argumentation, are crucial to evaluating norm decline. When it appears that a norm is in decline—non-compliance is increasing—the discursive dimension assumes even greater importance. Kirgis proposes a 'sliding scale' with respect to the relative roles of behavioural and discursive dimensions. Translating slightly from the CIL context,

[10] Friedrich V Kratochwil and John Gerard Ruggie, 'International Organization: A State of the Art on the Art of the State' (1986) 40 International Organization 753, 753.

[11] ibid.

[12] Lisbeth Zimmermann and Nicole Deitelhoff, 'Norms under Challenge: Unpacking the Dynamics of Norm Robustness' (2019) 4 Journal of Global Security Studies 2.

[13] Richard Price, 'Detecting Ideas and Their Effects' in Robert E Goodin and Charles Tilly (eds), *The Oxford Handbook of Contextual Political Analysis* (OUP 2006).

[14] I use the terms 'norm' and 'rule' interchangeably. Both are defined as standards of conduct. Some writers treat 'rules' as more formal or precise than 'norms', but that usage simply confirms that they are not different in kind, only in degree along some dimensions (precision, formality).

[15] Diana Panke and Ulrich Petersohn, 'Why International Norms Disappear Sometimes' (2001) 18 European Journal of International Relations 719.

[16] Ryder McKeown, 'Norm Regress: US Revisionism and the Slow Death of the Torture Norm' (2009) 23 International Relations 5, 10.

when state practice is highly consistent, not much evidence of belief in the validity of the norm is necessary. Similarly, strong and widespread belief that a norm exists and is valid is sufficient, even when rule-consistent behaviour declines. But when norm-consistent practice is declining, greater evidence of ongoing belief in the norm's validity is required.[17] In other words, as violations accumulate, what actors believe about the norm in question assumes crucial importance. The challenge then is how to assess actors' beliefs that a norm exists even in the face of rising non-compliance, that is, to focus on potential shifts in legal understanding and interpretation.[18] Those beliefs are revealed through normative disputes and argumentation.

## 3. Disputes, Argumentation, and Norm Viability

Equating non-compliance with norm decline involves an assumption that non-compliance can simply be observed. In fact, non-compliance—like beauty—exists in the eye of the beholder, and the 'beholders' who matter are those potentially affected by the conduct in question. The meaning and significance of alleged rule breaking depend on the interpretation placed on it by the relevant social community. Courts of law offer a highly formalized exemplar of this universal process. When Richard Nixon refused to hand over the White House tapes to the Watergate special prosecutor, was it a legitimate exercise of executive privilege or an obstruction of judicial process? It was what the Supreme Court decided it was, after the two sides presented their arguments.[19] Disputes over the meaning and practical application of international norms follow the same pattern, even though they usually take place outside of a courtroom and without a final dispute resolver.

### 3.1 Disputes Are Not Just 'Cheap Talk'

Disputes are crucial sites for deciphering shifts in the content and strength of international norms. They are crucial because they reveal information, in particular about the beliefs of relevant actors regarding the norms being contested. Those disputes can take place in the UN General Assembly, the Security Council, an international court, a regional organization, or in the daily flow of press conferences, official statements, diplomatic communications, and social media. In these episodes of argumentation, states and other actors announce their views about what the norms in question mean, how obligatory they are, and how they should be applied to specific acts. Disputes thus allow us to observe what is typically difficult to observe: actors' stated beliefs regarding the meaning and the weight of obligation of international norms.

A typical objection to the suggestion that normative discourses matter is that actors will say anything to obtain a better outcome. 'Talk is cheap'. But norm discourses are

[17] Frederic L Kirgis, 'Custom on a Sliding Scale' (1987) 81 The American Journal of International Law 146, 149.
[18] See Thomas Kleinlein, Chapter 4 in this book.
[19] *United States v Nixon*, 418 U.S. 683 (1974).

not always cheap talk, and verbal acts can be as important as other kinds of behaviour.[20] The arguments offered by states and other actors in normative disputes provide useful information regarding their beliefs about the obligatory status of norms, for three reasons.

First, states care not just about immediate outcomes but also about the rules of the game. Rules can advantage some interests and modes of conduct over others. Moreover, rules can be a source of influence and power, mobilizing political or legal action at domestic and international levels.[21] States and other actors, therefore, invest in shaping the rules of the international game. The arguments they offer in disputes express their preferences regarding those rules, and are, therefore, more than cheap talk.

Second, actors have an incentive to express their real preferences regarding the rules. They have little to gain from misrepresenting those preferences. The reason is that if a state expresses an insincere normative preference, and that norm gains supporters and becomes the rule, it can have real, undesired downstream consequences.[22]

Third, because actors care about rules, they also care about the discourses that shape and reshape the rules. The arguments they make in disputes affect those discourses, namely, the kinds of claims that can be influential.[23] Put differently, actors have an interest in shaping the argumentation frameworks surrounding norms they care about. Argumentation frameworks establish boundaries to the kinds of arguments that are considered legitimate and persuasive for a given type of normative dispute.[24] This point applies to normative disputes in general, but it is more visible in judicialized settings, where precedent is a form of congealed argumentation framework. Precedent, in formal terms, has no role in international courts and tribunals. Yet, international courts develop precedent and both judges and litigants invariably invoke it.[25] States, therefore, have an interest in shaping argumentation frameworks and their formalized instantiation in case law. As Pelc has shown in a study of the WTO Dispute Settlement Mechanism, countries invest strategically in WTO litigation in part to influence the development of precedent to their advantage.[26]

[20] Nicholas Greenwood Onuf, *World of Our Making: Rules and Rule in Social Theory and International Relations* (University of South Carolina Press 1989); Thomas Risse, '"Let's Argue!": Communicative Action in World Politics' (2000) 54 International Organization 1.

[21] Simmons (n 7).

[22] Thomas Risse, Steve C Ropp, and Kathryn Sikkink, *The Power of Human Rights: International Norms and Domestic Change* (CUP 1999); Risse, Ropp, and Sikkink, *The Persisting Power of Human Rights* (n 8); Simmons (n 7).

[23] Wayne Sandholtz and Alec Stone Sweet, 'Law, Politics, and International Governance' in Christian Reus-Smit (ed), *The Politics of International Law* (CUP 2004) 263.

[24] Alec Stone Sweet, 'Path Dependence, Precedent, and Judicial Power' in Martin Shapiro and Alec Stone Sweet (eds), *On Law, Politics, and Judicialization* (OUP 2002).

[25] Ingo Venzke, *How Interpretation Makes International Law: On Semantic Change and Normative Twists* (OUP 2012) 16–69; Armin von Bogdandy and Ingo Venzke, 'The Spell of Precedents: Lawmaking in International Courts and Tribunals' in Cesare PR Romano, Karen J Alter, and Chrisanthi Avgerou (eds), *The Oxford Handbook of International Adjudication* (OUP 2013).

[26] Krzysztof J Pelc, 'The Politics of Precedent in International Law: A Social Network Application' (2014) 108 American Political Science Review 547.

## 3.2 Dispute Dynamics

Disputes erupt out of actions that trigger condemnation on normative grounds; they provoke allegations that the act in question violated a norm. On one side, the author of the act in question must persuade others that her conduct complies with the group's norms. Critics of her behaviour will make the opposite argument. As actors argue about which rules apply and how they should be interpreted in the present context, the direct parties to a dispute (for instance, the United States and Afghanistan after the September 11th attacks) are not the only participants in the argumentation. Additional states with some perceived interest (whether material or normative) in the dispute will also join in. Actors make normative bids and counter-bids, attempting to gain support for their favoured interpretation of the rules. One side in a dispute may propose that the conduct being debated instantiates a new norm to replace the existing rule 'If other states reject the proposition, then the projected rule withers away and the original rule stands: reinforced by state practice and common acceptance.'[27]

In a judicialized setting like the International Court of Justice, the Court typically pronounces on which normative claims prevail. In the everyday world of IR, the normative arguments take place in the diplomatic and public spheres. Even when disputes involve the use of force, the contending sides always offer arguments as to why the use of force is legal under international law.

In these settings, actors may well be motivated by material interests and will argue strategically about norms, but to prevail they cannot argue that an outcome should be supported simply because it serves their interests. Indeed, the point is that actors must argue rather than merely assert self-interest. Persuading other parties requires normative arguments, which in turn require, as Elster points out, the ability to argue from a vantage point of at least minimal impartiality.[28] Disputes eventually reach a conclusion regarding the opposed normative claims, and that outcome modifies the rules. In IR, if a consensus emerges, one set of normative claims will be reinforced and perhaps clarified. If neither side 'wins', the norms in question will be left more ambiguous or weaker.

## 3.3 Non-Compliance, Disputes, and Norm Replacement

When non-compliance with a norm appears to be on the rise, the resulting disputes and the arguments they provoke are crucial for revealing how the relevant community views the violations. At a high level of non-compliance, belief in the rule's normativity and validity become crucial. If the norm continues to be broadly accepted it remains valid despite widespread non-compliance. But if acceptance of the norm's validity also declines, then it is in a process of weakening or decline. How do we recognize from disputes and arguments whether belief in a norm's validity is holding or is declining? The following criteria provide general guidance.[29] Whether a norm is being

[27] Malcolm N Shaw, *International Law* (5th edn, CUP 2003) 83.

[28] Jon Elster, 'Strategic Uses of Argument' in Kenneth J Arrow (ed), *Barriers to Conflict Resolution* (W. W. Norton 1995) 246.

[29] See also Price (n 13).

strengthened, maintained, or weakened depends on the degree to which participants in the dispute advance or support 'pro-norm' arguments. Pro-norm arguments acknowledge the validity of the norm and include the following:

---

*From states accused of violating a norm ('accused' states):*

1. Claiming the act actually complies with the existing norm as properly understood.
2. Claiming the act is permitted under a different norm.
3. Claiming the act is a permissible exception to the norm.
4. Claiming the act conflicts with the norm but should not incur liability because of extraordinary circumstances.

*From states alleging a violation ('accuser' states):*

1. Denying that the act complies with the existing norm.
2. Denying that the act is permitted by a conflicting norm, or claiming that the existing norm overrides the conflicting norm.
3. Denying that the act is a permissible exception.
4. Either accepting or rejecting the claim of extraordinary circumstances, which in itself acknowledges the existing norm.

---

Conversely, anti-norm arguments ('validity contestation' in Zimmermann and Deitelhoff's terms[30]) deny the premises underlying the pro-norm arguments. Anti-norm arguments simply reject the norm (claiming that the state is not bound by it), or dismiss its validity or legitimacy. The fewer the actors advancing or supporting pro-norm arguments, and the more numerous the actors endorsing anti-norm arguments, the weaker the norm is becoming.

In some accounts, the endpoint of rising non-compliance and declining belief in the norm's validity (as revealed in disputes and arguments) can lead to norm 'extinction' or 'death'. The idea of norm death is that a particular norm ceases to exist and is not replaced: it is no longer regarded as a norm and does not affect behaviour.[31] The language of norm death or extinction, I suggest, shifts attention away from the normative processes taking place. The term 'replacement' better captures what happens to norms as non-compliance increases and belief diminishes. Norm replacement occurs when an existing norm is no longer seen as valid or as guiding behaviour and actors accept a new or different norm to regulate conduct in that domain.[32]

In some discussions of norm death, extinction of a rule seems to imply that conduct that was formerly regulated becomes unregulated. But a domain of conduct that has been subject to rules cannot return to some pre-normative state of nature or void.[33] The state of nature exists only as a heuristic myth, not as a social reality. It is just as

[30] Zimmermann and Deitelhoff (n 12).

[31] Diana Panke and Ulrich Petersohn, 'Why International Norms Disappear Sometimes' (2012) 18 European Journal of International Relations 719.

[32] Wayne Sandholtz, 'Norm Contestation, Robustness, and Replacement' (2019) 4 Journal of Global Security Studies 139.

[33] David J Bederman, *International Law Frameworks* (3rd edn, Foundation Press 2010) 24.

impossible to replace regulation with non-regulation as it is to un-think a thought. A norm can only disappear in one circumstance: when the entire social system of which it is a part of also vanishes. Norms governing siege warfare disappeared when that mode of combat disappeared. Rules regulating international telegraphy vanished when the telegraph was replaced by telephones and other technologies (though rules on telephony borrowed from norms governing telegraphy). Outside of such contexts of large-scale social change, norms do not disappear but rather are replaced by a different, sometimes contrary, norm. The norm that permitted wartime plunder was replaced by one prohibiting it. The norm requiring declarations of war was based on the principle that wars should be grounded in legitimate reasons and justified.[34] That norm did not disappear but evolved into a requirement that wars must be *legally* justified, which also entails a public offering of legal reasons.

Instead of a normative void, the old or existing rule will continue as the default until it is replaced by a different rule. For instance, in a context in which torture is prohibited, a transition that results in torture being permitted (as some feared was happening in the 'war on terror') would imply a new permissive rule.

Non-compliance—even widespread—by itself does not indicate norm replacement, but it does trigger disputes about the content of norms. Non-compliance with an existing rule 'contains within itself the seeds of a new rule and if it is endorsed by other nations, the previous law will disappear *and be replaced*'.[35] But '[i]f other states reject the proposition [that the violation embodies a new norm], then the projected rule withers away and the original rule stands'.[36] Disputes thus open 'a dynamic [ ... ] marketplace of rules',[37] a marketplace that is both practical and discursive. Actors make normative bids and counter-bids, attempting to gain support for their favoured interpretation of the rules. Competing norms can exist, each with some support: 'there could be a period of time during which the two customs co-exist until one of them is generally accepted'.[38] The 'marketplace' metaphor is apt, but the discursive struggle over making and interpreting rules is also like an ongoing plebiscite in which members of a community define the rules under which they will live. Participants in the dispute try to win 'votes' for the rules and interpretations that they prefer. What share of votes does the new norm require in order to replace the old? No a priori standard is possible, but rules 'should to some extent mirror the perceptions of the majority of states'.[39] If argumentation fails to produce a broad agreement, the norms in question remain subject to continuing contestation.[40] The previous norm is abandoned when actors behave in accordance with the new norm and believe that it is a rule.

[34] Eric Grynaviski, 'The Bloodstained Spear: Public Reason and Declarations of War' (2013) 5 International Theory 238.
[35] Shaw (n 27) 86.
[36] ibid.
[37] Bederman (n 33) 20.
[38] Shaw (n 27) 86.
[39] ibid.
[40] Michael Byers, *Custom, Power, and the Power of Rules* (CUP 1999) 154.

## 4. Norm Resilience

Norms are necessarily resilient. Indeed, it accounts for their 'counterfactual validity'. Otherwise, we would be in a world in which, at some level of violations, the norm ceases to exist. Compliance and disputation clearly matter for the robustness of a norm, but the relationship is not linear and compliance is not the only determinant of norm strength (or decline). The other key determinant of norm robustness consists of actors' beliefs about the validity of the norm. As the rate of non-compliance mounts, the validity of the norm—as expressed by affected actors—assumes decisive importance. This leads to a key source of norm resilience: institutionalization. The more a norm is institutionalized—that is, the more it is incorporated into policy, procedures, law, and organizations—the stronger are the supports for the norm when it is challenged. Or, from a slightly different angle, the more institutionalized a norm is, the greater the political and discursive resources available to norm defenders, that is, to those who advance pro-norm arguments.

Institutionalization enhances norm resilience at both domestic and international levels. Institutionalization includes two key components: (Section 4.1) the embeddedness of norms in larger normative structures, and (Section 4.2) the incorporation of norms into policies, practices, law, and the standard operating procedures of states and other actors. The more norms are institutionalized in these senses, the more resilient they are. Law is a powerful form of institutionalization, not because law has magical properties but because it can channel disputes and argumentation in ways that are norm reinforcing.

### 4.1 Norms Embedded in Larger Norm Structures

International norms are always integrated into larger regimes. A particular norm (do not torture prisoners of war) is embedded in a regime (Geneva law), which in turn is embedded in a larger normative structure (humanitarian and human rights norms), which is embedded in the system of international law. When a norm is part of a broader regime, it both supports other regime norms and is reinforced by them. Those linkages keep individual norms from being abandoned, even when they are subject to non-compliance challenges. When international regimes include organized mechanisms for monitoring compliance, adjudicating disputes, or authorizing penalties, the norms embedded in that regime are buttressed by those supports. The more successful those organized mechanisms are, the more states and other actors come to rely on them and invest in them. States that have invested in a regime are more likely to support its norms when they are challenged. For instance, the former Trump administration in the US challenged international trade norms in a potentially fundamental way, leading to the suspension of the WTO Appellate Body. China, however, having invested heavily in the WTO, has signalled its willingness to continue wo work within the WTO framework.[41]

[41] Gregory Shaffer, 'Governing the Interface of U.S.-China Trade Relations' (2021) 115 American Journal of International Law 622.

Similarly, the prohibition of the use of force, codified in Article 2(4) UN Charter, is deeply integrated into broader norm structures that reinforce it and make it resilient to violations. The prohibition of the use of force is central to the sovereignty norms that are at the foundation of the international system and contribute to its stability. Without a prohibition of the use of force in relations among states, the rights associated with sovereign statehood would be undermined. Interrelated norms that sustain sovereignty—self-determination, non-interference in the internal affairs of other states, independence in foreign relations—also reinforce the prohibition of the use of force and are sustained by it.

More generally, a regime or complex of international rules is not like a sweater. Pulling on one yarn—one norm—will not unravel the whole garment.

## 4.2 Domestic Incorporation of Norms

The idea that international norms gain strength from being incorporated in domestic policies, practices, and law is well established in both IR and international law. One of Simmons's central findings with respect to international human rights treaties is that their most important effects occur domestically, enabling or empowering domestic actors to challenge state non-compliance either through political mobilization or litigation.[42] In the spiral model of human rights norms, the latter stages occur at the domestic level. Under certain conditions, state actors accept the validity of international norms and behaviour consistent with those norms becomes routinized.[43] The transnational legal process model similarly posits a process by which international legal norms are 'domesticated', that is, 'become incorporated into domestic legal systems'.[44] The domestication of international norms leads to 'internalized compliance', or 'obedience'.[45] In a parallel vein, Halliday and Shaffer show how the settling of rules at both domestic and trans- or international levels creates systems of transnational legal ordering.[46]

The upshot for our purposes is that the more broadly international norms are internalized in domestic systems, the more resistance there will be—at both domestic and international levels—to non-compliance. This does not mean that states with domesticated international norms will never violate them, only that countervailing, pro-norm forces will be more empowered to counteract violations. The case of torture in the 'war on terror' illustrates this.[47]

The anti-torture norm was institutionalized in multiple treaties (the Geneva Conventions, the International Covenant on Civil and Political Rights, the Convention

[42] Simmons (n 7).
[43] Risse, Ropp, and Sikkink, *The Persistent Power of Human Rights* (n 8).
[44] Harold Hongju Koh, 'The 1998 Frankel Lecture: Bringing International Law Home' (1998) 35 Houston Law Review 623, 627.
[45] ibid.
[46] Terence C Halliday and Gregory Shaffer, *Transnational Legal Orders* (CUP 2015).
[47] See also Max Lesch and Lisbeth Zimmermann, Chapter 6 in this book, and Dominik Steiger, Chapter 7 in this book.

Against Torture),[48] which were in turn embedded in the larger international human rights regime. Moreover, the anti-torture norm had been incorporated in domestic law and in the military codes of most countries, including the United States.[49] American torture of detainees thus triggered vigorous pro-norm arguments from other governments, NGOs, civil society, and from segments of the United States government itself. The international backlash to US torture, in the form of pro-norm arguments, was powerful. Equally important were the pro-norm efforts by activists, lawyers, and legislators within the United States. Their actions led to legislation and successful court challenges that pushed back the Bush administration's torture policies. It is sometimes overlooked that executive branch legal advisors, in multiple agencies, who were steeped in and committed to the law of armed conflict and international human rights law, also resisted the torture policies and helped to roll them back.[50] In other words, the domestic institutionalization of anti-torture norms, both internationally and domestically, supported pro-norm action. As a result, the anti-torture norm may well have emerged strengthened internationally.

## 4.3 Law and Institutionalization

The argument so far applies to international norms in general, including informal norms, CIL, and international treaty law. What difference does the codification of norms in formal law make? It may be useful to think of treaty law and its associated practices as a form of institutionalization. Legal norms are rules that are created, modified, and applied through pre-defined processes, namely, legal processes.[51] As Weber argued, legal rules constitute the characteristic form of authority in modern society.[52] Indeed, legal rationality is at the core of the modern world polity.[53] Law is thus a basic source of authority in modern IR.[54] In Franck's account, international norms

[48] Geneva Convention Relative to the Treatment of Prisoners of War (adopted 12 August 1949, entered into force 21 October 1950) 75 UNTS 31; International Covenant on Civil and Political Rights (adopted 16 December 1966, entered into force 23 March 1976) 999 UNTS 171; Convention against Torture and Other Cruel, Inhuman or Degrading Treatment or Punishment (adopted 10 December 1984, entered into force 26 June 1987) 1465 UNTS 85.

[49] 18 U.S. Code 113 C – Torture.

[50] Arturo Jimenez-Bacardí, 'The Double Life of Uncle Sam: The United States and the International Laws Banning Torture and Cruel, Inhuman, and Degrading Treatment' in Lucrecia García Iommi and Richard W Maass (eds), *The United States and International Law: Paradoxes of Support across Contemporary Issues* (University of Michigan Press, forthcoming).

[51] Herbert LA Hart, *The Concept of Law* (2nd edn, OUP 1994).

[52] Max Weber, 'Economy and Society: An Outline of Interpretive Sociology' in Guenther Roth and Claus Wittich (eds), *Economy and Society: An Outline of Interpretive Sociology* (University of California Press 1978); Max Weber, 'Politics as a Vocation' in Tony Waters (ed), *Weber's Rationalism and Modern Society* (Palgrave Macmillan 2015).

[53] John W Meyer, John Boli, and George M Thomas, 'Ontology and Rationalization in the Western Cultural Account' in George M Thomas and others (eds), *Institutional Structure: Constituting State, Society, and Individual* (Sage Publications 1987); John W Meyer and others, 'World Society and the Nation-State' (1997) 103 American Journal of Sociology 144.

[54] Jutta Brunnée and Stephen J Toope, *Legitimacy and Legality in International Law: An Interactional Account* (CUP 2010); Byers (n 40); Christian Reus-Smit, 'Politics and International Legal Obligation' (2003) 9 European Journal of International Relations 591; Christian Reus-Smit, 'The Politics of International Law' in Christian Reus-Smit (ed), *The Politics of International Law* (CUP 2004).

created through proper legal process carry legitimacy that exercises a 'compliance pull' on actors.[55] The effects of law on behaviour are thus not driven by enforcement but by legal obligation, which is 'internalized commitment'. And internalized commitment develops where the criteria of legality—right legal process embedded in social context—are present.[56] But even if one does not want to accept that international law has an inherent capacity to motivate compliance, other approaches grounded in rational individualism explain why international law—as law—influences behaviour.[57]

Law, like other forms of institutionalization, stabilizes norms and gives them a source of resiliency. This is not to argue that legal norms are fixed or permanent. They cannot be, as law must adapt to a changing world. In a sense, then, law is like a motion picture. At any given moment—in a particular frame—it appears still. This short-term fixity is necessary for actors, disputants, advocates, and judges to be able to identify and apply the law in a specific temporal context. It is necessary for law to fulfil its functions of guiding conduct, generating reliable expectations about the behaviour of others, solving collective action problems, and facilitating mutually beneficial exchange.

International treaty norms, I would argue, change according to the same general process described above. Violations trigger disputes, which give rise to pro-norm and anti-norm arguments, which in turn lead to revised interpretations of the rules. With legal norms, the disputes are channelled into legal modes of argumentation. In legal argumentation, the boundaries of legitimate discourses are more narrowly defined than in the world of non-legal (social) norms. Legal arguments are bounded by the text of the law, the interpretations arrived at in previous disputes (precedent), and general standards of legal discourse.[58] In any given legal domain, previous rounds of disputation generate argumentation frameworks, that is, shared understandings of the limits of acceptable arguments on either side of a legal question.[59] This channelling effect of formal law operates both in dyadic disputes (where the parties contest directly the meaning and application of a legal instrument) and in triadic dispute resolution (involving a judge or other dispute resolver).[60] Where disputes are resolved in courts or tribunals, argumentation frameworks are highly formalized and meticulously curated in the form of case law, and precedent disciplines the arguments and reasons available to both disputants and judges.[61] In short, formal law adds additional layers of institutionalization that can add resilience to challenged norms.

[55] Thomas M Franck, 'The Power of Legitimacy and the Legitimacy of Power: International Law in an Age of Power Disequilibrium' (2006) 100 American Journal of International Law 88; Thomas M Franck, *The Power of Legitimacy Among Nations* (OUP 1990).

[56] Brunnée and Toope (n 54) 20–55.

[57] Andrew T Guzman, *How International Law Works: A Rational Choice Theory* (OUP 2008).

[58] Lief Carter and Thomas Burke, *Reason in Law* (9th edn, University of Chicago Press 2016).

[59] Sandholtz and Stone Sweet (n 23).

[60] See also Adam Bower, Chapter 10 in this book.

[61] Marc Jacob, 'Precedents: Lawmaking through International Adjudication' in Armin von Bogdandy and Ingo Venzke (eds), *International Judicial Lawmaking: On Public Authority and Democratic Legitimation in Global Governance* (Springer 2012); Armin von Bogdandy and Ingo Venzke, 'Beyond Dispute: International Judicial Institutions as Lawmakers' in Armin von Bogdandy and Ingo Venzke (eds), *International Judicial Lawmaking: On Public Authority and Democratic Legitimation in Global Governance* (Springer 2012); Armin von Bogdandy and Ingo Venzke, 'The Spell of Precedents: Lawmaking in International Courts and Tribunals' in Cesare PR Romano, Karen J Alter, and Yuval Shany (eds), *The Oxford Handbook of International Adjudication* (OUP 2013).

## 5. Challenges Ahead

An array of international legal norms and institutions are currently under stress. The challenges arrive on both dimensions of norm robustness, compliance/non-compliance, and pro-norm/anti-norm discourse. Non-compliance does not necessarily indicate norm weakening, as it can also trigger more assertive defences of the norm in question. It has arguably done so with respect to torture, for example. In addition, as the rate of violations increases, the discursive dimension—the balance between actors offering pro-norm and anti-norm arguments—assumes greater importance. Disputes are, therefore, crucial sources of information about the degree to which actors continue to accept a given norm as valid. The current status of a norm would compare two quantities:

1. the number of states offering pro-norm arguments, with each state weighted by its relative power and the forcefulness of its arguments (the intensity of its preferences); and
2. the number of states offering anti-norm arguments, with each state weighted by its relative power and the forcefulness of its arguments (the intensity of its preferences).

In this heuristic formulation, a growing number of major states that express strong opposition to an existing norm (or support for a rival norm) would be evidence that a norm is weakening.[62]

A worrisome sign in recent years was that one of the world's leading powers—the United States—was challenging existing international norms and the institutions created to sustain them.[63] The United States was undermining norms and institutions dealing with trade, climate change, democracy, and basic human rights. Then-president Trump even hinted at rejecting the norm on non-first-use of nuclear weapons. These discourses weighed on the anti-norm side of the balance. But they were worrisome in two other ways. First, the United States has been one of the architects and main defenders—even if inconsistently—of core international norms. This subtracts from the pro-norm side of the equation. Second, to the extent that other states take advantage of US indifference or hostility to international norms and institutions to shift their own conduct and discourse away from those norms, the weakening of the norms and institutions of international governance could become more pronounced.

Three considerations offer some hope that the damage can be contained. First, the institutionalization of norms in international and domestic law and policy provides a source of resilience that could counteract the weakening. Second, to the extent that other major states step in to defend international norms and institutions, or to intensify their pro-norm discourses, that could counterbalance the weakening role of the United States. China, for instance, has indicated a willingness to take a stronger lead

[62] Of course, states are not the only actors who can challenge (or support) international norms. See Kleinlein, Chapter 4 in this book.

[63] For a more complete assessment of anti-torture norms, see Lesch and Zimmermann, Chapter 6 in this book.

in support of multilateral trade and climate change norms. Third, the norms and institutions that are under challenge do not represent merely altruistic, do-gooder wishful thinking. They provide material benefits to a broad range of actors in virtually every country. For instance, international trade norms make hundreds of millions of people around the world better off. Human rights norms likewise improve life for people, making societies more stable and productive. Of course, the gains from trade should be distributed more broadly and human rights must still be fulfilled for a large share of the world's population. But the point is that international norms and institutions serve real interests, and as those norms are challenged, those who benefit from them should be expected to defend them. Activist networks, civil society organizations, and committed advocates may well, in coming years, have to 'play more defence' in support of basic norms that are being challenged. In other words, just as there can be resistance and backlash against international norms, there can also be resistance and backlash against their erosion.

# 4

# Matters of Interpretation

## How to Conceptualize and Evaluate Change of Norms and Values in the International Legal Order

*Thomas Kleinlein**

## 1. Introduction

Change is a defining feature of international law. It is not coincidental that the notion figures prominently in the titles of important contributions to international law scholarship. Perhaps most prominently, Wolfgang Friedmann analysed 'The Changing Structure of International Law' in his 1964 monograph.[1] More recently, James Crawford entitled his 2013 General Course at The Hague Academy 'Chance, Order, Change: The Course of International Law'.[2] Right now, many of us sense that we are experiencing a fundamental change in the international legal order. Liberal values that appeared to be fairly established in international law seem to be on the retreat. A considerable number of multilateral institutions currently face serious challenges, from deep divisions at the United Nations Security Council (UNSC) and a stalemate at the World Trade Organization to severe budget cuts and difficult reform processes in a variety of organizations.[3] Even withdrawals from international organizations are no longer just a mostly theoretical option, as the developments in the International Criminal Court, the United Nations Educational, Scientific and Cultural Organization, or the European Union demonstrate. A far-reaching 'globalization fatigue', a new national egoism, incessant violations of the prohibition of the use of force, a worldwide increase in the flow of migrants and refugees, problems of the global economy, and ecological disasters all contribute to the impression that the international legal order is now in a new phase—and in a state of crisis.

Not so long ago, most of us witnessed another change of the international legal order, a change that gave cause for hope. It is a common understanding that, after the end of the Cold War, international law underwent significant transformations that led to a higher degree of institutionalization and a tighter network of rules. New

* I would like to thank Julian Kulaga for thoughtful comments on an earlier draft and the participants to the workshop of the Berlin Potsdam Research Group for their stimulating contributions to the discussion.

1 Wolfgang G Friedmann, *The Changing Structure of International Law* (Stevens 1964).

2 James Crawford, 'Chance, Order, Change: The Course of International Law' (2013) 365 Recueil des Cours de l'Académie de Droit International 13.

3 Joost Pauwelyn, Ramses A Wessel, and Jan Wouters, 'When Structures Become Shackles: Stagnation and Dynamics in International Lawmaking' (2014) 25 European Journal of International Law 733, 737.

Thomas Kleinlein, *Matters of Interpretation* In: *Tracing Value Change in the International Legal Order*. Edited by: Heike Krieger and Andrea Liese, Oxford University Press. © Thomas Kleinlein 2023. DOI: 10.1093/oso/9780192855831.003.0004

key multilateral treaties were concluded and many treaty regimes were flourishing. International law increasingly contributed to the legal protection of the individual and international adjudication was on the rise.[4] These developments prompted some scholars to claim that new layers were added to the 'geology'[5] of international law, while its structure has generally evolved from coexistence via cooperation to constitutionalization.[6]

However, it is far from clear what exactly should be the criteria to justify the claim that the international legal order has entered a new phase.[7] Our answers to this question depend on how we conceptualize and evaluate change of norms and values in the international legal order. While one scholar might get the impression that things are barely moving, others think that things are moving very fast. Stanley Fish, literary theorist and legal scholar, prominently cautions that if change could be understood at all, it was only in the context of a historical reconstruction of its empirical condition and not in the context of any (impossible) general account.[8]

This chapter analyses, from a methodological and theoretical perspective, how international legal method deals with change. Section 2 sets the stage, develops a legal perspective on change of norms and values in the international legal order, and distinguishes between structural change and norm change. This is followed in Section 3 and Section 4 by an examination of doctrinal categories that provide techniques to process change in international legal practice. International legal method is equipped with several techniques to process—and to conceptualize and evaluate—change: 'formal' norm change is a matter of the doctrine of sources. International law can also change 'informally' through the shifting meaning of norm texts. Both formal and informal change is a matter of interpretation. Therefore, Section 5 aims at theorizing interpretive change. It examines the relationship between the sources of law and legal interpretation as categories of change and analyses theoretical perceptions of interpretive change.

## 2. 'Change' in International Law

Change in international law occurs on a structural level (Section 2.1) and on the level of individual norms (Section 2.2).

[4] For a summary of these developments, see Heike Krieger and Georg Nolte, 'The International Rule of Law – Rise or Decline? – Approaching Current Foundational Challenges' in Heike Krieger, Georg Nolte, and Andreas Zimmermann (eds), *The International Rule of Law – Rise or Decline?* (OUP 2019) 5–6.

[5] Cf Joseph HH Weiler, 'The Geology of International Law – Governance, Democracy and Legitimacy' (2004) 64 Zeitschrift für ausländisches öffentliches Recht und Völkerrecht 547; James Crawford, 'The Current Political Discourse Concerning International Law' (2018) 81 The Modern Law Review 1, 2 and 21: 'sedimentary formation'.

[6] See, inter alia, Anne Peters, 'Global Constitutionalism Revisited' (2005) 11 International Legal Theory 39.

[7] See Stefan Kadelbach, 'Jenseits der Anarchie – Entwicklungstendenzen im Völkerrecht' in Heinrich Menkhaus and Midori Narazaki (eds), *Japanischer Vorkämpfer für die Rechtsordnung des 21. Jahrhunderts: Festschrift für Koresuke Yamauchi zum 70. Geburtstag* (Duncker & Humblot 2017).

[8] Stanley E Fish, *Doing What Comes Naturally: Change, Rhetoric, and the Practice of Theory in Literary and Legal Studies* (Clarendon Press 1989) 153.

## 2.1 Structural Changes in the International Legal Order

Structural changes of the international legal order bring about transformations of actors, processes, and outputs, as discussed in Friedmann's book *The Changing Structure of International Law*.[9] Structural changes can reflect changing values or fundamental principles,[10] as exemplified by the 'humanization'[11] and 'ecologization'[12] of international law since the early 1990s. The structural effect of these developments in the subject-matters of international law and their doctrinal expressions in the law of treaties and beyond are well captured in Bruno Simma's phrase 'from bilateralism to community interest'.[13] Beyond the emergence of new normative paradigms, the phenomena of fragmentation,[14] transnationalization,[15] deformalization,[16] and judicialization[17] have contributed to structural changes since the 1990s. As diverse as they are, these developments also include changes in international law-making processes,[18] which affect our understanding of the 'sources' of international law—ie, changes of the 'rules of change'—and changes in the rules of interpretation.[19] While evolutive interpretation was for a long time a method not frequently used by international courts,[20] more adjudication and more judicial decision-making have now increased the chances for reinterpretations and re-evaluations of previous decisions. Thus, the structural change of judicialization contributes to a trend towards more evolutive interpretation.[21]

How should legal scholars study structural changes? International lawyers have not only always observed whether and how legal rules form, identified contestations and

[9] Friedmann (n 1).

[10] Jochen Rauber, *Strukturwandel als Prinzipienwandel: Theoretische, dogmatische und methodische Bausteine eines Prinzipienmodells des Völkerrechts und seiner Dynamik* (Springer 2017).

[11] Theodor Meron, *The Humanization of International Law* (Martinus Nijhoff 2006).

[12] Rauber (n 10) 657ff.

[13] Bruno Simma, 'From Bilateralism to Community Interest' (1994) 250 Recueil des Cours 221.

[14] For an analysis, see Eyal Benvenisti and George W Downs, *Between Fragmentation and Democracy: The Role of National and International Courts* (CUP 2017).

[15] Dana Burchardt, 'Intertwinement of Legal Spaces in the Transnational Legal Sphere' (2017) 30 Leiden Journal of International Law 305.

[16] Joost Pauwelyn, Ramses A Wessel, and Jan Wouters (eds), *Informal International Lawmaking* (OUP 2012).

[17] Karen J Alter, *The New Terrain of International Law: Courts, Politics, Rights* (Princeton University Press 2014).

[18] Rüdiger Wolfrum and Volker Röben (eds), *Developments of International Law in Treaty Making* (Springer 2005).

[19] International Law Association Study Group on the Content and Evolution of the Rules of Interpretation, 'Preliminary Report Johannesburg' (Johannesburg 7–11 August 2016) <https://ila.vettoreweb.com/Storage/Download.aspx?DbStorageId=1401&StorageFileGuid=bcaa951e-ae3e-4ccb-9c80-248c98c741e3> accessed 25 November 2021; Michael Waibel, 'Demystifying the Art of Interpretation' (2011) 22 European Journal of International Law 571, 572.

[20] Paolo Palchetti, 'Interpreting "Generic Terms": Between Respect for the Parties' Original Intention and the Identification of the Ordinary Meaning' in Nerina Boschiero and others (eds), *International Courts and the Development of International Law: Essays in Honour of Tullio Treves* (Asser Press 2013) 91.

[21] For this trend, see Georg Nolte, 'Between Contemporaneous and Evolutive Interpretation: The use of "subsequent practice" in the judgment of the International Court of Justice concerning the case of Costa Rica v. Nicaragua (2009)' in Holger P Hestermeyer and Rüdiger Wolfrum (eds), *Coexistence, cooperation and solidarity: Liber amicorum Rüdiger Wolfrum* (Martinus Nijhoff 2012) 1679; Christian Djeffal, *Static and Evolutive Treaty Interpretation: A Functional Reconstruction* (CUP 2016) 5ff.

violations, but also have almost always felt responsible for giving overall assessments about the state of 'the law'.[22] Therefore, it is important that the history of international law does not develop into a separate sub-discipline that is no longer part of the more general legal discourse.[23] In the historiography of international law, structural changes can mark turning points and guide periodization. Yet, periods are interpretations of facts that allow for many possible approaches and there hardly exist any ambitious theoretical contributions to this aspect of how to conceptualize and evaluate change.[24] This complex issue and its far-reaching implications cannot be expounded in more detail in this chapter. Suffice it to say that future work on periodization in the historiography of international law is a rewarding task.

Legal historiography and periodization is certainly not the only approach to structural changes. It even implies a bias towards change. This becomes apparent in a comparison with a 'geological approach' to structural change that Joseph Weiler outlined some years ago. Weiler explains that, while history emphasizes change, geology stratifies and emphasizes accretion. By stratifying, geology folds the whole of the past into any given moment in time—that moment in which one examines a geological section.[25] Weiler continues: '[G]eology allows us to speak not so much about transformations but of layering, of change which is part of continuity, of new strata which do not replace earlier ones, but simply layer themselves alongside. Geology recognizes eruptions, but it also allows a focus on the regular and the quotidian.'[26] In my opinion, this is an effective approach to think about structural changes in the international legal order.

## 2.2 Change of Norms

Change occurs also on the level of individual norms. This again is a manifold phenomenon. Change can bring into existence a new legal norm that did not exist before. Sometimes, it is not entirely clear or uncontested whether norm-generative processes have actually resulted in a new legal norm. Examples of this uncertainty are the much-discussed Responsibility to Protect (R2P)—considered by some as an 'emerging norm' and as customary international law (CIL) by others[27]—or, less prominently, the odious debts doctrine, where the existence of relevant CIL is doubtful.[28] Beyond the question

[22] Krieger and Nolte (n 4) 18.
[23] Thomas Kleinlein, 'International Legal Thought: Creation of a Tradition and the Potential of Disciplinary Self-Reflection' (2016) 16 The Global Community: Yearbook of International Law and Jurisprudence 811, 826.
[24] Oliver Diggelmann, 'The Periodization of the History of International Law' in Bardo Fassbender and Anne Peters (eds), *The Oxford Handbook of the History of International Law* (OUP 2012) 999.
[25] Weiler (n 5) 549; for a critique, see Liliana Obregón, 'The Geological Strata of International Law: Response to Professor Weiler's "Geology of International Law"' (2006) 100 Proceedings of the American Society of International Law 103.
[26] Weiler (n 5) 551.
[27] Sven Simon, '15 Jahre Responsibility to Protect: Worin liegt die Schutzverantwortung?' (2016) 54 Archiv des Völkerrechts 1, 16ff, with further references.
[28] Sabine Michalowski and Juan P Bohoslavsky, 'Ius Cogens, Transitional Justice and Other Trends of the Debate on Odious Debts: A Response to the World Bank Discussion Paper on Odious Debts' (2009) 48 Columbia Journal of Transnational Law 59, 63.

of the mere existence of a certain norm, norm change can also affect norm diffusion—ie the legal subjects bound by a norm—or the broadness or narrowness of the norm's substantive scope of application. Change can also mean that existing norms become stronger (more robust) or weaker (or erode). Norm robustness and norm erosion are difficult to evaluate for international lawyers, who mostly require a threshold for a rule to be established as a legal norm. Yet, international lawyers are well aware that rules can change in their substantive content, their formality and specificity, and authoritativeness.[29] Perhaps most subtly, norm change arises if an existing legal norm shifts its meaning. Instances of this kind of change include the semantic shift of 'peace' in Article 39 United Nations Charter[30] or the transformation of the North Atlantic Treaty Organization Treaty after the end of the Cold War in the wake of the 'New Strategic Concept'.[31] The contested shift in meaning of the distinction between combatants and civilians in the law of armed conflict since the George W Bush administration introduced the notion of 'enemy combatant' provides a further example.[32] The contributions to this volume also exemplify the different categories of change. The diffusion of the nuclear taboo in arms control is contested; and in international human rights law, the prohibition of torture might be eroding, not to mention the classical candidate for a changing norm, the prohibition of the use of force. The examples also demonstrate that the categories of change are sometimes not clear-cut, especially due to the interaction of individual norms with other norms in the international legal system. This interaction sometimes makes it difficult to distinguish the emergence of new norms and semantic shifts of existing norms.

As the subsequent Section 3 and Section 4 of this chapter will demonstrate, international legal practice encompasses several doctrinal categories that offer techniques to deal with change. The doctrine of sources is the most obvious candidate to provide rules of change in international law. Beyond these modes of formal change, international treaty norms can change informally, through interpretation. My account of change from the *internal* perspective of legal practice or 'method' differs from other approaches to the change of (legal and non-legal) norms in the international legal order. In international relations, norm change or, more precisely, the inherent dynamism of norms and norm systems is a research area of its own,[33] and in linguistics, a whole sub-discipline analyses the change of language.[34] Legal practice or method is certainly not the only jurisprudential approach to norm change in the international

[29] For these phenomena, see Wayne Sandholtz and Kendall W Stiles, *International Norms and Cycles of Change* (OUP 2009) 6–7; see also Heike Krieger and Andrea Liese, Chapter 1 in this book.

[30] Nico Krisch, 'Article 39' in Bruno Simma and others (eds), *The Charter of the United Nations: A Commentary* (3rd edn, OUP 2012) paras 22–29.

[31] See BVerfGE 104, 151; Stefan Kadelbach, 'Domestic Constitutional Concerns with Respect to the Use of Subsequent Agreements and Practice at the International Level' in Georg Nolte (ed), *Treaties and Subsequent Practice* (OUP 2013) 147–48, with further references.

[32] Ingo Venzke, 'Legal Contestation about "Enemy Combatants": On the Exercise of Power in Legal Interpretation' (2009) 5 Journal of International Law and International Relations 155.

[33] For an overview, see Wayne Sandholtz, 'International Norm Change' in Robert B Thompson (ed), *Oxford Research Encyclopedia of Politics* (OUP 2017).

[34] See, inter alia, Lyle Campbell, *Historical Linguistics: An Introduction* (3rd edn, Edinburgh University Press 2013).

legal order. In particular, legal theory contributes significantly to its understanding and takes up the insights of other disciplines.

## 3. The Doctrine of Sources and Formal Norm Change

In the doctrine of sources, change has its place in international treaty law (Article 38(1)*(a)* of the Statute of the International Court of Justice (ICJ Statute)[35]) (3.1) and CIL (Article 38(1)*(b)* ICJ Statute) (3.2). Peremptory norms of international law (*ius cogens*) represent a special case, also in terms of their evolutive nature (3.3).

### 3.1 Change of Treaty Obligations

One obvious method to bring about a change of norms in the international legal order is the conclusion of new international conventions. Today, the practical significance of this instrument of change is limited. The number of international treaties has been stagnating, in terms of both quantity and quality, since the beginning of the new century.[36] The change of existing treaty rules is governed by the fundamental principle of *pacta sunt servanda*, as contained in Article 26 of the Vienna Convention on the Law of Treaties (VCLT).[37] Perhaps the least sophisticated way to bring about change in international treaty law is to replace the entire treaty by a new one on the same subject matter and comprising the same parties. Article 59 VCLT recognizes this option.[38] According to Article 59 para 1 VCLT, a treaty can, under certain circumstances, be considered as terminated if all the parties to it conclude a later treaty relating to the same subject matter. Alternatively, the parties to a treaty can supplement a treaty with an Additional Protocol.[39] A change can also occur if treaty obligations that are limited in time simply expire. This happened to disarmament obligations that expired and were not replaced immediately.[40]

The VCLT also comprises a number of methods of revision.[41] Part IV of the VCLT (Articles 39 et seq) contains rules on amendment and modification. An amendment denotes a formal agreement between the state parties to alter the provisions of a treaty with respect to all of them (Articles 39, 40 VCLT). Modification refers to an *inter se* agreement concluded between certain state parties and intended to vary provisions of

[35] Statute of the International Court of Justice (adopted 26 June 1945, entered into force 24 October 1945) UKTS 67 (1946).

[36] Pauwelyn, Wessel, and Wouters, 'When Structures Become Shackles' (n 3) 734.

[37] Vienna Convention on the Law of Treaties (adopted 23 May 1969, entered into force 27 January 1980) 1155 UNTS 331.

[38] Jan Klabbers, 'Treaties, Amendment and Revision' in Rüdiger Wolfrum (ed), *Max Planck Encyclopedia of Public International Law* (OUP 2008) para 13.

[39] Georg Nolte, 'Introduction' in Georg Nolte (ed), *Treaties and Subsequent Practice* (OUP 2013) 3.

[40] START I treaty expired in December 2009 while the new START between the US and Russia entered into force in February 2011 only. See Claire Mills, 'Nuclear Weapons: Disarmament and Non-Proliferation Regimes' (2016) House of Commons Library Briefing Paper 7634, 15–20 <https://commonslibrary.parliament.uk/research-briefings/cbp-7634/> accessed 5 December 2021.

[41] Gerhard Hafner, 'Subsequent Agreements and Practice: Between Interpretation, Informal Modification, and Formal Amendment' in Georg Nolte (ed), *Treaties and Subsequent Practice* (OUP 2013) 105.

a multilateral treaty in their mutual relations (Articles 39, 41 VCLT). The provisions of the VCLT are subject to modification by special rules on amendment and modification in the relevant treaty itself. In practice, amendment clauses in multilateral treaties show a great variety and state practice is very diverse.[42] Given this diversity of practice, treaty revision is a curiously under-analysed phenomenon. The reason for the lack of scholarly attention may be that revision is often seen as a matter for politics and diplomacy. Moreover, the widely diverging revision clauses reveal few generalities that may come to serve as normative guidance.[43] To generalize, however, it can be said that the revision regimes lead to a considerable rigidity of treaties, once adopted. Amendments often require unanimity or a qualified majority of the state parties, and the need for a new, formal round of parliamentary approvals makes treaty revision a cumbersome process that is rarely applied in practice.

In order to accommodate the need for flexibility and to facilitate revision, some modern treaties distinguish between the basic principles of a regime and more technical and detailed rules. While the basic principles are subject to strict amendment procedures, the technical elaborations, laid down in annexes, in later protocols or in the treaty itself, can be changed in less onerous procedures.[44] Furthermore, many multilateral treaties have created their own governance regimes, in the context of which (non-binding) rulemaking takes place through Conferences of the Parties, Meetings of the Parties, and other committees or working groups.[45] Under certain conditions, states may also denounce a treaty (Article 56 VCLT). In extreme cases, a party to a treaty may invoke a supervening impossibility of performance or a fundamental change of circumstances in order to terminate or suspend the operation of a treaty (Articles 61, 62 VCLT).[46]

## 3.2 Changes in Customary International Law

Since the process of change in treaty law is rather cumbersome, CIL could be the more important source in terms of change and provide for more flexibility than treaty law. The development of CIL may also affect treaty obligations. Individual treaty provisions may be superseded and entire treaties may become obsolete if new rules of CIL emerge. Still, this is not a significant mechanism of change and happens rather rarely, for instance with regard to the third Hague Convention relative to the Opening of Hostilities of 1907.[47]

More generally, CIL continues to be relevant, despite the flourishing of treaty law in the recent past. Some of the most crucial rules of international law—the prohibition of genocide and torture, the prohibition of slavery and piracy, the rules on state

[42] Kerstin von der Decken (formerly Odendahl), 'Article 39' in Oliver Dörr and Kirsten Schmalenbach (eds), *Vienna Convention on the Law of Treaties: A Commentary* (2nd edn, Springer 2018)paras 4 and 18.

[43] Klabbers (n 38) para 19.

[44] ibid para 17.

[45] Pauwelyn, Wessel, and Wouters, 'When Structures Become Shackles' (n 3) 740.

[46] Nolte, 'Introduction' (n 39) 3.

[47] Hague Convention (III) on the Opening of Hostilities (adopted 18 October 1907, entered into force 26 January 1910) 205 CTS 264; see Klabbers (n 38) para 16.

responsibility, and the no-harm rule—started as or continue to exist as CIL. The intensified international interaction of our day and age may lead to a more rapid formation of CIL in specific instances. On the other hand, today's preference of states for informal arrangements obviously also impacts upon CIL, as the essence of the *opinio iuris* component relates precisely to the legally binding character of an obligation. With fewer multilateral conventions being generated, it becomes harder to find strong evidence of *opinio iuris* confirmed by practice.[48]

While change in CIL sometimes takes several decades, the 'passage of only a short period of time is', in the words of the International Court of Justice (ICJ), 'not necessarily, or of itself, a bar to the formation of a new rule of customary international law' if state practice is 'both extensive and virtually uniform'.[49] In some circumstances, fundamental changes or paradigm-shifting developments can expedite the formation of CIL, and new rules and doctrines may emerge with unusual rapidity and acceptance. In this sense, it can be argued that the Nuremberg precedent and the universal and unqualified endorsement of the Nuremberg Principles by the United Nations General Assembly in 1946 resulted in an accelerated formation of CIL, including the mode of international criminal responsibility now known as Joint Criminal Enterprise liability.[50]

The continued existence of a rule of CIL depends on a continual state practice and a stable *opinio iuris*. If many states defect, a rule can lose its status of CIL. Compliance and change are thus entwined: a state that violates a rule of CIL creates a precedent that may lead the rule to change or disappear.[51] Different from treaties, CIL does not include flexibility provisions that allow a state to suspend or breach its obligations. A relatively small number of defections can slowly build up until they reach a critical mass and a tipping point, beyond which defections accelerate and the rule of CIL unravels.[52] An example of a major change in a rule CIL is provided by the transformation of sovereign immunity. The traditional rule of absolute immunity holds that states cannot be sued in the domestic courts of other states. Many states have switched to restrictive immunity, in which foreign states can be sued for their private or commercial activities, thus bringing about a change of the relevant CIL.[53] By contrast, the 'humanization' of international law mentioned in Section 2.1 is not (yet) reflected in a general customary rule on immunity exceptions in cases of grave human rights violations.[54]

[48] Pauwelyn, Wessel, and Wouters, 'When Structures Become Shackles' (n 3) 736.

[49] *North Sea Continental Shelf (Germany v Denmark and Netherlands)* (Judgement) [1969] ICJ Rep 3 with regard to the formation of a new rule of customary international law (CIL) on the basis of what was originally a purely conventional rule.

[50] Michael P Scharf, *Customary International Law in Times of Fundamental Change: Recognizing Grotian Moments* (CUP 2013) 63ff; for the more radical concept of 'instant' CIL, see Bin Cheng, 'United Nations Resolutions on Outer Space: "Instant" International Customary Law' (1965) 5 Indian Journal of International Law 23.

[51] Pierre-Hugues Verdier and Erik Voeten, 'How Does Customary International Law Change? The Case of State Immunity' (2015) 59 International Studies Quarterly 209, 209.

[52] Pierre-Hugues Verdier and Erik Voeten, 'Precedent, Compliance, and Change in Customary International Law' (2014) 108 American Journal of International Law 389, 395.

[53] Verdier and Voeten, 'How Does Customary International Law Change?' (n 51) 210.

[54] Heike Krieger, 'Between Evolution and Stagnation – Immunities in a Globalized World' (2014) 6 Goettingen Journal of International Law 177, 181ff.

### 3.3 The Evolutive Nature of *Ius Cogens*

Beyond treaty law and CIL, the evolutive nature of *ius cogens* is recognized in Articles 53 and 64 VCLT and unanimously accepted, though some doctrinal controversy regarding its source persists.[55] The emergence and evolution of peremptory norms is a two-level process.[56] According to the wording of the VCLT, a peremptory norm must first become general international law, ie CIL or a general principle of law pursuant to Article 38(1) ICJ Statute. In a second step, it can be elevated to *ius cogens* by the international community. Accordingly, a change of peremptory norms presupposes a new ordinary *opinio iuris* referring to the primary norms and an *opinio iuris cogentis* that is necessary for establishing the special character of peremptory norms.[57] First, the norm comes into existence in the same way as any 'ordinary' norm of general international law. No qualified procedure applies. Even the higher hierarchical status of *ius cogens* norms does not require a higher threshold for achieving that rank as opposed to the creation of 'ordinary' international rules.[58] Statements at the Vienna Conference highlight that acceptance by a very large majority of states would suffice to establish the peremptory character of a norm.[59] Yet, the wording of Article 53 VCLT and the understanding of state parties at the time reflects an unstable compromise. Therefore, some uncertainty persists with regard to the emergence of *ius cogens*. Remarkably, the supposedly most important norms are based on the most uncertain mechanism of norm change.[60]

The strong ethical underpinning of peremptory norms might be able to compensate for deficiencies in universal acceptance of these norms, either at the level of normative content or at the level of peremptory character.[61] Therefore, the threshold for the change of peremptory norms does not appear to be simply 'higher' than the

[55] Anne Lagerwall, 'Article 64 Convention of 1969' in Olivier Corten and Pierre Klein (eds), *The Vienna Conventions on the Law of Treaties: A Commentary* (OUP 2011) para 4. On the modest role of *ius cogens* and the fragility of the core values underlying it, see also Erika de Wet, Chapter 5 in this book; for a list of most widely recognized examples of *ius cogens* see International Law Commission (ILC), 'Fourth Report on Peremptory Norms of General International Law (jus cogens) by Dire Tladi, Special Rapporteur' (29 April–7 June, 8 July–9 August 2019) UN Doc A/CN.4/727, para 137.

[56] Thomas Kleinlein, 'Jus Cogens as the "Highest Law"? Peremptory Norms and Legal Hierarchies' (2015) 46 Netherlands Yearbook of International Law 173, 195–96.

[57] Władysław Czapliński, 'Jus Cogens and the Law of Treaties' in Christian Tomuschat and Jean-Marc Thouvenin (eds), *The Fundamental Rules of the International Legal Order: Jus Cogens and Obligations Erga Omnes* (Martinus Nijhoff 2005).

[58] Andreas L Paulus, 'Jus Cogens in a Time of Hegemony and Fragmentation: An Attempt at a Reappraisal' (2005) 74 Nordic Journal of International Law 297, 302–03.

[59] Iraqi Chairman of the Drafting Committee Yasseen, 'United Nations Conference on the Law of Treaties Official Records First Session' (26 March–24 May 1968) A/CONF.39/11, 472 para 12. Also, consider the statement by US delegate Kearney, who referred to the 'absence of dissent by any important element of the international community', 'United Nations Conference on the Law of Treaties Official Records Second Session' (9 April–22 May 1969) A/CONF.39/11/Add.1, 102 para 22. See Giorgio Gaja, 'The Protection of General Interests in the International Community: General Course on Public International Law (2011)' (2012) 364 Recueil des Cours 9, 56–57.

[60] Paulus (n 58) 325.

[61] Jure Vidmar, 'Norm Conflicts and Hierarchy in International Law: Towards a Vertical International System?' in Erika de Wet and Jure Vidmar (eds), *Hierarchy in International Law: The Place of Human Rights* (OUP 2012) 26.

threshold for 'ordinary' norms. State practice, by contrast, is seemingly irrelevant for establishing the peremptory status of a certain norm. The second sentence of Article 53 VCLT defines a peremptory norm of general international law as a norm *accepted and recognized* by the international community of states as a whole as 'a norm from which no derogation is permitted and which can be modified only by a subsequent norm of general international law having the same character'.[62] Different from the creation of CIL in general, the creation of the special status of a norm as *ius cogens* obviously does not depend on a consistent state practice, but only on an *opinio iuris cogentis*. The example of *ius cogens* demonstrates that we should not confuse normative strength and stability. Despite their normative strength, peremptory norms are not immune to change.

## 4. Interpretation and Informal Norm Change

Although less visible than formal norm change (see Section 4.1), the modes of informal norm change (Section 4.2) provide a significant mechanism of change in current international law.

### 4.1 Low Visibility of Interpretive Change

Apart from 'formal' changes in the sources of international law, international law can change through the shifting meaning of norm texts.[63] Interpretation can bring about 'informal' change by clarifying a previously unclear term, by reinterpreting a term or provision in a sense contrary to its original meaning, and even by reinterpretations that shade into modification.[64] Change through interpretation is mostly not very visible, for two reasons. First, the visibility of change is low simply because the words in the treaty stay the same while only their meaning is altered. Second, judicial interpreters tend to downplay their active role in order not to risk the legitimacy of their judgments. For example, the ICJ has insisted several times that it cannot 'legislate', but only 'ascertain' the existence of relevant legal principles and rules.[65] As Stanley Fish explains, '[t]he enterprise of the law [ ... ] is by definition committed to the ahistoricity of its basic principles. [ ... ] [T]he very point of the legal enterprise requires that its practitioners see continuity where others, with less of a stake in the enterprise, might feel free to see change'.[66] For international courts, it is all the more important to portray

[62] Emphasis added; on these criteria see ILC, 'Second Report on jus cogens by Dire Tladi, Special Rapporteur' (16 March 2017) UN Doc A/CN.4/706, 15–45.

[63] Ingo Venzke, 'Sources and Interpretation Theories: The International Lawmaking Process' in Samantha Besson and Jean d'Aspremont (eds), *Oxford Handbook on the Sources of International Law* (OUP 2017).

[64] Julian Arato, 'Subsequent Practice and Evolutive Interpretation: Techniques of Treaty Interpretation over Time and Their Diverse Consequences' (2010) 9 Law & Practice of International Courts and Tribunals 443, 457–58.

[65] *Legality of the Threat or Use of Nuclear Weapons* (Advisory Opinion) [1996] ICJ Rep 226; also, see *Fisheries Jurisdiction (UK v Iceland)* (Judgment) [1974] ICJ Rep 3.

[66] Fish, *Doing What Comes Naturally* (n 8) 157.

their practice as firmly based on the law as it stands because state consent, as expressed in the rules of treaty and CIL, is an important source of their legitimacy.[67]

Due to this 'outward show' of international courts as ascertaining and not developing or even changing the law, the view persists that interpretation uncovers the law that is already out there, contained and conserved in given norms.[68] While their presentation of legal argument conceals that interpretation actually and necessarily brings about change, it generally responds to expectations of other participants in legal discourse and has the aptitude to constrain and allow for critique. Argumentative standards in legal discourse can contribute to the normative legitimation of international adjudication.[69] Accordingly, the rule of interpretation in the VCLT (Articles 31 et seq) functions less as a hermeneutical guide for the interpreter to arrive at goals such as the intentions of the parties to the treaty and does not directly impact upon the interpretive result. Rather, it is best understood as a structure for international legal argument and its presentation. However, the VCLT forces the interpreter to make his or her arguments visible and thus requires a justification, which fosters the precedential value for future cases.[70]

Despite legitimacy concerns regarding 'law-making' by international judicial institutions, change is a necessary product of international adjudication. Since process of formal international law-making, described in Section 3, is cumbersome, international courts simply correspond to an existing social need for change. A specific legitimation problem of international judicial institutions still exists in an institutional asymmetry of legislation and adjudication. While—as a product of the 'judicialization' mentioned in the introduction—a highly developed judiciary exists at the international level, legislative power is decentralized and essentially exists at the level of individual states. Unlike domestic courts, international judicial institutions are regularly not embedded within an overall context of democratic politics. Domestic (parliamentary) control is therefore curtailed, and law-making by international courts largely evades the reach of national parliamentary bodies. As pointed out above, procedures for amending treaties or alternative mechanisms for 'overriding' a specific judicial interpretation often requires unanimity or a qualified majority of state parties, which is difficult to attain. The processes of negotiating international treaties are slow and protracted.[71] The democratic premise that judicial law-making can be politically corrected with democratic majorities is hardly respected with international adjudication. Therefore, the lack of a fully fledged political system at the international level creates a major problem of democratic legitimation.

[67] Ingo Venzke, 'The Role of International Courts as Interpreters and Developers of the Law: Working out the Jurisgenerative Practice of Interpretation' (2011) 34 Loyola of Los Angeles International and Comparative Law Review 99, 101.

[68] ibid 99.

[69] ibid 107.

[70] Djeffal (n 21) 352.

[71] Armin von Bogdandy and Ingo Venzke, *In Whose Name? A Public Law Theory of International Adjudication* (OUP 2014) 124.

## 4.2 Modes of Interpretive Change

Nonetheless, (judicial) interpretation is a significant mechanism of change in current international law. For this reason, the specific method of norm creation—like in the case of *ius cogens*—does not necessarily make norms more resistant to change. Dynamic or evolutive interpretation (in a broad sense) seeks to establish the meaning of a treaty at the time of its interpretation. Its effect is that while the words in a treaty stay the same, their meaning is altered.[72] By contrast, static or contemporaneous interpretation asks for the meaning of treaty provisions and the circumstances prevailing at the time of the conclusion of the treaty.[73] The decision between evolutive or static interpretation is a question of inter-temporal law.[74] Established rules and practice of interpretation include two basic modes of change via interpretation.[75] Both evolutive interpretation (in the narrow sense) and taking into account subsequent practice and agreements rest upon the intention of the parties that their treaty develops over time. Evolutive interpretation (in the narrow sense) is based on the *original* intention of the parties. This first mode of change is not a separate method, but rather the result of a proper application of the usual means of interpretation.[76] The second mode is based on the *later* intentions of the parties as expressed in subsequent conduct, namely subsequent agreements (Article 31(3)*(a)* VCLT) and subsequent practice (Article 31(3)*(b)* VCLT). 'Subsequent agreement' is a manifested agreement between the parties after the conclusion of a treaty regarding its interpretation or the application of its provisions. 'Subsequent practice' consists of conduct, including pronouncements, by one or more parties to the treaty after its conclusion regarding its interpretation or application.[77] The ICJ recognized these two types of interpretive change—one based on the original intention of the parties, and the other based on their later intentions—in the *Navigational Rights* Case. According to the Court, the subsequent practice of the parties can result in a departure from the original intent on the basis of a tacit agreement between the parties. Moreover, there are situations in which the parties' intent upon conclusion of the treaty was, or may be presumed to have been, to give some or all of the terms used a meaning or content capable of evolving, not one fixed once and for all, so as to make allowance for, among other things, developments in international law.[78] In such instances, the Court considered it to be 'indeed in order to respect the

[72] Djeffal (n 21) 19.

[73] Oliver Dörr, 'Article 31' in Oliver Dörr and Kirsten Schmalenbach (eds), *Vienna Convention on the Law of Treaties: A Commentary* (2nd edn, Springer 2018)para 23.

[74] Nolte, 'Between Contemporaneous and Evolutive Interpretation' (n 21) 1676.

[75] Moreover, founding treaties of international organizations may undergo change with the help of the doctrine of implied powers, cf Klabbers (n 38) 15.

[76] Georg Nolte, 'Report 1 – Jurisprudence of the International Court of Justice and Arbitral Tribunals of Ad Hoc Jurisdiction Relating to Subsequent Agreements and Subsequent Practice: Introductory Report for the ILC Study Group on Treaties over Time' in Georg Nolte (ed), *Treaties and Subsequent Practice* (OUP 2013) 188.

[77] ILC, 'Report of the International Law Commission. Seventieth Session' (2018) UN Doc A/73/10, para 52 Conclusion 4: definition of subsequent agreement and subsequent practice; cf ILC, 'Fifth Report on Subsequent Agreements and Subsequent Practice in Relation to Treaty Interpretation: by Georg Nolte, Special Rapporteur' (28 February 2018) UN Doc A/CN.4/715, para 52, Draft conclusion 4: definition of subsequent agreement and subsequent practice and the commentary thereto.

[78] *Dispute regarding Navigational and Related Rights (Costa Rica v Nicaragua)* (Judgment) [2009] ICJ Rep 2009, 213; cf Nolte, 'Report 1' (n 76) 184–85; Arato, 'Subsequent Practice and Evolutive Interpretation'

parties' common intention at the time the treaty was concluded, not to depart from it, that account should be taken of the meaning acquired by the terms in question upon each occasion on which the treaty is to be applied'.[79]

The 'bifurcation'[80] of evolutive interpretation (in the narrow sense) and taking into account subsequent conduct as two modes of interpretive change does not imply that they can be kept separately. Rather, evolutionary interpretation and the taking into account of subsequent conduct are in principle mutually complementary, and are often used that way in practice.[81] Notably, subsequent conduct can also limit evolutionary interpretation.[82]

## 5. Theorizing Interpretive Change

Although of relatively low visibility, informal change via interpretation clearly has its place in legal practice. This raises the question of how formal and informal change relate to each other and how interpretive change interacts with changing values and structural change (Section 5.1). Finally, this brings us to theoretical perceptions of interpretive change and attempts to accommodate interpretive change within the framework of legal positivism (Section 5.2).

### 5.1 Relationship Between Different Modes of Change

According to the outward show of international legal argument and its standard perception, change is taking place in terms of sources, and interpretation is uncovering what is already out there.[83] At this point, I should like to emphasize that both applying the doctrine of sources in order to ascertain the existence of rules, on the one hand, and interpreting these rules in order to determine their content, on the other, are matters of interpretation. When ascertaining the law, the judge, counsel, academic, activist, adviser, or observer necessarily interprets some pre-existing standards of identification of law. What qualifies as law itself involves an act of interpretation.[84]

(n 64) 445; Julian Arato, 'Treaty Interpretation and Constitutional Transformation: Informal Change in International Organizations' (2013) 38 Yale Journal of International Law 289, 307–48; Richard K Gardiner, *Treaty Interpretation* (2nd edn, OUP 2015) 317.

[79] *Dispute regarding Navigational and Related Rights* (n 78) 242–43; cf Eirik Bjorge, *The Evolutionary Interpretation of Treaties* (OUP 2014) 76–79.

[80] Bjorge (n 79) 77.

[81] Nolte, 'Report 1' (n 76) 184–88. See *Legal Consequences for States of the Continued Presence of South Africa in Namibia (South West Africa) notwithstanding Security Council Resolution 276 (1970)* (Advisory Opinion) [1971] ICJ Rep 16, para 53; *Aegean Sea Continental Shelf (Greece v Turkey)* (Judgment) [1978] ICJ Rep 3.

[82] Bjorge (n 79) 76–79.

[83] Venzke, 'The Role of International Courts' (n 67) 107.

[84] Jean d'Aspremont, 'Wording in International Law' (2012) 25 Leiden Journal of International Law 575, 580; highlighting (and criticizing) that practice even tends to blur the distinction between content-determination processes (or interpretation *stricto sensu*).

Legal method comprises different approaches as to how changes of overarching values can be reflected on the level of the interpretation of individual norms. Interpretative practice, particularly in some fields like human rights protection and international criminal law, increasingly invokes notions of fundamental values or community interests, which is possibly indicative of a deeper structural transformation of international society which influences understandings of interpretation.[85] In a meticulous study, Jochen Rauber has demonstrated the impact of legal values like human rights or the global environment, understood as legal principles, on the interpretation and judicial development of international law.[86] While Rauber offers a 'principle-based reconstruction', I have argued elsewhere that structural changes like the 'humanization' of international law and changing legal values actually find expression in certain 'burdens of justification'. International judicial institutions have placed new 'burdens of justification' on international actors like the UNSC and have developed legal presumptions of non-deviation that express fundamental values or 'constitutional concerns' such as human rights sensitivity or responsiveness to domestic preferences and subsidiarity.[87] Arguably, international lawyers' very awareness of an increasing intertwining of overarching values and individual norms makes them worry that international law is particularly vulnerable if liberal values are now on the retreat.

## 5.2 Theoretical Perceptions of Interpretive Change

In legal practice, interpretation is obviously an important mechanism of change. However, mainstream positivism has some difficulties conceptualizing interpretive change. It struggles to reconcile the idea that legal provisions are 'posited' and come with fixed meanings attached to them, only waiting to be uncovered, with the notion of interpretive change.[88] This understanding and even the notion that the norm is a 'frame' of possible meanings,[89] is difficult to uphold if one takes seriously central propositions of the linguistic turn in philosophy. In Ludwig Wittgenstein's formulation that would trigger the linguistic turn, words do not have a meaning other than that given to them by their use.[90] Semantic pragmatism teaches us that it is not possible to find meaning anywhere beyond the specific 'use of words'.[91] Consequently, law also only exists in its interpretative practice and is not something ready to be discovered. The content of legal expressions is shaped in the creative acts of interpretation.

[85] Venzke, 'The Role of International Courts' (n 67) 114.

[86] Rauber (n 10) 491ff (chs 4 and 5).

[87] Thomas Kleinlein, 'Between Myths and Norms: Constructivist Constitutionalism and the Potential of Constitutional Principles in International Law' (2012) 81 Nordic Journal of International Law 79, 112ff.

[88] Cf Emmanuel Voyiakis, 'International Law, Interpretative Fidelity and the Hermeneutics of Hans-Georg Gadamer' (2011) 54 German Yearbook of International Law 385, 400.

[89] Hans Kelsen, *Reine Rechtslehre: Einleitung in die rechtswissenschaftliche Problematik* (Deuticke 1934) 64–65.

[90] Ludwig Wittgenstein, *Philosophical Investigations* (3rd edn, MacMillan 1958) 43; cf Richard Rorty, *Essays on Heidegger and Others: Philosophical Papers* vol 2 (CUP 1991) 50–65.

[91] Venzke, 'The Role of International Courts' (n 67) 115.

Interpretive practice shifts meanings and offers new reference points for legal discourse thereby contributing to the change of norms.[92]

One attempt to reconcile this conception of interpretive practice with legal positivism is to distinguish between interpretation and mere application of the law, as suggested by Marko Milanovic.[93] According to him, 'interpretation' denotes the activity of establishing the linguistic or semantic meaning of a legal text. 'Application', by contrast, refers to the activity of translating that text into workable legal rules to be applied in a given case. This distinction enables Milanovic to claim that the meaning of the word has not changed with the passing of time. What has changed is only the application of that meaning.

Milanovic's approach cannot explain that the meaning of the norm is generally not affected by the changing application. If norms do exist only in practice, if they do not have a fixed meaning, this cannot be the case. In language theory, the very question of whether there is a language 'behind' speaking provides a criterion for structuring the debate of the twentieth century. The distinction between a universal scheme and the particular use serves as a criterion for sorting out those authors who plead for this methodological difference and those who reject it. On the one hand, we can identify proponents of a 'two-worlds model' of language, including Saussure and Chomsky, as well as Searle and Habermas. On the other hand, there are those philosophers, like Wittgenstein, Austin, Davidson, and Derrida, who reject the separation between scheme and use as a methodological strategy.[94] If we share an understanding of law as language, a theory of evolutive interpretation in law cannot simply ignore this 'logical geography'[95] of twentieth-century language theory and the fact that a 'two-worlds model' that distinguishes between 'abstract meaning' and 'application' does not make sense for a significant number of language philosophers, and tacitly side with the contested 'two-worlds model'.

For our purposes, the suggestion is also unsatisfying because change actually reaches beyond mere application in some prominent international law cases and is also presented in that way. In the case law of the ICJ, some of the Court's evolutive interpretations clearly go beyond mere changes in application. For example, the *Aegean Continental Shelf* Case raised the issue of the ICJ's jurisdiction under the General Act for the Pacific Settlement of International Disputes of 1928 (General Act). One of the intertemporal questions concerned the phrase 'domestic jurisdiction' in a reservation of Greece to the General Act, and whether it would apply to continental shelves. The ICJ opted for an evolutive interpretation that changed the very concept of territory and not only its application.[96]

[92] Venzke, 'Sources and Interpretation Theories' (n 63) 1.

[93] Marko Milanovic, 'The ICJ and Evolutionary Treaty Interpretation' (*EJIL:Talk!*, 4 July 2009) <www.ejiltalk.org/the-icj-and-evolutionary-treaty-interpretation/> accessed 5 December 2021.

[94] Sybille Krämer, 'Is there a Language "Behind" Speaking? How to Look at 20th Century Language Theory in an Alternative Way' in Volker Munz, Klaus Puhl, and Joseph Wang (eds), *Language and World, Part Two: Signs, Minds and Actions*, vol 15 (Ontos 2010) 39–40.

[95] ibid 39.

[96] *Aegean Sea Continental Shelf* (n 81) 33–34; cf Djeffal (n 21) 222–23; for further examples, see Djeffal (n 21) 219ff.

Eirik Bjorge offers a further solution to the problem of how to reconcile positivism and interpretive change. He argues that evolutive interpretation is entirely explainable by reference to the concept of the common intention of the parties. Their common intention at the time the treaty was concluded, correctly understood, can be that later interpreters take into account the meaning acquired by the terms in question upon each occasion on which the treaty is to be applied.[97] Bjorge defines the intention of the parties as the product of general rules of interpretation correctly applied. He himself admits that this approach, which relies on interpretation in order to decide on the question of intertemporal law of how to interpret, amounts to a circular definition and 'comes close to being a *petitio principii*'.[98]

While the idea that the task of good interpretation is to retrieve authorial or legislative intention is difficult to reconcile with taking the object of interpretation to be a living instrument,[99] a different understanding of interpretation reconciles insights of the linguistic turn and positivism. For positivists, interpretation need not necessarily refer to 'the intention of the parties'. In Emmanuel Voyiakis' terminology, there is, beyond positivism as 'intentionalism', a second strand of positivist understandings of interpretation: 'conventionalism'. 'Conventionalists' like Stanley Fish,[100] Detlef Vagts,[101] and Ian Johnstone[102] have taken on board many of the insights of twentieth-century philosophy into the intersubjective nature of language and the public character of the standards of its use. For them, legal meaning turns on the state of contemporary conventions. The interpreter's question then is what the interpretive convention is that members of this community currently share. Accordingly, evolutive interpretation is rather the rule and not the exception. It is the consensus in the profession—the invisible college of international lawyers[103]—that determines, at any moment, whether a particular argument is or is not persuasive, whether or not interpretive change is achieved.[104] Interpretation is the object of the semantic struggles[105] that take place

[97] Bjorge (n 79) 77.

[98] ibid 63; relying on ILC, 'Report of the International Law Commission on the work of its sixty-fifth session' (2013) UN Doc A/68/10, 27.

[99] Voyiakis (n 88) 400.

[100] Stanley E Fish, *Is There a Text in this Class? The Authority of Interpretive Communities* (6th edn, Harvard University Press 1980); Fish, *Doing What Comes Naturally* (n 8).

[101] Detlev Vagts, 'Treaty Interpretation and the New American Ways of Law Reading' (1993) 4 European Journal of International Law 472.

[102] Ian Johnstone, 'Treaty Interpretation: The Authority of Interpretive Communities' (1991) 12 Michigan Journal of International Law 371; Ian Johnstone, *The Power of Deliberation: International Law, Politics, and Organizations* (OUP 2011).

[103] For this prominent notion, see Oscar Schachter, 'The Invisible College of International Lawyers' (1977) 72 Northwestern University Law Review 217.

[104] Martti Koskenniemi, 'Methodology of International Law' in Rüdiger Wolfrum (ed), *Max Planck Encyclopedia of Public International Law* (OUP 2008) para 1; Jean d'Aspremont, 'The Multidimensional Process of Interpretation: Content-Determination and Law-Ascertainment Distinguished' in Andrea Bianchi, Daniel Peat, and Matthew Windsor (eds), *Interpretation in International Law* (OUP 2015) 114.

[105] Ingo Venzke, *How Interpretation Makes International Law: On Semantic Change and Normative Twists* (OUP 2012); Ralph Christensen and Michael Sokolowski, 'Recht als Einsatz im Semantischen Kampf' in Ekkehard Felder (ed), *Semantische Kämpfe: Macht und Sprache in den Wissenschaften*, vol 19 (De Gruyter 2006). Bourdieu has offered a view of law as a product of the struggle between different actors: Pierre Bourdieu, 'The Force of Law: Toward a Sociology of the Juridical Field' (1987) 38 Hastings Law Journal 814; cf Yves Dezalay and Mikael R Madsen, 'The Force of Law and Lawyers: Pierre Bourdieu and the Reflexive Sociology of Law' (2012) 8 Annual Review of Law and Social Science 433.

in the community. Identifying interpretive communities is not straightforward. Boundaries are fluid and intersecting and community members increasingly interact and overlap. International law has many different interpreters and associated perspectives: judges and arbitrators on international courts and tribunals, national courts, government legal advisers, the staff of international organizations, and a wide range of non-state actors.[106] Obviously, these challenges and uncertainties make it difficult to evaluate change. If nothing else, the concept of interpretive communities draws our attention to struggles about who is a relevant member of the community and thus, contestations about the modes of interpretative change,[107] as a further indication of instability.

Unlike the approaches discussed before, 'conventionalism' does not provide a complete structure for international legal argument and its presentation. Interpreters would not present their interpretation of the law by simply referring to the consensus of the profession. According to Article 31(1) VCLT, this consensus can indeed be relevant with regard to the 'ordinary meaning to be given to the terms of the treaty'. However, this is qualified by the context and object and purpose of the treaty (Article 31(2) and (3) VCLT). Consequently, 'conventionalism' rather aims at explaining 'interpretation' from a different perspective. Keeping these perspectives separately as 'internal' perspective of the interpreter and 'external' perspective of the theorist, however, is not that simple for the very ambition of the rules of interpretation themselves to determine the relevant interpretive communities.

The concept of interpretive communities explains why neither interpretation can produce one single stable meaning, nor can the theory of sources provide full stability in the process of law ascertainment. Meaning is constructed and not extracted through interpretation.[108] International law is not only a set of rules, but also an argumentative practice aimed at persuading target audiences.[109] Other members of the interpretive community may accept interpretive change because they are convinced by it, genuinely agree with it, or because they succumb to it as they either falsely agree or as they submit due to material forces at play. At the abstract level of theory, as well as in the study of specific instances of interpretative practice, it is necessary to account for both the possibility of reason and the role of power, rhetoric, and violence.[110] At this abstract level, the concept of interpretive communities offers a plausible explanation for the fact that change in international law is not easy to achieve even for the most powerful states. The complexity of interpretive communities and the plurality in

[106] Michael Waibel, 'Interpretive Communities in International Law' in Andrea Bianchi, Daniel Peat, and Matthew Windsor (eds), *Interpretation in International Law* (OUP 2015) 152 and 155.

[107] See, for example, the debate about the role of international organizations in the formation and determination of rules of CIL, Niels Blokker, 'International Organizations and Customary International Law' (2017) 14 International Organizations Law Review 1.

[108] d'Aspremont, 'The Multidimensional Process of Interpretation' (n 104) 114.

[109] Andrea Bianchi, 'The Game of Interpretation in International Law: The Players, the Cards, and Why the Game is Worth the Candle' in Andrea Bianchi, Daniel Peat, and Matthew Windsor (eds), *Interpretation in International Law* (OUP 2015).

[110] Venzke, 'Sources and Interpretation Theories' (n 63) 25. For interpretation as rhetoric and violence, respectively, see Ian Scobbie, 'Rhetoric, Persuasion, and Interpretation in International Law' in Andrea Bianchi, Daniel Peat, and Matthew Windsor (eds), *Interpretation in International law* (OUP 2015); Robert M Cover, 'Violence and the Word' (1986) 95 Yale Law Journal 1601.

the convictions of its members make international law resistant to sudden change. Yet, this does not mean that the legal character of a norm generally makes it more resistant to change.

## 6. Conclusion

International law scholarship is struggling with the problem of how to conceptualize and evaluate change. On the one hand, standard narratives on change like those presented in the introduction are widely shared. On the other hand, methodological uncertainty—and even a certain lack of scholarly attention—persists with regard to the question of how to perceive change. On the one hand, the notion of 'change' figures prominently in scholarly discourses. On the other hand, change is sometimes not directly visible because international lawyers have good reasons to downplay their own role in bringing about interpretive change. An examination of how international law changes demonstrates that the international legal order is less stable than the doctrine of sources and cumbersome processes of treaty revision suggest. Due to the restrictions in the avenues of formal change, the importance of informal change in interpretation as a mechanism of change should not be underrated. In any case, change is a matter of interpretation. In interpretation, changing values can play out at least in new or shifting burdens of justification and presumptions of non-deviation. To complicate further the conceptualization of change, structural and norm changes interact, mostly in legal interpretation, and the example of *ius cogens* teaches us that we cannot simply equate normative strength and stability. Precisely the informality of change might be a challenge for international lawyers, who are trained as formalists. However, if we take the interpretive community as the *locus* of interpretive change seriously, international lawyers should be well aware of their own role in the change of international legal norms and values.

# PART II
# PEREMPTORY NORMS SHIELDING VALUES FROM CHANGE?

# 5

# Entrenching International Values through Positive Law

## The (Limited) Effect of Peremptory Norms

*Erika de Wet**

## 1. Introduction

In domestic legal systems, some norms are of a constitutional nature and, thereby, hierarchically superior to ordinary norms.[1] This system of norm hierarchy, in accordance with which the higher norm will override the ordinary one in case of conflict, is underpinned by the value system of a certain constitutional polity.[2] International law, on the other hand, has traditionally been regarded as a horizontal system of legal norms.[3] It resembles a patchwork of treaty regimes and customary obligations that were adopted by multiple sovereign states.[4] These different normative regimes and the respective values embodied by them operate on an equal footing, in the sense that there is no formal hierarchy between them. As a consequence, it is difficult to resolve norm conflicts in international law on the basis of a normative hierarchy, that is, on the basis that the values underpinning a particular norm are of overriding importance.[5] Different treaty regimes, therefore, can be a reflection of competing values in a decentralized, pluralist international order in the absence of shared values that can guide judicial decision-making in case of a normative conflict.

Subsequent to the creation of the United Nations (UN) and against the backdrop of an increasingly organized international legal order, various collective interest treaties emerged that were premised on the existence of shared values across state parties. These treaties may be distinguished from multilateral treaties that contain 'bundles of bilateral' obligations,[6] that is, obligations of which the performance involves

* An earlier draft was published as (2019) KFG Working Paper Series No 25.

[1] See Hans Kelsen, *General Theory of Law and State* (Russell and Russell 1961) 115, arguing that national law is not a system of 'co-ordinated norms', operating side-by-side on the same level, 'but a hierarchy of different level of norms'.

[2] See Dinah Shelton, 'Normative Hierarchy in International Law' (2006) 100 American Journal of International Law 291.

[3] Erika de Wet and Jure Vidmar, 'Conflicts Between International Paradigms: Hierarchy Versus Systemic Integration' (2013) 2 Global Constitutionalism 196, 197.

[4] Maarten den Heijer and Harmen van der Wilt, 'Jus Cogens and the Humanization and Fragmentation of International Law' (2015) 46 Netherlands Yearbook of International Law 3, 15.

[5] ibid.

[6] An example in point would be art 22 of the Vienna Convention on Diplomatic Relations of 1961 (adopted 18 April 1961, entered into force 24 April 1964) 500 UNTS 95, where the obligation to protect the

Erika de Wet, *Entrenching International Values through Positive Law* In: *Tracing Value Change in the International Legal Order*. Edited by: Heike Krieger and Andrea Liese, Oxford University Press. © Erika de Wet 2023.
DOI: 10.1093/oso/9780192855831.003.0005

two individual states, even though the treaty framework in question establishes obligations applicable to all state parties.[7] Instead, collective interest treaties regulate interests in the protection of which all state parties at all times have a legal interest. A typical example would be human rights treaties, such as the UN Covenant on Civil and Political Rights of 1966,[8] as well as the UN Covenant on Economic, Social and Cultural Rights of 1966.[9] Furthermore, where the obligations stemming from such a collective interest treaty have been recognized as customary international law (CIL), these obligations arguably would have an *erga omnes* effect, that is, all states would have a legal interest in their protection.[10] The notion of obligations *erga omnes* has been endorsed by the International Court of Justice (ICJ) in the Barcelona Traction decision of 1970.[11] References to obligations towards the 'international community [of states] as a whole' has since also found its way into various treaties,[12] as well as the work of the UN International Law Commission (ILC).[13]

However, for the most part the recognition of the collective interest nature of certain norms did not result in their acquiring a hierarchically superior status vis-à-vis

premises of a diplomatic mission is owed by the individual receiving state to the individual sending state. See James Crawford, *The International Law Commission's Articles on State Responsibility. Introduction, Text and Commentaries* (CUP 2002) 258.

[7] Crawford, *International Law Commission's Articles on State Responsibility* (n 6) 257–58.

[8] International Covenant on Civil and Political Rights (adopted 16 December 1966, entered into force 23 March 1976) 999 UNTS 171.

[9] International Covenant on Economic, Social and Cultural Rights (adopted 16 December 1966, entered into force 03 January 1976) 993 UNTS 3.

[10] Pierre-Marie Dupuy, 'L'unité de l'ordre juridique international' (2002) 297 Collected Courses of the Hague Academy of International Law 382, 384; Crawford, *International Law Commission's Articles on State Responsibility* (n 6) 277–78. However, see International Law Commission (ILC), 'Third Report on Peremptory Norms of General International Law (jus cogens) by Dire Tladi, Special Rapporteur' (12 February 2018) UN Doc A/CN.4/714, para 4. Tladi is sceptical as to whether there can be any other *erga omnes* obligations than *jus cogens*. This point is taken up again below in Section 3.

[11] *Barcelona Traction, Light and Power Company Limited (Belgium v Spain)* (Judgment) [1970] ICJ Rep 3, 32. Subsequently the ICJ has reaffirmed the notion on several occasions, among others in *Legal Consequences of the Construction of a Wall in the Occupied Palestinian Territory* (Advisory Opinion) [2004] ICJ Rep 136, paras 15ff; *Accordance with International Law of the Unilateral Declaration of Independence in Respect of Kosovo* (Advisory Opinion) [2010] ICJ Rep 403, paras 89ff; *Questions Relating to the Obligation to Prosecute or Extradite (Belgium v Senegal)* (Judgment) [2012] ICJ Rep 422, para 103; and *Legal Consequences of the Separation of the Chagos Archipelago from Mauritius in 1965* (Advisory Opinion) [2019] ICJ Rep 95, para 180.

[12] See the Preamble of the Rome Statute of the International Criminal Court (adopted 17 July 1998, entered into force 1 July 2002) 2187 UNTS 3. It refers to 'the most serious crimes of concern to the international community as a whole'. See also arts 136 and 137 of the United Nations Convention on the Law of the Sea (adopted 10 December 1982, entered into force 16 November 1994) 1833 UNTS 397. It determines that the seabed and ocean floor that stretch beyond the limits of the national jurisdiction constitute the 'common heritage of mankind'. Rüdiger Wolfrum, 'Enforcing Community Interests through International Dispute Settlement: Reality or Utopia?' in Ulrich Fastenrath and others (eds), *From Bilateral to Community Interest. Essays in Honour of Judge Bruno Simma* (OUP 2011) 1136.

[13] See ILC, 'Report of the International Law Commission on the work of its fifty-third session (23 April–1 June and 2 July–10 August 2002)' (August 2001) Supplement No 10/(A/56/10) ch IV.E.1, arts 42 and 48 drew a distinction between breaches of bilateral obligations and obligations of a collective (community) interest nature, which include obligations towards the international community as a whole. See also ILC, 'Draft Conclusions on Identification and Legal Consequences of Peremptory Norms of General International Law (*Jus Cogens*) with Commentaries 2022. Report of the International Law Commission on the Work of its seventy third session (18 April–3 June and 4 July–5 August 2022)' Supplement no A/77/10 ch 4 .E.1, Conclusion 17.

other norms. Instead, it facilitated modest avenues for the invocation of state responsibility by third states in instances where such norms were violated.[14] Stated differently, the fact that a particular treaty or customary obligation is underpinned by values that are shared across states (or state parties) does not in and of itself imply that it would override any other conflicting international obligation binding on any of the parties. Some scholars have attempted to link the rise of international human rights protection through international and regional treaties to a process of constitutionalization. In line with this reasoning, obligations stemming from human rights would be concretizations of pre-existing constitutional rights and, therefore, would have a superior standing vis-à-vis other international obligations.[15] However, only a small number of norms have over time acquired hierarchical features. These notably include peremptory norms of international law (*jus cogens*), which consist of a small number of obligations representing the fundamental values underpinning the international legal order.[16] The ILC for its part has also indicated that peremptory norms 'reflect and protect fundamental values of the international community, are hierarchically superior to other rules of international law and are universally applicable'.[17]

The subsequent analysis will give an overview of the benchmarks of *jus cogens*. In so doing, it commences with an overview of the historical origins of peremptory norms in legal scholarship, followed by its endorsement by positive law and courts and tribunals. This analysis will illustrate that there are lingering uncertainties pertaining to the process of identification of peremptory norms. Even so, the concept has been invoked in state executive practice (although infrequently) and has been endorsed by various courts. However, such invocation thus far has had a limited impact from a legal perspective, including in the context of norm conflict resolution. The contribution further suggests that this limited impact results from the fact that the content of peremptory obligations is either very narrow or very vague. This, in turn, implies a lack of consensus amongst states regarding the content (scope) of *jus cogens*, including the values underlying these norms. As a result, it is questionable whether the construct of *jus cogens* is able to provide meaningful legal protection against the erosion of legal

[14] The purpose of the recognition of obligations *erga omnes (partes)* is to facilitate the invocation of state responsibility and not to establish a hierarchy of norms. See James Crawford, 'Responsibility for Breaches of Communitarian Norms: An Appraisal of Article 48 of the ILC Articles on Responsibility of States for Internationally Wrongful Acts' in Ulrich Fastenrath and others (eds), *From Bilateral to Community Interest. Essays in Honour of Judge Bruno Simma* (OUP 2011) 230. See also ILC, 'Conclusions 2022' (n 13) Conclusion 17.2. For an analysis of the different avenues for invoking state responsibility of *erga omnes (partes)* obligations in a decentralized legal order, see Erika de Wet, 'Invoking Obligations Erga Omnes in the Twenty-First Century: Progressive Developments since Barcelona Traction' (2013) 37 South African Yearbook of International Law 1.

[15] See the analysis by Stephen Baumgard, 'Human Rights as International Constitutional Rights' (2008) 19 European Journal of International Law 749, 757–58; see extensively also Alexander Orakhelashvili, *Peremptory Norms in International Law* (OUP 2006). See also the Dissenting Opinion of Judge Tanaka in the *South-West Africa Case (Ethiopia v South Africa; Liberia v South Africa)* (Judgment, Second Phase) [1966] ICJ Rep 6, 298.

[16] See Pierre-Marie Dupuy, 'Some Reflections on Contemporary International Law and the Appeal to Universal Values: A Response to Martti Koskenniemi' (2005) 16 European Journal of International Law 131, 133.

[17] ILC, 'Conclusions 2022' (n 13) Conclusion 2.

norms. It is too rudimentary in character to entrench and stabilize core human rights values as the moral foundation of the international legal order.[18]

## 2. A Contested Creature of Scholarship

While *jus cogens* only found its way into positive law via the Vienna Convention on the Law of Treaties (VCLT) in 1969,[19] the concept has since Roman times been present in legal writings.[20] It has predominantly been developed through scholarship in an attempt to limit the freedom of contract of states in order to protect fundamental international values.[21] It is also at the level of scholarship that most of the open contestation pertaining to the nature and scope of *jus cogens*, as well as the process for its identification, has taken place and is continuing to do so. Already at an early stage, scholars explored the possibility of curbing the power of states both nationally and internationally, through norms that could bind a state regardless of whether the state in question expressed its consent thereto.[22] For example, classic authors tended to distinguish between consensual law (*jus dispositivum*) and mandatory norms (*jus natural nessarium*) that bind a state independently of its will.[23] By the nineteenth century, the idea that certain agreements by states would be *contra bonos mores* gained ground within scholarship, as international law evolved into a distinct legal sub-discipline at universities.[24] This coincided with the first attempts at the humanization of international law (namely, codifying obligations closely linked to human dignity), as exemplified by the abolition of slavery and the development of the law of armed conflict.[25]

In the twentieth century, the claim that *jus cogens* protected values that were indispensable to the international community of states at any given time persisted against the backdrop of two world wars and the increased organization of international society.[26] Influenced also by the work of Alfred Verdross, the concept gained moral

[18] den Heijer and van der Wilt (n 4) 14–15; Jean d'Aspremont, 'Jus Cogens as a Social Construct Without Pedigree' (2015) 46 Netherlands Yearbook of International Law 85, 92. See also Thomas Kleinlein, Chapter 4 in this book, Section 3.3.

[19] Vienna Convention on the Law of Treaties (adopted 23 May 1969, entered into force 27 January 1980), 1155 UNTS 331 (VCLT). See also Dinah Shelton, 'Sherlock Holmes and the Mystery of Jus Cogens' (2015) 46 Netherlands Yearbook of International Law 23, 24, and 26.

[20] d'Aspremont (n 18) 90. See also Stefan Kadelbach, 'Genesis, Function and Identification of Jus Cogens Norms' (2015) 46 Netherlands Yearbook of International Law 147, 150, who notes that the term itself stems from nineteenth-century Pandectism.

[21] Shelton, 'Sherlock Holmes and the Mystery of Jus Cogens' (n 19) 24.

[22] ibid 25.

[23] See Alberico Gentili, *De Iure Belli Libri Tres* (1646); Hugo Grotius, *De Jure Belli ac Pacis Libri Tres* (1625); Chistian Wolff, *Jus Gentium Method Scientifica Petratctorum* (1764); Emer de Vattel, *Le Droit de Gens au Principes de la Loi Naturelle* (1758). See also ILC, 'Report of the Study Group of the International Law Commission, Fragmentation of International Law: Difficulties Arising from the Diversification and Expansion of International Law' (13 April 2006) UN Doc A/CN.4/L.682, para 361. The study group pointed to the Roman law distinction between *jus cogens* or *jus strictum* and *jus dispositivum* and the maxim *jus publicum privatorum pactis mutari non potest*. See also Shelton, 'Sherlock Holmes and the Mystery of Jus Cogens' (n 19) 26–27.

[24] Kadelbach (n 20) 150.

[25] ibid.

[26] den Heijer and van der Wilt (n 4) 19; d'Aspremont (n 18) 90; Shelton, 'Sherlock Holmes and the Mystery of Jus Cogens' (n 19) 28–29. As far as earlier authors are concerned, see William Hall, *A Treatise*

ground after the Second World War.[27] As of the 1950s, references to *jus cogens* became a constant feature in textbooks on international law.[28] Moreover, it made its way into the work of the ILC on the Law of Treaties that subsequently culminated in the VCLT.[29] References to the need for limiting the contractual freedom of states was already present in the work of the first ILC Rapporteur on the Law of Treaties.[30] The report of the ILC that was ultimately submitted to the Vienna Conference stated that it was increasingly difficult to argue that there is no rule of international law from which states cannot contract out.[31] In 1969, this reasoning was endorsed at the Vienna Conference through Article 53 VCLT, with the support of the (then) socialist and newly independent states and despite the reluctance of some Western states (notably France).[32] Article 53 determined:

> A treaty is void if, at the time of its conclusion, it conflicts with a peremptory norm of general international law. For the purposes of the present Convention, a peremptory norm of general international law is a norm accepted and recognized by the international community of States as a whole as a norm from which no derogation is permitted and which can be modified only by a subsequent norm of general international law having the same character.[33]

In addition, Article 64 VCLT declared that '[if] a new peremptory norm of general international law emerges, any existing treaty which is in conflict with that norm becomes void and terminates'.[34] More than three decades later, the ILC reaffirmed the existence of *jus cogens* in its Articles on Responsibility of States for Internationally Wrongful Acts of 2001, by acknowledging a category of serious breaches of obligations 'arising under a peremptory norm of general international law'.[35] In 2016, the ILC

*on International Law* (8th edn, Clarendon Press 1924) 382–83; Lassa Oppenheim, *International Law* (Longmans 1905) 528.

[27] See Alfred Verdross, 'Forbidden Treaties in International Law' (1937) 31 American Journal of International Law 571. See also Alfred Verdross, 'Jus Dispositivum and Jus Cogens in International Law' (1966) 60 American Journal of International Law 55.

[28] See eg Arnold McNair, *Law of Treaties* (Clarendon Press 1961) 213–14. In this classic work on the law of treaties, McNair found it difficult to imagine any society, whether of individuals or states, whose laws set no limit to freedom of contract. See also Kadelbach (n 20) 150; Shelton, 'Sherlock Holmes and the Mystery of Jus Cogens' (n 19) 24–25.

[29] d'Aspremont (n 18) 90; Giorgio Gaja, 'The Protection of General Interests in the International Community' (2012) 364 Collected Courses of The Hague Academy of International Law 9, 47.

[30] ILC, 'Report on the Law of Treaties by J.L. Brierly, Special Rapporteur' (14 April 1950) UN Doc A/CN.4/23, 246; ILC, 'Report by Mr Hersh Lauterpacht, Special Raporteur' (24 March 1953) UN Doc A/CN.4/63, paras 4–5. See also Shelton, 'Sherlock Holmes and the Mystery of Jus Cogens' (n 19) 31.

[31] ILC, 'Report of the International Law Commission on the Work of its Eighteenth Session' (4 May–9 July 1966) UN Doc A/CN.4/191, 247; Shelton, 'Sherlock Holmes and the Mystery of Jus Cogens' (n 19) 33.

[32] Eric Suy, 'Article 53: Treaties Conflicting with a Peremptory Norm of General International Law (jus cogens)' in Oliver Corten and Pierre Klein (eds), *The Vienna Convention on the Law of Treaties*, vol 2 (OUP 2011) 1225. See also Jure Vidmar, 'Norm Conflicts and Hierarchy in International Law: Towards a Vertical International System?' in Erika de Wet and Jure Vidmar (eds), *Hierarchy in International Law. The Place of Human Rights* (OUP 2012) 26. See Dupuy, 'Some Reflections' (n 16) 134.

[33] VCLT (n 19) art 53.

[34] ibid art 64.

[35] ILC, 'Report of the International Law Commission on the work of its fifty-third session (23 April–1 June and 2 July–10 August 2002)' (n 13) ch IV.E.2, Commentary on art 40, para 1.

once again engaged in a project on 'peremptory norms of general international law'. By 2022 the ILC had adopted 23 draft conclusions, inter alia relying on the definition of a peremptory norm in Article 53 VCLT as the point of departure for the identification of *jus cogens* norms.[36]

A striking feature of Article 53 VCLT is that it neither identifies any norms having peremptory status, nor clarifies the procedure whereby these norms were to be identified. The only reference to method was that the 'international community as a whole' had to identify those international law norms belonging to the category of peremptory norms.[37] In an annex to its 2022 draft conclusions, the ILC did however include a list of norms to which it has previously referred as having the status of *jus cogens*. This non-exhaustive list refers to (a) the prohibition of aggression; (b) the prohibition of genocide; (c) the prohibition of crimes against humanity; (d) the basic rules of international humanitarian law; (e) the prohibition of racial discrimination and apartheid; (f) the prohibition of slavery; (g) the prohibition of torture; and (h) the right of self-determination.[38] On these earlier occasions the ILC motived its choices with reference to municipal and international judicial decisions and authors, but without elaborating either on its own methodology for identification, or on the methodology of the sources it quoted.[39]

Scholars for their part have attempted to explain the method of identification as well as the origins of *jus cogens* with reference to private law, general principles of law, legal philosophy, and religion. For example, some scholars linked peremptory norms to public policy without which the preservation of the international community as such would not be possible.[40] Another line of reasoning described *jus cogens* as resulting from the logic of law that required compliance with essential rules on which the system of law itself was based.[41] Others claim that peremptory obligations are not grounded in the law itself, but in metaphysical principles of justification.[42] As a manifestation of the fundamental values of the international community, peremptory norms would exist independently from the will of states.[43] However, these scholarly explanations are all vulnerable to arbitrary conclusions as to what constitutes the 'essential' rules and the values underpinning them of the international community.[44]

[36] ILC, 'Conclusions 2022' (n 13) Conclusion 3; see also ILC, 'Second Report on jus cogens by Dire Tladi, Special Rapporteur' (16 March 2017) UN Doc A/CN.4/706, para 33; ILC, 'Third Report by Tladi' (n 10) para 4.

[37] Shelton, 'Sherlock Holmes and the Mystery of Jus Cogens' (n 19) 33; see also Kleinlein, Chapter 4 in this book, Section 3.3.

[38] See ILC, 'Conclusions 2022' (n 13) annex; see also ILC, 'Report Fragmentation of International Law' (n 23) para 374; ILC, 'Report of the International Law Commission on the work of its fifty-third session (23 April–1 June and 2 July–10 August 2002)' (n 13) ch IV.E.2, Commentary on art 40, paras 4–6.

[39] See for example ILC, 'Report of the International Law Commission on the work of its fifty-third session (23 April–1 June and 2 July–10 August 2002)' (n 13) ch IV.E.2, Commentary on art 40, paras 4–5.

[40] See ILC, 'Third Report of the Law of Treaties by Mr. G. G. Fitzmaurice, Special Rapporteur' (18 March 1958) UN Doc A/CN.4/115, 41. He claimed that *jus cogens* norms involved not only legal rules, but considerations of morals and of international good order. See also Shelton, 'Sherlock Holmes and the Mystery of Jus Cogens' (n 19) 30.

[41] Shelton, 'Sherlock Holmes and the Mystery of Jus Cogens' (n 19) 30.

[42] Glider Hernández, 'A Reluctant Guardian: The International Court of Justice and the Concept of "International Community"' (2013) 83 British Yearbook of International Law 13, 38–39.

[43] ILC, 'Report Fragmentation of International Law' (n 23) para 361.

[44] Gaja (n 29) 53–54; Kadelbach (n 20) 149; ILC, 'First report on jus cogens by Dire Tladi, Special Rapporteur' (8 March 2016) UN Doc A/CN.4/693, para 52.

They all allow for the subjective preferences of the scholars, practitioners, and judges to be elevated to 'higher law'.[45]

This (perceived) arbitrariness in the process of identification of *jus cogens* has provoked severe criticism. Critics of the legal construct of *jus cogens* fear that it facilitates the abuse of power by stronger states in the interests of a hegemonic endeavour.[46] In accordance with this reasoning, the dominant political powers of the time could deploy the notion of normative hierarchy in a manner that privileges themselves and imposes their ideological prejudices, undermining the pluralist values inherent to an international community consisting of multiple, diverse states.[47] This concern finds some support in the fact that most of the norms generally cited by authors as having a peremptory character have their roots in the Western liberal human rights tradition.

Another challenge common to most *jus cogens* theories is the difficulty in reconciling the existence of fundamental pre-existing norms with the notion of consent which has underpinned the international legal order since the nineteenth century.[48] In particular, it is not clear how in such a consent-based system, peremptory norms can bind those who object to the very idea of hierarchically superior norms, or to the idea that such norms can be identified and imposed by a large majority of states on 'persistent objectors'.[49] Modern international lawyers have attempted to explain this conundrum by emphasizing the role of state consent in the customary process by means of which peremptory norms come about.[50] In line with this reasoning, peremptory norms constitute a specific category of CIL.[51] In order to acquire peremptory status, a norm first has to be recognized as CIL, whereafter the international community of states as a whole further has to agree that it is a norm from which no derogation is permitted. Peremptory norms, therefore, would be subject to a process of 'double acceptance' by the international community of states as a whole.[52] Having consented to this process, states by implication consented to the consequence that a large majority

[45] Shelton, 'Sherlock Holmes and the Mystery of Jus Cogens' (n 19) 24; Gaja (n 29) 54. However, see Antonio Cançado Trindade, 'Jus Cogens: The Determination and the Gradual Expansion of its Material Content in Contemporary International Case Law' in Organización de los Estados Americanos (OEA) (ed), *XXXV Curso de Derecho Internacional* (Seretaría General de la OEA 2009), who supports the role of judges in identifying and developing jus cogens.

[46] d'Aspremont (n 18) 93; Martti Koskenniemi, 'International Law in Europe: Between Tradition and Renewal' (2005) 16 European Journal of International Law 113, 123; Prosper Weil, 'Towards Relative Normativity in International Law?' (1983) 77 American Journal of International Law 413.

[47] d'Aspremont (n 18) 93; den Heijer and van der Wilt (n 4) 15.

[48] Shelton, 'Sherlock Holmes and the Mystery of Jus Cogens' (n 19) 32, 34.

[49] ibid 34.

[50] See Michael Byers, 'Conceptualizing the Relationship between Jus Cogens and Erga Omnes Rules' (1997) 66 Nordic Journal of International Law 211, 228.

[51] See ILC, 'Conclusions 2022' (n 13) Conclusion 4, 5. While Conclusion 5(1) notes that CIL is the most common basis for peremptory norms, Conclusion 5(2) states that '[t]reaty provisions and general principles of law may also serve as bases for peremptory norms of general international law (*jus cogens*)'. See also ILC, 'Third Report by Tladi' (n 10) para 15. Tladi conceded that within the sixth committee of the UN General Assembly, the issue of sources generated much debate. Although most states supported the notion that CIL formed the basis of peremptory norms, several states did question the role of other sources. See also Byers (n 50) 225–26, 228. He points out that as national laws often also reflect concretizations of CIL, general principles of law and custom would often overlap.

[52] Such an explanation does find textual support in arts 53 and 64 VCLT, which refer four times to peremptory norms as a 'norm of general international law'. See Gaja (n 29) 54–55; Vidmar, 'Norm Conflicts and Hierarchy' (n 32) 25.

of states can bind a dissenter to a peremptory obligation.[53] On the whole, however, the role of state consent in the formation of peremptory norms as well as the process of identification remain a bone of contention amongst scholars.[54]

## 3. *Jus Cogens* in the Practice of State Executives and (International) Courts

Despite the controversies pertaining to the nature, origins, and identification of *jus cogens*, the construct has on occasion been invoked in the executive practice of states, although this does not often occur. International and domestic courts for their part have been more eager to invoke *jus cogens*, especially since the turn of the twentieth/twenty-first century. However, the invocation of the legal construct of *jus cogens* in these contexts did little to clarify the methods for identification of peremptory norms, as none of the states or judicial bodies in question explained their methodology for identifying *jus cogens*. At most, they appealed to the importance of the obligation in question, citing other case law and/or authors whose methodology in this regard was equally unclear.[55] In addition, the recognition of the peremptory status of the norm in question had no direct bearing on the legal outcome of the case, as is illustrated below.

As far as the invocation of *jus cogens* in executive practice is concerned, it occurred in relation to the potential invalidity of certain treaties.[56] It was thus invoked in the context in which *jus cogens* was initially developed, namely, the outlawing of immoral contracts. For example, in 1964 during a debate in the UN Security Council, Cyprus claimed that Article IV of the Treaty of Guarantee of 1960, as interpreted by Turkey, violated *jus cogens*, by allowing Turkey the right to unilateral military intervention.[57] Similarly, some Arab states argued that the Camp David Accords of September 1978[58] violated the right to self-determination of the Palestinian people, which had the status of *jus cogens*.[59] Also, in 1980 the United States stated that if the Treaty of Friendship between the Soviet Union and Afghanistan endorsed the type of military intervention by the Soviet Union in Afghanistan, it would be void because of a conflict with

[53] Byers (n 50) 222; Vidmar, 'Norm Conflicts and Hierarchy' (n 32) 26. The claim of the South African government that it was a persistent objector to the prohibition of racial discrimination and apartheid was universally rejected with the argument that peremptory law does not exempt persistent objectors.

[54] Kadelbach (n 20) 149.

[55] ibid 167.

[56] ibid 152; ILC, 'Third Report by Tladi' (n 10) para 31; Shelton, 'Sherlock Holmes and the Mystery of Jus Cogens' (n 19) 34.

[57] UN Security Council (UNSC), 'Official Records of the 19th session, 1098th meeting' (27 February 1964) UN Doc S/PV 1098, paras 94–95.

[58] Framework for Peace in the Middle East (Israel – Egypt) (17 September 1978) 1138 UNTS I-17853.

[59] ILC, 'Third Report by Tladi' (n 10) para 31; see also *East Timor (Portugal v Australia)* (Counter-Memorial of the Government of Australia) 1992, para 223 <www.icj-cij.org/public/files/case-related/84/6837.pdf> accessed 2 December 2021. Australia argued that if the ICJ were to accept the view of Portugal that the right to self-determination had peremptory status, and then found that the conclusions of the 'Timor Gap Treaty' were in conflict with this right, the treaty would be void, see Treaty between Australia and the Republic of Indonesia on the Zone of Co-operation in an Area between the Indonesian Province of East Timor and Northern Australia (Australia–Indonesia) (11 December 1989) <https://cil.nus.edu.sg/wp-content/uploads/formidable/14/1989-Australia-Indonesia-Timor-Gap-Treaty.pdf> accessed 2 December 2021.

a peremptory norm of international law, namely, Article 2(4) of the UN Charter.[60] However, in none of these instances did the invocation of *jus cogens* have any consequence for the validity of the treaty.[61]

Turning to court practice, an early reference to *jus cogens* can be found in the jurisprudence of the Permanent Court of International Justice, the predecessor of the ICJ. In his Separate Opinion in the 1934 *Oscar Chinn* case, Judge Schücking asserted that the League of Nations would not have embarked on the codification of international law:

> [I]f it were not possible, even today, to create a jus cogens, the effect of which would be that, once States have agreed on certain rules of law, and have given an undertaking that these rules may not be altered by some only of their number, any act adopted in contravention of that undertaking would be automatically void.[62]

The ICJ implicitly referred to peremptory norms in the 1949 *Corfu Channel* case, when referring to Albania's obligations with reference to well-recognized principles of humanity.[63]

As mentioned in Section 1 above, the 1970 Barcelona Traction decision recognized the concept of obligations with an *erga omnes* effect, that is, obligations in the realization of which all states would have a legal interest.[64] As was also mentioned, the recognition that all states can in principle invoke the responsibility of a state that breached an *erga omnes* obligation (for example by protesting through diplomatic channels) is not necessarily a manifestation of the hierarchically superior status of the obligation in question. Yet, the examples of *erga omnes* obligations cited by the ICJ coincided with those generally cited by authors as having peremptory status. As mentioned, these include the prohibition of the aggressive use of force, genocide, and the prohibition of slavery and racial discrimination.[65] Therefore, by referring to these specific obligations in the context of obligations that have an *erga omnes* effect, the ICJ implicitly also acknowledged the existence of *jus cogens*.[66] Subsequently in its 1986 Nicaragua decision, the ICJ once again implicitly endorsed the notion of *jus cogens* by referring

[60] Memorandum of Legal Advisor of the United State Department, Robert B Owen to the Acting Secretary of State, Warren Christopher, dated 29 December 1979, reproduced in Marian L Nash, 'Contemporary practice of the United States relating to international law' (1980) 74 American Journal of International Law 418, 419; ILC, 'Third Report by Tladi' (n 10) para 31.

[61] See Kadelbach (n 20) 152; Shelton, 'Sherlock Holmes and the Mystery of Jus Cogens' (n 19) 34.

[62] *The Oscar Chinn Case (UK v Belgium)* (Judgment, Separate Opinion of Judge Schücking) [1934] PCIJ Series A/B No 63, 149–150; Shelton, 'Sherlock Holmes and the Mystery of Jus Cogens' (n 19) 32–33; see d'Aspremont (n 18) 90.

[63] *Corfu Channel Case (UK v Albania)* (Judgment) [1949] ICJ Rep 4, 22; Shelton, 'Sherlock Holmes and the Mystery of Jus Cogens' (n 19) 31.

[64] *Barcelona Traction* (n 11) 32. Subsequently the ICJ has reaffirmed the notion on several occasions. It was also endorsed in the ASR (n 13). In arts 42 and 48, the ILC drew a distinction between breaches of bilateral obligations and obligations of a collective (community) interest nature, which include obligations towards the international community as a whole.

[65] *Barcelona Traction* (n 11) 34; Gaja (n 29) 25 and 55; Hernández (n 42) 41ff; Jochen A Frowein 'Collective Enforcement of International Obligations' (1987) 47 Zeitschrift für Ausländisches Öffentliches Recht und Völkerrecht 67, 71.

[66] All peremptory norms, therefore, have an *erga omnes* effect, even though not all obligations *erga omnes* would necessarily have the status of *jus cogens*. Gaja (n 29) 56; Dupuy, 'L'unité' (n 10) 385.

to the prohibition of the use of force as a 'cardinal' principle of CIL.[67] However, it took another 20 years for the ICJ to explicitly acknowledge the notion of *jus cogens* in a majority decision. In its 2006 decision on the Armed Activities in the Congo of 2006, the ICJ confirmed the peremptory status of the prohibition of genocide,[68] a position which it has since reaffirmed.[69] In 2012 it also acknowledged the peremptory status of the prohibition of torture in the *Habre* case.[70]

At this juncture, it is worth noting that these endorsements of the peremptory status of the obligations in question were merely declaratory and not decisive for the cases in question. First, the ICJ did not accept that the *jus cogens* status of an obligation in and of itself provides jurisdiction before it, nor does it have any other 'automatic' effect. The question whether the ICJ has jurisdiction instead depends on whether the relevant states have accepted the ICJ's jurisdiction as provided for in Article 36 of the ICJ Statute.[71] The fact that the violation of a peremptory obligation was at issue does not in and of itself compensate for the absence of such consent.[72] In addition, the ICJ has consistently refrained from attaching any overriding consequences to *jus cogens* norms, as inter alia became clear in the decision of Jurisdictional Immunities of the State.[73]

This case had its origins in the *Ferrini* case in which the Italian domestic courts attached significant weight to the values underpinning peremptory obligations and the need for enforcing these obligations and the values that they represent effectively.[74] However, when the *Ferrini* case subsequently culminated in proceedings between Germany and Italy before the ICJ in 2012, the ICJ explicitly rejected this line of argument. The ICJ saw no basis for the proposition that a rule lacking the status of a peremptory norm may not be applied even if that would hinder the enforcement of a peremptory norm.[75] While this decision remains controversial in

[67] *Military and Paramilitary Activities In and Against Nicaragua (Nicaragua v USA)* (Judgment) [1986] ICJ Rep 4, para 190.

[68] See *Armed Activities on the Territory of the Congo (New Application: 2002) (Democratic Republic of the Congo v Rwanda)* (Judgment) [2006] ICJ Rep 6, para 46.

[69] See *Application of the Convention on the Prevention and Punishment of the Crime of Genocide (Bosnia and Herzegovina v Serbia and Montenegro)* (Judgment) [2007] ICJ Rep 43, para 161.

[70] *Belgium v Senegal* (n 11) paras 99–100; Kadelbach (n 20) 155.

[71] *Armed Activities in the Congo* (n 68) paras 67 and 69.

[72] See also Jure Vidmar, 'Rethinking Jus Cogens after Germany v Italy: Back to Article 53?' (2013) 60 Netherlands International Law Review 1, 14ff.

[73] *Jurisdictional Immunities of the State (Germany v Italy: Greece Intervening)* [2012] ICJ Rep 99, para 95; *Armed Activities in the Congo* (n 68) paras 64, 125. See also Kadelbach (n 20) 155; Hernández (n 42); Stefan Talmon, 'Jus Cogens after Germany v Italy: Substantive and Procedural Rules Distinguished' (2012) 25 Leiden Journal of International Law 979, 987ff; see also Vidmar, 'Rethinking Jus Cogens' (n 72) 14ff.

[74] *Ferrini v Germany* No 5044/04 ILDC 19 (IT 2004); *Germany v Milde (Max Josef)* No 1072/09 ILDC 1224 (IT 2009); *Lozano (Mario Luiz) v Italy* No 31171/08 ILDC 1085 (IT 2008); see also *R ex parte Pinochet v Bartle and ors* [1999] UKHL 17; see also Riccardo Pavoni, 'Human Rights and the Immunities of Foreign States and International Organizations' in Erika de Wet and Jure Vidmar (eds), *Hierarchy in International Law: The Place of Human Rights* (OUP 2012) 86–87.

[75] *Jurisdictional Immunities of the State* (n 73) para 95; see also Philippa Webb, 'Human Rights and the Immunities of State Officials' in Erika de Wet and Jure Vidmar (eds), *Hierarchy in International Law: The Place of Human Rights* (OUP 2012) 122–23. As far as the enforcement of peremptory norms is concerned, the ICJ has essentially limited itself to general statements about the obligation of states to cooperate (in particular through the UN) to bring to an end serious violations of peremptory norms. See the Advisory Opinions on the *Construction of a Wall* (n 11) para 159 and the *Chagos Islands* Opinion (n 11) para 180. See also See ILC, 'Conclusions 2022' (n 13) Conclusion 19 and commentary.

Italy,[76] domestic and international courts on the whole remain reluctant to waive jurisdictional immunities of states, state officials, and international organizations for alleged human rights violations that constitute peremptory prohibitions under international law.[77] This is exemplified by the *Al-Adsani* decision of the European Court of Human Rights (ECtHR) of 2001,[78] as well as several subsequent decisions.[79]

At the beginning of the twenty-first century and lasting for almost a decade, the jurisprudence of the Inter-American Court of Human Rights (IACtHR)—due to its particular composition at the time—displayed an activist rhetoric towards *jus cogens*.[80] Whereas the ICJ and the ECtHR have attributed peremptory status to a small category of norms, notably the prohibition of torture and genocide, the IACtHR declared various norms as representing fundamental values and therefore having peremptory status.[81] This included the principle of non-discrimination, for being intrinsically related to the right to equal protection before the law and the dignity of the individual.[82] In addition, the IACtHR used *jus cogens* as an argument to stress the particularly grave character of certain human rights violations and the need to prosecute and punish the perpetrators thereof.[83] It held so in cases of widespread and consistent practice of extrajudicial executions, torture, rape, slavery, and involuntary servitude, as well as in a large number of decisions with respect to enforced disappearance.[84]

[76] In October 2014, the Italian Constitutional Court quashed legislation which the Italian government had adopted to give effect to the ICJ judgment. In the view of the Constitutional Court, the legislation did not give due consideration to Italian constitutional provisions pertaining to access to justice. Christian Tams, 'Let the Games Continue: Immunity for War Crimes Before the Italian Constitutional Court' (*EJIL:Talk!*, 24 October 2014) <www.ejiltalk.org/let-the-games-continue-immunity-for-war-crimes-before-the-italian-supreme-court/> accessed 2 December 2021. Recently, in February 2017, one of the judges of the United Kingdom Supreme Court also suggested that the domestic public policy exceptions to the foreign act of state doctrine should be interpreted in light of international *jus cogens*. See *Belhaj and Boudchar v Straw and others* [2017] UKSC 3, paras 249–80.

[77] See also Riccardo Pavoni, 'The Law of International Immunities after Germany v Italy, Mothers of Srebrenica and Jones: The Best is Yet to Come' (*ESIL Newsletter*, 13 March 2014) <https://esil-sedi.eu/wp-content/uploads/2013/02/March-2014.pdf> accessed 2 December 2021.

[78] *Al-Adsani v United Kingdom* App no 35763/97 (ECtHR, 21 November 2001). A minority of eight judges (against the majority of nine), however, did favour the value-driven argument that resulted in the lifting of the immunity in the Ferrini. See Joint Dissenting Opinion of Judges Rozakis and Caflisch, joined by Judges Wildhaber, Costa, Cabral Barreto, and Vajic. See also the Dissenting Opinions of Judges Cançado Trindade and Yusuf in *Jurisdictional Immunities of the State* (n 73).

[79] See eg *Stichting Mothers of Srebrenica v The Netherlands* App no 65542/12 (ECtHR, 11 June 2013); *Jones v UK* App no 34356/06 and 40528/06 (ECtHR, 14 January 2014).

[80] Shelton, 'Sherlock Holmes and the Mystery of Jus Cogens' (n 19) 43.

[81] ibid.

[82] *Juridical Condition and Rights of the Undocumented Migrants* (Advisory Opinion OC-18/03) Series A No 18 (IACtHR, 17 September 2003) 95–96 and 101. The IACtHR also recognized the fundamental nature of the right to life. See *Gomez Paquiauri Brothers v Peru* Series C No 110 (IACtHR, 8 July 2004) para 8. The Inter-American Commission on Human Rights has declared the right to life to be a norm of jus cogens in *Victims of the Tugboat '13 de Marzo' v Cuba*, Case 11.436, Inter-American Commission of Human Rights Report No 47/96 (16 October 1996) 146–47. See also Shelton, 'Sherlock Holmes and the Mystery of Jus Cogens' (n 19) 43–44 and 157; Kadelbach (n 20) 6.

[83] See also ILC, 'Third Report by Tladi' (n 10) para 115, who concludes that there is a duty to prosecute international crimes of a peremptory nature.

[84] See *La Cantuta et al v Peru* Series C No 162 (IACtHR, 29 November 2006); *Bayarri v Argentina* Series C No 187 (IACtHR, 30 October 2008) para 81; *Velez Loor v Panama* Series C No 218 (IACtHR, 23 November 2010) para 248; Shelton, 'Sherlock Holmes and the Mystery of Jus Cogens' (n 19); Kadelbach (n 20) 158.

Despite this activist rhetoric, closer scrutiny reveals that thus far the references in the IACtHR's jurisprudence to the peremptory character of the human rights obligations in question have merely been declaratory.[85] The various legal consequences to which the Court referred, such as the positive obligation to revert existing discriminatory situations, as well as to prosecute the perpetrators of widespread human rights violations, in any case were encompassed by the applicable treaty obligations. As a consequence, any contrary municipal law would in any case violate the applicable international law.[86] It also remains to be seen whether the IACtHR's elevating of the duty to prosecute various widespread human rights abuses to *jus cogens* status will result in the waiving of sovereign immunity. The question so far has not arisen before it.[87]

The declaratory rhetoric of the IACtHR to some extent has been reiterated by that of criminal courts and tribunals.[88] The International Criminal Tribunal for the Former Yugoslavia (ICTY), the first international tribunal to explicitly invoke *jus cogens*,[89] declared the prohibition of torture as having peremptory status. The ICTY underscored the importance of the values underpinning *jus cogens*, as a result of which it enjoyed a higher rank than treaty and 'ordinary' CIL.[90] Similarly, the International Criminal Court (ICC) underscored the gravity of international crimes with reference to their peremptory character. The ICC further justified the need for contravening domestic law to be set aside with the overriding character of peremptory norms.[91] Once again, these references added little from a legal perspective, as it is a general principle of treaty law that states cannot invoke the contravention of domestic law to justify the non-performance of an international obligation.[92] In addition, the statements by the ICC neither had any direct bearing on the outcome of the trials, nor on the type of punishment imposed.[93]

[85] Shelton, 'Sherlock Holmes and the Mystery of Jus Cogens' (n 19) 44.

[86] ibid 42.

[87] ibid 38.

[88] d'Aspremont (n 18) 96.

[89] At Nuremberg there were implicit references to the peremptory character of certain norms. For example, in the *Krupp* trial, one of the five indictments concerned forced labour of French prisoners of war in weapon factories, in contravention of the Geneva Convention Relative to the Treatment of Prisoners of War of 27 July 1929. The counsel for defendants invoked a treaty between Germany and the Vichy regime, facilitating such use, but without proof of its existence. The Military Tribunal held that even if such a treaty had existed, it would have been 'manifestly *contra bones mores* and hence void'. See *The Krupp Trial*, Case No 58 (US Military Tribunal, 31 July 1948) 144. See also Kadelbach (n 20) 153.

[90] *Prosecutor v Furundzija*, Case No IT-95-17/I-T (ICTY, 10 December 1998) para 153.

[91] Kadelbach (n 20) 160. See also ILC, 'Third Report by Tladi' (n 10) para 132, according to whom immunity ratione materiae does not apply to any offence prohibited by a peremptory norm of general international law. In addition, he submits that states have a duty to exercise jurisdiction over offences concerning peremptory norms of international law (*jus cogens*), where the offences were committed by the nationals of that state or the territory under its jurisdiction.

[92] VCLT (n 19) art 27.

[93] Shelton, 'Sherlock Holmes and the Mystery of Jus Cogens' (n 19) 45.

## 4. Limited Impact of *Jus Cogens* on Stabilization of Norms

It is fair to conclude from the above analysis that the main added value of the invocation of *jus cogens* during executive practice and, in particular, during court proceedings has been the strengthening of the moral appeal of the (underpinning values of the) obligations in question.[94] By appealing to the fundamental nature of the values at stake, the invocation of peremptory norms can increase the burden of the argument on those who are on the opposing side.[95] It further intensifies the political (moral) pressure on law makers, to give due consideration to the effective implementation of the obligations at stake and the values underpinning them.[96] Interestingly, this strategy is predominantly deployed in situations where state responsibility for human rights violations was at issue, or individual criminal responsibility for the commission of an international crime. This means that the invocation of *jus cogens* predominantly occurs beyond the context for which it was not originally intended, namely, the invalidation of immoral treaties.[97]

As far as the limited legal impact of the invocation of *jus cogens* is concerned, it is arguable that this relates to the uncertain content (scope) of these norms. First, it remains uncertain whether the scope of those peremptory norms which have found their way into court decisions extends beyond the prohibition of the conduct in question (that is, the negative obligation).[98] Despite the activist approach of the IACtHR in this regard, ancillary (positive) obligations that would enhance the enforcement of the respective peremptory prohibition are not broadly cited as having peremptory status. Second, even the scope of the respective negative obligations remains contested, including in those instances where the prohibition is absolute, as is the case with the prohibition of torture. The fact that no derogation from the obligation is allowed does not in and of itself clarify the scope of the prohibition, as it is still up to states to determine the conduct that would amount to torture.[99]

That being said, the uncertainty regarding the scope of a peremptory prohibition is likely to be even more pronounced where the prohibition allows for certain exceptions, as this provides additional avenues for the erosion of the scope of the obligation. This would, for example, be the case with the prohibition of the use of force in international relations in accordance with Article 2(4) of the UN Charter and CIL. A prominent exception to this prohibition is the right of states to resort to individual or collective self-defence in response to an armed attack.[100] Ever since the ICJ's Nicaragua decision

94 ibid 34–35 and 44, who notes that it was also driven by the natural law theories underpinning the reasoning of one particular judge on the court at the time.

95 Kadelbach (n 20) 169.

96 ibid; Shelton, 'Sherlock Holmes and the Mystery of Jus Cogens' (n 19) 46.

97 See extensively Gaja (n 29) 47ff. He inter alia mentions that it is the invocation of the concept in other areas of international law that has resulted in the identification of a limited number of peremptory norms by judicial bodies. See also Erika de Wet, 'The Prohibition of Torture as an International Norm of Jus Cogens and Its Implications for National and Customary Law' (2004) 15 European Journal of International Law 97, 98–99.

98 Vidmar, 'Norm Conflicts and Hierarchy' (n 32) 33–34.

99 For example, in *R (on the Application of Bary) v Secretary of State for the Home Department* [2009] EWHC 2068 (Admin); the House of Lords did not, under the circumstances, accept harsh prison conditions combined with the possibility of life without parole in a Florida prison as a bar to extradition.

100 The Charter of the United Nations of 26 June 1945, art 51, determines that '[n]othing in the present Charter shall impair the inherent right of individual or collective self-defence if an armed attack occurs

in 1986, the threshold requirements for the right to self-defence have remained highly contested amongst authors and in executive state practice.[101] This, in turn, has placed the scope of the prohibition under pressure, as an increasingly flexible interpretation of the exception to the prohibition implies less room for the application of the prohibition in the first place.[102]

In light of this vague nature of peremptory norms and the different interpretations as to their scope, some authors regard them as too elementary to preserve unity within and stability of the international legal order.[103] This, in turn, suggests that the notion of core values of the international community aspires to more unity than the highly diverse international legal order can accommodate.[104] A different but related criticism relates to the fact that the elevation of certain norms to a hierarchical superior may inadvertently lead to a devaluation of (the values underpinning) other obligations under international law.[105] For example, only a narrow category of human rights obligations (mainly prohibitions) have been recognized as peremptory. This raises the question as to whether other internationally recognized human rights obligations are of lesser importance. This, in turn, could result in the erosion of respect for these obligations and undermine their enforcement.[106] In summary, therefore, not only is the concept of peremptory norms too rudimentary to protect certain norms from erosion, but by elevating certain norms to a hierarchically superior position, the erosion of 'ordinary norms' is implicitly encouraged.

## 5. Conclusion

The concept of *jus cogens* is firmly established in international scholarship, the work of expert bodies of the UN, as well as in decisions of international and domestic courts. Yet, it remains an infrequent tool in the executive practice of states. It also remains unclear if and to what extent its invocation, either by the executive or by judicial bodies, has yielded concrete legal results. This modest impact of the notion of peremptory norms of international law almost 50 years after its endorsement in the VCLT suggests a lingering reluctance by state executives as well as courts to embrace the notion of a hierarchy of norms in international law.

This reluctance is not necessarily openly expressed by, for example, denying the *jus cogens* character of the prohibition of torture or genocide as such. It is more often than not implied by the unwillingness of governments to invoke the concept in their international relations, or by the refusal by most courts to attach any concrete consequences to peremptory obligations of international law. Stated differently, through a

against a Member of the United Nations, until the Security Council has taken measures necessary to maintain international peace and security'.

[101] See Dissenting Opinion of Judge Sir Robert Jennings, *Nicaragua Decision* (n 67) 543; similarly, Dissenting Opinion of Judge Schwebel, *Nicaragua Decision* (n 67) 268–69, 332ff.

[102] See extensively Tom Ruys, *'Armed Attack' and Article 51 of the UN Charter* (CUP 2010).

[103] Kadelbach (n 20) 167.

[104] ibid 169.

[105] de Wet, 'The Prohibition of Torture' (n 97) 118–19.

[106] ibid 119.

process of 'contestation by omission', states have expressed a reluctance to develop a well-developed hierarchy of norms in international law. This reluctance may in part be rooted in the uncertainties pertaining to the process of identification. It is also likely to be a reflection of the lack of consensus of the scope of peremptory norms and the values underpinning them. While these uncertainties and differences may in recent times have become more visible, in part due to the increased invocation of peremptory norms in litigation since the turn of the twentieth/twenty-first century, they have been ever present in the scholarly debate pertaining to *jus cogens*.

# 6

# There's Life in the Old Dog Yet

## Assessing the Strength of the International Torture Prohibition

*Max Lesch and Lisbeth Zimmermann**

## 1. Introduction

The prohibition of torture is at the heart of the international human rights regime. It is one of the core values of the international legal order.[1] In the early 2000s, the infamous 'enhanced interrogation techniques', used by United States (US) officials in counterterrorism efforts, became public. Concerns about 'fundamental human rights in crisis' and a change of the 'rules of the game' flared up.[2] In the field of international relations (IR), this sparked a vivid and ongoing debate about the potential erosion of international norms or even of the current international order.[3] At the same time, violations and contestations of the torture prohibition are not a new phenomenon.[4] Already in the 1990s, Israel, for instance, advanced a justification of the use of 'moderate physical pressure' in their fight against terrorism.[5] The torture prohibition is thus an exemplary case for studying the extent to which these challenges have affected the strength of the torture prohibition. In this way, it adds to the general objective of this book: exploring whether we are observing change or even metamorphosis of international law.

Assessments of the prohibition's strength vary widely—many of them state that a decay of the torture prohibition has occurred: focusing on non-compliance with the norm, Jutta Brunnée and Stephen Toope, for instance, concluded that the torture prohibition 'was close-to-moribund'[6] due to its being 'undermined by widespread

* We would like to thank Dominik Steiger and the participants in the KFG International Law: Rise or Decline Conference preceding this book for their helpful comments and suggestions. The empirical data on the torture prohibition draws on Lisbeth Zimmermann and others, *International Norm Disputes: The Link between Contestation and Norm Robustness* (OUP 2023 *forthcoming*), Chapter 2, and Max Lesch's dissertation, Max Lesch, *Dynamics of Deviance: Torture and Its Prohibition in World Politics* (Goethe University Frankfurt 2020). Matthew Harris provided helpful copy-editing assistance.

[1] Heike Krieger and Andrea Liese, Chapter 1 in this book.

[2] Tim Dunne, 'The Rules of the Game are Changing: Fundamental Human Rights in Crisis After 9/11' (2007) 44 International Politics 269.

[3] For a comprehensive overview, see Krieger and Liese, Chapter 1 in this book.

[4] Jamal Barnes, *A Genealogy of the Torture Taboo* (Routledge 2017).

[5] Catherine M Grosso, 'International Law in the Domestic Arena: The Case of Torture in Israel' (2000) 86 The Iowa Law Review 305.

[6] Jutta Brunnée and Stephen J Toope, *Legitimacy and Legality in International Law: An Interactional Account* (CUP 2010) 270.

Max Lesch and Lisbeth Zimmermann, *There's Life in the Old Dog Yet* In: *Tracing Value Change in the International Legal Order.* Edited by: Heike Krieger and Andrea Liese, Oxford University Press. © Max Lesch and Lisbeth Zimmermann 2023. DOI: 10.1093/oso/9780192855831.003.0006

contrary practice'.[7] Other studies focus on torture practices and highlight their historical continuity and transnationality, or argue that their prohibition has been replaced by alternative norms.[8] A third group focuses on discursive indicators—contestation—but with a strict focus on debate in the United States, and observes an at least potential decline in the prohibition of torture.[9] By contrast, a smaller strand in the debate concentrates solely on changes in the international discourse: here, compliance becomes irrelevant. Instead, discursive affirmation gives a norm legitimacy and strength.[10] Finally, combining the practice and discourse dimensions has led to a more differentiated assessment that shows how the norm seems to be resilient at the global level but has been weakened among those states participating in the United States rendition programme.[11] Beyond this division, what all these studies have in common, however, is that even if they adopt a comparative,[12] historical,[13] or global perspective,[14] they tend to assess the strength of the torture prohibition based on a few particular cases and reactions to them. A more general analysis of international norm strength is missing.

In this chapter, we will study the strength of the torture prohibition between 1990 and 2010 because two of the most fundamental challenges to the norm were made by Israel and the United States during these two decades. We will approach the question of value change in the international order by analysing the strength of the international torture prohibition over time, specifically examining state discourse (social validity) and practice (sphere of application).[15] As a starting point, we take the end of the Cold War, which was arguably a watershed in the history of international law development. In the 1990s, many longstanding projects in international law, including the field of

[7] ibid 266.

[8] Jonathan Luke Austin, 'Torture and the Material-Semiotic Networks of Violence Across Borders' (2006) 10 International Political Sociology 3; Jonathan Luke Austin, 'We Have Never Been Civilized: Torture and the Materiality of World Political Binaries' (2017) 23 European Journal of International Relations 49; Regina Heller, Martin Kahl, and Daniela Pisoiu, 'The "Dark" Side of Normative Argumentation: The Case of Counterterrorism Policy' (2012) 1 Global Constitutionalism 278; Regina Heller and Martin Kahl, 'Tracing and Understanding "Bad" Norm Dynamics in Counterterrorism: The Current Debates in IR Research' (2013) 6 Critical Studies on Terrorism 414.

[9] Ryder McKeown, 'Norm Regress: US Revisionism and the Slow Death of the Torture Norm' (2009) 23 International Relations 5; Kathryn Sikkink, 'The United States and Torture: Does the Spiral Model Work' in Thomas Risse, Stephen C Ropp, and Kathryn Sikkink (eds), *The Persistent Power of Human Rights: From Commitment to Compliance* (CUP 2013).

[10] Ian Hurd, 'Torture and the Politics of Legitimation in International Law' in Andreas Føllesdal, Johan Karlsson Schaffer, and Geir Ulfstein (eds), *The Legitimacy of International Human Rights Regimes: Legal, Political and Philosophical Perspectives* (CUP 2013); Jamal Barnes, 'The "War on Terror" and the Battle for the Definition of Torture' (2016) 30 International Relations 102. Michal Ben-Josef Hirsch and Jennifer M Dixon, 'Conceptualizing and Assessing Norm Strength in International Relations' (2021) 27 European Journal of International Relations 521.

[11] Averell Schmidt and Kathryn Sikkink, 'Breaking the Ban? The Heterogeneous Impact of US Contestation of the Torture Norm' (2019) 4 Journal of Global Security Studies 105, 118.

[12] Andrea Liese, 'Exceptional Necessity: How Liberal Democracies Contest the Prohibition of Torture and Ill-Treatment when Countering Terrorism' (2009) 5 Journal of International Law and International Relations 17.

[13] Barnes (n 4).

[14] Vincent Charles Keating, 'Contesting the International Illegitimacy of Torture: The Bush Administration's Failure to Legitimate its Preferences within International Society' (2014) 16 The British Journal of Politics & International Relations 1; Schmidt and Sikkink (n 11).

[15] For this focus on norm strength see Krieger and Liese, Chapter 1 in this book. For international relations and international law perspectives on the changing meaning of norms see Antje Wiener, Chapter 2 in this book, and Thomas Kleinlein, Chapter 4 in this book.

human rights, (re)gained salience and 'significantly manifested themselves in the international legal sphere'.[16] This also holds true for the prohibition of torture, with rapidly growing ratification rates of the International Covenant on Civil and Political Rights (ICCPR) as well as the United Nations (UN) Convention against Torture (CAT) after 1990.[17] By now, it is a truism that the optimistic outlook of the 1990s has remained elusive. But how does the strength of the torture prohibition fare when we take a long-term perspective? Are there signs of change or even metamorphosis?

We propose unpacking the notion of norm strength by taking stock of how it evolves in four dimensions: two which are more practice-oriented—compliance and implementation—and two which are more discourse-oriented—concordance and negative reactions to norm violations. This allows us to observe long-term trends in norm strength and avoids falling into what Wayne Sandholtz has identified as a 'compliance trap' in both IR and international law accounts of norm decline.[18] In doing so, we look beyond individual crises such as the challenges by Israel and the United States and extend the analysis to cover a longer timeframe and the global reach of norm strength from the 1990s until 2010.[19]

In the remainder of this chapter, we will first introduce an analytical framework that has recently been developed in IR norms research and will assess change at the level of norm strength. Second, we apply this framework to the case of the international prohibition of torture. After briefly discussing our understanding of this norm, we assess its strength by measuring trends in four dimensions—compliance, implementation, concordance, and negative reactions to norm violations—between 1990 and 2010. We find that the strength of the international torture prohibition did not change—at least not for the worse. We conclude with a discussion of explanatory factors for the norm's continuous strength despite the challenges it has been facing.

## 2. Assessing Norm Strength: An International Relations Perspective

Similar to IR research on normative decay more broadly,[20] research on the prohibition of torture usually discusses the strength of the norm either focussing on a behavioural dimension, in other words, compliance, or on a discourse dimension, that is, contestation.[21] However, such one-sided analyses—especially those focusing on compliance only—neglect 'the intersubjective nature of behaviour in relation to the law'.[22] Norms

[16] Heike Krieger and Georg Nolte, 'The International Rule of Law: Rise or Decline? Approaching Current Foundational Challenges' in Heike Krieger, Georg Nolte, and Andreas Zimmermann (eds), *The International Rule of Law: Rise or Decline?* (OUP 2019) 6.

[17] See Section 3.3 of this chapter.

[18] Wayne Sandholtz, Chapter 3 in this book.

[19] Krieger and Nolte (n 16) 17.

[20] This section draws on Nicole Deitelhoff and Lisbeth Zimmermann, 'Norms under Challenge: Unpacking the Dynamics of Norm Robustness' (2019) 4 Journal of Global Security Studies 2.

[21] Nicole Deitelhoff and Lisbeth Zimmermann, 'Things We Lost in the Fire: How Different Types of Contestation Affect the Robustness of International Norms' (2020) 22 International Studies Review 51, 53.

[22] Ian Clark and others, 'Crisis in the Laws of War? Beyond Compliance and Effectiveness' (2018) 24 European Journal of International Relations 319, 326.

are counterfactually valid and the meaning of norm violations, *ergo* compliance, depends on the assessment *of* and reactions *to* this behaviour by a community.[23] In this chapter, we combine a focus on practice and discourse dimensions in order to assess norm strength. We focus on how states, as the parties to international treaties and main norm addressees, comply with the norm, implement it domestically, concur with it in discourse and react negatively to norm violations.

*Compliance.* We understand compliance as behaviour conforming with a norm's prescription.[24] To assess compliance, we measure trends in the level of behaviour (in) consistent with the core normative claims.

*Implementation.* By implementation we mean the introduction of 'international norm's precepts into formal legal and policy mechanisms within a state or organization in order to routinize compliance'.[25] Such transfer into legal and policy mechanisms is related to efforts to address and improve compliance in itself.[26] Implementation can be achieved through formal legislation, institutionalization, or the adoption of specific policies.

*Concordance.* The degree to which norms are intersubjectively shared among their addressees is one of the crucial indicators involved in assessing the emergence of international norms.[27] Concordance describes 'how widely accepted the rules are in diplomatic discussions and treaties'.[28] For example, the ratification of human rights treaties is a discursive act which is 'rationally expressive'.[29] It expresses an actor's overall support of a norm. This means that high or increasing ratification rates are an indicator of a high or growing degree of intersubjective agreement. In addition, discursive affirmations demonstrate the existence and relevance of a norm to a social group and actors signal their general support of the norm.[30] This can be indicated by the salience of affirmations in public international discourse.

*Negative reactions to norm violations.* Norms have both a prescriptive and an evaluative dimension. The prescriptive dimension refers to the intersubjectively shared 'oughtness' of norms: prohibition norms, for instance, proscribe a certain behaviour. The evaluative dimension refers to norms as yardsticks through which actors evaluate

[23] Friedrich Kratochwil and John Gerard Ruggie, 'International Organization: A State of the Art on an Art of the State' (1986) 40 International Organization 753, 767; Richard Price, 'Detecting Ideas and their Effects' in Robert E Goodin and Charles Tilly (eds), *The Oxford Handbook of Contextual Political Analysis* (OUP 2006).

[24] Oran R Young, *Compliance and Public Authority: A Theory with International Applications* (Taylor and Francis 1979) 3; of course, what a norm violation is, is also based on intersubjective discourse and changes over time.

[25] Alexander Betts and Phil Orchard, 'Introduction: The Normative Institutionalization-Implementation Gap' in Alexander Betts and Phil Orchard (eds), *Implementation and World Politics. How International Norms Change Practice* (OUP 2014) 2.

[26] Beth A Simmons, 'Compliance with International Agreements' (1998) 1 Annual Review of Political Science 75, 77–78; see Sections 3.1 and 3.2 in this chapter.

[27] Martha Finnemore and Kathryn Sikkink, 'International Norm Dynamics and Political Change' (1998) 52 International Organization 887, 901.

[28] Jeffrey W Legro, 'Which Norms Matter? Revisiting the "Failure" of Internationalism' (1997) 51 International Organization 31, 35.

[29] Beth A Simmons, *Mobilizing for Human Rights: International Law in Domestic Politics* (CUP 2009) 64.

[30] Alexander Dukalksis and Robert C Johansen, 'Measuring Acceptance of International Enforcement of Human Rights: The United States, Asia, and the International Criminal Court' (2013) 35 Human Rights Quarterly 569, 576–77. Ben-Josef Hirsch and Dixon (n 10) 524–26.

behaviour.[31] Such reactions can be material and/or discursive. Whereas the former is usually referred to as 'economic' or 'military' sanctions, the latter can take a variety of forms, from official statements by states to decisions of international organizations, or judgements handed down by international courts. We will focus here on negative reactions voiced by states in public international discourse.

Ideally, this framework makes it possible to look beyond singular cases of norm violations and thus sketch global trends in norm strength over time. The following analysis is based on existing data sets, our own results of a qualitative content analysis of international discourses, as well as secondary literature. For each dimension we briefly introduce the specific material used in the analysis.

## 3. Norm Strength Trends of the Torture Prohibition

The prohibition of torture and cruel, inhuman, or degrading treatment or punishment became an international human rights norm with the adoption of the Universal Declaration of Human Rights in 1948.[32] Three decades later, the prohibition was codified in the ICCPR. This made the torture prohibition one of the few non-derogable norms in international human right law.[33] The CAT, which was adopted in 1984 and entered into force in 1986, is founded on this prohibition.[34] The aim was 'to *strengthen* the existing prohibition of such practices by a number of supportive measures'.[35] Building on the existing prohibition in international human rights law, the CAT codified a definition of torture, underlined the universality and non-derogability of the prohibition, and spelled out demands for universal jurisdiction, victim's rights, as well as the prevention of torture.[36] It established the UN Committee against Torture to oversee the implementation of the Convention. By the beginning of the 1990s, the prohibition of torture was deeply anchored in international human rights law. The development of this norm is reflected in regional human rights law, international humanitarian law, and international criminal law.[37] One of the notable and more recent developments is the entry into force of the Optional Protocol to the Convention against Torture (OPCAT) in 2006 and the establishment of the Sub-Committee on Prevention of Torture tasked with *in situ* visits to places of detention.[38]

[31] Finnemore and Sikkink (n 27) 891.

[32] Universal Declaration of Human Rights (adopted 10 December 1948) UNGA Res 217 A(III) art 5.

[33] International Covenant on Civil and Political Rights (adopted 16 December 1966, entered into force 23 March 1976) 999 UNTS 171 arts 4, 7.

[34] Convention against Torture, Cruel, Inhumane, and other Degrading Treatment and Punishment (adopted 10 December 1984, entered into force 26 June 1987) 1456 UNTS 85.

[35] J Herman Burgers and Hans Danelius, *The United Nations Convention Against Torture: A Handbook on the Convention Against Torture and Other Cruel and Inhuman or Degrading Treatment* (Martinus Nijhoff Publishers 1988) 1.

[36] Manfred Nowak, Moritz Birk, and Giuliana Monina, *The United Nations Convention against Torture and its Optional Protocol: A Commentary* (2nd edn, OUP 2019) 6–9.

[37] Nigel S Rodley and Matt Pollard, *The Treatment of Prisoners under International Law* (OUP 2009) 46–47; see also Dominik Steiger, Chapter 7 in this book.

[38] Optional Protocol to the Convention against Torture and Other Cruel, Inhuman or Degrading Treatment or Punishment (adopted 18 December 2002, entered into force 22 June 2006) 2375 UNTS 237.

In this chapter, we follow Martha Finnemore and Kathryn Sikkink's definition of a norm as 'a standard of appropriate behaviour' for actors in a social group.[39] Based on international human rights law, we will ground our analysis of the torture prohibition's strengths on the following understanding: the central negative obligation is that torture, as defined in CAT,[40] and inhumane treatment are each universally prohibited in war and peace time. This prohibition is not derogable under any circumstances. The prohibition of torture is, therefore, applicable to everyone at all times, and everywhere. In addition, state parties have a positive obligation to implement the norm and to take preventive measures domestically under CAT.

## 3.1 Compliance

In terms of the torture prohibition, rule-following behaviour would ideally mean the complete absence of torture practices under any circumstances (in member states of ICCPR and CAT). In this chapter, we are interested in the degree of norm violations on a global scale in order to assess compliance as one dimension of norm strength. This is a challenging task because comprehensive international data on torture practices is hard to come by. Since officials and perpetrators usually seek to conceal torture and ill-treatment from the public eye, studies on torture practices—quantitative data in particular—must rely on proxies for assessing (non)compliance with the prohibition of torture in order to track usually clandestine practices. Quantitative work on compliance with human rights norms takes the annual reports on human rights (violations) by Amnesty International and country reports by the US State Department as primary sources.[41] While there is legitimate criticism of such data sets,[42] the quantitative analysis of these resources has so far been the only comprehensive approach to analysing global trends in compliance with the prohibition of torture over time.

[39] Finnemore and Sikkink (n 27) 891.

[40] Article 1(1) CAT: 'For the purposes of this Convention, the term "torture" means any act by which severe pain or suffering, whether physical or mental, is intentionally inflicted on a person for such purposes as obtaining from him or a third person information or a confession, punishing him for an act he or a third person has committed or is suspected of having committed, or intimidating or coercing him or a third person, or for any reason based on discrimination of any kind, when such pain or suffering is inflicted by or at the instigation of or with the consent or acquiescence of a public official or other person acting in an official capacity. It does not include pain or suffering arising only from, inherent in or incidental to lawful sanctions.'

[41] David L Cingranelli and David L Richards, 'The Cingranelli and Richards (CIRI) Human Rights Data Project' (2010) 32 Human Rights Quarterly 401, 406; Courtenay R Conrad, Jillienne Haglund, and Will H Moore, 'Disaggregating Torture Allegations: Introducing the Ill-Treatment and Torture (ITT) Country-Year Data' (2013) 14 International Studies Perspectives 199, 201–202; Oona A Hathaway, 'Do Human Rights Treaties Make a Difference?' (2002) 111 Yale Law Journal 1934, 1969–70; Simmons, *Mobilizing for Human Rights* (n 29) 266–67. The Political Terror Scale (PTS) is based on the same material. It is, however, not possible to disaggregate the PTS for scales of torture only. Reed M Wood and Mark Gibney, 'The Political Terror Scale (PTS): A Re-introduction and a Comparison to CIRI' (2010) 32 Human Rights Quarterly 367, 375–76.

[42] For this debate, see for example Ann Marie Clark and Kathryn Sikkink, 'Information Effects and Human Rights Data: Is the Good News about Increased Human Rights Information Bad News for Human Rights Measures?' (2013) 35 Human Rights Quarterly 539; Emilie M Hafner-Burton and James Ron, 'Seeing Double: Human Rights Impact through Qualitative and Quantitative Eyes' (2009) 61 World Politics 360; Emilie M Hafner-Burton, David G Victor, and Yonatan Lupu, 'Political Science Research on International Law: The State of the Field' (2012) 106 The American Journal of International Law 47.

To date, David Cingranelli and David Richard's (CIRI) Human Rights Data Project provides the most comprehensive data on torture from 1981 to 2011. CIRI distinguishes three levels of torture: 'torture did not occur', 'torture occurred occasionally' (1 to 49 instances) and 'torture was practiced frequently' (50 and more instances).[43] It is important to note that the CIRI data set only measures *allegations* of torture—not actual behaviour.[44] In addition, this data set is biased by an 'information effect': as awareness of torture grows, national and international monitoring generates more and better information on the issue, creating 'a false perception that a phenomenon has increased in prevalence'.[45] Furthermore, the data set cannot control for the changing definitions of torture used in allegations.[46] Human rights reports include more cases of torture in 1999 than in 1989 because they employ a broader concept of torture.[47] Taken together, CIRI produces data that is biased towards showing negative trends because human rights reports note more norm violations as information improves and the concept of torture broadens over time.[48] Despite these caveats, CIRI offers the broadest means for assessing compliance with the prohibition of torture on a global and long-term scale.

What can the available quantitative data tell us? The CIRI data set, as visualized in Figure 1, suggests that full compliance with the prohibition of torture has remained roughly constant in about 20 per cent of all states. In other words, there are more than 80 per cent of states where torture is reported occasionally (which includes a single report) or frequently (50 and more reports). This applies similarly to the period before 1990, as the CIRI data and also several historical studies on torture practices demonstrate.[49] The presence of torture is a (sad and definitely unacceptable) historical constant.

Nonetheless, the overall trend in compliance rates is generally stable. While we can observe decreasing compliance numbers during the 1990s, they recovered during the early 2000s. In addition, this trend should be seen in the light of the caveats sketched out above. Christopher Fariss, for instance, shows that a 'changing standard of accountability' explains the stability in quantitative findings and argues that 'physical integrity practices have improved over time'.[50] In the case of torture, reported instances only appear to be on the rise compared with earlier numbers because 'monitoring agencies look harder for torture, look in more places for torture, and classify more acts as torture'.[51] From this perspective, trends in compliance with the prohibition of torture might have even increased in the period observed.

[43] The data sets compiled by Hathaway, Simmons, and Conrad and colleagues use more nuanced scales of torture.

[44] Conrad, Haglund, and Moore (n 41) 202.

[45] Clark and Sikkink (n 42) 542; see also Margaret E Keck and Kathryn Sikkink, *Activists beyond Borders: Advocacy Networks in International Politics* (Cornell University Press 1998) 194.

[46] Clark and Sikkink (n 42) 546.

[47] Clark and Sikkink (n 42) 543.

[48] Christopher J Fariss, 'Respect for Human Rights Has Improved Over Time: Modeling the Changing Standard of Accountability' (2014) 108 American Political Science Review 297.

[49] For a comprehensive overview see Darius Rejali, *Torture and Democracy* (Princeton University Press 2007).

[50] Fariss (n 48) 308. Emphasis omitted.

[51] ibid 309.

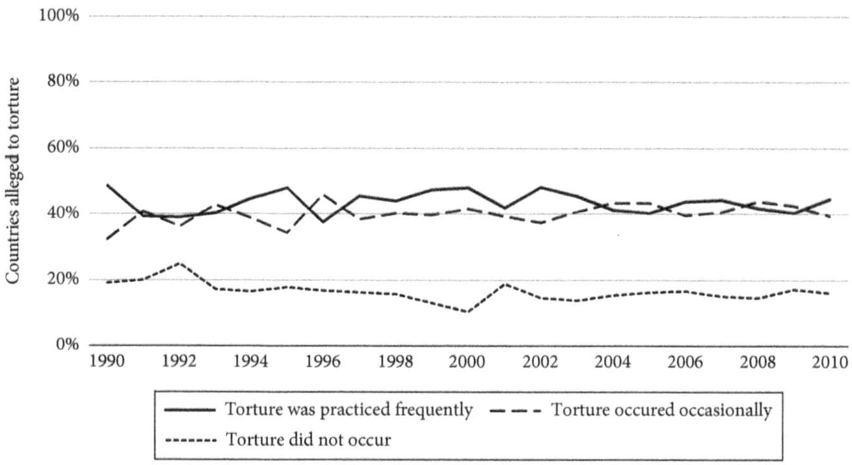


**Figure 1.** Percentages of countries reportedly practicing/not practicing torture, 1990–2010

*Source*: CIRI Human Rights Data Project. Version as of 14 April 2014.*

*The figure shows the percentage of countries coded with either 'torture did not occur' (no instances), 'torture occurred occasionally' (1 to 49 instances) and 'torture was practiced frequently' (50 and more instances) in each year. We excluded countries coded with missing data, state collapse, or occupation during war time. The dataset is available online: <www.humanrightsdata.com/p/data-documentation.html> accessed 04 April 2022.

In contrast to recent negative assessments of compliance trends, which often highlighted specific cases of non-compliance,[52] the long-term trend in behaviour complying with the torture prohibition is stable. At least after 2001 the trend has even been slightly positive. We acknowledge that this general finding does not rule out deteriorating compliance in particular states or among certain groups of states. Averell Schmidt and Kathryn Sikkink, for instance, show that compliance with the prohibition of torture decreased in those states that participated in the US rendition programme.[53] The CIRI data may not account well for stark increases in torture cases in individual countries. At the same time, it may also include many states with very few or only one case of reported torture allegations. And, finally, even though torture remains a widespread practice, it is often not a deliberate choice by a government to deviate from the norm but a consequence of problems in training and the absence of sufficient safeguards, and can thus be addressed through preventive measures.[54] In sum, we can see that, globally, concerns about a negative trend or even an erosion do not match compliance trends.

[52] The recent focus on US practices is only one example. Brunnée and Toope, for instance, cite long lists of reports on torture to demonstrate the lack of congruence between norm and practice. See Brunnée and Toope (n 6) 260–63. This does, however, neglect a comprehensive assessment of trends over time including positive cases.

[53] Schmidt and Sikkink (n 11) 114.

[54] See the contributions in Richard Carver and Lisa Handley (eds), *Does Torture Prevention Work?* (Liverpool University Press 2016).

## 3.2 Implementation

Implementation of the prohibition against torture describes the formal or institutional translation of international human rights treaties into domestic settings. In this section, we draw on different data sets collected in quantitative research projects on constitutional rights, domestic criminalization, and National Human Rights Institutions (NHRIs). Benedict Goderis and Mila Versteeg have compiled a data set on constitutional rights including the prohibition of torture for 188 states between 1948 and 2006.[55] Mark Berlin has developed a data set on the criminalization of torture in states since 1984 based on coding of criminal codes and documentation by the Committee against Torture.[56] Jacqueline DeMeritt, Ryan Welch and Courtenay Conrad have collected data on the establishment of NHRIs, in 153 countries with a population of more than one million between 1991 and 2012 and whether they have a mandate concerning the issue of torture.[57] NHRIs usually tasked with monitoring, promoting, and advising on human rights are important in facilitating the prevention of human rights violations on the ground.[58]

How has the implementation of the international prohibition of torture in domestic settings developed over time? First, human rights treaties have considerably affected national constitutions. In 2006, 84 per cent of 188 countries had included the prohibition of torture in their constitutional rights—an increase of 47 percentage points since 1946.[59] Building on this dataset, Mila Versteeg concludes that 'the entry into force of ECHR and CAT has inspired constitution makers around the globe, even in the absence of treaty ratification'.[60] Second, the national criminalization of torture 'has spread steadily since the adoption of the CAT in 1984'.[61] By 2010, almost half of all states had adopted at least a minimal prohibition of torture.[62] In addition, Mark Berlin has demonstrated that there is a clear trend towards the adoption of stronger anti-torture laws, often through the (at least partial) inclusion of the definition of torture from CAT.[63] However, the full implementation of the definition of torture from CAT into domestic criminal law remains one of the most contentious issues when the Committee against Torture reviews state reports. Third, the establishment of NHRIs

[55] Benedikt Goderis and Mila Versteeg, 'The Diffusion of Constitutional Rights' (2014) 39 International Review of Law and Economics 1, 4.

[56] Mark S Berlin, 'Does Criminalizing Torture Deter Police Torture?' (2021) American Journal of Political Science, 7–8 <https://papers.ssrn.com/sol3/papers.cfm?abstract_id=3606304> accessed 30 March 2022.

[57] Ryan M Welch, Jacqueline H R DeMeritt, and Courtenay R Conrad, 'Conceptualizing and Measuring Institutional Variation in National Human Rights Institutions (NHRIs)' (2021) 65 Journal of Conflict Resolution 1010. For an earlier dataset, see Jeong-Woo Koo and Francisco O Ramirez, 'National Incorporation of Global Human Rights: Worldwide Expansion of National Human Rights Institutions, 1966-2004' (2009) 87 Social Forces 1321.

[58] See Katerina Linos and Tom Pegram, 'Architects of Their own Making: National Human Rights Institutions and the United Nations' (2016) 38 Human Rights Quarterly 1109, 1118.

[59] Goderis and Versteeg (n 55) 6.

[60] Mila Versteeg, 'Law versus Norms: The Impact of Human-Rights Treaties on National Bills of Rights' (2015) 171 Journal of Institutional and Theoretical Economics 87, 108; see also Wayne Sandholtz, 'Domestic Law and Human Rights Treaty Commitments: The Convention against Torture' (2017) 16 Journal of Human Rights 25.

[61] Berlin (n 56) 8.

[62] ibid 9.

[63] ibid 8.

has consistently increased. Even though NHRIs already existed before 1990,[64] this is a trend which gained tremendous momentum after the end of the Cold War: whereas in 1990, 22 NHRIs existed around the world, this number was almost five times higher in 2006, when 101 NHRIs had been established.[65] Until 2010, however, the number of NHRIs stagnated.[66]

Taken together, the prohibition of torture has increasingly been implemented in domestic law and institutions. We can observe an increasing level of domestic implementation of the international torture prohibition. However, both indicators are rather static, as states rarely abolish institutions or erase fundamental rights from their constitutions. They can indicate the diffusion of legal and institutional means of addressing torture. Some might argue that these implementation efforts are only domestic manifestations of human rights paper tigers. However, many of the studies of implementation cited above find that it interacts positively with our other practice-based dimension—compliance: where states criminalize torture according to the CAT definition, torture is less likely to occur.[67] Similarly, the establishment of NHRIs makes it less likely that torture will be practised frequently and more likely that no torture occurs,[68] particularly if these states have also ratified CAT.[69] Beyond the domestic setting, NHRIs increase the performance of states in the self-reporting process with the human rights treaty bodies.[70] Finally, the concern and efforts of US allies in Afghanistan to limit the risk of becoming legally liable before national courts in the particular countries for US actions in the war on terror, illustrate how the national implementation of the prohibition of torture can have policy effects.[71]

In a nutshell, domestic implementation provides domestic channels for holding perpetrators accountable, furthering the prevention of torture, and even enforcing claims related to human rights.[72] There is growing evidence that implementation has positive effects on the prevention of torture.[73] If implementation has been rising in the period observed, it is likely that these efforts will bear fruit in the future.

## 3.3 Concordance

We trace concordance with the torture prohibition by analysing both ratification rates of the central human rights treaties based on official UN numbers and official state discourse at the UN. Taken together, the human rights treaties on torture at the global

[64] Koo and Ramirez (n 57) 1326.

[65] Welch, DeMeritt, and Conrad (n 57) 1014.

[66] This dataset covers data on NHRIs until 2012.

[67] Berlin (n 56) 11.

[68] Welch, DeMeritt, and Conrad (n 57) 1019–20.

[69] Ryan M Welch, 'National Human Rights Institutions: Domestic Implementation of International Human Rights Law' (2017) 16 Journal of Human Rights 96, 106–07.

[70] Cosette D Creamer and Beth A Simmons, 'Ratification, Reporting, and Rights: Quality of Participation in the Convention against Torture' (2015) 37 Human Rights Quarterly 579, 597.

[71] Schmidt and Sikkink (n 11) 111–12.

[72] Ryan M Welch, 'Domestic Politics and the Power to Punish: The Case of National Human Rights Institutions' (2019) 36 Conflict Management and Peace Science 385, 399.

[73] See the contributions of Carver and Handley (n 54).

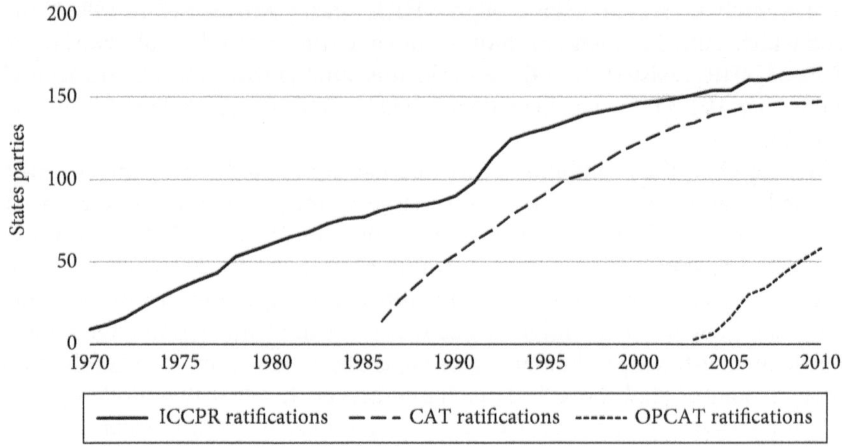


**Figure 2.** Ratification status of ICCPR, CAT and OPCAT based on the OCHR database on human rights treaty status.
*Source*: http://indicators.ohchr.org/

level enjoy widespread and growing membership (see Figure 2). The major international human rights treaty prohibiting torture is the ICCPR. In the first half of the 1990s, the ICCPR witnessed a rapid increase in membership—a trend that continued at a slower pace well into the early 2000s. Today, it is one of the most widely ratified human rights treaties, with 173 state parties. We see a similar trend in the still ongoing ratification of the CAT, with 173 state parties today. Finally, growing membership in OPCAT, which entered into force in the midst of the 'war on terror'. Today, it has 91 state parties.

Ratifications continued throughout the war on terror. The increasing ratification rates—even in times of perceived crisis—indicate the ongoing normative appeal of the prohibition of torture.[74] All three ratification trends are thus evidence of continuing concordance with the norm.

A more nuanced look at ratifications and opt-in clauses can tell us to what extent certain—often crucial—aspects of a treaty are also accepted by state parties. The CAT has three mechanisms under which the Committee can open inquiries beyond the state reporting system: inquiries on the initiative of the Committee (Article 20),[75] state-to-state complaints (Article 21), and individual communications (Article 22).[76] In 2010, 138 states (94 per cent) had accepted the inquiry system and 64 state members (44 per cent) of the Convention had accepted individual complaint communications.

[74] Liese (n 12) 35.

[75] So far, the Committee has compiled ten reports under the inquiry procedure. Office of the High Commissioner for Human Rights (OHCHR) data available at <https://tbinternet.ohchr.org/_layouts/15/TreatyBodyExternal/Inquiries.aspx> accessed 28 December 2021.

[76] As of August 2015, the Committee against Torture had received 697 and concluded 539 based on the individual communication procedure. OHCHR data available at <www.ohchr.org/Documents/HRBodies/CAT/StatisticalSurvey.xls> accessed 28 December 2021.

It is worth noting that the gap between the number of ratifications and state parties accepting the individual communications to CAT has been growing. In addition, several states—including the United States—have expressed reservations or made observations concerning the applicability and scope of the definition of torture in Article 1 of CAT.[77] These reservations are not going unchallenged. A group of European states, for instance, filed objections against them and similar 'far-reaching reservations', which also regularly become subject to criticism by the Committee against Torture.[78] As Schmidt and Sikkink observe, after 2000, opt-outs and reservations have been criticized more often than previously,[79] which in turn indicates the broader concordance with the prohibition of torture as codified in CAT.

Ratification does not automatically lead to better compliance with or implementation of a norm. In fact, Oona Hathaway even found a negative effect of ratification on compliance.[80] Others have, however, demonstrated the positive effect for partially democratic and transition regimes in particular,[81] and even for ratifying states in general.[82] However, similarly to rates of domestic implementation, ratification rates usually remain static, even if concordance weakens, because states only rarely withdraw from international treaties. If they dothis might be a strong indicator for a weakening of a norm, something that we have not observed in the case of torture yet. Ongoing increasing ratification rates even throughout times of perceived crisis might at least indicate the ongoing normative pull exerted by the treaty in question.

To obtain an impression beyond this rather formal and perhaps static trend, we studied general diplomatic interactions, specifically the role of norm affirmations at the UN. The following analysis is based on a qualitative content analysis of state statements in the Third Committee of the UN General Assembly (UNGA) dealing with human rights issues and the torture prohibition. We conducted a full-text search for affirmative statements of the prohibition of torture as well as affirmations of specific aspects of the prohibition, and coded each statement that contained a reference to torture (see Figure 3).

The results show that if states talk about torture in the UNGA, they increasingly also explicitly affirm its prohibition. It is noteworthy that states only began to include affirmations of the non-derogability or absoluteness of the torture prohibition after the US challenges to torture beginning in 2001 in which the United States tried to create exceptions to the prohibition.[83] For example, a Portuguese delegate underlined the European Union's 'firm stance regarding the *absolute* prohibition of torture and other cruel, inhuman or degrading treatment or punishment. International law *did not allow*

[77] Nowak, Birk, and Monina (n 36) 40–41; on the reasons and implications of human rights treaty reservations, see Kelebogile Zvobgo, Wayne Sandholtz, and Suzie Mulesky, 'Reserving Rights: Explaining Human Rights Treaty Reservations' (2020) 64 International Studies Quarterly 785.

[78] ibid 41; see also Steiger, Chapter 7 in this book.

[79] Schmidt and Sikkink (n 11) 109.

[80] Hathaway (n 41) 1983–84; for a critique of her findings, see Ryan Goodman and Derek Jinks, 'Measuring the Effects of Human Rights Treaties' (2003) 14 European Journal of International Law 171.

[81] Simmons, *Mobilizing for Human Rights* (n 29) 276.

[82] Fariss (n 48) 313. See Section 3.1 of this chapter.

[83] For a comprehensive summary of US contestation of the torture prohibition, see McKeown (n 9) and Sikkink (n 9). Israel advanced similar arguments, see Grosso (n 5). For a comparative perspective, see Liese (n 12).

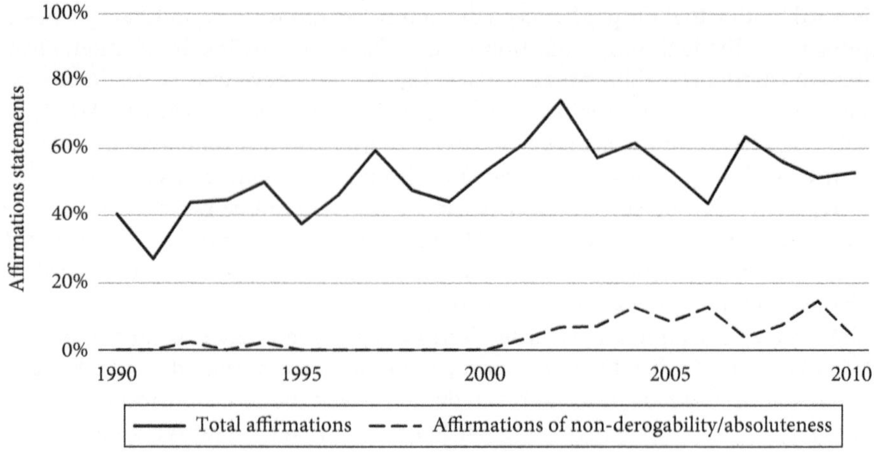


**Figure 3.** Norm affirmations of the torture prohibition and its non-derogability or absoluteness in 852 statements to UNGA's Third Committee between 1990 and 2010.
*Source*: International Norm Disputes Dataset: https://doi.org/10.7910/DVN/6VHFZK

*for any exceptions* to that prohibition'.[84] This shows that the prohibition was not only clearly present in UNGA debates, but that states also reacted to mounting challenges by explicitly re-affirming its absolute character. When affirmations decreased around 2006, negative reactions to norm violations increased.[85] In sum, we find concordance with the prohibition of torture increasing slightly in these debates during the observed timeframe.

This is also reflected in the persistent inclusion of torture and its prohibition in resolutions adopted by the UNGA. In the 1990s and early 2000s, states adopted on average about 13 resolutions each year that referred to torture.[86] In particular, this includes the annual, since 2013 biennial, general resolutions on the prohibition of torture which are adopted by consensus. The biennial resolutions support the overall concordance with the prohibition of torture. The debates and resolutions of the UNGA are evidence for the persistent belief in the legitimacy of the prohibition of torture among virtually all states. In a similar vein, 'Torture and other CID Treatment' is one of the most frequently raised issues in the Universal Periodic Review (UPR), a peer review-based mechanism under the auspices of the UN Human Rights Council. In their recommendations, states regularly criticize torture, use international human rights treaties as benchmarks, and demand their ratification (without reservation) and implementation.[87]

[84] UN General Assembly (UNGA) Third Committee (62nd Session) 'Summary record of the 22nd meeting' (24 October 2007) UN Doc A/C.3/62/SR.22, para 68. Emphasis added.
[85] See Section 3.4 of this chapter.
[86] This is based on a full-text search for torture in UNGA resolutions in the UN database <https://documents.un.org> accessed 28 December 2021.
[87] For an overview, see the UPR-Info database on recommendations <https://upr-info-database.uwazi.io/> accessed 28 December 2021.

In sum, torture was continuously a topic in general debates at the UN and states continued to rally behind its absolute prohibition. We observe increasing concordance with the prohibition of torture between 1990 and 2010. This concordance proved to be resilient in the face of human rights crises, as the majority of states continued to defend the belief in its legitimacy against challenges.

## 3.4 Negative Reactions to Norm Violations

Given that there are constant deviations from the international torture prohibition, it is also crucial to assess how the international community of states reacts to these norm violations. International norms remain particularly strong if non-compliance is met with negative reactions. In this section, we focus on negative reactions uttered by states in the Third Committee of the UNGA between 1990 and 2010.[88] In addition to coding general criticism of torture or of particular states, we have coded for specific negative reactions to norm violations by Israel and the United States because of their explicit challenges to the prohibition of torture in the 1990s and early 2000s, respectively.[89]

The results of our qualitative content analysis show that throughout the 1990s statements on torture included negative reactions to norm violations in about 40 per cent of the cases, reaching a peak in 1999 (Figure 4).[90] During this period, Nigeria, for example, 'condemned the practice of torture and other cruel, inhuman or degrading treatment or punishment, wherever or whenever they might occur'.[91] In the early 2000s, the European Union, for instance, expressed 'its concern about cases of alleged torture in a number of countries'.[92]

There is a significant drop after 2000 which most probably reflects relatively high compliance levels at the time.[93] However, the level of negative reactions quickly recovered, peaking again in 2006 when the enhanced interrogation techniques and the Abu Ghraib scandal became public. Only then did many states begin to openly and directly criticize US politics on torture. China, for instance, claimed that 'the United States was even attempting to legalize the use of torture'.[94] This trend is supported by evidence from an analysis of diplomatic cables between 2004 and 2008, when a parallel rise of criticism of US conduct is visible.[95] Israel faced a similar peak in negative

[88] This is based on the same data as in the qualitative content analysis used above. See Section 3.3 of this chapter.

[89] See Liese (n 12) 35.

[90] These results do not account for the fact that UN members have increasingly coordinated their statements in regional and other groups, which results in fewer coded statements to which, however, more states subscribe.

[91] UNGA Third Committee (45th Session) 'Summary record of the 37th meeting' (9 November 1990) UN Doc A/C.3/45/SR.37, para 42.

[92] UNGA Third Committee (59th Session) 'Summary record of the 24th meeting' (26 October 2004) UN Doc A/C.3/59/SR.24, para 69.

[93] See Section 3.1 of this chapter.

[94] UNGA Third Committee (60th Session) 'Summary record of the 33rd meeting' (2 November 2005) UN Doc A/C.3/60/SR.33, para 65.

[95] Schmidt and Sikkink (n 11) 109–12.

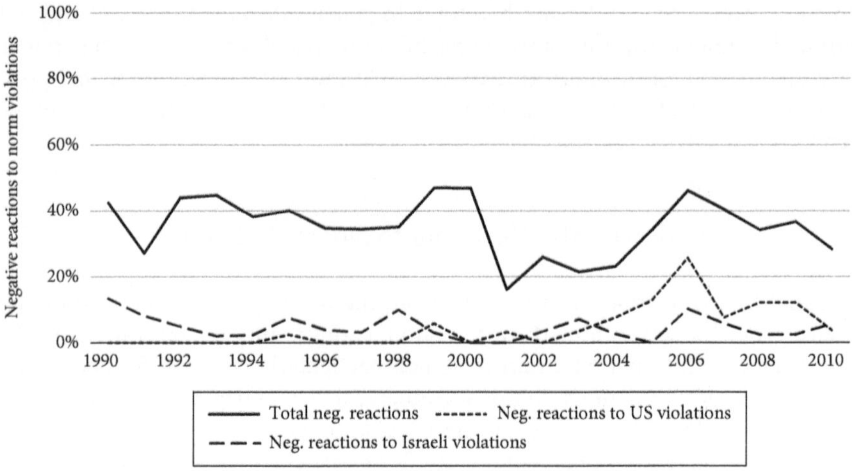


**Figure 4.** Negative reactions to all norm violations, and to norm violations by Israel and the US in 852 statements to UNGA's Third Committee between 1990 and 2010.
*Source*: International Norm Disputes Dataset: https://doi.org/10.7910/DVN/6VHFZK

reactions to norm violations at the beginning of the 1990s during the first *intifada*, during which a torture debate in Israel erupted.[96] Both trends show that contestations and norm violations do not go unchallenged in the debates at the UN, where states—however powerful—are criticized for norm-violating behaviour.

These findings are reflected in institutionalized means for addressing norm violations. As we have shown above,[97] torture is a consistent issue at the UPR, where shortcomings in compliance and implementation are addressed. During the two reviews of the United States in 2010 and 2015 within the UPR framework, 16 and 25 recommendations respectively related to the issue of torture.[98] While it might be argued that such negative reactions are nothing more than 'cheap talk', studies of the UN Economic and Social Council's human rights procedures and the reporting system of the human rights treaty bodies have recently demonstrated their effects on compliance by states under scrutiny. Marie Clark finds that 'external criticism positively influences human rights treaty compliance', particularly in the case of the CAT.[99] In a similar vein, Cosette Creamer and Beth Simmons show that state interaction with the Committee against Torture through the self-reporting procedures have positive effects on compliance with the prohibition of torture,[100] a finding that is generalizable

[96] Grosso (n 5)
[97] See Section 3.3 of this chapter.
[98] Recommendations for the United States in the 1st and 2nd cycle based on the UPR-Info Database <https://upr-info-database.uwazi.io/en/> accessed 28 December 2021.
[99] Ann Marie Clark, 'Laws, Talk, and Human Rights: The Impact of Treaty Ratification, UN Criticism, and Democratic Change on Torture' (2018) 17 Journal of Human Rights 418, 431.
[100] Cosette D Creamer and Beth A Simmons, 'Do Self-Reporting Regimes Matter? Evidence from the Convention against Torture' (2019) 63 International Studies Quarterly 1051, 1056–57.

**Table 1.** The strength of the prohibition of torture; our own compilation based on the above analysis.

| | Dimension | Data | Results |
|---|---|---|---|
| Practice | *Compliance* | Allegations of torture per country and year; based on CIRI human rights dataset on torture | *constant/slightly increasing* |
| | *Implementation* | Inclusion of the prohibition in national constitutions and criminal codes<br>Establishment of National Human Rights Institutions (NHRIs) | *increasing* |
| Discourse | *Concordance* | Ratification rates of ICCPR, CAT, OPCAT<br>State statements (affirmations) in official UN Debates (3rd Committee UNGA)<br>Relevance of torture in the Universal Periodic Review at the UN Human Rights Council | *increasing* |
| | *Negative reactions to norm violation* | State statements in official UN Debates (3rd Committee UNGA) | *constant* |

beyond the torture case.[101] In other words, one of the crucial dimensions of norm strengths—reactions to violations—can also positively affect compliance.

In the UN, torture has been consistently criticized as a violation of the prohibition of torture or human rights law more broadly. Except for the dip between 2001 and 2004, this trend appears—across the board—to be stable in the period observed.

## 3.5 No Norm Weakening in Sight: What Explains the Norm's Resilience?

Taking the four dimensions together, we conclude that the strength of the international torture prohibition did not significantly change between 1990 and 2010 globally. If anything, there are indications of an increase in the norm's strength. Of course, this does not exclude the possibility that individual states have seen a severe weakening of the ban. However, these instances did not spread internationally. Neither the challenges posed by the United States nor by Israel led to global norm decay, as some feared.[102] Although norm violations occur consistently, they are criticized. In addition, implementation of and concordance with the prohibition of torture are slightly increasing (Table 1).

[101] Cosette D Creamer and Beth A Simmons, 'The Proof Is in the Process: Self-Reporting under International Human Rights Treaties' (2020) 114 American Journal of International Law 1, 44–45.

[102] McKeown (n 9) 19–20.

Why did the norm weather the storm? We assume that a combination of three factors, suggested as explanatory factors for norm change in this book, was at play in the case of the torture prohibition. First, whereas 'anti-norm arguments'[103] were put forward by Israel in the 1990s and the United States in the early 2000s, their claims contested application rather than the validity of the torture prohibition.[104] Since validity contestation did not become dominant in their challenges, norm weakening remained unlikely.[105] Moreover, their contestation did not gain traction within the broader international discourse, as we and others have shown elsewhere,[106] and challenges were consistently met with 'pro-norm arguments'.[107] Second, the norm is deeply embedded in and at the core of not only international human rights law but also international humanitarian law, regional human rights treaties, and international criminal law. This makes it harder to target a single treaty because such an embedded norm might have higher legitimacy.[108] As we have shown, the norm has also been widely incorporated into domestic law.[109] This has opened several pathways for fighting back against challenges to the prohibition of torture. National courts, for instance, began to scrutinize the cooperation of European countries with the US rendition programme,[110] often facilitated by the work of transnational litigation networks.[111] Third, the role of legal institutionalization was crucial for fighting off norm change. Not only at the domestic but also at the international level, institutions such as the Committee against Torture provided for an exchange of competing interpretations of the prohibition. Moreover, the Committee against Torture was able to sort out the disputes and contribute to a stabilization of *opinio juris*.[112] Taken together, this explains the continuous strength of the torture prohibition—in the face of strong challenges.

## 4. Conclusion

Does the recent crisis of the international prohibition of torture indicate a value change or is it even a metamorphosis in international law? Based on a four-dimensional

[103] See Sandholtz, Chapter 3 in this book.

[104] Liese (n 12) 32.

[105] Deitelhoff and Zimmermann, 'Things We Lost in the Fire' (n 21) 57–58.

[106] Lisbeth Zimmermann and others, *International Norm Disputes: The Link Between Contestation and Norm Robustness* (OUP 2023), Chapter 2; Keating (n 14) 15; Schmidt and Sikkink (n 11) 109; Anette Stimmer, 'Beyond Internalization: Alternate Endings of the Norm Life Cycle' (2019) 63 International Studies Quarterly 270, 277.

[107] See Section 3.3 of this chapter on concordance with the norm. On the link between anti- and pro-norm arguments, see Sandholtz, Chapter 3 in this book.

[108] Sandholtz, Chapter 3 in this book; Sara V Percy and Wayne Sandholtz, 'Why Norms Rarely Die' (2022) European Journal of International Relations 934, 945. Jeffrey S Lantis and Carmen Wunderlich, 'Resiliency Dynamics of Norm Clusters: Norm Contestation and International Cooperation' (2018) 44 Review of International Studies 570, 579.

[109] See Section 3.2 of this chapter.

[110] Schmidt and Sikkink (n 11) 116–17.

[111] Antje Wiener, *Contestation and Constitution of Norms in Global International Relations* (CUP 2018) 159.

[112] Max Lesch 'From Norm Violations to Norm Development: Deviance, International Institutions, and the Torture Prohibition (2023) International Studies Quarterly. For a discussion of the stability in *opinio juris* regarding recent challenges, see Steiger, Chapter 7 in this book.

framework for studying the strength of international norms in discourse and practice, we argue that change remained at the level of individual cases of norm violations or contestations. Even when faced with challenges by powerful actors like the United States, global norm strength remained surprisingly stable, or might even show a slight strengthening during the 1990s and 2000s.

This, we argue, is mostly due to the specific institutionalization of the norm both domestically and internationally, which also helped curb existing challenges and their diffusion. Although institutionalization was highly important, it did not serve as a 'backstop' mechanism which protected the torture prohibition from challenges.[113] Instead, domestic and international institutions provide rules, processes and spaces to channel, react to and deal with challenges which arise in the international community of states—especially if these institutions have broad legitimacy among norm addressees.

Predicting the immediate doom of the international legal order in the current crisis may be premature: norm challenges cannot be equated with norm decay. At the same time, domestic and international institutions do need some legitimacy and support to fulfil the functions described above. While we are not yet observing direct challenges to the institutional institutions underlying the CAT,[114] several regional human rights systems are increasingly under attack and scholars have been investigating a wave of 'backlashes' against international courts, for example against the European Court of Human Rights and the Inter-American human rights system.[115] However, the recent growing financial strains on the human rights treaty bodies are also an example of how backlash can play out at the budgetary level, when states withdraw or hold back funds.[116] Consequently, future research should combine a focus on norm strength with institutional resiliency: how do international institutions (courts, expert commissions or other forms of institutionalized mechanisms, which manage norm applications and norm violations) react and deal with potential challenges to their authority?[117] This will vitalize and deepen the interdisciplinary project to study changes in the international legal order and provide a better understanding of the challenges to this order we are currently facing.

[113] For such an argument, see Miles Kahler, 'Conclusion: The Causes and Consequences of Legalization' (2000) 54 International Organization 661, 679.

[114] On challenges to the human rights treaty bodies see the report by the UN Secretary General 'Cooperation with the United Nations, Its Representatives and Mechanisms in the Field of Human Rights' (1 December 2021) UN Doc A/HRC/48/28.

[115] Mikael Rask Madsen, Pola Cebulak, and Micha Wiebusch, 'Backlash against International Courts: Explaining the Forms and Patterns of Resistance to International Courts' (2018) 14 International Journal of Law in Context 197; Ximena Soley and Silvia Steininger, 'Parting Ways or Lashing Back? Withdrawals, Backlash and the Inter-American Court of Human Rights' (2018) 14 International Journal of Law in Context 237.

[116] Courtney Hillebrecht, *Saving the International Justice Regime: Beyond Backlash Against International Courts* (CUP 2021) 112–13.

[117] Silvia Steininger, 'With or Without You: Suspension, Expulsion, and the Limits of Membership Sanctions in Regional Human Rights Regimes' (2021) 81 Heidelberg Journal of International Law 533.

# 7

# *Ex iniuria ius oritur*? Norm Change and Norm Erosion of the Prohibition of Torture

*Dominik Steiger*[*]

## 1. Introduction

At which point does a heap of grain stop to be a heap if one takes away one grain after another? This so-called 'paradox of the heaps' has kept philosophers busy ever since it was developed 2,400 years ago by Eubulides of Miletus. Some 2,390 years later, international relations (IR) scholars have started to tend to the question under the heading of 'norm erosion'. Mainly in reaction to the use of torture by the United States after the attacks of 9/11, they began asking under which circumstances the content of an international norm changes and at which point it becomes void of its normative content if it is repeatedly violated. This book takes this question one step further and asks whether we can observe a metamorphosis, ie a fundamental systemic change in which not only norms—which are understood as 'collective expectations about proper behaviour for a given identity'—, but also the underlying values change or are even renounced.[1]

While norm erosion by now has become an area of research in IR which has led to many new insights, international lawyers have until very recently not engaged with the current debate. This seems especially troublesome given the fact that international law provides for rules on norm change and also on the most extreme form of norm erosion, norm death, ie the termination of the validity of a norm.[2] Norm erosion, ie the process which leads to norm death or, as our editors define it in a more refined way, a re-interpretation of the norm's objective to protect a specific common value which may affect the rule's scope and effect,[3] is, however, not coded in a binary manner and thus more difficult to conceptualize with legal methods.[4]

Nevertheless, legal norms not only govern how norms of treaty law and customary international law (CIL) come into being, how treaties can be modified or renounced and how CIL can be changed but also how re-interpretation processes of a norm affect the rule's content, scope, and effect. These rules have been overlooked by most IR research which still has arrived at similar explanations under which circumstances norm

* The author thanks Martin Hock, Linus Mührel, and Lotta Kuhlmann for their valuable help.

[1] Ronald L Jepperson, Alexander Wendt, and Peter J Katzenstein, 'Norms, Identity and Culture in National Security' in Peter J Katzenstein (ed), *The Culture of National Security: Norms and Identity in World Politics* (Columbia University Press 1996) 54; Heike Krieger and Andrea Liese, Chapter 1 in this book, pp. 1–4.

[2] Wayne Sandholtz, Chapter 3 in this book, pp. 56–57.

[3] Krieger and Liese, Chapter 1 in this book, p. 8ff.

[4] ibid p. 8f.

Dominik Steiger, Ex iniuria ius oritur*? Norm Change and Norm Erosion of the Prohibition of Torture* In: *Tracing Value Change in the International Legal Order.* Edited by: Heike Krieger and Andrea Liese, Oxford University Press. 
DOI: 10.1093/oso/9780192855831.003.0007

change and norm erosion take place. Furthermore, IR research has developed criteria which allow to determine whether a certain norm is more robust and thus resilient to change and erosion. These criteria find a correspondence in the rules of international law and can be translated to and framed in international law terms. From a lawyer's perspective, such an exercise is fruitful as the robustness protects the validity and the normativity of a norm—and thus its underlying values—in times of non-compliance.

In general, lawyers are mainly concerned with a rule's validity and normativity[5] and IR scholars are concerned about state behaviour, ie compliance. In norm erosion research, these two concerns merge.[6] This makes an interdisciplinary approach especially rewarding as it allows to understand norm change and norm erosion in a more holistic manner and enriches both disciplines and their understanding of how norm change and norm erosion function. This chapter will show that the validity of mono-disciplinary findings can be strengthened by inter-disciplinary research.

In order to do so, this chapter will proceed as follows. First, it will briefly set the stage by highlighting the main findings of IR research (Section 2). Second, against this background, the chapter will engage with the rules of international law on modification and interpretation of international norms and will show that the prohibition of torture is highly robust. It will then demonstrate that the legal perspective reinforces the findings of IR research and that pure non-compliance does neither lead to norm change nor to norm erosion (Section 3).

## 2. Setting the Stage: An International Relations' Perspective on Norm Erosion

In the 1990s, IR scholars found that norm compliance relies on a norm's development, circulation, and internationalization.[7] As the prohibition of torture was widely regarded as an example of such a norm,[8] the 'return of torture'[9] after the terrorist attacks of 9/11 questions this model and spurred intensive research about norm change, norm erosion, and norm death, and thus about the validity of a norm and its normativity.[10] Two key elements in establishing whether norm change and norm erosion is taking place have been identified (Section 2.1). In addition, different criteria in order to measure the robustness and resilience of a norm have been established (Section 2.2).

[5] Jeffrey L Dunoff and Mark A Pollack, 'International Law and International Relations: Introducing an Interdisciplinary Dialogue' in Jeffrey L Dunoff and Mark A Pollack (eds), *Interdisciplinary Perspectives on International Law and International Relations. The State of the Art* (CUP 2013) 11–21.

[6] Robert O Keohane, 'International Relations and International Law: Two Optics' (1997) 38 Harvard International Law Journal 487, 489–94.

[7] Martha Finnemore and Kathryn Sikkink, 'International Norm Dynamics and Political Change' (1998) 52 International Organization 887, 895–905.

[8] Lucrecia García Iommi, 'Norm Internalisation Revisited: Norm Contestation and the Life of Norms at the Extreme of the Norm Cascade' (2020) 9 Global Constitutionalism 76, 95–99.

[9] Gerhard Beestermöller and Hauke Brunkhorst (eds), *Die Rückkehr der Folter. Der Rechtsstaat im Zwielicht?* (CH Beck 2006); Dominik Steiger, *Das völkerrechtliche Folterverbot und der 'Krieg gegen den Terror'*"" (Springer Verlag 2013).

[10] eg Regina Heller, Martin Kahl, and Daniela Pisoiu, 'The "Dark" Side of Normative Argumentation – The Case of Counterterrorism Policy' (2012) 1 Global Constitutionalism 278, 282; Ryder McKeown, 'Norm Regress: US Revisionism and the Slow Death of the Torture Norm' (2009) 23 International Relations 5, 10ff.

## 2.1 Non-Compliance + Contestation = Norm Change?

In the beginning, it was held that non-compliance, ie breaches of the norm, alone might lead to norm death.[11] Such a view, accurately named 'compliance trap',[12] has been given up by now as the counter-factual expectations of norms would else be obsolete.[13] Non-compliance is thus a necessary but not sufficient condition for norm erosion.[14]

Additionally, the changed attitude of the norm-violating state as well as third states[15] towards a norm must be expressed in public discourse.[16] Not every contestation leads to norm change, though, but may actually strengthen normativity and compliance.[17] Decisive for a differentiation is whether states directly contest the validity of a norm or whether they only contest its application in a given situation.[18] Direct contestation of the validity leads to a loss of the norm's scope and effect and, thus, to norm erosion.[19] Contestation of the application[20] of the norm in a given situation—and this is what a single act of non-compliance actually is—does not lead to norm erosion. Thus, if a state argues for an exception from the absoluteness of the prohibition of torture or for a redefinition of torture,[21] it weakens the norm. If the state justifies its act as a valid exemption or if other states condemn this behaviour, it actually strengthens the norm.[22]

[11] Michael J Glennon, 'How International Rules Die' (2005) 93 Georgetown Law Journal 939, 940, 959ff, and 975ff.

[12] Sandholtz, Chapter 3 in this book, p. 50ff.

[13] ibid p. 51f; cf Friedrich Kratochwil and John Gerard Ruggie, 'International Organization: A State of the Art on an Art of the State' (1986) 40 International Organization 753, 767.

[14] Kratochwil and Ruggie (n 13) 725f; Nicole Deitelhoff and Lisbeth Zimmermann, 'Things We Lost in the Fire: How Different Types of Contestation Affect the Validity of International Norms' (2013) PRIF Working Papers No 18, 4f <https://nbn-resolving.org/urn:nbn:de:0168-ssoar-455201> accessed 25 February 2022.

[15] McKeown, 'Norm Regress' (n 10) 11f; cf Heller, Kahl, and Pisoiu, 'The "Dark Side" of Normative Argumentation' (n 10) 299–302.

[16] Christopher Kutz, 'How Norms Die: Torture and Assassination in American Security Policy' (2014) 28 Ethics & International Affairs 425, 430.

[17] See for an overview Anja Jetschke and Andrea Liese, 'The Power of Human Rights a Decade After: From Euphoria to Contestation?' in Thomas Risse, Stephen C Ropp, and Kathryn Sikkink (eds), *The Persistent Power of Human Rights: From Commitment to Compliance* (CUP 2013) 35f; Clifford Bob, *The Global Right Wing and the Clash of World Politics* (CUP 2011).

[18] Deitelhoff and Zimmermann, 'Things We Lost in the Fire – Working Papers' (n 14) 5; see also Nicole Deitelhoff and Lisbeth Zimmermann, 'Things We Lost in the Fire: How Different Types of Contestation Affect the Robustness of International Norms' (2020) 22 International Studies Review 51, 57f.

[19] Deitelhoff and Zimmermann, 'Things We Lost in the Fire – Working Papers' (n 14) 1; Deitelhoff and Zimmermann, 'Things We Lost in the Fire' (n 18) 57f.

[20] Deitelhoff and Zimmermann, 'Things We Lost in the Fire – Working Papers' (n 14) 5; Deitelhoff and Zimmermann, 'Things We Lost in the Fire' (n 18) 57f; Lucrecia García Iommi, 'Norm Internalisation Revisited: Norm Contestation and the Life of Norms at the Extreme of the Norm Cascade' (2020) 9 Global Constitutionalism 76, 84, and 88f..

[21] Andrea Liese, 'Exceptional Necessity: How Liberal Democracies Contest the Prohibition of Torture and Ill-Treatment When Countering Terrorism' (2009) 5 Journal of International Law and International Relations 17, 22.

[22] Deitelhoff and Zimmermann, 'Things We Lost in the Fire – Working Papers' (n 14) 4; Wayne Sandholtz and Kendall W Stiles, *International Norms and Cycles of Change* (OUP 2009) 14f; Liese (n 21) 46; Sandholtz, Chapter 3 in this book, p. 55.

### 2.2 Robustness of a Norm Shields Against Norm Erosion

While non-compliance and contestation may lead to norm erosion, certain factors which may be summarized under the heading of the robustness of a norm strengthen the resilience of a norm and protect it against erosion. These five factors are the type of norm in question, concordance, implementation, embeddedness, and preciseness.

First, it makes a difference which kind of norm is being questioned. A fundamental norm, which entails the broadest possible moral reach, is far more difficult to change than a standardized rule which serves to implement fundamental norms.[23] Second, concordance refers to the number of treaty ratifications, including the acceptance of opt-in clauses and the non-use of opt-out-clauses.[24] Third, implementation is about whether domestic laws have been adopted and enforcement is ensured.[25] Fourth, norms embedded in larger norm clusters are more resilient because they are reinforced by and support other regime norms.[26] Fifth, the less precise a norm is, the easier it can be challenged and the harder it is to react to norm violations as the challenging state possesses more interpretative space to defend the legality of its actions.[27]

To summarize, IR scholarship has established that non-compliance and supporting arguments are necessary for norms to change and to erode. The more robust a norm is, however, the more resilient it is against norm change and norm erosion.

## 3. The Birth and Death of Norms: An International Law Perspective

International law provides for norms and means which determine whether a norm is still valid and which content, scope, and effect it has. In alignment with the findings of IR scholars, the elements of compliance and *opinio iuris* are of decisive importance to international law scholars as regards both the birth and death of norms. The same is true of a norm's robustness. Firstly, the birth of norms of public international law and the robustness of the absolute prohibition of torture in international law will be discussed (Section 3.1). Secondly, international law's approach to norm change and norm erosion will be analysed. Here, it will be shown that while the United States after 9/11 has not complied with the prohibition of torture in many instances, no norm change has taken place (Section 3.2).

[23] Antje Wiener, Chapter 2 in this book, p. 39f.

[24] Averell Schmidt and Kathryn Sikkink, 'Breaking the Ban? The Heterogeneous Impact of US Contestation of the Torture Norm' (2019) 4 Journal of Global Security Studies 105, 108; cf Max Lesch and Lisbeth Zimmermann, Chapter 6 in this book, p. 103; for a different understanding see Michal Ben-Josef Hirsch and Jennifer M Dixon, 'Conceptualizing and Assessing Norm Strength in International Relations' (2021) 27 European Journal of International Relations 521, 524.

[25] Schmidt and Sikkink (n 24) 115; cf Lesch and Zimmermann, Chapter 6 in this book, p. 103.

[26] Jeffrey S Lantis and Carmen Wunderlich, 'Resiliency Dynamics of Norm Clusters: Norm Contestation and International Cooperation' (2018) 44 Review of International Studies 570.

[27] Deitelhoff and Zimmermann, 'Things We Lost in the Fire – Working Papers' (n 14) 5; Deitelhoff and Zimmermann, 'Things We Lost in the Fire' (n 18) 57.

## 3.1 The Birth of a Norm of Public International Law: Treaty Law and Customary Law

From an international law perspective, the prohibition of torture is a very robust norm well established in treaty law (Section 3.1.1) and CIL alike (Section 3.1.2).

### 3.1.1 The Prohibition of Torture as Robust Treaty Norm

A norm of international treaty law comes into being according to the rules of the Vienna Convention on the Law of Treaties (VCLT).[28] With the ratification of a treaty, a state declares itself to be bound by it.[29] As soon as the treaty has entered into force—which is determined by the rules of the treaty itself[30]—it follows from this valid ratification that the treaty and its norms apply to the treaty parties and, thus, legally bind them. The following overview of the international prohibition of torture will show how well regulated this field is and that the prohibition of torture has become a very robust norm of treaty law.

The prohibition of torture protects personal integrity as well as human dignity[31] which is regarded by the Universal Declaration of Human Rights (UDHR) as the highest value[32] (protection of fundamental values) and is firmly rooted in international treaty law (concordance). The first prohibition of torture in international treaty law can be found in Article 4 of the annexed Regulations to the Hague Convention respecting the Laws and Customs of War on Land of 1907[33] which applies to prisoners of war. The first explicit general prohibition of torture is stipulated in Article 5 UDHR, while the first general treaty prohibition of torture at the universal level is contained in the International Covenant on Civil and Political Rights of 1966 (ICCPR), which has been ratified by 173 states. At the regional level, *inter alia* the European Convention on Human Rights (ECHR), the American Convention on Human Rights (ACHR), and the African Charter on Human and Peoples' Rights (Banjul Charter) which together have been ratified by 124 states, prohibit torture. All of these treaties prohibit derogations from the prohibition of torture and balancing it with other human rights considerations.[34] The prohibition of torture is thus considered to be absolute. In addition, international humanitarian law and international criminal law prohibit torture.[35]

[28] Vienna Convention on the Law of Treaties (adopted 23 May 1969, entered into force 27 January 1980) 1155 UNTS 331, arts 10–18 (VCLT).

[29] VCLT (n 28) arts 14, 16; see also art 2(1)(b).

[30] VCLT (n 28) art 24.

[31] David Luban, *Torture, Power and Law* (CUP 2014) 146f.

[32] See Universal Declaration of Human Rights (adopted 10 December 1948) UNGA Res 217 A(III) Preamble, para 1; Christopher McCrudden, 'Human Dignity and Judicial Interpretation of Human Rights' (2008) 19 European Journal of International Law 655, 665–72.

[33] Hague Convention respecting the Laws and Customs of War on Land (adopted 18 October 1907, entered into force 26 January 1910) reprinted in Georg Friedrich Martens, *Nouveau Recueil Général de Traités*, vol 3 (Dieterich 1843) 461.

[34] Manfred Nowak, Moritz Birk, and Giuliana Monina (eds), *The United Nations Convention Against Torture: A Commentary* (2nd edn, OUP 2018)art 2, para 59.

[35] eg Third Geneva Convention Relative to the Treatment of Prisoners of War (adopted 12 August 1949, entered into force 21 October 1950) 75 UNTS 135, arts 3, 13, 17, and 87; Rome Statute of the International Criminal Court (adopted 17 July 1998, entered into force 1 July 2002) 2187 UNTS 3, arts 7(1)(f), 7(1)(k), 8(2)(a)(ii), and 8(2)(c).

Since 1984, the United Nations Convention against Torture and Other Cruel, Inhuman or Degrading Treatment or Punishment (UNCAT),[36] which just as the ICCPR has been ratified by 173 states to date, reinforces and deepens these prohibitions. UNCAT provides a rather clear and precise definition of torture[37] which has been further refined by (international) courts (preciseness). That the prohibition is precise, is underlined by its, albeit contested, direct applicability in national law. Whether a norm of international law is directly applicable in national law depends on the formulation and content of the rule. If the wording is sufficiently clear, precise, and unconditional and thus capable of being applicable without the requirement of a further rule implementing the norm, the rule may be directly applicable by national courts and the executive.[38] This is the case for the prohibition of torture.[39]

UNCAT furthermore contains a complex body of rules to combat torture. It *inter alia* obliges the state parties to prevent torture, to investigate incidents of torture and to punish and prosecute torturers, even on the basis of the principle of universality (embeddedness).[40] The same is true for the general human rights treaties. While they do not expressly foresee a duty to investigate or prosecute, these duties are deduced from the right to an effective remedy and the undertaking to respect and ensure the right to be free from torture.[41] Furthermore, the prohibition of torture is protected through different supervisory systems which are highly institutionalized and provide for thorough means of dialogue. Both ICCPR and UNCAT provide for a mandatory reporting procedure, an inter-state-complaint as well as an individual-complaint procedure. More than 60 states have opted-in to these mechanisms.[42] The regional systems even provide for full judicial protection through human rights courts. Also, proactive supervisory mechanisms have been developed. In 2002, the Optional Protocol to the United Nations Convention Against Torture (OPCAT)[43] was adopted. OPCAT is a unique international human rights treaty, especially because it follows a new proactive approach by establishing a system of on-site visits as well as a dual supervisory mechanism which consists of an international committee, the UN Subcommittee on Prevention of Torture and the National Prevention Mechanisms.[44] OPCAT, which has been ratified by 91 states, is modelled on the Inter-American Convention to Prevent and Punish Torture of 1985[45] as well as the European Convention for the Prevention

[36] Convention against Torture and Other Cruel, Inhuman or Degrading Treatment or Punishment (adopted 10 December 1984, entered into force 26 June 1987) 1465 UNTS 81 (UNCAT).

[37] Liese (n 21) 40.

[38] Steiger (n 9) 504; Bernd Grzeszick, 'Rechte des Einzelnen im Völkerrecht' (2005) 43 Archiv des Völkerrechts 312, 318.

[39] Steiger (n 9) 530.

[40] Cf UNCAT (n 36) arts 2, 4, 5–8, 12f.

[41] Steiger (n 9) 381–90.

[42] See United Nations Treaty Collection, 'Chapter IV Human Rights Subchapter 9' <https://treaties.un.org/Pages/ViewDetails.aspx?src=TREATY&mtdsg_no=IV-9&chapter=4&clang=_en> accessed 25 February 2022.

[43] Optional Protocol to the Convention against Torture and Other Cruel, Inhuman or Degrading Treatment or Punishment (adopted 18 December 2002, entered into force 22 June 2006) 2375 UNTS 237.

[44] Lorena González Pinto, 'The United Nations Subcommittee on Prevention of Torture: The Effects of Preventive Action' (to be published 2022) Journal of Human Rights Practice.

[45] Inter-American Convention to Prevent and Punish Torture (adopted 9 December 1985, entered into force 28 February 1987) OAS Treaty Series No 67.

of Torture and Inhuman or Degrading Treatment or Punishment of 1987[46] which together have been ratified by 65 states.

Lastly, these norms have been adopted on a large scale in domestic law.[47] In the United States, for example, the Torture Convention Implementation Act[48] implements the UNCAT (implementation). Also, the direct applicability of the prohibition of torture strengthens the application of the norm on the domestic level as it allows the executive and the courts to apply the prohibition of torture without any implementation act by the legislature.

### 3.1.2 Customary International Law: Practice and *Opinio Iuris*

CIL comes into being through a completely different mechanism than treaty law. It requires state practice (*consuetudo*) and the conviction that the practice is being followed because it is law (*opinio iuris*).[49] If a norm forms not only part of treaty law but also of CIL,[50] it fortifies the robustness of the norm.

The objective element, ie practice, demands that certain acts have been practised consistently, generally and for a certain amount of time.[51] Consistency refers to the content of the norm. It does not imply that all states have to practise the rule in full consistency all of the time. Rather, the practice 'must be reasonably consistent'.[52] The generality of practice refers to states practising the norm. The practice needs to be 'both extensive and virtually uniform'[53], ie common to a significant number of states but not all of them.[54] Thus, one has to take into account the acts of not only the US after 9/11 but those of all states.

The subjective element, ie *opinio iuris*, demands that states must accept the practice as binding law.[55] The *opinio iuris* by states can *inter alia* be established by public statements of governments, domestic courts, and legislatures. Again, third states play a role, as their *opinio iuris* also needs to be taken into account. Furthermore, decisions of international courts[56] and declarations of international organizations[57] may provide evidence in finding existing *opinio iuris*. Lastly, treaty law may add to the

[46] European Convention for the Prevention of Torture and Inhuman or Degrading Treatment or Punishment (adopted 26 November 1987, entered into force 1 February 1989) ETS No 126.

[47] For criminal law see Antonio Marchesi, 'Implementing the UN Convention Definition of Torture in National Criminal Law (with Reference to the Special Case of Italy)' (2008) 6 Journal of International Criminal Justice 195, 196–201.

[48] US Torture Convention Implementation Act, 18 USC § 2340 A (b).

[49] See eg *Case Concerning the Continental Shelf (Libya v Malta)* (Judgement) [1985] ICJ Rep 13, para 27.

[50] That such an overlap is possible has been held by the International Court of Justice (ICJ), see inter alia *Military and Paramilitary Activities in and against Nicaragua (Nicaragua v USA)* (Judgement) [1986] ICJ Rep 14, para 177; *North Sea Continental Shelf (Germany v Denmark and Netherlands)* (Judgement) [1969] ICJ Rep 3, para 63.

[51] Cf Statute of the International Court of Justice (adopted 26 June 1945) 557 UNTS 143, art 38(1)(b); Martin Dixon, *Textbook on International Law* (7th edn, OUP 2013) 33.

[52] Dixon, *Textbook on International Law* (n 51) 33; International Law Commission (ILC), 'Identification of Customary International Law: Text of the draft conclusions as adopted by the Drafting Committee on second reading' (2018) UN Doc A/CN.4/L.908 Conclusion 8 para 1; *Military and Paramilitary Activities* (n 50) para 186.

[53] *North Sea Continental Shelf* (n 50) para 74.

[54] Dixon, *Textbook on International Law* (n 51) 34.

[55] ibid 34; ILC, 'Identification of Customary International Law' (n 52) Conclusion 9 para 1.

[56] ILC, 'Identification of Customary International Law' (n 52) Conclusion 13.

[57] ibid Conclusion 12.

coming-into-being of CIL, at least if the norm is widely ratified and of a fundamentally norm-creating character.[58]

Applying this background to the prohibition of torture, it becomes clear that widespread *opinio iuris* regarding the absolute prohibition of torture exists: no state has legalized torture;[59] states repeatedly stress the importance of the absolute prohibition of torture;[60] international[61] and national courts[62] regularly underline the prohibition of torture's absolute nature. In addition, the *opinio iuris* held in and by the United Nations (UN) supports the existence of a norm of CIL. The UN is condoning torture regularly and persistently.[63] Furthermore, the existence of so many different treaty law norms offers evidence that the norm is also regarded as a norm of CIL.

Lastly, the prohibition of torture is 'clearly accepted and recognized'[64] as *ius cogens*.[65] The ILC thus correctly stated the prohibition of torture reinforces the CIL status as ius cogens is based in CIL.[66]

Nevertheless, torture is still a widely used technique[67] which makes one wonder whether enough practice exists in order to speak of the prohibition of torture as a norm of CIL. However, these instances of torture have to be regarded as exceptions to a general practice of non-torture since states do not use torture on a regular basis. While omissions as such cannot be regarded as practice, the way certain omissions are practised could be regarded as practice if states are 'being conscious of having a duty to abstain'.[68] Since all states are bound by the prohibition of torture, they are conscious of the prohibition. By not torturing openly, ie without verbally justifying it, states then show that the omission of torture is the practice they find to be constitutive for the creation of CIL.[69] Even cases, in which states torture openly, may serve as evidence for a practice of not-torturing. The ICJ famously held in the *Nicaragua Case* that the prohibition of the use of force is founded in CIL, since even a state 'that act[s] in a way prima facie incompatible with a recognized rule, but defends its conduct by appealing to exceptions or justifications ... confirm[s] rather than ... weaken[s] the rule'.[70]

[58] *North Sea Continental Shelf* (n 50) paras 71–74.

[59] Lauri Hannikainen, *Peremptory Norms (Jus Cogens) in International Law: Historical Development, Criteria, Present Status* (Finnish Lawyers' Publication Company 1988) 502 with further references.

[60] See eg United Nations Committee against Torture, 'Consideration of reports Submitted by States parties under art 19 of the Convention: Second periodic reports of States parties due in 1999: United States of America' (13 January 2006) CAT/C/48/Add.3/Rev.1, para 5.

[61] See eg *El-Masri v The Former Yugoslav Republic of Macedonia* App No 39630/09 (ECtHR, 13 December 2012) para 195.

[62] See eg *R (Binyam Mohamed) v Secretary of State for Foreign and Commonwealth* [2010] EWCA Civ 65, para 14.

[63] See eg Declaration on the Protection of All Persons from Being Subjected to Torture and Other Cruel, Inhuman or Degrading Treatment or Punishment (9 December 1975) UNGA Res 3452(XXX) and the annual, by now biannual resolutions condoning torture.

[64] ILC, 'Report of the International Law Commission on the work of its fifty-third session' (2001) UN Doc A/56/10, 85 para 5.

[65] eg United Nations Human Rights Committee, 'General Comment No. 24' (4 November 1994) CCPR/C/21/Rev.1/Add.6, para 8; *Siderman de Blake v Argentina* 965 F2d 699 (9th Cir 1992) para 58.

[66] Thomas Kleinlein, 'Jus Cogens as the "Highest Law"? Peremptory Norms and Legal Hierarchies' (2015) 46 Netherlands Yearbook of International Law 173, 195.

[67] Human Rights Watch, 'World Report 2021' <www.hrw.org/sites/default/files/media_2021/01/2021_hrw_world_report.pdf> accessed 30 March 2022.

[68] *Case of the S.S. Lotus (France v Turkey)* (Judgement) [1927] PCIJ Rep Series A No 10, 28.

[69] Cf ILC, 'Identification of Customary International Law' (n 52) Conclusion 6 para 1.

[70] *Military and Paramilitary Activities* (n 50) para 186.

### 3.1.3 Summary: Prohibition of Torture as a Very Robust Norm

To summarize, the prohibition of torture is a very robust norm of international law: it protects fundamental values, it can be found in treaty law and CIL alike. Furthermore, the precisely framed prohibition of torture has also been implemented on the domestic plane.[71] It is embedded in other norms that only exist to fortify the prohibition and in well-institutionalized compliance mechanisms. In addition, the prohibition of torture is a *ius cogens* norm which protects fundamental values.[72] Furthermore, the definition of torture, while leaving room for interpretation and thus also room for arguments—as every definition does—is nevertheless clear and precise.[73] Not only is it one of the very few prohibitions that are legally defined (cf Article 1 UNCAT) but also (international) courts have helped in further defining it.

## 3.2 The Death of a Norm: State Practice and *Opinio Iuris*

Despite its high legal robustness, the prohibition of torture might have changed or even eroded over time. In general, this is perceivable: a norm's content may change during its life span and it might even cease to exist. This may take place through different means depending on whether a norm is based in treaty law (Section 3.2.1) or in CIL (Section 3.2.2). Aside formal amendments and modifications in treaty law, *opinio iuris* which will often be accompanied by practice is the decisive factor in norm change (Section 3.2.3).

### 3.2.1 Treaty Law: Modification, Renouncement, and Interpretation

One way to modify treaty law would be via an explicit agreement of the parties.[74] Such a modification would apply to all state parties. Treaty norms might also cease to apply in case a state renounces its status as a treaty party.[75] In this case, however, only the renouncing state would not be bound by the treaty norm anymore. With regard to torture, neither a formal modification nor any renouncement of any torture norm has been undertaken thus far. But there is another, subtler way to change the understanding of treaty law, ie via the methods of interpretation. However, interpretation must not lead to modifications of the content[76] as it has to stay within the interpretative boundaries set by the wording of the norm.[77] A proper modification can only be attained by changing the wording of a norm.

[71] For criminal law see Marchesi (n 47) 196–201.

[72] See eg Erika de Wet, 'Sources and the Hierarchy of International Law. The Place of Peremptory Norms and Article 103 of the UN Charter within the Sources of International Law' in Jean d'Aspremont, Samantha Besson, and Sèvrine Knuchel (eds), *The Oxford Handbook on the Sources of International Law* (OUP 2017) 630–34.

[73] Liese (n 21) 40.

[74] VCLT (n 28) arts 39ff.

[75] ibid arts 54ff.

[76] Christian Djeffal, *Static and Evolutionary Treaty Interpretation: A Functional Reconstruction* (CUP 2016) 15f; ILC, 'Subsequent agreements and subsequent practice in relation to the interpretation of treaties: Text of the draft conclusions adopted by the Drafting Committee on second reading' (2018) UN Doc A/CN.4/L.907, Conclusion 7 para 3.

[77] Anthony Aust, *Modern Treaty Law and Practice* (3rd edn, CUP 2013) 205–09.

Interpretation in international law in principle follows the lines of all legal interpretations. According to Article 31(1) VCLT a treaty shall be interpreted in good faith in accordance with the ordinary meaning to be given to the terms of the treaty and in the light of its object and purpose. Norm interpreters, eg international or national courts or the executive branch of each state, may interpret norms differently and according to their *opinio iuris*. However, the interpretation of a norm by one actor is not binding on others. The content, scope, and effect of a norm is left untouched.

This is only true to a certain extent, though. If a certain reinterpretation of a norm is taken up by all or most other norm interpreters[78] and thus becomes their *opinio iuris*, then a norm changes.[79] Just as IR research has underlined, the reactions of other institutions to a re-modelling of a norm play a highly relevant role in norm change and norm erosion. From this follows that the subjective understanding of the content of a norm is more important than state practice.

However, reinterpretation efforts will generally involve some practice. Interpretation by domestic courts is understood to be state practice[80] and the *opinio iuris* of a state's executive will usually lead to state practice. If the executive's interpretation is contrary to the norm as understood by others, the ensuing practice might be an act of non-compliance. According to Article 31(3)(b) VCLT which names 'subsequent practice establishing agreement' as one interpretative tool, this practice may change the meaning of treaties over time.[81] In this context, state practice is the means to establish a changed interpretation and can be described as the emanation of a changed interpretation which needs to be, albeit indirectly, agreed upon between the parties.[82] Since state practice needs to be 'concordant, common, and consistent',[83] it is rather difficult to change the content of a norm via subsequent practice. Furthermore, pronouncements of treaty bodies[84] which tend to be rather protective of the norm and its underlying values may also 'be relevant when assessing the subsequent practice of parties to a treaty'.[85]

### 3.2.2 Customary Law and Treaty Law: *Desuetude*

Another way to change international treaty law as well as CIL is via *desuetude*. *Desuetude*, which is 'defined as the rejection of a rule through subsequent non-enforcement or non-compliance',[86] is considered to be a ground for terminating a

[78] For the different actors that might be involved see Nico Krisch, 'The Dynamics of International Law Redux' (2021) 74 Current Legal Problems 269, 287.

[79] Cf Thomas Kleinlein, Chapter 4 in this book, p. 73f.

[80] See eg ILC, 'Report of the International Law Commission. Seventieth Session' (2018) UN Doc A/73/10, 32.

[81] For the difficulties involved in conceptualising interpretation, see Kleinlein, Chapter 4 in this book, p. 76ff.

[82] Aust, *Modern Treaty Law* (n 77) 214ff.

[83] Gerhard Hafner, 'Subsequent Agreements and Practice: Between Interpretation, Informal Modification, and Formal Amendment' in Georg Nolte (ed), *Treaties and Subsequent Practice* (OUP 2013) 112.

[84] ILC, 'Seventieth Session' (n 80) 39f.

[85] UN General Assembly, 'Subsequent agreements and subsequent practice in relation to the interpretation of treaties' (20 December 2018) UNGA Res/73/202, Conclusion 5(2).

[86] Jan Wouters and Sten Verhoeven, 'Desuetudo' in Rüdiger Wolfrum (ed), *Max Planck Encyclopedia of Public International Law* (online edn, OUP 2008) para 1 <http://opil.ouplaw.com/view/10.1093/law:epil/9780199231690/law-9780199231690-e1027?prd=EPIL> accessed 25 February 2022.

treaty and may be invoked for the abrogation of CIL.[87] Does that mean that in international law pure non-compliance by a sufficient number of states may lead to the death of a norm?[88]

Such a reading of *desuetude* is too far-reaching: *desuetude* has purposefully not been included in the VCLT, implying that non-compliance with a treaty cannot lead to the modification of a treaty[89]—for which the VCLT foresees explicit norms. Moreover, other authors speak of the 'non-application' of treaties,[90] which is quite different from 'non-compliance', especially with regard to human rights treaties which provide a supervisory mechanism that applies the treaty on a regular basis. Furthermore, it is not convincing that practice alone may change international law as the consent of states is decisive in creating as well as changing international law. Lastly, the counter-factual expectations by norms would become void if only (f)acts changed the norm.

Because of that, it is even argued that *desuetude* does not have a place in international law.[91] While this argument is too far-reaching, it is decisive that *opinio iuris* must also be considered when inquiring whether a norm has fallen into *desuetude*.[92] Even the above cited authors who seemingly only require state practice for *desuetude* refer to the importance of *opinio iuris* for *desuetude* several times.[93] Hence, in principle,[94] *desuetude* corresponds to subsequent practice interpretation: a new practice needs to emerge which is accompanied by a corresponding *opinio iuris*, ie a common understanding on what the law should say and, thus, on whether the new practice is legal. CIL is therefore changed in the same way it comes into being.[95] While breaching international law is problematic because a breach is illegal and engages the state's international responsibility, it can actually be a building block in creating new international law: *ex iniuria ius oritur* is indeed possible.[96] Pure non-compliance, however, does not suffice. Rather, states have to be convinced that the new practice mirrors a new status of the law.[97] Here, the *opinio iuris* of third states plays an important role as the change of international law can be precluded when

[87] ibid.

[88] Glennon (n 11) 940, 959–64, and 975–80; cf also Thomas Franck, 'Who Killed Article 2(4)? or: Changing Norms Governing the Use of Force by States' (1979) 64 American Journal of International Law 809.

[89] Marcelo G Kohen, 'Desuetude and Obsolescence of Treaties' in Enzo Cannizzaro (ed), *The Law of Treaties Beyond the Vienna Convention* (OUP 2011) 351.

[90] Karl Doehring, *Völkerrecht* (2nd edn, C.F. Müller 2004) 296; Mark Villiger, *Customary International Law and Treaties: A Manual on the Theory and Practice of the Interrelation of Sources* (Martinus Nijhoff Publishers 1997) 206.

[91] Kohen (n 89) 359.

[92] See also Maarten Bos, 'The Identification of Custom in International Law' (1982) 25 German Yearbook of International Law 9, 39; Kleinlein, Chapter 4 in this book, p. 70ff.

[93] Wouters and Verhoeven (n 86) paras 2, 10, 14.

[94] As mentioned above, subsequent practice is 'only' about re-interpretation. *Desuetude* in principle reaches further as it allows to overcome the strict boundaries of interpretation.

[95] Wouters and Verhoeven (n 86) para 14.

[96] Cf Antonio Cassese, 'Ex Iniuria Ius Oritur: Are We Moving Towards International Legitimation of Forcible Humanitarian Countermeasures in the World Community?' (1999) 10 European Journal of International Law 23, 27–30.

[97] ibid 29f.

states express their dissent with violations of or undertakings to change the prohibition of torture.[98]

### 3.2.3 Prohibition of Torture: Changing State Practice and *Opinio Iuris*?

As shown, practice but even more so *opinio iuris* are the decisive factors for norm erosion of international treaty law and CIL. Thus, from an international law perspective, IR scholars have aptly described how international law works by arguing that non-compliance is a necessary precondition for norm change, but not in itself sufficient as the attitude of states also needs to have changed. Consequently, in the following, after showing that the prohibition of torture has been violated in reaction to the terrorist attacks of 9/11 (Section 3.2.3.1), it will be analysed whether this (mal)practice is supported by a corresponding *opinio iuris* (Section 3.2.3.2).

#### *3.2.3.1 (Mal)Practice of torture*

Reported cases of torture and thus non-compliance are easy to find.[99] Especially, the United States is regarded as the most important actor in eroding the torture prohibition. For example, so-called no-touch torture was frequently employed during the 'War on Terror'. Its main elements are sensory deprivation and so-called self-inflicted pain.[100] The infamous photography of a prisoner of the Iraqi Abu Ghraib prison is a typical example of this practice: a prisoner is standing on a wooden box wearing a hood, with his arms extended and faked wired electrodes purporting to be used for the infliction of lethal electric shocks attached to his fingertips. But this method is not new: it was already developed in the 1950s,[101] *inter alia* used in the Vietnam War and taught at the School of the Americas from where it spread to Latin America.[102] In addition, the United States has only very reluctantly and not fully fulfilled its duty to investigate and prosecute allegations of torture as well as to compensate for cases of torture.[103]

#### *3.2.3.2* Opinio iuris*—new challenges to the torture prohibition?*

While non-compliance has indeed taken place, the question remains whether it was accompanied by corresponding *opinio iuris*. It is decisive whether states indeed want to change the torture prohibition and express an understanding which differs from accepted interpretations.[104] There are different avenues which could be taken in order

[98] Cf Helmut Aust and Mehrdad Payandeh, 'Praxis und Protest im Völkerrecht: Erosionserscheinungen des völkerrechtlichen Gewaltverbots und die Verantwortung der Bundesrepublik im Syrien-Konflikt' (2018) 73 Juristen-Zeitung 633, 633f, and 637f.

[99] See Human Rights Watch (n 67).

[100] Robert Duncan, 'Neuropsychological and Electronic "No-Touch Torture". The Spectrum of "Interrogation" and Torture Techniques Used by the US and its Allies' (*GlobalResearch*, 1 April 2015) <www.globalresearch.ca/neuropsychological-and-electronic-no-touch-torture-the-spectrum-of-interrogation-and-torture-techniques-used-by-the-us-and-its-allies/5454124> accessed 25 February 2022.

[101] Steiger (n 9) 252–60.

[102] Jennifer Harbury, *Truth, Torture, and the American Way: The History and Consequences of U.S. Involvement in Torture* (Beacon Press 2005) 103.

[103] Cf eg United Nations Committee against Torture, 'Concluding observations on the combined third to fifth periodic reports of the United States of America' (19 December 2014) CAT/C/USA/CO/3-5, paras 12, 29.

[104] But see Glennon (n 11) 976f.

to undertake such a change. A state could argue that the prohibition of torture is obsolete today (Section 3.2.3.2.1); it could try to change the definition of torture (Section 3.2.3.2.2); it could argue that derogations and justifications are possible (Section 3.2.3.2.3); or it could attack the ensuing duties of the torture prohibition, ie the duty to investigate, the duty to prosecute, and the duty to compensate (Section 3.2.3.2.4). A closer look at these different issues shall reveal whether the understanding of the torture prohibition and, thus, the *opinio iuris* of the torturing states as well as of third states has changed or is about to change (Section 3.2.3.2.5). Such a close-up look shall also reveal whether states challenge the validity of the norm or only its applicability and, thus, do not question the norm as such.

**3.2.3.2.1 No outright denial of the existence of a torture prohibition** An outright denial of the existence of the prohibition of torture would be a direct challenge to the existence of the norm. However, no state has yet argued that the prohibition of torture as such has become or should become obsolete.[105] On the contrary, even states that have tortured have simultaneously underlined the importance of the torture prohibition: 'I want to reaffirm yet again that the United States has very high values. We do not engage in torture. We are bound by the Convention against Torture ... [T]he United States government has never authorized torture.'[106] This lack of an outright denial of the validity of the torture prohibition shows that the prohibition of torture has not died. Furthermore, it is a first hint that the torture norm has not eroded.

**3.2.3.2.2 Re-defining torture?** According to the legal definition in Article 1 UNCAT, torture means 'any act by which severe pain or suffering, whether physical or mental, is intentionally inflicted on a person ... when such pain or suffering is inflicted by ... a public official'. While this definition is unique to UNCAT, it serves as a general interpretative guideline for the international prohibition of torture in general.[107] Although the torture definition is rather precise and clear,[108] it still is open to interpretation as every norm is—and states indeed use this space for interpretation. Especially the United States has engaged in a reinterpretation of the definition of torture by excluding no-touch torture from the definition of torture on the one hand[109] and through the notorious, quasi-legal Bybee Memorandum on the other hand which added a 'special intent' element,[110] allowing the United States to argue that torture to save human lives

[105] Liese (n 21) 32 for the US, 34 for Israel and the United Kingdom.
[106] Office of the Press Secretary, 'Press Briefing by White House Counsel Judge Alberto Gonzales, DoD General Counsel William Haynes, DoD Deputy General Counsel Daniel Dell'Orto and Army Deputy Chief of Staff for Intelligence General Keith Alexander' (*The White House*, 22 June 2004) <https://georgewbush-whitehouse.archives.gov/news/releases/2004/06/20040622-14.html> accessed 25 February 2022.
[107] See eg *Selmouni v France*, App No 25803/94 (ECtHR, 28 July 1999) paras 97–105; Manfred Nowak, *U.N. Covenant on Civil and Political Rights: CCPR Commentary* (NP Engel 2005) art 7 para 6.
[108] Liese (n 21) 40.
[109] Andrea Birdsall, 'But we don't call it "torture"! Norm contestation during the US "War on Terror"' (2016) 53 International Politics 176, 181; Tim Dunne, 'The Rules of the Game Are Changing: Fundamental Human Rights in Crisis After 9/11' (2007) 44 International Politics 269, 276–82.
[110] John Bybee, 'Memorandum for Alberto Gonzales. Re: Standards of Conduct for Interrogation under 18 U.S.C. §§ 2340–2340A, 1 August 2002' in Karen Greenberg and Joshua Dratel (eds), *The Torture Papers: The Road to Abu Ghraib* (CUP 2005) 174.

never constitutes torture in legal terms. Such changes in the interpretation of the torture definition may be one way how norms change.

However, both undertakings cannot be understood as arguments in favour of a changed *opinio iuris*. First, the special intent requirement was later retracted through another memorandum.[111] Second, the United States at the moment of the ratification of UNCAT had already declared via a so called 'interpretative declaration' that it does not understand no-touch torture to be included in the torture definition.[112]

But one might be inclined to ask, has the United States not started eroding the prohibition way before 9/11 by excluding no-touch torture from the ambit of the torture definition and thus narrowing down the definition of torture on the day it joined UNCAT? The answer depends on the legal effect of the United States' declaration. Interpretative declarations are a permissible instrument to express a state's understanding of a specific norm but do not aim to modify a state's obligations. Also, they do not bind any other treaty state.[113] Thus, their (re)interpretative value is rather low.

But the so-called declaration is in fact a reservation that aims at or purports to exclude or modify the legal effect of certain provisions of the treaty in their application to that state (Article 2(d) VCLT). Such a reservation has a greater legal impact—and this is exactly what the United States aimed at: it tried to modify the legal effect of UNCAT by narrowing down the content, scope, and effect of UNCAT. The United States was, however, not successful from a legal point of view as the reservation possesses no legal effect: a reservation is only legally binding as long as it is permissible, but the reservation at hand is incompatible with the object and purpose of the respective treaties.[114] It is thus impermissible (Article 19 VCLT). Such reservations need to be severed from the treaty which will be operative for the reserving party as though it had been concluded without the impermissible reservation.[115]

This debate about the definition of torture is nothing new. Rather, the United States questioned the content of the norm from the beginning and aimed—unsuccessfully—at changing it. This declaration can thus be seen as a constructive form of engaging with the prohibition of torture, but not as a sign of norm erosion. Contesting the exact content of a norm is a regular occurrence in international law and, as IR research

[111] Daniel Levin, 'Memorandum for James B. Comey Deputy Attorney General. Re: Legal Standards Applicable Under 18 U.S.C. §§ 2340–2340A' (30 December 2004) 12–17 <https://cdn.factcheck.org/UploadedFiles/DoJ-Memo-overriding-August-Memo.pdf> accessed 25 February 2022.

[112] Cf Alfred McCoy, *A Question of Torture, CIA Interrogation, from the Cold War to the War on Terror* (Hold Paperbacks 2006) 10.

[113] Cf ILC, 'Third report on reservations to treaties by Mr. Alain Pellet, Special Rapporteur' (1998) UN Doc A/CN.4/491/Add.4, para 352.

[114] Steiger (n 9) 351–57; cf United Nations Committee against Torture, 'Report of the Committee against Torture. Twenty third session and Twenty-fourth session' (November 1999 and December 2000) UN Doc A/55/44, para 179(a).

[115] *Belilos v Switzerland* App No 10328/83 (ECtHR, 29 April 1988) para 55; Rosalyn Higgins, 'Introduction' in JP Gardner (ed), *Human Rights as General Norms and a State's Right to Opt Out: Reservations and Objections to Human Rights Conventions* (British Institute for International and Comparative Law 1997) xv–xxix, xxvii; but see Ryan Goodman, 'Human Rights Treaties, Invalid Reservations, and State Consent' (2002) 96 American Journal of International Law 531.

underlines, even strengthens the norm as it contests its applicability and not its validity.[116]

**3.2.3.2.3 Relativizing the absolute prohibition of torture? Derogations, justifications, and necessity** No treaty that prohibits torture allows for derogations. Thus, no exceptional circumstances whatsoever, whether a state of war or a threat of war, internal political instability, or any other public emergency may allow for an interference with the prohibition of torture. Furthermore, as the prohibition of torture is of an absolute nature, a breach cannot be justified by protecting other norms such as the right to life[117] or by necessity which can never be brought up as a circumstance precluding wrongfulness in case a *ius cogens* norm has been breached.[118]

Nevertheless, after 9/11, it was argued that the prohibition of torture could either be derogated from or its violation could be justified, eg by arguing that necessity applies in order to protect from terrorism.[119] However, the argument that torture could be justified never left academic circles.[120] On the contrary, it was even explicitly stated by the Bush administration that '[t]he President has not directed the use of specific interrogation techniques. . . . There has been no presidential determination that circumstances warrant the use of torture to protect the mass security of the United States'.[121] Rather, the United States, as described above, undertook to redefine torture instead of justifying its use. Thus, '[i]n violating international norms on human rights, the US has sought to operate in secret and has not provided a public legitimation narrative'.[122]

But, as Andrea Liese rightly argues,[123] a combination of a change in the definition of torture and the introduction of a possible justification of acts of cruel, inhuman, or degrading treatment was indeed undertaken by some states, *inter alia* the United States and Israel. In Israel, the Landau Commission in 1987 argued that the necessity claims allow for a 'moderate measure of physical pressure' to be applied. However, the Israeli Supreme Court in 1999 declared this approach to be illegal: 'These prohibitions [of torture and cruel, inhuman, and degrading treatment] are "absolute." There are no exceptions to them and there is no room for balancing.'[124] Finally, the Bybee

[116] Deitelhoff and Zimmermann, 'Things We Lost in the Fire – Working Papers' (n 14) 5; Deitelhoff and Zimmermann, 'Things We Lost in the Fire' 2020 (n 18) 57f; Wiener, 'Norm(ative) Change in International Relations' (n 23) 11f.

[117] eg UN Committee Against Torture, 'Concluding observations' (n 103) paras 5ff.

[118] UN General Assembly, 'Responsibility of States for Internationally Wrongful Acts' (28 January 2002) UNGA Res 56/83, Annex art 26.

[119] Cf Jutta Brunnée and Stephen J Toope, *Legitimacy and Legality in International Law – An Interactional Account* (CUP 2010) 221.

[120] eg Winfried Brugger, 'May Government Ever Use Torture? Two Responses From German Law' (2000) 48 American Journal of Comparative Law 661.

[121] Office of the Press Secretary, 'Press Briefing by Alberto Gonzales' (n 106).

[122] Ian Hurd, 'Breaking and Making Norms: American Revisionism and Crises of Legitimacy' (2007) 44 International Politics 194, 200.

[123] Liese (n 21) 27–32. For the United Kingdom see Frank Foley, 'The (De)Legitimation of Torture: Rhetoric, Shaming and Narrative Contestation in Two British Cases' (2021) 27 European Journal of International Relations 102.

[124] *Public Committee Against Torture in Israel v Israel and General Security Service* (Judgement) Case No HCJ 5100/94 (6 September 1999) para 23.

Memorandum aimed at redefining torture and, in a second step, at justifying cruel, inhuman and degrading treatment by using a balancing act.[125] But again, this position was later retracted[126] and the United States stated that 'under U.S. law every U.S. official, wherever he or she may be, is prohibited from engaging in torture or in cruel, inhuman or degrading treatment or punishment, at all times, and in all places.'[127] Thus, no *opinio iuris* can be detected that questions the absoluteness of the prohibition of torture.

**3.2.3.2.4 The duties to investigate and prosecute torture—often breached but rhetorically upheld** In order to combat torture, duties that render the prohibition effective in practice, namely the duties to investigate and prosecute torture, have been introduced. During the 'War on Terror', the United States conducted several investigations into alleged cases of torture, some only superficially and incompletely, while others were carried out thoroughly and conscientiously.[128] Attempts to fulfil the duty to prosecute were only made in few cases.[129] While these attempts were by no means adequate,[130] the United States has not questioned the existence of these duties, but on the contrary has underlined their importance at the highest level. George W Bush affirmed that '[t]orture anywhere is an affront to human dignity everywhere. ... I call on all governments to join with the United States and the community of law-abiding nations in prohibiting, investigating, and prosecuting all acts of torture'.[131] A changing agreement about the existence or content of these norms does not exist.

**3.2.3.2.5 Reactions by third states—reaffirming the prohibition of torture** While the United States has indeed contested the definition of torture for a long time, it is important to widen the view to the other more than 190 states as practice and *opinio iuris* have to be widespread and generally consistent.[132] The United States on its own cannot erode the torture prohibition. Of particular importance is how third states have reacted to the United States' stance on torture: have they acquiesced in the United States' understanding of the prohibition of torture or have they even followed its example?

[125] Bybee (n 110) 172–222.
[126] Levin (n 111) 2, 5–15.
[127] United Nations Committee against Torture, 'Consideration of reports submitted by States parties under article 19 of the Convention pursuant to the optional reporting procedure: Third to fifth reports of States parties due in 2011: United States of America' (4 December 2013) CAT/C/USA/3-5, paras 36, 153, see also para 13.
[128] Steiger (n 9) 394–98.
[129] Kathryn Sikkink, 'The United States and Torture: Does the Spiral Model Work?' in Thomas Risse, Stephen C Ropp, and Kathryn Sikkink (eds), *The Persistent Power of Human Rights: From Commitment to Compliance* (CUP 2013) 156–60.
[130] Steiger (n 9) 438–41.
[131] Office of the Press Secretary, 'Statement by the President' (*The White House*, 26 June 2003) <https://georgewbush-whitehouse.archives.gov/news/releases/2003/06/20030626-3.html> accessed 25 February 2022.
[132] Hafner (n 83) 112, 117–20; for CIL, cf ILC, 'Identification of Customary International Law' (n 52) Conclusion 8 para 1.

Or, on the contrary, have they protested and thus defended the absolute prohibition of torture?

Only few governments have publicly justified torture by pointing to the United States.[133] Rather, governments protested and dissented.[134] Public inquiries into US torture cases were launched *inter alia* in Canada, Germany, Spain, and the United Kingdom, and also by the Parliament of the European Union and the Council of Europe.[135] Italy convicted 23 US officials *in absentia* for abducting a Muslim cleric in Milan and sending him to Egypt to be tortured.[136] Governments,[137] civil society,[138] courts such as the European Court of Human Rights,[139] and quasi-judicial bodies such as the Human Rights Committee[140] have made their dissent clear and reiterated an understanding of torture which *inter alia* leaves intact its interpretation and does not allow for any balancing act, even if the act in question does not constitute torture but 'only' cruel, inhuman, or degrading treatment.

To conclude, states and international organs have made their stance on the undertaking to change the absolute prohibition of torture clear. Even if some states have *de facto* supported torture by the United States, they have nevertheless *de iure* fortified the torture norm if they simultaneously opposed torture openly.

### 3.2.4 Summary: No Change in *Opinio Iuris*

Decisive for the question of norm erosion is whether the interpretation of the prohibition of torture and thus the *opinio iuris* has changed. This is not the case: while the prohibition of torture has been challenged by some, others have continued to support it. Even then-US President George W Bush sent positive signals in support of the prohibition of torture: 'The United States is committed to the worldwide elimination of torture and we are leading this fight by example.'[141] Moreover, then-US President Barack Obama stated in 2016: '[I] affirm the United States' abiding commitment to achieve a world without torture or other cruel, inhuman, or degrading treatment or punishment.'[142]

[133] Douglas A Johnson, Alberto Mora, and Averell Schmidt, 'The Strategic Costs of Torture. How "Enhanced Interrogation" Hurt America' (*Foreign Affairs*, September/October 2016) <www.foreignaffairs.com/articles/united-states/strategic-costs-torture> accessed 25 February 2022.

[134] Johnson, Mora, and Schmidt (n 133); Schmidt and Sikkink (n 24) 108–17; Lesch and Zimmermann, Chapter 6 in this book, p. 113.

[135] Johnson, Mora, and Schmidt (n 133).

[136] Sikkink (n 129) 157ff.

[137] Johnson, Mora, and Schmidt (n 133).

[138] eg Association for the Prevention of Torture, 'Defusing the Ticking Bomb Scenario: Why We Must Say No to Torture, Always' (2007) <www.acat.ch/__/frontend/handler/document.php?id=460&type=42> accessed 25 February 2022.

[139] *El-Masri v The Former Yugoslav Republic of Macedonia* (n 61) paras 195–99.

[140] See United Nations Human Rights Committee, 'Consideration of reports submitted by States parties under Article 40 of the Covenant: Concluding observations of the Human Rights Committee: United States of America' (18 December 2006) CCPR/C/USA/CO/3/Rev.1, para 13.

[141] Office of the Press Secretary, 'Statement by the President' (n 131).

[142] Office of the Press Secretary, 'Statement by the President on the International Day in Support of Victims of Torture' (*The White House*, 26 June 2006) <https://obamawhitehouse.archives.gov/the-press-office/2016/06/26/statement-president-international-day-support-victims-torture> accessed 25 February 2022.

While these statements supporting the absolute prohibition of torture stand in contrast to the United States' actions, the latter is not decisive. Thus, neither the norm as such nor its definition has been altered.

## 4. Conclusion: Why the Prohibition of Torture is Alive and Well and Remains Unchanged

To conclude, the prohibition of torture has been under attack by the United States and other states since 9/11 but has proven to be highly resilient. Why this is the case is answered by a collaborative effort of international law and IR scholarship: the prohibition of torture is highly institutionalized as many international and national organs exist that engage in a dialogue with each other and with states and other relevant actors.[143] Torture is constantly and consistently renounced by all kinds of actors. This dialogue and constant renouncement of torture strengthens the prohibition and helps in internalizing it. The prohibition is also embedded in an entire regime of norms that aim at preventing and remedying torture and which has been ratified by nearly all states. While these norms emanate on the international level they have also been implemented on the domestic level. Furthermore, the definition of torture, while leaving some room for interpretation, is clear and precise. Lastly, the prohibition of torture is a norm of *ius cogens* which gives it a special status in international law.[144] This special status is based on the understanding that *ius cogens* norms protect fundamental values of special importance to the international community as a whole.[145]

While these insights do not allow us to solve the paradox of the heaps, they show that the prohibition of torture is a norm which is very hard to erode and although torture takes place in many states on a regular basis, states, even the non-compliant ones, do not question the validity of the absolute prohibition of torture but, on the contrary, show their continued support for the prohibition of torture. To argue against the validity of the prohibition of torture, however, would be necessary (albeit not sufficient) to erode it as simple non-compliance cannot change a norm. Thus, although law can generally be born out of illegality, the prohibition of torture is not endangered normatively and cannot serve as an example for value change and the metamorphosis of international law.

[143] For the importance of institutionalization and dialogue in order to protect human rights in general, see Monica Hakimi, 'The Work of International Law' (2017) 58 Harvard International Law Journal 1; Gráinne de Burca, 'Human Rights Experimentalism' (2017) 111 American Journal of International Law 277.

[144] Kleinlein, Chapter 4 in this book, pp. 67–70.

[145] Alexander Orakhelashvili, *Peremptory Norms in International Law* (OUP 2006) 46f.

# 8

# The Prohibition on the Use of Force

## *Plus Ça Change*? Towards a Theory of Global Normative Change

*Theresa Reinold*

## 1. Introduction

The question of why the law changes—and why at times it resists change—is among the perennial puzzles of international relations (IR) theory and international law. Why, for instance, did the United States invasion of Iraq in 2003 fail to change the rules governing the use of force, whereas Washington's 2001 intervention in Afghanistan did initiate a process of normative change? While both situations were admittedly complex and varied in a number of important ways, a simple answer to this question can nonetheless be given: the invasion of Iraq was dissonant with the norms held by the international community at large, whereas the intervention in Afghanistan was not (even though both interventions were strictly speaking illegal at the time they were undertaken). The general conclusion that emerges from these and other instances of law-breaking in world politics is that the emergence of dissonance within a legal system—or in the system's relationship with its environment—is a driver of legal change. In this contribution, I propose to conceptualize international law as an equilibrium-maintaining system, and legal change as the process by which equilibrium is restored once it has been disturbed. Just as in human cognitive systems—for which the concept of dissonance reduction was originally developed—dissonance reduction also underlies the dynamics of global normative change, and is at the same time the foundation of international law's (partial) autonomy from politics. The concept of dissonance reduction was coined by Leon Festinger who argued that human beings constantly strive to avoid cognitive dissonance, ie 'the existence of non-fitting relations among cognitions'.[1] Cognitive dissonance may arise, for instance, when the law as it stands is at odds with important non-legal values, or when political acts are perceived as violating important legal norms. In the latter case, the perceived dissonance shields the law from usurpation by powerful actors, because the requirement of coherence, or dissonance reduction, respectively, forces even the most powerful actors to justify their actions within a framework of existing norms, and thus prevents self-serving changes of the law by unilateral fiat.

In this chapter, I conceptualize legal change as an alteration of the law's content, either because a new norm has emerged *in vacuo* or as a modification of an existing

[1] Leon Festinger, *A Theory of Cognitive Dissonance* (Stanford University Pres 1957) 3.

Theresa Reinold, *The Prohibition on the Use of Force* In: *Tracing Value Change in the International Legal Order*. Edited by: Heike Krieger and Andrea Liese, Oxford University Press. © Theresa Reinold 2023. DOI: 10.1093/oso/9780192855831.003.0008

norm.[2] I will focus on a contemporary example of state practice—international strikes against the Islamic State of Iraq and the Levant (ISIL) in Syria—in order to demonstrate how the desire to reduce dissonance between the law as it stood on the one hand, and the political imperative of effectively combating terrorism on the other hand, precipitated a process of legal change. Neither international lawyers nor IR theorists have developed a comprehensive theory of global normative change. IR theorists' explanations of global norm dynamics are heavily agent-centred, mostly focusing on the norm entrepreneurship of powerful states,[3] transnational advocacy networks,[4] epistemic communities,[5] etc. International legal scholars, for their part, have in the past generally shown less interest in causal analysis and have traditionally focused on description and prescription instead. Even though international legal scholars are increasingly engaging in causal analysis of legal dynamics,[6] all of these contributions tend to neglect the 'internal life of international law'.

In this chapter I shall argue that the psychological principle of dissonance reduction helps us understand why demands for changing the law of self-defence arose in the first place, and under which conditions these demands translated into changes in international legal structures. Now, why do we need to talk about dissonance reduction when examining the operation of the law? Well, law is, after all, a product of the human mind. It is human beings who make and remake the law, and who are subject to it. We cannot grasp the operation of the law if we do not understand the purposes it serves and the basic psychological needs it satisfies. As usual, there is no shortage of calls for interdisciplinary analysis: lon Fuller, for instance, urged decades ago that '[w]e must come to ... understand the ... psychological forces that underlie law generally and give it efficacy in human affairs'.[7] More recently, Tom Tyler noted that '[t]aking psychology seriously means linking our understanding of motivation and social influence in legal contexts to a broader psychological understanding of the person'.[8] However, these insights have thus far failed to make inroads into the disciplines of IR and international law. In the following, I will seek to fill this gap by theorizing the changes we are currently observing in the area of self-defence as an instance of dissonance reduction.

[2] Legal innovation—a term which I will use later—is a subcategory of the broader concept of legal change: the latter describes the entire process of norm emergence, consolidation, and possibly decay or termination, whereas legal innovation is limited to the stages of emergence and consolidation.

[3] See eg G John Ikenberry, *After Victory: Institutions, Strategic Restraint, and the Rebuilding of Order After Major Wars* (Princeton University Press 2001); G John Ikenberry and Charles A Kupchan, 'Socialization and Hegemonic Power' (1990) 44 International Organization 283.

[4] See eg Margaret Keck and Kathryn Sikkink, *Activists Beyond Borders. Advocacy Networks in International Politics* (Cornell University Press 1998).

[5] See eg Peter M Haas, 'Introduction: Epistemic Communities and International Policy Coordination' (1992) 46 International Organization 1.

[6] See eg Paul Diehl and Charlotte Ku, *The Dynamics of International Law* (CUP 2010); Andrew Guzman, *How International Law Works: A Rational Choice Theory* (OUP 2008); Pierre-Hugues Verdier and Erik Voeten, 'Precedent, Compliance, and Change in Customary International Law: An Explanatory Theory' (2014) 108 American Journal of International Law 389.

[7] Lon Fuller, *The Principles of Social Order* (Duke University Press 1981) 212.

[8] Tom Tyler, 'New Approaches to Justice in the Light of Virtues and Problems of the Penal System' in Margit Oswald, Steffen Bienek, and Joerg Hupfeld-Heinemann (eds), *Social Psychology of Punishment of Crime* (Wiley-Blackwell 2009) 19.

## 2. Counter-Terrorism Operations on Syrian Territory: The Facts of the Case

In this section I will use an example from recent state practice—the international effort to combat the ISIL in Syria—to show how dissonance reduction drives legal innovation. ISIL is increasingly viewed as a threat not only to the populations of Iraq and Syria, but also to the national interests of many states around the world—Muslim and non-Muslim, Western and non-Western.

Article 51 of the United Nations (UN) Charter lays down states' 'inherent right of individual or collective self-defense if an armed attack occurs against a Member of the United Nations'. Before the 9/11 terrorist attacks, this exception to the Charter's general prohibition on the use of force was construed narrowly. The norms of the Charter—including Articles 2(4) on the non-use of force and 2(7) on non-intervention—were thus explicated in light of the UN Charter's overarching concern with protecting the sovereign rights of its member-states. An equilibrium existed between the norms of the UN Charter and the international community's overriding concern with preventing the resurgence of inter-state war through a restrictive interpretation of Article 51. The international community at large agreed that states that had suffered a terrorist attack from abroad were not entitled to exercise their right to self-defence against non-state actors operating from the territory of states who were merely harbouring, but not effectively controlling, the terrorist actors.[9]

However, a small group of states had traditionally interpreted the right to self-defence much more broadly. The United States in particular had long argued that a state is responsible for the actions of private actors operating on its territory even if it does not exercise effective control over them, and that self-defence may therefore be exercised against the non-state actor and the state who is either unwilling or unable to reign in the militants.[10] Successive US administrations invoked this so-called harbouring doctrine to justify controversial military interventions abroad, which produced stark divisions among states, which for the most part rejected the US interpretation of the right to self-defence.[11] Because of this dissonance between the US harbouring doctrine and the majority interpretation of the UN Charter, the Charter's

[9] The jurisprudence of the International Court of Justice (ICJ) supported the majority's restrictive interpretation of Article 51: in the paradigmatic *Nicaragua* case, the Court ruled that the sending of armed bands by, or on behalf of, a state does qualify as an armed attack, whereas the mere provision of financial, military, logistical, or other support does not amount to an armed attack and thus does not give rise to the right to self-defence. Regarding the question of attribution, the ICJ established the 'effective control test'. According to the Court 'participation ... in the financing, organizing, training, supplying and equipping of the *contras* ... is still insufficient in itself ... for the purpose of attributing to the United States the acts committed by the *contras* ... For this conduct to give rise to legal responsibility of the United States, it would in principle have to be proved that that State had effective control of the military or paramilitary operations in the course of which the alleged violations were committed.' *Case concerning Military and Paramilitary Activities In and Against Nicaragua (Nicaragua v US)* (Merits) [1986] ICJ Rep 14 [115], [195]. The toleration of, or inability to prevent, wrongful nonstate activity thus does not meet the demanding attribution standard established by the ICJ.

[10] Memorandum for Edwin Meese III (Aug. 15, 1984) <www.washingtondecoded.com/files/nsdd.pdf> last accessed 15 October 2017.

[11] Christine Gray, *International Law and the Use of Force* (2nd edn, OUP 2004) 160–64.

rules governing the use of force remained largely intact throughout the Cold War and for about a decade thereafter.

The devastating 9/11 attacks triggered a shift in global attitudes regarding the proper balance between the objective of counter-terrorism on the one hand, and the principles of non-intervention and non-use of force on the other hand. The terrorist attacks exposed the dissonance between the then-prevailing sovereignty-friendly reading of Article 51 and the security interests of not just the United States, but the international community at large. As a result, a process of legal change was initiated. In this process, the notion that sovereignty entails responsibility for the effective control of one's territory and that failure to discharge this obligation legitimates a military response garnered increasing acceptance worldwide.[12] The toppling of the Afghan Taliban, which had neither directed nor controlled the perpetrators of 9/11, broke with traditional norms for attributing private action to a state but was nonetheless greeted with widespread approval or at least tacit acquiescence by the vast majority of states.[13]

Subsequent state practice has underlined that a highly restrictive interpretation of the right to self-defence has become untenable. Turkey's attacks on PKK bases in Iraq, Washington's use of force against militants in Pakistan an elsewhere, Israel's strikes against Hezbollah in Lebanon, Russia's pursuit of Chechen rebels in Georgia, Colombia's incursions into Ecuadorian territory in pursuit of FARC rebels, Kenya's repeated incursions into Somali territory in order to combat the Al-Shabaab militia, etc—all of these events failed to trigger the kind of emphatic denunciation that they would likely have provoked pre-9/11.[14] While often concerns were voiced regarding the necessity and/or proportionality of these actions, which have cost the lives of thousands of innocent civilians, it seems to be increasingly accepted that in principle states have a right to defend themselves against terrorist attacks emanating from the territory of states that are either unable or unwilling to effectively rein in the militants.[15]

This shift is also reflected in the rather muted international reaction to international airstrikes against ISIL targets in Syria. After ISIL had attacked the Iraqi army near Mosul, the US initiated strikes against ISIL targets on both Iraqi and Syrian territory, justifying this as an exercise of collective self-defence. Maintaining that ISIL operating on Syrian territory constitutes a threat to Iraq and many other countries including the United States, Washington went on to stress that states ought to be able to defend themselves in accordance with Article 51 of the UN Charter, 'when, as is the case here,

[12] Theresa Reinold, 'State Weakness, Irregular Warfare, and the Right to Self-Defense Post-9/11' (2011) 105 American Journal of International Law 244, 284–86.

[13] ibid 251–52.

[14] For a more detailed discussion of these interventions see eg Reinold, 'State Weakness' (n 12).

[15] In the scholarly literature, however, a schism can be observed separating so-called 'expansionists', who favour a broad interpretation of the rules governing the use of force from those who advocate for a more restrictive reading of Article 51. The expansionists, who have risen to dominance in recent years (see Raphael van Steenberghe, 'The Law of Self-Defence and the New Argumentative Landscape on the Expansionists' Side' (2016) 29 Leiden Journal of International Law 43), are found mainly in US academia, whereas the latter are predominantly from continental Europe. I will discuss these divergent views in more detail below.

the government of the state where the threat is located is unwilling or unable to prevent the use of its territory for such attacks'.[16]

UN Secretary-General Ban Ki-moon seemed to give his blessing to the US intervention when declaring that even though the strikes were not requested by the Syrian government, they did take place in a part of its territory that was no longer under Damascus' effective control. Ban Ki-moon moreover argued that it was beyond doubt that ISIL and other militant groups posed an 'immediate threat to international peace and security'.[17]

The anti-ISIL military alliance has in the meantime broadened to include states as diverse as the United Kingdom, Canada, the United Arab Emirates, Bahrain, Saudi Arabia, Qatar, Jordan, Turkey, Germany, and Morocco, who have all launched military operations on Syrian territory.[18] Furthermore, Egypt has struck targets in neighboring Libya after 21 Egyptian Coptic Christians had been massacred by fighters associated with ISIL on Libyan territory.[19] Interestingly, the Arab League expressed its 'full understanding' for the airstrikes and stressed states' 'right to defend themselves and protect their citizens'.[20]

Not all of the countries responding militarily to ISIL terrorism have put forward an explicit legal rationale for their interventions—interventions which have triggered remarkably little criticism worldwide, thus strengthening the assumption that the '"unwilling or unable" test is starting to seem less controversial and better settled as a doctrine'.[21] The only notable objection to the strikes came from Syria (unsurprisingly) and Russia (also predictably), 'although with less than the full-throated denunciations they usually aim at the American administration'.[22] The general international reaction is thus probably best described as tacit acquiescence.[23] Some academic commentators, however, contest this view. Paulina Starski, for instance, holds 'that remaining silent in the current context of legality-claims and reactions must not be interpreted as acquiescence'.[24] While Starski acknowledges that states have a responsibility to speak up, she maintains that silence should only be read as acquiescence under strict conditions:

[16] Michelle Nicols, 'United States Defends Syria Airstrikes in Letter to UN Chief' *Reuters* (London, 23 September 2014) <www.reuters.com/article/us-syria-crisis-un-usa-exclusive-idUSKCN0HI22120140923> accessed 25 November 2021.

[17] ibid.

[18] As of December 2021, the anti-ISIL coalition includes 84 states from all over the globe, cf 'Partners List' <https://theglobalcoalition.org/en/partners/> accessed 10 December 2021.

[19] 'Civilians Killed as Egypt Launches Airstrikes in Libya' *Aljazeera* (Doha, 17 February 2015) <www.aljazeera.com/news/2015/02/egypt-bombs-isil-targets-libya-mass-beheadings-150216063339037.html> accessed 10 December 2021.

[20] 'Arab League "Understands" Egypt Airstrikes in Libya, Qatar Raises Concerns' *Mada* (Cairo, 18 February 2015) <www.madamasr.com/en/2015/02/18/news/u/arab-league-understands-egypts-airstrikes-in-libya-qatar-raises-concerns/> accessed 15 February 2022.

[21] Ashley Deeks, 'The UK's Article 51 Letter on Use of Force in Syria' (*Lawfare Blog*, 2014) <www.lawfareblog.com/uks-article-51-letter-use-force-syria> accessed 25 November 2021.

[22] Sangwon Yoon, 'Obama's Syria Strikes Leave International Law Questions' *Bloomberg* (New York, 2 October 2014) <www.bloomberg.com/news/articles/2014-10-02/obama-s-syria-strikes-leave-international-law-questions> accessed 25 November 2021.

[23] ibid.

[24] Paulina Starski, 'Silence within the Process of Normative Change and Evolution of the Prohibition on the Use of Force – Normative Volatility and Legislative Responsibility' (2016) MPIL Research Paper No 2016-20, 43 <https://papers.ssrn.com/sol3/papers.cfm?abstract_id=2851809> accessed 10 December 2021.

> Such effects occur if other states and the international community can legitimately expect that a state makes its dissenting position known. The determination of such an expectation requires an overall assessment of numerous factors including: the determinacy of the legality claims made by the acting states, the capacity of silent states to act, the specific circumstances in which a claim was made, the determinacy of reactive claims of other actors, and questions of time, as well as the nature of the affected rules.[25]

Starski maintains that 'mere passivity in light of the legality-claims currently made with regard to Coalition airstrikes against ISIL positions in Syria does not amount to "acquiescence"'.[26] Yet other scholars, including the present author, beg to differ: as Karol Wolfke pointed out decades ago, 'in view of the growth in international relations and the growing knowledge of the consequences of tolerating international practice, the presumption of a practice having been accepted as law has become increasingly justified'.[27] Tom Ruys and Luca Ferro echo this view in their analysis of states' reaction to the anti-ISIL campaign in Syria. After a thorough examination of 'the alleged transatlantic divide with regard to the content and relevance of the *jus ad bellum*', Ruys and Ferro conclude that a closer analysis of states' positions indicates a gradual acceptance of the unable and unwilling test.[28] The view that an expansive reading of Article 51 is increasingly uncontroversial is echoed by Ashley Deeks who observes that in general, '[s]tates seem to be making fewer efforts these days to discuss their international justifications for using force (with a few exceptions), and few other states are demanding clear explanations for the use of force'.[29] The lack of efforts at justification and the absence of demands for such justifications could be another indicator that the defensive use of force on the soil of states harbouring terrorists is increasingly seen as non-controversial.

Even before the terrorist attacks in Paris on 13 November 2015, the French foreign minister had declared that '[a]s soon as it is established that from Syrian territory ... Daesh forces ... are threatening French interests, both outside and inside France, it is perfectly legitimate that we defend ourselves'.[30] After France had initiated air strikes against ISIL targets in Syria, the French prime minister echoed the justification previously offered by his foreign minister, claiming that '[w]e are striking Daesh in Syria because this terrorist organization prepares and organizes attacks in France from Syria, from these sanctuaries. We are therefore acting in self-defense, which

[25] ibid, abstract.

[26] ibid.

[27] Karol Wolfke, 'Some Persistent Controversies Regarding Customary International Law' (1993) 24 Netherlands Yearbook of International Law 1, 8–9.

[28] Tom Ruys and Luca Ferro, 'Divergent Views on the Content and Relevance of the Jus ad Bellum in Europe and the United States? The Case of the U.S.-Led Military Coalition against "Islamic State"' (2016) 2, 4 <http://papers.ssrn.com/sol3/papers.cfm?abstract_id=2731597> accessed 25 November 2021,

[29] Deeks (n 21).

[30] Quoted in 'France Invokes Self-Defense for Syria Air Strikes' *The Express Tribune* (Karachi, 11 September 2015) <http://tribune.com.pk/story/955050/france-invokes-self-defence-for-syria-air-strikes/> accessed 25 November 2021.

Article 51 of the United Nations Charter permits us to do'.[31] While this claim has been widely accepted in principle, questions have been raised regarding the air strikes' conformity with fundamental ius in bello precepts.[32] In response to the Paris terrorist attacks as well as a previous ISIL attack on a Russian jetliner, which left 224 people dead, the UN Security Council (UNSC) unanimously adopted resolution 2249.[33] In it, the UNSC determines that ISIL is 'a global and unprecedented threat to international peace and security,' and called for 'all necessary measures' to 'eradicate the safe haven (ISIL) established' in Syria. Proponents of a broadened right to self-defence have adduced this resolution as exhibit A to make a case for a fundamental transformation of the *ius ad bellum*,[34] whereas others view it as a product of the UNSC's deliberate 'strategy of ambiguity': as Christian Marxsen writes:

> [The] Council acted in a way that gives ammunition to those supporting an extended right to self-defence, and those rejecting it. … the Council called on states to act against the Islamic State of Iraq and Syria (ISIS), but only within the constraints of international law – herewith leaving it open whether international law allowed states to take action in self-defence, but somehow implying that taking measures was justified under international law.[35]

Overall, the conclusion seems warranted that the strikes against ISIL in Syria as well as previous uses of force in response to terrorist attacks demonstrate that 'there is considerable state practice based on the understanding that where an armed attack is caused by a non-state actor self-defence is lawful. This practice is quite widespread'.[36] Even Olivier Corten, one of the advocates of a more restrictive interpretation of Article 51, acknowledges that in unilateral and regional practice, many states have carried out military operations based on a broad conception of self-defence.[37] Seeking to account

[31] Quoted in Aurelien Breeden, 'France Says Its Airstrikes Hit an ISIS Camp in Syria' *The New York Times* (New York, 27 September 2015) <www.nytimes.com/2015/09/28/world/europe/france-says-it-has-struck-at-isis-in-syria.html?_r=0> accessed 25 November 2021.

[32] See eg the post-Paris debate on EJIL Talk, where authors such as Tilman Rodenhaeuser have urged a consideration of the necessity dimension of the counter-terrorism operations against ISIS (Tilman Rodenhaeuser, 'Self-Defense Operations Against Armed Groups and the Ius in Bello' (*EJIL:Talk!*, 16 December 2015) <www.ejiltalk.org/self-defense-operations-against-armed-groups-and-the-jus-in-bello/> accessed 25 November 2021).

[33] UN Security Council Resolution 2249 (20 November 2015) UN Doc S/RES/2249.

[34] Michael Scharf, 'How the War against ISIS Changed International Law' (2016) 48 Case Western Reserve Journal of International Law 1, 15.

[35] Christian Marxsen, 'A Note on Indeterminacy of the Law on Self-Defence against Non-State Actors' (2017) 77 Zeitschrift für ausländisches öffentliches Recht und Völkerrecht (ZaöRV) 91.

[36] Jochen A Frowein, 'Article 51 and the Realities of the Present Day World' (2017) 77 ZaöRV 47.

[37] Olivier Corten, 'Has Practice Led to an "Agreement Between the Parties" Regarding the Interpretation of Article 51 of the UN Charter?' (2017) 77 ZaöRV 15, 17; Corten's otherwise restrictive interpretation of art 51 is shared by some other (mostly European) legal scholars, which contributed to a symposium held at the Max Planck Institute for Comparative Public Law and International Law in 2016, whose conveners concluded that 'even those who do not share the belief in a turning point must concede that the dynamism makes it even more difficult than usually in international law to pinpoint what the law actually "says". … The essays assembled in this focus section represent greatly differing views and approaches to the question of self-defence against non-state actors. They disagree profoundly on the state and the interpretation of the law', Anne Peters and Christian Marxsen, 'Editors' Introduction: Self-Defence in Times of Transition' (2017) 77 ZaöRV 3, 8, and 12.

for this shift in state practice, Michael Scharf argues that the 2015 ISIL attacks against a Russian jetliner and various targets in Paris triggered a 'Grotian Moment' which persuaded previously sceptical states that a more expansive reading of the right to self-defence was required. According to Scharf, states' reactions to these events marked the tipping point in the debate about an expanded right to self-defence against dangerous non-state actors: 'The October 31 and November 13 ISIS attacks were a game changer, killing and injuring over 824 nationals of Russia, France, and twenty-two other countries ... Moreover, Russia was now just as much a target as the West.'[38] Scharf concludes that 'the international community's response to ISIS in Syria has provided the final push necessary to bring the Grotian Moment to fruition'.[39] The exact scope of the expanded right to self-defence against non-state actors, however, remains to be defined.

Now, how can the transformation of the rules governing the use of force described in this chapter be grasped conceptually? In the following I will offer a theoretical explanation that zeroes in on the concept of dissonance reduction as a driver of legal change.

## 3. The Theoretical Literature on Legal Change: An Overview

Most existing accounts of legal change—with the exception of the theory of autopoiesis—tend to privilege agency over structure: the Law and Society movement, for instance, emphasizes the importance of political variables in the (trans)formation of legal structures: 'Law is not impartial, timeless, classless; it is not value-free. It reflects the distribution of power.'[40] Legal change is seen as resulting from a disturbance of the law's equilibrium by outside forces—shifts in the distribution of power, wars, the introduction of new technologies, economic crises, etc: when these factors trigger a change in social relations, 'legal change follows rapidly, obediently, thereafter'.[41] Changing societal norms and attitudes may also exert pressure on the legal system to adapt itself.[42] Underlying this argument is the assumption that dissonance—exposed, for instance, as a result of external shocks or changed intersubjective understandings—initiates a process of legal change. Yet Law and Society theorists do not elaborate on how exactly the legal system responds to political influences.

The legal system's internal wiring is at the heart of the concept of legal autopoiesis. While legal systems may be irritated from the outside and are thus 'cognitively open', they remain 'normatively closed' and therefore evolve only in accordance with their internal logic.[43] The notion of normative closure means that the law itself sets the parameters for legal change, and *not* powerful actors participating in the legal process.

[38] Scharf (n 34) 64.
[39] ibid 66.
[40] Lawrence Friedman, *The Legal System. A Social Science Perspective* (Russell Sage Foundation 1975) 178.
[41] ibid 307.
[42] ibid.
[43] Niklas Luhmann, 'The Unity of the Legal System' in Gunther Teubner (ed), *Autopoietic Law: A New Approach to Law and Society* (Walter de Gruyter 1988) 20.

This self-referentiality is the very basis of the law's autonomy.[44] The legal system thus (re)produces its elements according to its own logic, ie according to the secondary rules governing the (trans)formation, application, interpretation, and termination of primary rules.[45] Its rules of recognition, for instance, define the sources of law and thereby separate law from non-law. By making this distinction between legal and illegal the legal system asserts its autonomy vis-à-vis political actors. The law's autonomy is imperiled, however, when the binary distinction between legal and illegal is diluted.[46]

In international legal scholarship, a few recent contributions have engaged in causal analysis of global norm dynamics. Ku and Diehl use a model of legal change which is heavily centred on the role of political agents and external shocks.[47] Pierre-Hugues Verdier and Erik Voeten in turn use a rational choice-based approach focused on the signaling effects of precedent, which, however, gives short shrift to the law's autonomy from politics.[48] A somewhat more structure-sensitive account has been proposed by Wayne Sandholtz, who has equally contributed to a chapter to this book, and who conceptualizes international legal dynamics as a process of discursive exchanges, in which notions of fit, analogy, etc, loom large: 'The idea is ... that ... there is a powerful inclination for participants in normative systems to seek consistency'.[49] Sandholtz thus acknowledges the force of dissonance reduction yet does not elaborate on this point. In the following Section 4 I will therefore draw on insights from psychological theories in order to illuminate why the law's addressees have such a strong desire for consistency, as noted by Sandholtz and others.

## 4. Dissonance Reduction and the Changing Law of Self-Defence

Reflecting on the theory of legal autopoiesis, Richard Lempert writes that if this theory is not falsified by examples of legal norms that have changed as a result of extralegal factors, the theory:

> should, ideally, offer us a mechanism which explains how extralegal norms and values come to influence legal norms ... This is particularly important for a general theory of legal systems since many of the most interesting questions in the contemporary sociology of law ... depend on understanding the mechanisms which render

[44] Gunther Teubner, 'Evolution of Autopoietic Law' in Gunther Teubner (ed), *Autopoietic Law: A New Approach to Law and Society* (Walter de Gruyter 1988) 222.

[45] On the distinction between primary and secondary rules, see Herbert LA Hart, *The Concept of Law* (Clarendon Press 1961) 78–79.

[46] Niklas Luhmann, 'Closure and Openness: On Reality in the World of Law' in Gunther Teubner (ed), *Autopoietic Law: A New Approach to Law and Society* (Walter de Gruyter 1988) 347.

[47] Diehl and Ku (n 6) 75.

[48] Verdier and Voeten (n 6).

[49] Wayne Sandholtz, 'Explaining International Norm Change' in Wayne Sandholtz and Kendall Stiles (eds), *International Norms and Cycles of Change* (OUP 2009) 17.

law partially autonomous – that is both independent to some degree and open to extra-legal influences.[50]

In this section I offer such an explanation which zeroes in on the concept of dissonance reduction, which is at the same time a driver of normative change and the foundation of international law's (partial) autonomy. The concept of cognitive dissonance was coined by Leon Festinger, who studied the ways in which human beings try to make sense of their behaviour and their environment. This environment also includes the (legal and non-legal) norms that govern people's daily lives. Festinger argues that human beings constantly strive to avoid cognitive dissonance, ie 'non-fitting relations among cognitions', which he defines as 'any knowledge, opinion, or belief about the environment, about oneself, or about one's behavior'.[51] Human beings therefore want to perceive the legal system which they are subjected to as a more or less coherent set of rules, ie as one that does not exhibit major dissonance neither as regards its internal make-up, nor as regards the fit of legal rules with important political and moral values.

The study of law and legal behaviour has in the past decades taken a 'cognitive turn',[52] with a growing number of scholars using the above-mentioned insights into the workings of the human mind in order to explain legal phenomena such as judicial behaviour. Based on the assumption that people try to make sense of the world by constructing coherent narratives from events, Nancy Pennington and Reid Hastie, for instance, demonstrate that jurors organize the evidence in a jury trial in the form of a coherent causal story, and that the story jurors create predicts their verdict in the trial.[53] The same can be said of judges' behaviour: as Dan Simon argues, when deciding a hard case, the judge's thought process 'evolves naturally towards a state of coherence. That is, the cognitive system imposes coherence on the arguments so that the subset of arguments that supports one outcome becomes more appealing to the judge and the opposite subset … turns less favorable'.[54] Thus, human behaviour, including the behaviour of judicial actors, displays a 'coherence bias'.[55] It has been called the 'most gripping observation' made by theorists of cognitive dissonance that humans have a marked tendency to change the elements that constitute their cognitive structure in order to reduce dissonance among them, and thus restore coherence.[56] Dissonance is a highly uncomfortable state: if a balanced, ie coherent state does not exist, 'then forces toward this state will arise'.[57]

[50] Richard Lempert, 'The Autonomy of Law: Two Visions Compared' in Gunther Teubner (ed), *Autopoietic Law: A New Approach to Law and Society* (Walter de Gruyter 1988) 187.

[51] Festinger (n 1) 3.

[52] See eg Pierre Schlag, 'Missing Pieces: A Cognitive Approach to Law' (1989) 67 Texas Law Review 1195; Dan Simon, 'A Psychological Model of Judicial Decision-Making' (1998) 30 Rutgers Law Journal 1; Steven L Winter, 'The Metaphor of Standing and the Problem of Self-Governance' (1988) 40 Stanford Law Review 1371; Steven L Winter, 'Transcendental Nonsense, Metaphoric Reasoning, and the Cognitive Stakes for Law' (1989) 137 University of Pennsylvania Law Review 1105.

[53] Nancy Pennington and Reid Hastie, 'Evidence Evaluation in Complex Decision Making' (1986) 51 Journal of Personality and Social Psychology 242, 245.

[54] Simon (n 52) 20.

[55] ibid.

[56] Fritz Heider, 'Attitudes and Cognitive Organization' (1946) 21 Journal of Psychology 107, 108.

[57] ibid.

Now, how does this help us understand the dynamics of global normative change? The thesis defended here is that the desire to reduce dissonance is a driver of legal innovation, and that we ought to conceptualize the international legal system as a dynamic social process in which not only inconsistencies within the legal system, but also contradictions between legal and important non-legal norms provide an impetus for legal change. These evolutionary processes present a dilemma for the rule of law: even though the rule of law implies a certain presumption in favour of stability and constancy over time this does not mean that the law can afford to stand still. On the contrary, the rule of law must reconcile the conflicting demands of stability and change, predictability, and adaptability. If the gap between the law as it stands and the law as it ought to be from the point of view of its addressees becomes too large, this creates pressure on the legal system to adapt itself in order to reduce the gap between legality and legitimacy.[58] While change in and of itself is not a threat to the rule of law, the absence of agreed-upon procedures providing for an orderly modification of existing law would be. In 'advanced' legal systems, secondary rules perform this function by regulating how primary rules are to be modified or reinterpreted, if changed political circumstances so require.[59] Secondary rules are thus instrumental to the rule of law because they help to maintain the law's overall coherence, thereby bolstering its legitimacy in the eyes of the legal subjects, and hence its ability to effectively govern human conduct.

In legal theory, the notion of coherence, or dissonance reduction, respectively, is generally viewed as a central factor in strengthening the rule of law. Whilst there may be differences in nuance, concepts such as 'law as integrity',[60] 'systematicity',[61] and 'consistency'[62] are all rooted in the same (mostly unacknowledged) fundamental assumption about human nature, namely that there exists a universal human need to perceive the legal rules which structure social life as a more or less coherent set of norms which, when taken together, make sense, in that these rules do not oblige the addressees of the law to pursue mutually inconsistent overall objectives. Ronald Dworkin, for instance, points out that most people would intuitively reject 'checkerboard laws' that fail to treat like cases alike.[63] Whence this seemingly universal tendency to regard checkerboard laws as illegitimate? Dworkin notes that 'our instincts condemn it'[64] but fails to explain why this is so. Neil MacCormick equally argues that there is something about the law's drive towards dissonance reduction which cannot be explained by cultural factors (which differ across legal systems), but that this drive is rooted in psychological instincts that are common to all human beings.[65] Coherence in reasoning about the law, MacCormick writes, goes beyond logical consistency in a technical sense. It requires not only non-contradiction among the rule in question and

[58] See also Thomas Kleinlein, Chapter 4 in this book, especially 20–21.
[59] Hart (n 45) 90ff.
[60] Ronald Dworkin, *Law's Empire* (Harvard University Press 1986) 179.
[61] Jeremy Waldron, 'The Concept and the Rule of Law' (2008) The NYU Public Law & Legal Theory working paper No 08–50 <http://ssrn.com/abstract=1273005> accessed 25 November 2021.
[62] Niklas Luhibmann, *Das Recht der Gesellschaft* (Suhrkamp 1993) 18–19, 222–23, 272, 368–72.
[63] Dworkin (n 60) 179ff.
[64] ibid 180.
[65] Neil MacCormick, *Legal Theory and Legal Reasoning* (OUP 1978) 152.

other legal rules, but additionally that 'the multitudinous rules of a developed legal system should "make sense" when taken together'.[66] Any given legal rule must satisfy the test of coherence with the overarching principles or goals of the legal system. Thus, 'to explicate the principles is to rationalize the rules'.[67]

This drive towards unity of principle, or overall coherence, is a universally cherished quality of persuasive legal arguments, as has been demonstrated in a large-scale comparative study of legal interpretation across a range of different legal systems.[68] This psychological process of 'making-sense' of a set of legal rules is what Joseph Raz describes when he points out the difference between the point of view of an observer external to a particular legal system, and the perspective of an insider. While the outsider may regard any given legal system as an incoherent assemblage of norms, and may be objectively justified to do so, the latter cannot possibly do this: 'It makes no sense to accept an assemblage of norms as one's own norms unless one regards them as valid and justified, and one cannot regard them as justified unless they form a coherent body'.[69]

Coherence implies not only that the law presents itself as an internally consistent set of rules, but moreover requires consistency of the law with important non-legal norms held by society at large, as law is, 'by its very nature ... deeply implicated in the practices and conventions of the communities it governs'.[70] Hence, we should not view international law as a closed and static system which is immune to political impetuses, but rather understand it as a dynamic social process in which inconsistencies within the legal system, but also contradictions between legal and important non-legal norms provide an impetus for legal change.

Now, according to the theory of legal autopoiesis, only law can change the law. Theorists of legal autopoiesis accept that the initial impetus for legal change usually comes from the political sphere; however, the process of translating political preferences into legal substance is governed by the secondary rules of the legal system. This is seen as ensuring the law's autonomy from political usurpation.[71] Yet international law defies the autopoietic notion of normative closure. Does this mean that international law enjoys no autonomy from political power? Not necessarily. I submit that it only means that international law has different ways of securing its autonomy, namely through the requirement of dissonance reduction, respectively. This principle imposes constraints upon powerful agents seeking to change international law. Normative structures cannot be changed by unilateral fiat; instead, even the most powerful actors in the system must make sure that their actions are not perceived as being dissonant with intersubjectively agreed norms—legal and/or non-legal. If they fail to do so, their norm entrepreneurship will not be successful and international law will resist change. Thus, even though the secondary rules of the international legal system do not rule out the possibility that violations of the law may change its substance, these rules nonetheless require that attempts at legal innovation be consistent

[66] ibid 152.
[67] ibid 155, 157.
[68] Neil MacCormick, *Rhetoric and the Rule of Law: A Theory of Legal Reasoning* (OUP 2005) 124ff.
[69] Joseph Raz, *Ethics in the Public Domain. Essays on the Morality of Law and Politics* (OUP 1994) 281.
[70] Gerald Postema, 'Implicit Law' (1994) 13 Law and Philosophy 361, 377.
[71] Niklas Luhmann, *Rechtssoziologie* (Westdeutscher Verlag 1987) 143–44.

with the values of the international community at large. If a particular breach of the law is not met with nearly universal support or at least tacit acquiescence, this breach will not trigger changes in the international legal system. This bars powerful actors from unilaterally changing the substance of the law to legitimize their parochial interests, thereby ensuring the partial autonomy of the law.

Even though the principle *ex iniuria ius non oritur* is commonly believed to shield the law from political manipulation, in customary international law, non-compliant behaviour is actually an important source of legal innovation, because breaches of the law initiate a process of claims and counter-claims in the course of which states' *opinio juris*, and thus the customary norm in question, potentially undergo modification. Nonetheless, international lawyers have long held onto the fiction that illegal behaviour cannot give rise to new law: when the Statute for the Permanent Court of International Justice was drafted after for First World War, an enigmatic formula was adopted that continues to puzzle those analysing the dynamics of customary law evolution. This formula was enshrined in Article 38(1)(b) of the Statute of the Court, which states that the Court 'shall apply . . . international custom, as evidence of a general practice accepted as law'. However, if a particular practice has to be 'accepted as law' this implies that breaches of the law cannot give rise to new legal rules, as any deviating practice will initially be at odds with existing law. This in turn would prevent the law from adapting to changing political circumstances and would risk the emergence of major dissonance between the norms of the legal system and its political environment, which would in turn endanger the law's legitimacy. Scholars such as Anthony D'Amato therefore defend a conception of customary law that allows for the transformation of *opinio juris*—triggered by states violating existing norms—which eventually leads to a modification of these norms: '[A]n illegal act by a state contains the seed of a new legality. When a state violates an existing rule . . . the illegal act itself becomes a disconfirmatory instance of the underlying rule ... eventually a new line of conduct will replace the original rule by a new rule'.[72]

What is critical to note is that non-compliance will only have law-generating effects if it not only does not evoke significant dissonance but, on the contrary, is perceived as reducing dissonance between the law as it stood before the violation occurred, and the values of the majority of participants in the legal process. Thus, to put it in D'Amato's somewhat metaphorical terms, the 'seed' sown by a law-violating state will not always lead to the 'blossoming' of a new rule. If this were indeed the case, international law would cease to perform its stabilizing function, that is, to guarantee a modicum of predictability in an otherwise very unpredictable world. Thus, while it is true that the law needs to be responsive to state interests in order not to slip into insignificance, it is also true that legal norms that are infinitely pliable cease to perform their legitimizing function, and that the coherence requirement precludes self-serving changes of the law by powerful actors.

The basic causal mechanism underlying change in customary international law for a given rule A thus looks as follows: after a period of equilibrium, in which rule A is seen

[72] Anthony D'Amato, *The Concept of Custom in International Law* (Cornell University Press 1971) 97.

as being consistent with fundamental values held by the international community at large, changes in the environment of the legal system give rise to a perception of dissonance between rule A and important non-legal values and interests. Subsequently, one or more actors expose this dissonance, for instance by issuing statements demanding that the law be changed, or by creating facts, ie by violating rule A in the hope that the breach will be hailed as the 'seed of a new rule'. Other participants to the legal process may share the law-breaker's view, and therefore endorse or, at a minimum, fail to oppose this violation of the law. In light of the acquiescence or active support of significant parts of the international community, a new intersubjective consensus emerges which reduces the perceived dissonance between the legal system and its environment. A new equilibrium is thereby reached, which will exist as long as the law remains consonant with fundamental preferences and intersubjective understandings of the international community.

An alternative scenario would be that the perception of dissonance is *not* shared by the majority of members of the international system; instead, it is merely perceived by an individual, yet powerful actor B. In this case, if the latter decides to break rule A, this will provoke emphatic denunciation by the international community, as in this case what is perceived as dissonant with widely held values is not rule A, but state B's violation of this rule. This perception of dissonance in turn prevents state B from changing the law to suit its particularistic interests.

The case of the anti-ISIL military alliance nicely illustrates the causal mechanism of legal change outlined above: until 9/11 an equilibrium existed between a restrictive reading of Article 51 and the norms of the international community at large, especially the prohibition of the use of force as a peremptory norm of international law, the exceptions (Article 51 being one of them) to which were construed rather narrowly. However, due to an exogenous shock—the devastating terrorist attacks of 11 September 2001—the privileging of the harbouring state's sovereignty over the victim state's national security concerns was increasingly seen as being dissonant with the international community's fundamental values and interests: most states realized that transnational terrorism had become that large of a threat to their populations that countering this threat justified trumping traditional sovereignty rights including those to non-interference and the non-use of force. A restrictive reading of Article 51 was seen as preventing states from responding effectively to terrorist attacks and thus the majority of states acquiesced when the US took the lead in challenging a restrictive reading of the right to self-defence by intervening in Afghanistan, and removing the regime from power that had provided a safe haven to the perpetrators of 9/11. Technically a breach of existing law, the intervention was greeted with widespread approval, thus consolidating a new intersubjective consensus supporting a more expansive reading of the right to self-defence. The generally muted international reaction to military strikes against ISIL targets in Syria is another indicator that the law of self-defence has been adapted to a changing geopolitical context, even though the exact contours of the law continue to be unclear. The relaxing of the constraints on the use of force thus reduced the perceived dissonance between black letter international law on the one hand, and a rapidly changing geopolitical environment on the other hand. More and more actors now subscribe to an expansive reading of the right to self-defence that responds to their most pressing national security concerns. Had international law not evolved in sync with the new political exigencies, it would most likely have been condemned to irrelevance.

Acknowledging the law-generating effects of non-compliance obviously raises difficult questions from a rule of law perspective, as it challenges the presumption that the law ought to be complied with. International law's mechanisms for adapting its rules to changing political circumstances are somewhat underdeveloped, and while compliance should be the norm, occasional departures from this norm are sometimes necessary to 'modernize' the law, ie ensure its continued relevance in a changing geopolitical context. Having established that international law is not normatively closed in the sense that domestic legal systems are—does this mean that international law is not autonomous? After all, according to theorists of legal autopoiesis, the autonomy of the law critically depends on in its normative closure. However, the thesis defended in this chapter is that it would be wrong to assume that the international legal system's openness to political stimuli means it lacks autonomy—on the contrary, it is precisely *because* of international law's ability to adapt itself to a changing environment that the law retains its (partial) autonomy, legitimacy, and ultimately its compliance pull.

To be sure, autonomy and legitimacy are two different concepts, yet there is a close connection between them. The requirement of dissonance reduction immunizes the law—at least to a certain extent—against political usurpation and thereby bolsters its legitimacy. Only a law that maintains a certain independence from political power will be regarded as legitimate, and—in the absence of an international enforcement mechanism—legitimacy will be critical in ensuring compliance. If legal structures are viewed as being merely an expression of the particularistic interests of powerful agents, all the while being dissonant with the intersubjective understandings held by international society at large, this will undermine the law's legitimacy. Consequently, attempts by powerful agents to reshape legal structures which evoke dissonance with fundamental values of the international community will leave existing legal structures intact.

Hence the requirement of dissonance reduction not only explains how and why international law changes—and, at times resists change—it also forms the basis of international law's partial autonomy from power politics, and hence its legitimacy. Contra Luhmann and associates I would thus argue that it is not the law's normative closure that accounts for its autonomy, but the requirement of dissonance reduction. This requirement implies a certain degree of normative openness, as dissonance reduction refers not only to the law's internal coherence, but also to its consistency with fundamental extra-legal values held by societal majorities—what Gerald Postema has called 'implicit law'.[73] While it is true that the law 'venerates tradition, precedent, pedigree' and is 'suspicious of innovation, discontinuities, (and) "paradigm shifts"'[74] it can only absorb a certain amount of dissonance between positive law and societal values before it must yield to the forces of change.

[73] Postema (n 70).

[74] Richard A Posner, 'Past-Dependency, Pragmatism, and Critique of History in Adjudication and Legal Scholarship' (2000) 67 University of Chicago Law Review 573.

## 5. Conclusion

Human beings tend to perceive cognitive dissonance as a highly uncomfortable state, and will therefore engage in efforts aimed at reducing this dissonance. The (legal, political, and moral) norms governing human conduct are one of various potential sources of dissonance, and the thesis defended in this chapter is that the emergence of dissonance within a legal system—or in the system's relationship with its environment—is driver of legal change. The principle of dissonance reduction not only explains why demands for changing the law arise in the first place, but also why these demands are sometimes successful, triggering global normative change, and why they sometimes fail, leaving the existing legal regime intact. The principle of dissonance reduction also explains why international law—even though it does not meet the autopoietic criterion of full normative closure—nonetheless enjoys a certain degree of autonomy from political power.

Now, one might argue that in the empirical example discussed in this chapter power and norms happened to coincide, which renders it difficult to make a case for the autonomy of the law from power politics. However, there are other instances of the use of force—the 2003 invasion of Iraq mentioned in the introduction is a case in point—where power and norms did *not* coincide, and which clearly demonstrate the autonomy international law enjoys from politics: since the various rationales the US offered for the invasion were patently at odds with black letter international law and did not resonate with the values of the international community at large, the intervention was widely condemned and did not alter the law as it stood. On the contrary: it reaffirmed states' commitment to the prohibition on the use of force and consequently the US was forced to shoulder the burden of its illegal preventive war largely by itself. This in turn stands in stark contrast to its 1991 intervention in Iraq, where the United States led a broad-based international coalition *because* the intervention was perceived as giving effect to important values of the international community. These interventions demonstrate that the insights emerging from the anti-ISIL campaign in Syria discussed in this chapter are broadly applicable to other instances of the use of force in world politics: legal change occurs if, and only if, an intervention is seen as reducing dissonance between black letter international law and the values of the international community at large. If, by contrast, a military intervention is seen as being at odds with the values of the majority of relevant actors, the law will not undergo modification. On the contrary: it is the intervenor's actions that will be perceived as being dissonant with the norms of the international community, which will in turn lead to an affirmation of these norms.

What does this imply for the transformation of international law as conceptualized in the present edited book? In the introductory chapter Heike Krieger and Andrea Liese proposed a set of indicators for capturing the 'metamorphosis' of the international legal order. According to the editors, there are three proxies for grasping the kind of fundamental transformation that would justify the label metamorphosis, two of which are change of legally protected values as well as the latter's loss of social validity. Applying these yardsticks to the law of self-defence suggests that indeed profound changes are taking place. As the restrictive, sovereignty-friendly interpretation of Article 51 had lost its social validity in light of the terrorist threat materializing in the context of 9/11 and its aftermath, the right to self-defence subsequently underwent a broadening that Krieger and Liese would describe as substantive value change. In light of this, the use of the label metamorphosis seems quite justified to grasp the profound changes we are currently observing in the area of the rules governing the use of force.

# 9

# Changing Perceptions on the Right of Self-Defence

## Reflections from a Third World Perspective

*Srinivas Burra*

The right of self-defence arguably has been attracting more attention in the last two decades than any other matter relating to the use of force in international law. Primarily, the United Nations (UN) Charter determines international legal rules on the use of force and the right of self-defence. The textual position of the UN Charter on these matters has not changed since the adoption of the UN Charter in 1945. However, states in their contextual application ascribe varying meanings to it. The prohibition of the use of force under Article 2(4) of the UN Charter, the powers of the UN Security Council (UNSC) under Chapter VII of the UN Charter and the right of self-defence have been under strain even prior to the more recent developments concerning the right of self-defence.[1] However, in the recent past, particular attention has been drawn to the legality of invoking the right of self-defence in the context of the use of force by a state against non-state actors operating from another state. This issue attracted attention and assertion from states and scholarly reflections. Both state positions and scholarly opinion seem divided at the doctrinal level as well as in the application to specific cases.[2]

This chapter deals with the question of value change with regard to the right of self-defence.[3] It engages with its UN Charter meaning, application, changing perceptions, and possible critique from a Third World perspective. It primarily focuses on the use of force against non-state actors in another state. It evaluates the issue by underlining various changes in the interpretation and application of the right of self-defence, particularly in the last three decades. It attempts to present possible premises of critique from a Third World methodological perspective. Accordingly, the chapter consists of four sections. Section 1 deals with the right of self-defence under the UN

[1] See David Wippman, 'The Nine Lives of Article 2(4)' (2007) 16 Minnesota Journal of International Law 387.

[2] eg see Anne Peters and Christian Marxsen (eds), 'Self-Defence Against Non-State Actors: Impulses from the Max Planck Trialogues on the Law of Peace and War' (2017) 77 Zeitschrift für ausländisches öffentliches Recht und Völkerrecht 1; Statements at the Arria-formula meeting convened by Mexico, on the theme 'Upholding the collective security system of the Charter of the United Nations: the use of force in international law, non-State actors and legitimate self-defence' held on 24 February 2021, Letter dated 8 March 2021 from the Permanent Representative of Mexico to the United Nations addressed to the Secretary-General and the President of the Security Council, <https://digitallibrary.un.org/record/3905536?ln=en#record-files-collapse-header> accessed 15 April 2022.

[3] On the relation between norms and values, see Heike Krieger and Andrea Liese, Chapter 1 in this book.

Srinivas Burra, *Changing Perceptions on the Right of Self-Defence* In: *Tracing Value Change in the International Legal Order*. Edited by: Heike Krieger and Andrea Liese, Oxford University Press. © Srinivas Burra 2023.
DOI: 10.1093/oso/9780192855831.003.0009

Charter. Section 2 focuses on the changing perceptions of the right of self-defence. Section 3 provides the reflections from a Third World perspective and Section 4 offers a conclusion.

## 1. The Right of Self-Defence under the UN Charter

The use of force is arguably comprehensively dealt with in the UN Charter. Article 2(4) is considered as providing the comprehensive prohibition of the use of force in international law. This provision 'constitutes by necessity the basis of any discussion of the problem of the use of force'.[4] The UN Charter itself provides exceptions to this comprehensive prohibition, and they come in two forms: a collective security system in Chapter VII of the UN Charter incorporates an exception to this prohibition. In addition to it, the right of self-defence is included in Article 51. While these two forms of use of force are considered exceptions to the general prohibition under Article 2(4), they are not considered alternative forms of exceptions from which states can exercise option on which exception they choose. Rather, it is the UNSC's collective security which is considered as the main exception to Article 2(4). The unilateral use of force as the right of self-defence under Article 51 is considered an exception to the authorization of force by the UNSC under Chapter VII of the UN Charter and not as an exception to Article 2(4).[5] Consequently, the right of self-defence under Article 51 is resorted to where the UNSC's authorization has not taken place.[6] Thus, Article 51 is an exception to an exception to Article 2(4).[7] While this reflects the carefully structured legal framework on the use of force, effectively both these legal channels act as exceptions to the general prohibition on the use of force under Article 2(4) of the UN Charter.

Article 51 of the UN Charter spells out the content and context of the right of self-defence fairly clearly when it says that '[n]othing in the present Charter shall impair the inherent right of individual or collective self-defence if an armed attack occurs against a Member of the United Nations, until the Security Council has taken measures necessary to maintain international peace and security'.[8] While this provision is explicit in its plain reading, it has been relied upon to generate varying interpretations. Particularly, two aspects are highlighted in the context of the claims of a right of self-defence against non-state actors. Firstly, the proponents of the right of self-defence against non-state actors underline that the provision's language is silent on the originator of the armed attack—as it only reads 'if an armed attack occurs against a Member of the United Nations'. They argue that the provision omitted to specify from where the

[4] Oliver Dörr and Albrecht Randelzhofer, 'Purposes and Principles, Article 2(4)' in Bruno Simma and others (eds), *The Charter of the United Nations: A Commentary Volume I* (3rd edn, OUP 2012).

[5] Dire Tladi, 'The Use of Force in Self-Defence Against Non-State Actors: Decline of Collective Security and the Rise of Unilateralism: Whither International Law?' in Mary O'Connell, Christian Tams, and Dire Tladi (eds), *Self-Defence against Non-State Actors* (Max Planck Trialogues) (CUP 2019) 31.

[6] ibid.

[7] See Adil Ahmad Haque, 'The United Nations Charter at 75: Between Force and Self-Defense — Part Two' *Just Security*, 24 June, 2020 <https://www.justsecurity.org/70987/the-united-nations-charter-at-75-between-force-and-self-defense-part-two/> accessed 5 March 2022.

[8] Article 51 UN Charter.

attack may originate mainly to extend the right of self-defence even against the acts committed by non-state actors. Therefore, in the proponents' view, the provision itself provides the right of self-defence against non-state actors.[9] This position is contested on the ground that Article 51 is essentially inter-state in nature—just as the whole legal framework governing the use of force in the UN Charter.[10] Secondly, the proponents of the right of self-defence against non-state actors further point out that Article 51 language provides that the right of self-defence exists outside Article 51 and the provision itself recognizes the same as it refers to 'inherent right' of self-defence. This reference to 'inherent right' is noted as intended to convey that Article 51 acknowledges the existing customary international law (CIL) that provides for the self-defence against armed attacks from non-state actors.[11] This view is also equally critiqued based on the historical analysis of doctrinal developments.[12]

While Article 51 is a part of comprehensive treaty law that addresses the right of self-defence in general, arguments in favour of the right of self-defence against non-state actors go beyond this provision. It is also important to note that the arguments for the right of self-defence against non-state actors are not an isolated incident of purported norm change as law on the use of force, in general, has been the subject of similar discussions. Before offering any critique on the claims of the right of self-defence against non-state actors, it is imperative that broad arguments in favour of norm change on the right of self-defence are analysed in their doctrinal context.

## 2. Changing Perceptions of the Right of Self-Defence

Even though the text of the law on the use of force and self-defence remains static, it is argued that law relating to the use of force either changed or needs to change either in the form of treaty interpretation or CIL. Dapo Akande and Kelie A Johnson identified changes in four aspects.[13] First, the UNSC's authorization of the use of force under Chapter VII of the UN Charter has undergone changes. In contrast to what it was at the time of the adoption of the UN Charter, the UNSC now has the competence to act in internal matters and in humanitarian crises, which differs from the Charter understanding of inter-state conflicts. The second change stems from arguments in favour of anticipatory or preemptive self-defence. This view asserts that even though Article 51 of the UN Charter clearly provides that a state has the right to individual and collective self-defence once an armed attack occurs, it is lawful to exercise the right of self-defence even before the armed attack occurs. The third change—and subject matter of this chapter—is the exercise of the right of self-defence in response to attacks by non-state actors operating from another state. The fourth change is that the use of force is permitted even in the absence of UNSC authorization to stop or prevent

[9] For relevant views see Dire Tladi, 'The Extraterritorial Use of Force against Non-State Actors' (2021) 418 Recueil des cours l'Académie de Droit International 283–84.

[10] See ibid 299–315.

[11] For discussion on it, see ibid 284–86.

[12] See ibid 296–99.

[13] Dapo Akande and Katie A Johnston, 'Implications of the Diversity of Rules on the Use of Force for Change in the Law' (2021) 32 European Journal of International Law 679, 681–83.

a humanitarian tragedy which is often referred to as humanitarian intervention. The reasoning for humanitarian intervention puts forth the view that a new exception to the prohibition on the use of force emerges in addition to the two exceptions provided in the UN Charter. However, this reasoning is countered by those arguing that no such new exception to the use of force can be justified under current international law.[14] Similarly, a justification of humanitarian intervention under the rules of state responsibility is rejected.[15]

Even if each of the above-stated changes can be persuasively countered, they point to the fact that various aspects of law on the use of force in general are under strain for some time now. One of these perceived changes, which is the subject matter of this chapter, is the exercise of the right of self-defence in response to the attacks by non-state actors operating from another state. This change is observed as taking place mainly after the 9/11 incidents of 2001 and that the momentum that started with the 9/11 incidents took a decisive shape in the context of use of force against ISIS in Syria.[16] The developments that followed the 9/11 incidents created the grounds for arguing that the law has changed permitting the use of force as self-defence against non-state actors operating from another state as Teresa Reinold argues in her chapter to this book.[17] The rapid development that created this impetus following the 9/11 incident was the adoption of UNSC resolutions 1368[18] and 1373.[19] These resolutions recognized the 'inherent right of individual or collective self-defence in accordance with the Charter'. As both resolutions were adopted in response to the non-state actor 9/11 attacks, reference to the right of self-defence is interpreted as permitted in such situations which involved non-state actors. This argument is underlined by some of the International Court of Justice (ICJ) judges' individual opinions.[20] In their view, law on self-defence has undergone a transformation in light of developments after the 9/11 incident, particularly with the adoption of the UNSC resolutions 1368 and 1373.[21]

Indeed, these UNSC resolutions, in their preambular paragraphs, recognize and reaffirm the inherent right of individual or collective self-defence in accordance with the Charter. These paragraphs do not qualify the right of self-defence as available against states or non-state actors. However, both resolutions address states only, which is generally the case with UNSC resolutions. Instead of reading the preambular paragraphs

[14] Kevin Jon Heller, 'The Illegality of "Genuine" Unilateral Humanitarian Intervention' (2021) 32 European Journal of International Law 613.

[15] For a discussion see Federica I Paddeu, 'Humanitarian Intervention and the Law of State Responsibility' (2021) 32 European Journal of International Law 649.

[16] Christian Marxsen and Anne Peters are of the view that the revival of the debate has taken place since 2014 and observe that the 'debate about whether and under what conditions self-defence is lawful against (certain types of) non-State attacks has received renewed attention since 2014 due to the interventions of numerous States in the armed conflict in Syria'. Christian Marxsen and Anne Peters, 'Dilution of Self-Defence and its Discontents' in Mary O'Connell, Christian Tams, and Dire Tladi (eds), *Self-Defence against Non-State Actors* (Max Planck Trialogues) (CUP 2019) 7.

[17] Teresa Reinold, Chapter 8 in this book.

[18] UNSC Res 1368 (12 September 2001) UN Doc S/RES/1368.

[19] UNSC Res 1373 (28 September 2001) UN Doc S/RES/1373.

[20] See separate opinion of judge Pieter H Kooijmans and Declaration by Thomas Buergenthal, *Legal Consequences of the Construction of the Wall in Occupied Palestinian Territory* (Advisory Opinion) [2004] ICJ Rep 136.

[21] See Tladi, 'The Extraterritorial Use of Force against Non-State Actors' (n 9) 300–09.

as independent of operative paragraphs, it is judicious to read them in relation to the obligations of states as provided in the operative paragraphs. Such a reading would take these paragraphs closer to the established position of attribution of acts of non-state actors to states. Most importantly, Resolution 1373 states explicitly that 'every State has the duty to refrain from organizing, instigating, assisting or participating in terrorist acts in another State or acquiescing in organized activities within its territory directed towards the commission of such acts'.[22] This paragraph reaffirms the obligations of states, and if states act contrary to those obligations, then the right of self-defence can be invoked as stated in the preambular paragraph. This is a reasonable reading, at least going by the text of both the resolutions. However, contrary to this, these two preambular paragraphs are often read independently and understood as permitting the right of self-defence against the acts of non-state actors without linking them to states from where they operate. Moreover, the language of these paragraphs seems to follow Article 51 which says '*inherent right of individual or collective self-defence*'. Therefore, it is difficult to accept the argument that these resolutions changed the position of law on the right of self-defence. Instead, reading them in their totality reveals the established position of law which requires the attribution of actions of non-state actors to states.

As mentioned earlier, there has not been any change in the text of law on the use of force and self-defence as provided in the UN Charter. As is the case with any text of law, the provisions on the use of force and self-defence in the UN Charter have been subject to interpretations and contending views[23] in cases involving adjudication by adjudicatory bodies, particularly the ICJ.[24] These cases directly or indirectly dealt with the right of self-defence. The *Nicaragua Case* made lasting observations on the right of self-defence and non-state actors. The Court, in this case, underlined the legal position that armed attack by regular armed forces leads to the right of self-defence of the victim state.[25] However, the Court also reflected on the involvement of non-state actors and their relation to the right of self-defence. Accordingly, based on the UN General Assembly resolution on the crime of aggression[26], the Court observed that 'it may be considered to be agreed that an armed attack must be understood as including not merely action by regular armed forces across an international border, but also "the sending by or on behalf of a State of armed bands, groups, irregulars or mercenaries, which carry out acts of armed force against another State of such gravity as to amount to" (inter alia) an actual armed attack conducted by regular forces, "or its substantial

[22] UNSC Res 1373 (28 September 2001) UN Doc S/RES/1373.

[23] For the role of legal change through informal means of interpretation, see Thomas Kleinlein, Chapter 4 in this book.

[24] eg *Case Concerning Military and Paramilitary Activities in and against Nicaragua (Nicaragua v United States of America)* (Judgment) [1986] ICJ Rep 4; *Case Concerning Oil Platforms (Iran v United States)* (Judgment) [2003] ICJ Rep 161; *Construction of the Wall in Occupied Palestinian Territory* (n 20); *Case Concerning the Armed Activities in the Territory of the Congo (Democratic Republic of the Congo v Uganda)* (Judgement) [2005] ICJ Rep 168.

[25] *Nicaragua Decision* (n 24) para 195.

[26] Art 3, paragraph (g) of the Definition of Aggression annexed to General Assembly resolution 3314 (XXIX) reads as follows: 'The sending by or on behalf of a State of armed bands, groups, irregulars or mercenaries, which carry out acts of armed force against another State of such gravity as to amount to the acts listed above, or its substantial involvement therein.' UNGA Res 3314 (XXIX) (14 December 1974).

involvement therein"'.[27] The Court made it clear that these non-state actors are either sent by or act on behalf of a state. Further, to establish the link between the state and the non-state actors the Court established a test to evaluate the role of the former in the activities of the latter. The Court observed that the activities undertaken by non-state actors should be attributed to the state for the latter to be held accountable to the activities of the former. This attribution cannot happen without the effective control of the state over the non-state actors. Thus, the Court stated that 'it would in principle have to be proved that that State had effective control of the military or paramilitary operations in the course of which the alleged violations were committed'.[28]

The above-stated position of the ICJ in the *Nicaragua Case* is not in any manner a deviation from the text of the UN Charter on the right of self-defence because it looks at the issue as an inter-state relation. It is not just the activities of the non-state actors alone but also the level of control exercised by the state on the activities of the non-state actors which determines the involvement of the state and the right of self-defence. The Court's understanding here clearly includes two states opposing each other, though one of them is operating through a non-state actor. This position seems to have been adopted by the ICJ in its later judgments. This case remarkably 'set the standard for attribution that would be followed in subsequent decisions of the Court'.[29] The cases that followed mainly are *Oil Platforms Case*,[30] *Wall Advisory Opinion*,[31] and *Armed Activities in Congo Case*.[32] Commentators critical of this position of the ICJ in successive cases view it as echoing the cold war orthodoxy.[33] Some point to it as a reflection of a 'considerable degree of uncertainty about the proper understanding of self-defence'.[34] These views contend that the majority decisions in *Wall Advisory Opinion* and *Armed Activities in Congo Case* have given short shrift to post-Cold War practice.[35] Further, they are of the view that individual judges differed from majority opinions. Thus, it is observed that 'the recent ICJ jurisprudence is fairly difficult to make sense of . . ., the closer one looks, the more blurred the picture appears'.[36]

While it is a fact that the treaty rules in the UN Charter on the use of force have not been formally altered in a Charter reform, the arguments on the perceived change in rules presented above rely upon state practice. Their emphasis on state practice is meant to underline that despite the static nature of treaty law, state practice changed over time leading to the creation of legal rules different from the provisions in the UN Charter. Those who perceive the change in the rules on the use of force and self-defence refer to different rules from different sources of international law, in particular subsequent state practice and customary international law.[37] This part does not intend

[27] *Nicaragua Decision* (n 24) para 195.
[28] ibid para 115.
[29] Tladi, 'The Extraterritorial Use of Force against Non-State Actors' (n 9) 303.
[30] *Case Concerning Oil Platforms* (n 24).
[31] *Construction of the Wall in Occupied Palestinian Territory* (n 20).
[32] *Case Concerning the Armed Activities in the Territory of the Congo* (n 24).
[33] Christian Tams, 'Self-Defence against Non-State Actors: Making Sense of the "Armed Attack" Requirement' in Mary O'Connell, Christian Tams, and Dire Tladi (eds), *Self-Defence against Non-State Actors* (Max Planck Trialogues) (CUP 2019) 156.
[34] ibid 158.
[35] ibid.
[36] ibid.
[37] Akande and Johnston (n 13) 681–83.

to analyse in doctrinal terms whether state practice, judicial opinions, and scholarly commentaries reflect the formation of CIL or led to the change in the interpretation of Article 51 of the UN Charter. It is only intended to present the debate around it to understand the wide-ranging views on the current legal position.

The law on the use of force is not only located in the Charter rules but also in sources beyond treaty law, and particularly those who argue that there is a change in the law on the use of force either count on CIL or on subsequent practice in the interpretation of a treaty. Chiefly, these arguments rely on the state practice. State practice constitutes a necessary component, along with opinion juris, in forming CIL.[38] State practice also contributes to the interpretation of treaties in a particular way under Article 31(3)(b) of the Vienna Convention on the Law of Treaties of 1969.[39] Hence, state practice plays the dual role of contributing to the formation of CIL and to provide a particular interpretative meaning to a treaty provision. However, state practice needs to be carefully and separately evaluated to assess whether it led to any change in CIL or treaty law. CIL and treaty law need a separate evaluation because, as it is convincingly argued, 'a norm from one source of international law cannot affect the validity of a norm of another source, even where they conflict'.[40] Arguments for norm change on the use of force refer to the practice of states to underline the change while not often explicitly mentioning the law from which source has changed. The CIL nature of the right of self-defence against non-state actors is traced back to its long presence in international law.[41] This historical presence is often substantiated with the well-known example of *Caroline* incident.

The *Caroline* incident took place in 1837 involving United Kingdom and the United States.[42] As Canada was under UK control then, insurgents opposing UK sometimes carried out attacks from the US territory. *Caroline*, a vessel used in one of those attacks, was destroyed by the United Kingdom in US waters. The ensuing communication between Daniel Webster of the United States and Lord Ashburton of the United Kingdom arguably established the CIL on the right of self-defence. The particular point that is emphasized by those who rely on CIL in relation to non-state actors is that the attack involved in this context was committed by non-state actors on the UK

[38] 'Customary international law is unwritten law deriving from practice accepted as law... Article 38, paragraph 1, of the Statute of the International Court of Justice, ... refers, in subparagraph (b), to "international custom, as evidence of a general practice accepted as law". This wording reflects the two constituent elements of customary international law: a general practice and its acceptance as law (the latter often referred to as *opinio juris*).' International Law Commission, 'Draft conclusions on identification of customary international law, with commentaries 2018' Adopted by the ILC at its seventieth session, in 2018, and submitted to the General Assembly as a part of the Commission's report covering the work of that session (A/73/10). Footnotes in the original are omitted here.

[39] Art 31(3)(b) Vienna Convention on the Law of Treaties (adopted 23 May 1969 entered into force 27 January 1980) (VCLT) states: any subsequent practice in the application of the treaty which establishes the agreement of the parties regarding its interpretation.

[40] ibid; Akande and Johnston (n 13) 685.

[41] For example, the US says: '[f]or centuries, States have invoked the right of self-defense to justify taking action on the territory of another State against non-State actors'. US statement at the Arria-formula meeting of the UNSC on the theme 'Upholding the collective security system of the Charter of the United Nations: the use of force in international law, non-State actors and legitimate self-defence', held on 24 February 2021, <https://undocs.org/en/S/2021/247>.

[42] On the *Caroline* incident see Abraham Sofaer, 'On the Necessity of Pre-Emption' (2003) 14 European Journal of International Law 209, 209.

and hence the understanding of self-defence since its inception in the *Caroline* incident involved actions of non-state actors. Hence, the conclusion is that even if not the UN Charter, CIL provides the right of self-defence against the actions of non-state actors. While underlining that there is 'no reason to limit a state's right to protect itself to an attack by another state',[43] the Chatham House principles say that this 'conclusion is supported by reference to the *Caroline* case; the criteria in *Caroline* were enunciated in the context of a marauding armed band, not orthodox state-to-state conflict'.[44] Therefore, the marked assertion is that the state practice that started with the *Caroline* incident further only concretized with the subsequent similar state practice without any deviation.

In addition to the developments on the right of self-defence against non-state actors at the fora involving states and international organizations, there are also individual and scholarly initiatives in the form of explanatory policy principles. These are the Chatham House Principles,[45] the Leiden Policy Recommendations,[46] and the Bethlehem Principles.[47] These policy principles are extensively commented upon.[48] In varying ways, they support the view that self-defence against non-state actors on the territory of a non-consenting state is lawful if the territorial state is either unwilling or unable to prevent attacks by non-state actors emanating from its territory.[49]

The most recent reflections of states on the arguably changing nature of the law on the use of force, particularly on the right of self-defence against non-state actors come from the statements made at the informal 'Arria formula' meeting of the UNSC convened by Mexico on 24 February 2021.[50] The opinions expressed by states on the topic are divided, and it is difficult to draw any direct conclusion as a dominant opinion of the meeting. While analysing the statements made at the meeting, one commentator convincingly argues that 'subsequent practice in the application of the Charter has

[43] Elizabeth Wilmshurst, 'The Chatham House Principles of International Law of the Use of Force in Self-Defense' (2006) 55 International and Comparative Law Quarterly 963, 969–70.

[44] ibid.

[45] ibid 963–72. These Principles were drawn up as a result of a study undertaken by Chatham House in 2004/2005.

[46] Nico Schrijver and Larissa van den Herik, 'Leiden Policy Recommendations on Counter-Terrorism and International Law' (2010) 57 Netherlands International Law Review 531–50. This set of policy recommendations emanates from a consultative process led by Nico Schrijver and Larissa van den Herik, which was concluded on 1 April 2010.

[47] Daniel Bethlehem, 'Self-Defense against an Imminent or Actual Armed Attack by Nonstate Actors' (2012) 106 American Journal of International Law 770 (the 'Bethlehem Principles'; with 'Principles Relevant to the Scope of a State's Right of Self-Defense against an Imminent or Actual Armed Attack by Nonstate Actors' at 775). Bethlehem Principles are a set of principles drawn up by Daniel Bethlehem.

[48] eg see Said Mahmoudi, 'Self-Defence and "Unwilling or Unable" States' (2022) 422 Recueil des cours l'Académie de Droit International 249–399; Mary Ellen O'Connell, 'Dangerous Departures' (2013) 107 American Journal of International Law 380; Gabor Rona and Raha Wala, 'No Thank You to a Radical Rewrite of the Jus Ad Bellum' (2013) 107 American Journal of International Law 386; Elizabeth Wilmshurst and Michael Wood, 'Self-Defense against Nonstate Actors: Reflections on the "Bethlehem Principles"' (2013) 107 American Journal of International Law 390; Dire Tladi, 'The Nonconsenting Innocent State: The Problem with Bethlehem's Principle 12' (2013) 107 American Journal of International Law 570.

[49] Marxsen and Peters (n 16) 5–6.

[50] Arria-formula meeting was convened by Mexico, on the theme 'Upholding the collective security system of the Charter of the United Nations: the use of force in international law, non-State actors and legitimate self-defence' on 24 February 2021. In addition to Mexico, a total of 33 Member States expressed their positions at the meeting.

not established the agreement of the parties regarding its interpretation or application with respect to the use of inter-state force against non-state actors'.[51] Similarly, with regard to CIL, it is also observed based on the statements that 'there is no general, widespread, representative, or consistent state practice accepted as law regarding cross-border force against non-state actors'.[52] The states' positions in the meeting reflect a divided opinion on the issue. Some states adopt a restrictive approach, a few go for the expansive view, some other states' statements are ambiguous, and a few states are changing their position from the past.[53] While the divided opinions do not point to any uniform view, they also reflect differences on what the existing law says on the use of force as self-defence against non-state actors.

The above discussion demonstrates that the treaty law on the use of force and self-defence has been static but there have been constant attempts to present the modified understanding of the existing legal framework. Having presented broad views on the issue the chapter will now turn to offer a critique on the purported norm change in the following section.

## 3. Reflections from a Third World Perspective

The prohibition of the use of force in the UN Charter marks a significant development in international law.[54] However, it is important to contextualize this prohibition in the post-Second World War world order. Despite being the product of the post-Second World War world order, driven by dominant states' interests, the legal framework of the general prohibition of the use of force has limited the unilateral use of force by states. Subsequent to this, any instance of the use of force requires that states justify any exception on the basis of law to signal their compliance.[55] A Third World critical perspective[56] would, mainly engage with the historical context in which this prohibition and its exceptions became part of the UN Charter and, equally importantly, it would analyse the textual application of these provisions critically.[57] As discussed in the previous sections, the textual position of Article 51 of the UN Charter and its application to certain contexts involving non-state actors are fairly clear examples for arguing in favour of norm change. This process of norm change is often presented by the mainstream international law discussions as a progressive development of law's application to suit the changing circumstances and new challenges like

[51] Adil Ahmad Haque, 'The Use of Force against Non-State Actors: All over the Map' (2021) 8 Journal on the Use of Force and International Law 278, 289.

[52] ibid 290.

[53] See ibid. Also see Srinivas Burra, 'India's decisive turn on the right of self-defence' *Opinio Juris*, 22 March 2021 <https://opiniojuris.org/2021/03/22/indias-decisive-turn-on-the-right-of-self-defence/> accessed 19 February 2022.

[54] For a general overview see Marc Weller (ed), *The Oxford Handbook of the Use of Force in International Law* (OUP 2015).

[55] On these mechanisms see Wayne Sandholtz, Chapter 3 in this book.

[56] On TWAIL criticism of hegemony and value-orientation in international law, see also Krieger and Liese, Chapter 1 in this book.

[57] For extensive TWAIL bibliography reflecting TWAIL perspectives see James Thuo Gathii, 'The Promise of International Law: A Third World View' (2021) 36 American University International Law Review 377.

terrorism and the threat posed by non-state actors. The use of force as self-defence against non-state actors is defended based on textual and doctrinal positions and the evolving state practice. However, these arguments are further based on the need to deal with the growing threat of grave challenges of terrorism and non-state actors.[58] Even if these threats dwindle after some time, the arguments for norm change will in all probability last unless there is an express rejection or amendment to this understanding in the form of codification or judicial pronouncements. Hence, the purported change, though driven by a necessity to deal with specific circumstances, will last beyond that.

In this regard, a point to make is that the law that deals with the use of force in the UN Charter is essentially a product of a legal positivist framework. Similarly, the changes that are being sought in this regard are also a product of the same process of positivist norm creation. In other words, the law that exists today in the form of UN Charter and the changes that are being brought are the product of similar processes and remain similar in their normative nature. From a conceptual standpoint, a critique from a critical Third World perspective on the law of self-defence as it exists in the UN Charter and the attempts to change the same may not fundamentally differ from each other. Both the law that 'is' and the law that is sought to be made primarily are formalist norms and do not address the fundamental concerns of the Third World. With this critical backdrop and in an attempt to offer a comprehensive critique, a critical Third World stance can reflect on this purported norm change broadly from three strands: critiquing historical continuities; defence of textual position; and law and critique as contingent on dominant narratives. I will address these in turns.

## 3.1 Historical Critique

A historical critique of international law on the use of force from a Third World perspective would emphasize the colonial continuities in international law in general and on the law on the use of force and the right of self-defence against non-state actors in particular. This effort is to demonstrate the reenactment of the past hierarchies and to underline the structural bias international law carries against the Third World peoples. This has been perceptibly shown in the context of debates on the preemptive right of self-defence. Antony Anghie observes that 'pre-emption, as articulated and acted upon by the Bush doctrine and the example of Iraq, resurrects a very old set of ideas that were articulated at the beginning of the modern discipline of international law'.[59] He is of the view that the 'reemergence of these themes disturbingly illuminates the imperial dimensions of international law, and the enduring impact of imperialism in the international system'.[60] In this critique, historical continuities in international law's development and application are linked to the imperialist ambitions of those

[58] For the manner in which these claims work in order to bring about norm change see Reinold, Chapter 8 in this book.

[59] Antony Anghie, 'The War on Terror and Iraq in Historical Perspective' (2005) 43 Osgoode Hall Law Journal 45, 46.

[60] ibid 46.

dominant states who are at the forefront of invoking arguments like pre-emptive self-defence.

The historical critique is equally important in debunking the 'unprecedentedness' or 'newness' of recent developments. The right of self-defence against the attacks by non-state actors is contextually justified by arguing that the threat from terrorism and from organized non-state actors that we witness today, particularly after the 9/11 incidents, is unprecedented. The claim is that the newness of the threat requires a nuanced application of international law. These new realities are engendered by these modern forms of terrorism and the situation 'poses a new set of challenges for the rule of law'.[61]

Another view acknowledges that the right of self-defence against attacks by non-state actors was already discussed earlier, however, asserts that 9/11 incidents 'sharpened its focus and gave it greater operational urgency'.[62] Further, these attacks are perceived as 'megaterrorist' creating a new global environment.[63] By presenting the gravity and scale of these terrorist attacks, these arguments underline these events' newness and their unprecedented impact on global affairs. Foregrounding these arguments with their newness creates the ground for responses with equal newness to be effective. Without meticulous and critical scrutiny of the historical events, these arguments present the current terrorist threats without any comparable past. Hence, they significantly rely on history to claim the newness of these current events. Therefore, debunking the newness of these events necessitates the critical scrutiny of these claims with historical sources.

Obiora Chinedu Okafor engages with the newness argument head-on in the context of the 9/11 attacks and questions the selectivity in employing this argument.[64] While it is important to underline that the gravity and the loss of life in the 9/11 attacks are massive, the same are conflated with unprecedentedness and newness. The call for normative changes to face these challenges emanated from foregrounding them as new. The triple consequences of this newness argument are that firstly, it erases from history the past violent incidents in which human loss and tragedy were equal or more than 9/11 incidents. Secondly, it serves the purpose of expunging from history the catalyst role played by the dominant states in inflicting similar violence on Third World peoples historically. Thirdly, the newness argument justifies the calls for new normative responses to counter future such terrorist threats. Okafor deftly challenges this rhetoric of newness as imperialist manoeuvring and demonstrates with examples how similar violent attacks in Third World states failed to attract similar attention and newness arguments.[65] He points out that the newness argument is deployed in the past as well to promote the expansionist ambitions of the dominant states. He sums up that the 'structure of the newness argument that has been made in support of the

[61] Thomas Franck, 'Criminals, Combatants, or What? An Examination of the Role of Law in Responding to the Threat of Terror' (2004) 98 American Journal of International Law 686, 688.

[62] Bethlehem (n 47) 770.

[63] Richard A Falk, *The Great Terror War* (Olive Branch Press 2003).

[64] Obiora Chinedu Okafor, 'Newness, Imperialism, and International Legal Reform in Our Time: A Twail Perspective' (2005) 43 Osgoode Hall Law Journal 171, 180.

[65] He says that '[t]housands of innocent civilians have been deliberately or at least recklessly killed in U.S.- led, U.S.-sponsored, and U.S.-supported conflicts... This has been the case in Angola, El Salvador, Mozambique, and so on'. ibid 184.

imperial-style international law reforms that have been urged by the United States and some of its allies bears an unnerving resemblance to the structure of the kinds of newness claims that European powers deployed in the sixteenth and nineteenth centuries, and even much later, as they sought to legitimize their imperial conquests and occupations of the Third World'.[66]

The way the newness argument is employed after the 9/11 attacks is redeployed in the context of arguments in favour of the right of self-defence against non-state actors.[67] It is, in other words, an extension of the same reasoning that works for the invocation of the right of self-defence against non-state actors. The newness argument also eclipses the well-established legal concepts which were seen as part of the progressive development of international law. Today, almost every form of non-state actors' violence is conflated with terrorist violence. This was not the case a few decades ago. Anne-Charlotte Martineau shows how the violence of non-state actors gained legitimacy and legality through various developments.[68] She observes that during the 1960s–1980s, one could speak about non-intervention and legitimate forms of non-state violence, which is not possible today.[69] She is of the view that to understand the law on the use of force, one has to look at its evolution and its transformations. She states that a 'postcolonial analysis invites us to examine the trajectories of legal concepts such as non-intervention, aggression, and self-determination'.[70] While violence is intrinsic in these concepts, its legality is determined based on the legal status of these concepts. However, recent debates on terrorism have deconceptualized and decontextualized the violence, particularly the non-state actor violence. Therefore, the right of self-defence against non-state actors needs to be contextualized as part of these developments.

### 3.2 Defence of Textual Position

A defence of the textual position of law implies drawing the meaning of relevant treaty law based on the general meaning attributed to the text of the provision.[71] However, the meaning of the rule is determined by the methodology applied. It is fairly observed that '[w]hether a positivist, natural law, realist or critical approach is adopted will have a significant impact on how the rule is defined and how the exceptions are circumscribed'.[72] Formal rules of interpretation do provide the possibility of going beyond the text of the provision in the event of ambiguity and absurdity.[73] However, critical perspectives, particularly those that question international law's foundational aspects, go beyond these interpretative techniques to challenge international law's making and

[66] ibid 187.
[67] Tladi, 'The Use of Force in Self-Defence Against Non-State Actors' (n 5) 82.
[68] Anne-Charlotte Martineau, 'Concerning Violence: A Post-Colonial Reading of the Debate on the Use of Force' (2016) 29 Leiden Journal of International Law 95.
[69] ibid 108.
[70] ibid 112.
[71] Art 31 VCLT.
[72] Tladi, 'The Extraterritorial Use of Force against Non-State Actors' (n 9) 245.
[73] Art 32 VCLT.

application.[74] The theoretical perspectives that focus on foundational aspects generally look at the law as it exists as the product of the legal positivist framework and most of the critical perspectives tend to be critical of the positivist notion of international law. The Third World approaches to international law in its dominant variant is not different from these perspectives. However, it cannot be overlooked that the law as it is, ie, *lex lata*, provides a particular meaning and sets a particular policy into action. While that *lex lata* is the subject of critique of a particular critical perspective, it looks contradictory to defend the same law from the same critical perspective, which challenges it for its historical and foundational biases. While this contradiction is substantive and irreconcilable, a critical perspective's defence of the law as it is, is not always irreconcilable if the same is resorted to when the dominant forces tend to deviate from the same. It is beyond the simplistic binary of the law 'as it is' is bad and the law that 'ought' to be is good. A defence of the textual position is not necessarily a defence of the conceptual framework within which that particular law is made, in this case, the positivist methodological framework. Further, a defence of the textual position does not mean that the law in question does not require any change. Even further, the defence of textual position does not mean that the existing law is an apt normative framework. The critical aim of engaging in the defence of textual position is to inform a particular meaning of the existing law and to highlight how the meaning or interpretation offered by certain states and other actors is contrary to the textual meaning. This critical defence of textual position may not have any particular critical perspective of eliciting the textual meaning. It rather relies on the same interpretative tools that mainstream legal framework provides.

A counterargument to this can be: what is critical about this defence? The critical part of this defence is not squarely relevant for international law. However, it would make an important political point that states and other actors, who are expected to uphold the law as it is, are misinterpreting or deviating from the textual position. The purpose of underlining it is not just to show they are violating the law, but also to emphasize implicitly that the law as it exists is not even being followed by those who are proponents of the same general legal system. The critical part here is not to engage in legal argumentation of critically dissecting the relevant provision or doctrine but to seek the compliance of relevant actors to the textual position and underline their inability to do the same. This defence also intends to show that attempts on the part of the relevant actors to provide a different meaning demonstrates the susceptibility of the mainstream international law to the maneuverings of the power and the powerful. Thus, from a critical perspective, the defence of the textual position is not to uphold the infallible nature of the relevant provision or doctrine but to expose its limits in its everyday application. From a critical perspective, the defence of the textual position also contextually serves to expose the limits of the existing law.

While the critical perspectives, including the Third World perspective, predominantly tend to engage in meta critique of the mainstream, they cannot remain

[74] For critical theoretical perspectives and methods in international law, see, Andrea Bianchi, *International Law Theories: An Inquiry into Different Ways of Thinking* (OUP 2016); Anne Orford and Florian Hoffmann (eds), *The Oxford Handbook of the Theory of International Law* (OUP 2016); Rossana Deplano and Nicholas Tsagourias, *Research Methods in International Law: A Handbook* (Edward Elgar 2021).

unconcerned with the micro critique of a specific legal norm or a doctrine. However, there may be a significant difference between these two. A meta critique may predominantly adopt a rejectionist stance with mainstream international law. In contrast, a micro critique of a legal norm or a doctrine may often adopt a dual stance of tactical alliance and rejection as the consequences of their application may align with the critical perspectives.

The defence of the textual position of the provisions of the right of self-defence resorts to the defence of law as it exists. This implies that the law as it exists is a product of democratic processes reflecting the concerns of all, and its use against non-state actors is a deviation from law's objective and unbiased existence. This truncates the Third World perspective as critique of misinterpretation and as a defence of the textual position. This truncated view further implies that the Third World critique of historical injustice is limited to the past and that the post-colonial project of international law textually is sound and anti-hierarchical. While these implications have limited merit, not engaging in such a critique makes the Third World and other critiques outsiders with certain ideological priorities and least concerned with the disciplinary nuances. On the other hand, engaging in textual and doctrinal critique can reveal how constrained the arguments of the proponents of the right of self-defence against non-state actors are. It is appropriately stressed that the purported change in the law on the right of self-defence is, in reality, based on a sparse practice and involving a limited number of players. A few states are actively involved in the unable and unwilling arguments on the right of self-defence against non-state actors and there is a curious case of mutual referencing between a few states, state officials, and commentators.[75] In such a situation, it is equally important to engage with a textual and doctrinal counter critique of the proponents of the rights of self-defence against non-state actors.

### 3.3 Law and Critique as Contingent

It is evident from the analysis above on the changing perceptions on the law of self-defence that there are serious attempts—some with underlining the existing doctrinal coherency and some others seeking doctrinal coherency and a few others for some other reasons—to expand the scope of the existing law on the right of self-defence to accommodate the legality of self-defence against non-state actors. It is also evident that each of these assertions are challenged on similar grounds and, wherever possible, by pointing out the inconsistencies. A plausible conclusion from this position can be the uncertainty of law on the expansion of self-defence against non-state actors. However, there are substantial scholarly opinions claiming that the law on the use of force and self-defence has been the subject of different interpretations in state practice from time to time. These interpretations in state practice are often either self-serving or serving the geopolitical interests of the state offering such expositions. There is a dominant view that the right of self-defence against non-state actors took a decisive

[75] Jutta Brunnée and Stephen J Toope, 'Self-Defence Against Non-State Actors: Are Powerful States Willing but Unable to Change International Law?' (2018) 67 International and Comparative Law Quarterly 263, 266.

turn after the 9/11 attacks as the language of the UNSC resolutions 1368[76] and 1373[77] refer to the inherent right of self-defence and prior to that, there was a fairly settled position of *Nicaragua Case* which emphasized the attributability of acts of non-state actors to states. The ICJ jurisprudence after the *Nicaragua Case* arguably followed the same path despite the differences expressed in the individual opinions. However, a contrary view argues that Article 51 permits self-defence against non-state actors. The subsequent practice on the issue 'recognises that there is in principle room for self-defence against non-state actors: this has been the position during most of the Charter's history, overshadowed only during the dominance of the *Nicaragua* judgment; and it clarifies that States supporting "private" armed attacks can be targets in self-defence'.[78] These views point to an important aspect that continuity and change in the meaning and interpretation of law are not static and it is a continuous process.[79] International lawyers may see this as a familiar feature of international law in general, mainly because of the interpretation of treaty law as well as the formation of new CIL. If one extends the same logic to the right of self-defence, then the perceived changes or the arguments for change and expansion of the right of self-defence against non-state actors will seem as a natural progression. However, the change in the law is not a neutral and natural process. There are catalyst actors and factors for every change and each change is intended to serve a particular aim or set of aims.[80] The catalyst actors are primarily states and catalyst factors are the interests of these states. However, it is neither that all states that play this role nor that those states that play this role represent the interests of all states. Therefore, from a Third World perspective, the critique would deal with the questions of who these actors are, and what is at the centre of the debate. It is not just the substantive law that is the subject of the critique. It would also include the processes and the actors involved in the exercise of purported change in the law.

Unlike historical and textual doctrinal critique, approaching the law and critique as contingent helps to reveal, at every stage of development in the law, which are the states that played the pivotal role and which are the international institutions and other commentators who contributed to this process. Studies have shown that primarily a few Western states are clearly willing to change the law.[81] To facilitate this process, a series of academic 'articles by former government lawyers had appeared after 11 September 2001, setting the stage for the unwilling or unable standard of necessity'.[82] These aspects cannot be captured by engaging in the historical critique or pointing to the deviation from textual and doctrinal coherence. Critiquing who the actors are and what the factors are, reveals the prime players and their interests in making and applying international law in general. Framing critique contingent on each aspect of law and exploring the actors and factors behind such law also helps to evaluate the changing positions of states including Third World states. For example, the recent

[76] UNSC Res 1368 (12 September 2001) UN Doc S/RES/1368.
[77] UNSC Res 1373 (28 September 2001) UN Doc S/RES/1373.
[78] Tams (n 33) 168.
[79] See Kleinlein, Chapter 4 in this book.
[80] For the relevance of actor's engagement for norm change see Krieger and Liese, Chapter 1 in this book.
[81] Brunnée and Toope (n 75) 286.
[82] ibid 283.

Arria formula statements reflect that a few Third World states are moving towards claiming the right of self-defence against non-state actors, which differs from their past positions.[83] It is astutely observed that a Third World Approach to International Law (TWAIL), while focusing on history, 'occasionally overemphasizes continuity over rupture, as well as the ability of hegemonic states to determine unilaterally the content of international law'.[84] To avoid this history centrism, it is necessary to expand the critique to contemporary geopolitical and global economic considerations by way of focussing on actors and factors. In that respect looking at the law and critique as contingent may necessitate the defence of textual position, which otherwise would not be possible within the framework of historical critique.

Further, assessing law and critique as contingent helps to capture the norm change trajectory and their long-term impact. The above analysis shows that a group of influential Western states are in support of the right of self-defence against non-state actors and are supported by some voices in academic literature. Will these views prevail over the opposing positions and will this norm change get concretized? The answer cannot be a straightforward yes or no. It depends on how these arguments of a few Western states are carried around to convince other states. It is also possible that this may not be pursued further. It may become insignificant because of changed circumstances. It is not the first time this kind of change is pushed forward. There have been debates on the questions of proportionality and necessity. During the Iraq war, anticipatory and preemptive self-defence was brought forward. In addition to these assertions, it is argued with examples that even prior to 9/11 incidents, the right of self-defence against non-state actors was invoked on several occasions.[85] These arguments have not led to any apparent change in the applicable law, nor have the arguments entirely disappeared. They are resurrected as and when found relevant by the dominant states.[86] Similarly, arguments around the right of self-defence against non-state actors have not changed the law unequivocally and may not succeed in the near future. However, they armour international law language of some states for a long time.

## 4. Conclusion

The right of self-defence against non-state actors operating from another state gained importance after the incidents of 11 September 2001 and has received renewed attention in the context of Syria since 2014. Arguments of those who point to the existence of the right of self-defence against non-state actors defend their position based

[83] For example, for India's changing position, see, Srinivas Burra, 'India's decisive turn on the right of self-defence' *Opinio Juris*, 22 March 2021 <https://opiniojuris.org/2021/03/22/indias-decisive-turn-on-the-right-of-self-defence/> accessed 19 February 2022; Srinivas Burra, 'Use of Force as Self Defence against Non-State Actors and TWAIL Considerations: A Critical Analysis of India's State Practice' (2018) 24 Asian Yearbook of International Law 106.

[84] Ntina Tzouvala, 'TWAIL and the "Unwilling or Unable" Doctrine: Continuities and Ruptures' (2015) 109 AJIL Unbound 266.

[85] Tams (n 33) 136–39.

[86] One may observe this from the US statement at the Arria formula meeting, which refers to the possibility of the right of self-defence against attacks and related acts, similar to anticipatory or preemptive self-defence. Also see, Haque, 'The Use of Force against Non-State Actors' (n 51) 282.

on multiple assertions. Whereas the treaty law position on the use of force and self-defence has remained static in the form of UN Charter and still does not expressly provide for this right, there are indications that the law on the right of self-defence has either undergone or is undergoing change. Those arguing that the legal norm of self-defence has changed, explain change in multiple ways: they range from justifying it on the basis of the textual position of Article 51 of the UN Charter, which does not explicitly require that the attack should come from states only, to relying on the state practice to contend the formation of CIL as well as to give a particular interpretation of the treaty provisions through subsequent state practice. A few Western states prominently contend these changes, supported by a few scholars. It is difficult to conclude that the law has changed decisively based on this. Having said that, it is essential to note that those who argue for the applicability of the right of self-defence against non-state actors, even if not substantial in number, maintain a considerable sway over the discussion around it. This is very much facilitated through the pliability of structures of international law like the state practice. Proponents of the right rely on state practice to present the modifications in the form of CIL and treaty interpretation. Consequently, a critique from a Third World perspective needs to go beyond the historical account of identifying continuities and evaluate the textual position as well as hold law and critique as contingent. It is evident that there is no unambiguous change in the law accommodating the right of self-defence against non-state actors. It is equally evident that the proponents of this change continue to sway the discourse on the issue.

[illegible] position of the [illegible]

# PART III
# REVERSING POST-COLD WAR TRENDS OF NORM DEVELOPMENT?

# 10

# The International Criminal Court

## Between Sovereignty and the Internationalized Fight Against Impunity

*Adam Bower*

## 1. Introduction

The International Criminal Court (ICC) appears by many accounts to be in crisis.[1] Early hostility from the United States receded during the final years of the Bush administration and subsequent Obama presidency but resurfaced during the Trump administration in the context of the ICC's preliminary examination and subsequent investigation concerning Afghanistan.[2] At the same time, leaders of some African states have characterized the ICC as a biased institution that prioritizes allegedly 'Western' conceptions of justice over more local considerations, impedes regional solutions to complex conflicts, and further replicates unfairness at the heart of the international system.[3] Concerns also persist regarding the ICC's case selection and prosecutorial strategy,[4] trial procedures and judgments,[5] and the broader political relationship with states that shapes the Court's operations and efficacy.[6] These various perspectives have led some observers to worry—and in some cases hope—that the ICC may be in the midst of a serious challenge to its legitimacy.

These critiques coexist with, and are often spurred by, important institutional developments as the ICC has expanded its membership and legal activities. As the first permanent global court tasked with investigating and prosecuting the most serious violations of international humanitarian and human rights law, the ICC is widely identified as a key feature of a 'justice cascade' transforming global politics.[7] The ICC can be understood as a focal point for the development of a global norm of anti-impunity that reflects an expectation that all individuals should be equally

[1] The analysis presented in this chapter is current to May 2018.

[2] For detailed discussion of US opposition to the ICC, see Malcolm Jorgensen, Chapter 11 in this book.

[3] Kamari M Clarke, Abel S Knottnerus, and Eefje de Volder (eds), *Africa and the ICC: Perceptions of Justice* (CUP 2016); Kurt Mills and Alan Bloomfield, 'African Resistance to the International Criminal Court: Halting the Advance of the Anti-Impunity Norm' (2018) 44 Review of International Studies 101.

[4] Alana Tiemessen, 'The International Criminal Court and the Politics of Prosecutions' (2014) 18 The International Journal of Human Rights 444.

[5] Carsten Stahn (ed), *The Law and Practice of the International Criminal Court* (OUP 2015).

[6] David Bosco, *Rough Justice: The International Criminal Court's Battle to Fix the World, One Prosecution at a Time* (OUP 2014).

[7] Kathryn Sikkink, *The Justice Cascade: How Human Rights Prosecutions Are Changing World Politics* (WW Norton & Company 2011).

Adam Bower, *The International Criminal Court* In: *Tracing Value Change in the International Legal Order*. Edited by: Heike Krieger and Andrea Liese, Oxford University Press. © Adam Bower 2023. DOI: 10.1093/oso/9780192855831.003.0010

subject to criminal accountability proceedings for acts of alleged atrocity. Its jurisdictional arrangement and independent powers also represent a substantial transfer of authority from the state to a supranational institution, raising important questions about the relationship between sovereignty, political authority, and the provision of collective goods. Indeed, given the sensitivities that surround judgments of responsibility for mass violence, it is unsurprising that the expansion of the ICC's institutional capacity has revealed profound disagreements concerning the globalized pursuit of accountability.

The ICC thus offers a compelling case study by which to evaluate this book's concern with norm change and the rise or decline in the international rule of law.[8] In this chapter I argue that the ICC is emblematic of a fundamental tension between sovereignty and collective aspirations for accountability for acts of atrocity that has characterized the international criminal justice regime since its inception. The widespread adoption of the Rome Statute and rhetorical endorsement of the anti-impunity norm has not translated into a settled consensus concerning the appropriate balance between domestic and supra-national legal authority. Yet from the perspective of constructivist international relations (IR) theorizing, this enduring contestation is unsurprising, since intersubjective phenomena norms are always subject to expansion, contraction, and transformation in relation to other ideational structures. Sovereignty and accountability are not diametrically opposed and irreconcilable values but rather discursive resources that actors draw upon to frame, justify, and adjudicate their policies. The particular institutional solution embodied in the Rome Statute provides the architecture for pursuing a global criminal accountability mandate while simultaneously engendering a series of focal points for contestation. Contemporary clashes are therefore animated by competing accounts of when and how (and how much) to prioritize one over the other in particular circumstances.

I do not wish to understate the significant challenges facing the Court, but rather relate these confrontations to the broader move towards accountability that the ICC is held to embody.[9] There are a range of ways in which states have sought to exempt their nationals from ICC jurisdiction, which has had the effect of constricting the capacity and authority of the Court. These are serious impediments but are not necessarily indicative of fundamental *decline* in the anti-impunity norm, because the norm was never fully consolidated in the first place. A more appropriate framing is one of continued *transformation* where the most likely near-term outcome is the modest narrowing of the norm's scope. Most contestation takes place within and through international law, and this widespread reliance on legal practices can serve to reinforce an international rule of law, even as specific features are in dispute.

[8] My analysis draws inspiration from the valuable discussion of crisis and change in the international legal order provided in Heike Krieger and Andreas Liese, Chapter 1 in this book.

[9] This chapter draws on arguments developed in Adam Bower, 'Contesting the International Criminal Court: Bashir, Kenyatta, and the Status of the Nonimpunity Norm in World Politics' (2019) 4 Journal of Global Security Studies 88.

## 2. Studying International Norm Change

Scholars of IR and international law are often portrayed as tilling separate intellectual fields, frequently addressing similar concerns from distinct and not necessarily complementary directions. Yet increasing efforts at interdisciplinary dialogue can be detected, as the present book and other recent initiatives attest.[10] One such starting point for engagement is to conceptualize law as a cornerstone of a multifaceted international social system as has been most explicitly undertaken by constructivist IR scholars.[11] This literature yields four general insights that are of particular relevance here.

First, from a constructivist perspective international law is *inherently normative* in the sense that it serves as a primary means by which actors constitute the legitimate participants and acceptable modes of conduct in an international system.[12] In this view, law is distinguished from other—political, economic, or moral—modes of action by its distinctive form of principled justification rather than a discrete set of binding rules made authoritative through regular enforcement, as with rationalist 'hard law' approaches.[13]

Second, international law offers the *dominant language* for articulating conceptions of rightful action among members of the international community.[14] When states invoke international law they are simultaneously pursuing their own interests within a distinctive social context and set of constraints—by validating particular actions as conforming to, or violating, established principles, rules, and norms—and contributing to the further reification of legal process and criteria as the highest standard of justification. These efforts do not occur in a vacuum but are structured by the parameters of legal argumentation which frames possible claims in reference to previously articulated rules and procedures. In employing legal discourses as a strategic resource, political action is thus constrained by intersubjectively accepted practices and linguistic structures. Legalization does not represent a teleological end-point for normative development, and institutionalization in a legal form does not inherently lead to stronger norms in all cases. However, the resort to law does alter the ways in which a norm may be discussed and serves as a privileged—and given law's intersubjective authority, especially potent—pathway for remaking social standards.

Third, norms are the product of intersubjective social processes and are therefore necessarily *dynamic* rather than static phenomena.[15] Norms both constitute actors

[10] Jeffrey L Dunoff and Mark A Pollack (eds), *Interdisciplinary Perspectives on International Law and International Relations: The State of the Art* (CUP 2013).

[11] Jutta Brunnée and Stephen J Toope, *Legitimacy and Legality in International Law: An Interactional Account* (CUP 2010); Martha J Finnemore and Stephen Toope, 'Alternatives to Legalization: Richer Views of Law and Politics' (2001) 55 International Organization 743; Christian Reus-Smit (ed), *The Politics of International Law* (CUP 2004).

[12] Christian Reus-Smit, 'Politics and International Legal Obligation' (2003) 9 European Journal of International Relations 591; Shirley Scott, 'International Law as Ideology: Theorizing the Relationship between International Law and International Politics' (1994) 5 European Journal of International Law 313.

[13] Kenneth W Abbott and others, 'The Concept of Legalization' (2000) 54 International Organization 401.

[14] Friedrich Kratochwil, *The Status of Law in World Society: Meditations on the Role and Rule of Law* (CUP 2014); Ian Hurd, *How to Do Things with International Law* (Princeton University Press 2017).

[15] Wayne Sandholtz and Kendall Stiles, *International Norms and Cycles of Change* (OUP 2008); Antje Wiener, 'Contested Compliance: Interventions on the Normative Structure of World Politics' (2004) 10 European Journal of International Relations 189.

and forms of action and are themselves transformed through forms of agency. In other words, norms are perpetually in motion, even as they appear to be more or less stable—and thereby provide guidance for actors by informing their identities and resulting interests—at particular moments in time.[16]

Fourth, contestation is inherent in politics and can be understood as a vital feature of a pluralistic international society.[17] From this vantage point norms are always subject to processes of interrogation as actors reason about the meaning, limits, and legitimacy of their obligations in the context of prevailing social expectations. Moreover, norms—whether institutionalized in legal rules or not—are by definition the product of social interaction and thus necessarily contain some allowance for interpretation and indeterminacy. Norms do not exist as discrete entities but are instead deeply entwined in overlapping ideational structures; in a given social context, therefore, actors have multiple reference points by which to justify their actions. As such, *tensions* between connected norms provide key pathways through which actors interpret, challenge, and in some cases seek to modify or supplant these standards. Sandholtz and Stiles conceptualize this as a cyclical process in which '[t]he inevitable gap between general rules and specific actions ceaselessly casts up disputes, which in turn generate arguments, which then reshape both rules and conduct'.[18] Norm change thus often proceeds through forms of strategic action in which nascent norms—or alternative interpretations of existing norms—are promoted via deliberate linkage to more established and widely accepted standards. These processes are not random but emerge from and are conditioned by the prevailing social environment in which the discourses and practices of international law provide powerful sources of justification.

The presence of such disputes does not necessarily suggest an ineffective or illegitimate institution. Contestation can potentially lead to the modification or replacement of a norm but can equally stimulate forms of counter-mobilization seeking to reaffirm the referent norm. Assessing norm status and trajectory must therefore account for the inherently intersubjective quality of norms and the complex ways that norms structure and constrain action. '[B]ecause they are collective understandings and not abstract principles … norms derive their strength from the degree of consensus they enjoy and the level of commitment they engender'.[19] This demands a careful consideration of patterns of conformance and violation and the ways that actors describe these actions—and equally, the responses these actions yield from other actors.[20]

In sum, the international legal order is by its nature always in transformation, but it is not infinitely malleable: at any given point in time, actors still operate in relation to the existing institutions. The existence of multiple sources of authority generates

[16] Sandholtz and Stiles (n 15) 1.

[17] Antje Wiener, *The Invisible Constitution of Politics: Contested Norms and International Encounters* (CUP 2008); Jonas Wolff and Lisbeth Zimmermann, 'Between Banyans and Battle Scenes: Liberal Norms, Contestation, and the Limits of Critique' (2016) 42 Review of International Studies 513. For detailed discussions concerning the relationship between contestation and norm change, see the Wayne Sandholtz, chapter 3 in this book and Antje Wiener, chapter 2 in this book.

[18] Sandholtz and Stiles (n 15) 3.

[19] Ward Thomas, *The Ethics of Destruction: Norms and Force in International Relations* (Cornell University Press 2001) 30.

[20] Richard Price, 'Detecting Ideas and Their Effects' in Robert E Goodwin and Charles Tilly (eds), *The Oxford Handbook of Contextual Political Analysis* (OUP 2006).

interpretive dilemmas which in turn facilitate contestation. Yet the structure of international law provides a framework through which the pursuit of policy goals, and the more fundamental reconstruction of international social standards, can take place.

## 3. The ICC Between Sovereign States and Globalized Anti-Impunity

The ICC represents a complex and wide-ranging intervention in international politics. The ICC is a global institution founded by states and ultimately subject to forms of direct and indirect state oversight and influence. At the same time, the Court is an independent judicial institution whose legitimacy and authority is in no small measure drawn from its ostensible separation from state power.[21] By virtue of its structure, functions, and scope, therefore, the Court sits uneasily between a state-based legal order that is grounded in concerns for sovereign equality and calls for responses to major collective action problems—such as the response to mass atrocity—that require empowered institutions and active cooperation between state and non-state actors. Sandholtz and Stiles have shown the macro dynamics of international norm change to be driven by cycles of interaction between 'sovereignty' norms that constitute states as the primary units of an international system and 'liberal' norms that enshrine the inherent moral value of individual human beings and collectives as subjects of protection.[22] This pattern is evident in the case of the ICC.

A conception of sovereignty is a foundational element underpinning all systems of political order. Sovereignty 'defines the social identity of the state and, in turn, constitutes the basic institutional practices of international society'.[23] Expressions of sovereignty are fundamentally normative—in that they define boundaries of acceptable actors and forms of organization—and emerge through historically and culturally contingent processes of social construction concerning recognition, physical territory, and political authority.[24] In the modern state system this principle of sovereign statehood is composed of a set of interconnected norms, the most important of which are (i) territorial integrity and exclusive jurisdiction over internal affairs (and concomitant non-interference in a state's domestic relations), (ii) formal legal equality and independence in external relations, and (iii) the right to provide or withhold consent for international obligations. Sovereignty has never been absolute, of course, as the Westphalian state system is suffused with forms of inequality and hypocrisy that have seen the political autonomy of the principal units frequently transgressed.[25] At the same time, the international order is characterized by extensive transfers of decision-making power from states to supranational and increasingly, non-state, actors. Yet

[21] Karen J Alter, 'Agents or Trustees? International Courts in Their Political Context' (2008) 14 European Journal of International Relations 33.

[22] Sandholtz and Stiles (n 15) 19–24.

[23] Christian Reus-Smit, 'The Constitutional Structure of International Society and the Nature of Fundamental Institutions' (1997) 51 International Organization 555, 556.

[24] Thomas J Biersteker and Cynthia Weber (eds), *State Sovereignty as a Social Construction* (CUP 1996).

[25] Stephen Krasner, *Sovereignty: Organized Hypocrisy* (Princeton University Press 1999); Antony Anghie, *Imperialism, Sovereignty, and the Making of International Law* (CUP 2007).

despite these ambivalences, the idea of sovereign statehood provides a powerful rhetorical frame for the articulation of rights and responsibilities in international society.

As a central institutional expression of global justice, the ICC is animated by a belief that 'the most serious crimes of concern to the international community as a whole must not go unpunished'.[26] What I term the 'anti-impunity norm' is characterized by four core components. The norm regards individual human beings as the appropriate subjects of accountability that is primarily realized via judicialized procedures of investigation, trial, and punishment through incarceration. Individualization, criminalization, and retribution are thus the intellectual lodestars of the global response to mass atrocity.[27] The norm is also universal in nature in that it is supposed to apply equally to all people irrespective of their position or status. Article 27 of the Rome Statute reaffirms the position of international tribunals since 1945 in subjecting senior state officials to criminal accountability.[28] The subject matter to which the norm applies is more constrained, however, encompassing the 'core crimes' of genocide, crimes against humanity, war crimes, and aggression which are understood to constitute the most serious forms of violence;[29] other criminal activities, such as drug trafficking and terrorism, are excluded from this international justice regime. Finally, the norm is officially agnostic concerning the location of accountability processes. The ICC is a court of last resort and complementary to national jurisdictions, with states retaining the primary responsibility for investigating and prosecuting atrocity crimes.[30] The ICC can be regarded as the primary global expression of the anti-impunity norm, but it is only one prominent manifestation of a broader shift towards criminal prosecutions for mass human rights abuses that has emerged in national, regional, and international settings over the past 40 years.[31]

These general objectives can imply very different configurations of rights and responsibilities, however, and the particular structure of the Rome Statute represents one of a variety of potential mechanisms for countering impunity in the international system. The creation of a permanent international court 'represents a remarkable transfer of authority from sovereign states to an international institution'[32] and thus poses distinct challenges to accepted notions of sovereignty and non-interference. The advent of the ICC means that national processes are undertaken in view of internationally agreed standards of criminal law and with the oversight of a supranational

[26] United Nations General Assembly Rome Statute of the International Criminal Court (adopted 17 July 1998, entered into force 1 July 2002) 2187 UNTS 3 (Rome Statute) preamble para 4.

[27] Mark A Drumbl, *Atrocity, Punishment, and International Law* (CUP 2007).

[28] The irrelevance of official capacity is articulated in the founding statutes of the Nuremberg (Article 7), Tokyo (Article 6), ICTY (Article 7(2)), ICTR (Article 6(2)), and Special Court for Sierra Leone (Article 6(2)), among others.

[29] An amendment to the Rome Statute operationalizing the crime of aggression was adopted at the 2010 Review Conference in Kampala, Uganda and activated via a resolution at the ICC Assembly of States Parties in December 2017, see ICC, 'Activation of the Jurisdiction of the Court over the Crime of Aggression' (14 December 2017) ICC-ASP/16/Res.5 <https://asp.icc-cpi.int/iccdocs/asp_docs/Resolutions/ASP16/ICC-ASP-16-Res5-ENG.pdf> accessed 25 February 2022. The ICC will be able to exercise jurisdiction over the crime of aggression from 17 July 2018.

[30] Rome Statute (n 26) art 17.

[31] Gary Jonathan Bass, *Stay the Hand of Vengeance: The Politics of War Crimes Tribunals* (Princeton University Press 2001); Sikkink (n 7).

[32] Bosco (n 6) 2.

legal body that is able to step in when state authorities are unwilling or unable to act. In this respect the principle of complementarity holds important implications for state policy since it subjects national legal processes to external monitoring and provides strong incentives towards harmonization of domestic law in line with the international standard.[33]

The ICC's ability to investigate and prosecute senior political, military, and security officials, as well as those from non-state armed groups allied with or in opposition to the government, thus exposes states to considerable potential scrutiny. The ICC can consider alleged violations occurring either on the territory of a State Party or committed by the national(s) of a Party, leaving open the possibility that nationals from non-member states may be subject to ICC prosecution even though their governments do not accept the Court's authority.[34] Ongoing preliminary examinations and investigations concerning Afghanistan, Georgia, Palestine, and Ukraine raise the prospect that American, Israeli, and Russian nationals may soon face scrutiny. The same is true for ICC members like Canada and the United Kingdom that have thus far supported the Court's work. Notably, the prospect of ICC investigation of US nationals has animated US opposition to the Court since its inception.[35] The Rome Statute also gives the Prosecutor the power to initiate investigations *proprio motu*—under his or her own initiative—a form of jurisdiction that weakens state control over the institution. The temporal and geographic scope of the Court substantially constrains the ability of states to choose whether and when to pursue criminal justice, and major shift from the prior model wherein the state and its agents retained sole responsibility for ensuring accountability.[36] Taken together, this amounts to a dramatic sea change in how states conceive of their domestic and international responsibilities concerning the punishment of atrocity.

Yet the Rome Statute does contain notable concessions to state sovereignty and the established international order. First, the Statute does not enact a form of universal jurisdiction even as it enables the investigation and prosecution of non-party nationals under some circumstances. Second, through Article 98 the Statute accommodates established international obligations *between states* concerning diplomatic immunities, meaning that the universality of the anti-impunity norm under the ICC remains contentious.[37] Third, while the ICC is constituted as an independent entity it retains some connections to the United Nations (UN) system. Most especially, the Security Council (UNSC) is accorded the ability to both refer situations to the ICC Chief Prosecutor (Article 13(b)) and defer ongoing investigations and prosecutions under its Chapter VII powers (Article 16). Finally, the Rome Statute creates an institution with invasive

[33] Carsten Stahn and Mohamed M El Zeidy (eds), *The International Criminal Court and Complementarity: From Theory to Practice* (CUP 2011).

[34] Rome Statute (n 26) art 12(2).

[35] William Lietzau, 'International Criminal Law after Rome: Concerns from a U.S. Military Perspective' (2001) 64 Law and Contemporary Problems 119; David Scheffer, 'The United States and the International Criminal Court' (1999) 93 The American Journal of International Law 12, 18–19. For further discussion see Jorgensen, Chapter 11 in this book.

[36] Beth A Simmons and Allison Danner, 'Credible Commitments and the International Criminal Court' (2010) 64 International Organization 225, 226.

[37] Dapo Akande, 'International Law Immunities and the International Criminal Court' (2004) 98 The American Journal of International Law 407.

powers but without its own enforcement capacities and so the Court remains reliant on external assistance to finance its operations, facilitate investigations and prosecutions, and enforce punishments. As a consequence, the ICC is vulnerable to challenges and must be continually attentive to its legitimacy.[38] While empowered as an impartial legal actor the Court must also operate in the world of politics and navigate between state power and institutional autonomy, with the attendant compromises and limitations that this entails.[39] As will be shown, this has provided a variety of means by which states have sought to restrict the Court's authority.

## 4. Tracing Challenges to the ICC's Legal and Political Status

In light of the above, one might regard the rapid negotiation and entry into force of the Rome Statute as evidence of the broadening acceptance of the anti-impunity norm. Nicole Deitelhoff has argued that the diplomacy leading to the creation of the ICC was characterized by a fundamental shift in state interests from an institution that was initially envisaged as subservient to state consent and power politics—with the UNSC retaining sole responsibility for authorizing investigations—to one that enjoys considerable independence as described.[40] From the outset, therefore, ICC proponents were convinced that an international court could only realize its objectives if it was empowered as an autonomous and impartial legal entity whose structure promised some insulation from political considerations.

### 4.1 The Expansion of the Anti-Impunity Norm

From this perspective, 'the normative basis of the Court's appeal is what made negotiation of the Statute possible in the first place ... converging international normative commitments against impunity continue to be the ICC's primary basis of support'.[41] One hundred and twenty-three states have joined the Rome Statute,[42] with strong regional representation in Africa, Europe, Latin America, and the Caribbean. A rhetorical commitment to accountability generally, and the ICC's specific justice mandate more specifically, is widely apparent in state discourse. This is especially notable among those states—including Afghanistan, Colombia, Democratic Republic of the Congo, Palestine, the Philippines, and Uganda—that joined the Court in the midst of internal armed conflicts or the aftermath of systematic violence and societal

[38] Lee JM Seymour, 'The ICC and Africa: Rhetoric, Hypocrisy Management, and Legitimacy' in Kamari M Clarke, Abel S Knottnerus, and Eejfe de Volder (eds), *Africa and the ICC: Perceptions of Justice* (CUP 2016) 110–12.

[39] Bosco (n 6); Leslie Vinjamuri, 'The International Criminal Court and the Paradox of Authority' (2016) 79 Law and Contemporary Problems 275.

[40] Nicole Deitelhoff, 'The Discursive Process of Legalization: Charting Islands of Persuasion in the ICC Case' (2009) 63 International Organization 33.

[41] Benjamin N Schiff, *Building the International Criminal Court* (CUP 2008) 166.

[42] As of May 2018. This figure takes into account the recent withdrawal of Burundi, which took effect on 27 October 2017.

instability, and others like Argentina and Chile that undertook human rights prosecutions after the end of authoritarian regimes, where ICC membership is presented as evidence of domestic political transformations.[43] The decision by six states[44] to refer violence on their territories to the Court has been held up by the respective governments as further demonstration of their commitment to accountability—though one can equally regard these developments as part of a strategy to instrumentalize international justice by targeting opponents of the state.[45] Even the vast majority of ICC non-parties, including some of the Court's most vocal critics like China, Russia, and the United States, routinely express support for the ICC's objective of ending impunity despite enduring unease concerning the particular institutional formulation enshrined in the Rome Statute.[46] The association of the ICC with an international consensus against impunity goes deeper than state structures, however, and is also seen in the extensive engagement of domestic civil society groups in the development of international criminal law norms, and favourable public opinion polling in many countries including those currently experiencing ICC investigations and prosecutions.[47]

Yet this apparent consensus regarding accountability can mask important contestation over the more particular meaning and application of the anti-impunity norm and its relationship to, and implications for, a state-based international order. Debates over the content and structure of the ICC ultimately revolve around competing visions for the legal scope and political independence of the institution and as a consequence 'the conflict between the universal nature of the Statute's normative claims and the particularistic nature of national sovereignty is at the root of opposition to the Court'.[48] It is therefore possible to observe an enduring and arguably widening gap between more abstract and aspirational statements of support for the *idea* of a permanent global criminal court, and practical commitment to observe the demands of the actually-existing ICC in its real-world operations.[49]

## 4.2 Targets of International Justice

A central question in the development of international criminal law concerns the scope of legal accountability, and specifically whether there are any permissible exceptions to the ICC's mandate to investigate and prosecute the individuals most responsible for the perpetration of atrocity crimes. The collision between sovereignty

[43] Adam Bower, *Norms Without the Great Powers: International Law and Changing Social Standards in World Politics* (OUP 2017) 127–31.

[44] Uganda, Democratic Republic of the Congo, Central African Republic, C ôte D'Ivoire, Mail, and Palestine.

[45] Tiemessen (n 4).

[46] Bower, *Norms Without the Great Powers* (n 43) 154–55.

[47] Beth A Simmons and Hyeran Jo, 'Measuring Norms and Normative Contestation: The Case of International Criminal Law' (2019) 4 Journal of Global Security Studies 18.

[48] Schiff (n 41) 166.

[49] I do not claim to provide a comprehensive accounting of debates relating to the ICC. Additional concerns for, among other things, trial processes and outcomes and conceptions of international justice (the prospect of deterrence, use of trials as symbolic responses to mass atrocity, and appropriate role for victims and affected communities) are also of great legal, political, and normative consequence. Yet these debates are less directed towards the key cleavage here between sovereignty and accountability.

and accountability norms has featured prominently in objections to the Court's ability to exercise jurisdiction over the citizens of ICC non-member states, as provided for in Article 12(1)(a) of the Rome Statute. Prominent ICC opponents including China, India, Russia, and the United States maintain that this arrangement violates the foundational tenet of international law that states cannot be bound by rules to which they do not consent.[50] The most obvious manifestation of this contestation came during the Bush administration, when the United States undertook an active campaign to curtail the ability of Court to gain custody of US nationals.[51] This involved domestic legislative measures aimed at both prohibiting cooperation with the ICC and, most provocatively, pre-emptively authorizing the US President to use diplomatic and military means to free any Americans that may come to be held by the Court. At the same time, the United States attempted to secure blanket immunities for their nationals by concluding bilateral non-surrender agreements with over 100 governments and by inserting language into successive UNSC resolutions that permanently exempted non-party nationals from ICC jurisdiction in the context of peacekeeping operations in Bosnia and the referral of the Darfur and Libyan situations to the Court.

Interestingly, US officials explicitly sought to portray their diplomatic efforts as consistent with Article 98 of the Rome Statute which recognizes the right of states to observe established immunities owed to the citizens of other states.[52] Despite their apparent near-term success, US invocation of the Rome Statute had the effect of implicitly legitimizing the ICC's legal regime and provided a rhetorical opening by which ICC supporters were able to limit the extent of US exceptions.[53] Debates over the exposure of non-party nationals thus illustrate both the prospective utility of contestation through law and the unanticipated ways that such efforts can motivate and empower counter-contestation aimed at upholding the ICC's anti-impunity norm.

The ICC arrest warrants, in 2009 and 2010, for Sudanese President Omar al-Bashir reinvigorated debates concerning the ability of an international court to impose obligations on non-party states.[54] The Bashir case became the focal point for a much broader process of contestation from within the African continent, a region which includes a diverse range of views concerning the Court and the objectives of international justice

[50] Bower, *Norms Without the Great Powers* (n 43) 155–59. Detailed treatments of this topic include Dapo Akande, 'The Jurisdiction of the International Criminal Court over Nationals of Non-Parties: Legal Basis and Limits' (2003) 1 Journal of International Criminal Justice 618; Dapo Akande, 'The Immunity of Heads of States of Nonparties in the Early Years of the ICC' (2018) 112 AJIL Unbound 172; Robert Cryer, 'The ICC and Its Relationship to Non-States Parties' in Carsten Stahn (ed), *The Law and Practice of the International Criminal Court* (OUP 2015); and Jorgensen, Chapter 11 in this book.

[51] Bower, *Norms Without the Great Powers* (n 43) 172–82; Judith Kelley, 'Who Keeps International Commitments and Why? The International Criminal Court and Bilateral Nonsurrender Agreements' (2007) 101 The American Political Science Review 573; Ifran Nooruddin and Autumn Lockwood Payton, 'Dynamics of Influence in International Politics: The ICC, BIAs, and Economic Sanctions' (2010) 47 Journal of Peace Research 711.

[52] ibid.

[53] Adam Bower, 'Arguing with Law: Strategic Legal Argumentation, US Diplomacy, and Debates over the International Criminal Court' (2015) 41 Review of International Studies 337.

[54] *The Prosecutor v Omar Hassan Ahmad Al Bashir* (First Arrest Warrant) ICC-02/05-01/09-1 (4 March 2009); *The Prosecutor v Omar Hassan Ahmad Al Bashir* (Second Arrest Warrant) ICC-02/05-01/09-95 (12 July 2010).

more broadly.[55] Here too the language of consent, equality, and non-interference have provided rhetorical frames for challenging ICC authority.[56] The Court has repeatedly asserted that the UNSC's referral of the Darfur situation both brings Sudan and its nationals under ICC jurisdiction and obliges all states to comply with ICC requests stemming from that investigation. This assertion rests on a claim that the UNSC's powers as vested by the UN Charter—as a quasi-constitutional text—take precedence over norms emphasizing state autonomy and the consensual basis of legal obligation. The indictment of a sitting Head of State also highlighted the controversial status of immunities under international criminal law. African states individually, and collectively via the African Union (AU), have rejected the validity of the Bashir arrest warrants on both of these grounds, with frequent reference made to Article 98 and a claim that an individual treaty cannot override customary international legal norms for states that do not consent. These actors seized upon this issue as evidence of supranational interference but have also used the controversy as a means of protecting regional players like Bashir and, later, Kenyan President Kenyatta from legal scrutiny. These actors continue to deny any legal obligation to arrest and surrender President Bashir and have refused to cooperate with the arrest warrants, as discussed below. This concern is not confined to Africa, however, and AU contestation has provided an opening for other states—most notably China and Russia—to reiterate support for the view that Heads of State retain immunity from international criminal prosecution.[57]

The interface between sovereignty and accountability has also provided the impetus for a series of attempts to restrict the legal scope and practical effect of the anti-impunity norm under the Rome Statute. In reference to the Kenyatta indictment the AU sought support for a proposed change to Article 27 that would provide for immunity for democratically elected leaders during their term in office.[58] Kenya and its supporters presented this initiative as a modest correction to the ICC immunities standard that would recognize domestic popular will. This position has not been endorsed within the ICC Assembly of States Parties and instead only a modest change to the Rules of Procedure and Evidence has been adopted which permits senior state officials to be excused from constant attendance at trial.[59] As with the US immunities

[55] Clarke, Knottnerus and de Volder (n 3); Anton du Plessis and Ottilia A Maunganidze, 'The ICC and the AU' in Carsten Stahn (ed), *The Law and Practice of the International Criminal Court* (OUP 2015); Charles Chernor Jalloh and Ilias Bantekas, eds. *The International Criminal Court and Africa* (OUP 2017); Mills and Bloomfield (n 3).

[56] For further discussion see Bower, 'Contesting the ICC' (n 9).

[57] Russian Federation, 'Statement of the Russian Federation Delivered by Ms. Diana Eloeva, First Secretary of the Legal Department of the Ministry of Foreign Affaires' (12 December 2014) presented at the Thirteenth Assembly of States Parties of the Rome Statute of the International Criminal Court in New York <http://asp.icc-cpi.int/iccdocs/asp_docs/ASP13/GenDeba/ICC-ASP13-GenDeba-Russian-ENG.pdf> accessed 17 November 2021; People's Republic of China, 'Statement by Mr. MA Xinmin, Deputy Director-General of the Department of Treaty and Law of the Ministry of Foreign Affairs' (8 December 2014) presented at the Thirteenth Assembly of States Parties of the Rome Statute of the International Criminal Court in New York <http://asp.icc-cpi.int/iccdocs/asp_docs/ASP13/GenDeba/ICC-ASP13-GenDeba-China-ENG.pdf> accessed 17 November 2021.

[58] ICC, 'Report of the Working Group on Amendments' (7 December 2014) ICC-ASP/13/31 Annex I sec VI.B. <https://asp.icc-cpi.int/iccdocs/asp_docs/ASP13/ICC-ASP-13-31-ENG.pdf> accessed 25 February 2022.

[59] ICC, 'Amendments to the Rules of Procedure and Evidence' (27 November 2013) ICC-ASP/12/Res.7 <https://asp.icc-cpi.int/iccdocs/asp_docs/Resolutions/ASP12/ICC-ASP-12-Res7-ENG.pdf> accessed 25 February 2022.

effort discussed above, the invocation of salient norms and more specific ICC rules has thus facilitated modes of contestation and provided resources for resisting erosions of the anti-impunity standard. The consequences of these disputes are more far-reaching than in the US case, however, as the indictments of Bashir and Kenyatta, coupled with the lack of action on African initiatives relating to Head of State immunity, has spurred further anger towards the Court among Sudan, Kenya, and their allies leading to more provocative and damaging forms of overt non-compliance that are addressed later (Section 4.5).

## 4.3 The ICC's Position in the International Order

Closely connected to the question of who may be legitimately subject to international criminal accountability is how the ICC is situated within the international system. A chief tension going back to the negotiation of the Rome Statute in the late 1990s concerned the independence of a new international court and its relationship to the UN. The US has been the most vocal proponent of the view that any international court must be subordinate to the UNSC in recognition of the prevailing political reality in which the UNSC retains the ultimate responsibility for ensuring peace and security.[60] The majority of states, by contrast, rejected this position during the negotiations as a deliberate attempt to 'politicize' international justice by giving the five permanent members of the UNSC the ability to block any inconvenient ICC investigations. The outcome was a court that is empowered to act independent of state direction through the Prosecutor's *proprio motu* powers.

Two permanent UNSC members—France and the United Kingdom—did ultimately join the 'Like-minded Group' advocating for an independent ICC and ratified the Rome Statute. Yet the Permanent five members (P5) have shown greater solidarity in seeking practical means of preserving UNSC pre-eminence and thus their own special prerogatives.[61] On the one hand, the Council has guarded its referral and deferral powers jealously, authorizing ICC investigations in two instances—Darfur and Libya—where its own political objectives aligned (or were not at odds with) ICC action, and failing to act in other instances—such as Myanmar, North Korea, or Syria—where one or more permanent members opposed international legal scrutiny. At the same time, the Council has not seen fit to act on requests from *other* states to pause ongoing ICC investigations as permitted under Article 16. Interestingly, this was a feature of US efforts to exempt their servicemembers from ICC jurisdiction discussed above and was rejected on the merits by other Council members,[62] as also experienced by African states discussed further in a moment.

On the other hand, the P5 have sought to protect their own privileged position in the international order by restricting the scope of ICC jurisdiction on matters of

[60] William A Schabas, 'United States Hostility to the International Criminal Court: It's All About the Security Council' (2004) 15 European Journal of International Law 701; Deborah Ruiz Verduzco, 'The Relationship between the ICC and the United Nations Security Council' in Carsten Stahn (ed), *The Law and Practice of the International Criminal Court* (OUP 2015).

[61] Bosco (n 6).

[62] Bower, 'Arguing with Law' (n 53).

particular concern, most notably with respect to the inclusion of the crime of aggression under the Rome Statute.[63] These states have long resisted any innovation that would transfer responsibility for determining the existence of an illegal use of armed force away from the UNSC, thereby diminishing its role as the ultimate arbiter of international peace and security—and with it the ability of these states to conduct military operations free from the threat of legal condemnation. These power-political concerns have clearly influenced the scope of the ICC's authority, as the P5 and their allies successfully lobbied ICC State Parties to enact a jurisdictional arrangement on the crime of aggression that permanently excludes the nationals of non-party states and generally sets a high bar for judgments concerning the aggressive use of force.[64]

Concerns about the relationship between the ICC and UNSC are not limited to the major powers. As part of the broader strategy of countering the indictments against Bashir and Kenyatta, the AU sought separate deferrals in relation to the Sudan and Kenya investigations which it presented as striking a balance between a commitment to countering impunity—via the legal procedures established by the Rome Statute—and respect for the constitutional duties of state leaders and national-level responses to violence and political instability.[65] Similar calls have been made to end ICC investigations in Central African Republic and Uganda in order to facilitate nascent peace processes. Yet such efforts are always careful to emphasize the AU's 'unflinching commitment to combating impunity'.[66] But here again the invocation of the anti-impunity norm and more particular Rome Statute rules has proved a double-edged sword as it provided an avenue for contestation that was seized upon by UNSC members to reject the deferral requests.[67] From the perspective of Council members, the ICC legal processes against Bashir and Kenyatta did not constitute a threat to international peace and security necessary to warrant the invocation of Article 16. The language of accountability was privileged, in other words, with justice and peace mutually reinforcing rather than sequentially ordered. At the same time, the inclusion of the UNSC drew attention to concerns for sovereignty, fairness, and stability in the international order. In response, the AU has sought to shift the primary international forum for *political* deliberations regarding accountability from the UNSC to the General Assembly (UNGA)—a setting where they possess greater decision-making authority—by amending Article 16 to empower the UNGA to authorize deferrals in the face of UNSC inaction.[68] Such a change could usher in an expanded use of deferrals (which have never been invoked by the UNSC); but as with other initiatives the proposal has received little support among other ICC members.

[63] Carrie McDougall, *The Crime of Aggression Under the Rome Statute of the International Criminal Court* (CUP 2013).

[64] Bower, *Norms Without the Great Powers* (n 43) 168–72.

[65] African Union (AU) (Assembly of the AU), 'Decision on the Implementation of the Decisions of the International Criminal Court Doc. EX.CL/639(XVIII)' (AU Addis Ababa 31 January 2011) Assembly/AU/Dec.334(XVI) para 6; AU (Assembly of the AU), 'Decision on Africa's Relationship with the International Criminal Court (ICC)' (AU Addis Ababa 12 October 2013) Ext/Assembly/AU/Dec.1-2(Oct.2013) and Ext/Assembly/AU/Decl.1-4 para 10 ii, ix–xi.

[66] AU (Peace and Security Council), 'Communiqué of the 175th Meeting of the Peace and Security Council' (AU Addis Ababa 5 March 2009) PSC/PR/Comm.(CLXXV)Rev.1.

[67] Bower, *Norms Without the Great Powers* (n 43) 143, 147–48; Bower, 'Contesting the ICC' (n 9) 96.

[68] ICC, 'Report of the Working Group on Amendments' (n 58) Annex I sec V.

## 4.4 Location of Accountability Processes

A key consequence of the UNSC's selective employment of its powers has been to further sharpen critiques amongst African states who have taken the episodes as evidence of a fundamental lack of respect for regional perspectives and the needs of local populations.[69] A range of African leaders complain that the targeting of Bashir and later Kenyan President Uhuru Kenyatta is emblematic of a fundamental bias in the ICC's case selection in which African conflicts are singled-out for scrutiny while other potential situations elsewhere are ignored. This unfair skewing in the geographic distribution of ICC operations is said to reinforce 'racist' attitudes toward Africa amounting to a further imposition of 'neo-colonial' control over African states and the diminishment of their sovereign independence.

The sub-text of these disputes ultimately concerns the most appropriate venue for addressing atrocity, and the interaction between justice and sovereignty has often revolved around the conditions under which criminal accountability should be pursued. While the Rome Statute creates a new global institution it also seeks to stimulate a revolution in accountability at the domestic level. The preamble and Article 17 thus enshrine an expectation that the ICC will be complementary to national jurisdictions, but that the Court ultimately retains the final say in determining the capacity and willingness of state and sub-state actors to effectively investigate and prosecute atrocity crimes. Yet the Statute remains vague with respect to the criteria used to evaluate state progress, making it difficult to render judgments about the proper balance between international and national authority in the abstract.[70] Moreover, governments typically resist oversight of their national security policies and domestic legal processes even in instances where they have previously ceded some sovereign control by joining institutions like the ICC.

Given these sensitivities, complementarity has become a further battleground upon which states have sought to exert influence over the legal processes in current and prospective ICC situations. For example, both Sudan and Kenya engaged with the ICC at the outset of the investigations and sought to convince the Court that national processes—which included the creation of new legislation and domestic tribunals, and the initiation of investigations—met the standard of complementarity.[71] In both instances, the Court determined that the complementarity standard was not met.[72] Complementarity has also proven a useful tool for the Court to manage its caseload

[69] Benson Chinedu Olugbuo, 'The African Union, the United Nations Security Council and the Politicisation of International Justice in Africa' (2014) 7 African Journal of Legal Studies 351; Abel S Knottnerus, 'The AU, the ICC, and the Prosecution of African Presidents' in Kamari M Clarke, Abel S Knottnerus, and Eefje de Volder (eds) *Africa and the ICC: Perceptions of Justice* (CUP 2016); Bower, *Norms Without the Great Powers* (n 43) 159–67.

[70] Stahn and El Zeidy (n 33).

[71] *The Prosecutor v William Samoei Ruto, Henry Kiprono Kosgey and Joshua Arap Sang and the Prosecutor v Francis Kirimi Muthaura, Uhuru Muigai Kenyatta and Mohammes Hussein Ali* (Application) ICC-01/09-01/11-19 (31 March 2011); ICC, 'Statement by the Delegation of The Sudan, as Observer. Delivered by Ambassador Sirajuddin Hamid Yousuf, Director, Department of International Law and Treaties, MFA, Sudan' (23 December 2006) <https://asp.icc-cpi.int/iccdocs/asp_docs/library/asp/ICC-ASP5_Statement_sudan.pdf> accessed 26 February 2022.

[72] *Situation: Situation in the Republic of Kenya* (Appeals Chamber Decision) ICC-01/09-78 (12 August 2011).

through the adoption of 'positive complementarity' in which the threat of ICC action can encourage national transformations in places like Colombia.[73] Most obviously, the decision of the Pre-Trial Chamber that the case against Abdullah Al-Senussi was inadmissible before the ICC as there was a credible ongoing investigation against the defendant in Libya seems hard to defend on the legal merits.[74] A similar determination was not forthcoming with respect to another key ICC indictee, Saif Al-Islam Gaddafi, despite the government of Libya's claim that a domestic prosecution should take precedence.[75]

The international criminal justice regime admits no exceptions, at least with respect to those bearing greatest responsibility for alleged crimes, but a persistent theme of the ICC's first 15 years has been whether and when any allowances should be made for other approaches to accountability. Criminal punishment might therefore be unsuited to specific circumstances in which mass violence is not easily linked to the actions of discrete individuals.[76] Nothing in the Rome Statute forecloses the employment of alternative mechanisms such as lustration, truth-and-reconciliation, or community-based remedies alongside criminal processes. But in some circumstances, such efforts might be judged to be preferable to *any* form of prosecution. In addition, governments may wish to utilize amnesties or asylum in order to incentivize the cessation of hostilities, facilitate the integration of former belligerents, or simply avoid legal scrutiny altogether. The emphasis on trials thus partially constrains the policy options available to states in dealing with complex societal challenges. In Uganda, for example, the leadership of the Lord's Resistance Army has previously demanded the withdrawal of ICC arrest warrants against Joseph Kony and his associates as a pre-condition for their surrender and participation in a peace process. The government of Uganda has agitated for ICC to honour this demand, something the Court has refused to consider.[77] Consequently, at least some resistance to ICC investigations among African governments stems from a frustration at losing control over the political process of which these alleged crimes are a part.

In light of these and other disputes the AU has expanded the jurisdiction of the African Court of Human and People's rights to encompass ICC crimes.[78] This might be viewed as a positive development that enhances criminal justice capacity within the African region, thereby alleviating some of the ICC's burden while at the same time ameliorating concerns for domination by a supranational institution. Yet this alternative location for accountability also represents a challenge to the anti-impunity norm

[73] Diego Acosta Arcarazo, Russell Buchan, and Rene Ureña, 'Beyond Justice, Beyond Peace? Colombia, the Interests of Justice, and the Limits of International Criminal Law' (2015) 26 Criminal Law Forum 291; René Urueña, 'Prosecutorial Politics: The ICC's Influence in Colombian Peace Processes, 2003–2017' (2017) 111 American Journal of International Law 104.

[74] This ruling was subsequently upheld on appeal. *The Prosecutor v Saif Al-Islam Gaddafi and Abdullah Al-Senussi* (Judgement) ICC-OI/II-OI/IIOA6 (24 July 2014) <www.icc-cpi.int/CourtRecords/CR2014_06755.PDF> accessed 20 February 2022.

[75] ICC, 'Decision on the admissibility of the case against Saif Al-Islam Gaddafi' (31 May 2013) ICC-01/11-01/11 <www.icc-cpi.int/CourtRecords/CR2013_04031.PDF> accessed 26 February 2022.

[76] Drumbl (n 27).

[77] Bower, *Norms Without the Great Powers* (n 43) 141–42.

[78] AU (Assembly of the AU), 'Protocol on Amendments to the Protocol on the Statute of the African Court of Justice and Human Rights' (adopted 27 June 2014, not yet entered into force) 18–25, 38–39.

as embodied in the Rome Statute, since the revised African Court's jurisdiction explicitly exempts senior state officials during their time in office.[79]

## 4.5 Non-Compliance and International Response

Lee Seymour[80] has argued that '[t]he diplomatic campaign waged by African states against the ICC can be understood as a form of rhetorical action premised on the exposure of hypocrisy'. The AU has on a number of occasions decried '[t]he obstinacy of ... the Prosecutor, the Registrar and the President of the ICC, which continues to privilege the views of civil society over clearly held positions of African Member States parties to the Rome Statute'.[81] The perceived incongruities between an invasive supranational legal order and respect for regional and national prerogatives has generated a range of discursive challenges, the instrumentalization of legal resources, and attempted institutional renegotiation—as discussed already—and has further given rise to overt disobedience.

The most obvious—and damaging—manifestation of this is found in the AU's policy opposing cooperation with the Bashir and Kenyatta investigations.[82] This challenge to ICC authority has been enabled both inside and outside of the African continent. President Bashir visited over 20 non-parties and ICC member states as a show of deliberate defiance of his arrest warrant.[83] The majority of states civil society actors expressed concern over and opposed any modification of the ICC's anti-impunity norm, but neither the ICC Assembly of States Parties nor the UNSC have taken any action to enforce compliance with ICC obligations. Obstruction by Sudan, Kenya, and their allies—and the subsequent failure to back public statements of support for the ICC with practical action—undermined the ICC investigations leading to a suspension of the investigation in Darfur and the outright collapse of the cases against Mr Kenyatta and his deputy Mr Ruto.[84] The more recent AU proposal for a mass exodus of African states from the Rome Statute, mirrored in Burundi's recent withdrawal and similar threats from Kenya, South Africa, and The Gambia, are similarly troubling.[85] This, in turn, has created political conditions whereby a de facto exemption for sitting Heads of State may coalesce, a point I return to briefly in the Conclusion.

Yet here I depart from the more despairing analyses that regard the ICC as in the midst of a potentially terminal decline. While current contestation surrounding the Court is indeed serious, the forms of challenge also contain within them the possibility

[79] ibid art 46A *bis*.

[80] Seymour (n 38) 116.

[81] AU (Assembly of the AU), 'Decision on the International Criminal Court – Doc. EX.CL/952(XXVIII)' (AU Addis Ababa, 31 January 2016) Assembly/AU/Dec.590(XXVI) para 9 i.

[82] AU (Assembly of the AU), 'Decision on the Meeting of African States Parties to the Rome Statute of the International Criminal Tribunal (ICC)' (AU Sirte 3 July 2009) Assembly/AU/Dec.245(XIII) Rev.1 para 10; AU (Assembly of the AU) 2016 (n 81) para 2 iv.

[83] All Africa, 'Sudan: 75 Trips to 22 Countries in 7 Years – an Indicted War Criminal's Travels' (*Nuba Reports*, 7 March 2016) <https://allafrica.com/stories/201603071669.html> accessed 06 December 2021.

[84] ICC, 'Press Release: Trial Chamber V(B) Terminates the Proceedings' (13 March 2015) ICC-CPI-20150313-PR1099 <https://www.icc-cpi.int/pages/item.aspx?name=pr1099> accessed 20 February 2022.

[85] AU, 'Decision on the International Criminal Court' (n 81) para 10 iv.

for resisting norm erosion and even reinvigorating the ICC as a global justice project. Elsewhere I have argued that engagements between states and the Court are complex and by no means uniform even within regional groupings like the African Union.[86] In the face of dramatic contestation from (some) governments, concerted pressure from domestic and transnational civil society has provided an alternative narrative insisting on fidelity to impartial and universal justice. In some cases—such as South Africa and Kenya—these public efforts have spurred national deliberations that have meaningfully constrained state action by forcing governments to cancel or abbreviate visits by Mr Bashir and subjecting proposed withdrawal processes to legal scrutiny that has stalled these efforts. Indeed, after much initial clamour it appears—for the moment, at least—that the threat of mass withdrawal has receded and with it one major existential threat to the Court.

## 5. Conclusion: Pathways of Norm Change

The ICC is clearly facing a number of serious challenges to its legitimacy, only a few of which have been detailed here. The emergence and widespread adoption of the Rome Statute has not resolved foundational concerns for how the sovereign affairs of the state can be preserved but also meaningfully constrained within a supranational legal order. As has been shown, there remain multiple overlapping disagreements concerning the practical meaning and limits of the anti-impunity norm in global politics. While this chapter has sought first and foremost to identify these main cleavages, it also advanced some theoretically informed assumptions concerning the relationship between forms of contestation and norm change. Most broadly, the interaction of competing sovereignty and accountability norms have provided rhetorical resources by which actors contest the implications of a universalist conception of anti-impunity. States have on various occasions sought to resist inconvenient applications of ICC authority by invoking norms of non-interference, legal equality, and consent as justification for constraining the Court's jurisdiction.

I am not convinced that this amounts to a fundamental erosion of the ICC's normative mandate or the wider international rule of law, however.[87] Here an important distinction needs to be made between widespread rejections of the norm as such, and efforts aimed at interrogating its features.[88] Challenges to the underlying foundations of a norm are more damaging because they raise questions concerning the norm's legitimate basis within the wider international system. The campaign by (some) African states and the African Union to discredit the Court thus raises the prospect of a fundamental rupture in the international response to atrocity. Yet the more visceral attacks on the ICC's institutional legitimacy have not been widely endorsed outside the African continent; within the region too there are many examples of mobilization by

[86] Bower, 'Contesting the ICC' (n 9) 99.

[87] My brief analysis here draws on arguments presented in Bower, 'Contesting the ICC' (n 9).

[88] This distinction is developed in Nicole Deitelhoff and Lisbeth Zimmermann, 'Norms under Challenge: Unpacking the Dynamics of Norm Robustness' (2019) 4 Journal of Global Security Studies 2; Nicole Deitelhoff and Lisbeth Zimmerman, 'Things We Lost in the Fire: How Different Types of Contestation Affect the Robustness of International Norms' (2020) 22 International Studies Review 51.

governments, civil society, and domestic publics in support of the ICC even as many of these same actors recognize the pervasive imbalances in the international system. And even the contesting states themselves continue to officially reaffirm their commitment to ending impunity—albeit under revised conditions.

Instead, the more plausible pathway for norm change involves the gradual and informal narrowing of the anti-impunity norm to recognize some exceptions. The ultimate purpose of many of the episodes described above has been to place international accountability under greater state control, most especially by creating exemptions for senior state officials and further privileging national-level responses. Instrumental invocations of ICC rules have in some instances facilitated the avoidance of inconvenient constraints, as when the Bush administration temporarily gained international acquiescence with its bilateral non-surrender initiative and African states sought to limit the scope of the immunities regime to exclude sitting Heads of State. In many of the more consequential cases, however, this strategy ultimately backfired because it provided the rhetorical means to mobilize counter-contestation, as seen in the US experience and the efforts of African states to secure deferrals via the UNSC. The lack of progress in forcing institutional amendments has led aggrieved states to open defiance, and it is this alloying of argument and action that holds the greatest prospect for altering the anti-impunity norm. The refusal of the international community to systematically address persistent non-compliance has opened the possibility that inaction will harden into a de facto modification of the norm which effectively excludes sitting Heads of State from the ICC's legal scope. This would constitute a blow to the ICC's promise to prosecute those bearing greatest responsibility and represent a partial rebalancing in favour of sovereign prerogatives at the expense of universal accountability.

Forms of contestation are inherent to global politics and norms are consequently subject to regular disputes involving interpretation, challenge, and reinforcement. These intersubjective processes can lead to the expansion or contraction of social standards—even ones articulated in formal legal texts. This chapter has argued that enduring tensions in the operationalization and prioritization of state sovereignty and accountability represent one key source of political and legal friction in the ICC's first decades. While challenges can weaken the anti-impunity norm—especially when disputes become entrenched—forms of contestation by their nature also provide opportunities for other actors to resist a narrowing of the ICC's accountability mandate. Rather than assessing the fate of global justice through discrete episodes, scholars and practitioners are therefore well advised to take a long-term view. Equally, those seeking to uphold or transform the ICC's scope must remain vigilant in working to bolster their preferred manifestation of the non-impunity norm that, despite the many disagreements and inconsistencies, retains broad aspirational appeal in the contemporary international system.

# 11
# Ideological Values and Norm Contestation in the ICC
## The Afghanistan Investigation and American Opposition to Article 12(2)(a) Jurisdiction

*Malcolm Jorgensen*

## 1. Introduction

On 20 November 2017, former International Criminal Court (ICC) prosecutor Fatou Bensouda took the historic step of formally requesting authorization from the Pre-Trial Chamber (PTC) of the Court to investigate alleged crimes committed in connection with the war in Afghanistan (2001–2021).[1] Particularly noteworthy was that the investigation would include alleged crimes by United States (US) military and official personnel, including the following:[2]

> War crimes of torture, outrages upon personal dignity and rape and other forms of sexual violence, by members of the US armed forces on the territory of Afghanistan and members of the CIA in secret detention facilities both in Afghanistan and on the territory of other States Parties, principally in the 2003-2004 period.

The ICC appeared to enter uncharted territory by, for the first time, setting its authority and hard-fought judicial independence against the Court's most powerful and persistent critic and was lauded accordingly, for upholding a conception of international criminal accountability in which 'no one is above the law'.[3] Yet, less than four years later, Bensouda's successor Karim Khan announced that the investigation would proceed only in relation to allegations against the Taliban and the Islamic State, effectively terminating investigation of US (and Afghan) personnel, but while framing that decision as consistent with ICC commitment to 'promote accountability efforts'.[4]

[1] International Criminal Court (ICC), 'Situation in Afghanistan: Summary of the Prosecutor's Request for Authorisation of an Investigation Pursuant to Article 15' (20 November 2017) <www.icc-cpi.int/itemsDocuments/Afghanistan/171120-afgh-art_15-app-summ_ENG.pdf> accessed 4 February 2022.

[2] ibid 6; ICC, 'Report on Preliminary Examination Activities' (14 November 2016) 44, 47 <www.icc-cpi.int/itemsDocuments/2020-PE/2020-pe-report-eng.pdf> accessed 4 February 2022.

[3] Katherine Gallagher, 'International Crimes Committed in Afghanistan: Towards ICC Prosecutions of All Operating Forces?' (*Center for Constitutional Rights*, 3 November 2017) <https://ccrjustice.org/home/press-center/press-releases/international-crimes-committed-afghanistan-towards-icc-prosecutions> accessed 3 February 2022.

[4] Karim AA Khan, 'Statement of the Prosecutor of the International Criminal Court, Karim A. A. Khan QC, following the application for an expedited order under article 18(2) seeking authorisation to

Malcolm Jorgensen, *Ideological Values and Norm Contestation in the ICC* In: *Tracing Value Change in the International Legal Order*. Edited by: Heike Krieger and Andrea Liese, Oxford University Press. © Malcolm Jorgensen 2023.
DOI: 10.1093/oso/9780192855831.003.0011

The present chapter explores this arc of shifting assertions of ICC jurisdiction over US personnel in the Afghanistan investigation, which presents a crucial case for examining evidence for norm and value change in the international legal order. The central claim is that ideologies held by legal policymakers have structured conflicted interpretations of the underlying values of global order from the beginning, such that the Rome Statute was never founded on any true universality in the value conceptions of negotiating states. Competing interpretations of ICC legal norms have, in consequence, divided American policymakers from global counterparts and American policymakers from one another. Understanding this ideological contestation can illuminate what Patryk Labuda has described as the 'growing philosophical disagreement within the ICC about the institution's future priorities'.[5] The Afghanistan investigation has crystallized ideational divisions into a substantive conflict, with the fate of this most consequential international criminal justice institution offering systemic insights into the dynamics of value change in the legal order as a whole.

The chapter begins by identifying the competing ideological values at the foundations of the ICC project, which are drawn from prior interdisciplinary research in international law and international relations (IR).[6] This work demonstrates that American legal policymakers interpret international legal accountability as having a positive relationship with robust US national sovereignty, which directly contradicts the beliefs of global counterparts committed to accountability through ICC independence. The second section of the chapter explores the implications of ideology in the Afghanistan case, in which divided value interpretations have manifested in conflicted interpretations of ICC jurisdiction over nationals of non-parties to the Rome Statute. The case demonstrates the ways in which ideologically informed values enable but also constrain the agency of international lawyers in developing ICC legal norms toward less contested interpretations. The chapter concludes by turning to consider the influence of US practice on the ICC itself, which is increasingly evident in a turn to 'pragmatism' in the exercise of jurisdictional power. Confirmation of such a trend will force fundamental questions about the values and future authority of the Court.

## 2. Ideology and Underlying Values of the ICC

A commitment to the international 'rule of law' has been held out for more than a generation as the common focal point for states and actors contributing to the ICC

resume investigations in the Situation in Afghanistan' (27 September 2021) <www.icc-cpi.int/Pages/item.aspx?name=2021-09-27-otp-statement-afghanistan> accessed 3 February 2022.

[5] Patryk I Labuda, 'A Neo-Colonial Court for Weak States? Not Quite. Making Sense of the International Criminal Court's Afghanistan Decision' (*EJIL: Talk*, 13 April 2019) <www.ejiltalk.org/a-neo-colonial-court-for-weak-states-not-quite-making-sense-of-the-international-criminal-courts-afghanistan-decision/> accessed 3 February 2022.

[6] See Malcolm Jorgensen, *American Foreign Policy Ideology and The International Rule of Law: Contesting Power Through the International Criminal Court* (CUP 2020) 9–11.

project. At the conclusion of the Rome Statute in 1998, Antonio Cassese saw the Court as heralding 'a new world order based on the rule of international law',[7] while at a United Nations (UN) meeting on the rule of law over a decade later, the UN Secretary General described the ICC as 'the centre of the new system of international criminal justice'.[8] US officials have expressed parallel sentiments, with former Ambassador at Large for War Crimes David Scheffer, and one of the most significant American officials in ICC history, describing support for the ICC as making credible US claims that it 'took the rule of law seriously'.[9] Yet the history of the Court has remained one of persistent tension between US and non-US legal policymakers, with common critiques of American practice as 'a high-profile rejection of a major initiative for the rule of law in international affairs'.[10] US refusal to join the ICC 'despite its seeming reification of American values' remains a source of frustration among global counterparts.[11]

The first part of this chapter seeks to explain these tensions through interdisciplinary research from the IR subfield of Foreign Policy Analysis (FPA), which corresponds with the level of analysis necessary to identify the underlying values of the ICC as understood by real policymakers.[12] It is thus useful to restate the objectives of this exchange between disciplines, which share an overlapping 'territory' but are separated by distinct 'tribal cultures'.[13] The shared territory is a basic concern about forms of governance in the international system, but, as historical cycles of convergence and divergence demonstrate, these remain 'distinct disciplines because their fundamental objectives differ. In international relations, the objective is to understand behaviour. In international law, the objective is to direct behaviour'.[14] The objective of the present chapter is thus not to dissolve disciplinary identity but, rather, to assess legal scholarship on its own terms and identify limitations that can be addressed by political science.[15] Particularly relevant is Thomas Kleinlein's observation that 'mainstream positivism has some difficulties conceptualizing interpretive change'.[16] Precisely because of legal scholarship's conscious distance from empirical methods, it remains reliant on political science to explain the causes and dynamics of contestation.[17]

[7] Antonio Cassese, 'On the Current Trends Towards Criminal Prosecution and Punishment of Breaches of International Humanitarian Law' (1998) 9 European Journal of International Law 2, 8.

[8] United Nations Security Council (UNSC), 6849th Meeting (17 October 2012) UN Doc S/PV.6849, 2.

[9] David J Scheffer, *All the Missing Souls: A Personal History of the War Crimes Tribunals* (Princeton University Press 2012) 172.

[10] Abram Chayes and Anne-Marie Slaughter, 'The ICC and the Future of the Global Legal System' in Sarah B Sewell and Carl Kaysen (eds), *The United States and the International Criminal Court: National Security and International Law* (Rowman & Littlefield Publishers 2000) 238.

[11] Harlan G Cohen, 'The American Challenge to International Law: A Tentative Framework for Debate' (2003) 28 Yale Journal of International Law 551, 572.

[12] See generally Valerie M Hudson and Benjamin S Day, *Foreign Policy Analysis: Classic and Contemporary Theory* (3rd edn, Rowman & Littlefield 2020).

[13] Tony Becher and Paul Trowler, *Academic Tribes and Territories: Intellectual Inquiry and the Cultures of Disciplines* (Open University Press 2001) 25, 60.

[14] Charlotte Ku, *International Law, International Relations, and Global Governance* (Routledge 2012) 26.

[15] Douglas W Vick, 'Interdisciplinarity and the Discipline of Law' (2004) 31 Journal of Law and Society 163, 165.

[16] Thomas Kleinlein, Chapter 4 in this book, 25.

[17] Edward L Rubin, 'Law and the Methodology of Law' (1997) Wisconsin Law Review 521, 521, 553.

## 2.1 Conceptualizing Ideology in Legal Scholarship

An important point of commencement for this book is the widespread sense in the immediate post-Cold War years that ever-growing forms of multilateralism evidenced 'a deeper normative consensus that had been reached within the international community'.[18] Yet, any attempts to specify and define the content of international community values—especially of the 'rule of law' itself—must confront the reality that 'everyone is for it, but have contrasting convictions about what it is'.[19] Critical here is Fallon's observation that it becomes:

> impossible even to make sense of the ideal of the Rule of Law without reference to values or purposes that it serves. And those values or purposes, once specified, inevitably furnish the ground for contestable arguments that the Rule of Law could be most fully realized only if the substantive law assumed a particular content.[20]

Here FPA offers a useful analytical approach, since its primary focus is not on the behaviours that exist *between* states (as in orthodox IR), but rather on the agency of 'human decision-makers' *within* each state as bearers of specific ideologies and legal beliefs.[21] Here David Davis's definition of ideology is apposite, as 'an integrated system of beliefs, assumptions, and values, not necessarily true or false, which reflects the needs and interests of a group or class at a particular time in history'.[22] Jonathan Zasloff notes that, by accepting this definition, legal policymakers' beliefs cannot be dismissed as merely 'a cynical cover for the naked pursuit of self-interest'. Rather, 'ideologies carry power precisely because they allow people to believe that they are acting properly while at the same time serving their own interests. Legitimation, then, is directed more at the producer of ideology than at the consumer'.[23] Thus, the norms of legal order do not emerge from a mere process of logical deduction from universal values, but rather through the particularistic interests and worldviews of its authors.[24]

The present author has previously adopted this approach to segment American legal policymakers' conceptions of international law into four competing ideological interpretations drawn from FPA, each of which corresponds with divisions evident in legal scholarship and diplomatic history.[25] In Max Weber's terms, each such

[18] Heike Krieger and Andrea Liese, Chapter 1 in this book, 2.

[19] Brian Z Tamanaha, *On the Rule of Law* (CUP 2004) 3; see Anthea Roberts, *Is International Law International?* (OUP 2017) 2.

[20] Richard H Fallon Jr., '"The Rule of Law" as a Concept in Constitutional Discourse' (1997) 97 Columbia Law Review 1, 54.

[21] Valerie M Hudson, 'Foreign Policy Analysis: Actor-Specific Theory and the Ground of International Relations' (2005) 1 Foreign Policy Analysis 1, 2; see generally Joel H Westra, 'International Law and Foreign Policy' in *Oxford Research Encyclopedia of Politics* (24 May 2017) <https://doi.org/10.1093/acrefore/9780190228637.013.439> accessed 28 March 2022.

[22] David B Davis, *The Problem of Slavery in the Age of Revolution, 1770–1823* (Cornell University Press 1975) 14.

[23] Jonathan M Zasloff, 'Law and the Shaping of American Foreign Policy: From the Gilded Age to the New Era' (2003) 78 New York University Law Review 239, 248. Citations removed.

[24] Fallon (n 20) 7, 17.

[25] These ideal types are identified as 'liberal internationalism', 'illiberal internationalism', 'liberal nationalism', and 'illiberal nationalism': see Jorgensen (n 6) 74, 88.

ideology constitutes an 'ideal type', in the sense of being analytical constructs that usefully capture patterns of observed behaviour, without claiming to be an account of any particular person's belief system.[26] Nevertheless, identifying these ideal ideological types allows for an understanding of dynamics of norm change at the level of US international legal policy which, when disaggregated from global trends, can be observed to switch and revert between a finite number of pre-determined tracks—reminiscent of Weber's famous railway analogy.[27] Thus, although the words and actions of all states might explicitly or implicitly support the value of 'accountability' in international criminal law, the evidence shows that, even at the height of US support for the ICC, the substantive interpretation of that value has been shaped by divergent and shifting ideological understandings of what that means in terms of norms of international law.

### 2.2 Prevailing Conceptions: Negative Relationship Between Sovereignty and Accountability

There has of course been significant divergence in the value conceptions of the many states opposing US ICC policy, but a largely united approach has consolidated over time between the so called 'Like Minded States' (LMS) as a bloc of over 60 countries, the European Union, and the Coalition for the ICC, as the peak body for the Non-Governmental Organizations (NGOs) that have occupied such a uniquely influential and officially sanctioned role.[28] These voices have consistently advocated for accountability through norms that separate ICC judicial powers from 'executive' and 'legislative' type global governance powers, which are exercised directly by states, or indirectly through international organizations such as the UN Security Council (UNSC). No domestic legal system based on the rule of law would vest executive control over the judiciary, nor would it allow citizens to determine the legality of their own actions under the state's criminal jurisdiction. Likewise, international law must seek to constrain the discretion of states to determine their own global privileges and obligations.[29] Because the political foundations of the ICC remain embedded in the consent of sovereign states, there is an ever-present risk posed by 'their self-interested agendas [that] are still often at odds with international accountability'.[30]

Advocates of this conception of accountability have sought to diminish sovereign prerogatives in favour of a range of alternative normative foundations for the Court. French jurist Robert Badinter argued that depoliticization would ultimately be upheld

[26] Max Weber, *The Methodology of the Social Sciences* (The Free Press 1949) 90.

[27] Jorgensen (n 6) 261; Max Weber, 'The Social Psychology of the World Religions' in Hans H Gerth and C Wright Mills (eds), *From Max Weber: Essays in Sociology* (OUP 1946) 280.

[28] See M Cherif Bassiouni, *The Legislative History of the International Criminal Court: Introduction, Analysis, and Integrated Text of the Statute, Elements of Crimes and Rules of Procedure and Evidence* (Transnational Publishers 2005) 74–75.

[29] Rosalyn Higgins, *Themes and Theories: Selected Essays, Speeches, and Writings in International Law* (OUP 2009) 1330–31.

[30] Emanuela Piccolo Koskimies, *Norm Contestation, Sovereignty and (Ir)responsibility at the International Criminal Court: Debunking Liberal Anti-Politics* (Springer 2022) 134.

by 'NGOs dedicated to humanitarian action' and 'public opinion',[31] while others have emphasized the claimed absence of great power aspirations among LMS: 'Because they were not global powers, they thought of themselves as more able to construct international architecture that would be perceived as fair and legitimate by the rest of the world'.[32] The ICC itself has responded to strident US objections to the Afghanistan investigation by reiterating its character as 'an independent and impartial institution' that, 'as a court of law, will continue to do its work undeterred, in accordance with those principles and the overarching idea of the rule of law'.[33] A prevailing conception can thus be identified, according to which accountability requires the transcendence of sovereignty through ICC independence from national politics.

## 2.3 US Conceptions: Positive Relationship Between Sovereignty and Accountability

The entire history of US engagement with the ICC demonstrates that appeals to the rule of law based on the separation of sovereignty and accountability have had limited resonance. The US has contested such conceptions not through bare denials of the value of accountability itself, but through ideologically informed arguments about America's 'exceptional' status and role in promoting this value.[34] Hilary Charlesworth defines 'American exceptionalism' in this context as a belief that 'while other states should comply with international legal norms, it is not appropriate to subject the United States to the same regime'. The reasons for this include a belief that 'the United States is already an exemplary international citizen and its domestic legal system can be relied on to provide appropriate accountability and/or the expectation that international law will inevitably be used in a politicized way to discriminate against the United States'.[35] The aforementioned four ideal ideological types each offer a distinct understanding of American uniqueness that, when taken together, represent the different faces of 'American exceptionalism'.[36] Two in particular, termed here 'liberal internationalism' and 'illiberal internationalism', well illustrate the normative assumptions that underpin seemingly contradictory US engagement with the ICC.

Adherents of *liberal* internationalism have perceived the rule of international law as the externalization of American constitutional government to establish a system of transnational law, with international and national legal systems reinforcing universal

[31] Robert Badinter, 'International Criminal Justice: From Darkness to Light,' in Antonio Cassese, Paola Gaeta, and John RWD Jones (eds), *The Rome Statute of the International Criminal Court: A Commentary* (OUP 2002) 1934.

[32] David Bosco, *Rough Justice: The International Criminal Court's Battle to Fix the World, One Prosecution at a Time* (OUP 2014) 39.

[33] ICC, 'The ICC Will Continue Its Independent and Impartial Work, Undeterred' (12 September 2018) <www.icc-cpi.int/Pages/item.aspx?name=pr1406> accessed 3 February 2022.

[34] See generally Byron E Shafer, 'American Exceptionalism' (1999) 2 Annual Review of Political Science 445.

[35] Hilary Charlesworth, *No Country is an Island: Australia and International Law* (University of New South Wales Press 2006) 147.

[36] See Jorgensen (n 6) 68–69.

liberal values.[37] Although this ideology thus supports an ever-deeper framework of international institutions governing global politics, it does so privileging American power and values as central to the project. The significance of this distinction is that robust US sovereignty remains complementary and even necessary to an effective system of international criminal accountability. Slaughter pithily asserts the central belief of 'liberal internationalism' as being that: 'the global rule of law depends on the domestic rule of law'.[38] There is no mechanism in the primitive structure of the international legal system to ensure that international courts determine rights and duties solely on a principled basis, and thus they cannot rest on mere good faith of its participants, or the strength of institutional design. American constitutional government is seen to provide that political foundation, such that the 'backstopping' function of international courts is understood as a check on other national legal systems more than the US itself.[39] Harold Koh, US State Department legal adviser under President Barack Obama, remains a prominent voice for liberal internationalist beliefs, including recognition of an exceptional US role in promoting the values that make international law work.[40] This is a commitment to liberalism that carries with it the justifications for setting aside 'absolutist, formalist, textualist, originalist' legal interpretations in favour of political recognition that 'international law should serve human purposes'.[41]

The beliefs of *illiberal* internationalism likewise recognize the value of active US engagement with global rules and institutions, but diverge in doing so foremost to facilitate US strategic autonomy and to incorporate diplomatic justifications within the law.[42] Most relevant for understanding ICC policy, this ideological approach favours a 'pragmatist' method that treats the development of international law as 'a multifaceted method of problem-solving rather than a formula for finding a single, correct solution'.[43] According to this view, 'reliance upon formal legalist categories masks the decision-making process that actually occurs, which is situationally contingent'.[44] Applying this principle to the vexed question of whether the Geneva Conventions applied to Al-Qaeda and Taliban detainees during the war in Afghanistan, Michael Glennon considered the full range of factors, including the negative reactions of US allies and the status of US prisoners of war seeking reciprocal protections. For Glennon, '[w]hether such factors are, strictly speaking, legal or political is, to the pragmatist lawyer, beside the point: in the real world, these are, to varying degrees,

[37] Anne-Marie Burley, 'Regulating the World: Multilateralism, International Law, and the Projection of the New Deal Regulatory State' in John Gerard Ruggie (ed), *Multilateralism Matters: The Theory and Praxis of an Institutional Form* (Columbia University Press 1993) 144.

[38] Anne-Marie Slaughter and Jose E Alvarez, 'A Liberal Theory of International Law' (2000) 94 Proceedings of the Annual Meeting (American Society of International Law) 240, 246.

[39] The terminology of 'backstopping' in international law is from Slaughter, who applies it specifically to describe the ICC complementarity regime: See Anne-Marie Slaughter and William Burke-White, 'The Future of International Law Is Domestic (or, the European Way of Law)' (2006) 47 Harvard International Law Journal 327, 339–40.

[40] See Harold H Koh, 'On American Exceptionalism' (2003) 55 Stanford Law Review 1479.

[41] Harold H Koh, *The Trump Administration and International Law* (Oxford University Press 2019) 129–30.

[42] Jorgensen (n 6) 101.

[43] Michael J Glennon, *The Fog of Law: Pragmatism, Security, and International Law* (Woodrow Wilson Center Press 2010) 2.

[44] ibid 3.

the kinds of factors that international lawyers do take into account'.[45] In so doing, pragmatism 'serves to protect international law from itself', which is threatened by formalism to become 'ever more internally "pure" but ever more disconnected from the world of international politics where, ultimately, it must live'.[46] John Bellinger, State Department legal adviser under President George W Bush, is an exemplar of this legal approach, having argued that the administration's 'general approach to international courts and tribunals is pragmatic'. By this he meant that international courts were foremost 'potential tools to advance shared international interests in developing and promoting the rule of law, ensuring justice and accountability, and solving legal disputes'.[47]

Ideology thus dissolves any clear binary opposition 'between sovereignty and the internationalized fight against impunity', which is at the heart of contestation over the rule of law values most fundamental to the ICC.[48] Certainly, significant divisions have existed between US policymakers and agencies influenced by different ideological commitments, but they have been as one, and unmoved, on the principle that the Court's jurisdictional reach must remain subject to forms of US oversight. Jamison Borek, as deputy legal adviser at the State Department, specifically acknowledged criticism that US demands for a controlling UNSC role over the ICC might appear to have the effect of 'unduly tainting the independence of a judicial body'. She responded however that, under alternative proposals, 'the initiation of cases would be subject to whatever political agenda a particular State may have, rather than a collective decision by the Council that in fact would be less likely to reflect a political bias than that of an individual State'.[49] This was not merely a rejection of a particular institutional design, but of the very compatibility of robust ICC independence with the rule of law. These dynamics indicate the extent to which today's obvious lack of contemporary agreement on ICC norms can be traced back to fragmented conceptions of accountability, which have been present since the beginning.

## 3. The Afghanistan Investigation and US Opposition to Article 12(2)(a) Jurisdiction

The jurisdictional regime of the ICC was designed to be one based foremost on state consent to jurisdiction by virtue of court membership, but with the extension of that jurisdiction to all crimes committed in the territory of member states under Article 12(2)(a)—irrespective of whether an accused was a national of a member

[45] ibid 20.

[46] Kenneth Anderson, 'Readings: Michael Glennon on the "Incompleteness" of International Law Governing the Use of Force' (*Lawfare*, 13 May 2013) <www.lawfareblog.com/readings-michael-glennon-incompleteness-international-law-governing-use-force> accessed 3 February 2022.

[47] John B Bellinger III, 'International Courts and Tribunals and the Rule of Law' in Cesare PR Romano (ed), *The Sword and the Scales: The United States and International Courts and Tribunals* (CUP 2009) 2.

[48] See Adam Bower, Chapter 10 in this book.

[49] Jamison S Borek, 'Agenda Item 142: Establishment of An International Criminal Court' (1 November 1995) 3 <https://2009-2017.state.gov/documents/organization/65827.pdf> accessed 4 February 2022.

state.[50] The ICC's claim of jurisdiction in the Afghanistan investigation thus rested on Afghanistan's accession to the Rome Statute on 10 February 2003.[51] Defenders of Article 12(2)(a) have long noted that the right to exercise jurisdiction for crimes committed in a state's own territory is 'fundamental' since at least the landmark *Lotus Case* and the principle that, because there is no specific rule against delegation: 'Restrictions upon the independence of States cannot therefore be presumed.'[52] Moreover, as Cherif Bassiouni argues, this is a right 'to transfer jurisdiction to another state that has jurisdiction over an accused, *or to an international adjudicating body*'.[53] The claimed ICC norm is therefore an analogous 'delegation' of territorial jurisdiction to an international court that does not turn on additional state consent beyond that required in cases of extradition.[54]

US legal policymakers from across the political and ideological spectrum have been united from the beginning in rejecting the legality of any such exercise of jurisdiction, which has been described as the 'single most problematic part of the Rome Treaty'.[55] The right of Afghanistan to 'delegate'[56] its inherent territorial jurisdiction to the ICC under Article 12(2)(a) has crystallized the controversy over the positive or negative relationship between sovereignty and accountability, with the US warning that to proceed would be contrary to the Court 'exercising its power judiciously within the limits of international law'.[57] In particular, US legal policymakers have argued that the rights of US military and civilian personnel in Afghanistan are already governed by a series of overlapping Status of Forces Agreements (SOFA),[58] including a January 2002 agreement between the Interim Security Assistance Force and the then interim Afghanistan government.[59] That agreement stipulated that relevant personnel 'will

[50] Rome Statute of the International Criminal Court (adopted 17 July 1998, entered into force 1 July 2002) UN Doc A/CONF.183/9, art 12(2)(a). Jurisdiction is also established without the direct consent of a State where the UNSC refers a matter to the prosecutor under its Chapter VII powers: art 13(b). Jurisdiction in all cases remains subject to the principle of 'complementarity': art 17(1)(a).

[51] Instrument of ratification deposited on 10 February, 2003: See Rome Statute (n 50) art 126(2).

[52] See *S.S. Lotus, The (France v Turkey)* (Judgement) PCIJ Series A No 10, 18; Gerhard Hafner and others, 'A Response to the American View as Presented by Ruth Wedgwood' (1999) 10 European Journal of International Law 108, 117.

[53] Cherif M Bassiouni, *The Legislative History of the International Criminal Court: Introduction, Analysis, and Integrated Text of the Statute, Elements of Crimes and Rules of Procedure and Evidence* (Transnational Publishers 2005) 136; emphasis added.

[54] Antonio Cassese, Paola Gaeta, and John RWD Jones, 'The Rome Statute: A Tentative Assessment' in Antonio Cassese, Paola Gaeta, and John RWD Jones (eds), *The Rome Statute of the International Criminal Court: A Commentary* (OUP 2002) 1911.

[55] David J Scheffer, 'The International Criminal Court: The Challenge of Jurisdiction' (1999) 93 Proceedings of the Annual Meeting (American Society of International Law) 68, 69.

[56] Alternatively 'cede jurisdiction': Gennady M Danilenko, 'ICC Statute and Third States' in Antonio Cassese, Paola Gaeta, and John RWD Jones (eds), *The Rome Statute of the International Criminal Court: A Commentary* (OUP 2002) 1881.

[57] United States of America, 'Statement on Behalf of the United States of America' (16th Session of the Assembly of States Parties, 8 December 2017) <https://asp.icc-cpi.int/iccdocs/asp_docs/ASP16/ASP-16-USA.pdf> accessed 4 February 2022.

[58] For a useful overview see: Beth Van Schaack, 'Can the Int'l Criminal Court Try US Officials?–The Theory of "Delegated Jurisdiction" and Its Discontents (Part I)' (*Just Security*, 6 April 2018) <www.justsecurity.org/54578/intl-criminal-court-officials-the-theory-delegated-jurisdiction-discontents-part-i/> accessed 3 February 2022.

[59] See Michael A Newton, 'How the International Criminal Court Threatens Treaty Norms' (2016) 49 Vanderbilt Journal of Transnational Law 371, 406, n 144.

under all circumstances and at all times be subject to the exclusive jurisdiction of their respective national elements in respect of any criminal or disciplinary offences which may be committed by them on the territory of Afghanistan'. These arrangements were reconfirmed in September 2002 when the US concluded an 'Article 98 agreement,' with Afghanistan explicitly asserting the primacy of existing treaty arrangements over ICC jurisdiction.[60] These US legal arguments have been contested and revisited over subsequent years, but have not relented to ICC jurisdiction. Moreover, persistent US opposition may now be driving contestation within the ICC itself, with institutional disagreements over jurisdictional powers challenging any consensus over the meaning of 'accountability' in international criminal justice.

## 3.1 Tracing Ideology and US Practice

The US has not denied the authority of legal normativity in the case of delegated jurisdiction but, rather, has consistently defended its position as 'grounded in law'.[61] For David Scheffer, the prevailing position depended on a customary international law (CIL) assumption to the effect that states have a right to delegate territorial (and universal) jurisdiction to an international court. He 'lit a firestorm among international law scholars' by responding that, although it was 'indisputable' that municipal courts could exercise jurisdiction, CIL did not yet recognize the equal status of an international court.[62] Moreover, a state exercising territorial jurisdiction over a US national has 'no legal right to extradite' to a third state 'which has no connection to the crime or the suspect . . . for the sake of political expediency'. Therefore, neither did that right exist in relation to the ICC absent 'the consent of the non-party state'.[63] The difference thus came down to a question of whether and how the ICC was distinguished from national courts for delegation purposes.

The jurisprudence of the US legal position was developed from the academic work of Professor Madeline Morris, whose critique of the delegation analogy was picked up and promulgated by Scheffer.[64] Up to that point, the US government had relied chiefly on treaty interpretation arguments that, as a 'third state', the US could not be bound by obligations it had not consented to.[65] The legal objections were more fundamental for Morris, however, and went to the limits of institutionalized global judicial power. Whereas the 'jurisdictional structure of the ICC is based on a view of the ICC as a criminal court, *tout court*', which adjudicates over individuals, the nature of ICC cases would necessarily also adjudicate official acts of states. In these cases, 'the ICC's role

[60] ICC, 'Article 98 Agreement between the United States of America and Afghanistan' (20 September 2002) <www.state.gov/wp-content/uploads/2019/02/03-0823-Afghanistan-UN-and-Related-Organization-International-Criminal-Court-9.20.2002.pdf> accessed 4 February 2022.

[61] See Sally J Cummins and David P Stewart (eds), *Digest of United States Practice in International Law: 1991-1999* (International Law Institute 2005) 635.

[62] ibid 635, 638.

[63] Scheffer, *All the Missing Souls* (n 9) 234.

[64] Madeline Morris, Personal Communication with Author (16 March 2018); Scheffer, *All the Missing Souls* (n 9) 478, n 13.

[65] Vienna Convention on the Law of Treaties (adopted 23 May 1969, entered into force 27 January 1980) 1155 UNTS 331 (VCLT) art 34.

as an adjudicator of interstate disputes is not adequately accounted for in the Court's jurisdictional design'.[66] Existing CIL rights could not therefore be delegated to an international court, which would carry 'an authoritative weight and resulting political impact of a categorically different nature' to those of municipal courts. Moreover, the ICC held 'the power to create international law in a manner disproportionate to that of any state', which was not easily amended through domestic legislative processes.[67]

These are intriguing arguments, since the precise factors cited by Morris are those that global counterparts have cited as evidence of the ICC *upholding* the rule of law. From an alternative perspective, the listed concerns have been interpreted as evidence of accountability achieved through the protection of independent international judicial power against partisan national interests.[68] The US position has been criticized as politically compromised, with Georg Nolte arguing that 'it can be comparatively easily refuted'[69] and Cassese claiming that, as 'a legal objection, this is easily dismissed'.[70] Philippe Sands more forcefully rejected the 'absurd notion that it is contrary to international law for the ICC to exercise jurisdiction over Americans who commit international crimes on the territory of countries that have joined the ICC'.[71] Such divergence, on what should be a matter of legal interpretation from established norms, presents a striking case for identifying the reception and contestation of international law through competing ideological commitments.

It matters that US interpretations originated in the intervention of Professor Morris speaking as an independent scholar bound by legal convention, and not as a government advocate.[72] Morris herself has argued that US concerns could not be dismissed as irrelevant to law, since the legality of customary obligations is itself constituted by consistent state practice. Thus, these are 'not "mere policy concerns" but are, in fact, of fundamental *legal* significance'.[73] The division opened by US policy represented 'a genuine dilemma – not excuses or pretexts, but legitimate concerns on each side'.[74] Foreign policy ideology provides a compelling explanation for such divergent yet firmly held legal interpretations: that US and non-US legal policy have determined the integrity of international judicial power through competing conceptions of underlying values and that they have remained coherent in these terms. David Wippman recognizes that, as between the US and its opponents, 'the dispute was framed as a disagreement over competing legal values'. These were respectively 'accountability' and 'independence and impartiality', upon which '[e]ach side claimed the legal high

[66] Madeline Morris, 'High Crimes and Misconceptions: The ICC and Non-Party States' (2001) 64 Law and Contemporary Problems 13, 14–16.

[67] Equally applicable in cases of delegated universal and delegated territorial jurisdiction: ibid 30–33, 45.

[68] See Dapo Akande, 'The Jurisdiction of the International Criminal Court over Nationals of Non-Parties: Legal Basis and Limits' (2003) 1 Journal of International Criminal Justice 618, 625–34.

[69] Georg Nolte, 'The United States and the International Criminal Court' in David Malone and Yuen Foong Khong (eds), *Unilateralism and US Foreign Policy: International Perspectives* (Lynne Rienner Publishers 2003) 76.

[70] Cassese, Gaeta, and Jones (n 54) 1911.

[71] Philippe Sands, *Lawless World: Making and Breaking Global Rules* (Viking 2006) 244.

[72] Morris, Personal Communication (n 64). Morris has served as a legal adviser and counsel to the US government, but not at the time of her intervention, or on this particular issue.

[73] Madeline Morris, 'The Jurisdiction of the International Criminal Court over Nationals of Non-Party States' (2000) 6 ILSA Journal of International & Comparative Law 363, 366, original emphasis.

[74] ibid 369.

ground'.[75] That Morris's interpretation resonated so readily with US legal policy-makers speaks to the power of shared ideological international law attitudes, which has manifested in principled jurisprudential terms.[76]

This interpretive dispute persists more than twenty years later, with the failure to gain acceptance beyond a narrow circle of US policymakers and academics eroding much of the strategic value in maintaining the argument.[77] Scheffer has more recently acknowledged that his historical position now holds 'very little credibility' and should be reconsidered in light of the 'evolution of international criminal law' (and perhaps also reflects the altered parameters of Scheffer's own post-government perspective).[78] Further iterations of US legal policy can be expected to remain constrained by ideological beliefs however, which continue to determine the interpretive tracks down which ICC norms can travel. US scholar Michael Newton progressed the debate in 2017 by dismissing the conventional position as an 'inaccurate legal conclusion',[79] yet did so reaffirming US opposition to ICC jurisdiction in the Afghanistan case. Newton accepted that 'the act of transferring territorial jurisdiction over a state that is not party to the Rome Statute can be done perfectly consistent with the VCLT',[80] but only '*if the territorial state has a colourable claim to jurisdiction at the time of the alleged offense*'.[81] In circumstances where Afghanistan previously relinquished jurisdiction over US personnel, the maxim '*nemo plus iurius transferre potest quam ipse habet*' governed the situation: 'No one can transfer to another more rights than he has himself'.[82] Any purported delegation of territorial jurisdiction by Afghanistan to the ICC was thus ultra vires and without legal effect.[83]

Especially relevant here is that, even in offering a path to moderate the absolute nature of US jurisdictional opposition, Newton reaffirmed broader ideological values. The exceptionalist warning was repeated that undermining SOFA protections will 'paradoxically threaten to undermine international peace and security because they would without doubt disincentivize UN peacekeeping and peace-enforcement operations'.[84] This is perverse reasoning for lawyers situated outside the American ideological context, with Richard Goldstone once retorting that: 'What the US is saying is, "In order to be peacekeepers ... we have to commit war crimes"'.[85] The apparent hypocrisy is resolved only by an ideological faith that the foundation of accountability lies within the normative commitments of US constitutional government, which offer

[75] David Wippman, 'The International Criminal Court' in Christian Reus-Smit (ed), *The Politics of International Law* (CUP 2004) 173.

[76] See Jorgensen (n 6) 155.

[77] See Carsten Stahn, 'The ICC, Pre-Existing Jurisdictional Treaty Regimes, and the limits of the *Nemo Dat Quod Non Habet* Doctrine—A Reply to Michael Newton' (2016) 49 Vanderbilt Journal of Transnational Law 443, 444, n 5.

[78] David J Scheffer, 'The Self-Defeating Executive Order Against the International Criminal Court' (*Just Security*, 12 June 2020) <www.justsecurity.org/70742/the-self-defeating-executive-order-against-the-international-criminal-court/> accessed 3 February 2022.

[79] Newton (n 59) 385, n 48.

[80] VCLT (n 65).

[81] Newton (n 59) 399; original emphasis.

[82] ibid 374, 398, 407.

[83] ibid 415.

[84] ibid 428.

[85] Farhan Haq, 'Goldstone: US Stance Contradictory' *Terra Viva* (17 June 1998) 7 <www.legal-tools.org/doc/f83fcc/pdf/> accessed 28 March 2022.

protection against the 'politicized exploitation' of jurisdiction.[86] Ideology thus continues to constrain evolution towards less contested interpretations of jurisdictional norms, which must overcome US beliefs in a positive relationship between sovereignty and accountability that have been present since the creation of the ICC.

## 3.2 Tracing US Practice and Change in the ICC

The analysis has thus far been focused at the level of normative argumentation proposed by, and in response to, US international legal practice. The decentralized nature of the international legal order ensures that a focus on the legal positions of individual states and their representatives remains a central component of identifying the ICC's operative norms and values. However, the turbulent history of the Afghanistan investigation now includes striking examples of the ICC appearing to encompass US preferences and value conceptions within its own institutions and jurisprudence, with resulting internal contestation demonstrating pressures for change at the level of legally protected values.

### 3.2.1 Pre-Trial Chamber Decision, 2019

Prosecutor Bensouda's request for authorization of the Afghanistan investigation had been considered all but assured by observers,[87] and so it was with significant controversy that the PTC refused authorization in April of 2019, as contrary to 'interests of justice'.[88] Speculation followed that the ICC had caved to US pressure, by interpreting the statutory requirement to encompass a pragmatic assessment of whether successful and timely prosecution would be possible; the chamber concluded this was unlikely in circumstances of 'scarce cooperation' by the US and other parties.[89] Thus, although relevant requirements for jurisdiction and admissibility were met, the PTC rendered the geopolitical dimensions of sustaining 'the overall credibility of the Court, as well as its organizational and financial sustainability' as a legally relevant bar to proceeding.[90] The PTC never explicitly cited US opposition to the ICC, but the chamber's intent was clear in its emphasis on adverse 'changes within the relevant political landscape', including 'in key States' not party to the Rome Statute.[91] The subsequent appeal of the decision by the Office of the Prosecutor singled out the 'undue weight' given to the importance of US cooperation relative to other states.[92] Labuda observed that, 'in

[86] Newton (n 59) 416.

[87] See Alex Whiting, 'An ICC Investigation of the U.S. in Afghanistan: What does it Mean?' (*Opinio Juris*, 3 November 2017) <www.justsecurity.org/46687/icc-investigation-u-s-afghanistan-mean/> accessed 3 Feburary 2022.

[88] ICC, 'Decision Pursuant to Article 15 of the Rome Statute on the Authorisation of an Investigation into the Situation in the Islamic Republic of Afghanistan' (12 April 2019) ICC-02/17, [87]–[96] <www.icc-cpi.int/CourtRecords/CR2019_02068.PDF> accessed 4 February 2022.

[89] ibid [91].

[90] ibid [91]; see Emanuela Piccolo Koskimies, *Norm Contestation, Sovereignty and (Ir)responsibility at the International Criminal Court: Debunking Liberal Anti-Politics* (Springer 2022) 72–73.

[91] ICC, 'Decision Pursuant to Article 15 of the Rome Statute' (n 88) [94].

[92] See ICC, 'Request for Leave to Appeal the "Decision Pursuant to Article 15 of the Rome Statute on the Authorisation of an Investigation into the Situation in the Islamic Republic of Afghanistan"' (7 June 2019) ICC-02/17 <www.icc-cpi.int/CourtRecords/CR2019_03060.PDF> accessed 4 February 2022.

avoiding a clash with the world's superpower, this decision serves primarily the ICC's own institutional self-interest'[93]—which, for Luis Moreno Ocampo, 'thus transformed a political consideration into a legal requirement'.[94] Unless one accepts the premise of an exceptional US role in promoting accountability, the PTC decision appeared to narrow the meaning of 'equality' and 'accountability' in ways detrimental to the rule of law.

Unsurprisingly, the decision was condemned by legal voices committed to ICC independence while being praised by US legal policymakers, with each claiming the mantle of fidelity to the rule of law. In particular, the PTC's turn to pragmatic reasoning mirrored the type of policy-conscious jurisprudence evident in US approaches to the ICC, with John Bellinger arguing in 2018 that the Afghanistan investigation was 'counterproductive and would only hurt the Court and the cause of international justice in the long run'.[95] Objections to ICC jurisdiction cut across ideological lines: Harold Koh warned that states that dismissed US concerns in favour of legalistic ideals should remain mindful of the necessity of 'making international criminal law for the real world'.[96] Despite divergent ideological positions, in other words, these leading advocates of engagement with the ICC both rejected claims that existing US privileges in relation to the Court ipso facto constitute a form of impunity that undermines the ICC's objectives. These critiques transformed into decidedly hostile opposition through the illiberal nationalist worldview of the Trump administration, with the president framing the decision not to investigate American personnel as 'a major international victory, not only for these patriots, but for the rule of law. We welcome this decision and reiterate our position that the United States holds American citizens to the highest legal and ethical standards'.[97] That assertion was contrary to the PTC finding that the US failed to discharge its complementarity obligations.[98] Yet, even in his illiberal and nationalist defence of the rule of law, Trump was compelled to invoke US claims to implement superior prosecutorial and judicial power at the domestic level as evidence for accountability.

The PTC decision did not stand long, with the Appeals Chamber setting it aside on 5 March 2020, holding that there was simply no entitlement to assess 'interests of justice' (however defined), which remained the sole province of the independent prosecutor.[99] In so deciding, the Appeals Chamber returned to a vision of substantive

[93] Labuda (n 5).

[94] Luis Moreno Ocampo, 'Deconstructing the Int'l Criminal Court's Decision on Afghanistan' (*Just Security*, 24 April 2019) <www.justsecurity.org/63746/deconstructing-the-intl-criminal-courts-decision-on-afghanistan/> accessed 3 February 2022.

[95] John B Bellinger III, 'The Trump Administration Throws Down the Gauntlet to the ICC. The Court Should Decline The Challenge' (*Lawfare*, 10 September 2021) <www.lawfareblog.com/trump-administration-throws-down-gauntlet-icc-court-should-decline-challenge> accessed 3 February 2022.

[96] Harold H Koh, 'Statement at the Review Conference of the International Criminal Court' (4 June 2010) <https://2009-2017.state.gov/s/l/releases/remarks/142665.htm> accessed 3 February 2022.

[97] Donald J Trump, 'Statement from the President' (12 April 2019) <www.govinfo.gov/content/pkg/DCPD-201900224/pdf/DCPD-201900224.pdf> accessed 3 February 2022.

[98] ICC, 'Request for Leave' (n 92) paras [78]–[79]. See Rome Statute (n 50) art 17(1)(a).

[99] ICC, 'Judgment on the Appeal against the Decision on the Authorisation of an Investigation into the Situation in the Islamic Republic of Afghanistan' (5 March 2020) ICC-02/17 OA4 <www.icc-cpi.int/CourtRecords/CR2020_00828.PDF> accessed 3 February 2022.

equality for all states in terms of the Court's jurisdictional regime. Kevin Jon Heller endorsed the reassertion of ICC independence from global power distribution, warning that a contrary decision 'would have signaled the end of the ICC as a meaningful international institution'.[100] The Trump administration imposed various sanctions and visa restrictions on ICC personnel soon after,[101] with then National Security Advisor John Bolton declaring the ICC to constitute 'a direct assault on the concept of national sovereignty, especially that of constitutional, representative governments like the United States'.[102] In doing so, Bolton reiterated the perceived positive relationship between robust US sovereignty and accountability: 'We believe in the rule of law, and we uphold it. We don't need the ICC to tell us our duty, or second-guess our decisions.'[103] It was thus to little avail that the ICC president responded by pleading that the Court's jurisdictional regime 'does the very opposite of usurpation of national sovereignty. It actually prides and underscores national sovereignty'.[104]

This outcome demonstrated the fragmented value and norm conceptions that have conspicuously separated the Court from the US, but which have also created divisions among US policymakers and potentially among members of the ICC judiciary itself. It was thus something of a reprieve when the entire investigation was suspended immediately after the Appeals Chamber decision, following a request from the Afghan government for deferral to domestic legal processes—reportedly following pressure from US officials.[105] The investigation thus remained dormant until shortly after the fall of the government to Taliban forces in August 2021 and the appointment of the new ICC Prosecutor.[106]

### 3.2.2 Prosecutor Khan's Statement, 2021

Prosecutor Khan's 2021 announcement of a renewed investigation likely renders the entire confrontation between the ICC and US moot, with the investigation to proceed in relation to alleged crimes of the Taliban and the Islamic State, but accompanied by an intent to 'deprioritise other aspects of this investigation' including those relating

[100] Kevin Jon Heller, 'The Appeals Chamber Got One Aspect of the Afghanistan Decision Very Wrong' (*Opinio Juris*, 9 March 2020) <http://opiniojuris.org/2020/03/09/the-appeals-chamber-got-one-aspect-of-the-afghanistan-decision-very-wrong/> accessed 3 February 2022.

[101] 'Blocking Property of Certain Persons Associated With the International Criminal Court' (Executive Order 13928, 11 June 2020) <www.govinfo.gov/content/pkg/FR-2020-06-15/pdf/2020-12953.pdf> accessed 4 February 2022.

[102] John R Bolton, 'The Hague Aims for U.S. Soldiers' *The Wall Street Journal* (20 November 2017) <www.wsj.com/articles/the-hague-tiptoes-toward-u-s-soldiers-1511217136> accessed 3 February 2022.

[103] John R Bolton, 'Protecting American Constitutionalism and Sovereignty from International Threats' (*The Federalist Society*, 10 September 2018) <www.lawfareblog.com/national-security-adviser-john-bolton-remarks-federalist-society> accessed 3 February 2022.

[104] Chile Eboe-Osuji, ICC President's Keynote Speech 'A Tribute to Robert H. Jackson – Recalling America's Contributions to International Criminal Justice' (Annual Meeting of American Society of International Law, March 2019) <www.icc-cpi.int/Pages/item.aspx?name=190329-stat-pres> accessed 3 February 2022.

[105] Alice Speri, 'How The U.S. Derailed an Effort to Prosecute its Crimes in Afghanistan' (*The Intercept*, 5 October 2021) <https://theintercept.com/2021/10/05/afghanistan-icc-war-crimes/> accessed 3 February 2022; see ICC, 'Notification on Status of the Islamic Republic of Afghanistan's article 18(2) deferral request' (16 April 2021) ICC-02/17-142 <www.icc-cpi.int/CourtRecords/CR2021_03504.PDF> accessed 3 February 2022.

[106] ICC, 'Notification on Status' (n 105).

to US personnel (as well as allies including the former Afghan government).[107] The announcement noted the 'gravity, scale and continuing nature of alleged crimes by the Taliban and the Islamic State' but, echoing the PTC decision, incorporated a pragmatic assessment of what was possible in global justice. The question of jurisdiction has loomed large among critical legal responses, with Sophie Duroy noting that 'the ICC's jurisdictional opportunity in relation to the US global war on terror was unique', such that the decision likely 'buries most hopes that US officials will be held accountable'.[108] Duroy accordingly rejects the merits of the claimed pragmatism of the decision, arguing that:

> when the Prosecutor of a universal court, with a mandate to end impunity for all persons without any distinction, decides to pursue a one-sided investigation and to deprioritise the crimes committed by the most powerful perpetrators, the resulting impression is more one of double standards than pragmatism.[109]

Amnesty International likewise noted the ICC's 'clear territorial jurisdiction' over relevant US nationals, and therefore the 'unfathomable' decision of the prosecutor to align with the objectives of the most forceful US critics.[110] As with the PTC decision, the 2021 statement did not explicitly endorse US normative commitments, but nevertheless conspicuously aligned with US prioritization of pragmatism in apparently delinking ICC political independence from global accountability. All commentators have noted the irony of the ICC effectively acquiescing to US preferences at precisely the moment when the Biden administration ended the Trump era sanctions—in the interests of 'engagement'.[111] This act was reportedly done in the context of a 'tacit understanding' that investigation of US personnel would not resume.[112]

Of greatest consequence is what these combined decisions say about the meaning of 'accountability', as a core rule of law value institutionalized in the Court. Unsurprisingly, US statements have welcomed the prioritization of resources 'to focus on the greatest of allegations and atrocity crimes' in the name of ensuring 'accountability'.[113] In response, Jennifer Trahan observes that, although '[f]ailing to pursue the

[107] Khan (n 4).

[108] Sophie Duroy, 'Pragmatism and power at the ICC: US crimes not a priority' (*EUIdeas*, 11 October 2021) <https://euideas.eui.eu/2021/10/11/pragmatism-and-power-at-the-icc-us-crimes-not-a-priority/> accessed 3 February 2022.

[109] ibid.

[110] Amnesty International, 'Afghanistan: ICC Prosecutor's statement on Afghanistan jeopardises his Office's legitimacy and future' (5 October 2021) <https://hrij.amnesty.nl/afghanistan-icc-prosecutors-statement-on-afghanistan-jeopardises-his-offices-legitimacy-and-future/> accessed 3 February 2022.

[111] Antony J Blinken, 'Ending Sanctions and Visa Restrictions against Personnel of the International Criminal Court' (Press Statement, 2 April 2021) <www.state.gov/ending-sanctions-and-visa-restrictions-against-personnel-of-the-international-criminal-court/> accessed 3 February 2022; Jennifer Trahan, 'Prosecutor De-Prioritizes ICC Investigation of US Torture Program' (*Opinio Juris*, 1 October 2021) <https://opiniojuris.org/2021/10/01/prosecutor-de-prioritizes-icc-investigation-of-us-torture-program/> accessed 3 February 2022.

[112] Speri (n 105).

[113] US Department of State, 'Department Press Briefing – September 27, 2021' (27 September 2021) <www.state.gov/briefings/department-press-briefing-september-27-2021-2/> accessed 3 February 2022.

rule of law equally' may make political and financial sense, the turn to pragmatism nevertheless:

> represents a clear backslide for the notion of global accountability—that the rule of law must apply to all—something that is proving very difficult to achieve, but must be attempted notwithstanding. If the ICC cannot strive to do so, then who can? This was precisely the mandate of the ICC and the new Prosecutor has made a misstep in entrenching impunity for US nationals.[114]

Kelebogile Zvobgo likewise views the reinterpretation of accountability in these terms as perilous, since it 'is not a voluntary exercise'.[115] The most consequential trend that appears to be emerging from these cases is that the meaning of 'accountability' as a value protected by the ICC is becoming functionally more aligned with the conceptions held by American policymakers.[116] Here Rocío Lorca usefully distinguishes between a 'thin' concept of impunity, concerned with ensuring criminal punishment, and a 'thick' concept, concerned more with equal application of the law.[117] The ICC's prioritization of the thin concept—that to 'punish some may be better than punishing none'—likely has substantive consequences for thicker conceptions, since 'when the selection aligns with power, impunity is deepened and consolidated'.[118] The divergent implications can be illuminated by inverting the focus of Khan's statement, to consider what it means to deny 'Americans an opportunity to see their own government held accountable for the crimes it committed in their name'.[119] Here Shaharzad Akbar, former chair of Afghanistan's Independent Human Rights Commission, argues that the investigation has never been only about Afghan victims, but also addresses 'the U.S. military in its deep and systematic problems. Americans who care about the U.S. should care about this'.[120] The announcement of Prosecutor Khan effectively deprioritizes equal application of the law in the investigation, replicating the normative preferences of US legal policymakers, while simultaneously championing what remains of accountability as a value worthy of this peak judicial institution.

## 4. Conclusion

This chapter's emphasis on ideological constraints should not suggest that the international legal order cannot be greater than the sum of its parts, but rather demonstrates

[114] Trahan (n 111).

[115] Kelebogile Zvobgo, 'The ICC's Flawed Afghan Investigation: Why the Court Shouldn't Let America Off the Hook' *Foreign Affairs* (3 November 2021) <www.foreignaffairs.com/articles/afghanistan/2021-11-03/iccs-flawed-afghan-investigation> accessed 4 February 2022.

[116] See Julian Elderfield, 'Uncertain Future for the ICC's Investigation into the CIA Torture Program' (*Just Security*, 12 November 2021) <www.justsecurity.org/79136/uncertain-future-for-the-iccs-investigation-into-the-cia-torture-program/> accessed 3 February 2022.

[117] Rocío Lorca, 'Impunity Thick and Thin: The International Criminal Court in the Search for Equality' (2022) 35 Leiden Journal of International Law 421, 422–25.

[118] ibid 431.

[119] Speri (n 105).

[120] Cited ibid.

that international law does remain an artefact of real decision-makers and their underlying values. A cross-cutting study on norm and value change must accordingly take account of empirical evidence at the level of the foreign policy beliefs of the states and policymakers who author international law's rules and institutions. Identifying the structure of competing American ideological beliefs allows for better understanding of why partisan divides in US politics will likely have the effect of 'pushing the ICC firmly into that category of international organizations ... whose standing in U.S. officialdom will depend very much on U.S. presidential elections'.[121] This yields a disconcerting dynamic for US global counterparts, whereby American international law policy switches between opposing internationalist and nationalist tracks pegged to electoral politics, yet exhibits bipartisan continuity in resisting ICC jurisdiction.

The sui generis commitments of American ICC policy were clearly demonstrated in the transition from the Trump administration to that of President Joe Biden, and more recently in US responses to the 2022 Russo-Ukrainian War. Biden conspicuously distinguished himself from his predecessor by a commitment to 'repair our alliances and engage with the world once again',[122] and yet has remained guided by his long adherence to a liberal internationalist worldview. In a July 1998 hearing before the US Senate Committee on Foreign Relations, then Senator Biden voiced his strong objections to 'purported de facto universal jurisdiction' under Article 12, recommending that allies be threatened with a review of SOFAs in order to 'get them to focus on aspects of the treaty I suspect they have not really fully focused on'.[123] In the context of Biden's broader ideological commitments, Article 12 remained inconsistent with accountability under international law and its perceived dependence on an exceptional American military role. The ideological rather than empirical foundations for this worldview appeared to be conspicuously laid bare with the victory of Taliban forces in the 20-year war in Afghanistan, which profoundly undercut US claims to be an indispensable and effective guarantor of global legal order.[124]

Yet the war in Ukraine has reinforced the durability of ideological exceptions, with the US Senate passing a unanimous resolution on 2 March 2022 that endorsed an ICC investigation of Russian nationals for alleged war crimes, despite Russia not being party to the Rome Statute.[125] The resolution sought to square the circle of differentiated jurisdiction over non-party states by framing the ICC as 'an international tribunal that seeks to uphold the rule of law, *especially in areas where no rule of law*

[121] David Bosco, 'Bolton Barked at the ICC, But With How Much Bite?' (*Lawfare*, 11 September 2018) <www.lawfareblog.com/bolton-barked-icc-how-much-bite> accessed 3 February 2022.

[122] Joseph R Biden, 'Inaugural Address by President Joseph R. Biden, Jr' (20 January 2021) <www.whitehouse.gov/briefing-room/speeches-remarks/2021/01/20/inaugural-address-by-president-joseph-r-biden-jr/> accessed 3 February 2022.

[123] Committee on Foreign Relations, *Is a U.N. International Criminal Court in the U.S. National Interest?* (1998).

[124] See Andrew Hilland and Catherine Gilfedder, 'The International Criminal Court and Afghanistan' (*Just Security*, 3 September 2021) <www.justsecurity.org/78080/the-international-criminal-court-and-afghanistan/> 3 February 2022.

[125] Expressing the Sense of The Senate Condemning The Russian Federation, President Vladimir Putin, Members of The Russian Security Council, The Russian Armed Forces, and Russian Military Commanders for Committing Atrocities, including Alleged War Crimes, against The People of Ukraine and Others, S. Res. 546, 117th Cong. (2022), <https://www.congress.gov/117/bills/sres546/BILLS-117sres546ats.pdf> accessed 24 April 2022.

*exists*'.[126] Thus, from an ideological perspective, jurisdiction was not enlivened merely because Russian actions had 'severely undermined the international rule of law' but, crucially, because 'Vladimir Putin and his regime have destroyed the rule of law in Russia'.[127] Senator Lindsay Graham accordingly introduced the resolution by asserting that, although the 'court doesn't make sense when it comes to America or Israel', it 'makes perfect sense when it comes to places where there is no rule of law'.[128] Bellinger, along with former Democratic Senator and leading ICC advocate Christopher J Dodd,[129] correspondingly wrote that to proceed therefore 'would not constitute a double standard or be inconsistent with U.S. objections to the court's claimed jurisdiction over U.S. personnel'.[130]

Identifying internal consistency in US policymakers' ideological conceptions of accountability thus offers a degree of analytical clarity, yet it is an entirely different matter to establish meanings of accountability that are capable of broad external acceptance. Ideology maintains a powerful hold over American international legal policy precisely because it has 'helped to reconcile imperial power with republican traditions and universal principles'.[131] It is undeniable that American resistance to an expansive jurisdictional regime aligns with its geopolitical interests. The purpose of SOFAs is to 'define the legal status of U.S. Department of Defense (DoD) personnel, activities, and property in the territory of another nation and set forth rights and responsibilities between the United States and the host government'.[132] They are thus the bedrock of the legal framework necessary for US capacity to act as a globally engaged power. Equally, the opponents of US legal arguments have a clear rational interest in an international legal system that diminishes advantages of hegemonic power and any 'exceptional' role that it brings. Indeed, commentators have even sought to argue that the Afghanistan investigation meets necessary thresholds for gravity precisely *because* the US 'see themselves as untouchable'.[133] In each case, the operation of ideology frames understandings of law in ways that reconcile legal values and global power from particularistic standpoints, which invariably yields competing and often incompatible legal norms.

More recent evidence of a pragmatic turn in ICC norms requires close monitoring, since there is a real possibility that it is not merely ICC jurisdictional norms being

[126] ibid 2; emphasis added.

[127] ibid 3, 4.

[128] Cited in Ryan Goodman, 'Top Cover: Congressional Republicans Pave Way for US Policy Shift on Int'l Criminal Court', (*Just Security*, 13 April 2022), <https://www.justsecurity.org/81093/top-cover-congressional-republicans-pave-wave-for-us-policy-shift-on-intl-criminal-court/> accessed 24 April 2022.

[129] See Jorgensen (n 6) 134–35, 185–86.

[130] Christopher J Dodd and John B Bellinger III, 'Opinion: How the U.S. Can Support a War Crimes Investigation into Russia', *The Washington Post* (5 April 2022), <https://www.washingtonpost.com/opinions/2022/04/05/us-international-criminal-court-russia-war-crimes-putin-ukraine/> accessed 24 April 2022.

[131] Benjamin A Coates, *Legalist Empire: International Law and American Foreign Relations in the Early Twentieth Century* (OUP 2016) 3.

[132] International Security Advisory Board, 'Report on Status of Forces Agreements' (16 January 2015) 1 <https://2009-2017.state.gov/documents/organization/236456.pdf> accessed 3 February 2022.

[133] Carla Ferstman, 'The International Criminal Court Prosecutor's Preliminary Examination on Afghanistan and Possible Impacts on Accountability for Secret Detention and Rendition' in Elspeth Guild, Didier Bigo, and Mark Gibney (eds), *Extraordinary Rendition: Addressing the Challenges of Accountability* (Routledge 2018).

contested, but the underlying values protected by the international legal system. The fact that the Court's jurisdictional and administrative decisions have elicited such consternation among Court watchers is itself a sign of the deeper, hidden rifts in value conceptions. Recent decisions remain far from settled and may well be superseded by competing conceptions,[134] as was the case with the Appeals Chamber reversal of the PTC decision. Indeed, in this case it was the PTC who issued a warning to prosecutor Khan that '[n]ot only impartiality, but also *appearance of impartiality*, is a *sine qua non* requirement for justice to contribute to peace and reconciliation' and that, to this end, prosecutorial discretion must be exercised foremost by reference to 'the duties and obligations as regards victims' rather than states.[135] Nevertheless, understood in ideological context, neither the 2019 PTC decision, nor the statement of Prosecutor Khan, can be simply dismissed as ICC decisionmakers dispensing with notions of accountability. Rather, a more complex and potentially subversive process is taking place, in which Court personnel are guided by particularistic yet sincerely held conceptions of accountability. If the turn to ICC pragmatism stabilizes as a trend—'even a hidden and implicit one'[136]—that may ultimately signal a change in the substantive meaning of 'accountability' as a protected value in international criminal justice.

[134] See ICC, 'Decision pursuant to article 18(2) of the Statute authorising the Prosecution to resume investigation' (31 October 2022) ICC-02/17-196, [58] <https://www.icc-cpi.int/sites/default/files/CourtRecords/CR2022_06500.PDF> accessed 27 February 2023.

[135] ICC, 'Decision on submissions received and order to the Registry regarding the filing of documents in the proceedings pursuant to articles 18(2) and 68(3) of the Statute' (8 November 2021) ICC-02/17-171, [15] <www.icc-cpi.int/CourtRecords/CR2021_10257.PDF> accessed 4 February 2022; original emphasis.

[136] Krieger and Liese, Chapter 1 in this book, 38.

# 12
# Authoritarian Regimes and Nuclear Nonproliferation Norms

*Alexandros Tokhi*[*]

## 1. Introduction

Since its 'discovery', nuclear energy has confronted the world with a difficult dilemma: how to enable the peaceful uses of atomic fission while avoiding catastrophe. This inherent tension runs through all international efforts to regulate nuclear energy, as states seek to reconcile the value of international peace and security with the value of equal access to (new) technologies. The Treaty on the Non-Proliferation of Nuclear Weapons (NPT), as the key institution of the global nonproliferation regime, reflects and adds to this tension through the asymmetry of the status of its state parties and their obligations. The NPT recognises five official Nuclear Weapon States (NWS) that may retain their nuclear weapons, while all other states accede to the treaty as Non-Nuclear Weapon States (NNWS), thereby renouncing the pursuit and acquisition of nuclear weapons and accepting international verification. The asymmetry of status raises issues of fairness and distributional justice.[1] Moreover, the central norms of the treaty—nonproliferation, peaceful uses, and disarmament—are differently legalised, with the most precise and binding provisions on nonproliferation and the least specific and more aspirational provisions on disarmament. The asymmetry of legal obligations, in turn, raises concerns about the treaty's ability to protect the values that states seek to advance. It is not surprising, therefore, that the NPT and its norms have become an object of normative contestation and challenge, leading to debates about their implications for the treaty and its norms.[2]

'All normative structures generate disputes.'[3] However, not all disputes and normative challenges have the capacity to undermine international norms and their

[*] For helpful comments I thank Jelena Cupac, Andrea Liese, and Heike Krieger.

[1] Nina Tannenwald, 'Justice and Fairness in the Nuclear Nonproliferation Regime' (2013) 27 Ethics and International Affairs 299.

[2] Nina Tannenwald and James Acton, *Meeting the Challenges of the New Nuclear Age: Emerging Risks and Declining Norms in the Age of Technological Innovation and Changing Nuclear Doctrines* (American Academy of Arts & Sciences 2018); Scott D Sagan and Jane Vaynman, 'Conclusion: Lessons Learned from the 2010 Nuclear Posture Review' (2011) 18 Nonproliferation Review 237; Jeffrey W Knopf, 'After Diffusion: Challenges to Enforcing Nonproliferation and Disarmament Norms' (2018) 39 Contemporary Security Policy 367.

[3] See Wayne Sandholtz, 'Dynamics of International Norm Change: Rules Against Wartime Plunder' (2008) 14 European Journal of International Relations 101, 105. Wayne Sandholtz, Chapter 3 in this book; Wayne Sandholtz, 'Norm Contestation, Robustness, and Replacement' (2019) 4 Journal of Global Security Studies 139.

Alexandros Tokhi, *Authoritarian Regimes and Nuclear Nonproliferation Norms* In: *Tracing Value Change in the International Legal Order*. Edited by: Heike Krieger and Andrea Liese, Oxford University Press. 
DOI: 10.1093/oso/9780192855831.003.0012

underlying values. Indeed, in many cases, dissatisfied states have formulated their specific demands and criticisms during the NPT's quinquennial review conferences, inspiring necessary reform debates.[4] By contrast, behavioural contestation, which is related to what states do rather than what they say,[5] may be more likely to jeopardise the NPT. The refusal of states to commit to stricter rules or their failure to comply with the treaty's norms can weaken its effectiveness and legitimacy and thus contribute to the gradual erosion of its norms.[6]

This chapter focuses on behavioural contestation and, specifically, on compliance with the NPT's highly legalised nonproliferation norm. This norm is violated when NNWS seek to acquire nuclear weapons, including the relevant know-how and materials to build them. Noncompliance with the treaty does not necessarily indicate normative decay or invalidate the nonproliferation norm.[7] However, norm violations are more than just an attempt by states to express their dissatisfaction with the NPT. This is because violations of the nonproliferation norm can directly threaten international peace and security, one of the values upon which the nuclear nonproliferation regime is built. Moreover, to the extent that NNWS are able to evade monitoring and acquire relevant know-how, violations of the NPT can undermine the confidence of State Parties in each other's intentions, which is essential for maintaining security cooperation.[8] Finally, non-adherence to the nonproliferation norm may have negative consequences for the peaceful uses and disarmament norms of the treaty, as some state parties may seek to restrict access to civilian nuclear technology or become even more reluctant to pursue nuclear disarmament.[9]

Noncompliance with the nonproliferation norm has the potential to undermine the normative fabric of the NPT and its underlying values. Curiously, all violations of the nonproliferation norm have been committed by authoritarian regimes.[10] Authoritarian regimes differ from democracies in important ways, not least in their emphasis on national sovereignty and non-interference[11], and the weakness of their domestic institutions,[12] which often explain why autocracies are more likely than

[4] Maria Rost Rublee and Avner Cohen, 'Nuclear Norms in Global Governance: A Progressive Research Agenda' (2018) 39 Contemporary Security Policy 317; Harald Müller and Alexandros Tokhi, 'The Contestation of the Nuclear Non-Proliferation Regime' in Matthew D Stephen and Michael Zürn (eds), *Contested World Orders: Rising Powers, Non-Governmental Organizations, and the Politics of Authority Beyond the Nation-State* (OUP 2019).

[5] For the distinction between discursive and behavioural contestation see Heike Krieger and Andrea Liese, Chapter 1 in this book and Sandholtz, Chapter 3 in this book.

[6] Martha Finnemore and Kathryn Sikkink, 'International Norm Dynamics and Political Change' (1998) 52 International Organization 887; Scott D Sagan, 'Nuclear Power, Nuclear Proliferation and the NPT' (paper presented at the APSA Annual Meeting, Washington DC, September 2010); Tannenwald and Acton (n 2).

[7] See Sandholtz, Chapter 3 in this book.

[8] Robert Jervis, 'Cooperation Under the Security Dilemma' (1978) 30 World Politics 167; Thomas C Schelling, 'Confidence in Crisis' (1984) 8 International Security 55.

[9] Jeffrey W Knopf, 'Nuclear Disarmament and Nonproliferation: Examining the Linkage Argument' (2012) 37 International Security 92; Tannenwald and Acton (n 2).

[10] Following the habit of comparative politics, this chapter uses dictatorships, autocracy, and authoritarian regimes interchangeably to designate non-democratic polities.

[11] Tom Ginsburg, 'Authoritarian International Law?' (2020) 114 American Journal of International Law 221.

[12] Brett Ashley Leeds, 'Domestic Political Institutions, Credible Commitments, and International Cooperation' (1999) 43 American Journal of Political Science 979.

democracies to seek nuclear weapons and ignore nonproliferation norms.[13] However, the fact that autocracies generally lack respect for international law and domestic constraints cannot explain why several autocratic NNWS respect the NPT's nonproliferation norm. Given that authoritarian regimes pose a challenge to international law,[14] this chapter seeks to understand why some authoritarian regimes engage in the behavioural contestation of the NPT by violating its nonproliferation norm while others do not.

To shed light on this question, this chapter focuses on the internal dynamics of authoritarian politics. Institutions in authoritarian regimes can constrain foreign policies when the domestic distribution of power between the dictator and his ruling elite is balanced.[15] Unlike in democracies, however, institutional constraints can and often do change in response to power struggles within the authoritarian elite. It is this dynamic of shifting internal constraints that drives NPT compliance choices of authoritarian regimes. To the extent that the distribution of power between the dictator and his elite is balanced and remains stable, authoritarian institutions can constrain foreign policy choices and thus moderate NPT compliance by authoritarian regimes. Under these conditions, elite factions with either a material or an ideational stake in nonproliferation can use their political clout to avert nuclear policies that may be costly to them. However, as power becomes more concentrated, particularly within the same regime over time, authoritarian institutions lose their constraining effect as fewer factions are able to limit discretionary authority. As a result, the chances of compliance with the NPT diminish.

The theoretical argument identifies the conditions under which authoritarian regimes are more or less likely to comply with the NPT's nonproliferation norm. This has implications for the policy responses of the treaty's norm defenders.[16] Because nuclear decision-making is subject to authoritarian power struggles, international strategies to address NPT violations will be more successful if they tilt the domestic balance of power towards those factions that need international cooperation in order to survive politically within the regime. Bringing NNWS back into norm adherence requires well-designed policies that set the right domestic incentives and that also refer to other norms of the NPT, such as peaceful uses. Resolving noncompliance cases through diplomatic means can thus attenuate some of the regime's normative conflicts and thus make the NPT more robust and protect its values.

The chapter proceeds as follows. The first section chronicles the normative evolution of the NPT, discussing the values and initial norms of the early atomic age and how superpower confrontation shaped their institutionalisation. The chapter then discusses the central normative conflicts in the NPT, paying particular attention to the objects and types of contestation. Many normative challenges surround the NPT, of which noncompliance with the Treaty's nonproliferation norm is a particularly

[13] Matthew Fuhrmann and Jeffrey Berejikian, 'Disaggregating Noncompliance: Abstention versus Predation in the Nuclear Nonproliferation Treaty' (2012) 56 Journal of Conflict Resolution 355.

[14] See Krieger and Liese, Chapter 1 in this book.

[15] Milan W Svolik, *The Politics of Authoritarian Rule* (CUP 2012); Jennifer Gandhi, *Political Institutions Under Dictatorship* (CUP 2008); Joseph Wright, 'Do Authoritarian Institutions Constrain? How Legislatures Affect Economic Growth and Investment' (2008) 52 American Journal of Political Science 322.

[16] See Sandholtz, Chapter 3 in this book and Sandholtz, 'Norm Contestation' (n 3).

important one. The third section describes patterns of NPT noncompliance and discusses the distinct challenges posed by the contestation behaviour of authoritarian regimes. After proposing an explanation for the variation in noncompliance by authoritarian regimes, the argument is illustrated by the Iranian nuclear crisis. The conclusion reviews recent international responses to Iranian noncompliance and discusses the conditions under which these may strengthen the norms and underlying values of the nuclear nonproliferation regime.

## 2. The Normative Evolution and Contestation of the NPT

The nuclear bombing of Hiroshima and Nagasaki not only overturned all previously held beliefs about the destructive power of weapons, but also revealed a difficult dilemma, involving two different values: how to make nuclear energy accessible to every state while preventing its hostile use. In a first attempt to reconcile the values of equal access to technology and international peace and security, the United Nations General Assembly (UNGA), at its first session, established the UN Atomic Energy Commission (UNAEC) with a mandate to propose specific measures on four normative objectives:[17] first, to find ways for 'extending between all nations the exchange of basic scientific information for peaceful ends'. Second, to develop 'the control of atomic energy to the extent necessary to ensure its use only for peaceful purposes'. Third, the UNAEC should work on 'the elimination from national armaments of atomic weapons and all other major weapons adaptable to mass destruction'. Finally, the UNAEC should provide 'for effective safeguards by way of inspection and other means to protect complying States against the hazards of violations and evasions'.

With the adoption of the resolution and the subsequent endorsement by the P5,[18] the United Nations consensualized two foundational norms of the nuclear age: peaceful uses and security. The *peaceful uses* norm is reflected in the first two goals of the UNGA resolution, which proposes *controlled* access to civilian nuclear energy for *every* state. *Security* is reflected in the third and fourth goals, and is thus subdivided into *security through disarmament* and *security through nonproliferation*, respectively. The former should be achieved through the elimination of nuclear weapons and the latter through international inspections that would protect non-nuclear states.

The institutionalisation of these norms through specific legal provisions took more than twenty years because it dependent primarily on the relationship between the United States (US) and the Soviet Union. In the early years of the atomic age, the US proposed far-reaching measures for the global regulation of atomic energy in the Acheson-Lilienthal Report and Baruch Plan. In essence, the proposal was to create an intrusive international authority under whose auspices the US would place all its

[17] Establishment of a Commission to Deal with the Problem Raised by the Discovery of Atomic Energy (adopted 24 January 1946) UNGA Res 1 (I).

[18] The permanent five UN Security Council members, or P5, which are also the official NWS, are: the USA, Russia, France, the UK, and the People's Republic of China. The UNAEC comprised the P5 (and Taiwan instead of China), plus Canada.

fissile material, and eventually eliminate its nuclear weapons stockpile.[19] However, as Cold War tensions grew, the Soviet Union demanded that the US first eliminate its stockpile before placing all other states under international safeguards to prevent proliferation. These discussions, as the UNAEC itself, came to an end with the first Soviet nuclear test in 1949.

After the United Kingdom (UK) 'went nuclear' in 1952, and in an effort to halt the further spread of nuclear technology, US President Dwight D. Eisenhower proposed the creation of an International Atomic Energy Agency (IAEA) in his 'Atoms for Peace' speech to the UNGA in 1953. This Agency—finally established in 1957—was conceived as a fuel bank to which the nuclear haves (the United States, the USSR, and the United Kingdom) would gradually transfer their fissile material. Other states could 'borrow' this material to produce nuclear energy, under IAEA safeguards.[20] 'Atoms for Peace' reflects the norms of peaceful uses and security through nonproliferation. In terms of *security through disarmament*, however, the initiative retreated from earlier aspirations by focusing on gradual disarmament through the fuel bank mechanism rather than the elimination of nuclear weapons.[21] Moreover, as in the Bretton Woods institutions, the three nuclear haves would have a greater voting weight in the IAEA than others.

But unlike the Bretton Woods institutions, the realisation of 'Atoms for Peace' required Soviet cooperation and consent. At the end of the negotiations, the IAEA had only partial control over nuclear transfers and safeguarded only a few selected nuclear facilities.[22] Importantly, the idea of a fuel bank did not materialise, so systematic efforts at even incremental disarmament were halted. Instead, the nuclear haves demanded safeguards for the transfer of material, thereby prioritizing nonproliferation over disarmament—a development further reinforced by bilateral nuclear cooperation agreements between the superpowers and other countries.[23] And while the nuclear haves did not get veto rights or greater voting weights, they did get reserved seats on the IAEA's governing body.[24] The IAEA thus foreshadowed the shape of the future nuclear world order. Despite its creation, however, efforts to halt nuclear proliferation were unsuccessful. The Soviet–American arms race reached new heights, while France (1960) and the People's Republic of China (1964) acquired nuclear weapons. It was only after the Cuban missile crisis that the superpowers came together and began a series of negotiations that eventually led to the NPT.

[19] The Baruch plan proposed an international organisation with unprecedented authority that would dismantle nuclear weapons and control compliance, circumventing also the P5's veto power.

[20] Safeguards are rules and procedures whose goals is to avoid the diversion of nuclear material and facilities from peaceful to military uses; David Fischer, *History of the International Atomic Energy Agency: The First Forty Years* (International Atomic Energy Agency 1997).

[21] Paul C Szasz, *The Law and Practice of the International Atomic Energy Agency* (IAEA 1970) 22.

[22] Fischer (n 20) 34.

[23] Szasz (n 21); Fischer (n 20).

[24] Patrick M Cottrell, *The Evolution and Legitimacy of International Security Institutions* (CUP 2016) 133–78; Szasz (n 21).

## 2.1 Norms and Rules in the NPT

Superpower agreement, or even collusion as some argue,[25] was crucial to the negotiation of the NPT.[26] However, halting the spread of nuclear weapons and the associated security benefits for many states came at a price.[27] Despite pressure for more balanced treaty obligations,[28] the nuclear priorities of the US and the Soviet Union, together with their combined leverage over states, ultimately resulted in a treaty that institutionalized inequality, both in the status of state parties and in the legal status of individual norms.[29]

In terms of status, the NPT recognises five official NWS, which are allowed to retain their nuclear weapons.[30] All other states would join the treaty as NNWS and renounce the possession and acquisition of nuclear weapons. Relatedly, the treaty institutionalises a hierarchy of norms with a corresponding imbalance of rights and obligations.[31] The *security through nonproliferation norm* is highly codified, establishing baselines of legitimate behaviour and delegating monitoring authority to the IAEA. The *peaceful uses* norm is moderately institutionalized in the form of a conditional right to nuclear energy. However, the provisions are neither precise enough nor do they delegate exclusive authority to a central international organization. Finally, *security through disarmament* is the least institutionalised norm and, judging from the treaty text alone, more aspirational than constraining.

Articles I, II, and III set out the main objective of the NPT, which is to prevent the proliferation of nuclear weapons. Under Article I, NWS undertake not to transfer nuclear weapons, including their control, or to assist or encourage others to acquire them. Article II requires NNWS to renounce the possession, development, and acquisition of nuclear weapons, including seeking or receiving assistance from anyone in this regard. Article III of the NPT, which is the longest and most detailed provision, is directly related to nonproliferation in that it obliges all NNWS to conclude a safeguards agreement with the IAEA 'for the exclusive purpose of verification of the fulfillment of its obligations assumed under this Treaty with a view to preventing diversion of nuclear energy from peaceful uses to nuclear weapons'. The NPT mandates the IAEA to monitor compliance with Article II. The verification

[25] Andrew J Coe and Jane Vaynman, 'Collusion and the nuclear nonproliferation regime' (2015) 77 Journal of Politics 983.

[26] The UN's Eighteen Nations Disarmament Committee, composed of five Western (US allies), five Eastern (Soviet allies), and eight non-aligned states, started NPT negotiations in 1965. The treaty was adopted in 1968 and entered into force in 1970.

[27] Lora Anne Viola, *The Closure of the International System* (CUP 2020).

[28] UNGA Res 2028 (XX) (adopted 19 November 1965) recommends that the NPT balances obligations, takes steps towards disarmament, ensures the treaty's effectiveness, assures credible nonproliferation, and enables Nuclear Weapon Free Zones.

[29] ELM Burns, 'The Nonproliferation Treaty: Its Negotiation and Prospects' (1969) 23 International Organization 788; Gro Nystuen and Torbjørn Graff Hugo 'The Nuclear Non-Proliferation Treaty' in Gro Nystuen, Stuart Casey-Maslen and Annie Golden Bersagel (eds), *Nuclear Weapons under International Law* (CUP 2014).

[30] The NWS are all states that tested a nuclear explosive device before 1967 and thus are: the United States; the USSR/Russia; the United Kingdom; France; and the People's Republic of China. These also form the P5.

[31] See also Mirko Sossai, Chapter 13 in this book.

'burden' thus falls on the NNWS, while the NWS are generally exempt from IAEA verification.[32]

The above three main articles codify the norm of *security through nonproliferation* by prohibiting proliferation and creating an international mechanism to assure state parties of each other's compliance. The highly legalised nonproliferation norm reflects the preferences of the superpowers. They had tabled a joint, identical draft to the NPT negotiators that focused exclusively on nonproliferation. While the US and the Soviet Union were the main proponents, many non-nuclear states, including members of the non-aligned movement (NAM), also called for a strong nonproliferation norm, concerned about nuclear weapon transfers from NWS to NNWS and credible nonproliferation verification mechanisms.[33] The main articles create behavioural standards and expectations by distinguishing between legitimate and illegitimate activities.[34] They also create incentives for compliance by making nonproliferation commitments centrally monitored and enforceable.[35] These are important prerequisites for the functioning of any security institution. At the same time, the main articles establish an asymmetry of obligations, with NNWS bearing significantly higher implementation costs than NWS.

Many developing non-nuclear states were concerned about their access to civilian nuclear technology and material.[36] Eventually, with the issue of verification resolved, the superpowers agreed to include 'compensatory articles',[37] of which Article IV is one. It states that all state parties have the 'inalienable right' to research, produce, and use nuclear energy for peaceful purposes and in compliance with Articles I and II of the NPT. The article also encourages cooperation on the civilian applications of nuclear energy between nuclear advanced states and developing nations through bilateral and multilateral fora, including international organizations.

Article IV takes up the norm of peaceful use. It provides for nondiscriminatory access to nuclear knowledge and technology. However, this right is conditional upon state parties complying with Article II, with the consequence that all nuclear activities, facilities, and material in a country are subject to safeguards. What is less clear is what this 'inalienable right' to nuclear energy actually means in practice. For example, Uranium enrichment and spent fuel reprocessing can be used not only for peaceful purposes, but also to produce fissile material for nuclear weapons. Mastery of these sensitive technologies could create a latent nuclear capacity, allowing states to 'go nuclear' when conditions permit.[38] This ambiguity gives rise to conflicting

[32] As transfers of nuclear material are also safeguarded, the NWS are indirectly monitored in their Article I obligations, see Nystuen and Hugo (n 29). The IAEA does not monitor compliance with the entire treaty, but only with Article II.

[33] Dimitris Bourantonis, 'The Negotiation of the Non-Proliferation Treaty, 1965–1968: A Note' (1997) 19 International History Review 347, 351.

[34] Maria Rost Rublee, *Nonproliferation Norms: Why States Choose Nuclear Restraint* (University of Georgia Press 2009).

[35] Formally, the IAEA can determine if a country is in noncompliance with safeguards and refer the case to the UN Security Council. Informally, the superpowers also enforce the treaty's nonproliferation obligation, see Coe and Vaynman (n 25).

[36] Cottrell (n 24).

[37] Burns (n 29).

[38] Scott D Sagan, 'Nuclear Latency and Nuclear Proliferation' in William C Potter and Gaukhar Mukhatzhanova (eds), *The Little Known Story of Deproliferation: Why States Give Up Nuclear Weapons Activities* (Stanford University Press 2010).

interpretations of whether or not states have a right to enrichment. Moreover, having the IAEA serve as a focal point for civil nuclear cooperation—as originally envisioned in the UNAEC and 'Atoms for Peace'—is an option, but not an explicit mandate.

Avoiding firm commitments, the superpowers accommodated demands for the NPT to be a step towards disarmament,[39] and agreed to the inclusion of Article VI. All state parties—both NWS and NNWS—commit themselves to negotiate in good faith on nuclear and general disarmament, ultimately under the supervision of international actors. The NAM states in particular pressed the superpowers on the issue of disarmament. However, the non-aligned position was not unitary. While India and Brazil argued that without verified disarmament the NPT would cement the NWS' nuclear monopoly,[40] more moderate voices such as Mexico linked progress on nonproliferation to future progress on disarmament.[41] The latter position eventually prevailed, leading to Article VI. To pressure the NWS to start negotiations under Article VI, a withdrawal clause (Article X paragraph 1), a 25-year duration limit, and a provision for regular treaty reviews—the quinquennial Review Conferences (Article VIII paragraph 3)—were added to the NPT.

Article VI appeals to *security through disarmament*. The imprecise language of Article VI has led to recurring debates about whether the NWS are obliged only to negotiate or to actually disarm. In 1996, one year after the indefinite extension of the NPT, the ICJ found that there was an obligation both to negotiate and to disarm through further agreements.[42] Because of its weak formalisation, disarmament is a matter of inter-state interpretations at the NPT's Review Conferences and not, like safeguards, a clearly defined rule monitored by an international organisation. In the history leading up to the NPT, the meaning of the disarmament norm changed quite significantly. It began with demands for the elimination of nuclear weapons (UNAEC), then changed to gradual disarmament ('Atoms for Peace'), and finally to good-faith negotiations in the NPT.

## 2.2 Normative Conflicts

With the advent of the atomic age and even before its entry into force, the NPT and the nuclear legal norms it codifies have been challenged and contested. The treaty's asymmetric institutional design has distributional consequences and fuels normative contestation around its 'three pillars': nonproliferation, peaceful uses, and disarmament. It is the unequal implementation of the three pillars, rather than the pillars and their normative content, that is the object of contestation. However, not every normative challenge or type of contestation has the capacity to erode the treaty and its normative fabric. Some types of contestation, especially discursive ones, can inspire

[39] Bourantonis (n 33); Daniel H Joyner, 'The legal meaning and implications of Article VI of the Non-Proliferation Treaty' in Gro Nystuen, Stuart Casey-Maslen, and Annie Golden Bersagel (eds), *Nuclear Weapons under International Law* (CUP 2014).

[40] Burns (n 29) 797.

[41] Nystuen and Hugo (n 29).

[42] However, the legal scope of the ICJ's opinion remains disputed among experts, see Joyner (n 39) 405.

normative change and ultimately contribute to strengthening the treaty.[43] By contrast, what threatens to undermine the treaty and its central nonproliferation norm is behavioural contestation by states. Failure to comply with the nonproliferation norm not only threatens international peace and security, but also undermines the treaty's most fundamental bargain: a mechanism by which NNWS can credibly assure each other that they have indeed renounced nuclear weapons. Accordingly, this section discusses which of the NPT's many normative challenges have the capacity to threaten the regime and its norms.

Before turning to the different types of NPT contestation (discursive and behavioural), I use the 'grand bargain' perspective to discuss the NPT's central normative conflicts and their dynamics. According to the 'grand bargain' perspective, NNWS renounce nuclear weapons in exchange for further disarmament by the NWS and access to nuclear technology, materials, and knowledge for civilian purposes. However, the uneven implementation of this bargain across the treaty's three pillars, creates strong tensions between nonproliferation on the one hand and peaceful uses and disarmament on the other, threatening the treaty's effectiveness and stability. The demands of many developing NNWS for access to nuclear technology and material compete with concerns, prominently voiced by NWS, over the dangers of repurposing civilian nuclear applications to serve military ends. Many developing NNWS perceive their side of the bargain as unfulfilled, as they do not have direct, let alone exclusive, access to nuclear cooperation and the sharing of knowledge and technology.[44] Rather, nuclear suppliers seem to prefer bilateral nuclear cooperation agreements,[45] with the 2008 US–India nuclear deal causing considerable frustration because an NWS indirectly legitimated a non-NPT nuclear weapon state. By contrast, civilian nuclear cooperation—either bilateral or through the IAEA's technical cooperation—has enabled some NNWS, such as Iraq or North Korea, to pursue and acquire nuclear weapons.[46] To reduce proliferation risks, many state parties, especially the NWS, are calling for strengthened safeguards, limitations on indigenous nuclear fuel cycles (eg no enrichment), and restrictions on nuclear trade. The institutionalised priority of nonproliferation over disarmament leads to regular confrontations between NWS and NNWS over the relative weight of the norms. The ambiguity of Article VI raises questions about the identification of legitimate behaviour and implementation of the norm.[47] Several NNWS, and in particular many NAM, interpret it as obliging NWS to disarm, while the latter emphasise the importance of strong nonproliferation and the obligation of *all state parties* to enter into disarmament negotiations. Despite

[43] Wayne Sandholtz, 'Dynamics of International Norm Change' (n 3); Rublee and Cohen (n 4); Müller and Tokhi (n 4).

[44] Recent evidence finds no difference between NNWS and non-NPT states in receiving nuclear assistance, see Matthew Kroenig, 'Exporting the Bomb: Why States Provide Sensitive Nuclear Assistance' (2009) 103 American Political Science Review 113; see also Sossai, Chapter 13 in this book.

[45] Matthew Fuhrmann, 'Spreading Temptation. Proliferation and Peaceful Nuclear Cooperation Agreements' (2009) 34 International Security 7.

[46] Fuhrmann and Berejikian (n 13); Robert L Brown and Jeffrey M Kaplow, 'Talking Peace, Making Weapons: IAEA Technical Cooperation and Nuclear Proliferation' (2014) 58 Journal of Conflict Resolution 402.

[47] Knopf, 'After diffusion' (n 2); Kenneth W Abbott and others, 'The Concept of Legalization' (2000) 54 International Organization 401.

significant reductions in Russian and US nuclear weapon stockpiles,[48] many NNWS criticise the failure to formalise and implement the disarmament norm, while their nonproliferation obligations are supposed to be deepened through the adoption of strengthened safeguards in the IAEA's Additional Protocol.[49] In this respect, agreement or even implementation of practical disarmament steps has too often been subject to political developments outside the NPT and the specific dynamics of the Review Conferences. For example, while the end of the Cold War created new momentum for disarmament,[50] the revelation of several clandestine nuclear programs and the shifting priorities of the George W. Bush administration in the United States halted further progress.[51] Even President Obama's disarmament initiatives could not prevent the conflict from becoming, at least discursively, one of the most 'acrimonious' normative conflicts in nuclear politics.[52] Some NNWS, especially Middle Eastern states that had violated their nonproliferation obligations (eg Iran), even accused the NWS of NPT noncompliance.[53] Such accusations—despite their apparent strategic use—can still undermine nonproliferation efforts if they feed perceptions of double standards in the implementation of the NPT's security norms.[54] As some argue, these perceived double standards and the unavailability of other institutional levers may explain why some NNWS condition their acceptance of stronger nonproliferation on prior NWS disarmament.[55]

The grand bargain metaphor leads to gloomy expectations. The institutionalised power asymmetries and perceived double standards raise questions of fairness and justice.[56] From a rationalist perspective, NNWS would have entered into the worst of all possible bargains: forced to give up their nuclear sovereignty and be closely monitored, while receiving little or no economic (peaceful uses) or security benefits (disarmament) in return. The empirical record, however, is difficult to reconcile with these expectations. The NPT is one of the few global institutions with near- universal membership.[57] Moreover, recent evidence shows that the NPT has been effective in curbing proliferation.[58] The grand bargain metaphor provides an incomplete reading of normative conflicts in the NPT, because it pays insufficient attention to the NPT's

[48] From over 70,000 nuclear weapons during the Cold War to about 11,000 today, see Hans M Kristensen, Matt Korda, and Robert Norris, 'Estimated Global Nuclear Warhead Inventories 1945-2021' (*Federation Of American Scientists*, 2021) <https://fas.org/issues/nuclear-weapons/status-world-nuclear-forces/> accessed 28 January 2022.

[49] Rublee and Cohen (n 4); Tannenwald and Acton (n 2); Müller and Tokhi (n 4).

[50] US–Russian bilateral disarmament and China's and France's NPT accession in 1992 facilitated the negotiation and adoption of 13 practical steps toward disarmament at the 2000 Review Conference.

[51] For example, the 2001 Nuclear Posture Review called for the development of new nuclear weapons, see Scott D Sagan, 'Shared responsibilities for nuclear disarmament' (2009) 138 Daedalus 157.

[52] Rublee and Cohen (n 4) 326.

[53] Tanya Ogilvie-White, 'International Responses to Iranian Nuclear Defiance: The Non-Aligned Movement and the Issue of Non-Compliance' (2007) 18 European Journal of International Law 453.

[54] Knopf, 'Nuclear disarmament and nonproliferation' (n 9).

[55] Rublee and Cohen (n 4); Knopf, 'After diffusion' (n 2).

[56] Tannenwald (n 1).

[57] Out of all UN member states, 97 per cent are NPT state parties. India, Pakistan, and Israel that all possess nuclear weapons never joined the treaty. North Korea withdrew in 2003 and acquired nuclear weapons in 2006.

[58] See Matthew Fuhrmann and Yonatan Lupu, 'Do Arms Control Treaties Work? Assessing the Effectiveness of the Nuclear Nonproliferation Treaty' (2016) 60 International Studies Quarterly 530.

most fundamental 'bargain': reciprocal nonproliferation. The establishment of an institution capable of monitoring nuclear compliance and enforcing rules has solved a serious problem of international security cooperation.[59] The relatively intrusive nonproliferation provisions, criticised by some NNWS, actually give NNWS the means to bind their neighbours to stringent and enforceable nonproliferation obligations. Rather than deterring neighbours or adversaries with their own nuclear weapons, NNWS can use the NPT to ensure that others do not proliferate, or at least are prevented from doing so.[60] The NPT can thus provide significant security benefits for most NNWS. Indeed, during the drafting of the NPT, many NNWS called for a credible verification mechanism to ensure that other NNWS comply with nonproliferation rules and for a ban on nuclear weapon transfers from NWS to NNWS.[61] Ultimately, most NNWS believe to gain from the NPT in terms of their security.[62]

The fact that most states are concerned about their security from proliferating neighbours changes the assessment of normative contestation. Rather than focusing on a perennial antagonism between unitary NNWS concerned with peaceful uses and NWS pushing for tighter nonproliferation controls, all state parties are concerned with peaceful uses, nuclear disarmament, and nonproliferation. Because these norms and rules are interdependent rather than isolated pillars, they create important trade-offs. For example, easier access to nuclear technology offers development opportunities but also raises proliferation risks for many NNWS if controls are too weak. Similarly, while nuclear disarmament strengthens international security, it also requires more stringent nonproliferation measures to prevent the emergence of future nuclear-armed states.[63] *All* states parties must therefore balance different nuclear policy goals. To the extent that states gain, or at least do not lose, in terms of their security, they will recognize the NPT as a legitimate institution and try to prevent its disintegration, despite its shortcomings. This does not mean that their concerns about peaceful uses or nuclear disarmament become irrelevant. Rather, whether or not states recognise an institution has implications for how they challenge and contest it.

In this regard, recent research on norm contestation shows that, with the exception of the Middle Eastern states, most NNWS, and especially the NAM, engage constructively with the NPT during Review Conferences.[64] They put forward concrete reform proposals to promote peaceful uses and refrain from delegitimizing the NPT. This contestation behaviour aims to gradually change practices and rules in the institution and presupposes the recognition of the treaty's core norms and an acceptance of their underlying validity. Otherwise, states would not engage constructively with the institution in the first place. The majority of State Parties do not contest the validity of the

[59] Robert Jervis, 'Security Regimes' (1982) 36 International Organization 357; Coe and Vaynman (n 25).
[60] Sagan and Vaynman (n 2); Coe and Vaynman (n 25).
[61] Sagan and Vaynman (n 2); Nystuen and Hugo (n 29).
[62] Knopf, 'Nuclear disarmament and nonproliferation' (n 9); Cottrell (n 24); Coe and Vaynman (n 25).
[63] On the necessity of strong nonproliferation measures for effective disarmament, see Chester I Barnard and others, 'The Acheson-Lilienthal Report on the International Control of Atomic Energy' (1946) <https://fissilematerials.org/library/ach46.pdf> accessed 28 January 2022; Knopf, 'Nuclear disarmament and nonproliferation' (n 9); Scott D Sagan, 'Shared responsibilities' (n 51); Sossai, Chapter 13 in this book.
[64] Müller and Tokhi (n 4).

NPT's norms, but rather express concerns and demands regarding the often (unequal) application of these norms.[65]

Many analysts have noted that the non-ratification of the IAEA's Additional Protocol (AP) represents behavioural contestation. Indeed, some NNWS refuse to ratify the AP with enhanced IAEA verification, unless the NWS disarm. For many, this represents an entrenched conflict in the regime, akin to noncompliance with the non-proliferation norm.[66] On closer inspection, however, this conflict is neither noncompliance nor entrenched. First, the AP is a voluntary instrument and still more than 80 per cent of NNWS have ratified it.[67] Second, and more importantly, more than two thirds of the AP's non-ratifiers are from the Middle East, including countries that have violated their NPT safeguards agreements (eg Egypt, Iran, or Syria). By refusing to ratify the AP, they may be trying to avoid intrusive inspections or using it for strategic reasons, in particular to force Israel into the NPT as an NNWS. In sum, this contestation strategy is not widespread and is more likely to be driven by idiosyncratic state interests.

The violation of the NPT's nonproliferation norm, however, has the capacity to unravel the treaty and its central goals. While it has been argued that noncompliance does not automatically lead to norm erosion or invalidation if other states do not support such behaviour,[68] it is questionable whether this is true for security treaties in general and the NPT in particular. Running a secret nuclear weapons program or ignoring NPT safeguards is a major threat to the NPT's stability. This is because such noncompliance weakens not only *security through nonproliferation*, but also the treaty's entire normative fabric through the interdependence of its norms. In particular, attempts to obtain nuclear weapons by violating the NPT undermine the norm against the possession of nuclear weapons.[69] With respect to disarmament, noncompliance could lead NWS to reconsider their nuclear weapons strategies and reject any further steps toward disarmament. As nuclear energy promises climate-friendly emissions, civilian nuclear energy programmes will become more popular, making compliance even more important to prevent hostile use. Repeated violations could result in the imposition of further restrictions on materials and technologies to other states, exacerbating existing distributional conflicts. Most importantly, NPT violations undermine confidence in the treaty's protection against nuclear weapons, threatening the very functioning of the regime.[70] Violations of the NPT can thus erode the regime, even if few other states share the justifications of noncompliant NNWS.

[65] For the distinction between applicatory and validity contestation, see Krieger and Liese, Chapter 1 in this book.

[66] Rublee and Cohen (n 4); Knopf, 'After diffusion' (n 2).

[67] Even proponents of this linkage argument, such as the New Agenda Coalition, seem split. Out of their seven members, only two—Brazil and Egypt—refuse to ratify the AP.

[68] See Krieger and Liese, Chapter 1 in this book.

[69] Tannenwald and Acton (n 2) 16.

[70] Heike Krieger, 'A Nuclear Test for Multilateralism–Challenges to the Non-Proliferation Treaty as a Means of Arms Control' (2006) 49 German Yearbook of International Law 17; Scott D Sagan, 'The Causes of Nuclear Weapons Proliferation' (2011) 14 Annual Review of Political Science 225; Thomas C Schelling, 'A World without Nuclear Weapons?' (2009) 138 Daedalus 124.

## 3. NPT Violations by Authoritarian States

Given the consequences of NPT violations for state security, it is crucial to understand why states comply with or violate the NPT. However, unlike the issue of nuclear weapons acquisition, NPT (non-)compliance has received comparatively little attention in the literature. One reason for this is the debate over an appropriate indicator of NNWS noncompliance.[71] For example, the most obvious violation of the NPT's nonproliferation norm would be the testing of a nuclear weapon by an NNWS, which has never happened. Judged by this indicator, all NNWS are in compliance with the NPT. The pursuit of nuclear weapons in a clandestine program, short of actual proliferation, is another indicator of NPT violations. Three states have violated the NPT in this respect: North Korea, Iraq, and Libya. However, focusing only on these extreme and historically rare forms of NPT violations underestimates the true extent of noncompliance. Rather, NPT compliance should be judged by whether NNWS comply with the legally binding safeguards agreement that operationalises the NPT's nonproliferation norm. Whether it is an undeclared laboratory-scale experiment or a secret nuclear weapons program, all such actions require one or more violations of safeguards, which ultimately undermine the IAEA's capacity to verify that nuclear activities remain peaceful. If NPT compliance is defined in terms of adherence to safeguards, the number of NNWS that have violated their obligations in the history of the treaty grows from three to eight.[72]

In order to better assess the extent and dynamics of NPT violations, Figure 1 shows the share of non-complying state parties to all state parties over time. Immediately after the NPT's entry into force in 1970, Libya, and soon after Iraq, committed their first treaty violations. In the late 1980s and 1990s, when North Korea started its nuclear weapons programme and South Korea or Egypt failed to declare proliferation-sensitive experiments (e.g. enrichment), the proportion of noncompliant states rose to five percent. Of note, all violations have been revealed only gradually, and mostly through third-party reports.[73] From the mid-1990s to the early 2000s, the share of noncomplying state parties decreases significantly, following increased efforts by the IAEA and many NPT state parties to bring the NPT violators back into compliance. By 2020, only Iran is not complying with its safeguards obligations and additional provisions.

Importantly, all documented NPT safeguards violations have been committed by authoritarian regimes. South Korea, Libya, or Romania were all non-democracies at the time they violated their safeguards agreements. Other nondemocratic NNWS, however, such as Algeria or Jordan in the Middle East, or Vietnam or Indonesia in Asia were in compliance with the NPT. This raises an important but so far unsolved puzzle: why do some nondemocracies violate the nonproliferation norm while others abide by it? Violations of the NPT endanger international peace and security because

[71] Fuhrmann and Berejikian (n 13).

[72] In terms of percentage change, the noncompliance cases grow by 166 per cent when taking as benchmark compliance with NPT-mandated safeguards.

[73] In Iraq, for example, the IAEA failed to detect nuclear weapon sites that were often situated next to safeguarded facilities. The Additional Protocol is therefore a response to the IAEA's limited verification capacities in the past.

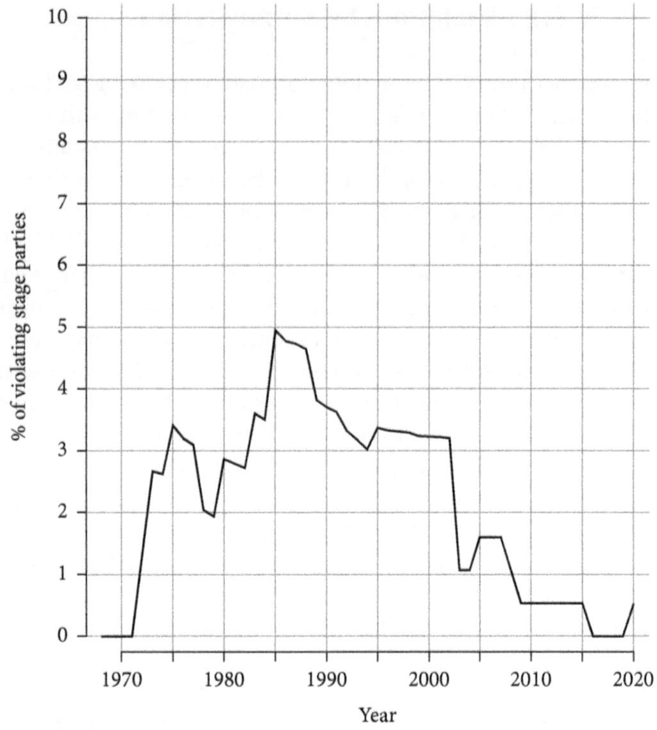


**Figure 1.** Share of noncomplying NNWS to all NNWS from 1970 to 2020.
*Source:* Fuhrmann and Berejikian (2012) and own coding.

they may serve to acquire a (latent) nuclear capability and can thus contribute to an increase in nuclear weapons (eg North Korea).

Violations of the NPT do not necessarily invalidate the norm of nuclear nonproliferation, because few, if any, states approve of these violations.[74] However, noncompliance, undermines an important mechanism by which states cooperate on security issues: Trust.[75] When state parties evade NPT verification and succeed in building a nuclear (breakout) capability, it undermines the belief of compliant NNWS that the NPT is capable of ensuring *security through nonproliferation*.

Given the consequences of NPT violations for the value underlying the treaty (international peace and security) and the effectiveness of its highly legalised nonproliferation norm, existing explanations cannot fully explain why some authoritarian regimes abide by the treaty, while others break it. Security threats, especially when posed by a nuclear-armed rival, certainly feature into authoritarian leaders' calculations. Yet they do not uniformly affect compliance decisions as some dictatorships that were little threatened have tried to acquire nuclear weapons (eg Libya). Similarly, the

[74] See Krieger and Liese, Chapter 1 in this book and Sandholtz, Chapter 3 in this book.
[75] Schelling, 'A world without nuclear weapons' (n 71).

NPT's asymmetric institutional design affects all state parties alike, yet their behavioural contestation of the treaty varies.[76] Rather, it appears that the main driver for NPT compliance choices lies in the dynamics of authoritarian politics. Recent contributions have therefore unpacked the category of authoritarian regimes to argue that those dictatorships with few decision-making constraints are more likely to proliferate than other regime types.[77] Building on this literature, I propose to focus on the internal power dynamics of authoritarian regimes and how these alter state incentives for NPT compliance.

## 3.1 The Dynamics of Authoritarian Politics

To better understand why dictatorships would follow or reject international law,[78] it is important to develop a clear understanding of what a dictatorship is. Unlike democracies, dictatorships prevent free, regular, and competitive elections to fill legislative and executive offices.[79] Because authoritarian elites exclude the population from public affairs and monopolise political authority, they also deprive themselves of a mechanism for monitoring and enforcing political promises among themselves. As a result, authoritarian elites, consisting of the dictator and the ruling coalition, cannot credibly promise to honour mutual agreements.[80] This distinct authoritarian commitment problem fuels elite power struggles, with important implications for the stability of domestic institutional arrangements.

Institutions in autocracies typically help to maintain power-sharing arrangements between the dictator and the ruling elite when the balance of power between them is approximately balanced.[81] Under these conditions, authoritarian institutions will constrain and moderate policy choices, including treaty compliance, because they involve different political actors with the necessary political power to pursue and realise their preferences. However, authoritarian power-sharing arrangements and the institutions that sustain them are precarious. In the absence of a central third-party enforcer of political agreements (the people via elections), neither side can credibly promise not to oust a member of the elite in the future. Incentives to renege on power-sharing arrangements are therefore abundant. The dictator, as the regime's central authority, has the strongest incentives to reduce potential threats from the ruling elite and will try to gradually amass more power for himself.[82] If the ruling coalition is too weak,

[76] The treaty's institutionalised asymmetry of status and obligations is often used as a justification, or rather excuse, for one's own noncompliance, see Tanya Ogilvie-White, 'The Defiant States: The Nuclear Diplomacy of North Korea and Iran' (2010) 17 The Nonproliferation Review 115.

[77] Christopher Way and Jessica Weeks, 'Making it Personal. Regime Type and Nuclear Proliferation' (2014) 58 American Journal of Political Science 705.

[78] Ginsburg (n 11).

[79] Adam Przeworski and others, *Democracy and Development. Political Institutions and Well-Being in the World, 1950–1990* (CUP 2000).

[80] Gandhi (n 15); Svolik (n 15).

[81] Gandhi (n 15); Carles Boix and Milan W Svolik, 'The Foundations of Limited Authoritarian Government: Institutions, Commitment, and Power-Sharing in Dictatorships' (2013) 75 The Journal of Politics 300.

[82] Svolik (n 15); Beatriz Magaloni, 'Credible Power-Sharing and the Longevity of Authoritarian Rule' (2008) 41 Comparative Political Studies 715.

it risks being eliminated from power-sharing, often literally. As a result, institutions lose their constraining effect when members of the elite are removed from decision-making. This dynamic of authoritarian politics has implications for treaty compliance. Whether institutions in authoritarian regimes will contribute to treaty compliance will thus depend on (changes in) the balance of power among authoritarian elites. To the extent that the ruling coalition balances the dictator's power, power sharing will persist and institutions are likely to constrain decision-making. Conversely, as power becomes increasingly concentrated around a small elite, institutions may continue to exist on paper but without constraining effect as the political arrangement that sustains them diminishes. In short, only if members or factions from the ruling coalition have the clout to *keep* their seat at the table, can they effectively constrain political choices.

Persistent power sharing is the political precondition for effective institutional constraints in dictatorships. But what is the mechanism that ultimately leads to honouring the NPT? When power is shared, different members of the elite, often organised in factions, can make their preferences count.[83] Depending on their sources of income that sustain their power base, factions will differ in their nuclear policy preferences, and NPT (non-)compliance creates different opportunities to maintain or expand their position within the regime. Factions that rely on international trade will seek to attract foreign investments and exploit the developmental promises of nuclear energy.[84] Alternatively, other factions may seek to enhance their diplomatic prestige and thus their country's reputation.[85] On the other hand, factions with domestic sources of income may prefer a nuclear programme for reasons of national prestige or energy independence. The military may even wish to acquire a nuclear capability and thus knowledge of sensitive nuclear processes (eg enrichment and reprocessing). Compliance with safeguards, for example, would limit the military's access to nuclear material and technologies. Violations of the NPT, which almost always lead to sanctions, in turn reduce revenue of pro-trade factions and thus their domestic power to avert unfavourable policies. More generally, NPT compliance has distributional consequences that can shift the domestic balance of power. Anticipating these consequences, factions will seek to prevent their removal from power, and compliance will be decided according to each faction's stake in compliance and its relative strength in the authoritarian power-sharing game.

## 3.2 The Iranian Nuclear Crisis

For two decades, Iran's nuclear programme has dominated the international nonproliferation agenda. In contrast to many other cases, Iran has alternated between close cooperation with the IAEA and provocative outright noncompliance, raising serious doubts about its nuclear intentions. The explanation offered in this chapter sheds

[83] George Tsebelis, *Veto Players. How Political Institutions Work* (Princeton University Press 2002)

[84] Etel Solingen, *Nuclear Logics. Contrasting Paths in East Asia and the Middle East* (Princeton University Press 2007).

[85] Rublee (n 34).

light on Iran's NPT (non-)compliance behaviour and provides important insights for evaluating the international responses aimed at restoring Iranian compliance.

In 2002, an Iranian opposition group revealed the existence of a secret Uranium enrichment facility at Natanz and a heavy water reactor at Arak.[86] Both facilities, well hidden from the IAEA, can be used to produce fissile material for nuclear weapons. Together with the declared facilities and a series of other activities revealed by the IAEA, Iran was found to develop the entire nuclear fuel cycle, with considerable advances in some critical areas, most notably in Uranium enrichment.

Since then, Iranian nuclear decision-making has been characterised by intense conflict between the various factions of the regime. Before tracing the power struggles and their eventual outcomes, it is important to discuss the regime's institutional set-up and the relevant factions. The founding principle of the Islamic Republic (Velayat-e Faqih) provides for two tiers of political institutions, a republican and a clerical one. The clerical layer is headed by the Supreme Leader, Ayatollah Ali Khamenei. Two other clerical institutions are the Guardian Council, which can veto the decisions of republican institutions, and the Assembly of Experts, which elects and supervises the Supreme Leader. The parliament and president (as head of government) represent the republican layer. Both institutions are elected by the population.[87] Finally, some mixed-form institutions, such as the Expediency Council, mediate between republican and clerical bodies in cases of conflict. While this formal institutional structure appears constraining, whether it ultimately limits leaders' discretionary authority depends largely on how the different factions use these institutions to achieve their strategic goals. Often, decisions by one body are either ignored or contested by another. For example, the clerical Guardian Council vetoes many decisions made by republican institutions. In turn, its veto can be overriden by the Expediency Council.

What matters, therefore, is which political factions occupy which institutions and how they seek to extend their influence. At the beginning of the nuclear crisis in 2002, three different factions were relevant. The parliament and the government were dominated by the so-called reformers around then president Mohammed Khatami. This faction pursued the economic, political, and cultural opening of the country and sought to overcome the country's international pariah status after the 1979 Islamic Revolution.[88] The clerical institutions were largely controlled by the conservative establishment under Supreme Leader Ayatollah Khamenei. The conservatives are socially and economically supported by traditional merchants and religious foundations, which are de facto financial institutions active in the domestic, inward-oriented industry.[89] The conservatives therefore have little interest in opening up the country's economy and seek to shield their support base from foreign economic competition.[90] The leadership of Iran's Revolutionary Guards, a paramilitary elite organisation, is

[86] Alireza Jafarzadeh, 'Remarks by Alireza Jafarzadeh on New Information on Top Secret Projects of the Iranian Regime's Nuclear Program' (*Iran Watch*, 14 August 2002) <www.iranwatch.org/library/ncri-new-information-top-secret-nuclear-projects-8-14-02> accessed 28 January 2022.

[87] Note that these are not free and fair elections as the Guardian Council vets candidates for the parliament and presidency.

[88] Nikki R Keddie, *Modern Iran. Roots and Results of Revolution* (2nd edn, Yale University Press 2006).

[89] Ali Gheissari and Vali Nasr, 'The Conservative Consolidation in Iran' (2005) 47 Survival 175.

[90] Ray Takeyh, 'Iran: From Reform to Revolution?' (2004) 46 Survival 131; Keddie (n 89).

tied to the clerical conservative establishment. The Revolutionary Guards operate a large defensive industry, including significant parts of the nuclear program, and have a significant share in the country's petrochemical industry. Finally, the pragmatist faction around Hashemi Rafsanjani was represented in some secondary secular (Supreme National Security Council) and clerical institutions (Assembly of Experts and Expediency Council). They represent the country's industrial non-oil elite and opt for a Chinese model of governance—fostering strong economic growth to ensure regime survival.[91]

Obstruction and concealment characterized Iranian nuclear politics from 2002 until 2003. The conservative-dominated Atomic Energy Organization of Iran (AEOI) and the government's foreign ministry battled over nuclear authority, with the latter preferring cooperation with the IAEA and the former concealing the scope of the country's nuclear programme.[92] That year saw a peak in Iranian violations as the AEOI deliberately obstructed international verification. After the IAEA called on Iran to cooperate and restore compliance, the nuclear dossier was referred to the country's Supreme National Security Council (SNSC). The council represented conservatives, pragmatists, and reformists, with a slight majority of the latter two factions. The SNSC's secretary, Hassan Rohani, who was a close ally of the pragmatist Rafsanjani, was tasked with coordinating nuclear policy and negotiating with the IAEA. As a result of the institutional dominance of the reformist-pragmatist camp, Iran cooperated with the IAEA from late 2003 to early 2005, suspending Uranium enrichment, disclosing relevant information, and even provisionally implementing the IAEA's Additional Protocol.[93] The rationale for cooperation with the IAEA was described by Rohani himself in a rare piece of evidence on Iranian nuclear decision-making.[94] The pragmatist-reformist majority in the SNSC wanted to avoid UN sanctions against Iran, as this would cut-off the country's, and thus this faction's own, sources of (foreign) revenue. Instead, they saw NPT compliance as a means to open negotiations with the 'EU three' (E3—France, the UK, and Germany) on closer economic ties,[95] in the hope of one day joining the World Trade Organization. Their position was strongly challenged by the conservatives, who accused the government and the SNSC of betraying Iranian interests, particularly by agreeing to the AP ,[96] which would not only diminish the country's prestige but also limit the AEOI's and Revolutionary Guards' access to nuclear processes, knowledge, and capabilities. Having won a majority in Iran's parliament in 2004, the conservatives stepped up their opposition to the country's official nuclear policy, for example by passing legislation that prohibited

[91] Hossein S Seifzadeh, 'The Landscape of Factional Politics and Its Future in Iran' (2003) 57 Middle East Journal 57; Ray Takeyh, *Hidden Iran: Paradox and Power in the Islamic Republic* (NY Times Books 2006).

[92] William A Samii, 'The Iranian Nuclear Issue and Informal Networks' (2006) 59 Naval War College Review 63.

[93] Iran signed the Additional Protocol in 2004 and applied it provisionally until its parliament would officially ratify it. Until today, the AP has not been ratified and is at times applied, but not at others.

[94] Hassan Rohani, 'Beyond the Challenges Facing Iran and the IAEA Concerning the Nuclear Dossier' (2005) 1–39 <www.iranwatch.org/sites/default/files/rahbord-rohani-093005_0.pdf> accessed 28 January 2022.

[95] ibid 6.

[96] ibid 4.

the suspension of uranium enrichment[97]. Nevertheless, the reformist and pragmatist factions were powerful enough to pursue their interests and cooperate with the IAEA, either by ignoring domestic opposition or by referring controversial legislation to the Expediency Council, which Rafsanjani himself chaired at the time.

However, Iran's nuclear policies was soon radically overturned. While the conservatives gradually consolidated their power,[98] the most significant reduction in the number of competing factions occured with the election of Mahmood Ahmadinejad to the Iranian presidency in 2005. Representing an ultraconservative faction based on the support of Islamic militants (eg the Basij militia), radical clerics, and lower-ranking Revolutionary Guards, the newly elected president resumed and expanded Uranium enrichment and severely obstructed the IAEA's work. Together with the conservatives, the ultraconservatives successfully removed reformers from Iranian politics and limited the pragmatists to the Assembly of Experts. As Iranian violations increased, the UN Security Council imposed several sets of economic sanctions against the country. However, the sanctions had little effect on Iranian policies because the economic base of the ruling conservatives and ultraconservatives was domestic and thus largely insulated from foreign influences.

Instead, by reducing non-oil revenues, sanctions have reduced the revenues and hence the power of the factions opposed to Ahmadinejad. As a result, Ahmadinejad's efforts to consolidate his power were met with little resistance, resulting in the violent suppression of public protests against the rigged 2009 presidential elections, the open persecution of reformist politicians and clerics (notably Ahmadinejad's contenders in the 2009 presidential election, Mir-Hossein Mousavi and Mehdi Karubi), and an belligerent foreign policy (eg threatening the destruction of Israel). Ultimately, however, the violent expansion of ultraconservatives' power threatened the very survival of the conservatives at the helm of the regime. With domestic protests and foreign pressure mounting, the economy deteriorating, and the president openly challenging the conservative establishment, the Supreme Leader turned against the ultraconservatives and publicly disapproved of Ahamdinejad.[99] Ultraconservative hardliners were gradually removed from public office and the conservatives increased their majority in the parliament. In 2013, the candidate of the pragmatists and reformists, Hassan Rohani, won the presidential elections. In addition to their growing influence in clerical bodies, these factions have once again taken over the country's government.

The domestic political conditions were thus favourable for a solution to the decades-long nuclear standoff. In this respect, the sanctions worked more indirectly by mobilising those factions that wanted to overcome international economic sanctions by changing nuclear policies. Rohani also transferred the nuclear dossier from the SNSC back to the foreign ministry, reducing conservatives' influence on nuclear policies.[100] In contrast to 2003/2004, when the Iranian government only talked to the E3 while

[97] Ali Akbar Dareini, 'Iranian Parliament Approves Bill Requiring Government to Resume Uranium Enrichment' (2004) <https://eu.heraldtribune.com/story/news/2004/11/01/iran-lawmakers-ok-resuming-uranium-enrichment/28822124007/> accessed 7 March 2022.

[98] Gheissari and Nasr (n 90).

[99] Ariane M Tabatabai, 'Negotiating the "Iran Talks" in Tehran: The Iranian Drivers that Shaped the Joint Comprehensive Plan of Action' (2017) 24 Nonproliferation Review 225.

[100] ibid.

the Bush administration put Iran on the axis of evil, the Obama administration actively sought to resolve the nuclear issue. Together with the other permanent members of the Security Council plus Germany (the P5+1), the Obama administration began formal negotiations with the new Iranian leadership in autumn 2013. Eventually, the parties signed the Joint Comprehensive Plan of Action (JCPoA), commonly referred to as the 'Iran nuclear deal'. The agreement obliges Iran to curb its enrichment activities, dismantle its stockpile of moderately enriched Uranium, and reconfigure its heavy water reactor to prevent the production of Plutonium for a nuclear weapon. The possible routes to the bomb would thus be severely constrained. Moreover, Iran would agree to a comprehensive and unprecedented verification mandate of the IAEA, going well beyond the Additional Protocol and setting new standards for NPT compliance control.[101] Upon confirmation of Iran's compliance, UN and European sanctions would be phased out and the US would refrain from imposing secondary sanctions.[102] Following the adoption of the JCPoA, Iran complied with the terms of the agreement,[103] resolving within the broader nonproliferation regime and through diplomatic negotiations a conflict that had threatened international and regional security.

By contrast, the unilateral renunciation of the JCPoA by US President Donald Trump in 2016 carries significant dangers for the stability of Iranian compliance and for the robustness of the NPT. Notwithstanding the IAEA's confirmation of Iranian compliance, President Trump revoked the Iran deal and reimposed secondary sanctions.[104] Trump's decision could damage pro-compliance factions in Iran and thus strengthen hardliners with aggressive foreign policy stances and a preference for a nuclear capability (eg Revolutionary Guards). The nuclear hawks in Iran had already condemned the JCPoA, accusing the pragmatist-reformist government once again of betraying Iran and delivering the country to the whims of the US and international organisations.

As has happened in the past, in an authoritarian power-sharing equilibrium, domestic anti-compliance factions may be strengthened as their rivals lose influence. This increases the chances of NPT noncompliance. And indeed, the reimposed sanctions have weakened the pro-compliance faction by reducing its revenues and by growing street protests against the government due to the deteriorating economic situation. In response, pressure from hardline conservative factions is growing, once again raising the threat of pragmatists' removal from power. With few options left to stave off growing domestic opposition from rival factions, Rohani's government appears to have partly capitulated by resuming Uranium enrichment in 2020. The election of Ebrahim Raisi as Iran's president in 2021 effectively removed the pro-compliance factions from power. The new hardline conservative leadership not only resumed Uranium enrichment, but accelerated the pace of its nuclear program and its

[101] Mark Fitzpatrick, 'Assessing the JCPOA' (2017) 57 Adelphi Series 19.

[102] In the context of its nonproliferation policy, the US can impose sanctions on states that trade with noncomplying NPT state parties.

[103] International Atomic Energy Agency, 'IAEA and Iran - IAEA Reports' <www.iaea.org/newscenter/focus/iran/iaea-and-iran-iaea-reports> accessed 28 January 2022.

[104] The Trump administration with its many critics of the Iran deal, 'have laboured to create a narrative of Iranian violations' see Fitzpatrick (n 102) 43.

efforts to acquire a nuclear deterrent in open defiance of its nuclear nonproliferation commitments.

## 4. Conclusion

In an attempt to understand the varying NPT compliance behaviour of authoritarian states, the theoretical discussion and the Iranian case suggest that authoritarian politics should be viewed as a power struggle between competing domestic factions. These factions are endowed with varying political resources and opportunities to gain political influence at the expense of others. Accordingly, shifts in the regime-internal distribution of power happen often and have, in turn, important consequences for dictatorships' respect for international law, including the NPT. To the extent that domestic pro-compliance factions are powerful enough to partake in nuclear decision-making, they can use their political clout to achieve NPT compliance. Conversely, factions seeking to enhance their prestige or build a latent nuclear capability raise the odds for NPT violations if they are not challenged by domestic rivals. Compliance with the NPT will therefore vary in response to changes in the distribution of power among elite factions in authoritarian regimes.

The insights of this account have implications for the NPT and the robustness of its norms and underlying values, because knowing when and why authoritarian regimes comply can help evaluate international strategies to avoid NPT violations, and thus increase confidence in the treaty's central security promise to stop proliferation. In this respect, the JCPoA can be described as a historic agreement within the nonproliferation regime. It ensured NPT compliance of an authoritarian state with dubious nuclear ambitions, because it set incentives in a way that generated strong domestic support from influential factions of the authoritarian elite. Importantly, the successful operation of the deal would provide the pro-trade factions with the economic resources necessary to maintain and even expand their domestic power against their rivals. Moreover, as the economy grows, popular opposition would diminish and, further stabilizing the rule of pro-compliance factions. As argued and shown, empowering factions with a stake in international cooperation can weaken others in authoritarian power sharing, thus creating the domestic conditions for treaty compliance by authoritarian regimes.

The JCPoA was part of President Obama's international nonproliferation and disarmament efforts, as summarised in his Prague Speech of 2009.[105] The new nuclear policy of the United States focused on strong nonproliferation measures, promoting peaceful uses, strengthening the security of nuclear materials and facilities against terrorism, and, importantly, promoting disarmament. Prior to the JCPoA, the US concluded the New START treaty with Russia in 2010, signaling the willingness of NWS to disarm. In the case of Iran, the Obama administration's new policy also indirectly weakened conservative critics of the NPT and the West. More importantly, the new

[105] The White House Office of the Press Secretary, 'Fact sheet: The Prague Nuclear Agenda' (*The White House President Barack Obama*, 11 January 2017) <https://obamawhitehouse.archives.gov/the-press-office/2017/01/11/fact-sheet-prague-nuclear-agenda> accessed 28 January 2022.

policy and the conclusion of the JCPoA demonstrated that severe and persistent conflicts can be peacefully settled within the institution. Furthermore, the strong verification measures provided for by the JCPoA serve as a template for safeguarding civilian nuclear programmes, thereby reassuring other states that nuclear energy remains peaceful, even though Iran has been allowed some enrichment activity.[106] This is an important precondition for facilitating civilian nuclear cooperation, which could further the NPT goals of nonproliferation and peaceful uses. In sum, the JCPoA has restored Iranian compliance and strengthened the nonproliferation norm.[107]

However, President Trump's revocation of the Iran nuclear deal in 2016 has jeopardized this success. Domestically, it creates strong motivations and justifications for Iranian nuclear hawks to fight the pragmatist-reformist leadership. As happened before in 2004/2005, pro-compliance factions risk losing influence, while the factions that seek an Iranian nuclear deterrent gain ground. As a result, the risk of regional proliferation as a hedge against a nuclear Iran grows (eg Turkey or Saudi Arabia). This, in turn, could put an end to disarmament negotiations and make peaceful nuclear cooperation even more difficult. More importantly, abrogating a functioning agreement, where the IAEA has consistently confirmed Iranian compliance, severely undermines the confidence of state parties in the NPT as an institution that provides for security through nonproliferation. Accusations of unfair treatment and double standards in the application of norms and rules may now resonate more strongly with some NNWS, particularly when they fail to reciprocate a state's compliance while honouring an NPT violator with nuclear weapons (North Korea) through direct talks.

Despite the experience of the past four years, the core NPT norms are not eroding in the sense of losing their social or legal validity. However, the discussion in this chapter has also shown that the resilience of the treaty's nonproliferation norm depends on understanding the behaviour of authoritarian NPT violators and on the response of norm defenders to such fundamental challenges.[108] Recognizing that compliance depends on authoritarian power struggles requires well-designed policies that empower domestic actors with an interest in NPT compliance. By contrast, unilateral and selective policies can have adverse effects by weakening potential allies among authoritarian elites and thereby strengthening one's adversaries.

[106] George Perkovich, 'Implications of the Joint Comprehensive Plan of Action' (2017) 1898 AIP Conference Proceedings <https://aip.scitation.org/doi/abs/10.1063/1.5009224> accessed 28 January 2022.
[107] Tannenwald and Acton (n 2).
[108] Sandholtz, 'Norm Contestation' (n 3).

# 13
# Arms Control
## Between the NPT and the Nuclear Taboo?

*Mirko Sossai*

## 1. Introduction

The gradual emergence of a normative stigma vis-à-vis nuclear weapons has been the cornerstone of the argument developed by Nina Tannenwald to explain the most significant achievement of the atomic age so far: the 'nuclear taboo', 'a widespread inhibition on the use of nuclear weapons, stemming from a powerful sense of revulsion associated with such destructive weapons'.[1] In challenging the realist assumption that mutual deterrence is the key factor for the non-use of this typology of weapons since 1945, the term 'taboo' emphasizes not only the profound moral dimensions of the debate over nuclear weapons but also the absolute character of the prohibitionary norm.

It is not by chance that the concept of 'nuclear taboo'—in its strong version as prohibition 'never under any circumstance' to use—has not much penetrated into international legal scholarship: the most obvious reason is that in the last 25 years any legal debate on the use or threat of use of nuclear weapons has been framed around the main findings of the International Court of Justice (ICJ) in the 1996 Advisory Opinion. In a split 7 to 7 decision, with the President casting the deciding vote, the Court concluded 'that the threat or use of nuclear weapons would generally be contrary to the rules of international law applicable in armed conflict, and in particular the principles and rules of humanitarian law', but that it could not 'conclude definitively whether the threat or use of nuclear weapons would be lawful or unlawful in an extreme circumstance of self-defence, in which the very survival of a State would be at stake'.[2]

Although it does not prohibit nuclear weapons for the time being, the Treaty on the Non-Proliferation of Nuclear Weapons (NPT) has undoubtedly contributed to establish a taboo on use, as it is aimed at minimizing the risk of nuclear war by limiting the spread of nuclear weapons and by providing for their ultimate complete destruction. The obligations under the NPT reflected a balance between the principle of peaceful coexistence between the two superpowers, and the emerging trends of the protection of certain fundamental values (namely international peace and security). At the end of the Cold War, the existing nuclear non-proliferation regime seemed to remain an effective tool to preserve peace and to safeguard humanity in the new century.

However, only few years later, new threats raised doubts about whether the NPT still represented a suitable answer to the challenges posed by nuclear weapons. The

[1] Nina Tannenwald, 'How Strong Is the Nuclear Taboo Today?' (2018) 41 The Washington Quarterly 89.
[2] *Legality of the Threat or Use of Nuclear Weapons* (Advisory Opinion) [1996] ICJ Rep 226, 266.

Mirko Sossai, *Arms Control* In: *Tracing Value Change in the International Legal Order*. Edited by: Heike Krieger and Andrea Liese, Oxford University Press. © Mirko Sossai 2023. DOI: 10.1093/oso/9780192855831.003.0013

point is made that cases of non-compliance with the NPT have been just one of the factors determining normative evolution in this context.[3] The combination of formal and informal regulatory initiatives taken in the first decade of this century—such as the Proliferation Security Initiative (PSI) and the UN Security Council (UNSC) Resolution 1540 (2004)—reflected both the perceived new threat represented by the acquisition of weapons of mass destruction (WMD) by non-state actors or 'rogue states' with terrorist intentions as well as the specific political culture of the United States (US) administration, manifesting a preference for the creation of multilateral initiatives and partnerships, which were not based on legally binding instruments.

The success of the nuclear non-proliferation regime has depended on its capacity to ensure an adequate balance of interests of all parties. In this regard, the issue of good faith adherence to the NPT obligations is not limited to the nuclear ambitions of certain countries. Since 2014, reciprocal allegations of treaty violations by the United States and Russia have eroded the legal framework for nuclear disarmament. The fate of the INF Treaty—the 1987 bilateral agreement on the elimination of intermediate-range and shorter-range missiles—is paradigmatic: the United States decided first to suspend its obligations and later to withdraw from the treaty,[4] due to material breach by Russia, on the basis of the *inadimplenti non est adimplendum* principle enshrined in Article 60 of the Vienna Convention on the Law of Treaties (VCLT).[5] Therefore, more recent developments—including the adoption and the entry into force of the Treaty on the Prohibition of Nuclear Weapons (TPNW)—need to be understood against the background of the frustration manifested by non-nuclear states with respect to the implementation of the NPT provisions on nuclear disarmament. Undoubtedly, the Humanitarian Initiative, with its emphasis on the protection of core humanitarian values, has contributed to change the dynamics of the debate on nuclear non-proliferation and disarmament. One might wonder how giving priority to those values is having implications on the lawfulness of the possession and use of nuclear weapons, towards a globally recognized taboo.

## 2. The Legacy of the 1996 Advisory Opinion: The Implications of the 'Rule of Law' Argument

In 1996 the ICJ was indeed divided on the matter of whether non-recourse to nuclear weapons over the past 50 years constitutes the expression of an *opinio juris*. Much criticism was levelled against the relationship between *jus ad bellum* and *jus in bello* set by the opinion; others, including dissenting judges,[6] qualified the formula chosen

[3] Cf Alexandros Tokhi, Chapter 12 in this book.

[4] US Department of Defense, 'Statement from Secretary of Defense Mark T. Esper on the INF Treaty' (2 August 2019) <www.defense.gov/Newsroom/Releases/Release/Article/1924386/statement-from-secretary-of-defense-mark-t-esper-on-the-inf-treaty/> accessed 30 January 2022.

[5] The deterioration of the nuclear arms control framework was further exacerbated by Russia's decision to suspend the 2010 New Strategic Arms Reduction Treaty (New START) in February 2023, the last remaining treaty limiting US and Russian strategic nuclear arsenals. The suspension was part of the campaign of nuclear warnings that Russia started since the invasion of Ukraine one year earlier.

[6] Cf *Legality of the Threat or Use of Nuclear Weapons*, Dissenting Opinion of Judge Higgins [1996] ICJ Rep 583.

by the Court as a problematic *non liquet*. The point was made that such a finding was discriminatory in that it only applied to the NPT nuclear-weapon states (NWS) and to those states which are not party of the NPT regime. For all other states, the normative significance of the NPT was clear: 'the threat or use of nuclear weapons is illegal, since treaty law specifically and explicitly prohibits it'.[7]

The difficulties of the Court were, on the one hand, in prescribing absolute rules (affirming an absolute prohibition is in fact a taboo argument), and on the other, in developing a rational argument aimed at assessing whether a prohibition on the use of nuclear weapons could be deduced from their contrariety with formal rules and general principles of international law.[8] The conclusion, by eleven votes to three, was that '[t]here is in neither customary nor conventional international law any comprehensive and universal prohibition of the threat or use of nuclear weapons as such'.[9] In other words, the Court did not affirm the absence of applicable law (quite the contrary, there were even too many norms): rather, it could not find a specific rule prohibiting the relevant conduct.[10]

The 'rule of law' was an important argument throughout the proceedings: the opposite views regarding the question whether the Court should deliver its opinion, claimed that their position was based on the need to promote and ensure the 'rule of law' in international relations (IR). Whereas some states maintained that an answer by the Court was essential, as the law was 'the defence par excellence for the weak',[11] namely the small non-nuclear weapons states (NNWS), others pointed out that 'it would be destabilizing to the rule of law and to confidence in international negotiations if those treaties were now interpreted in such a way as to prohibit the use of nuclear weapons'.[12] In the view of other countries, the questions presented to the Court were even beyond the law and merely political. As is well known, the ICJ concluded that there existed no 'compelling reasons' which 'would lead the Court to exercise its discretion not to do so'.[13]

In any case, the 1996 Advisory Opinion has paved the way towards a discussion regarding the nature of international law as a normative system. By posing the question of whether the legitimacy of an *ad bellum* cause may ever justify the use of nuclear weapons in violation of *jus in bello*, the Court seemed to challenge the conceptual separation between the rules on the use of force in IR and international humanitarian law (IHL). The implications of a 'conflationist' approach are both theoretical and practical: it has been argued that the long-term consequence would be

[7] Timothy LH McCormack, 'A Non Liquet on Nuclear Weapons - The ICJ Avoids the Application of General Principles of International Humanitarian Law' (1997) 37 International Review of the Red Cross 76, 80.

[8] Martti Koskenniemi, 'Faith Identity, and the Killing of the Innocent: International Lawyers and Nuclear Weapons' (1997) 10 Leiden Journal of International Law 137.

[9] *Nuclear Weapons* (Advisory Opinion) (n 2) para 28.

[10] Mariano J Aznar-Gomez, 'The 1996 Nuclear Weapons Advisory Opinions and Non Liquet in International Law' (1999) 48 The International and Comparative Law Quarterly 3, 14.

[11] See the statement by Mexico in ICJ, 'Public Sitting' (3 November 1995) CR 95/25, 50, 55 <www.icj-cij.org/public/files/case-related/95/095-19951103-ORA-01-00-BI.pdf> accessed 30 January 2022.

[12] *Nuclear Weapons* (Advisory Opinion) (n 2) para 28.

[13] ibid para 19.

an incorrect merging of the proportionality principles under *jus ad bellum* and *jus in bello*.[14]

In addition, the proceedings and the Advisory Opinion showed the existence of a strong tension between different visions of the judicial function of the ICJ[15] and, more generally, of international law, 'in particular between a "state-oriented" approach and a more "humanist" approach'.[16] The Court first identified and then confronted the 'elementary considerations of humanity' at the basis of the 'intransgressible principles' of IHL, on the one hand, and the 'fundamental right of a State to its own survival', on the other. The indecisiveness of the Court was strongly criticized insofar as it could not find any criterion to prioritize one interest over the other, in order to solve what constituted only an 'apparent' lacuna. For others, instead, the conclusion of the Court seemed to constitute an attempt to use the method of balancing two general principles of law formed within the international legal system: the principle underlying the prohibition on the use of indiscriminate weapons would generally prevail over the principle ensuring the exigencies of self-defence; however in extreme circumstances, an inversion of priority would be possible, in favour of the principle of self-defence.[17]

The assumption of legal positivism is the completeness of international law as a whole,[18] in which the existence of lacunae is disputable, including in the field of nuclear non-proliferation and disarmament.[19] Of course, this does not exclude gaps in specific prescriptions. The newly adopted TPNW[20] definitely fills a regulatory gap, as it introduces a comprehensive ban on the use, in accordance with the formula 'never under any circumstances': the contribution towards a clear-cut prohibition 'of its own impact' encounters the open opposition to it of the NWS and their allies. Still, it is important to consider to what extent the multiplicity of legal regimes governing nuclear weapons continues to serve the purpose of promoting certain fundamental values, the protection of which is a legal interest of the international community as a whole.

[14] See Jasmine Moussa, 'Nuclear weapons and the separation of jus ad bellum and jus in bello' in Gro Nystuen, Stuart Casey-Maslen, and Annie Golden Bersagel (eds), *Nuclear Weapons under International Law* (CUP 2014) 78.

[15] Gleider I Hernandez, *The International Court of Justice and the Judicial Function* (OUP 2014) 266–76.

[16] Laurence Boisson de Chazournes and Philippe Sands, 'Introduction' in Laurence Boisson de Chazournes and Philippe Sands (eds), *International Law, the International Court of Justice and Nuclear Weapons* (CUP 1999) 13–14.

[17] Enzo Cannizzaro, *Diritto internazionale* (5th edn, Giappichelli 2020) 140.

[18] On this topic, see the debate between Hersch Lauterpacht, 'Some Observations on the Prohibition of Non liquet and the Completeness of the Law' in *Simbolae Verzijl* (Martinus Nijhoff 1958) 196 and Julius Stone, 'Non liquet and the Function of Law in the International Community' (1959) 35 British Yearbook of International Law 124; cf Jörg Kammerhofer, 'Gaps, the "Nuclear Weapons" Advisory Opinion and the Structure of International Legal Argument between Theory and Practice' (2009) 80 British Year Book of International Law 333.

[19] See Dieter Fleck, 'State responsibility consequences of termination of or withdrawal from non-proliferation treaties' in Daniel H Joyner and Marco Roscini (eds), *Non-Proliferation Law as a Special Regime* (CUP 2012) 250.

[20] Treaty on the Prohibition of Nuclear Weapons (adopted 7 July 2017, entered into force 22 January 2021) UN Doc A/CONF.229/2017/8.

## 3. Is the NPT Still a Suitable Answer to the Challenge Posed by Nuclear Weapons?

In the last 50 years, the NPT has been the cornerstone of international efforts to address the problem of the horizontal proliferation of nuclear weapons. On the basis of the distinction between NWS and NNWS, the balance of duties and rights included therein are usually considered under three pillars, which constitutes the 'Grand Bargain' of the NPT: non-proliferation, the peaceful use of nuclear energy, and disarmament. The preamble of the TPNW confirms the centrality of the NPT, which 'has a vital role to play in promoting international peace and security'.

### 3.1 The NPT as a Means for the Maintenance of International Peace and Security

The NPT negotiations need to be understood in the wider context of the arms control and non-proliferation efforts which characterized the bipolar confrontation during the 1960s: since the aim of the nuclear dissuasion was the stabilization of the balance of power, arms control instruments usually included measures consisting of mutual limitations of armaments or the freeze of their number at a given level. The aim of such initiatives was to ensure predictability and stability in IR, in order 'to avert the danger' of a nuclear war: cooperation, reciprocity, and inclusiveness[21] were the major features of an approach that promoted confidence building among states as the most effective tool to prevent the risk of surprise or accidental attacks, by avoiding misperceptions. The preamble of the NPT establishes a bridge between its obligations and the maintenance of the international peace and security, based on the ban on the use of force in IR under the UN Charter. The obligations under the NPT indicate the point of synthesis which reconciled the principle of peaceful coexistence in the mutual relations between the two superpowers and the emerging trends at the time of its adoption towards the protection of certain fundamental values. As other authors have observed, the regime against the proliferation of nuclear weapons is concerned with collective interests of the international community as a whole—namely international peace and security—while at the same time dealing with cardinal particularistic interests of major powers.[22]

The NPT crystallizes the situation in 1968 regarding the number of declared NWS. The instrument is founded on a basic distinction between those five countries (China, France, Russia, United Kingdom, United States) and the other NNWS. There is no doubt that the NPT was negotiated with the expectation that future progress on nuclear disarmament would be necessary to ensure the treaty's sustainability.[23] The

[21] See Heike Krieger, 'A Nuclear Test for Multilateralism – Challenges to the Non-Proliferation Treaty as a Means of Arms Control' (2006) 49 German Yearbook of International Law 17.

[22] Andreas L Paulus and Jörn Müller, 'Survival Through Law. Is there a Law Against Nuclear Proliferation?' (2007) 18 Finnish Yearbook of International Law 83.

[23] Matthew Harries, 'Disarmament as Politics: Lessons from the Negotiation of NPT Article VI' (2015) Chatham House Research Paper <www.chathamhouse.org/sites/default/files/field/field_document/20150512DisarmamentPoliticsNPTHarriesUpdate2.pdf> accessed 29 January 2022.

disarmament pillar of the NPT is represented by Article VI: it was included as a concession to the NNWS in an attempt to balance the essential discriminatory nature of the rights and obligations under the treaty. Article VI contains a duty 'to pursue negotiations in good faith on effective measures relating to cessation of the nuclear arms race at an early date and to nuclear disarmament, and on a Treaty on general and complete disarmament'. Should Article VI be removed from the NPT, the remaining obligations of the NWS could not be deemed to create an adequate reciprocal commitment for the renunciation of nuclear weapons by NNWS.[24]

### 3.2 NPT Structural Deficits and the Counter-Proliferation Efforts

Non-proliferation as a means of arms control and disarmament through a universal treaty regime seemed a successful approach,[25] at least in the first years after the end of the Cold War, as confirmed by the indefinite extension of the NPT in 1995.[26] However, the changes in the international security scenario were of such magnitude that only after a decade the question became whether the NPT suffered structural deficits and whether the legal regime for the non-proliferation of nuclear weapons—with NPT at its core—could still be considered as a suitable answer to the challenge posed by nuclear weapons in the new century. Lack of universality, reciprocity, and compliance were identified as the main deficits of the non-proliferation regime.[27] As for universality of ratifications, although the NPT was an effective non-proliferation tool after the dissolution of the Soviet Union, as all the former federal Republics except Russia adhered to the treaty as NNWS, India, Israel, and Pakistan have not yet ratified the NPT and North Korea withdrew from it in 2003: there is evidence that all these countries have nuclear-weapon capabilities, and this cannot but affect the security and stability of their respective regions.

Concern for lack of compliance was related not only to the North Korean withdrawal but also to the Iranian nuclear programme. Iran has always claimed that its nuclear activities represented the exercise of its right 'to develop research, production and use of nuclear energy for peaceful purposes', in accordance with Article IV of the NPT.[28] Moreover, at the beginning of the twenty-first century, the most frightening scenario was identified in the acquisition of nuclear materials and technology by non-state actors: states individually or collectively took several initiatives in reaction to that perceived threat, representing a move towards a reconfiguration of the paradigm developed during the Cold War. In an attempt to classify these developments, some authors have employed the notion of counter-proliferation, which encompasses all the

[24] Harald Müller, David Fischer and Wolfgang Kötter, *Nuclear Non-Proliferation and Global Order* (OUP 1994) 7.

[25] Krieger (n 21) 19.

[26] United Nations, 'Final Document on Extension of the Treaty on the Non-Proliferation of Nuclear Weapons' (1995) 34 International Legal Materials 959.

[27] Richard Leaver, 'The Failing NPT: the Case for Institutional Reform' (2005) 59 Australian Journal of International Affairs 417.

[28] See eg 'Statement by the Iranian Government and visiting EU Foreign Ministers, Full text: Iran declaration' *BBC News* (London, 21 October 2003) <http://news.bbc.co.uk/1/hi/world/middle_east/3211036.stm> accessed 29 January 2022.

initiatives taken to ensure that WMD do not fall into the hands of non-state actors, including terrorists, or irresponsible governments.[29] The major factors of this paradigm shift have been, on the one hand, the sanctions regimes imposed by the UNSC against Iran and North Korea and, on the other hand, the cooperation through multilateral fora created within the framework of informal initiatives, such as the PSI, aimed at countering the illicit trafficking of WMD. In this period, the term 'coalitions of the willing' became part of the vocabulary of the arms control discourse. The concept certainly reflected a peculiar understanding of international cooperation: in response to the threats of global terrorism and the spread of WMD, the administration of George W Bush manifested a preference for the creation of multilateral initiatives and partnerships, which were not based on legally binding instruments.[30]

Significantly, a non-legally binding agreement, establishing political commitments, was the instrument chosen by the participants of the negotiations with the purpose of concluding the decade of international tensions with respect to Iran's nuclear programme: the political nature of the Joint Comprehensive Plan of Action—the nuclear deal reached by Iran and the E3/EU+3 (China, the Russian Federation, the United States, France, Germany, the United Kingdom with the European Union) in July 2015[31]—seems to find confirmation in its specific title, as well as in the circumstance that the participants did not sign it. The difficulties encountered in the implementation of the nuclear deal, particularly after the US decision to abandon it, have been certainly related to the complex dynamics between the participants. Still, it is important to stress the inherent ambivalence of an accord oscillating between bilateralism and community interests: based on 'reciprocal commitments', it is also aimed at contributing to 'regional and international peace and security'.

## 3.3 The Growing Frustration of NNWS on the Lack of Implementation of Article VI

Throughout the history of the NPT, the inequality between the NWS and NNWS as well as the issue of the relations of priority among the three pillars of the treaty have represented the main source of conflict.[32] In the past two decades, the focus of NWS has been on nuclear non-proliferation rather than disarmament. The cyclical nature of the review conferences—alternating between success and failure every five years—reflected the frustration of many NNWS with the lack of progress on reducing nuclear arms levels and the belief that the NWS are not fulfilling their obligations under Article VI to negotiate disarmament in good faith.

[29] Daniel H Joyner, *International Law and the Proliferation of Weapons of Mass Destruction* (OUP 2009); Michael Bothe, 'Weapons of Mass Destruction, Counter-Proliferation', *Max Planck Encyclopedia of Public International Law* (2016).

[30] See, in general, Alejandro Rodiles, *Coalitions of the Willing and International Law* (CUP 2018).

[31] 'Joint Comprehensive Plan of Action' (2015) <www.europarl.europa.eu/cmsdata/122460/full-text-of-the-iran-nuclear-deal.pdf> accessed 29 January 2022.

[32] See Harald Müller, Una Becker-Jakob, and Tabea Seidler-Diekmann, 'Regime Conflicts and Norm Dynamics: Nuclear, Biological and Chemical Weapons' in Harald Müller and Carmen Wunderlich (eds), *Norm Dynamics in Multilateral Arms Control* (University of Georgia Press 2013) 55.

Much has been written in recent years on the content of Article VI of the NPT: it has been one of the most debated and contested provisions of the treaty because of its vague language and however high aspiration. While disagreement persists regarding the precise nature and scope of the obligation in this provision, Article VI is a binding legal obligation, not merely a goal. In the *Nuclear Weapons* Advisory Opinion, the ICJ adopted an expansive interpretation of the legal obligation: 'The legal import of that obligation goes beyond that of a mere obligation of conduct; the obligation involved here is an obligation to achieve a precise result – nuclear disarmament in all its aspects – by adopting a particular course of conduct, namely, the pursuit of negotiations on the matter in good faith'.[33] In the Court's view, there is not only an obligation of conduct, a *pactum de negotiando*, but also an obligation to achieve the desired result, a *pactum de contrahendo*. Furthermore, in dispositive F in the Advisory Opinion, the judges of the ICJ stated, unanimously, that 'there exists an obligation to pursue in good faith and bring to a conclusion negotiations leading to nuclear disarmament in all its aspects under strict and effective international control'.

Less clear is the position of the ICJ on whether this obligation forms part of customary international law (CIL). President Bedjaoui famously declared that the obligation had also 'acquired a customary character'.[34] Legal scholarship appears divided on this issue:[35] while the point has been made that disarmament obligations are 'part of customary international law or at least evolving custom' and 'are valid *erga omnes*, as they affect the international community as a whole rather than a particular State or group of States',[36] those in disagreement observe that it is difficult to see how Article VI can become CIL without considering the practice and *opinio juris* of those states that possess nuclear weapons and to which the provision is primarily addressed. In their view, the fact that Article VI does not reflect CIL is confirmed in the 1996 Advisory Opinion where the Court states that the obligation 'formally concerns the 182 states parties to the Treaty on the Non-Proliferation of Nuclear Weapons'. However, this remains a crucial aspect: although in 2016 the ICJ decided that it could not proceed on the merits,[37] CIL had played an important role in the applications submitted by the Marshall Islands to the ICJ, particularly in those against the NWS not parties to the NPT.

Such longstanding frustration of most NPT parties with the non-compliance of NWS with the NPT's disarmament provisions[38] has been one of the driving forces

[33] *Nuclear Weapons* (Advisory Opinion) (n 2) para 99.

[34] *Legality of the Threat or Use of Nuclear Weapons*, Declaration of President Bedjaoui [1996] ICJ Rep 268, 274, para 23.

[35] Cf Daniel H Joyner 'The legal meaning and implication of Article VI of the non-proliferation treaty' in Gro Nystuen, Stuart Casey-Maslen, and Annie Golden Bersagel (eds), *Nuclear Weapons under International Law* (CUP 2014) 413–17; Daniel Rietiker, *Humanization of Arms Control Paving the Way for a World Free of Nuclear Weapons* (Routledge 2017).

[36] International Law Association (ILA) Committee on Nuclear Weapons, Non-Proliferation and Contemporary International Law, 'Second Report: Legal Aspects of Nuclear Disarmament' in International Law Association Report of the 76th Conference in Washington DC (2014) 7.

[37] *Obligations Concerning Negotiations Relating to Cessation of the Nuclear Arms Race and to Nuclear Disarmament (Marshall Islands v Pakistan)* (Jurisdiction of the Court and Admissibility of the Application) [2016] ICJ Rep 552.

[38] This is to be understood as a dynamic of conflict with respect to the implementation of disarmament obligation by NWS: cf Heike Krieger and Andrea Liese, Chapter 1 in this book.

behind the adoption of a UN General Assembly resolution to convene a conference in 2017 to negotiate 'a legally binding instrument to prohibit nuclear weapons, leading towards their total elimination'.[39] The other trend is represented by the emergence of a new perspective on nuclear weapons through a humanitarian lens, that focuses on the devastating impact that such weapons would have on humanity, should they ever again be used in conflict.

The next paragraph will situate the issue of the 'catastrophic humanitarian consequences of any use of nuclear weapons' within the context of the 2010 NPT Review Conference. That gave impetus to the series of conferences under the Humanitarian Impacts of Nuclear Weapons Initiative, which brought together more than 150 states and civil society groups. Even the most traditional methodological approach cannot but recognize the role of NGOs in this process, as confirmed by the 2017 Nobel Prize.

## 3.4 Review Conferences as Subsequent Practice: The Humanitarian Impact as part of the Disarmament Pillar

The NPT Review Conferences have been the forum in which debate (and tension) emerged with regard to the lack of implementation of Article VI. As other arms control and disarmament treaties, Article VIII (3) of the NPT establishes a timeframe for convening a review conference on a regular basis, 'with a view to assuring that the purposes of the Preamble and the provisions of the Treaty are being realised'. The Review Conferences have represented an opportunity to apply pressure over disarmament: this was also facilitated by the reference in the text of Article VIII to 'the purposes of the preamble', which contains expansive language on disarmament, in comparison with Article VI. The outcome of the Review Conference is a final document: it is usually composed of a political declaration, which may be complemented by a more elaborate instrument on substantive issues. From a strictly legal perspective, these texts as such are not legally binding. In any case, since final documents are the product of a specific 'cooperative context', they reflect state practice and may be invoked for the interpretation of the NPT, as provided by Article 31 of the VCLT.[40]

The non-proliferation regime confirms that review conferences 'perform a crucial function for the adaptation of the treaties to factual developments'.[41] When states met in 1995 to decide whether or not to extend the NPT indefinitely, it was important to obtain a serious commitment to disarmament steps by the NWS. In fact, it is doubtful that the NPT would have been extended indefinitely in 1995 without such a commitment. The 2000 NPT Review Conference carried on this process of multilateral cooperation. The final document included 'the thirteen practical steps' for further progress towards nuclear disarmament: a comprehensive list of commitments, such as the entry into force of the Comprehensive Nuclear-Test-Ban Treaty, the drafting

[39] 'Taking forward multilateral nuclear disarmament negotiations' (11 January 2017) UN Doc A/RES/71/258.

[40] Guido den Dekker, *The Law of Arms Control: International Supervision and Enforcement* (Nijhoff 2001) 141.

[41] Georg Nolte, 'Third Report for the ILC Study Group on Treaties over Time' reproduced in Georg Nolte (ed), *Treaties and Subsequent Practice* (OUP 2013) 370.

of a fissile material cut-off treaty, the principle of irreversibility to apply to nuclear disarmament, and nuclear and other related arms control and reduction measures.[42] Step 6 is of particular relevance for our purposes: 'An unequivocal undertaking by the nuclear-weapon States to accomplish the total elimination of their nuclear arsenals leading to nuclear disarmament, to which all States parties are committed under article VI.'

After the failure of the 2005 NPT Review Conference to produce a final document, the relevance of final document adopted at the subsequent meeting in 2010 lies in the combination of substantive language on the interpretation of Article VI and the affirmation, in the same context, of the humanitarian impact of any use of nuclear weapons: not only did it express the 'deep concern at the catastrophic humanitarian consequences of any use of nuclear weapons and reaffirms the need for all States at all times to comply with applicable international law, including international humanitarian law', but it also contained the commitment of the NWS 'to accelerate concrete progress on the steps leading to nuclear disarmament . . . in a way that promotes international stability, peace and undiminished and increased security'.[43]

Unfortunately, the 2015 Review Conference failed to reach a consensus final document. It is worth looking at what went wrong in the negotiation process, particularly in the specific focus-group on disarmament. The biggest issue was how the conference could take into account the wide support received by the Humanitarian Impact of Nuclear Weapons Initiative. By the end of the conference, it was clear that there was a big difference between the position taken by Austria on behalf of 159 States and that of the NWS, including the NATO allies, with regard to nuclear deterrence.[44] In more specific terms, the most contentious issues were related to the very concept of 'effective measures' under Article VI NPT, including the issue of transparency and reporting by the nuclear states on their implementation of disarmament commitments. Interestingly, many states supporting the TPNW see it as an implementation of Article VI of the NPT on nuclear disarmament.

## 4. Guaranteeing the Taboo: Verification and Safeguards

NPT Review Conferences have consistently recognized that nuclear disarmament requires safeguards that are rigorous as well as universal. The extent to which compliance with a rule of international law can be supervised is an important factor determining the effectiveness of that rule. Verification regimes constitute essential tools for enhancing stability and predictability: in the absence of an indisputable violation, ie

[42] '2000 Review Conference of the Parties of the Treaty on Non-Proliferation of Nuclear Weapons Part I and II' (2000) NPT/CONF.2000/28.

[43] '2010 Review Conference of the Parties to the Treaty on the Non-Proliferation of Nuclear Weapons (Vol 1)' (2010) NPT/CONF.2010/50.

[44] Surprisingly, the polarization of the debate on nuclear disarmament did not play a role in the failure of the 2022 NPT Review Conference to adopt a final document. The main reason why delegations were unable to reach consensus on the draft document was indirectly related to the invasion of Ukraine, as Russia refused to accept the wording regarding nuclear safety matters at Ukraine's Zaporizhzhia nuclear power plant, which Russia had occupied since March 2022.

the *smoking gun* scenario, they substantially reduce the uncertainty on whether a state is adhering to its obligations.

Critics of the TPNW have argued that it risks undermining NPT and, more specifically, 'the IAEA Safeguards regime which supports it'.[45] Indeed, both Switzerland and Sweden—while voting in favour of the adoption of the Treaty at the Diplomatic Conference—expressed the concern that the provisions on the verification system could weaken the Treaty's credibility.[46] Under Article 3, non-nuclear possessor states 'shall, at a minimum, maintain' their International Atomic Energy Agency (IAEA) safeguards obligations in force at the time of entry into force of the TPNW. The problem is that the minimum standard for states that are not yet party to any such agreement is the Comprehensive Safeguards Agreement (CSA)[47] rather than the more intrusive instrument in terms of inspections, ie the Additional Protocol.[48] One could concur with the idea that it is unfortunate that the TPNW does not extend the most accurate and all-encompassing verification mechanism to all state parties: only where both the CSA and the Additional Protocol are in force 'the IAEA has sufficient information and access to provide credible assurances to the international community of both the non-diversion of nuclear material and the absence of undeclared nuclear material and activities'.[49] Other commentators stressed that the TPNW creates a counterproductive situation of discrimination by requiring Parties having possessed nuclear weapons after 7 July 2017 to adopt the highest standard of safeguards.[50]

However, it seems that the fears of an indulgent TPNW vis-à-vis the verification system in comparison with an onerous NPT are exaggerated.[51] The one under the Additional Protocol is not yet the compulsory standard under the NPT: therefore, both treaties take the same approach by imposing upon NNWS the obligation to negotiate and agree a safeguards agreement. Moreover, the ban Treaty goes beyond the NPT, by imposing parties to maintain their existing standards, thus making the Additional Protocol mandatory for states that are bound by it when the TPNW enters into force.

[45] 'North Atlantic Council Statement on the Treaty on the Prohibition of Nuclear Weapons' (20 September 2017) Press Release (2017) 135 <www.nato.int/cps/en/natohq/news_146954.htm> accessed 30 January 2022.

[46] 'Sweden, Explanation of vote' (7 July 2017) <www.alliansfriheten.se/karnvapenforbud-sweden-explanation-of-vote-7-july-2017-s3-amazonaws-com/> accessed 30 January 2022.

[47] International Atomic Energy Agency (IAEA), 'The Structure and Content of Agreements Between the Agency and States Required in Connection with the Treaty on the Non-proliferation of Nuclear Weapons' (1 June 1972) INFCIRC/153/(Corrected) <www.iaea.org/sites/default/files/publications/documents/infcircs/1972/infcirc153.pdf> accessed 30 January 2022.

[48] IAEA, 'Model Protocol Additional to the Agreement(s) Between State(s) and the International Atomic Energy Agency for the Application of Safeguards' (1 September 1997) INFCIRC/540 <www.iaea.org/sites/default/files/infcirc540.pdf> accessed 30 January 2022.

[49] IAEA, 'Safeguards Implementation Report (SIR)' (14 June 2017) <www.iaea.org/sites/default/files/statement_sir_2016.pdf> accessed 30 January 2022.

[50] John Carlson, 'Nuclear Weapon Prohibition Treaty: A Safeguards Debacle' (2017) 158 Vertic Trust & Verify 1.

[51] Marco Pedrazzi, 'The Treaty on the Prohibition of Nuclear Weapons: A Promise, a Threat or a Flop?' (2018) 27 Italian Yearbook of International Law 215.

## 5. 'State Survival' vs 'Humanitarian Impact': a Persisting Dichotomy?

Article 1 of the TPNW contains the formula which characterizes the most recent efforts in disarmament law in establishing a 'taboo': the wording 'never under any circumstances' indicates the comprehensive and totally binding character of the ban, which prohibits the use, including by way of reprisals, and obliges parties not to employ such weapons against non-parties.[52] The 'never under any circumstances' formulation makes clear that the treaty ban applies to both international and non-international armed conflicts.

One of the most contentious issues at the diplomatic conference was the content of the saving clause on the relationship with other international agreements, including the NPT. When the first draft provided that the TPNW did not affect 'the rights and obligations of the States Parties' under the NPT, it was argued that this would have allowed NWS to ratify the new Treaty while retaining nuclear weapons. The final wording of Article 18 TPNW is framed as a harmonization clause regarding obligations under existing international agreements. The key element is the last phrase: 'where those obligations are consistent with the Treaty'. Conflict between the TPNW and the NPT cannot be excluded: for instance, whereas the 'double-key system' has so far justified—from the view-point of NATO countries—the compliance with the NPT provisions by NNWS, on the territory of which US nuclear weapons are stationed,[53] Article 1(g) of the new Treaty provides that no state party shall '[a]llow any stationing, installation or deployment of any nuclear weapons or other nuclear explosive devices in its territory or at any place under its jurisdiction or control'. In the explanation of its negative note, the Netherlands made clear that 'the obligations in Article 1 are incompatible with our commitments as a NATO state. We attempted to rhyme these facts with the spirit of the treaty by introducing a temporality clause, but most delegations here could not reconcile that with their views on a nuclear weapons ban'.[54]

The International Committee of the Red Cross (ICRC) and International Federation of Red Cross and Red Crescent Societies welcomed the new treaty as 'a truly historic treaty', which 'clearly and comprehensively prohibits nuclear weapons on the basis of international humanitarian law. It acknowledges that any use of nuclear weapons would be abhorrent to the principles of humanity and the dictates of public conscience'.[55] Significantly, the Permanent Representatives to the United Nations of the US, United Kingdom, and France made a clear statement on the day of the adoption of the treaty: 'a purported ban on nuclear weapons that does not address the security

[52] Treaty on the Prohibition of Nuclear Weapons (adopted 7 July 2017, entered into force 22 January 2021) UN Doc A/CONF.229/2017/8.

[53] See inter alia Paolo Foradori, 'Tactical Nuclear Weapons in Italy: Striking a Balance between Disarmament Aspirations and Alliance Obligations' (2012) 19 The Non-Proliferation Review 13.

[54] Kingdom of the Netherlands, 'Explanation of Vote of the Netherlands on Text of Nuclear Ban Treaty' (7 July 2017) <https://s3.amazonaws.com/unoda-web/wp-content/uploads/2017/07/Netherlands-EoV-Nuclear-Ban-Treaty.pdf> accessed 30 January 2022.

[55] International Committee of the Red Cross (ICRC), 'Joint Statement of the International Committee of the Red Cross and the International Federation of Red Cross and Red Crescent Societies on the adoption of the Treaty on the Prohibition of Nuclear Weapons' (7 July 2017) <www.icrc.org/en/document/joint-statement-adoption-treaty-prohibition-nuclear-weapons> accessed 30 January 2022.

concerns that continue to make nuclear deterrence necessary cannot result in the elimination of a single nuclear weapon and will not enhance any country's security, nor international peace and security'. Moreover, 'we would not accept any claim that this treaty reflects or in any way contributes to the development of customary international law'.[56] NATO allies have further clarified that 'seeking to ban nuclear weapons through a treaty that will not engage any state actually possessing nuclear weapons will not be effective'; on the contrary, 'it risks doing the opposite by creating divisions and divergences' at a time of growing threats, 'in particular the grave threat posed by North Korea's nuclear programme'.[57]

These statements manifestly show the rift between the humanitarian approach and the doctrine of 'nuclear deterrence', which is still based on a 'secure second-strike capability', as the only way to ensure the state's survival in case of a threat of nuclear attack. In the Advisory Opinion, the ICJ did not take position on the 'policy of deterrence' and offered an ambiguous assessment regarding the relationship between deterrence and threat of the use of force. However, the ILA Committee on nuclear weapons could not but observe that 'many States do not perceive nuclear deterrence as a global security umbrella, but as a threat for peace and security', and that 'a policy of deterrence from nuclear attack as the "sole purpose" of nuclear weapons may be considered as further raising the threshold for nuclear weapons even beyond the policy of "no first use" of nuclear weapons which was of certain influence during the Cold War'.[58] In this regard, suffice here to recall the role that regional nuclear-weapon free zones[59] have played vis-à-vis the progressive delegitimization of nuclear deterrence, given their gradual and incremental approach to disarmament by slowly and painstakingly ruling out portions of the planet for nuclear deployment and use.[60]

## 5.1 Nuclear Weapons and the Principle of 'State Survival'

The Court's use of the notion of survival in the Advisory Opinion has been described as obscure:[61] it is recognized as a 'fundamental right' of every state.[62] Although the

[56] 'Joint Press Statement from the Permanent Representatives to the United Nations of the United States, United Kingdom, and France Following the Adoption of a Treaty Banning Nuclear Weapons' (7 July 2017) <https://usun.usmission.gov/joint-press-statement-from-the-permanent-representatives-to-the-united-nations-of-the-united-states-united-kingdom-and-france-following-the-adoption/> accessed 30 January 2022.

[57] See 'North Atlantic Council Statement' (n 45).

[58] ILA Committee (n 36) 7.

[59] There are currently five NWFZ treaties: the Treaty of Tlatelolco for Latin America and the Caribbean, the Treaty of Rarotonga for the South Pacific, the Treaty of Bangkok for South-east Asia, the Treaty of Pelindaba for Africa, and the Treaty of Semipalatinsk in Central Asia: see Marco Roscini, 'International Law, Nuclear Weapon-free Zones and the Proposed Zone Free of Weapons of Mass Destruction in the Middle East' in Gro Nystuen, Stuart Casey-Maslen, and Annie Golden Bersagel (eds), *Nuclear Weapons under International Law* (CUP 2014) 321.

[60] Elizabeth Mendenhall, 'Nuclear-Weapon-Free Zones and Contemporary Arms Control' (2020) 14 Strategic Studies Quarterly 122, 126.

[61] Marcelo G Kohen, 'The Notion of "State Survival" under International Law' in Laurence Boisson de Chazournes and Philippe Sands (eds), *International Law, the International Court of Justice and Nuclear Weapons* (CUP 1999) 293.

[62] *Nuclear Weapons* (Advisory Opinion) (n 2) para 96.

ordinary meaning is related to the existence or the preservation of states, state survival, as a term of art, had no precedent in the case-law of the ICJ: Judge Koroma pointed out that state survival was 'a concept invented by the Court'.[63] On the other hand, President Bedjaoui declared that '[a] State's right to survival is also a fundamental law, similar in many respects to a "natural" law'.[64] Interestingly, the theory of 'fundamental rights of the States' characterized the international legal scholarship at the beginning of the twentieth century, having a clear natural law foundation.[65] However, it was then argued that 'it has since become out-dated; in particular the idea of a right of "self-preservation" has been completely abandoned'.[66]

The ICJ refrained from an analysis of the concept of state survival: in the proceedings, only the UK referred to it in the context of the discussion of the role of proportionality in the exercise of self-defence, to demonstrate that the use of nuclear weapons would respect that principle, if 'essential to the survival of a State which was under attack'.[67] One might wonder whether 'state survival' deserves its own particular treatment by law, for instance as a new kind of circumstance precluding wrongfulness. One possible reading of the Court's conclusions is that, 'while the right of self-defence in "ordinary" circumstances may be founded on and limited by positive law, its exercise in extreme circumstances where the very survival of the state is at stake rests on other more fundamental grounds that escape regulation by positive law'.[68] Authors tend to exclude that 'a right to survival' could even be separate to the right to self-defence.[69]

It is disputed that 'state survival' might be seen as a fundamental value which deserves protection under international law; however, even assuming that the existence of states is a basic individual value, it has been correctly observed that 'the existence of one State cannot be considered more important than the existence of any other, and even less, than the existence of the whole international community'.[70] This has lead another author to claim that:

> whenever community interests are protected under international law and are considered to be fundamental to the system, the general trend shall be towards their

[63] Cf *Legality of the Threat or Use of Nuclear Weapons*, Dissenting Opinion of Judge Koroma [1996] ICJ Rep 556, 571.

[64] *Legality of the Threat or Use of Nuclear Weapons*, Declaration of President Bedjaoui (n 34) 273 para 22.

[65] See inter alia Arrigo Cavaglieri, *I diritti fondamentali degli Stati nella Società internazionale: saggio critico* (Drucker 1906); Gilbert Gidel, 'Droits et devoirs des Nations. La théorie classique des droits fondamentaux des Etats' (1925) 10 RCADI 537.

[66] Roberto Ago, 'Eight Report on State Responsibility: Addendum' in *ILC Yearbook* vol 2 (1980) part I, 16.

[67] Foreign and Commonwealth Office, 'Letter dated 16 June 1995 from the Legal Adviser to the Foreign and Commonwealth Office of the United Kingdom of Great Britain and Northern Ireland, together with Written Comments of the United Kingdom' (16 June 1995) 54 para 3.71 <www.icj-cij.org/public/files/case-related/95/8802.pdf> accessed 30 January 2022.

[68] Daniel H Joyner and Marco Roscini, 'Is There Any Room for the Doctrine of Fundamental Rights of States in Today's International Law?' (2015) 4 Cambridge Journal of International and Comparative Law 467, 473.

[69] See Dino Kritsiotis, 'Theorizing International Law on Force and Intervention' in Anne Orford and Florian Hoffmann (eds), *The Oxford Handbook of the Theory of International Law* (OUP 2016) 682; Nikolas Stürchler, *The Threat of Force in International Law* (CUP 20) 88.

[70] Kohen (n 61) 312.

prevalence over competing individual interests in those cases in which the continued preservation of the latter may undermine the common good.[71]

On a more profound level, because of the changing strategic environment, the 'extreme circumstances of self-defence' argument risks to be even counterproductive for the preservation of both individual state survival and collective peace and security, in the long run. The argument was mainly aimed at justifying a fundamental pillar of nuclear deterrence: the secure second-strike capability of NWS, sufficient to prevent an attack in the first place. However, both interpretative torsions of the scope of self-defence under international law[72] as well as the developments in the accuracy of nuclear attacks represent challenges to the stability of the international system, to the extent they increase the likelihood of a first strike.[73]

## 5.2 Nuclear Weapons and the 'Humanitarian Impact'

The resolution approved by the Council of Delegates of the International Red Cross and Red Crescent Movement in 2011 on 'working towards the elimination of nuclear weapons'[74] has been recognized as one of the defining moments of the Humanitarian Initiative. On many occasions in past years the ICRC moved from the premise that '[w]hile IHL does not specifically prohibit nuclear weapons, their use is restricted by IHL's general rules regulating the conduct of hostilities, which apply to the use of all weapons in armed conflict'.[75]

In the Advisory Opinion, the Court assessed nuclear weapons against 'cardinal principles ... constituting the fabric of humanitarian law':[76] the principle of distinction, which imposes an obligation to never make civilians the object of attack and a prohibition on the use of indiscriminate weapons, and the prohibition against causing unnecessary suffering to combatants, which includes a prohibition to use weapons causing them such harm or uselessly aggravating their suffering. The point has been made that the question posed by the UN General Assembly placed the ICJ 'in an

[71] Santiago Villalpando, 'The Legal Dimension of the International Community: How Community Interests Are Protected in International Law' (2010) 21 European Journal of International Law 387, 415.

[72] See Albrecht Randelzhofer and Georg Nolte, 'Article 51' in Bruno Simma and others (eds), *The Charter of the United Nations: A Commentary* (3rd edn, OUP 2012) 1424.

[73] In this respect, the US *Nuclear Posture Review 2018* explicitly states that the US could employ nuclear weapons in response to 'significant non-nuclear strategic attacks'. This includes, but is not limited to, 'attacks on the U.S., allied, or partner civilian population or infrastructure, and attacks on US or allied nuclear forces, their command and control, or warning and attack assessment capabilities'.

[74] ICRC, 'Council of Delegates 2011, Resolution 1: Working towards the elimination of nuclear weapons' (26 November 2011) <www.icrc.org/eng/resources/documents/resolution/council-delegates-resolution-1-2011.htm> accessed 30 January 2022.

[75] ICRC, 'International Humanitarian Law and the Challenges of Contemporary Armed Conflicts' Report prepared for the 32nd International Conference of the Red Cross and Red Crescent (8-10 December 2015 (31 October 2015) <www.icrc.org/en/document/international-humanitarian-law-and-challenges-contemporary-armed-conflicts> accessed 30 January 2022.

[76] *Nuclear Weapons* (Advisory Opinion) (n 2) para 78.

exceptionally difficult position, because it could not possibly consider all the combinations of circumstances in which nuclear weapons might be used or their use threatened'.[77]

If there has been an evolution in the last two decades, it was the vigorous attempt to gather evidence as regard the conformity of nuclear weapons with IHL. Several studies[78] have been published to support the conclusion that it is 'difficult to envisage how a use of nuclear weapons could be compatible with the rules of international humanitarian law'.[79] The position taken by the ICRC is grounded on two pillars: 'the exercise of the right of self-defence – even in an extreme situation where the very survival of a State is at stake – can on no account release that State from its obligations under IHL'; 'the new evidence and information that has emerged in recent years ... cast further doubt on whether nuclear weapons could ever be used in accordance with the above-mentioned rules of IHL'.[80]

Commentators argued that low-yield nuclear weapons could be compatible with the rules of IHL in the exceptional situations of 'a strike upon troops and armor in an isolated desert region with a low-yield air-burst in conditions of no wind'[81] or of 'detonating "clean" nuclear weapons against an enemy fleet in the middle of the ocean'.[82] The counterarguments developed by the ICRC are based on the risk of nuclear escalation as well as 'the impact of radiation on combatants, the radiological contamination of the environment, and the eventual spread of radiation to civilian areas'.[83] Others have observed that, even assuming that a limited tactical use of a nuclear weapon would not violate the cardinal principle of proportionality, 'it would nonetheless be contrary to the customary obligation to choose means that avoid or, in any event, minimize incidental effects upon the civilian population'.[84]

It is noteworthy that, even though the ICJ affirmed that the applicability of the Martens Clause 'is not to be doubted' and that it has 'proved to be an effective means of addressing the rapid evolution of military technology',[85] there has been a limited recourse to the 'principles of humanity and the dictates of public conscience' in recent legal analysis. By the way, this has not prevented Judge Cançado Trindade to resort to the Martens Clause in his dissenting opinion on the Marshall Islands case, in order to argue that '[e]ven if there was a "gap" in the law of nations in relation to nuclear

[77] Christopher Greenwood, 'Jus ad bellum and jus in bello in the Nuclear Weapons Advisory Opinion' in Laurence Boisson de Chazournes and Philippe Sands (eds), *International Law, the International Court of Justice and Nuclear Weapons* (CUP 1999) 249.

[78] See inter alia Daniel Thürer and Martin Zobl, 'Are Nuclear Weapons Really Legal? Thoughts on the Sources of International Law and a Conception of the Law Imperio Rationis instead of Ratione Imperii' in Ulrich Fastenrath and others (eds), *From Bilateralism to Community Interest: Essays in Honour of Judge Bruno Simma* (OUP 2011).

[79] ICRC, 'Working towards the elimination' (n 74).

[80] ICRC, 'International Humanitarian Law' (n 75) 59.

[81] Michael N Schmitt, 'The International Court of Justice and the Use of Nuclear Weapons' (1998) 362 Naval War College Review 91, 108.

[82] Yoram Dinstein, *The Conduct of Hostilities Under the Law of International Armed Conflict* (3rd edn, CUP 2016) 86.

[83] ICRC, 'International Humanitarian Law' (n 75) 58.

[84] Marco Sassoli, *International Humanitarian Law: Rules, Controversies, and Solutions to Problems Arising in Warfare* (Elgar 2019) 396.

[85] *Nuclear Weapons* (Advisory Opinion) (n 2) paras 87, 78.

weapons, which there is not, it is possible to fill it by resorting to general principles of law'.[86]

In this regard, when the Humanitarian Pledge—the document endorsed by the third conference on the humanitarian impact of nuclear weapons, in Vienna—referred to the existence of a 'legal gap',[87] this expression needs to be understood not in terms of a lacuna in the legal order as a whole, but of a specific regulation on the point. Significantly, the preamble of the TPNW not only affirms that 'any use of nuclear weapons would be contrary to the rules of international law applicable in armed conflict'[88] but also reaffirms the application of the Martens Clause: 'any use of nuclear weapons would also be abhorrent to the principles of humanity and the dictates of public conscience'.

## 6. Conclusion

There is no single mechanism that has driven normative change in the nuclear non-proliferation and disarmament regime. The logic of inequality between NWS and NNWS and the delicate compromise, that characterizes the NPT obligations, between national interests and the emerging community interests are key factors explaining dynamics of conflict that led to norm development. At the beginning of the twenty-first century, the preference for informal partnerships over legally binding initiatives—with the significant exception of UNSC decisions—was an expression not only of the new challenge posed by the risk of WMD terrorism but also of a specific political perspective and a peculiar understanding of international cooperation, according to which capability and willingness are closely related. 'Coalitions of the willing' indeed reflected a representation of the world as divided between states that shared certain values and were willing to defend them and unwilling or unable actors.

The current crisis of the nuclear non-proliferation regime reveals its structural character: whereas arms control efforts of the major powers have so far been devoted to maintaining the legacy of the Cold War, recent developments, including the re-emergence of strategic tensions between the United States and Russia, highlight the deterioration of the existing system based on legal and political commitments. In the wake of the 2022 invasion of Ukraine, whereas Russia's nuclear warnings were perceived as eroding the nuclear taboo, the widespread aversion to nuclear weapons among public opinions and world leaders could, on the contrary, contribute to its reinvigoration, given that even a limited use could trigger a global escalation and that nuclear deterrence would be ultimately unsustainable and dangerous.

[86] *Obligations concerning Negotiations (Marshall Islands v Pakistan)*, Dissenting Opinion of Judge Cançado Trindade [2016] ICJ Rep 615, para 191.

[87] 'Humanitarian Pledge' (9 December 2014) <www.bmeia.gv.at/fileadmin/user_upload/Zentrale/Aussenpolitik/Abruestung/HINW14/HINW14vienna_Pledge_Document.pdf> accessed 30 January 2022.

[88] See the Report of the first meeting of States parties to the TPNW (TPNW/MSP/2022/6, 21 July 2022, para 4), in which they stressed that 'any use or threat of use of nuclear weapons is a violation of international law, including the Charter of the United Nations.'

One of the main driving factors of the recent norm change efforts with respect to nuclear weapons has been a dynamic of contestation due to the non-implementation of the disarmament obligations, which has been simultaneously accompanied by a re-orientation of the focus on values, in the sense of placing the 'catastrophic humanitarian consequences of any use of nuclear weapons' at the centre of the discourse. In this respect, the TPNW should not be seen as a point of arrival, but as an expression of a trend towards the progressive elimination of nuclear weapons.

Already in the 1970s, an attempt was made to affirm the existence of a customary rule prohibiting the use of nuclear weapons in armed conflicts as a necessary implication of the principle of the coexistence of the members forming the international community. The proponent eventually changed his mind, in consideration of both the conduct and the will of NWS, but this argument deserves to be mentioned: an essential task of the international legal order would be that of guaranteeing the very subsistence of the international society, for which and in which it lives.[89]

After 25 years, one might wonder whether—if the issue of the legality of the threat or use of nuclear weapons were to come back before the ICJ now—a similar Advisory Opinion could be expected, in terms of analysis and conclusions: perhaps, the current position of the most powerful states, with respect to the maintenance of both their nuclear arsenals and their associated deterrence policies, might still lead the judges to conclude that there is a lack of general practice recognized as law indicating a customary prohibition on threat and use.[90] In 2021 the leaders of the five NWS issued a joint statement on 'preventing nuclear war and avoiding arms races' in which they affirmed the principle that 'a nuclear war cannot be won and must never be fought'.[91] That language evokes the 1985 joint statement of US president Ronald Reagan and Soviet general secretary Mikhail Gorbachev, which led to the two superpowers' disarmament push at the end of that decade.[92]

Nonetheless, the above analysis has sought to offer a contribution on the issue of the legality on the use of nuclear weapons from a different perspective, that assesses the function that general principles of international law might have for the promotion of fundamental values within the international community.[93] The question is not simply whether an explicit customary prohibition exists but how these general principles apply to the threat and use of nuclear weapons and how different principles coordinate themselves. The controversial findings of the Court could be read as an attempt to strike a balance between the cardinal principles of IHL and that of state survival.

[89] See Giuseppe Barile, *Lezioni di diritto internazionale* (CEDAM 1977) 50–51.

[90] See William H Boothby and Wolff Heintschel von Heinegg, *Nuclear Weapons Law: Where Are We Now?* (CUP 2022) 195–96.

[91] The White House, 'US-Russia Presidential Joint Statement on Strategic Stability' (16 June 2021) <www.whitehouse.gov/briefing-room/statements-releases/2021/06/16/u-s-russia-presidential-joint-statement-on-strategic-stability/> accessed 30 January 2022.

[92] 'Joint Soviet-United States Statement on the Summit Meeting in Geneva' (21 November 1985) <www.reaganlibrary.gov/archives/speech/joint-soviet-united-states-statement-summit-meeting-geneva> accessed 30 January 2022.

[93] See Marcelo Vázquez-Bermúdez, 'Second Report on General Principles of Law' (9 April 2020) UN Doc A/CN.4/741, 43 para 134, quoting the position of Norway according to which the Martens clause 'was an example of a principle that had been formed within the international legal system'.

Interestingly, the Declaration of President Bedjaoui, attached to the 1996 Opinion, evoked the possibility 'dans certaines circonstances, une opposition irréductible, une collision frontale de principes fondamentaux dont l'un ne saurait se réduire à l'autre'.[94] Still, he recognized that 'the use of nuclear weapons by a State in circumstances in which its survival is at stake risks in its turn endangering the survival of all mankind, precisely because of the inextricable link between terror and escalation in the use of such weapons'.[95] Judge Higgins doubted about the existence of 'antinomies' in international law, observing that 'the judicial lodestar … must be those values that international law seeks to promote and protect'.[96]

The idea of international law as a unitary system permeates the evolution of the international legal scholarship; particularly, the assumption that it has an autonomous regulatory capacity, based on a set of fundamental principles. As such principles are closely intertwined, they support one another, but also condition each other's application.[97] The well-known method of 'balancing' two or more principles is an exercise of weighting them and determining their respective importance: this does not exclude that the balance could change, depending on modifications in the international society.[98] One might wonder whether, a quarter century after the 1996 Opinion, the use of argumentative techniques based on applicable general principles of international law could create, rather than a stalemate, a dynamic of change leading to a finding of the definitive illegality of the threat or use of atomic weapons. Not only new factual evidence on both the characteristics of nuclear devices and on the humanitarian, environmental, and societal consequences of detonations offers further elements for an assessment of the lawfulness of their use on the basis of the cardinal principles of IHL but, most importantly, changes in the priority of values within the international community might have an impact in determining a new balance of general principles, with a further prevalence those of humanitarian nature.

[94] *Legality of the Threat or Use of Nuclear Weapons*, Declaration of President Bedjaoui (n 34) 273 para 22.
[95] ibid (official translation).
[96] *Legality of the Threat or Use of Nuclear Weapons*, Dissenting Opinion of Judge Higgins (n 6) para 41.
[97] See Paola Gaeta, Jorge Viñuales, and Salvatore Zappalà, *Cassese's International Law* (3rd edn, OUP 2020) 75.
[98] Cf Thomas Kleinlein, Chapter 4 in this book.

# 14
# International Women's Rights
## Progress Under Attack?

*Conny Roggeband*

## 1. Introduction

During the second half of the twentieth century, international legislation on the rights of women started to develop, the most comprehensive being the United Nations (UN) Convention on the Elimination of Discrimination against Women (CEDAW).[1] In particular, the 1990s marked a period of unprecedented progress in global gender equality rights. Women's rights activists successfully used the available human rights framework to target international organizations with the claim that 'women's rights are human rights' which culminated in the adoption of a number of conventions like the Declaration on the Elimination of Violence against Women,[2] the Inter-American Convention for the Prevention, Punishment and Elimination of Violence against Women (Belém do Pará Convention),[3] the Universal Declaration on Democracy,[4] and the Optional Protocol to the Convention on the Elimination of All forms of Discrimination against Women.[5]

While some voices have argued that this expanding body of international law is not necessarily effective at improving human rights conditions on the ground, other studies point to its significant impact. Simmons demonstrates that the ratification of human rights treaties positively influences state-society relations, empowering domestic actors to press for treaty implementation. International treaties make an important positive contribution to advancing women's rights, particularly in partially democratic and transitional contexts.[6] Also, CEDAW is shown to have a statistically significant and positive effect on women's rights, in particular their political rights and to a lesser extent their social rights, despite its weak enforcement mechanisms.[7]

[1] United Nations Convention on the Elimination of Discrimination against Women (adopted 18 December 1979, entered into force 3 September 1981) 1249 UNTS 13.

[2] Declaration on the Elimination of Violence against Women (20 December 1993) UN Doc A/RES/48/104.

[3] Inter-American Convention on the Prevention, Punishment, and Eradication of Violence against Women (adopted 9 June 1994, entered into force 5 March 1995) <www.oas.org/juridico/english/treaties/a-61.html> accessed 15 December 2021 (Belém do Pará Convention).

[4] Inter-Parliamentary Union, 'Universal Declaration on Democracy' (16 September 1997) <www.refworld.org/docid/48abd598d.html> accessed 15 December 2021.

[5] 1999 Optional Protocol to the 1979 Convention on the Elimination of All Forms of Discrimination against Women (adopted 6 October 1999, entered into force 22 December 2000) 2131 UNTS 83.

[6] Beth A Simmons, *Mobilizing for Human Rights: International Law in Domestic Politics* (CUP 2009).

[7] Neil A Englehart and Melissa K Miller, 'Empirical Study Demonstrates Positive Impact of International Human Rights Law' (2016) 4 Insights to a Changing World Journal 39.

Conny Roggeband, *International Women's Rights* In: *Tracing Value Change in the International Legal Order*. Edited by: Heike Krieger and Andrea Liese, Oxford University Press. © Conny Roggeband 2023. DOI: 10.1093/oso/9780192855831.003.0014

The global progress in the adoption of women's rights legislation in the mid-1990s was noted with dismay by conservative and religious state and non-state actors who started to mobilize to contest these rights. At the 1995 Beijing conference they made some small but significant inroads, including blocking the inclusion of sexuality rights in outcome documents.[8] This created the impetus to seek further collaboration between conservative actors within the framework of the UN conferences. An alliance between a wide range of conservative groups such as fundamentalist religious groups, both Christian and Islamic, and states with conservative governments[9] that share a particular conservative and traditional perspective on gender issues emerged seeking to contest, undermine, and prevent further progress of women's rights internationally.[10] This coalition operates and mobilizes both at the transnational and national level to act in favour of traditional family values and roles for men and women and thus counteract gender equality progress.

Over the last decade, oppositional forces have become stronger and better organized.[11] Since 2009, the UN Human Rights Council adopted several resolutions calling for reinterpretation of human rights in accordance with traditional values, challenging the right of women to equality in the family, established in the Universal Declaration of Human Rights (UDHR).[12, 13] The successful transnational counter mobilization of conservative and religious non-state and state actors potentially threatens existing international agreements and commitments and may undermine the work of international organizations and treaty monitoring bodies.[14] As a result of this threat, women's organizations have to invest most of their time and energy in protecting rather than expanding on the status quo reached in Beijing.[15]

This chapter explores current contestations against women's rights and the implications thereof. First, I discuss norm diffusion as an inherently contentious process of change, stepping away from norm diffusion theories that stress compliance or norm internalization. Instead, I stress norms as sense-making processes or

[8] Louise Chappell, 'Contesting Women's Rights: Charting the Emergence of a Transnational Conservative Counter-Network' (2006) 4 Global Society 491.

[9] According to Chappell this coalition included states (countries with a strong Roman Catholic heritage, governments with strong Islamic orientation, and the United States under the Bush administration), state-like actors (including the Vatican, the League of Arab Countries, and the G77), and non-state actors like Christian Right groups.

[10] Chappell (n 8).

[11] Clifford Bob, *The Global Right Wing and the Clash of World Politics* (CUP 2012); Ruth Halperin-Kaddari and Marsha A Freeman, 'Backlash Goes Global: Men's Groups, Patriarchal Family Policy, and the False Promise of Gender-Neutral Laws' (2016) 28 Canadian Journal of Women and the Law 182; Anne Marie Goetz, 'The New Competition in Multilateral Norm-Setting: Transnational Feminists & the Illiberal Backlash' (2020) 149 Daedalus 160.

[12] Universal Declaration of Human Rights (adopted 10 December 1948) UNGA Res 217 A(III).

[13] Frances Raday, 'Recent Developments in the UN Human Rights Council: Traditional Values and Women's Right to Equality in the Family' (*Oxford Human Rights Hub*, 2 September 2015) <http://ohrh.law.ox.ac.uk/recent-developments-in-the-un-human-rights-council-traditional-values-and-womens-right-to-equality-in-the-family/> accessed 15 December 2021; Halperin-Kaddari and Freeman (n 11).

[14] Philip Alston, 'Human Rights under Siege' (2017) 25 SUR-International Journal on Human Rights 267.

[15] Carolyn Hannan, 'Feminist Strategies in International Organizations: The United Nations Context' in Gülay Caglar, Elisabeth Prügl, and Susanne Zwingel (eds), *Feminist Strategies in International Governance* (Routledge 2013); Goetz (n 11).

'works-in-progress'[16] that are constantly renegotiated and change as they travel. Next, I examine the concerted efforts by conservative state and non-state actors to oppose women's rights norms, the strategies and counterframes that these deploy and the political arenas they use. I then move on to argue how current political developments create favourable opportunities for these oppositional actors to amend or revert women's rights. I ask what the implications of these developments are for gender equality norms at the national and international level. Do we see a regression in women's rights? How resilient are existing international norms in face of the strong transnational opposition to gender equality and unfavourable opportunity structures to further advance a women's rights agenda?

## 2. Norm Diffusion as Contentious Processes of Change

Translation of international norms to national policy making always implies transformation of such norms.[17] Not only is the emergence and negotiation of international women's rights subject to political struggle, but this struggle continues after the adoption of international norms.[18] Much of the norm diffusion literature treats international treaties or agreements as well-defined 'fixed' products to be ratified, adopted and internalized at the national level.[19] Processes of meaning making, interpretation, and contestation are only seen to be part of the norm emergence stage.[20] Yet, the adoption of international norms in general and gender equality norms in particular 'may initiate rather than resolve struggles over its exact content'.[21]

Gender equality norms challenge existing gender norms and require deep regime change.[22] Norms about gender relations and sex roles are embedded in social systems that link and structure ideas and practices and tend to reproduce themselves. Gendered inequalities and resistances to women's rights are often justified by referring to existing norms and beliefs.[23] Attempts to end violence against women, for example, challenge the classic political division between public and private, question what is acceptable and unacceptable behaviour, and how rules and procedures need to be altered to protect women, and men, from gender-based violence. Such regime change is likely to meet with resistance from the actors whose principles and norms are challenged.

[16] Mona L Krook and Jaqui True, 'Rethinking the Life Cycles of International Norms: The United Nations and the Global Promotion of Gender Equality' (2012) 18 European Journal of International Relations 103, 104.

[17] Anouka van Eerdewijk and Conny Roggeband, 'Gender Equality Norm Diffusion and Actor Constellations: A First Exploration' in Anna van der Vleuten, Anouka van Eerdewijk, and Conny Roggeband (eds), *Gender Equality Norms in Regional Governance: Transnational Dynamics in Europe, South America and Southern Africa* (Palgrave Macmillan 2014). Also see Antje Wiener, Chapter 2 in this book and Wayne Sandholtz, Chapter 3 in this book.

[18] ibid.

[19] Krook and True (n 16).

[20] Kees van Kersbergen and Bert-Jan Verbeek, 'The Politics of International Norms: Subsidiarity and the Imperfect Competence Regime of the European Union' (2007) 13 European Journal of International Relations 217.

[21] Krook and True (n 16) 110.

[22] van Eerdewijk and Roggeband (n 17).

[23] ibid.

Consequently, it requires dealing with power relations and processes, and with resistances and resilience, not only in the emergence but also in the diffusion of norms.[24]

Understanding diffusion of norms in terms of normative change or regime change resonates well with views in which policy processes are seen as contests where actors compete over different definitions of problems, causes, and solutions. This view is well captured by the notion of framing processes, because the meaning of norms is not exogenously given, but subject to 'politics of signification'.[25] Defined as standards of appropriateness, norms are inherently contested, and their meaning is negotiated in and between the frames employed by the variety of actors engaged in these processes.[26] These framing processes result in the 'stretching' and 'bending' of norms.[27] Processes of framing are central to all stages of norm production and diffusion, as they all entail negotiation and change, and are contentious because the process generates frames that not only differ from but also challenge existing ones.

International women's rights are not unequivocally defined and leave room for different interpretations. The content of international norms tends to be vague and at times even contradictory. The human rights framework, which presumably is an organic whole that spells out conditions for life in dignity, contains important internal tensions.[28] There are also tensions between international norms, for instance between norms on trade liberalization and gender mainstreaming.[29] This ambiguity, on the one hand, facilitates the spread of international norms to different places and arenas because it allows different actors to inscribe them with their own interpretations.[30] On the other hand, it also makes norms open to continuous amendments and (re) interpretations. Norms are thus *by definition* unsteady, as Zwingel argues, and this unsteadiness has to be studied in movement between different contexts and actors.[31]

## 3. Opposing Women's Rights

The development of an international women's rights framework has been contested all along[32] and the Holy See has been among the first and most prominent leaders of this opposition.[33] Over time, opposition and protests against gender equality and sexual rights have become more vocal, more global, and better organized. Actors include

[24] Margaret E Keck and Kathryn Sikkink, *Activists beyond Borders: Advocacy Networks in International Politics* (Cornell University Press 1998) 35.

[25] Robert D Benford and David A Snow, 'Framing Processes and Social Movements: An Overview and Assessment' (2000) 26 Annual Review of Sociology 611, 613.

[26] ibid 614.

[27] Emanuela Lombardo, Petra Meier, and Mieke Verloo (eds), *The Discursive Politics of Gender Equality: Stretching, Bending and Policy-making* (Routledge 2009).

[28] Suzanne Zwingel, *Translating International Women's Rights: The CEDAW Convention in Context* (Palgrave Macmillan 2016).

[29] Emilie Hafner-Burton and Mark A Pollack, 'Mainstreaming International Governance: The Environment, Gender, and IO Performance in the European Union' (2010) 5 Review of International Organizations 285; van Eerdewijk and Roggeband (n 17).

[30] Krook and True (n 16).

[31] Zwingel (n 28) 19.

[32] Chappell (n 8); Zwingel (n 28).

[33] Chappell (n 8).

religious groups and conservative liberal actors, right-wing populist and nationalist groups, and more recent actors such as the anti-gender ideology movements[34] and men's rights groups.[35] What these actors share is a conservative and patriarchal view of gender relations, stressing that men and women are different and have different roles in the family and public sphere. They defend heterosexual marriage and family relationships as a divine or natural norm. This motivates their struggle against the expansion of international women's rights and gender equality.[36] In this section, I discuss what this opposition to gender equality norms looks like, addressing key questions such as, who are the actors that oppose women's rights transnationally, how are they organized, and what are the tactics and frames they use?

The origin of a transnational network against the expansion of gender equality norms can be traced back to the mid-1990s, when the Vatican first allied with Muslim countries. During the preparations of the 1994 Cairo International Conference on Population and Development (ICPD), the Vatican sought the support from Libya and Iran to oppose language on women's rights and reproductive rights in the document.[37] To explain this move, the Vatican spokesman, Joaquin Navarro Valls, said that '[t]he positions of some of the delegations going to Cairo, coming from different countries, different backgrounds, and certainly not from a Catholic and even Christian background, are now closer to the position of the Holy See'.[38] During the 1995 Fourth World Conference on Women (FWCW) in Beijing and the two follow-up Beijing Conferences held in New York in 2000 and 2005, opposition forces became increasingly obvious and organized.[39] A fluid coalition emerged comprising states (countries with a strong Roman Catholic heritage, governments with an Islamic orientation, and the United States under the Bush administration), state-like actors and international organizations (including the Vatican, the Organisation for Islamic Cooperation (OIC), the League of Arab Countries, and the UN Africa group), and non-state actors like Christian Right and pro-family groups that joined forces to block the further advancement of international women's rights.[40] Chappell labels this transnational conservative

[34] Religious and conservative actors have called 'gender' an ideological tool used by 'radical' feminists and LGBT activists to establish a post-gender society, destroying masculinity and femininity, and the divine or natural notion of complementarity of men and women. This is perceived as a threat to the 'natural family', see Roman Kuhar and David Paternotte (eds), *Anti-Gender Campaigns in Europe: Mobilizing Against Equality* (Rowman & Littlefield International 2017) and Agnieszka Graff, Ratna Kapur, and Suzanna Danuta Walters, 'Introduction: Gender and the Rise of the Global Right' (2019) 44 Signs: Journal of Women in Culture and Society 541.

[35] Melissa Blais and Francis Dupuis-Déri, 'Masculinism and the Antifeminist Countermovement' (2012) 11.1 Social Movement Studies 21; Kuhar and Paternotte (n 34); Conny Roggeband, 'The Good, the Bad, and the Ugly: Making Sense of Opposition to Feminisms from a Social-Movement Perspective' in Mieke Verloo (ed), *Varieties in Opposition to Gender Equality in Europe* (Routledge 2018).

[36] Chappell (n 8); Rebecca Sanders, 'Norm Spoiling: Undermining the International Women's Rights Agenda' (2018) 94 International Affairs 271.

[37] Chappell (n 8).

[38] John Tagliabue, 'Vatican Seeks Islamic Allies in U.N. Population Dispute' *New York Times* (New York City, 18 August 1994) <www.nytimes.com/1994/08/18/world/vatican-seeks-islamic-allies-in-un-populat ion-dispute.html> accessed 15 December 2021.

[39] ibid.

[40] Chappell, following Buss and Herman, describes these actors as Christian Right, mainly North American conservative and orthodox religious groups who formed a coalition 'around an orthodox Christian vision and defense of the traditional nuclear-family formation' (cited in Chappell (n 8) 494).

networking against gender equality an 'unholy alliance', because the actors in the coalition 'differed on many fundamental matters of international politics, and because it includes representatives of two of the world's major religious blocs—Christianity and Islam—which have diametrically opposing views on many issues'.[41]

Often in tandem with the Vatican, the OIC acted as a powerful player opposing gender equality. OIC is an international organization with 57 member states that holds biannual conferences on Women's Role in the Development of OIC member states.[42] These conferences underline the important role of women in OIC states, in particular within the family. While the conference documents recognize some issues of gender inequality like high levels of poverty among women or violence against women, they oppose the recognition of women's reproductive and sexual rights. OIC has used UN forums such as the Human Rights Council (and its predecessor, the Commission on Human Rights) to (unsuccessfully) undermine the Human Rights Council's resolution 15/23 on the elimination of discrimination against women by proposing to insert wording that would have allowed states with effective discriminatory laws to maintain that status quo. Together with the Vatican, OIC blocked a resolution in the Commission on Human Rights that would have recognized sexual orientation as a possible source of discrimination.[43]

Another source of opposition are conservative pro-family non-governmental organizations (NGOs), which are principally US and Canada-based organizations that focus either on national-cultural tradition (eg the Heritage Foundation), religious and family values (eg the Catholic Family and Human Rights Institute, and conservative evangelical organizations like the World Family Policy Center, the Howard Center, and the Family Research Center), or promoting an 'alternative female voice' to counter the perceived dominance of 'radical feminists' (eg Concerned Women for America and REAL Women of Canada). These conservative North American NGOs have forged coalitions with NGOs in Islamic, Catholic, and post-Soviet states. For instance, the World Congress of Families, a loose coalition of pro-family and pro-marriage Christian organizations from around the globe, was launched in Moscow in 1995 by North American and Russian sociologists. It organized biannual world conferences in Prague, Geneva, Mexico City, Warsaw, Amsterdam, Madrid, and Sydney. In 2017, this congress was held in Hungary, where the populist right-wing prime minister Orbán opened the conference. In 2016, the World Congress of Families formalized its structure and now operates under the name International Organization for the Family, which is headquartered in the United States and links organizations from North America, Latin America, and post-Soviet countries. The conservative Spanish organization HazteOir, founded in 2001, launched the international platform Citizengo in 2013 that has local branches in Europe, Latin America, and the Russian Federation (Russia). The platform coordinates large-scale e-petitions to influence national politics in relation to reproductive and sexual issues in 2013. In 2015, Belarus, Egypt, and Qatar established the Group of Friends of the Family (GoFF). On the occasion of the International Day of the Family in March 2016, GoFF organized the Uniting

[41] Chappell (n 8) 492.
[42] Zwingel (n 28).
[43] ibid.

Nations for a Family Friendly World event at the UN Economic and Social Council (ECOSOC) Chamber to promote the family as the 'natural and fundamental group unit of society' and to remind the UN of their obligations 'in binding international human rights instruments to protect and safeguard the family formed by the union of a man and a woman in marriage'.[44] This event was supported by the Center for Family and Human Rights (C-Fam), The Family Research Council, HazteOir and CitizenGo. Many of these NGOs have a consultative status with ECOSOC.

What these oppositional actors share is that they do not acknowledge CEDAW as a legitimate document and refuse to accept the CEDAW Committee as an authoritative interpreter on the meaning of women's rights.[45] Yet, somewhat paradoxically, they strategically employ the language of international human rights declarations and treaties to actively oppose women's rights or propose alternative interpretations of existing norms.[46] These state and non-state actors are effectively using the platforms provided by the UN conferences to become better organized, develop new information channels and structures, and create shared counter frames.

## 4. Counterframing

Conservative activists have increasingly adopted human rights frames and terminology they previously rejected to influence the international agenda.[47] Human rights have become a central site of normative contestation, where both women's rights activists and conservative actors promote contrasting interpretations of human rights. Both camps position themselves as proponents of human rights, but refer to different human rights in support of their own positions.[48] Conservative and religious actors that oppose women's rights often refer to some specific elements of the UDHR like 'the right to life' (Article 3 UDHR), and 'the family as the natural and fundamental group unit of society' that 'is entitled to protection by society and the State' (Article 16(c) UDHR). These human rights are interpreted in ways that oppose certain elements of CEDAW or other international conventions.

The Article on the right to life has been used to resist the inclusion of reproductive rights in human rights conventions. CEDAW affirms women's rights to reproductive choice: women should be able 'to decide freely and responsibly on the number and spacing of their children and to have access to the information, education and means to enable them to exercise these rights' (Article 16(e) CEDAW). The CEDAW Committee has operated cautiously to avoid major confrontations about this issue. Accordingly, it adopted the position that women's reproductive health includes good coverage of their reproductive needs during pregnancy and as mothers and that women should be

44 Group of Friends of the Family and others, 'Uniting Nations for a Family Friendly World: Special High-Level Event' (New York, 16 May 2016) <http://www.un.org/webcast/pdfs/160516am-family-belarus.pdf> accessed 15 December 2021.

45 Zwingel (n 28).

46 Sanders (n 36).

47 Goetz (n 11); Sanders (n 36); Chappell (n 8).

48 Clifford Bob, *The Global Right Wing and the Clash of World Politics* (CUP 2012); Christopher McCrudden, 'Transnational Culture Wars' (2015) 13 International Journal of Constitutional Law 434.

able to determine the number and spacing of children.[49] The Committee also used the concept of *unwanted* pregnancies and views both teenage pregnancies and abortions as an expression of this, framing it as a violation of women's reproductive rights. Also, the Committee frequently recommended making emergency contraception available, as a means that some abortion opponents are willing to accept.[50] In relation to abortion, the Committee has mainly argued for decriminalization.[51] Yet, in 2015, the UN Human Rights Committee drafted General Comment No. 36 on Article 6 of the International Covenant on Civil and Political Rights (ICCPR)[52] (on the right to life), that explicitly takes up the issue of abortion. According to the draft text:

> any legal restrictions on the ability of women to seek abortion must not, inter alia, jeopardize their lives or subject them to physical or mental pain or suffering which violates article 7. States parties must provide safe access to abortion to protect the life and health of pregnant women, and in situations in which carrying a pregnancy to term would cause the woman substantial pain or suffering, most notably where the pregnancy is the result of rape or incest or when the fetus suffers from fetal impairment. States parties may not regulate pregnancy or abortion in a manner that runs contrary to their duty to ensure that women do not have to undertake unsafe abortions. … Nor should States parties introduce humiliating or unreasonably burdensome requirements on women seeking to undergo abortion. The duty to protect the lives of women against the health risks associated with unsafe abortions requires States parties to ensure access for women and men, and, in particular, adolescents, to information and education about reproductive options, and to a wide range of contraceptive methods. States parties must also ensure the availability of adequate prenatal and post-abortion health care for pregnant women.[53]

This text was opposed by conservative states and NGOs. Russia and the United States both argued it was inappropriate to include abortion in this General Comment. Poland argued that Article 6 ICCPR was envisioned to 'protect the life of every human being in every stage of its development, as the inherent dignity of a human person starts with the very first moment of its existence'.[54] Along the same line, conservative NGOs advocated an interpretation of the right to life as a right that starts at the moment of conception. For instance, the International Organization for the Family advocated a 'language acknowledging the inherent right to life of unborn children'.[55]

[49] Zwingel (n 28).
[50] ibid.
[51] ibid.
[52] International Covenant on Civil and Political Rights (adopted 16 December 1966, entered into force 23 March 1976) 999 UNTS 171.
[53] CCPR, 'General Comment No. 36 on article 6 of the International Covenant on Civil and Political Rights, on the right to life' (30 October 2018) UN Doc CCPR/C/GC/36 advance unedited version.
[54] Poland, 'Remarks of Poland to the General Comment No 36 on article 6 of the International Covenant on Civil and Political Rights, on the right to life' <www.ohchr.org/EN/HRBodies/CCPR/Pages/GC36-Article6Righttolife.aspx> accessed 15 December 2021.
[55] International Organization of the Family, 'Statement regarding: Draft of General comment No. 36 on article 6 of the International Covenant on Civil and Political Rights, on the right to life' <www.ohchr.org/EN/HRBodies/CCPR/Pages/GC36-Article6Righttolife.aspx> accessed 15 December 2021.

The NGO Culture of Life Africa claimed that the draft 'completely ignores the right to life of the unborn child, who is no less a member of the human family than an infant, a prepubescent, pubescent, adolescent, or an adult. S/he forms part of the continuity of human life, and to ignore children in the womb is discriminatory'.[56] Also, several NGOs questioned the authority of the Committee to 'reinterpret' Article 6 ICCPR. C-Fam argued that '[abortions] are not issues that should be decided or resolved by an unelected, unaccountable, and mostly obscure committee of experts in Geneva'[57] and CitizenGo declared that 'reinterpreting—as is pretended—that the treaties appeal to the "right" of abortion is against the literalness of these and implies a ABUSE OF AUTHORITY OF THE MANDATE'.[58] In the final version of the General Comment adopted 3 September 2019[59] some of the more contentious elements have been removed like the passage that abortion would be allowed in case the foetus suffers from foetal impairment. Also, language is obfuscated by using the word 'should' in clarifying the measures to be taken as a result of the 'duty' to ensure that States take measures to eradicate unsafe abortions.[60]

Another article of the UDHR frequently used to argue against gender equality is Article 16(c) UDHR that positions the family as 'the natural and fundamental group unit of society' entitled to protection by society and the state. The preamble of CEDAW acknowledges the crucial contribution of women to the wellbeing of family and society, but calls for a change in the traditional role models for men and women, especially concerning the education of children.[61] Article 5 CEDAW obliges states parties to modify social and cultural patterns based on the inferiority or superiority of either sex and ensure the common responsibility of men and women in the upbringing of their children.

Many state and non-state actors oppose this idea and instead argue for complementary male and female roles in marriage and family.[62] For instance, the Moroccan delegation at the Beijing conference argued that the notion of equal rights did not acknowledge the complementary roles of men and women in the family that 'had arisen in the deep consciousness of the human race' and that a clear distinction between the two was 'necessary for the physic and moral balance of children'.[63] The delegation of Iran argued that:

[56] Culture of Africa, 'Submission on the Draft General Comment on Article 6 of the International Covenant on Civil and Political Rights by United Nations Human Rights Committee' <www.ohchr.org/EN/HRBodies/CCPR/Pages/GC36-Article6Righttolife.aspx> accessed 15 December 2021.

[57] C-Fam and Civil Society for the Family, 'Observations on draft general comment 36' <www.ohchr.org/EN/HRBodies/CCPR/Pages/GC36-Article6Righttolife.aspx> accessed 15 December 2021.

[58] Translated from Spanish: 'Reinterpretar -como se pretende- que en los tratados se apela al "derecho" al aborto es contrario a la literalidad de los mismos y supondría una clara EXTRALIMITACIÓN DE MANDATO' in CitizenGO Foundation, 'Opinion ante el comentario general No 36 al art. 6 del pacto de derechos civiles y políticos' <www.ohchr.org/EN/HRBodies/CCPR/Pages/GC36-Article6Righttolife.aspx> accessed 15 December 2021.

[59] CCPR, 'General Comment No. 36 (2019) on Article 6 of the International Covenant on Civil and Political Rights, on the right to life' (3 September 2019) UN Doc CCPR/C/GC/36.

[60] Sarah Joseph, 'Extending the right to life under the International Covenant on Civil and Political Rights: General Comment 36' (2019) 19 Human Rights Law Review 352.

[61] Zwingel (n 28).

[62] ibid.

[63] UNGA, 'Summary Record of the 70th Meeting' (6 December 1979) UN Doc A/C.3/34/ SR, para 11.

> [t]he concept of equality in our interpretation takes into account the fact that although women are equal in their human rights and dignity with men, their different roles and responsibilities underlie the need for an equitable system of rights where particular priorities and requirements of the woman in her multiple roles are accounted for.[64]

The Holy See 'considers women and men as being of equal dignity in all areas of life, but without this always implying an equality of roles and functions'.[65] These different roles and functions refer to what is seen by many of the opposing actors as the 'natural' place for women in the family, carrying out a primary role as mothers and caretakers. In addition, pro-family frames define the 'natural family' as a heterosexual marriage in which men and women adhere to traditional gender roles.[66] The Canadian pro-family NGO REAL Women of Canada defines the family as 'being related by blood, heterosexual marriage or adoption, for the spiritual, emotional, economic and social well-being of the nation'.[67] The 2016 Cape Town Declaration of the International Organization for the Family points to this as a 'universal' ideal:

> Spanning the globe, we have no common tongue, culture, or creed. We are divided by history and geography, by social customs and forms of government. But in foundations, we are united. We are of one mind on the bedrock of civil society, on the basis of that first and primordial community called the family: We affirm the dignity of marriage as the conjugal bond of man and woman. We embrace it not as the parochial practice of any sect or nation or age, but as the patrimony of all mankind.[68]

Heterosexuality is seen as threatened by the concept of gender. The Holy See advanced this view in its reservations to the Beijing Platform for Action: the term 'gender' is understood by the Holy See as grounded in biological sexual identity, male or female. Furthermore, the Platform for Action itself clearly uses the term 'both genders'. 'The Holy See thus excludes dubious interpretations based on world views which assert that sexual identity can be adapted indefinitely to suit new and different purposes.'[69] This also became a key issue during the 1998 negotiations surrounding the inclusion of the term 'gender' in the International Criminal Court's (ICC's) Rome Statute.[70] This dispute was then resolved by the adoption of an ambiguous and strategically malleable definition of gender.[71]

[64] 'Report of the Fourth World Conference on Women' (Beijing, 4–15 September 1995) UN Doc A/CONF.177/20/Rev.1, 164.

[65] Cited in Chappell (n 8) 512.

[66] Chappell (n 8).

[67] Real Women of Canada, 'Definition of the Family – 1993' (18 December 2015) <www.realwomenofcanada.ca/definition-of-the-family-1993/> accessed 15 December 2021.

[68] International Organization for the Family, 'The Cape Town Declaration: Universal Declaration on the Family and Marriage' (2016) <www.upf-deutschland.de/files/The_Cape_Town_Declaration_on_the_Family_and_Marriage-2016.pdf> accessed 15 December 2021.

[69] 'Report of the Fourth World Conference on Women' (n 64) 162.

[70] Rome Statute of the International Criminal Court (adopted 17 July 1998, entered into force 1 July 2002) 2187 UNTS 3.

[71] Valerie Oosterveld, 'Constructive Ambiguity and the Meaning of "Gender" for the International Criminal Court' (2014) 16 International Feminist Journal of Politics 563.

A final important element in the counterframes of oppositional actors are references to state sovereignty and the protection of traditional values.[72] Sovereignty is defended 'in the face of the expansion of international human rights norms, especially where they are seen to conflict with traditional cultural and religious practices'.[73] This is clear in the reservations made by Egypt stating that its compliance with the Beijing Platform for Action 'will be conditional on complete respect for the rights of national sovereignty and various moral and religious values'.[74] Iran, Iraq, Libya, Morocco, and Tunisia made similar reservations to the document.[75] This language is also adopted by NGOs, for instance the NGO Concerned Women for America points to a number of affairs in which the Commission on the Status of Women 'injects itself into domestic social and political affairs of sovereign nations', such as 'indoctrination of children', referring to Article 10 CEDAW on the elimination of sexist stereotypes from school curricula and textbooks, 'mandatory sex education and contraception, including information and advice on family planning'.[76] More recently, oppositional actors also deploy anti-colonial discourses arguing against the universal character of women's rights and instead representing these as a Western construct promoted by radical feminists.[77] These Western products stand at odds with traditional norms and values. The lobby to protect traditional norms and values has become more powerful. Since 2009, a traditional values debate led by Russia has developed in the UN Human Rights Council and several resolutions calling for a reinterpretation of human rights in accordance with traditional values have been adopted. Resolution 16/3, adopted in 2011, stated 'that all cultures and civilizations in their traditions, customs, religions and beliefs share a common set of values that belong to humankind in its entirety, and that those values have made an important contribution to the development of human rights norms and standards'.[78] Many advocates and states claim this to be an attempt to undermine progress in equal family relations, thus limiting the rights of women.[79]

Conservative and religious state and non-state actors thus act as norm entrepreneurs promoting frames to defend the 'natural family' and 'the right to life', but they also act as 'antipreneurs',[80] actively resisting the norm of gender equality. They do this by contesting, blocking or reversing women's rights or proposing their alternative interpretations of human rights norms. Sanders labels this strategy as 'norm spoiling': 'norm spoiling is the process through which actors directly challenge existing norms with the aim of weakening their influence'.[81] She considers spoiling to be

[72] Chappell (n 8); Sanders (n 36); Zwingel (n 28).
[73] Chappell (n 8) 513.
[74] ibid.
[75] ibid.
[76] Zwingel (n 28) 147.
[77] Sanders (n 36).
[78] UN Human Rights Council, 'Resolution adopted by the Human Rights Council 16/3: Promoting human rights and fundamental freedoms through a better understanding of traditional values of humankind' (8 April 2011) UN Doc A/HRC/RES/16/3, 2.
[79] The resolutions received strong criticism of the Office of the High Commissioner for Human Rights, Treaty Bodies, and Special Procedures Mandate Holders, as undermining women's right to equality. Also, several states and the European Union expressed their concern over the potential misuse of the concept of traditional values (Raday (n 13); Halperin-Kaddari and Freeman (n 11)).
[80] Alan Bloomfield and Shirley V Scott (eds), *Norm Antipreneurs and the Politics of Resistance to Global Normative Change* (Routledge 2017).
[81] Sanders (n 36) 272.

a short-term strategy, complementing the long-term strategy of establishing conservative norms that can revert the existing women's rights framework. Vinjamuri talks about a strategic backlash to human rights now that countries like Russia adopted an active strategy of counter norming designed to circumvent and undermine Western norms.[82]

## 5. Explaining Resistances to Gender Equality

According to social movement theory, the emergence and strengthening of these oppositional networks is a predictable reaction to the significant international success to spread gender equality norms.[83] Social movement theory has labelled this the 'countermobilization dynamics'. The central idea is that movements that are successful in terms of visibility, force, and making progress will generate opposition from the groups whose interests are threatened. Yet, this opposition will only take the form of a countermovement when other, more effective formal political routes are not open to them. Institutional actors such as elected officials, religious actors, or other elites may also want to keep their efforts to resist gender equality change invisible by mobilizing other (social movement) actors to act on their behalf. They do this by using 'an already highly aligned constituency' as well as pre-existent political, institutional, civic, and religious organizations to mount their opposition to a particular social movement.[84] The emergence of a significant countermovement often implies that movement and countermovement become engaged in sustained interaction not just with institutional politics, but also with one another.[85] Countermobilization is particularly successful when oppositional actors portray the conflict as one that entails larger value cleavages in society.[86] This argument is highly relevant to the emergence of conservative activism against the progress of women's rights. As Chappell argues, it would be difficult to find a set of issues more morally contentious than those with which women's rights activists and conservative activists are engaged.[87]

To understand the dynamics of international norm diffusion, we thus have to take into account the oppositional dynamics between norm promotors and their counterforces that promote competing norms. This is a useful perspective to understand ups and downs in advancing (international) women's rights. It explains how the progress in international gender equality norms was contested by multiple conservative actors at different levels. A social movement approach also draws attention to the role of political opportunity structures in explaining the resonance and success of both positions. To understand the current success of forces that oppose international women's rights, I want to point to two interrelated political developments: democratic

[82] Leslie Vinjamuri, 'Human Rights Backlash' in Stephen Hopgood, Jack Snyder, and Leslie Vinjamuri (eds), *Human Rights Futures* (CUP 2017).
[83] Roggeband (n 35).
[84] Tahi L Mottl, 'The analysis of countermovements' (1980) 27 Social Problems 620, 626.
[85] David S Meyer and Suzanne Staggenborg, 'Movements, Countermovements and the Structure of Political Opportunity' (1996) 101 American Journal of Sociology 1628.
[86] ibid.
[87] Chappell (n 8).

backsliding,[88] often led by (right-wing and left-wing) populist and nationalist governments, and the closure of civic space.[89]

First, the positions of actors contesting gender equality norms are currently increasingly backed by populist and right-wing regimes that promote state projects to enforce heteronormative and patriarchal family models, in which women are situated as reproducers of the nation.[90] Such agendas pose restrictions on the reproductive and sexual rights of women but also affect their position on the labour market and in politics. Women's rights are particularly vulnerable in fragile and nascent democracies where such rights have been established only recently and where the space of civil society actors to defend such rights is limited and even shrinking.[91] The current wave of hollowing and backsliding democracies in Central and Eastern European countries,[92] but also Turkey, the United States, and Latin American countries like Brazil, Nicaragua, and Venezuela where populist and nationalist projects prevail may therefore lead to the erosion of women's rights both at the national and international level. Case study evidence indicates that backsliding democracy indeed negatively affects gender equality policies.[93] The Hungarian right-wing populist Fidesz government that took office in 2010 immediately stalled the implementation of the 2010 National Gender Equality strategy after the elections. Funds were diverted from gender equality objectives towards objectives opposing it. For example, funds coming from the EU Progress Fund were used for an anti-abortion campaign in ways that were challenged by EU Commissioner Viviane Reading.[94] In Poland, the right-wing populist Euro-sceptic Law and Justice Party (PiS) government that took office in October 2015 set out to reform the democratic institutional setting of Poland. Democratic backsliding in Poland has reached the threat of an Article 7 TEU procedure from the EU. A central element of this de-democratization process is a strong anti-gender

[88] Nancy Bermeo, 'On Democratic Backsliding' (2016) 27 Journal of Democracy 5; Bela Greskovits, 'The Hollowing and Backsliding of Democracy in East Central Europe' (2015) 6 Global Policy 28.

[89] Thomas Carothers and Saskia Brechenmacher, 'Closing Space: Democracy and Human Rights Support Under Fire' (Carnegie Endowment for International Peace 2014) <https://carnegieendowment.org/files/closing_space.pdf> accessed 15 December 2021; Douglas Rutzen, 'Civil Society under Assault' (2015) 26 Journal of Democracy 28.

[90] Andy Baker and others, 'Maintaining Civic Space in Backsliding Regimes' (22 September 2017) USAID Research and Innovation Grants Working Papers Series <www.usaid.gov/sites/default/files/documents/1866/Maintaining_Civic_Space_in_Backsliding_Regimes_-_Research_and_Innovation_Grants_Working_Papers_Series.pdf> accessed 15 December 2021; Kate Bishop, 'Standing Firm: Women- and Trans-Led Organisations Respond to Closing Space for Civil Society' (Mama Cash and Urgent Action Fund, July 2017) <www.mamacash.org/media/publications/mc_closing_space_report_def.pdf> accessed 15 December 2021.

[91] Carothers and Brechenmacher (n 89); Rutzen (n 89); Baker and others (n 90).

[92] Greskovits (n 88); Andrea Krizsan and Conny Roggeband, 'Towards a Conceptual Framework for Struggles over Democracy in Backsliding States: Gender Equality Policy in Central Eastern Europe' (2018) 6 Politics and Governance 90.

[93] Conny Roggeband and Andrea Krizsán, 'Democratic Backsliding and the Backlash against Women's Rights: Understanding the Current Challenges for Feminist Politics' (2020) The UN Women discussion paper series No 35 June 2020 <www.unwomen.org/sites/default/files/Headquarters/Attachments/Sections/Library/Publications/2020/Discussion-paper-Democratic-backsliding-and-the-backlash-against-womens-rights-en.pdf> accessed 15 December 2021.

[94] See 'EU Funds used for Hungarian Anti-Abortion Campaign' *EURACTIV* (17 June 2011) <www.euractiv.com/section/justice-home-affairs/news/eu-funds-used-for-hungarian-anti-abortion-campaign/> accessed 15 December 2021.

equality rhetoric[95] in which 'gender ideology' is featured as a major threat to Polish society and Catholic family values.[96] The government has dismantled some existing reproductive rights and domestic violence policies.[97] Funds for the National Action Plan on Domestic Violence were suspended and access to contraception was made more difficult. Also, the government proposed a total ban of abortion which it had to withdraw after massive protest.[98] Not only right-wing regimes attack women's rights, also populist left-wing regimes have been referring women back to traditional roles as caretakers, and dismantling existing gender equality policies and arrangements.[99] The late Venezuelan president Chavez frequently asserted that mothers were the foundations of the Bolivarian Revolution. The Ecuadorian left-wing president Correa held conservative ideas on reproductive rights and opposed a parliamentary proposal to decriminalize abortion in case of rape. Also, Correa dismantled the National Women's Council that had been in place since 1998 and that served as the central intermediate between the state and women's organizations.[100] The Nicaraguan president Ortega implemented a pro-natalist agenda and dismantled feminist advances to reposition himself as a Catholic populist leader.[101]

A second development related to democratic backsliding is the diminishing civic space. Civil society organizations and in particular those defending human rights are facing increasing pol.itical restraints all over the world, including restrictive legislation to control their activities and to ban or restrict foreign funding.[102] Since 2012, over 100 laws aimed at restricting funding, operations, and registration of civil society organizations have been passed in different countries.[103] State hostility not only entails threats to the rights of civil society but also repressive or even violent actions ranging

[95] For example Minister of Labour Rafalska spoke against the Istanbul Convention and consequences in terms of gender (Robert Kowalski, 'Rząd PiS przygotowuje wypowiedzenie konwencji antyprzemocowej' (2 December 2016) <https://oko.press/rzad-pis-przygotowuje-wypowiedzenie-konwencji-antyprzemocowej/> accessed 15 December 2021); president Duda spoke against the Istanbul Convention (Joanna Podgórska, 'Duda o konwencji antyprzemocowej: "Nie stosować". Niech prezydent wyjaśni to kobietom potrzebującym pomocy' (3 February 2017) <www.polityka.pl/tygodnikpolityka/kraj/1692956,1,duda-o-konwencji-antyprzemocowej-nie-stosowac-niech-prezydent-wyjasni-to-kobietom-potrzebujacym-pomocy.read> accessed 15 December 2021).

[96] Barbara Gaweda, 'The Recent Uprising against Gender Equality: Exploring the Discursive Construction of the «War on Genderism» in Poland' (2017) 18 Comunicazione Politica 251; Conny Roggeband and Andrea Krizsán, 'Democratic Backsliding and the Backlash against Women's Rights: Understanding the Current Challenges for Feminist Politics' (2020) (n 93)..

[97] Andrea Krizsan and Conny Roggeband, *Politicizing Gender and Democracy in the Context of the Istanbul Convention* (Palgrave Macmillan 2021)

[98] ibid.

[99] Karen Kampwirth (ed), *Gender and Populism in Latin America: Passionate Politics* (Pennsylvania State University Press 2010).

[100] Amy Lind, '"Revolution with a Woman's Face"? Family Norms, Constitutional Reform, and the Politics of Redistribution in Post-Neoliberal Ecuador' (2012) 24 Rethinking Marxism <www.researchgate.net/publication/263252591_Revolution_with_a_Woman's_Face_Family_Norms_Constitutional_Reform_and_the_Politics_of_Redistribution_in_Post-Neoliberal_Ecuador> accessed 15 December 2021.

[101] Kampwirth (n 99).

[102] Darin Christensen and Jeremy M Weinstein, 'Defunding Dissent: Restrictions on Aid to NGOs' (2013) 24 Journal of Democracy 77; Carothers and Brechenmacher (n 89); Rutzen (n 89); Annika E Poppe and Jonas Wolff, 'The Contested Spaces of Civil Society in a Plural World: Norm Contestation in the Debate about Restrictions on International Civil Society Support' (2017) 23 Contemporary Politics 469.

[103] Freedom House, 'Freedom in the World 2019' (2019) <https://freedomhouse.org/sites/default/files/Feb2019_FH_FITW_2019_Report_ForWeb-compressed.pdf> accessed 15 December 2021.

from disproportionate auditing as a means of control to policing and physical attacks against activists.[104] What is somewhat less noticed is how this closure of civic space is a gendered phenomenon that particularly affects women's rights activism. Women's rights activists are not only targeted because of the focus of their work that is often viewed as endangering 'traditional values', but opposition to women's rights also uses gendered mechanisms to restrict and repress organizations that promote such rights, including gender-based violence, harassment, and intimidation.[105] Next, closure is a selective process in which the space of specific civil society organizations defined as anti-state and anti-government is limited, while simultaneously the space and state support to organizations identified as pro-government is expanded.[106] The disempowerment and exclusion of women's rights organizations is accompanied by the empowerment and inclusion of organizations with opposite values and goals. In their efforts to restrict women's rights (activism), governments are sponsoring oppositional movements and use them to influence the realm of civil society in a way that directly supports state power.[107] Public funding of women's organizations is redirected to pro-government NGOs and the positions that women's rights activists previously held in policy processes is now given to pro-family or children's rights organizations.[108] Nationalist and populist regimes use conservative, religious, anti-feminist, anti-gay, or anti-immigration organizations to reinforce traditional gender norms and to recreate a traditional hierarchical patriarchal or exclusionary model of civil society.[109] Civil society becomes an ideological device to promote and justify a vision of the state promoting patriarchal family models rather than gender equality rights.[110] The closure of the civic space for women's rights defenders not only obstructs them in exercising their rights, but also limits their role in safeguarding existing gender equality policies and arrangements and preventing erosion.[111]

While the implications of this dual dynamic are particularly visible at the national level, some international effects are visible too. The processes of democratic backsliding in the Central and Eastern European (CEE) region and the related attacks on women's rights and women's rights activism has also spilled over to the international arena particularly affecting the Council of Europe (CoE) Convention on Preventing and Combating Violence against Women and Domestic Violence (Istanbul Convention).[112]

[104] Conny Roggeband and Andrea Krizsan, 'The Selective Closure of Civic Space' (2021) 12 Global Policy 23.

[105] ibid.

[106] Andrea Krizsan and Conny Roggeband, 'Reconfiguring State–Movement Relations in the Context of De-democratization' (2021) 3 Social Politics: International Studies in Gender, State & Society 604.

[107] Roggeband and Kriszan, 'The Selective Closure of Civic Space' (n 104).

[108] ibid; Krizsan and Roggeband 'Reconfiguring State–Movement Relations in the Context of De-democratization' (n 106).

[109] Dara Z Strolovitch and Erica Townsend-Bell, 'Sex, Gender, and Civil Society' in Georgina Waylen and others (eds), *The Oxford Handbook of Gender and Politics* (OUP 2013).

[110] Jude Howell, 'Gender and Civil Society' in Marlies Glasius, Mary Kaldor, and Helmut Anheir (eds), *Global Civil Society 2005/6* (Sage 2006).

[111] Dorothy McBride and Amy Mazur, *The Politics of State Feminism: Innovation in Comparative Research* (Temple University Press 2010); Roggeband and Kriszan 'The Selective Closure of Civic Space' (n 104).

[112] Council of Europe Convention on Preventing Violence against Women and Domestic Violence (adopted 11 May 2011, entered into force 1 August 2014) CETS 210.

This binding treaty was adopted by the CoE Committee of Ministers on 7 April 2011 and entered into force 1 August 2014. While the Convention on the one hand can be considered a success because almost all member states with the exception of Azerbaijan and Russia have signed the Convention, it has on the other hand also raised major opposition now blocking ratification processes in the CEE region. Religious leaders, conservative NGOs, and populist politicians claim that there is an intention of introducing the concept of gender in national laws through the ratification of the Convention. In response to a wave of protests against so-called 'gender ideology', The Constitutional Court in Bulgaria blocked ratification on 27 July 2018 and in Hungary the parliament blocked ratification on 5 May 2020. Poland, which ratified the Convention in April 2015, now threatens to back out.[113] Turkey withdrew from the Convention on 1 July 2021. These developments highlight widespread resistance to the perceived imposition of liberal values in general and gender equality in particular. The Slovak Prime Minister Fico explained he considered the Convention contrary to the constitutional definition of marriage as a heterosexual union, because of the use of the concept of gender in the Convention. In Latvia, which has not ratified the Convention yet, religious leaders have claimed that the Convention opens the door for imposing on Latvia a social transformation project based on gender ideology that would run counter to the constitution of the Republic of Latvia.[114] These resistances seem to be symptomatic of a wider backlash against women's rights in Europe and the ratification of the Istanbul Convention will be an important litmus test for the strength and resilience of international women's rights.

## 6. The Quality of Norms and Implications for Resilience

The quality of international norms on gender equality differs greatly, both in their substantive character and in whether they are legalized or not, and to what degree. The quality of gender equality norms can be assessed using two criteria.[115] First, norms differ to the extent to which gender issues are related to gender inequality. The gendered quality of an international norm is related to a structural understanding of gender inequality and implies that the envisioned change is also systematic, comprehensive, and long term.[116] A gendered framing is usually also enhanced with the inclusion of women's voices in the policy process. The second criterion concerns the character of the norm. Here we can distinguish between obligatory status (hard versus soft law) and different enforcement mechanisms, the precision of the rule and delegation of its interpretation and application to a third-party tribunal.[117] Abbott and

[113] Andrea Krizsan and Conny Roggeband, *Politicizing Gender and Democracy in the Context of the Istanbul Convention* (note 97).

[114] Michael Mustillo, 'Latvia Bristles against the Istanbul Convention Combating Violence against Women' *The Baltic Times* (28 February 2018) <www.baltictimes.com/latvia_bristles_against_the_istanbul_convention_combating_violence_against_women/> accessed 15 December 2021.

[115] van Eerdewijk and Roggeband (n 17).

[116] From 2013: Andrea Kriszan and Emanuela Lombardo, 'The Quality of Gender Equality Policies: A Discursive Approach' (2013) 20 European Journal of Women's Studies 77.

[117] Kenneth W Abbott and Duncan Snidal, 'Hard and Soft Law in International Governance' (2000) 54 International Organization 421.

Snidal claim that states often 'deliberately choose softer forms of legalization as superior institutional arrangements'.[118] They argue that different factors condition states' choice of soft law, including transaction costs, uncertainty, implications for national sovereignty, divergence of preferences, and power differentials.[119] More constructivist scholars argue that soft law creates a crucial framework for conversation, in which states gradually may alter their conception of their interests and even identity. This eventually makes agreement on harder rules possible.

Do legal rules affect behaviour differently from non-legal rules, or, more broadly, from norms? And are legal rules more resilient than non-legal rules? Scholars that work in the field of gender and politics have argued that soft law on gender equality tends to be more transformative, yet hard law may result to be more resilient. In a study on the diffusion and implementation of regional gender equality norms on violence and gender mainstreaming in trade and aid, Roggeband, van Eerdewijk, and van der Vleuten concluded that stronger norms had developed in the field of violence against women that seem to account for successful diffusion processes.[120] International hard law has been developed to deal with the issue of violence against women, like the Inter-American Convention for the Prevention, Punishment and Elimination of Violence against Women, and more recently the CoE Istanbul Convention. Gender mainstreaming norms of the EU, SADC, and Mercosur were often a combination of soft and hard law arrangements that were poorly implemented. Norms on gender mainstreaming in aid were somewhat better abided by compared to similar norms in the field of trade. This indicates that not only the quality of the norm is important but also the field in which it is issued. More systematic comparison of compliance to hard and soft norms is necessary to predict resilience.

## 7. Conclusions

Contestation over women's rights is a far from new phenomenon, but over the past two decades, opposition to gender equality has become better organized at the transnational level, mobilizing a dispersed set of state and non-state actors, and is becoming more successful in halting the progress of women's rights. I have argued that the position of oppositional actors vis-à-vis women rights activism appears to be strengthened by two recent political developments: democratic backsliding and the closure of civic space. Some preliminary findings show how these interrelated developments lead to an erosion of women's rights at the national level, but so far we lack systematic research into how the oppositional strategies of counterframing and blocking are playing out at the international level.

[118] ibid 423.

[119] ibid.

[120] Conny Roggeband, Anouka van Eerdewijk, and Anna van der Vleuten, 'Reconceptualizing Gender Equality Norm Diffusion and Regional Governance' in Anna van der Vleuten, Anouka van Eerdewijk, and Conny Roggeband (eds), *Gender Equality Norms in Regional Governance: Transnational Dynamics in Europe, South America and Southern Africa* (Palgrave Macmillan 2014).

Also, we need more studies that examine the consequences of the closure of civic space for the actor constellations that support international women's rights. Available research points to the central role of national and transnational women's rights activists in enhancing compliance.[121] National and transnational actors often form compliance constituencies that may include feminist activists, critical actors in legislative, judiciary, and civil society, but also lawyers, judges, and academics.[122] Such advocacy networks play a central role in monitoring, safeguarding, and advancing national legislation in line with international law. If such advocacy networks cannot sustain their advocacy, there is a serious danger of non-compliance but also reversal and erosion of previous progress.

Finally, we need to understand the puzzle of symbolic compliance and façade policies.[123] This is often the case in nascent and fragile democracies. On the surface, states seem to be complying with international law and formal policies appear to be in place that tick all the boxes. Yet, looking beyond the existence of legislation and policies into the implementation arrangements, institutions, and budgets, we see a different picture. This is, I think, the prominent threat in current waves of backlash against gender equality. Reluctant or oppositional governments do not necessarily (have to) withdraw from conventions or change laws to transform policies into dead letters.[124] We see a prevalence of low-key tactics to dismantle institutional and implementation arrangements.[125] In addition, we see strategies to get women's organizations sidelined but also some very open and even physical attacks on civil society organizations like in Poland or Hungary.[126] Without strong domestic actors monitoring compliance, the chances of backsliding on international commitments are much higher.

121 van Eerdewijk and Roggeband (n 17); Mala Htun and Laurel S Weldon, *The Logics of Gender Justice: State Action on Women's Rights Around the World* (CUP 2018); Conny Roggeband and Andrea Krizsan, 'Reversing Gender Policy Progress: Patterns of Backsliding in Central and Eastern European New Democracies' (2018) 1 European Journal of Politics and Gender 367.

122 van Eerdewijk and Roggeband (n 17).

123 Gerda Falkner, Oliver Treib, and Elisabeth Holzleithner, *Compliance in the Enlarged European Union: Living Rights or Dead Letters?* (Ashgate 2008).

124 ibid.

125 Roggeband and Kriszan, 'Reversing Gender Policy Progress: Patterns of Backsliding in Central and Eastern European New Democracies' (n 121)..

126 Human Rights First, 'Poland's New Front A Government's War against Civil Society' (August 2017) <www.humanrightsfirst.org/sites/default/files/Poland-Report-August-2017.pdf> accessed 15 December 2021.

# 15

# The Status of International Women's Rights

## Are Women's Rights in Danger?

*Lea Barbara Kuhlmann*

In October 2020, 34 states signed the Geneva Consensus Declaration, an initiative aimed at protecting the traditional family unit and limiting women from accessing abortion.[1] It was initiated by the United States under the Trump administration. Poland, Brazil, Egypt, Bahrain, and South Sudan were among the signatory states. The Geneva Consensus Declaration represents another attack on women's rights, especially their reproductive rights. It joins phenomena like domestic regresses in women's access to abortion in the United States[2] and Poland,[3] or Turkey's withdrawal of the Council of Europe (CoE) Convention on preventing and combating violence against women and domestic violence (Istanbul Convention).[4], [5] Conny Roggeband, approaching the progress of women's rights from the political science perspective, argues that oppositional actors vis-á-vis women's rights and gender equality have become better organized and more successful in halting progress in the last three decades.[6] This chapter posits that, from the legal perspective, women's rights have always been precarious in international law. The threats and attacks against them are not a new phenomenon. Especially women's reproductive rights and the concept of gender have been controversial and contested since their emergence in the 1990s. Nevertheless, there are also indicators of resilience and even progress in the work of United Nations human rights bodies.

Women's rights are rooted in gender equality and non-discrimination. Women's rights are enshrined in binding—hard law—and non-binding—soft law—instruments.

[1] United Nations General Assembly (UNGA), 'Letter dated 2 December 2020 from the Permanent Representative of the United States of America to the United Nations addressed to the Secretary-General' (7 December 2020) UN Doc A/75/626 Annex; see also Nathan P Southern and Lindsey Kennedy, 'Trump's Legacy is a Global Alliance against Women's Rights' (*Foreign Policy*, 20 January 2021) <https://foreignpolicy.com/2021/01/20/trump-anti-abortion-global-alliance-legacy/> accessed 4 February 2022.

[2] Elizabeth Nash and Sophia Naide, 'State Policy Trends at Midyear 2021: Already the Worst Legislative Year Ever for U.S. Abortion Rights' (*Guttmacher Institute*, 1 July 2021) <www.guttmacher.org/article/2021/07/state-policy-trends-midyear-2021-already-worst-legislative-year-ever-us-abortion> accessed 4 February 2022.

[3] 'Poland enforces controversial near-total abortion ban' *BBC News* (London, 28 January 2021) <www.bbc.com/news/world-europe-55838210> accessed 4 February 2022.

[4] Council of Europe Convention on preventing and combating violence against women and domestic violence (adopted 11 May 2011, entered into force 1 August 2014) CoETS 210 (Istanbul Convention).

[5] Denunciation contained in a Note Verbale from the Representation of Turkey to the Council of Europe (22 March 2021) Council of Europe (CoE), 'Reservations and Declarations for Treaty No. 210' <www.coe.int/en/web/conventions/full-list?module=declarations-by-treaty&numSte=210&codeNature=0> accessed 4 February 2022.

[6] See also Conny Roggeband, Chapter 14 in this book.

Lea Barbara Kuhlmann, *The Status of International Women's Rights* In: *Tracing Value Change in the International Legal Order*. Edited by: Heike Krieger and Andrea Liese, Oxford University Press. © Lea Barbara Kuhlmann 2023.
DOI: 10.1093/oso/9780192855831.003.0015

The universal instrument protecting women's rights is the Convention on the Elimination of All Forms of Discrimination against Women (CEDAW).[7] Moreover, there are regional and/or more specific treaties, including the Istanbul Convention. Among the significant soft law documents is the outcome document of the Fourth World Conference on Women (FWCW), the Beijing Platform for Action.[8] As a non-binding document, it only provides policy agendas and aspirational standards for states. However, it also impacts and guides the interpretation of human rights codified in treaties. While these instruments address all aspects of women's lives and despite many advances in the last decades, there are still many aspects where inequalities remain prevalent. These include equality in the workplace and equal pay, violence against women and gender-based violence, access to education, or sexual and reproductive rights.

This chapter analyses if there has been a change in the protection and the contestations[9] of gender equality—signifying a change to the norm development. It seeks to answer whether women's rights are in danger or if there are indications of resilience. The chapter addresses contestations to women's rights treaties in form of reservations to and the non-ratification of these treaties (Section 1). It then focuses on women's reproductive rights (Section 2) as an especially contested area.

## 1. Contestations to Women's Rights Treaties

CEDAW and the Istanbul Convention represent important codifications of women's rights. As binding treaties, they have positively impacted the protection of women's rights and the realization of gender equality.[10] However, international law does not guarantee the full implementation of these treaties. States can circumvent certain provisions and even underlying concepts by entering impermissible reservations upon their accession to CEDAW (Section 1.1). The Istanbul Convention has received similar reservations disguised as declarations and is faced with the non-ratification or even withdrawal by CoE member states (Section1.2).

### 1.1 CEDAW and Impermissible Reservations

Reservations to treaties are rooted in state sovereignty and are a fundamental principle of international treaty law. They are entered upon ratification or accession to a treaty and offer states the possibility to join the treaty with the option to exclude or modify the legal effect of provisions to the treaty in their application to the state.[11]

[7] Convention on the Elimination of All Forms of Discrimination against Women (adopted 18 December 1979, entered into force 3 September 1981) 1249 UNTS 13 (CEDAW).

[8] UN Woman, 'Beijing Declaration and Platform for Action | Beijing+5 Political Declaration and Outcome' (UN 1995, Reprinted by UN Women in 2014) (Beijing Platform for Action).

[9] See on the concept of 'contestation' Heike Krieger and Andrea Liese, Chapter 1 in this book, 13–20.

[10] See Roggeband, Chapter 14 in this book, 2.

[11] Vienna Convention on the Law of Treaties (adopted 22 May 1969, entered into force 27 January 1980) 1155 UNTS 331 (VCLT) art 2(1)(d); Christian Walter, 'Article 19 VCLT' in Oliver Dörr and Kirsten

Over time, the states can adopt and adapt local and domestic laws and customs to the treaty's standards and remove the reservation in due course. However, reservations compromise the treaty's integrity by hollowing out its norms and obligations.[12] They raise the question of how authoritative and accepted the provisions are, especially if several states have entered reservations on them. Moreover, states could enter a reservation with no intention of withdrawal, thus remaining a treaty party without having to adhere to the entire treaty. These dangers are especially prevalent in the context of human rights conventions and their core provisions.[13]

CEDAW has many of these compromising reservations. They are mostly associated with Muslim states with a strong foundation in Sharia law. These states enter these reservations despite prohibitions under CEDAW and international treaty law. Article 28(2) CEDAW prohibits reservations incompatible with its object and purpose. Incompatibility ensues when the reservation affects an essential element of CEDAW in such a way that it impairs its raison d'être.[14] Several Muslim member states have formulated either a general reservation[15] or one on Articles 1 to 5.[16] They limit the application of CEDAW for any provisions they deem inconsistent with sharia law. Thus, the reservations demonstrate a disregard for gender equality as provided for by CEDAW.[17] They are incompatible with CEDAW's object and purpose and are impermissible. Other states without a predominantly Muslim culture have also entered reservations that contradict the concept of gender equality. For example, several monarchies have formulated reservations protecting male primogeniture for royal or chief title succession.[18]

The phenomenon of impermissible reservations accompanies CEDAW since its entry into force in 1981. That year, Egypt formulated the first 'Sharia reservation'. Most

Schmalenbach (eds), *Vienna Convention on the Law of Treaty A Commentary* (2nd edn, Springer Verlag 2018) 264.

[12] Walter (n 11) 264.

[13] eg Liesbeth Lijnzaad, *Reservations to UN-Human Rights Treaties – Ratify and Ruin?* (Nijhoff 1995); Daniel W Hill, 'Avoiding Obligations: Reservations to Human Rights Treaties' (2016) 60 Journal of Conflict Resolution 1129; Heather E McKibben and Shaina D Western, '"Reserved Ratifications": An Analysis of States' Entry of Reservation Upon Ratification Treaties' (2018) 50 British Journal of Political Science 687; Kelebogile Zvobgo, Wayne Sandholtz and Suzie Mulesky, 'Reserving Rights: Explaining Human Rights Treaty Reservations' (2020) 64 International Studies Quarterly 785.

[14] International Law Commission (ILC), 'Guide to the Practice on Reservation on Treaties' (2011) II (Part Two) Yearbook of the ILC 26, 32 Rule 3.1.5.

[15] eg Reservations of Brunei Darussalam, Mauritania, or Oman; CEDAW (n 7) Declarations and Reservations 4–5, 7, 9.

[16] eg Reservations of Egypt, Morocco, or Niger; CEDAW (n 7) Declarations and Reservations 5, 8.

[17] Committee for the Elimination of All Forms of Discrimination against Women (CEDAW Committee), 'General Recommendations made by the Committee on the Elimination of Discrimination against Women' (1994) <www.un.org/womenwatch/daw/cedaw/recommendations/recomm.htm> accessed 4 February 2022, General Recommendation No. 21; UNGA, 'Report of the Committee on the Elimination of Discrimination against Women' (1998) UN Doc A/53/38/Rev.1, 47–48; see also Christine M Chinkin, 'Reservations and Observations to the Convention on the Elimination of All Forms of Discrimination against Women' in JP Gardner (ed), *Human Rights as General Norms and a State's Right to Opt Out* (British Institute for International and Comparative Law 1997) 68, 70; Rebecca J Cook, 'Reservations to the Convention in the Elimination of All Forms of Discrimination Against Women' (1990) 30 Virginia Journal of International Law 643, 692.

[18] Reservations of Lesotho, Monaco, Morocco, New Zealand, Spain, or the United Kingdom; CEDAW (n 7) Declarations and Reservations 7–10.

of them were added in the 2000s.[19] Unlike more specific reservations, these impermissible ones rarely get withdrawn by states.[20] Reservations on gender equality is also almost exclusive to CEDAW. Other human rights treaties only have very few comparable reservations. Of the 60 CEDAW member states with one or more reservations, 26 have formulated one on gender equality. There are only four similar reservations for the International Covenant on Civil and Political Rights (ICCPR):[21] one regarding the succession to the throne of Liechtenstein and three regarding Sharia law.[22]

Impermissible reservations are null and void.[23] Regardless, the high number and longevity of CEDAW's impermissible reservations affect the treaty's efficacy and reputation. They create the impression that women's rights are valued less than other human rights.[24] They also prevent the Committee for the Elimination of All Forms of Discrimination against Women (CEDAW Committee) from assessing the progress of states' implementation, thereby limiting its mandate.[25] Consequently, with their reservations, states contest and have been contesting the validity of women's rights and gender equality, in the context of binding law.

Other CEDAW member states do not remain passive and regularly object to these reservations because they deem them incompatible with CEDAW's object and purpose.[26] The objection precludes the application of the provision between the two states.[27] They also are regularly criticized by the CEDAW Committee.[28]

## 1.2 The Istanbul Convention

The Istanbul Convention's objective is inter alia the elimination of all forms of violence against women.[29] It identifies gender inequality as a cause of the prevalence of violence against women and gender-based violence and gender equality as one of the tools to combat it.[30] The Convention faces opposition for the definition of gender as a social construct, the so-called 'gender ideology'.[31] This opposition manifests itself in

[19] Marijke de Pauw, 'Women's Rights: From Bad to Worse? Assessing the Evolution of Incompatible Reservations to the CEDAW Convention' (2013) 29 Merkourios 51, 61.

[20] An exception would be Malawi's general reservation referencing traditional customs and practices which was withdrawn in 1991; CEDAW (n 7) Declarations and Reservations 52.

[21] International Covenant on Civil and Political Rights (adopted 16 December 1966, entered into force 23 March 1976) 999 UNTS 171 (ICCPR).

[22] ibid. Declarations and Reservations 4, 8, 9.

[23] ILC, 'Guide to the Practice on Reservation of Treaties' (n 14) chapter 4.5.1.

[24] Belinda Clark 'The Vienna Convention Reservations Regime and the Convention on Discrimination against Women' (1991) 85 American Journal of International Law 281, 317–20.

[25] UNGA, 'Report of the CEDAW Committee' (n 17) 48–49.

[26] CEDAW (n 7) Declarations and Reservations, objections 11–45; objections are formulated predominately by states of the Global North.

[27] VCLT (n 11) art 21(3); ILC, 'Guide to the Practice on Reservation of Treaties' (n 14) chapter 2.6.1.

[28] CEDAW Committee (n 17) General Recommendation No. 4 (1987); CEDAW Committee (n 17) General Recommendation No. 20 (1992); CEDAW Committee, 'Concluding observations on the combined third and fourth reports of Saudi Arabia' (14 March 2018) UN Doc CEDAW/C/SAU/CO/3-4.

[29] Istanbul Convention (n 4) art 1.

[30] Istanbul Convention (n 4) Preamble.

[31] See also Roggeband, Chapter 14 in this book, 30.

impermissible reservations disguised as declarations and in the non-ratification of or the withdrawal from the treaty.

### 1.2.1 The Istanbul Convention and Impermissible Reservations Disguised as Declarations

The Istanbul Convention's reservation regime is stricter than CEDAW's. Articles 78 and 79 provide a prohibition-exception model: reservations are permitted if they concern an aspect enumerated in Article 78(2) and (3) Istanbul Convention. Each reservation is only valid for five years and states must justify its continuance to the Group of experts on action against violence against women and domestic violence (GREVIO).

*Prima facie, this seems to prevent a high number of impermissible reservations.* Of the 34 member states, 21 have made reservations to the Istanbul Convention and all except one fulfil the criteria of the Convention's reservation regime.[32] The exception is Poland's reservation on Article 30(2) Istanbul Convention.[33] Yet, states have formulated interpretative declarations which would be impermissible as reservations. Declarations are unilateral statements to clarify or specify the meaning or scope of a treaty or certain provisions.[34] In contrast to reservations, they do not purport to exclude or modify the legal effect of the treaty.[35] The distinction between declarations and reservations often remains unclear. The ILC suggests interpreting the statement in good faith and according to the ordinary meaning of the terms.[36]

Poland, Lithuania, Latvia, and Croatia entered declarations stating that they will apply the Istanbul Convention in conformity with their respective constitutions.[37] For example, Croatia addresses gender ideology and they object to obligations to introduce gender ideology to their domestic legal and educational systems.[38] These declarations are aimed at modifying and even limiting the applicability of the Istanbul Convention. They are reservations disguised as a declaration. Reservations with this content would be impermissible under Article 78(1) Istanbul Convention because it is incompatible with the object and purpose of the Istanbul Convention. Austria, Finland, Netherlands, Norway, Sweden, and Switzerland have formulated objections to the Polish declaration arguing that the declaration seems to constitute a reservation as it limits the scope of the Istanbul Convention.[39] Nevertheless, since the Istanbul Convention does not have a specific declarations regime and specifically does not prohibit interpretative declarations or a binding assessment by GREVIO, the declarations

[32] See for a list of all member states with reservations CoE, 'Reservations and Declarations for Treaty No. 210' <www.coe.int/en/web/conventions/full-list?module=declarations-by-treaty&numSte=210&codeNature=0> accessed 4 February 2022.

[33] Wojciech Burek, 'Reservations and Declarations under the Istanbul Convention' in Johanna Niemi, Lourdes Peroni, and Vladislava Stoyanova (eds), *International Law and Violence against Women Europe and the Istanbul Convention* (Routledge 2020) 288–89.

[34] ILC, 'Guide to the Practice on Reservation of Treaties' (n 14) 1.2.

[35] ibid 1.3.

[36] ibid 1.3.1.

[37] CoE, 'Reservations and Declarations for Treaty No. 210' (n 32).

[38] This is detailed in the Croatian declaration: ibid. CoE, 'Reservations and Declarations for Treaty No. 210' (n 32); see also David Paternotte and Roman Kuhar, 'Disentangling and Locating the "Global Right": Anti-Gender Campaigns in Europe' (2018) 6 Politics and Governance 6, 8–9.

[39] CoE, 'Reservations and Declarations for Treaty No. 210' (n 32).

remain valid.[40] Thus, the application of the Istanbul Convention in those countries may be limited to their domestic law. However, that does not automatically mean the exclusion of the concept of gender or gender equality. In June 2020, the Latvian Constitutional Court held that the Istanbul Convention complies with the Latvian Constitution.[41]

### 1.2.2 Non-Ratification Of and Withdrawal From the Istanbul Convention

Several CoE member states have not signed, halted steps towards ratification of, or have recently withdrawn from the Istanbul Convention. Armenia, Bulgaria, the Czech Republic, Hungary, Latvia, Lithuania, Moldova, the Slovak Republic, the United Kingdom, and Ukraine have signed the Istanbul Convention without following up with ratification.[42] The United Kingdom is nine years after its signature, still in the process of ratification.[43] Other states simply refuse to do so: Hungary's parliament has refused to ratify the Istanbul Convention.[44] Bulgaria's Constitutional Court declared the Istanbul Convention unconstitutional.[45] Under international law, signatory states to a treaty are not obligated to ratify that treaty. They are, however, obliged to refrain from acts that would defeat the object and purpose of the Istanbul Convention.[46] Like the concept of reservations, the two-step ratification process provides time to adapt the domestic legal order to the standards of a treaty.[47]

Russia and Azerbaijan have not signed the Istanbul Convention at all.[48] Turkey has withdrawn from the Istanbul Convention in 2021. Poland has announced its intention to withdraw.[49] Again, there is no international obligation to sign a treaty or remain a member, not even for members of international organizations and their treaties. As states may voluntarily join a treaty and submit to its rules,[50] they may—*a contrario*—also not join a treaty.

The state behaviour towards the Istanbul Convention suggests that states oppose the Istanbul Convention based on gender and 'gender ideology', a fundamental part of women's rights.[51] They are also willing to sacrifice women's rights and protection

[40] For a detailed discussion see Burek (n 33) 291–94.

[41] CoE Newsroom, 'The Latvian Constitutional Court finds that the provisions of the Istanbul Convention comply with the Latvian Constitution' (7 June 2020) <https://go.coe.int/FzyR9> accessed 4 February 2022.

[42] CoE, 'Chart of signatures and ratifications of Treaty 210' <www.coe.int/en/web/conventions/full-list?module=signatures-by-treaty&treatynum=210> accessed 4 February 2022.

[43] UK House of Commons Debate (26 May 2021) vol 696 col 137-141WH. During the debate Home Office Minister Victoria Atkins has stated that they are doing everything they can to ensure ratification as soon as possible.

[44] Kovács Zoltán, 'Hungarian Parliament refuses to ratify the Istanbul Convention for its asylum provisions and inclusion of gender' (*Index*, 5 May 2020) <https://index.hu/english/2020/05/05/istanbul_convention_rejected_parliament_hungary_fidesz_kdnp/> accessed 4 February 2022.

[45] Hillary Margolis, 'Speak out to protect Bulgaria's women' (*Human Rights Watch*, 10 October 2018) <www.hrw.org/news/2018/10/10/speak-out-protect-bulgarias-women> accessed 4 February 2022.

[46] VCLT (n 11) art 18(a).

[47] Cf Home Office Minister Atkins on why the UK has taken so long to ratify the Istanbul Convention. UK House of Commons Debate (n 43).

[48] CoE, 'Chart of signatures and ratifications of Treaty 210' (n 42).

[49] 'Istanbul Convention: Poland to leave European treaty on violence against women' *BBC News* (London, 25 July 2020) <www.bbc.com/news/world-europe-53538205> accessed 4 February 2022.

[50] *The Case of the SS Lotus (France v Turkey)* (Judgment) PCIJ Rep Series A No 10, 18.

[51] Cf Beijing Platform for Action (n 8).

from violence in the name of preventing the spread of this 'ideology'. Consequently, women's rights and gender equality are not fully accepted, even in Europe. While the sudden announcement of Turkey's withdrawal from the Istanbul Convention has reinforced this assessment, the announcement was also met with criticism and protest from politicians and civil society.[52]

### 1.3 Are Women's Rights Treaties in Danger?

Roggeband argues that the resistance to the Istanbul Convention is connected to democratic backsliding and diminishing civic space and that it may be symptomatic of a wider backlash against women's rights in Europe.[53] However, states not (fully) accepting human rights treaties on women's rights and gender equality has a four-decade-long tradition in international law. Consequently, the concepts and values have never been fully accepted by many states across the world and the phenomena discussed are only new in terms of their actors and/or motivation. Roggeband also addresses 'symbolic compliance and façade policies' of reluctant and oppositional governments as the prominent threat in current backlashes against gender equality.[54] While she focuses on domestic, low-key tactics, states also very openly create façades of compliance. With no intention to fully accept gender equality, they join treaties with impermissible reservations or do not follow up with ratification after signature. This leads to the question of whether women's rights are more protected when states fully participate in the treaties, with potentially fewer member states, or to accept the caveats of reservations and have more comprehensive ratification. While it is desirable to have far-reaching and full ratifications of these treaties,[55] their effect on the protection of women's rights and gender equality is still palpable. With 189 member states, CEDAW remains one of the most ratified human rights treaties. Additionally, there are positive developments despite reservations, non-ratification, or withdrawal: Saudi Arabia has allowed women to obtain a driver's license and has abolished the requirement of permission by a male guardian to have access to government procedures.[56] Ukraine has started to reform its laws regarding domestic violence without ratification

[52] CoE Newsroom, 'Secretary General responds to Turkey's announced withdrawal from the Istanbul Convention' (20 March 2021) <https://go.coe.int/mOunb> accessed 4 February 2022; CoE Newsroom, 'Council of Europe leaders react to Turkey's announced withdrawal from the Istanbul Convention' (21 March 2021) <www.coe.int/en/web/istanbul-convention/-/council-of-europe-leaders-react-to-turkey-s-announced-withdrawal-from-the-istanbul-convention> accessed 4 February 2022; Esra Yalcinalp, 'Turkey Erdogan: Women rise up over withdrawal from the Istanbul Convention' *BBC News* (London, 26 March 2021) <https://www.bbc.com/news/world-europe-56516462> accessed 4 February 2022.

[53] Roggeband, Chapter 14 in this book, 30–31.

[54] ibid 34.

[55] The CEDAW Committee regularly calls on states with impermissible reservations to withdraw them, eg CEDAW Committee, 'Concluding observations on Saudi Arabia' (n 28). Similarly, the CoE has set the goal of all CoE member states to become a state party to the Istanbul Convention, German Federal Minister for Family Affairs, Senior Citizens, Women and Youth Franziska Giffey and CoE Secretary-General Marija Pejčinović Burić, 'Joint Statement for UN International Women's Day (5 March 2021) <https://rm.coe.int/final-version-8-march-joint-statement/1680a1a5dc> accessed 4 February 2022.

[56] CEDAW Committee, 'Concluding observations on Saudi Arabia' (n 28).

of the Istanbul Convention.[57] Turkey has added in its withdrawal announcement that women's rights and their security from violence remain a priority.[58] The Istanbul Convention is still considered an innovative legal tool for the protection of women and girls from violence[59] and CEDAW remains the most important human rights instrument for gender equality and women's rights.

## 2. Women's Reproductive Rights and Access to Abortion: Indications of Resilience?

Women's reproductive rights have their origin in the women's rights and women's health movements of the 1960s and 1970s as a response to coercive population planning policies and population control. Internationally, they were first recognized at the 1994 International Conference on Population and Development (ICPD) in Cairo and then immediately reaffirmed at the 1995 FWCW in Beijing. After long negotiations, the delegates in Cairo agreed on a definition of reproductive rights 'bearing in mind the ... definition [of reproductive health[60]] and embrac[ing] human rights that are already recognized in national laws, international human rights documents, and other consensus documents',[61] anchoring them in reproductive health and human rights law. Hence, reproductive rights are comprised of established human rights, mainly the right of all couples and individuals to decide freely and responsibly the number, spacing, and timing of their children and to have the information and means to do so,[62] the right to attain the highest standard of sexual and reproductive health,[63] and the right to make decisions concerning reproduction free of discrimination, coercion, and violence.[64] Reproductive rights are also rooted in the right to life and health and their corporal integrity and autonomy and are inherently connected to gender equality. Access to safe and legal abortion is one of the most contested aspects of

[57] Ukrainian Independent Information Agency, 'Domestic violence now criminal offence in Ukraine' (7 December 2017) <www.unian.info/society/2285764-domestic-violence-now-criminal-offense-in-ukraine.html> last accessed 4 February 2022; Kateryna Semchuk, 'Ukraine's legislation on domestic violence gets a reboot – but is it enough?' (*Open Democracy*, 4 March 2019) <www.opendemocracy.net/en/odr/ukraines-legislation-on-domestic-violence-gets-a-reboot-but-is-it-enough/> accessed 4 February 2022.

[58] Turkish Directorate of Communication, 'Statement regarding Türkiye's withdrawal from the Istanbul Convention' (21 March 2021) <www.iletisim.gov.tr/english/haberler/detay/statement-regarding-turkeys-withdrawal-from-the-istanbul-convention> accessed 4 February 2022.

[59] German Federal Minister Franziska Giffey and CoE Secretary General M Pejčinović Burić (n 55).

[60] Reproductive health is a state of complete physical, mental, and social wellbeing and not merely the absence of disease or infirmity, in all matters relating to the reproductive system and to its functions and processes; UN Population Fund, 'Programme of Action of the International Conference on Population and Development' (20th Anniversary edn, United Nations Population Fund 2014) 7.2 (Cairo Programme of Action).

[61] ibid 7.3.

[62] CEDAW (n 7) art 16(1)(e).

[63] International Covenant on Economic, Social and Cultural Rights (adopted 16 December 1966, entered into force 3 January 1976) 999 UNTS 3 art 12 (ICESCR).

[64] Cairo Programme of Action (n 60) 7.3. Reproductive rights are not exclusive to women as human reproduction concerns everyone, regardless of gender or sexual orientation. Nevertheless, women are disproportionately affected by inadequate reproductive rights protection, as numbers of maternal deaths or deaths after unsafe abortion show. Besides the reproductive rights of women, the question of protecting the reproductive rights of trans- or non-binary persons or same-sex couples are increasingly discussed.

reproductive rights.[65] Anti-abortion actors clash with sexual and reproductive health and rights (SRHR) proponents over a right to life from the moment of conception versus the reproductive rights of the pregnant person.[66] The Cairo Programme of Action approaches the access to abortion from a health perspective: as the impact of unsafe abortion[67] is a major public health concern, governments are urged to reduce recourses to abortion, for example with access to family planning services, or to improve post-abortion care.[68] Additionally, in cases where abortion is not against the law, such abortion should be safe.[69]

Traditionally, reproductive rights are addressed at UN development agendas, like the Cairo Programme of Action or the 2030 Agenda for Sustainable Development.[70] Increasingly, reproductive rights are also included in human rights treaties[71] and the work of UN human rights treaty monitoring bodies (treaty bodies). Nevertheless, reproductive rights remain very controversial and contested at the UN as anti-abortion activists equate reproductive rights language with the promotion of abortion. The section discusses the inclusion of reproductive rights language at post-Cairo UN development documents (Section 2.1), reservations on reproductive rights (Section 2.2), and reproductive rights in the work of treaty bodies (Section 2.3) as examples for these contestations.

## 2.1 Inclusion of Reproductive Rights Language in UN Documents

After the success of the Cairo consensus on reproductive rights, many SRHR activists had hoped for the future inclusion of reproductive rights language without lengthy negotiations and to build on the agreed language. However, this hope only lasted for a few years and towards the end of the 1990s, the inclusion of agreed-upon language was already threatened.

The momentum of the Cairo consensus was palpable at the FWCW. With overlapping preparation periods, the delegates in Beijing could include and thereby affirm the language agreed on in Cairo with little to no opposition. The Holy See announced early on that it did not want to contest the ICPD language. Moreover, the Beijing Platform for Action adds to the ICPD wording on abortion 'to consider reviewing laws containing punitive measures against women who have undergone illegal abortions'.[72] However, at the first follow-up of the ICPD, a first shift in the negotiation dynamics towards anti-abortion actors was noticeable. The ICPD+5's premise

[65] Other contentious aspects include sexual rights and sexual and reproductive health and rights for adolescents.

[66] See Roggeband, Chapter 14 in this book, 13 for the key actors opposing women's reproductive rights and their strategy of counterframing.

[67] The Cairo Programme of Action defined unsafe abortion as a procedure for terminating an unwanted pregnancy either by persons lacking the necessary skills or in an environment lacking the minimal medical standards, relying on the WHO definition; Cairo Programme of Action (n 60) note 20.

[68] ibid 8.25.

[69] ibid 8.25.

[70] UNGA, 'Transforming our world: the 2030 Agenda for Sustainable Development' (21 October 2015) UN Doc A/RES/70/1 (Sustainable Development Goals).

[71] eg Convention on the Rights of Person with Disabilities (adopted 13 December 2006, entered into force 3 May 2008) 2515 UNTS 3, art 25; Rome Statute of the International Criminal Court (adopted 17 July 1998, entered into force 1 July 2002) 2187 UNTS 3, art 7(1)(g).

[72] Beijing Platform for Action (n 8) 106(k).

was to review and appraise the first five years of implementation. The renegotiation of the original agreement's terms was explicitly excluded from the session's scope.[73] This prevented a regression of the original language. Nevertheless, SRHR actors had to actively work against attempts to deteriorate the Cairo consensus.[74] Even attempts to add agreed-on issues of the Beijing Platform for Action to the ICPD follow-up document failed. ICPD+5 does not include the addition of reviewing punitive laws for women who have undergone illegal abortions.

This trend of a shift in the negotiation dynamics intensified in the new millennium. The first major setback for reproductive rights was the Millennium Development Goals[75] (MDGs) based on the 2000 Millennium Declaration.[76] The original MDGs did not even include a separate goal on universal access to reproductive health, despite this being part of the draft goals.[77] Instead, they focused on promoting maternal health, paradoxically without addressing access to safe abortion, and combatting the HIV/AIDS pandemic. Anti-abortion states were threatening to block the entire project as universal access to reproductive health could, in their view, be interpreted to include access to abortion.[78] Hence, the goal was cut from the final Declaration. After many high-level initiatives,[79] universal access to reproductive health was added in 2007 as a sub-goal of reducing maternal mortality.[80] Furthermore, pro-SRHR states, NGOs, and the UN Population Fund feared that the new power balance could lead to a renegotiation of the Cairo Programme of Action.[81] Consequently, its 10-year review took place in a reduced format with mainly regional meetings and a review of the implementation of the Commission on Population and Development.[82] Overall, the early 2000s were marked by preventing backlashes on the consensus of Beijing and Cairo, rather than pushing the SRHR agenda forward. However, towards the end of the decade, the environment became less hostile for reproductive rights and a new optimism was palpable at the ICPD's 15-year review.[83]

[73] UNGA, 'Population and Development' (4 February 1998) UN Doc A/RES/52/188, 4(3).

[74] Alexandra Garita and Françoise Girard, 'Negotiating sexual and reproductive health and rights at the UN: a long and winding road' in Gita Sen and Marina Durano (eds), *The Remaking of Social Contracts: Feminists in a Fierce New World* (Zed Books 2014) 166–68.

[75] UNGA, 'Road map towards the implementation of the United Nations Millennium Declaration – Report of the Secretary-General' (6 September 2001) UN Doc A/56/326 Annex.

[76] UNGA, 'United Nations Millennium Development Declaration' (18 January 2000) UN Doc A/RES/52/2.

[77] David Hulme, 'Reproductive Health and the Millennium Development Goals: Politics, Ethics, Evidence and an "Unholy Alliance" (2010) BWPI Working Paper No 105 <https://papers.ssrn.com/sol3/papers.cfm?abstract_id=1545907> accessed 4 February 2022.

[78] Garita and Girard (n 74) 171.

[79] eg UNGA, '2005 World Summit Outcome' (24 October 2005) UN Doc A/RES/60/1, 57(g), 58(c); UNGA, 'In larger freedom: towards development, security and human rights for all' (21 March 2005) UN Doc A/59/2005, 40, 44.

[80] UNGA, 'General Assembly Official Records sixty-second session Supplement No.1' (2007) UN Doc A/62/1.2007 Annex II.

[81] Françoise Girard, 'Advocacy for Sexuality and Women's Rights: Continuities, Discontinuities, and Strategies Since ICPD' in Laura Reichenbach and Mindy J Roseman (eds), *Reproductive Health and Human Rights: The Way Forward* (University of Pennsylvania Press 2009) 174.

[82] See for both: International Conference on Population and Development, *ICPD at Ten – The World Reaffirms Cairo Official Outcomes of the ICPD at Ten Review* (United Nations Population Fund 2005).

[83] Commission on Population and Development, 'Resolution 2009/1 The contribution of the Programme of Action of the International Conference on Population and Development to the internationally agreed development goals, including the Millennium Development Goals' (30 March 2009) UN Doc E/CN.9/2009/10; Garita and Girard (n 74) 171–72.

The 2010s continued the back and forth on the inclusion of the reproductive rights language at UN development documents. At the 2012 UN Conference on Sustainable Development in Rio de Janeiro, the term 'reproductive rights' was cut from the final document.[84] Moreover, the wording for equal access of women to health care was reduced from 'ensure' to 'promote'.[85] Three years later, for the post-2015 development agenda, states included universal access to reproductive healthcare services as part of the goal on health and reproductive rights to achieve gender equality.[86]

Reproductive health and rights have been caught in a constant back-and-forth since the 1990s. Significantly, the Cairo Programme of Action institutionalized reproductive rights only to a certain degree. While the definitions and the concept of reproductive health are generally accepted, the inclusion of reproductive rights language in development documents has remained precarious after the ICPD.

## 2.2 Reservations on Reproductive Rights and the Access to Abortion

States also revert to reservations to limit reproductive rights and access to abortion. They do so for both treaties and non-binding instruments. Article 16(1)(e) CEDAW has two reservations concerning access to abortion: Malta, acceding to CEDAW in 1991, and Monaco, acceding in 2005, do not consider themselves bound by the paragraph to extent that it be interpreted to impose the legalization of abortion.[87] Noticeably, other states with (previously) strict abortion laws, like Ireland or Latin American states, did not enter a similar reservation. Moreover, the sections on reproductive rights, especially on the access to abortion, in the Cairo Programme of Action and the Beijing Platform for Action have received multiple 'reservations'. The VCLT and its reservation regime do not apply to non-binding documents. Hence, those 'reservations' pose several questions regarding their validity. However, the conference procedures allowed states to submit oral and written statements on the just-agreed outcome document.[88] In their statements, states regularly used the term 'reservation' and intended their statements to modify and limit the scope of outcome documents.

There were 23 statements on the Cairo Programme of Action at the last plenary meetings.[89] Only one does not address reproductive rights. Among the statements that do, there were general reservations on passages that, in the view of the state, contradicted the principles of Islam, comparable to CEDAW's 'sharia reservations'.[90] The Holy See and other Catholic states addressed abortion. They excluded abortion

[84] UNGA, 'The Future we want' (11 September 2012) UN Doc A/RES/66/288, 145, 146, 241.

[85] ibid 241; Rebecca Lefton, 'Assault on reproductive rights and gender equality at Rio+20' (*Center for American Progress*, 21 June 2012) <www.americanprogress.org/issues/green/news/2012/06/21/11804/assault-on-reproductive-rights-and-gender-equality-at-rio20/> accessed 4 February 2022.

[86] Sustainable Development Goals (n 70) Goal 3.7, Goal 5.6.

[87] CEDAW (n 7) Declarations and Reservations 7–8.

[88] eg Reservations and Interpretative Statements on the Cairo Programme of Action (n 60) explanatory note 187.

[89] Since 1994, El Salvador and Argentina have withdrawn their reservations.

[90] eg Statements and reservations of the United Arab Emirates or Djibouti; Reservations and Interpretative Statements on the Cairo Programme of Action (n 60) 193–94.

from reproductive health terms, denied the concept of legal and/or safe abortions, and emphasized that there is no human right to abortion.[91] The Holy See placed a general reservation on Chapters VII, VIII.[92] The Beijing Platform for Action has similar numbers. Twenty-nine states formulated reservations and only six did not restrict reproductive rights and abortion.

Entering 'reservations' on conference outcome documents utterly contradicts the just negotiated consensus. Moreover, the documents' recommendations are not binding on the states. The Cairo Programme of Action even recognizes that 'the implementation of the recommendations contained in [it] is the sovereign right of each country, consistent with national laws and development priorities, with full respect for the various religious and ethical values and cultural backgrounds of its people'.[93] Nevertheless, many states saw the need to limit women's reproductive rights.

## 2.3 Reproductive Rights at Human Rights Treaty Bodies

Treaty bodies monitor the implementation of their respective treaty.[94] Their main pronouncements are observations to the State Reports, Individual Communications, a quasi-judicial process to address individual violations, and General Comments, to guide the treaty's interpretation.[95] Below, the work of the Human Rights Committee (CCPR), the Committee on Economic, Social and Cultural Rights (CESCR), and the CEDAW Committee in Individual Communications and General Comments/Recommendations on reproductive rights and the access to abortion are illustrated.

By 2022, the CEDAW Committee and the CCPR have assessed five complaints claiming human rights violations in the denial of abortions. In the first one, the CCPR considered the failure to provide a therapeutic abortion to a minor with an anencephalic foetus a violation of her right to be free of cruel, inhuman, or degrading behaviour, her right to privacy, and discrimination against her based on her age.[96] The CCPR affirmed in later following communications these considerations for unviable foetuses and confirmed similar violations for denial of abortion after rape or incest.[97] The

[91] eg Statements and reservations of Honduras or the Dominican Republic; Reservations and Interpretative Statements on the Cairo Programme of Action (n 60) 194–95.

[92] Written Statement by the Holy See, Cairo Programme of Action (n 60) 198–202; The Holy See did the same for the Beijing Platform for Action; Reservations and Interpretative Statements on the Beijing Platform for Action (n 8) 12.

[93] Cairo Programme of Action (n 60) 11.

[94] See Janina Barkholdt and Nina Reiners, 'Pronouncements of Expert Treaty Bodies: From "Black Boxes" to "Key Catalysts" in International Law?' KFG Working Paper Series No 40 <https://papers.ssrn.com/sol3/papers.cfm?abstract_id=3507386> accessed 4 February 2022; Heike Krieger, Georg Nolte, and Andreas Zimmermann (eds), *The International Rule of Law: Rise or Decline?* (Oxford Scholarship Online 2019).

[95] Alice M Miller and Mindy J Roseman, 'Sexual and Reproductive Rights at the United Nations: Frustrations or Fulfillment?' (2011) 19 Reproductive Health Matters 102, 107, and 112.

[96] International Covenant on Civil and Political Rights (CCPR), 'Communication No. 1153/2003' (22 November 2005) UN Doc CCPR/C/85/D/1153/2003, 6.3–6.6.

[97] CCPR, 'Communications No. 1608/2007' (28 April 2011) UN Doc CCPR/C/101/D/1608/2007; CCPR, 'Views adopted by the Committee under article 5 (4) of the Optional Protocol, concerning communication No, 2324/2013 (Mellet v. Ireland)' (17 November 2016) UN Doc CCPR/C/116/D/2324/2013; CCPR, 'Views adopted by the Committee under article 5 (4) of the Optional Protocol concerning communication No. 2425/2014 (Whelan v. Ireland)' (11 July 2017) UN Doc CCPR/C/116/D/2425/2014.

CEDAW Committee considered the denial of a therapeutic abortion for a pregnancy caused by rape a violation of her equal rights regarding health and health care.[98]

There are four key General Comments on reproductive rights and access to abortion. The CEDAW Committee's 1999 General Recommendations on women and health states inter alia that 'it is discriminatory for a State party to refuse to provide for the performance of certain reproductive health services for women'.[99] The Committee also called on states to amend legislation criminalizing abortion when possible.[100] Furthermore, the CESCR has addressed reproductive rights in its General Comment on the rights to health in 2000. In line with the Cairo Programme of Action, the topic of abortion is alluded to in 'access to appropriate health care services in the context of safe pregnancies'.[101] In 2016, the CESCR issued its General Comment on sexual and reproductive health.[102] There, the Committee determines that the full enjoyment of sexual and reproductive health is an integral part of the right of everyone to the highest attainable physical and mental health but remains a distant goal, especially for women and girls. Additionally, it addresses the issues specifically from a gender and equality perspective. Regarding access to abortion, the Comment mentions the availability of medicines for abortion and post-abortion care, accessible information on safe abortion and post-abortion care, and good quality medications for abortions as elements of sexual and reproductive health. Furthermore, it calls on states to prevent unsafe abortions by inter alia liberalizing restrictive abortion laws, guaranteeing women and girls access to safe abortion services, and respecting the right of women to make autonomous decisions about their sexual and reproductive health. In its 2019 General Comment on the right to life,[103] the CCPR confirmed the access to abortion as part of women's and girls' rights to life and recognized a right to therapeutic abortion in cases where the life and health of the pregnant women or girl is at risk, or where carrying a pregnancy to term would cause the pregnant woman or girl substantial pain or suffering, in cases of pregnancy as a result of rape or incest or where the pregnancy is not viable.[104] The Comment does not address or determine the beginning of life or the beginning of the legal protection of life.

The early General Comment and Recommendation followed the consensuses of Cairo and Beijing. After these first pronouncements, it took a treaty body almost 10 years to address reproductive rights and health in a Comment again. However, in the interim, the Committees began to recognize a right to access to safe abortion in

[98] CEDAW Committee, 'Communication No. 2272009 (L.C. v. Peru) Views adopted by the Committee at its fifth session, 3 to 21 October 2011' (25 November 2011) UN Doc CEDAW/C/50/D/22/2009.

[99] CEDAW Committee, 'General Recommendation No. 24: Article 12 of the Convention (women and health)' (1999) UN Doc A/54/38/Rev.1, 11.

[100] ibid 31(c).

[101] Committee on Economic, Social and Cultural Rights (CESCR), 'General Comment No. 14 (2000) The right to the highest attainable standard of health (article 12 of the International Covenant on Economic, Social and Cultural Rights)' (11 August 2000) UN Doc E/C.12/2000/4.

[102] CESCR, 'General Comment No. 22 (2016) on the right to sexual and reproductive health article 12 of the International Covenant on Economic, Social and Cultural Rights' (2 May 2016) UN Doc E/C.12/GC/22.

[103] CCPR, 'General Comment No. 36 Article 6: the right to life' (3 September 2019) UN Doc CCPR/C/GC/36.

[104] ibid 8.

certain circumstances in the communications procedures. This provided a basis for the more comprehensive Comments of the 2010s. The Committees relied on their previous decisions, cross-referencing to other treaty bodies' work, and referencing soft law instruments. The opposition in the drafting processes, especially by pro-life civil society organizations,[105] remained unfruitful. The treaty bodies solidified and advanced women's reproductive rights and access to safe and legal abortion, at least in certain circumstances, as human rights. Consequently, current international human rights law provides for access to abortion to save the woman's health and/or life (therapeutic abortion), abortion to terminate the pregnancy with a non-viable foetus, abortion after rape or in cases of incest, and the right not to die from unsafe abortion.

Besides this positive development for human rights standards on access to abortion, the treaty bodies work also impacted domestic changes. For example, after the two communications, Ireland commenced taking steps to reform the Irish abortion law.[106] In 2018, a referendum overturned the abortion ban.[107] Subsequently, Ireland did not only allow abortions for non-viable pregnancies and other health-related grounds but opened it up to the request of the pregnant woman.[108]

## 2.4 Indications for Resilience and even Progress?

Reproductive rights have faced opposition and contestation since their inception on the international agenda in 1994. The Cairo Programme of Action is often considered a milestone for women's reproductive rights, especially for the paradigm shift from population policies to reproductive health and rights.[109] However, the course of the negotiations and the 'reservations' suggests that the term 'consensus' is a misnomer in this context. While reproductive rights were part of the formal consensus, their validity remained precarious, as seen by the constant topicality of reproductive rights and the constant attempts to weaken the agreed-upon language in subsequent negotiations. However, another significant impact of the Cairo Programme of Action was in anchoring reproductive rights in international human rights law. Consequently, treaty bodies could monitor their implementation and expand their scope. Both are signs of resilience and even progress. Sandholtz discussed institutionalization as a factor of norm resilience.[110] Roggeband furthermore considered the quality of a

[105] See CESCR, 'Summary record of the 49th meeting' (26 November 2010) UN Doc E/C.12/2010/SR.49 (CESCR Summary Record); Roggeband, Chapter 14 in this book, 14–16.

[106] CCPR, 'Follow-up progress report on individual communications' (29 May 2018) UN Doc CCPR/C/112/R.2, 13–15.

[107] 'Irish abortion referendum: Ireland overturns abortion ban' *BBC News* (London, 26 May 2018) <www.bbc.com/news/world-europe-44256152> accessed 4 February 2022.

[108] Health (Regulation of Termination of Pregnancy) Act 2018 (Ireland). A pregnant women may request an abortion until the 12th gestational week.

[109] C Alison McIntosh and Jason L Finkle, 'The Cairo Conference on Population and Development: A New Paradigm?' (1995) 21 Population and Development Review 223, 223; Mindy J Roseman and Laura Reichenbach, 'Global Reproductive Health and Rights: Reflecting on the ICPD' in Laura Reichenbach and Mindy J Roseman (eds), *Reproductive Health and Human Rights: The Way Forward* (University of Pennsylvania Press 2009).

[110] Sandholtz, Chapter 3 in this book, 25–28.

norm, especially their binding nature, as another factor for norm resilience.[111] Both elements can be detected in the resilience of reproductive rights. Additionally, due to their nature as a composite right, reproductive rights include many different rights and aspects. Thus, their protection is spread out over different treaties and multiple treaty bodies can address and monitor their implementation. Addressing one of the elements of reproductive rights, like the right to life, to health, to privacy, or to be free of cruel, inhuman, or degrading treatment, strengthens them overall. Hence, women's reproductive rights to not just exhibit resilience, but even progress.

Lastly, when looking at domestic jurisdictions, the impact the international developments also becomes visible. Since the 1990s, many states have decriminalized abortion fully or legalized abortion in certain circumstances.[112] This has accelerated in the 2010s and is happening despite orchestrated efforts against women's reproductive rights.[113] This reflects a growing global consensus that access to safe and legal abortion is not just a public health imperative but also a human right. Recent examples of the decriminalization of abortion or steps towards decriminalization include Ireland, South Korea,[114] Columbia,[115] or the October 2021 referendum in San Marino.[116] This global development outweighs regression in some jurisdictions, like Poland or within the United States.

## 3. Are Women's Rights in Danger?

Women's rights have always been precarious in international law. They are constantly met with contestations, regardless of their legal character. Binding treaties and non-binding instruments face similar, if not the same, contestations. As such, there is no new level of danger to women's rights detectable. Rather, any new developments or new adversaries joins the tradition of contesting women's rights. The number of reservations limiting women's rights suggests that there is no universal acceptance of gender equality (yet), especially in the context of women's reproductive rights. Furthermore, there are few signs of change in the anti-women and anti-abortion actors and their strategies: the impermissible reservations to CEDAW have been prevalent since the 1980s, there has been widespread opposition to women's reproductive rights since the 1990s, and some of the Istanbul Convention signatory states have delayed ratification since the 2010s.

[111] Roggeband, Chapter 14 in this book, 31–33.

[112] Center for Reproductive Rights, 'Accelerating Process: Liberalizing of Abortion Laws since ICPD' <https://reproductiverights.org/wp-content/uploads/2020/12/World-Abortion-Map-AcceleratingProgress.pdf> accessed 4 February 2022. Nearly 50 countries have taken steps towards the decriminalization of abortion.

[113] ibid.

[114] Amnesty International, 'South Korea: Top Court orders reform of abortion laws in a historic victory for women's rights' (11 April 2019) <www.amnesty.org/en/latest/press-release/2019/04/south-korea-abortion-ruling/> accessed 4 February 2022.

[115] Julie Turkewitz, 'Colombia decriminalizes abortion, bolstering the trend across the region' *The New York Times* (New York, 22 February 2022) <www.nytimes.com/2022/02/22/world/americas/colombia-abortion.html> accessed 6 March 2022.

[116] 'San Marino votes to legalize abortion in referendum' *BBC News* (London, 26 September 2021) <www.bbc.com/news/world-europe-58701788> accessed 4 February 2022.

The opposition to women's rights is not organized across traditional geopolitical blocs and alliances. It is not a conflict between the Global North and South. Rather, the actors can be organized according to social values. Actors in opposition to women's rights share a foundation of conservative values, often rooted in religion, whereas the supporters align progressive, liberal values.[117]

Nevertheless, the case study of women's reproductive rights and the access to safe and legal abortion demonstrates aspects of resilience and even progress. The anchoring in international human rights law with its enforcement mechanisms has secured and advanced the original Cairo standards.

Concerning the overarching question of the book, norm change or metamorphosis, it is difficult to attest to a change regarding women's rights and gender equality. Rather, they remain suspended between advances and regresses, a constant back and forth. The Geneva Consensus Declaration also depicts this phenomenon. While the project was signed under the Trump administration, the United States has already withdrawn from the Declaration under the Biden administration. President Biden has declared new support for women's reproductive rights in the United States and abroad.[118] It remains to be seen what impact the Geneva Consensus Declaration without the United States has on women's reproductive rights in the future.

[117] See also Roggeband, Chapter 14 in this book, 8.

[118] US White House, 'Memorandum on protecting women's heath at home and abroad' (28 January 2021) <www.whitehouse.gov/briefing-room/presidential-actions/2021/01/28/memorandum-on-protecting-womens-health-at-home-and-abroad/> accessed 4 February 2022.

# 16

# The Future We Want? Interlinking Global Sustainability Norm Change, Technology Innovation, and Regime Complexity

*Sandra Schwindenhammer*

## 1. Introduction

The editors of this book convincingly argue that changing values and the idea of their legal protection are embedded in structures and institutions of the legal system which are increasingly put under pressure by norm contestation to develop new practices in order to remain capable of acting, also with recursive consequences for legal structures.[1] This chapter deals with two challenges that put particular pressure on the international legal order in the domain of sustainability governance—regime complexity and technology innovation. Since the late 1980s, the *value of sustainable development* has become legally protected by norms embedded in international environmental regimes and regime complexes. The basic elements of sustainable development originate from the Brundtland report which stresses the interconnection between the three dimensions of environmental, economic, and social sustainability and the postulate of intragenerational and intergenerational justice.[2] In 2015, the United Nations adopted 17 Sustainable Development Goals (SDGs) as part of the global 2030 Agenda for Sustainable Development[3] which have since served as the global normative reference framework for sustainability.

Sustainability norms are a collection of connected, but distinct, norms that relate to the same value (sustainable development), but address different aspects (eg ensuring global health, food security, biodiversity) and contain specific obligations. They are embedded in the patchwork of environmental institutions differing in character (organizations, regimes, and implicit norms), constituencies (public and private), spatial scope (from bilateral to global), and subject matter (from specific policy fields to universal concerns).[4] In this context, sustainability norm dynamics are highly dynamic, exceed one international regime, and are influenced by *institutional complexity*. They lack a central actor with sufficient authority to orchestrate complexity and to set

[1] Cf Heike Krieger and Andrea Liese, Chapter 1 in this book.

[2] United Nations (UN) World Commission on Environment and Development (ed), *Our Common Future* (OUP 1987).

[3] UN General Assembly, 'Transforming our World: The 2030 Agenda for Sustainable Development' (25 September 2015) UN Doc A/RES/70/1.

[4] Cf Frank Biermann and others, 'The Fragmentation of Global Governance Architectures: A Framework for Analysis' (2009) 9 Global Environmental Politics 14, 16.

Sandra Schwindenhammer, *The Future We Want? Interlinking Global Sustainability Norm Change, Technology Innovation, and Regime Complexity* In: *Tracing Value Change in the International Legal Order.* Edited by: Heike Krieger and Andrea Liese, Oxford University Press. © Sandra Schwindenhammer 2023. DOI: 10.1093/oso/9780192855831.003.0016

(legal) norms across different issues, scales, and institutions. *Technology innovation* is another and, as yet, widely neglected challenge for the legal order of sustainability governance. It is politically promoted for enabling more efficient use and reuse of natural resources and the transformation towards more sustainable production systems.[5] Technology innovation and (legal) norms reveal a complex interplay. Today, advances in technology enable the rethinking and redesign of entire biological systems and raise new regulatory challenges and normative issues.[6] While (legal) norms are challenged, changed, or even made obsolete by the rise of new technologies, new technologies can be encouraged, facilitated, regulated, or inhibited by (legal) norms.[7] The reinforcing effect of technology innovation on sustainability norm dynamics relates to *norm entrepreneurs* which strategically promote new normative frames.[8] Whether a norm is being strengthened, maintained, or weakened depends on the degree to which participants in norm contestation advance or support pro-norm arguments.[9] Norm entrepreneurs can contest norms in the face of new technologies to develop new practices, also with consequences for sustainability norm change. This points to the question raised by the editors of this book: do new technologies create fundamental challenges for the international legal order, fuel norm dynamics, and thereby prompt value change?[10]

Building on (critical) norm research in international relations (IR), regime complex theory, and research on technological change, this analysis serves three purposes in the light of the ongoing debate on value change in the international legal order: (1) to trace value change in norm dynamics, ie between norms that exceed one single international regime; (2) to show that global sustainability norm dynamics occur after global norm contestation and regime complexity; and (3) to conceptualize technology innovation as a driver of global norm dynamics. The chapter starts by discussing sustainability norm dynamics fuelled by norm contestation, regime complexity, and technology innovation (Section 2). Then, the chapter presents findings from a qualitative case study analysis of genetically modified (GM) insect technology (Section 3). It reveals the influence of private norm entrepreneurship by the company Oxitec, norm dynamics in the fields of global food and agriculture, health, and biosafety, and norm contestation over the distribution of responsibility, the provision of transparency, and risk assessment and the (re)interpretation of the precautionary principle. The analysis detects an imbalance between public and private authority and the representation of different types of knowledge in norm dynamics and, thus, an unequal access to norm contestation. Technology innovation adds uncertainty to norm contestation

[5] Sandra Schwindenhammer and Denise Gonglach, 'SDG Implementation through Technology? Governing Food-Water-Technology Nexus Challenges in Urban Agriculture' (2021) 9 Politics and Governance 176.

[6] Victor Galaz, *Global Environmental Governance, Technology and Politics: The Anthropocene Gap* (Edward Elgar 2014); Sandra Schwindenhammer, 'The Rise, Regulation and Risks of Genetically Modified Insect Technology in Global Agriculture' (2020) 25 Science, Technology and Society 124.

[7] Cf Lyria Bennett Moses, 'Agents of Change' (2011) 20 Griffith Law Review 763, 767.

[8] Martha Finnemore and Kathryn Sikkink, 'International Norm Dynamics and Political Change' (1998) 52 International Organization 887.

[9] Wayne Sandholtz, Chapter 3 in this book.

[10] Cf Krieger and Liese, Chapter 1 in this book.

and raises new legal challenges for the international legal order of sustainability governance which deserve more attention in IR norm research (Section 4).

## 2. Sustainability Norm Dynamics Fuelled by Regime Complexity and Technology Innovation

Building on (critical) IR norm research and regime complex literature, the following section defines sustainability norm dynamics and conceptualizes norm contestation, regime complexity, and technology innovation as potential drivers of value change.

### 2.1 Sustainability Norm Dynamics and Contestation

Global norms are generally defined as intersubjective presumptions about the social world guiding the behaviour of actors with a given identity[11] and ideas of varying degrees of abstraction.[12] They are 'dynamic and contested, even as they become embedded in institutional practices in myriad settings across the international system'.[13] Following Wiener, three norm types can be distinguished according to their respective moral reach and expected degree of contestation[14]: *fundamental norms* (type 1) at the macro-scale of the global order are based on values. They entail the broadest possible moral or ethical reach and the lowest degree of contestation. *Organizing principles* (type 2) at the meso-scale leave a relatively broad margin for negotiation with reference to procedures and institutions and enable issue-related value-based policy strategies generated through practice. *Standardized rules* (type 3) at the micro-scale provide the details for implementing fundamental norms. They have a limited moral or ethical reach, yet with a high probability of contestation on local sites. This analysis focuses on the interplay of global sustainability norm dynamics and technology innovation in the field of synthetic biotechnology (GM insect technology). In doing so, the analysis deals with a specific segment of the legal order of sustainability governance which covers the fundamental norms of ensuring food security and sustainable agriculture, biodiversity, and human health (type 1), the precautionary principle (type 2), and standards and guidelines of distributing responsibility, providing transparency, and conducting a risk assessment of living modified organisms (LMOs) (type 3).

To assess sustainability norm dynamics, this analysis refers to (critical) IR norm research which draws a general distinction between the classical global norm diffusion perspective and the critical transnational perspective.[15] The *global norm diffusion*

[11] Finnemore and Sikkink (n 8) 891.

[12] Mona Lena Krook and Jacqui True, 'Rethinking the Life Cycles of International Norms: The United Nations and the Global Promotion of Gender Equality' (2012) 18 European Journal of International Relations 103, 103.

[13] ibid 106.

[14] Antje Wiener, Chapter 2 in this book.

[15] Susanne Zwingel, 'How Do Norms Travel? Theorizing International Women's Rights in Transnational Perspective' (2012) 56 International Studies Quarterly 115, 116. See also Sandra Schwindenhammer, 'The New Regionalism in Global Organic Agricultural Governance through Standards: Results from a Cross-Regional Comparison' (2018) 18 Global Environmental Politics 86, 90–92.

*perspective* treats international norms as causes that produce effects within domestic contexts (or fail to do so).[16] Norm life-cycle models[17] or the world culture model[18] cover general tendencies of international norm development. While for Finnemore and Sikkink, the success of a global norm depends on whether it reaches wide acceptance, Meyer and others see transnational forces at work that lead to structural similarities and isomorphism.[19] In this book, Antje Wiener conducts an excellent tracing of key historical developments in IR norm research showing that norm generation was predominantly studied as a formal rather than a socio-cultural process with a separation between norm-following and norm-generative behaviour.[20] Rather than focusing on practices of contestation and their effect on normative change, norm research prioritized studying compliance with norms and largely left research on contestation and therewith details of the variety of norm-generative practices to international lawyers.[21]

The *transnational perspective* criticizes the global norm diffusion perspective in several respects. Top-down-assumptions do not pay sufficient attention to processes of local norm creation and appropriation that shape value systems and institutional set-ups to make global norms applicable to different contexts, cultures, and national traditions.[22] While Acharya points to norm localization,[23] which implies regional actors reconstructing foreign norms to create congruence with existing regional beliefs, Zimmermann stresses the importance of discursive processes, frames, and existing worldviews in norm translation,[24] and Großklaus highlights the dialectic relationship between foreign and domestic ideas and their 'contextualisation and re-contextualisation into existing structures'.[25]

The content of global norms can be shaped in norm discourses and thus varies between different institutional settings, cultural practices, and over time.[26] This analysis conceptualizes global sustainability norm dynamics as the result of ongoing *norm contestation* defined as 'the range of social practices, which discursively express disapproval of norms'.[27] Through the lens of the global norm diffusion perspective, norm contestation indicates the questioning of the validity of a global norm.[28] Different norm understandings collide in global regime complexes and cause problems and negative spillover effects, such as policy incoherence or inconsistencies, inefficiencies,

[16] Cf Zwingel (n 15) 116.
[17] Finnemore and Sikkink (n 8).
[18] John W Meyer and others, 'World Society and the Nation-State' (1997) 103 American Journal of Sociology 144.
[19] Finnemore and Sikkink (n 8) 895–96; Meyer and others (n 18) 148.
[20] Antje Wiener, Chapter 2 in this book.
[21] ibid.
[22] Zwingel (n 15) 120.
[23] Amitav Acharya, 'Transnational Civil Society as Agents of Norm Diffusion' in Rodney Bruce Hall (ed), *Reducing Armed Violence with NGO Governance* (Routledge 2014) 100.
[24] Lisbeth Zimmermann, 'Same Same or Different? Norm Diffusion between Resistance, Compliance, and Localization in Post-Conflict States' (2016) 17 International Studies Perspectives 98, 106.
[25] Mathias Großklaus, 'Appropriation and the Dualism of Human Rights: Understanding the Contradictory Impact of Gender Norms in Nigeria' (2015) 36 Third World Quarterly 1253, 1257.
[26] Amitav Acharya, 'How Ideas Spread: Whose Norms Matter? Norm Localization and Institutional Change in Asian Regionalism' (2004) 58 International Organization 239.
[27] Antje Wiener, *A Theory of Contestation* (Springer 2014) 1.
[28] Zimmermann (n 24).

additional cost, and imperfect allocation of human and financial resources.[29] Through the lens of the transnational perspective, norm contestation is a productive force. It is the condition for a shared understanding over meanings of norms, generates norm legitimacy, and allows for identifying pathways to participation.[30] Norm contestation enables contextual sense-making, norm clarification, and refinement processes. States and other actors announce their views about what norms mean, how obligatory they are, how they should be applied to specific acts, and thereby reveal their specific beliefs regarding the meaning and the weight of obligation of international norms.[31]

Many of the norms that substantiate global sustainability governance are open to different conflicting and sometimes mutually exclusive interpretations. In a globalized economy, divergent responses to local sustainability challenges—drought, water stress, loss of biodiversity—create competitiveness tensions and add further pressure to the international legal order.[32] Actors interpret sustainability norms differently and pursue distinct or even mutually exclusive norm understandings.[33] While environmentally motivated trade restrictions are considered as undesired interference with international trade from the perspective of the World Trade Organization (WTO), which aims at liberalizing international trade and seeks to abolish trade obstacles, the same measures are appreciated as effective means for enforcing international environmental standards from the perspective of international environmental regimes.[34] The precautionary principle provides an illustrative example. As Stoll in this book shows, the WTO Agreement on Sanitary and Phytosanitary Measures (SPS) employs a more limited concept of precaution than Principle 15 of the Rio Declaration on Environment and Development.[35] Article 5.7 of the SPS widely neglects that scientific uncertainty may prevail for an unforeseeable amount of time, reflects the endeavour to open up markets, and to curb national regulatory policies in this regard.[36]

## 2.2 Regime Complexity

Scholars in global environmental politics have significantly contributed to the development of regime complex studies. Raustiala and Victor were the first to show that

[29] Katja Biedenkopf, 'Relations between International Organisations in Combating Climate Change' in Rafael Biermann and Joachim A Koops (eds), *Palgrave Handbook of Inter-organizational Relations in World Politics* (Palgrave Macmillan 2017); Maria Ivanova and Natalia Escobar-Pemberthy, 'The UN, Global Governance and the SDGs' in Raimund Bleischwitz and others (eds), *Routledge Handbook of the Resource Nexus* (Routledge 2020).

[30] Nicole Deitelhoff, 'What's in a Name? Contestation and Backlash Against International Norms and Institutions' (2020) 22 The British Journal of Politics and International Relations 715; Wiener, Chapter 2 in this book.

[31] Cf Sandholtz, Chapter 3 in this book.

[32] Ivanova and Escobar-Pemberthy (n 29).

[33] Helmut Breitmeier and others, 'Politicized Sustainability and Agricultural Policy: Comparing Norm Understandings of International Organizations' (2021) 23 Journal of Comparative Policy Analysis: Research and Practice 625.

[34] Sebastian Oberthür and Thomas Gehring, 'The Causal Mechanisms of Interaction Between International Institutions' (2009) 15 European Journal of International Relations 125.

[35] Peter-Tobias Stoll, Chapter 17 in this book.

[36] ibid.

regimes which were previously seen as distinct (biodiversity and trade) had begun to overlap and to produce rule inconsistencies.[37] Classical regime complex studies focus on interstate regimes that develop legal norms and assess interdependent and complex institutional interactions and related norm dynamics.[38] A global regime complex constitutes a non-hierarchical and loosely coupled set of specific regimes[39] that involve 'implicit or explicit principles, norms, rules, and decision-making procedures around which actors' expectations converge in a given area of international relations'.[40]

A central feature of regime complexes is *institutional complexity*. Institutional complexity is the 'diversity of international institutions that legally or functionally overlap in addressing a given issue area of global governance'.[41] It emerges from the proliferation of different organizations, norms, implementation mechanisms, and operational activities.[42] Global sustainability regime complexes reveal high institutional complexity and, even though they have become embedded in an overarching normative script (SDG framework), they 'always exhibit a degree of divergence regarding the principles, norms, rules, or procedures of their elemental regimes'.[43] Zelli and others distinguish three levels of institutional complexity analysing the global climate-energy nexus: the *macro level* captures the overarching institutional fragmentation for a given domain of global governance and its respective complex, the *meso level* zooms into specific subfields of such a domain and the institutional complexes thereof, and the *micro level* involves interlinkages among (at least) two individual institutions on specific questions.[44] Sustainability regime complexes are particularly decentralized with most organizations emerging from bottom up and pursuing governance goals with little if any central coordination.[45] In the absence of a central actor with sufficient authority to orchestrate institutional complexity, there are cross-institutional opportunities for strategic behaviour which also impact norm dynamics. Different regime actors, such as states,[46] business actors,[47] non-governmental organizations

[37] Kal Raustiala and David G Victor, 'The Regime Complex for Plant Genetic Resources' (2004) 58 International Organization 277.

[38] See eg Robert O Keohane and David G Victor, 'The Regime Complex for Climate Change' (2011) 9 Perspectives on Politics 7; Sebastian Oberthür and Thomas Gehring, 'Institutional Interaction: Ten Years of Scholarly Development' in Sebastian Oberthür and Olav Schram Stokke (eds), *Managing Institutional Complexity: Regime Interplay and Global Environmental Change* (The MIT Press 2011); Raustiala and Victor (n 37).

[39] Keohane and Victor (n 38) 7.

[40] Stephen D Krasner, 'Structural Causes and Regime Consequences: Regimes as Intervening Variables' (1982) 36 International Organization 185, 186.

[41] Fariborz Zelli, Ina Möller, and Harro van Asselt, 'Institutional Complexity and Private Authority in Global Climate Governance: The Cases of Climate Engineering, REDD+ and Short-lived Climate Pollutants' (2017) 26 Environmental Politics 669, 670.

[42] Kenneth W Abbott, 'The Transnational Regime Complex for Climate Change' (2012) 30 Environment and Planning C: Government and Policy 571.

[43] Amandine Orsini, Jean-Frédéric Morin, and Oran Young, 'Regime Complexes: A Buzz, a Boom, or a Boost for Global Governance?' (2013) 19 Global Governance: A Review of Multilateralism and International Organizations 27, 29.

[44] Cf Fariborz Zelli and others, *Governing the Climate-Energy Nexus: Challenges to Coherence, Legitimacy, and Effectiveness* (CUP 2020) 23.

[45] Abbott (n 42).

[46] Benjamin Faude and Thomas Gehring, 'Regime Complexes as Governance Systems' in Wayne Sandholtz and Christopher A Whytock (eds), *Research Handbook on the Politics of International Law* (Edward Elgar 2017).

[47] Zelli, Möller, and van Asselt (n 41).

(NGOs),[48] and international organizations (IOs)[49] shape their preferences and adopt their norm-related behaviour against the backdrop of overlapping institutions. Regime complex studies model strategic inter-institutional interaction as either co-operative or competitive.[50] States use or create institutional overlaps for strategic purposes,[51] eg through forum-shopping[52] or regime-shifting.[53] Such strategic behaviour puts functionally overlapping institutions under continuing competitive pressure[54] and thus challenges the integrity of international law.[55] These findings speak to norm scholars who argue that norm disputes open up discursive and practical marketplaces which allow for discursive struggles over making and interpreting rules.[56] Following this perspective, actors in sustainability regime complexes have an interest in shaping the argumentation surrounding norms they care about and in establishing boundaries to the kinds of arguments that are considered legitimate in normative disputes.[57] Recent research on the agency of IOs in regime complexes reveals that IOs initiate and undertake own political strategies in response to decisions taken at other parts of the regime complex.[58] This involves cooperation among IOs towards joint norms by coordinating policies and operational activities, pooling resources, and/or engaging in joint decision-making. For example, the secretariats of the Cartagena Protocol on Biosafety and the WTO increasingly share information and pool expertise to prevent non-compliance by states.[59]

### 2.3 Technology Innovation

Different worldviews, norm understandings, and organizational self-perceptions shape the way in which actors appraise the appropriateness of technology innovation to ensure sustainability.[60] The 2030 Agenda for Sustainable Development emphasizes the importance of technology as a pillar for the implementation of the SDGs.[61]

[48] Orsini, Morin, and Young (n 43).

[49] Rafael Biermann and Joachim A Koops, 'Studying Relations Among International Organizations in World Politics: Core Concepts and Challenges' in Rafael Biermann and Joachim A Koops (eds), *Palgrave Handbook of Inter-organizational Relations in World Politics* (Palgrave Macmillan 2017).

[50] ibid.

[51] Faude and Gehring (n 46).

[52] Marc L Busch, 'Overlapping Institutions, Forum Shopping, and Dispute Settlement in International Trade' (2007) 61 International Organization 735.

[53] Laurence R Helfer, 'Regime Shifting in the Intellectual Property System' (2009) 7 Perspectives on Politics 39.

[54] Oberthür and Gehring, 'Institutional Interaction' (n 38).

[55] Faude and Gehring (n 46).

[56] Sandholtz, Chapter 3 in this book.

[57] ibid.

[58] Breitmeier and others (n 33); Matias E Margulis, 'Intervention by International Organizations in Regime Complexes' (2021) 16 The Review of International Organizations 871; Biermann and Koops (n 49).

[59] Jingjing Zhao, 'The Role of International Organizations in Preventing Conflicts between the SPS Agreement and the Cartagena Protocol on Biosafety' (2020) 29 Review of European, Comparative & International Environmental Law 271.

[60] Galaz (n 6) 13.

[61] UN Interagency Task Team on Science, Technology and Innovation for the SDGs, 'Policy Briefs #1 Science, Technology and Innovation for SDGs Roadmaps – Framework and Working Method' (2018) <https://sdgs.un.org/documents/policy-brief-1-science-technology-and-innovation-sdgs-roadmaps-framework-and-working> accessed 15 November 2021.

Stratospheric aerosol geoengineering is promoted to mitigate Arctic permafrost carbon loss,[62] drone technology as early warning tool for countries at risk from natural disasters[63], and GM insect technology for more effective insect pest control and the transformation to sustainable agri-food systems.[64]

This analysis regards (legal) norms and technology innovation as mutually connected and conceptualizes technology innovation as a driver of global norm dynamics. (Legal) norms are challenged, changed, or even made obsolete by the rise of new technologies. Technology innovation can cause governance trade-offs[65] and new legal dilemmas and thus fuels demand for legal norms to keep pace with technological change to better reflect the current technological capacity.[66] But technology innovation distributes risks and costs across time, space, and social groups in ways that sometimes are difficult to predict in advance.[67] In doing so, it adds uncertainty to sustainability norm contestation. Relevant information for priori rational choice calculations regarding technology innovation is often not fully available due to unknown risks, knowledge gaps, and a lack of appropriate coping strategies and assessment guidelines.[68]

Technology innovation spawns new legal specialties[69] and substantiates the need for balancing between old and new norms which likely leads to norm change.[70] Technology innovation can facilitate the replacement of old norms with new ones or the discursive reframing, development, and interlinking of established norms with new ones.[71] According to Krieger and Liese, younger treaty norms are likely to be less contested and show only few changes because they mirror recent state consensus and more recent commitment.[72] Older norms, whether derived from practice or treaty law, are more likely to come under pressure when global power structures, state preferences, societal expectations, or the underlying problems change.[73] In global sustainability regime complexes, technology innovation fuels new norm dynamics and contestation which can lead to conflict but also to norm clarification and refinement processes on procedural and substantive grounds. *Norm entrepreneurs* strategically act as meaning managers and establish 'new ways of talking about and understanding issues'.[74] Public and private norm entrepreneurs

[62] Yating Chen, Aobo Liu, and John C Moore 'Mitigation of Arctic Permafrost Carbon Loss through Stratospheric Aerosol Geoengineering' (2020) 11 Nature Communications Article No 2430. <www.nature.com/articles/s41467-020-16357-8> accessed 8 November 2021.

[63] UN Food and Agriculture Organization (FAO), 'Drones Help Farmers in the Philippines Prepare for Climate Disasters' (25 April 2016) <www.fao.org/emergencies/fao-in-action/stories/stories-detail/en/c/411841/> accessed 8 November 2021.

[64] Schwindenhammer, 'The Rise, Regulation and Risks of Genetically Modified Insect Technology' (n 6).

[65] Schwindenhammer and Gonglach (n 5).

[66] Bennett Moses (n 7) 765–68.

[67] Galaz (n 6).

[68] Igor Linkov and others, 'Comparative, Collaborative, and Integrative Risk Governance for Emerging Technologies' (2018) 38 Environment Systems and Decisions 170.

[69] Bennett Moses (n 7) 764.

[70] Mathias Großklaus, 'Friction, Not Erosion: Assassination Norms at the Fault Line between Sovereignty and Liberal Values' (2017) 38 Contemporary Security Policy 260.

[71] Schwindenhammer, 'The Rise, Regulation and Risks of Genetically Modified Insect Technology' (n 6).

[72] Krieger and Liese, Chapter 1 in this book.

[73] ibid.

[74] Finnemore and Sikkink (n 8) 897.

exert political authority[75] and build new discursive links in norm debates in order to reinterpret and reshape established norms in the light of new knowledge.[76] NGOs and local people's movements are considered to represent local, traditional, and indigenous knowledge.[77] Private companies and scientific actors possess (scientific) expert knowledge which is especially relevant in norm contestation regarding technology innovation. But the boundaries between the academic and the economic sphere of (scientific) expert knowledge production are blurred. When companies spin off from universities, conflicts can arise between private business claims for the protection of proprietary data and patent rights and the aim of a transparent and independent scientific evaluation of new technologies.[78]

## 3. Norm Dynamics through Technology Innovation: The Case of GM Insects

The following empirical results are derived from a qualitative case study analysis of norm entrepreneurship and norm dynamics in the field of GM insect technology. They reveal that the private company Oxitec has managed to become a key norm entrepreneur in the field and that GM insect technology fuels norm dynamics in the subfields of global food and agriculture, health, and biosafety as well as norm contestation over the distribution of responsibility, provision of transparency, and risk assessment and (re)interpretation of the precautionary principle.

### 3.1 The Rise of GM Insect Technology

In the late 1990s, scientists from the University of Oxford and the University of Manchester laid the scientific foundation for the commercialization of GM insect technology investigating the Release of Insects Carrying a Dominant Lethal (RIDL)[79] technology in *Drosophila*.[80] In August 2002, Oxitec was spun off from the University of Oxford with support of the Wellcome Trust and the Bill and Melinda Gates Foundation.[81] Oxitec soon became the most important private norm entrepreneur

[75] Sandra Schwindenhammer, 'Authority Pooling and Regional Organic Agriculture Standard-Setting: Evidence from East Africa' (2016) 18 Journal of Environmental Policy & Planning 102; Annegret Flohr and others, *The Role of Business in Global Governance: Corporations as Norm-entrepreneurs* (Palgrave Macmillan 2010).

[76] Großklaus, 'Friction, Not Erosion' (n 70).

[77] Jan Sändig, Jochen von Bernstorff, and Andreas Hasenclever, 'Affectedness in International Institutions: Promises and Pitfalls of Involving the Most Affected' (2018) 3 Third World Thematics: A TWQ Journal 587.

[78] Graciela R Ostera and Lawrence O Gostin, 'Biosafety Concerns Involving Genetically Modified Mosquitoes to Combat Malaria and Dengue in Developing Countries' (2011) 305 JAMA 930.

[79] RIDL uses genetically modified male insects that carry a dominant lethal gene which is intended to pass on after mating with wild females to the offspring so that larvae are killed before they reach adulthood.

[80] Dean D Thomas and others, 'Insect Population Control Using a Dominant, Repressible, Lethal Genetic System' (2000) 287 Science 2474.

[81] Oxitec, 'Paper provided to the House of Lords Select Committee on Science and Technology call for evidence on genetically modified insects. Written evidence (GMI0016)' (18 September 2015)

in GM insect technology exerting political authority in norm debates based on exclusive expert knowledge.[82] Oxitec successfully promoted GM insect technology as a pillar for the implementation of the global norms of food security and global health.[83] The company developed and patented RIDL for several species and tested it in laboratory greenhouse, field cage, and open field trials between 2009 and 2014.[84] While Oxitec had to withdraw applications for cage trials in Europe due to political disputes and time delays,[85] its leading commitment has met with more success in the United States. After an environmental assessment that found no significant impact, the US Department of Agriculture's Animal and Plant Health Inspection Service (APHIS) permitted Cornell University the open field release of Oxitec's Diamondback moth OX4319L at the Cornell New York State Agricultural Experiment Station in July 2017.[86] Today, Oxitec's RIDL technology is the most advanced GM insect approach worldwide.

## 3.2 Norm Dynamics in Global Food and Agriculture, Health, and Biosafety

The rise of GM insect technology amplifies new norm dynamics in the subfields of global food and agriculture, health, and biosafety and ongoing norm contestation in the context of specific regulatory frameworks.

In *global food and agriculture*, GM insect technology links to norm debates on SDG 2 to end hunger, achieve food security and improved nutrition, and promote sustainable agriculture. Insect pests cause reduced agricultural production, loss of export markets, and/or costs of establishing phytosanitary measures.[87] They are difficult to control effectively using traditional methods such as biocides or insecticides.[88] Insecticide resistance jeopardizes conventional insect pest control approaches in nearly all parts of the world.[89] The integrated SDG 2 requires a change in traditional normative frameworks and policies in such a way that environmental or social goals are regarded as

<www.parliament.uk/documents/lords-committees/science-technology/GMInsects/GMInsectsevidence.pdf> accessed 8 November 2021.

[82] The presented findings in Section 3 draw on a more comprehensive case study analysis of private norm entrepreneurship in global GM insect regulation, see Schwindenhammer, 'The Rise, Regulation and Risks of Genetically Modified Insect Technology' (n 6).
[83] Oxitec, 'Paper provided to the House of Lords' (n 81).
[84] Philip T Leftwich, Michael Bolton, and Tracey Chapman, 'Evolutionary Biology and Genetic Techniques for Insect Control' (2015) 9 Evolutionary Applications 212.
[85] R Guy Reeves and Martin Phillipson, 'Mass Releases of Genetically Modified Insects in Area-Wide Pest Control Programs and Their Impact on Organic Farmers' (2017) 9 Sustainability 59.
[86] APHIS, 'USDA announces final EA, FONSI, and permit for GE diamondback moth' (6 July 2017) <https://content.govdelivery.com/accounts/USDAAPHIS/bulletins/1a80b62> accessed 8 November 2021.
[87] FAO, 'Averting risks to the food chain: A compendium of proven emergency prevention methods and tools' (2017) <www.fao.org/emergencies/resources/documents/resources-detail/en/c/471520/> accessed 15 November 2021.
[88] Leftwich, Bolton, and Chapman (n 84).
[89] World Health Organization (WHO) Global Malaria Programme, 'Global plan for insecticide resistance management in malaria vectors' (2012) <https://apps.who.int/iris/handle/10665/44846> accessed 15 November 2021.

basic prerequisites for food security.[90] Oxitec frames GM insect technology as a sustainable alternative to established insect pest control approaches. GM insects 'protect people from mosquito borne diseases, have the potential to reduce pesticide use, and contribute to sustainable agriculture'.[91] In 2016, Oxitec proclaimed a paradigm shift in mosquito control.[92] The company promotes GM insect technology as an approach that allows the reduction of the use of chemical insecticides and avoids related negative environmental impacts. GM insect technology is powerful where pests have become resistant to other crop protection products.[93] However, GM insect technology also fuels norm debates in the subfield of food and agriculture. While proponents promote GM insect technology as a sustainable innovation that addresses threats to food security in new ways, critics warn of unintended environmental, social, and health effects. GM insect technology poses risks to environmental safety. Unintended effects can include harm to other species and disruption of ecological communities and ecosystem processes.[94] Other risks relate to monopoly ownership rights and the mutual exclusiveness of different agricultural production systems. Organic farmers fear cross-pollution and losing their organic reputation, certification, and economic benefits.[95]

In *global health*, pest insects are targeted as vectors for serious infectious diseases, such as dengue fever or malaria. Threats from pests impede the achievement of SDG 3 (global health), especially regarding the prevention of infectious diseases. Insect pest control has a long history in the subfield of global health. Since the 1950s, the sterile insect technique (SIT) has been applied in pest insect control.[96] The SIT relies on the production and mass release of sufficient sterile male insects to induce sterility in the wild females, which, over time, causes the target population to decline.[97] According to the UN Food and Agriculture Organization (FAO), SIT is one of the most successful insect pest control methods ever developed, but obstacles remain that give rise to the spread of GM insect technology.[98] Sterilization by irradiation often has harmful impact on the insects' fitness. For several species, large-scale sex separation is not feasible without genetic methods.[99] GM insect technology is seen as a technological advance of SIT building on programmes employing release of radiation-sterilized insects.[100] After the outbreak of a mosquito-borne disease in French overseas territories, France's High Council for Biotechnology published a supportive position on the use

[90] Breitmeier and others (n 33).

[91] Oxitec, 'Paper provided to the House of Lords' (n 81) 190.

[92] Oxitec, 'Press Release' (21 November 2016) <www.oxitec.com/en/news/board-of-florida-keys-mosquito-control-district-approves-investigational-agreement-for-effectiveness-trial-of-oxitecs-friendly-mosquitoes-in-monroe-county-florida> accessed 8 November 2021.

[93] Cf Oxitec, 'Paper provided to the House of Lords' (n 81) 190.

[94] Convention on Biological Diversity (CBD), 'Guidance on Risk Assessment of Living Modified Organisms and Monitoring in the Context of Risk Assessment' (14 September 2016) UNEP/CBD/BS/COP-MOP/8/8/Add.1.

[95] Reeves and Phillipson (n 85).

[96] ibid.

[97] Rosemary Susan Lees and others, 'Back to the Future: The Sterile Insect Technique against Mosquito Disease Vectors' (2015) 10 Current Opinion in Insect Science 156.

[98] Cf FAO, 'Averting risks to the food chain' (n 87).

[99] Camilla Beech and others, 'Genetically Modified Insects: Science, Use, Status and Regulation' (2012) 6 Collection of Biosafety Reviews 66.

[100] WHO, 'Guidance framework for testing of genetically modified mosquitoes' (2014) first edition <www.who.int/tdr/publications/year/2014/guide-fmrk-gm-mosquit/en/> accessed 15 November 2021.

of Oxitec's *Aedes aegypti* OX513A for vector control in June 2017. In July 2017, the National Institute for Public Health and the Environment of the Dutch Ministry of Health, Welfare and Sport evaluated the potential release of *Aedes aegypti* OX513A on the island of Saba, a Dutch Caribbean island. The final assessment concluded that the potential adverse effects on human health and the environment are considered to be negligible.[101] These risk assessment results are in line with the positive evaluations of Oxitec's GM insects by the National Technical Biosafety Commission in Brazil (2014), the US Food and Drug Administration (2016), and the US Department APHIS (2017). However, GM insect technology fuels global norm debates on new risks to human safety. Unintended effects of GM insects may include the spread of new or more vigorous pests, especially those that have adverse effects on human health.[102] The World Health Organization (WHO) Guidance Framework for Testing of Genetically Modified Mosquitoes provides quality standards for assessing the safety and efficacy of GM insects and addresses legal, ethical, social, and cultural issues that arise during their development and deployment.[103] The first edition of the framework was developed by a multi-stakeholder working group led by the WHO and the Foundation for the National Institutes of Health (2010–2014). The development process involved a public comment period and the consultation of experts. Two Oxitec scientists belonged to the group of contributors that were consulted by the WHO for information and advice during the development of the draft guidance framework.[104] Both self-identified a commercial interest in GM insects.[105] The final guidance document includes several references to publications from Oxitec scientists and simultaneously declares promoting a science-based regulatory process 'that is publicly transparent, without conflict of interest, contains minimal confidential business information, and provides allowance for public stakeholder input'.[106]

In global *biosafety*, GM insect technology touches on SDG 15 to protect, restore, and promote sustainable use of terrestrial ecosystems and to halt biodiversity loss. The Cartagena Protocol on Biosafety to the Convention on Biological Diversity (CBD) is the international agreement that ensures safe handling, transport, and use of LMOs resulting from modern biotechnology that may have adverse effects on biological diversity.[107] The protocol encourages the parties to establish national regulatory systems to manage LMOs—usually including a central competent authority for implementation—and to pursue capacity-building measures for developing countries. The protocol includes the Nagoya–Kuala Lumpur Supplementary Protocol on Liability and Redress addressing response measures in the event of damage caused by the transboundary movement of LMOs. GM insect technology amplifies new norm dynamics in the subfield of biosafety. In December 2016, the parties decided

[101] Debora C M Glandorf, 'Technical evaluation of a potential release of OX513A Aedes aegypti mosquitoes on the island of Saba' (2017) RIVM Letter report 2017–0087, 68.
[102] CBD, 'Guidance on Risk Assessment' (n 94).
[103] WHO, 'Guidance framework' (n 100).
[104] Schwindenhammer, 'The Rise, Regulation and Risks of Genetically Modified Insect Technology' (n 6).
[105] WHO, 'Guidance framework' (n 100) 131.
[106] ibid 94.
[107] Cartagena Protocol on Biosafety to the Convention on Biological Diversity (adopted 29 January 2000, entered into force 11 September 2003) 2226 UNTS 208 (Cartagena Protocol).

on the additional Guidance on Risk Assessment of Living Modified Organisms and Monitoring in the Context of Risk Assessment, giving emphasis to specific issues that may need special consideration for the environmental release of LM mosquitoes.[108] Based on its exclusive technical knowledge, Oxitec provided background material and participated in the discussions of the Open-Ended Online Forum on the development of further guidance on new topics of LMO risk assessment and management. In 2018, the Conference of the Parties to the CBD set out an intersessional process for developing a post-2020 global biodiversity framework and established the Open-Ended Working Group on the Post-2020 Global Biodiversity. This process led to the publication of a zero-draft document, stressing that past and ongoing rapid declines in biodiversity and ecosystem functions mean that most international societal and environmental goals, such as the SDGs, 'will not be achieved on the basis of current trajectories'.[109] Biodiversity norms for 2030 'may only be achieved through transformative changes across economic, social, political and technological factors'.[110] Advances in synthetic biotechnology, such as GM insect technology, play a major role in further developing the post-2020 global biodiversity framework. They impact strategic, financial, and ecosystem-related issues of relevance to the implementation of the CBD, the Cartagena Protocol on Biosafety, and the Nagoya Protocol on Access and Benefit-sharing. Hence, the intersessional process to deliberate on the post-2020 global biodiversity framework involves, inter alia, an extended online forum and *Ad Hoc* Technical Expert Group on synthetic biology. The zero-draft document stresses that the impacts of such technology innovation 'need to be assessed carefully to ensure they do not have unintended negative impacts, including locking society into unsustainable development paths'.[111] Current debates also touch upon different national regulatory styles and frameworks and substantiate the need for more issue-specific biosafety governance at the national and global levels. GM insects challenge existing legal categories since they are not a plant pest, pesticide, food, or drug and can cause confusion about which national regulatory agency exercises jurisdiction.[112] Moreover, GM insects cross national boundaries and may alter entire ecosystems with unprecedented and far-reaching consequences,[113] thus substantiating the need for issue-specific global norm debates.

### 3.3 Norm Contestation in the Context of Specific Regulatory Frameworks

GM insect technology has been scientifically and politically criticized from its very beginning. One can observe contestation over the distribution of responsibility, the

[108] CBD, 'Guidance on Risk Assessment' (n 94) 82.

[109] CBD, 'Zero Draft of the Post-2020 Global Biodiversity Framework' (6 January 2020) CBD/WG2020/2/3.

[110] ibid.

[111] ibid 3.

[112] Cf Albert C Lin, 'Mismatched Regulation: Genetically Modified Mosquitoes and the Coordinated Framework for Biotechnology' (2017) 51 University of California Davis Law Review 205, 215–16.

[113] Cf Leftwich, Bolton, and Chapman (n 84) 213.

provision of transparency, and risk assessment and the (re)interpretation of the precautionary principle in the context of the two most important global regulatory frameworks in the field—the Cartagena Protocol on Biosafety to the CBD (2000) and the WHO Guidance Framework for Testing of Genetically Modified Mosquitoes (2014). The empirical findings reveal that norm dynamics privilege scientific expert knowledge over local knowledge and foster unequal access to norm contestation.

### 3.3.1 Contestation Over the Distribution of Responsibility

GM insects can cross national borders through either human-assisted or natural mechanisms. The transboundary movement of GM insects fuels contestation over the distribution of responsibility. The human-assisted transboundary movement includes the trade of GM insects. It is regulated under Articles 8, 10, and 12 of the Cartagena Protocol, which outline the procedure for dealing with the transboundary movement of LMOs.[114] Annex I specifies the information that must be provided, including a risk assessment report consistent with Annex III.[115] These provisions have already been incorporated into national regulations and form the basis of regulatory approval for GM insect research and development.[116] The natural movement of GM insects is a necessary prerequisite for successfully suppressing pest populations, but once GM insects are released, they do not stop at national borders.

The regulatory needs concerning the natural movement exceed the regulatory capacity and authority of single states. No state acting by itself can regulate the potential transboundary movement of GM insects.[117] Classical measures to limit the flow of GM materials like the use of buffer zones have no effect.[118] According to the WHO, it is appropriate in cases of potential transboundary movement to 'seek the views of authorities in neighbouring countries on hazards'.[119] To date, GM insect technology is primarily being developed for use in low- to middle-income countries.[120] GM insect technology control includes research and development, regulatory approval, implementation operations and training, monitoring, reporting, and responses to unintended outcomes.[121] The potential of low- to middle-income countries for managing GM insect technology is at least uncertain and points to the issues of improved transnational cooperation, assistance, and empowerment.

Moreover, it is contested among IOs, states, and private companies who should be responsible for overseeing the development of GM insect technology and the implications of its use. The Nagoya–Kuala Lumpur Supplementary Protocol on Liability and Redress outlines administrative response measures in the event of damage resulting from transboundary movements of LMOs. According to Article 5, the national competent authority shall identify the operator that has caused the damage, evaluate the

[114] Cf Cartagena Protocol (n 107).
[115] ibid.
[116] Hector Quemada, 'Regulation of Transgenic Mosquitoes' in Zach N Adelman (ed), *Genetic Control of Malaria and Dengue* (Academic Press 2016).
[117] Ostera and Gostin (n 78).
[118] Reeves and Phillipson (n 85).
[119] WHO, 'Guidance framework' (n 100) 59.
[120] ibid 11.
[121] John D Mumford and L Roman Carrasco, 'Economics of Transgenic Insects for Field Release' in Mark Q Benedict (ed), *Transgenic Insects* (CABI 2014).

damage, and determine which response measures should be taken by the operator.[122] Several countries have set out criteria to address damage in their domestic laws, including the attribution of responsibility to certain parties. The existence of legal provisions that expose scientists or companies to liability for damage fuels contestation over barriers to development in science, technology, and innovation. Critics argue that new technologies can be inhibited by strict (legal) norms. Legal liability provisions are an important consideration for any actor who might be contemplating working with LMOs.[123] In the words of Oxitec: 'If we over-regulate we alienate entrepreneurial innovation and value creation.'[124]

### 3.3.2 Contestation Over the Provision of Transparency

The provision of transparency regarding GM insect technology is another contested issue in norm dynamics. Several global regulatory schemes provide open access to scientific information about biosafety, eg the FAO GM Foods Platform, the Organisation for Economic Co-operation and Development (OECD) BioTrack Product Database, or the Biosafety Clearing-House (BCH) mechanism set up by the Cartagena Protocol.[125] But, to date, the FAO GM Foods Platform and the OECD BioTrack Product Database only provide information on food safety assessments of GM plants and are, thus, not suited for GM insects. The BCH mechanism set up under Article 20 of the Cartagena Protocol facilitates the exchange of scientific, technical, environmental, and legal information on LMOs intended for deliberate release.[126] The parties are mandated to provide information about national biosafety laws and regulations, risk assessments, and decisions. Since the BCH collects information on all types of LMOs, it is suitable for GM insects. However, some countries with significant involvement in GM insect technology, such as the United States, are not party to the Cartagena Protocol. Their low level of commitment limits the authority and power of the Cartagena Protocol to stipulate discursive exchange in norm debates and find common ground regarding the transparency of biosafety.

GM insect technology not only exceeds the regulatory scope of most global schemes of data collection and information sharing; it also involves that governance actors consider the relevance of provided information differently. Information is considered relevant if it is linked to norms of protection or assessment end-points, or if it contributes to the identification and evaluation of potentially adverse effects of the LMO, outcome of the risk assessment, or decision-making.[127] The Cartagena Protocol's guidance on risk assessment of LMOs suggests giving more weight to validated studies conducted according to international standards and peer-reviewed literature than to technical reports, specialist literature, and government reports.[128] However, in many

[122] Nagoya–Kuala Lumpur Supplementary Protocol on Liability and Redress to the Cartagena Protocol on Biosafety (adopted 15 October 2010, entered into force 5 March 2018) UNEP/CBD/BS/COP-MOP/5/17 <https://bch.cbd.int/protocol/NKL_text.shtml> accessed 15 November 2021.

[123] Quemada (n 116).

[124] Oxitec, 'Paper provided to the House of Lords' (n 81) 189.

[125] FAO, 'Report on the webinar on the international databases on biosafety' (2015) <www.fao.org/documents/card/en/c/856f86a1-7e1e-4223-8a10-7d2b1afa5573/> accessed 15 November 2021.

[126] Cartagena Protocol (n 107).

[127] CBD, 'Guidance on Risk Assessment' (n 94).

[128] ibid 18.

developing countries, few studies have been conducted to examine gene flow among disease-transmitting vectors, their mating behaviour, interactions among vectors sharing one habitat, or how pathogens respond to the introduction of new vectors.[129] Norm dynamics related to GM insect technology have to deal with unequal levels of knowledge and context-specific knowledge gaps, especially in the global South, which emerge from information-poor environments. Information-poor environments stem from economic constraints restricting the access to information, arise from political constraints on information collection, processing, spreading, access, and use, relate to poor organizational conditions and capacities, and can be implicated in specific cultural contexts where dominant interpretative frames or hegemonic institutional practices limit the meanings of information.[130] Unequal levels of knowledge and knowledge gaps inhibit norm contestation on an equal footing and involve the risk of excluding local and traditional perspectives in norm dynamics. According to the Cartagena Protocol's guidance on risk assessment of LMOs, information from national and international standards and guidelines as well as knowledge and experience of farmers, growers, scientists, regulatory officials, indigenous peoples, and local communities may be used in the risk assessment of GM insects.[131] There is a need for local empowerment and additional training in vector biology procedures and/or biosafety among public actors to ensure that decision-makers, especially in developing countries, competently assess GM technology and to reach definitive and defensible conclusions.[132] But, inevitably, the applicants of a GM insect technology will always know more about it than anyone else.[133]

### 3.3.3 Contestation Over Risk Assessment and the Precautionary Principle

Conventional risk governance is only applicable when risks are well understood, possible effects are known or can potentially be known, and the exposure to such effects can be quantified and reliably controlled.[134] Variations in political judgement among states and business actors lead to differing opinions and contestation over the risk–benefit assessment of GM insect technology. The effects of any genetic manipulation of insects are difficult to assess before release. Moreover, natural and social systems 'have lags between the time when actions are taken and when changes become apparent'.[135] These lags need to be 'considered in the design of targets and the actions to achieve them'.[136] Hence, some degree of uncertainty is always an inherent element of risk assessment.[137] The importance assigned to uncertainty in public discourse varies across national jurisdictions. While some countries advocate withholding

[129] ibid 82.

[130] Cf Arthur PJ Mol, 'Environmental Governance through Information: China and Vietnam' (2009) 30 Singapore Journal of Tropical Geography 114, 115.

[131] CBD, 'Guidance on Risk Assessment' (n 94).

[132] WHO, 'Guidance framework' (n 100).

[133] Luke Alphey and Camilla Beech, 'Appropriate Regulation of GM Insects' (2012) 6 PLOS Neglected Tropical Diseases e1496.

[134] Timothy Malloy, Benjamin D Trump, and Igor Linkov, 'Risk-Based and Prevention-Based Governance for Emerging Materials' (2016) 50 Environmental Science & Technology 6822, 6822.

[135] CBD, 'Zero Draft' (n 109) 3.

[136] ibid.

[137] CBD, 'Guidance on Risk Assessment' (n 94) 19.

regulatory approval until absolute assurance of the absence of risk is available, others feel that potential benefits and other contextual factors should be considered in risk assessment.[138]

Norm contestation among different states, NGOs, companies, and scientific actors prevails regarding to what extent the risks of GM insect technology should be weighed against the potential benefits.[139] The different actors express disapproval of the particular application of risk assessment with regard to the specific characteristics of GM insect technology. According to Oxitec, regulation should focus on the proportionate evaluation of safety and environmental issues and equally consider the relevant risks and benefits of GM insect technology.[140] The WHO guidelines have embedded mechanisms to balance risk and benefit evaluation that correspond to the position of Oxitec that regulation should 'give appropriate consideration to potential benefits as weighed against risks, and potentially the cost of not using the intervention'.[141] According to the WHO, regulation must consider the differences between GM insect technology and other GM technologies to avoid creating barriers, high costs, and extended indecision on regulatory approvals.[142] The WHO proposes conducting economic evaluations to compare alternative courses of action as a basis for weighing the options and making sound decisions.

Contestation over the application of a norm entails potential for norm refinement and strengthening, but permanent contestation of that kind can also weaken a norm when actors fail to achieve renewed consensus.[143] The latter seems to be the case regarding contestation over the risk-benefit assessment of GM insect technology. The risks associated with the release of GM insects vary regarding the type of GM insect strategy,[144] targeted species, and geographical context. In December 2017, the Conference of the Parties to the CBD noted that the general principles and methodologies for risk assessment under the Cartagena Protocol provide a good basis for risk assessment of living organisms developed through synthetic biology, but might need to be updated and adapted.[145] Existing risk assessment considerations might not be sufficient or adequate to assess and evaluate the risks that might arise from organisms containing *engineered gene drives*—expected to persist in the natural environment and to increase in frequency and geographical range—due to limited experience and the complexity of the potential far-reaching impacts.[146] The WHO suggests to proceed risk assessments on a case-by-case basis and proportionate to the particular phase of

[138] Cf WHO, 'Guidance framework' (n 100) 10.

[139] John M Marshall, 'The Cartagena Protocol and Genetically Modified Mosquitoes' (2010) 28 Nature Biotechnology 896.

[140] Oxitec, 'Paper provided to the House of Lords' (n 81) 189.

[141] ibid 175.

[142] WHO, 'Guidance framework' (n 100).

[143] Nicole Deitelhoff and Lisbeth Zimmermann, 'Things we Lost in the Fire: How Different Types of Contestation Affect the Robustness of International Norms' (2020) 22 International Studies Review 51.

[144] In self-sustaining strategies, wild insect populations are replaced with genetically modified populations while the genetic modification is expected to persist in the environment. In self-limiting strategies, GM insects are introduced to the pest population while the novel genetic trait is expected to disappear from the environment after the release, see WHO, 'Guidance framework' (n 100) 3–5.

[145] CBD, 'Report of the Ad Hoc Technical Expert Group on Synthetic Biology' (9 December 2017)CBD/SYNBIO/AHTEG/2017/1/3.

[146] ibid.

testing.[147] However, the more fundamental challenge is that a 'balance must be sought between the precautionary principle, respect for sovereignty of states and ethical mandate to prevent disease on a global scale'.[148] According to the WHO, the adoption of a strict interpretation of the precautionary principle could mean that regulatory approvals would not be granted until all possible safety issues are resolved, regardless of societal needs and potential benefits.[149] The evaluation of risks and benefits should include issues which are not covered by Annex III of the Cartagena Protocol, such as potential social, economic, cultural, and health benefits associated with the use of GM mosquitoes.[150] Moreover, the (further) development of guidelines on risk assessment of organisms containing engineered gene drives by the CBD, other international organizations, national governments, and professional bodies would be useful in that regard.[151] Decision-making bodies approving biosafety testing should have the capacity to formulate the risk problem, to define appropriate end points for risk, to interpret the character of risk components, and to understand the efficacy and uncertainty related to proposed measures.[152] Since this capacity is not always available at the national level, 'efforts should be made to obtain independent international expertise, and to strengthen the necessary national expertise in the longer term'.[153]

## 4. Conclusion

This analysis has contributed to the ongoing debate on value change in the international legal order through conducting research on sustainability norm dynamics that exceed one single international regime, locating global sustainability norm dynamics within the context of conceptual debates about global norm contestation and regime complexity, and conceptualizing technology innovation as a potential driver of global norm dynamics. In doing so, it contributes to answer the question whether new technologies create fundamental challenges for the international legal order, fuel norm dynamics, and thereby prompt value change.[154]

The findings indicate that GM insect technology raises some fundamental legal challenges. It exceeds the regulatory capacity and authority of single states as well as single environmental regimes. GM insect technology adds uncertainty to norm debates and unveils the difficulty to identify and resolve new legal issues stemming from new technologies soon after they arise. GM insect technology induces rapid environmental change, while the underpinnings of normative shifts in the global domain of sustainability governance are subject to rather slow and incremental change. It necessitates the balancing of old and new norms in the light of the new technology and poses new challenges which are barely covered by established normative frameworks,

[147] WHO, 'Guidance framework' (n 100) 62.
[148] Marshall (n 139) 897.
[149] WHO, 'Guidance framework' (n 100) 104.
[150] CBD, 'Guidance on Risk Assessment' (n 94) 94.
[151] CBD, 'Report of the Ad Hoc Technical Expert Group' (n 145) 7.
[152] WHO, 'Guidance framework' (n 100).
[153] ibid 62.
[154] Krieger and Liese, Chapter 1 in this book.

eg, a gene drive that persists in the environment and increases rapidly in frequency and geographic range after GM insect release. In this regard, Galaz convincingly stresses the need for a norm dialogue on the fundamental question: how do we interpret the precautionary principle in the global context of rapid and interacting technological change capable of altering entire ecosystems?[155]

The empirical findings show that GM insect technology amplifies norm dynamics in the subfields of global food and agriculture, health, and biosafety, and norm contestation in the context of specific regulatory frameworks—over the distribution of responsibility, the provision of transparency, and risk assessment and the (re)interpretation of the precautionary principle. The central entrepreneurial involvement of Oxitec in the norm dynamics confirms the general trend in the international legal order that public and private norm entrepreneurs increasingly contest the validity of legal norms, lobby for a substantial change, and/or reinterpret specific norms.[156] Oxitec has used its outstanding position in the field to promote, produce, and distribute GM insects and has commented on draft regulatory frameworks and participated in public expert hearings and dialogues. The company managed to become a source of exclusive and patent-protected expert knowledge political representatives draw upon.

The resulting imbalance between private and public authority and representation of different types of knowledge (scientific expert knowledge over local knowledge) in the norm dynamics leads to an unequal access to norm contestation. Conflicts arise between the aims of an inclusive and fair representation of interests, transparent and independent scientific evaluation, and the protection of proprietary data and patent rights. Leaving political authority in norm dynamics related to new technologies to business corporations from the global North, based on their claimed expert knowledge, seems to honour the rationality of professional expertise—and market interests—over that of democratic checks and balances.[157] As yet, GM insect technology is primarily being developed for use in developing countries. The findings point to the need for further research on the conditions that warrant the independency, transparency, and legitimacy of (scientific) knowledge generation[158] and the pathways to equal participation in norm contestation, especially by actors from the global South. All in all, technology innovation turns out as a potential driver of value change in the international legal order that deserves more attention in both future theory development and empirical studies in IR norm research.

[155] Galaz (n 6) 101–03.
[156] Krieger and Liese, Chapter 1 in this book.
[157] Flohr and others (n 75).
[158] Galaz (n 6).

# 17

# Precaution and Genetically Modified Organisms

## A Healthy Legal Environment?

*Peter-Tobias Stoll*

## 1. Introduction

With their impressive and unprecedented achievements in the first half of the 1990s, the 1992 Rio Conference and the 1995 establishment of the World Trade Organization (WTO), international economic and environmental law are perfect candidates to probe the rise or decline of the international law quest. With high flying expectations, the concept of sustainable development, which aims at marrying economic and social development and environmental protection, has become a milestone and the adoption of the 2015 Sustainable Development Goals might be seen as a proof of its enduring momentum. Indeed, this part of international relations (IR) and law has been seen as promoting and taming globalization and, in this way, to fulfil the aspirations of Article 55 of the Charter of the United Nations about the 'creation of conditions of stability and well-being which are necessary for peaceful and friendly relations among nations'. Indeed, apparently, there has been a 'rise' of international law in this area. But: how impressive is this 'rise' and is there some 'decline', too?

This chapter will approach this question by way of a case study. It will shed light on the inauguration of the principle of sustainable development and the principle of precaution by the Rio Declaration and examine how these two principles have impacted the very detailed international regulation on trade in genetically modified organisms (GMOs) in the course of further legal developments, how the issue came to the fore in WTO dispute settlement, and what this might mean in terms of a rise or decline of international law.

## 2. The 1992 Rio Conference and the Principles of Sustainable Development and Precaution

In terms of a rise of international law, the 1992 United Nations Conference on the Environment and Development (UNCED) can be certainly considered as an especially rich source of new international norms and legal developments in the areas of environmental protection and development. At the UNCED, two major international

Peter-Tobias Stoll, *Precaution and Genetically Modified Organisms* In: *Tracing Value Change in the International Legal Order.* Edited by: Heike Krieger and Andrea Liese, Oxford University Press. 
DOI: 10.1093/oso/9780192855831.003.0017

environmental agreements, namely the Convention on Biological Diversity (CBD)[1] and the Framework Convention on Climate Change (UNFCCC)[2] were adopted and opened for signature. Each formed the basis for further developments in their respective fields of global environmental policies and law.

To the more, the UNCED adopted a declaration and a work programme, the so-called Rio Declaration[3] and the Agenda 21.[4] The Rio Declaration is particularly worth noting in this context, as it introduced the principle of sustainable development. The inauguration of the principle roots back to the so-called Brundlandt Report of 1987,[5] which has inspired further developments in the UN, particularly further UN conferences and instruments, including most recently the 2015 adoption of the UN sustainable development goals.[6] Also, it has not only been incorporated in the two Rio conventions and in various further international agreements, but was referred to by international courts and tribunals. In the text of the Rio Declaration, 'sustainable development' has been mentioned in different contexts and its rich concept and exact meaning has only evolved over time. It certainly represents a 'moral principle … or shared idea … of a desirable "good"' and thus a value in the way, the term is used in this book.[7] In the context of this chapter, it is suffice to highlight that sustainable development first and foremost implies that economic and social development and environmental protection have to be understood as three pillars of an overarching concept in which these pillars can and should mutually support each other.

Next to sustainable development, which is generally assumed to be the overarching one, the Rio Declaration spelt out a number of further principles concerning development and environmental protection. In this context, the principle of precaution shall be highlighted. Originally, the precautionary principle had emerged as a principle of environmental policy in the 1970s.[8] It has been incorporated into the legislation of a number of countries[9] and by way of the 1992 Maastricht Treaty[10] now is explicitly mentioned in Article 191 para 2 of the Treaty of the Functioning of the European

[1] Convention on Biological Diversity (adopted 5 June 1992, entered into force 29 December 1993) 1760 UNTS 79 (CBD).

[2] United Nations Framework Convention on Climate Change (adopted 9 May 1992, entered into force 21 March 1994) 1771 UNTS 107 (UNFCCC).

[3] Rio Declaration on Environment and Development (12 August 1992) UN Doc A/CONF.151/26 (vol I).

[4] Agenda 21 (June 1992) UN Doc A/CONF.151/26 (vol I).

[5] Report of the World Commission on Environment and Development (4 August 1987) UN Doc A/42/427 (Brundtland Report). The Report is named after the chair of the commission, Gro Harlem Brundtland.

[6] United Nations General Assembly, 'Transforming our World: The 2030 Agenda for Sustainable Development' (25 September 2015) UN Doc A/RES/70/1.

[7] See Heike Krieger and Andrea Liese, Chapter 1 in this book, Section 3.1.

[8] About the development of the concept see Jonathan B Wiener, 'Precaution' in Daniel Bodansky, Jutta Brunnée, and Ellen Hey (eds), *The Oxford Handbook of International Environmental Law* (OUP 2007) 597, 599–601; Akawat Laowonsiri, 'Application of the Precautionary Principle in the SPS Agreement' (2010) 14 UNYB 565, 568–69; for the origin in German law see Peter-Tobias Stoll, 'Of Fear and Prudence: Precaution Through Better Regulation and Innovation' in Lorenzo Squintani and others (eds), *Managing Facts and Feelings in Environmental Governance* (Edward Elgar 2019).

[9] For example: Gene Technology Act 2000 (Australia); Hazardous Substances and New Organisms Act 1996 No 30 (New Zealand); Supreme Court of India, *Vellore Citizens' Welfare Forum v Union of India and Others* (28 August 1996) AIR 1996 SC 2715.

[10] Treaty on European Union [1992] OJ C191/1.

Union (TFEU),[11] the introductory provision of the TFEU's chapter on environmental protection, and has enfolded a considerable impact on European Union (EU) legislation and jurisprudence.[12]

In the Rio Declaration, Principle 15 reads:

> In order to protect the environment, the precautionary approach shall be widely applied by States according to their capabilities. Where there are threats of serious or irreversible damage, lack of full scientific certainty shall not be used as a reason for postponing cost-effective measures to prevent environmental degradation.

In substance, the precautionary principle is about decision-making in terms of timing, facts, and data and about the final decision to take. Notwithstanding its procedural character, the precautionary principle very well can be seen as a value, as it well describes an idea about a desirable 'good', which ultimately is about the proper protection of the environment. It can be considered to be closely related to the value of sustainable development.

## 3. From the Rio Principles to a Rise of International Law

Being adopted by a UN conference, the Rio Declaration did not intend to create a legally binding effect in itself. Also, the format of a declaration of principles as commonly used in the UN and IR more generally can hardly be understood to refer to Article 38 para 1 lit. c of the Statute of the International Court of Justice in a technical way and to situate the declaration in the system of sources of international law. While not carrying a legally binding effect in themselves, the Rio principles and more generally UN declarations may establish an *opinio iuris* in the course of creating rules of customary international law (CIL) and many inform the decisions of international courts and tribunals and the application and interpretation of existing rules. Even more importantly, they often enfold a momentum and direct further developments in treatymaking and the formation of customary rules. Nevertheless, and depending on the approach taken, it may be doubtful whether such UN declarations, which are often labelled as 'soft law', really form part of proper international law. However, it would be difficult to ignore the Rio Declaration and its adoption in the context of a 'rise' of international law. The idea of a 'rise' and also of a 'decline' is to find out about the advances and downfalls of international law seen in an evolutionary/devolutionary perspective. UN declarations have been an important driver of developments of modern international law. Their adoption is part of the picture of the evolution of international law. Yet, of course, they are not law in themselves, but are still situated more in the realm of politics than of law. We may label them as imperfect norms or 'potential'

[11] Consolidated version of the Treaty on the Functioning of the European Union [2007] OJ C115/47.

[12] See for a comprehensive overview Nicolas de Sadeleer, 'The Precautionary Principle in EC Health and Environmental Law' (2006) 12 European Law Journal 139; José Luís da Cruz Vilaça, 'The Precautionary Principle in EC Law' (2004) 10 European Public Law 369.

norms. Keeping in mind its imperfect normativity but also its potential in the process of evolution of international law, the Rio Declaration and its adoption may be seen as a 'rise' of international law in a somewhat preliminary or conditional way, where a more definite judgement and an assessment of the magnitude of such 'rise' depends on the extent, to which the Rio principles actually produce legal effects. In formal perspective, such legal effect could come about by way of incorporation into agreements by informing the decisions of international courts and tribunals and by guiding state practice, which could ultimately result in the creation of new rules of CIL.

Indeed, the Rio Declaration and its two aforementioned principles had quite an impact. Not only did the CBD and the UNFCCC, both adopted at the Rio Conference, reflect the principles explicitly or implicitly. First, the UNFCCC refers to the principle explicitly in Article 3 para 3.[13] Second, the CBD, without explicitly using the term, nevertheless alludes to the text of Principle 15 of the Rio Declaration in its preamble.[14]

Also, the sustainable development principle but also the precautionary principle have subsequently been incorporated in numerous international agreements. Furthermore, at times, international courts and tribunals referred to them. Arguably, they may be also seen as emerging nascent or already manifest rules of CIL.[15]

However, given their abstract and even somehow vague wording, the significance of the principles in terms of a rise of international law also requires examining whether they make a difference in substance. This is particularly so, as the principles relate to development, economic affairs, and environmental protection which are the subject of existing and extensive parts of international law. A closer look is merited to detect how and to what extent the two principles bring about a change in substantive terms in such a complex legal environment. Altogether, this calls for a substantial assessment in view of whether and how the principles in their rather principled wording—so to speak on a macro level—really impact regulations and their operation on the ground, which may be seen as a micro level.

The regulation of trade in GMOs is a well-suited case to study these questions. It is related to trade and to the environment and the respective regimes in international law, which each follow distinct and at times conflicting objectives and interests but should be brought together closer as called for by the principle of sustainable development. Also, trade in GMOs raise questions as to environmental risks and scientific certainty, which are at the core of the precautionary principle.

[13] Art 3 para 3 UNFCCC reads: 'The Parties should take precautionary measures to anticipate, prevent or minimize the causes of climate change and mitigate its adverse effects. Where there are threats of serious or irreversible damage, lack of full scientific certainty should not be used as a reason for postponing such measures, taking into account that policies and measures to deal with climate change should be cost-effective so as to ensure global benefits at the lowest possible cost.'

[14] Preambular para 9 of the CBD reads: 'Noting also that where there is a threat of significant reduction or loss of biological diversity, lack of full scientific certainty should not be used as a reason for postponing measures to avoid or minimize such a threat.'

[15] See about the question of the precautionary principle as a norm of customary international law, Owen McIntyre and Thomas Mosedale, 'The Precautionary Principle as a Norm of Customary International Law' (1997) 9 Journal of Environmental Law 221.

## 4. The WTO: Legalization and Judicialization of Trade Liberalization—and Some Idea of Sustainable Development

After the Rio Conference, international law has seen quite some developments in the area of trade and the environment, which are relevant for international trade in GMOs and for the more general question as to a rise or decline of international law. The first such development certainly has been the establishment of the WTO[16] in 1995. The WTO importantly expanded and consolidated the international rulebook for world trade and added a strong institutional frame, including a highly effective and ambitious system of dispute settlement.[17] Building on the General Agreement on Tariffs and Trade 1947 (GATT 1947),[18] the WTO importantly expanded international law on trade, now covering some 400 pages of legal text in more than forty agreements, all integrated in the WTO framework of substantial law and the related institutional frame. These new rules improve existing GATT 1947 rules and cover new issues as, for instance, trade in services and intellectual property rights.[19] While the GATT 1947 had been operating on the basis of provisional application for more than four decades, complemented by some additional agreements with different and often poor membership,[20] the WTO and its rulebook were construed as a single undertaking. Parties, or precisely: 'members', have to accept the whole set of agreements as a bundle and fully ratify it. To the more, in contrast to the GATT 1947, which had 'borrowed' secretariat capacities from the UN, the WTO is a separate international organization with full legal status. Finally, the WTO dispute settlement system must be mentioned, which comprises a two-tier compulsory procedure, where panels—designated for each case—and the Appellate Body, a standing judiciary body hear complaints or appeals by WTO members and can decide without a veto option for disputing parties as existed before.[21] The rules on standing come close to an *actio popularis* in allowing

[16] Marrakesh Agreement Establishing the World Trade Organization (adopted 15 April 1994, entered into force 1 January 1995) 1867 UNTS 154.

[17] See for the establishment of the WTO, Peter-Tobias Stoll and Frank Schorkopf, *Max Planck Commentaries on World Trade Law - Volume 1: World Economic Order, World Trade Law* (Brill 2005) 11–30; Mitso Matsushita and others, *The World Trade Organization - Law, Practice and Policy* (3rd edn, OUP 2015) 9–11.

[18] General Agreement on Tariffs and Trade (adopted 30 October 1947, entered into force provisionally 1 January 1948) 55 UNTS 194.

[19] General Agreement on Tariffs and Trade 1994, Annex 1A to the Marrakesh Agreement Establishing the World Trade Organization (adopted 15 April 1994, entered into force 1 January 1995) 1867 UNTS 187; General Agreement on Trade in Services, Annex 1B to the Marrakesh Agreement Establishing the World Trade Organization (adopted 15 April 1994, entered into force 1 January 1995) 1869 UNTS 183; Agreement on Trade-Related Aspects of Intellectual Property Rights, Annex 1C to the Marrakesh Agreement Establishing the World Trade Organization (adopted 15 April 1994, entered into force 1 January 1995) 1869 UNTS 299.

[20] An overview of the GATT 1947 can be found in Ilka Neugärtner, 'GATT 1947' in Meinhard Hilf and Stefan Oeter (eds), *WTO-Recht, Rechtsordnung des Welthandels* (Nomos 2005) 77–86.

[21] About the Panel Process see Werner Zdouc, 'The Panel Process' in Patrick FJ Macrory, Arthur E Appleton, and Michael G Plummer (eds), *The World Trade Organization: Legal, Economic and Political Analysis - Volume I* (Springer 2005) 1233–73; with regard to the Appellate Body see Victoria Donaldson, 'The Appellate Body: Institutional and Procedural Aspects' in Patrick FJ Macrory, Arthur E Appleton, and Michael G Plummer (eds), *The World Trade Organization: Legal, Economic and Political Analysis - Volume I* (Springer 2005) 1279–335.

members to complain about violations of their fellow WTO members in the common interest.[22] Furthermore, the implementation of decisions is monitored by the dispute settlement institutions, which may even allow complaining parties to take 'trade sanctions', where defending parties fail to implement properly. So far, around 500 disputes have been settled in this way.

Even though the recent blockade of the WTO Appellate Body[23] has considerably damaged the system and doubtlessly constitutes a decline of international law in itself, the WTO can nevertheless still be seen as a remarkable step in the legalization and judicialization of international law in the area of trade. In this way, it could also be seen to importantly accommodate the principle of sustainable development. Indeed, the preamble of the WTO agreement largely reflects the principle of sustainable development in para 1, which reads:

> Recognizing that [the Parties'] relations in the field of trade and economic endeavour should be conducted with a view to raising standards of living, ensuring full employment and a large and steadily growing volume of real income and effective demand, and expanding the production of and trade in goods and services, while allowing for the optimal use of the world's resources in accordance with the objective of sustainable development, seeking both to protect and preserve the environment and to enhance the means for doing so in a manner consistent with their respective needs and concerns at different levels of economic development.

The preamble, which has been relied on in a number of decisions in dispute settlement, certainly can be seen as an incorporation of the Rio principle of sustainable development in a formal perspective and might in this perspective even be counted as a 'rise' in international law. However, it is quite clear that beyond these few disputes and a Committee on Trade and Environment, the WTO has little to offer to accommodate the principle in substantial terms. It is hardly equipped with mechanisms or meaningful institutions to effectively create synergies between trade and environmental protection, as called for by the principle of sustainable development. Overall, it is fair to conclude that in substantial perspective, the WTO serves importantly to strengthen one pillar of sustainable development only, which is economic development and thus can hardly be seen as accommodating the principle of sustainable development in its entirety.

In terms of a 'rise' of international law, it may be concluded that the explicit incorporation of the principle of sustainable development in the preamble of the WTO agreement adds to the body of binding international law in a formal perspective. However, in view of substance, this effect is likely to be very limited, as no more concrete rules, mechanisms, or procedures are at hand which could help to accommodate the principle. In a sense, the incorporation of 'sustainable development' in the preamble in general terms is a macro-level reinstatement, which lacks contextualization at the micro-level.

[22] See also Yuji Iwasawa, 'WTO Dispute Settlement as Judicial Supervision' (2002) 5 Journal of International Economic Law 287, 294.

[23] See Wayne Sandholtz, Chapter 3 in this book, Section 1.2.

## 5. Special WTO Rules on GMO Trade and the Precautionary Principle

In regard to trade in GMOs, the WTO contains specific rules on aspects of agricultural trade in its Agreement on Sanitary and Phytosanitary Measures (SPS), which might be more apt to help a Rio principle to effectively contribute to a rise of international law in substantial terms. The liberalization of trade in agricultural goods has been an essential element in the negotiation and conclusion of the WTO.[24] In fact, both, developing states and a number of agricultural exporting states such as the US, Canada, New Zealand, Australia, Brazil, and Argentina have been pushing for better access to foreign markets, in particular to the markets of the EU, Switzerland, and Japan. Access to those markets has traditionally been quite restricted to protect domestic farmers and/or to secure high standards on public health, consumer safety or environmental standards. Particularly contested were the EU policies on GMO imports, which effectively barred exports of a number of food crops.

The WTO Agreement on SPS[25] is seen as an important additional stronghold against protectionism, as it disciplines the use of certain measures for the protection of human, animal, and plant health.[26] To that end, it sets out a number of conditions, requirements, and procedures for the sanitary and phytosanitary measures. Most importantly, '[m]embers shall ensure that their sanitary or phytosanitary measures are based on an assessment, as appropriate to the circumstances, of the risks to human, animal or plant life or health', Article 5.1 SPS.

Also, '[in] the assessment of risks, Members shall take into account available scientific evidence', Article 5.2 SPS. They must 'take into account the objective of minimizing negative trade effects', Article 5.4 SPS, and 'shall ensure that such measures are not more trade-restrictive than required to achieve their appropriate level of sanitary or phytosanitary protection', Article 5.6 SPS. Even further, '[w]ith the objective of achieving consistency ... each Member shall avoid arbitrary or unjustifiable distinctions in the levels it considers to be appropriate in different situations, if such distinctions result in discrimination or a disguised restriction on international trade', Article 5.5 SPS.[27]

In accordance with the general focus of the WTO, the SPS agreement thereby clearly disciplines the exercise of a right to regulate. Most importantly it does so by requiring a high threshold of scientific certainty for taking restrictive measures.[28]

[24] See Matsushita and others (n 17) 251–98.

[25] Agreement on the Application of Sanitary and Phytosanitary Measures, Annex 1A to the Marrakesh Agreement Establishing the World Trade Organization (adopted April 15 1994, entered into force 1 January 1995) 1867 UNTS 493.

[26] See for an overview of the Agreement Denise Prévost and Peter Van den Bossche, 'The Agreement on the Application of Sanitary and Phytosanitary Measures' in Patrick FJ Macrory, Arthur E Appleton, and Michael G Plummer (eds), *The World Trade Organization: Legal, Economic and Political Analysis – Volume I* (Springer 2005) 231–370.

[27] About the limits and the SPS Agreement see Steve Charnovitz, 'The Supervision of Health and Biosafety Regulation by World Trade Rules' (2000) 13 Tulane Environmental Law Jounal 271.

[28] WTO, 'EC- Measures Concerning Meat and Meat Products (Hormones) - Report of the Appellate Body' (16 January 1998) WT/DS26/AB/R, WT/DS48/AB/R para 177 ('*EC-Hormones*'). See for the risk assessment in art 5 SPS Matsushita and others (n 17) 474–85.

As the case for detrimental environmental effects of GMOs is still disputed among scientists, trade restrictions in view of GMOs could hardly stand. This, however, is not the end of the story as the SPS agreement contains an additional rule, which envisages that '[i]n cases where relevant scientific evidence is insufficient, a member may provisionally adopt sanitary or phytosanitary measures on the basis of available pertinent information'.

Evidently, this alludes to the precautionary principle[29] as stated in Principle 15 of the Rio Declaration, which is about a 'lack of scientific certainty'. However, while Principle 15 states that 'lack of full scientific certainty shall not be used as a reason for postponing cost-effective measures to prevent environmental degradation', Article 5.7 SPS is about provisional measures only. Furthermore, the provision entails the obligation to 'seek to obtain the additional information necessary for more objective assessment of risk' and that 'the sanitary or phytosanitary measures [shall be reviewed] accordingly within a reasonable period of time'.[30]

As compared to Principle 15 of the Rio Declaration, Article 5.7 SPS thereby implicates a remarkable concept of precaution. It is obviously based on the understanding that a definite and complete scientific answer and justification for measures can be given and that the information necessary for an objective assessment can be produced in a certain amount of time. This understanding is remarkable because it implies that there can be scientific certainty, whereas many others maintain that scientific uncertainty is something which cannot be totally eliminated. Furthermore, the concept of Article 5.7 suggests that this kind of a scientific certainty can be achieved in every case by a certain amount of effort and time. The idea that scientific uncertainty may prevail for an unforeseeable amount of time is neglected. More clearly, this means that the justification for provisional measures will lapse after such reasonable time, if no new findings or information show up.[31]

From a 'rise of international law' point of view, Article 5.7 SPS is remarkable, as it goes beyond simply incorporating language of the Principle 15 of the Rio Declaration in adding substance by defining conditions, measures, and procedures. Indeed, it has the potential to make a more 'macro-level' principle work on the micro level of a well applicable and tightly drafted set of operational rules. However, as seen, Article 5.7 SPS employs a definitely more limited concept of precaution than is true for Principle 15 of the Rio Declaration. Article 5.7 SPS is situated in a trade context and clearly reflects the endeavour to open up markets and to curb national regulatory policies in this regard.

[29] '*EC-Hormones*' (n 28) para 124; Peter-Tobias Stoll and Lutz Strack 'Art. 5 SPS' in Rüdiger Wolfrum, Peter-Tobias Stoll, and Anja Seibert-Fohr (eds), *Max Planck Commentaries on World Trade Law – Volume 3: Technical Barriers and SPS Measures* (Brill 2007) 458–60.

[30] See for the limits Prévost and Van den Bossche (n 26) 306–8; Laowonsiri (n 8) 577–81.

[31] Stoll and Strack (n 29) 462; see for further critical points Andrew TF Lang, 'Provisional Measures under Article 5.7 of the WTO's Agreement on Sanitary and Phytosanitary Measures: Some Criticisms of the Jurisprudence so far' (2008) 42 Journal of World Trade 1085.

## 6. Precaution in Environmental Perspective: the Cartagena Protocol

Possibly also to correct this 'trade bias', initiatives were taken soon after to address quite a similar issue by way of an environmental agreement. Modern international environmental law includes a number of agreements, which provide for mechanisms to secure an informed decisions-making for imports of hazardous substances such as waste,[32] chemicals and pesticides,[33] and persistent organic pollutants.[34] Along these lines the Cartagena Protocol on Biosafety to the Convention on Biological Diversity (Cartagena Protocol) was concluded in 2000[35] on the basis a mandate contained in Article 19 para 3 of the CBD.[36]

The Cartagena Protocol acknowledges that the transboundary movements of living modified organisms—similar to GMOs[37]—involve a risk and calls upon parties to ensure that such risks are prevented or reduced. To this end, the Cartagena Protocol envisages that such transboundary movements shall take place on an advance informed agreement by the importing party to enable it to take an informed decision. The advance informed agreement procedure requires exporting parties or exporters to notify the importing parties' competent national authority prior to the movement of organisms. Parties to the agreement shall designate such authority[38] and are obliged to undertake a proper risk assessment before taking decisions.[39]

The precautionary principle plays a prominent role in the Cartagena Protocol and Principle 15 of the Rio Declaration is expressly referred to as the basis for the instrument as a whole[40] and in view of decision-making. Article 10.6 Cartagena Protocol reads:

[32] Basel Convention on the Control of Transboundary Movements of Hazardous Waste (adopted 22 March 1989, entered into force 5 May 1992) 1673 UNTS 57.

[33] Rotterdam Convention on the Prior Informed Consent Procedure for Certain Hazardous Chemicals and Pesticides in International Trade (adopted 10 September 1998, entered into force 24 February 2004) 2244 UNTS 337.

[34] Stockholm Convention on Persistent Organic Pollutants (adopted 22 May 2001, entered into force 17 May 2004) 2256 UNTS 119.

[35] For details of the negotiation history of the Cartagena Protocol, see Convention on Biological Diversity, Report of the Extraordinary Meeting of the Conference of the Parties for the Adoption of the Protocol on Biosafety to the Convention on Biological Diversity (20 February 2000) UNEP/CBD/ExCOP/1/3; Peter-Tobias Stoll, 'Controlling the Risks of Genetically Modified Organisms: The Cartagena Protocol on Biosafety and the SPS Agreement' (1999) 10 Yearbook of International Environmental Law 82, 86–87.

[36] Art 19 para 3 of the CBD reads: 'The Parties shall consider the need for and modalities of a protocol setting out appropriate procedures, including, in particular, advance informed agreement, in the field of the safe transfer, handling and use of any living modified organisms resulting from biotechnology that may have adverse effects on the conservation and sustainable use of biological diversity.'

[37] For a definition of the terms see Markus Böckenförde, *Grüne Gentechnik und Welthandel - Das Biosafety-Protokoll und seine Auswirkungen auf das Regime der WTO* (Springer 2004) 122, 148–52.

[38] Art 19 Cartagena Protocol on Biosafety.

[39] See about the risk assessment and the AIA-procedure, Cosima Erben, *Das Vorsorgeprinzip im Völkerrecht* (Duncker & Humblot 2005) 145–48, 150–52; Stoll 'Controlling the Risks of Genetically Modified Organisms' (n 35) 94–96; Böckenförde (n 37) 170–94.

[40] The Preamble of the Cartagena Protocol reads: 'Reaffirming the precautionary approach contained in Principle 15 of the Rio Declaration on Environment and Development.'

> Lack of scientific certainty due to insufficient relevant scientific information and knowledge regarding the extent of the potential adverse effects of a living modified organism on the conservation and sustainable use of biological diversity in the Party of import, taking also into account risks to human health, shall not prevent that Party from taking a decision, as appropriate, with regard to the import of the living modified organism ... in order to avoid or minimize such potential adverse effects.

This language fully reflects Principle 15 of the Rio Declaration. In terms of a 'rise' of international law, it must be noted from a formal point of view that again here the principle is translated into international treaty language. In view of substance, the Cartagena Protocol reflects the principle comprehensively. Also, chiefly by introducing the advance informed agreement procedure and requiring to establish a national competent authority, the Cartagena Protocol adds institutional and procedural detail for the principle to work in practice. Indeed, taken as such, the Cartagena Protocol contributes considerably to a 'rise'.

Even more and on first glance, it might appear as a welcome addition or completion of the WTO SPS agreement. Indeed, both rules have much in common and the various institutional and procedural elements of the Cartagena Protocol could well apply in parallel to the WTO rules. However, it must not be forgotten that there are differences in view of the approach to precaution. In line with its general orientation as a trade agreement, the SPS agreement clearly follows a much more restricted approach as to precaution and more generally in view of policy space for controlling imports of GMO. As an environmental agreement, the Cartagena Protocol is more open in this regard. In short, the Cartagena Protocol would allow for measures which may be prohibited under the SPS agreement. This gap between the agreements did hardly happen by accident. The political tension around the conclusion of the Cartagena Protocol is witnessed by the fact, that the United States, Canada, and Argentina—all agricultural exporting countries, where farmers extensively grow GMO crops—did refuse to sign or respectively ratify it.

In terms of a 'rise' of international law, the Cartagena Protocol may be seen as good news, because a great deal of states and the EU concluded international treaty provisions which fully accommodate Principle 15 of the Rio Declaration and go beyond the SPS agreement for the special, but highly relevant case of controls for the import of GMOs. On the other hand, all parties to the Cartagena Protocol are members of the WTO at the same time and remain bound to the WTO SPS agreement. Members to both agreements are obliged to observe them fully and to prevent conflicts, which could arise in a given case. Even after a remarkable report of the WTO panel in EU Biotech, the interrelationship between the two agreements is far from clear, as not least the ILC found in its report on the fragmentation on international law.

Seen in this perspective, the parties to the Cartagena Protocol, while aiming to make progress in signing Principle 15 into treaty law, did cause some fragmentation.[41] It would be difficult to speak of a 'rise of international law' in substantial terms without

[41] See for the relevance of fragmentation in this context Thomas Kleinlein, Chapter 4 in this book, Section 2.1 and Sandra Schwindenhammer, Chapter 16 in this book, Section 2.1.

considering the aspect of coherence in international law. Thus, the Cartagena Protocol may look much less than a 'rise' or even as a 'decline'.

## 7. The WTO *EC-Biotech* Panel

The conflicting views on precaution and trade in the area of GMOs came to dispute in 2003 when Argentina, Canada, and the United States initiated complaints in WTO dispute settlement.[42] *EC-Biotech*, as the dispute is called in WTO parlance, met with high flying expectations into the ability of a WTO panel to bridge the gap between those divergent legal developments and to give a coherent answer as to how the emerging principle of precaution could be coherently applied. In terms of a rise or decline of international law, the dispute has been seen as an opportunity to overcome the fragmentation between the two agreements.

In view of such expectations, the WTO panel report was a harsh disappointment. Possibly because the EU explicitly relied on it, the WTO panel addressed the Cartagena Protocol and the question whether it could and should be taken into account in the dispute.[43] The need to address this issue was far from obvious, as none of the complaining members were parties to the Cartagena Protocol. Nevertheless, the WTO panel extensively discussed the question whether the Cartagena Protocol should be taken into account in the interpretation of the WTO rules at hand according to Article 31 (3) lit. c of the VCLT.[44], [45] It concluded that for 'rules of international law applicable in the relations between the parties' to be taken into account in the interpretation of a treaty it would be necessary that all parties to the agreement to be interpreted—eg all WTO members—would also be parties to the agreement to be taken into account—that is the Cartagena Protocol.[46] In the case at hand, therefore, the WTO panel rejected to take the Cartagena Protocol into account as not all WTO members were parties to it.[47] As has surfaced soon after, this requirement can hardly ever be met in the case of the WTO, as next to states and regional economic integration organizations, WTO membership includes a number of what are called 'customs territories', such as Hong Kong and Taiwan, which hardly ever are parties to other international agreements. Most observers correctly interpreted this to mean that it would be practically impossible to get WTO dispute settlement to consider other agreements and that therefore the WTO would be in a situation of splendid isolation.[48] Also, the WTO panel rejected the EU's

[42] WTO, 'European Communities – Measures Affecting the Approval and Marketing of Biotech Products' (29 September 2006) WT/DS291/R, WT/DS292/R, WT/293/R ('*EC-Biotech*'); for an analysis of the case see Margaret A Young, 'The WTO's Use of Relevant Rules of International Law: An Analysis of the Biotech Case' (2007) 56 International & Comparative Law Quarterly 907.

[43] *EC-Biotech* (n 42) [7.49]–[7.96].

[44] Vienna Convention on the Law of Treaties (adopted 23 May 1969, entered into force 27 January 1980) 115 UNTS 331 (VCLT).

[45] *EC-Biotech* (n 42) [7.65]–[7.71].

[46] ibid [7.68]

[47] ibid [7.75]

[48] See with regard to the question also Lorenz Franken and Jan-Erik Burchardi, 'Beyond Biosafety – An Analysis of the EC-Biotech Panel Report' (2007) 62 Aussenwirtschaft 77, 81–84.

claim that Principle 15 of the Rio Declaration would already represent a rule of CIL, which would override Article 5.7 SPS.

In sum, *EC-Biotech* did not overcome the divide between Article 5.7 SPS and the Cartagena Protocol. Even more, it concluded in more general terms that environmental agreements could hardly ever be taken into account in the interpretation of WTO rules. With this, *EC-Biotech* added to fragmentation and could even be seen as an incident of decline in international law.

## 8. Conclusion

After the fall of the Berlin Wall, the Rio Conference of 1992 initiated a broad development of international law in the field of the economy and the environment. The principles contained in the legally non-binding Rio Declaration contributed to a rise of international law in various ways. At times, they have been taken up in international court decisions and some see them reflected in nascent or even already manifest rules of CIL. Also and importantly, the two aforementioned principles have driven the development of international treatymaking. Particularly the principle of sustainable development has been frequently referred to in agreements. Such incorporation of the principle adds to the body of international law and may be seen as a 'rise' in formal terms. Also, we might indeed understand the Rio Conference and related developments as having brought about a value change in that they helped to establish the value of sustainable development and of precaution in environmental matters. From this point of view, we can see the subsequent treatymaking and developments in CIL as a sort of legalization of these newly established values. However, as seen, the legalization of the value of precaution took place by way of two agreements with slightly conflicting treaty terms, which even became the subject of a dispute settlement procedure. This procedure hardly helped to reconcile the two diverging treaty provisions. In the end, the fragmentation remains and we are left in a situation of stagnation. We could understand the WTO contracting parties' version of precautionary principle in the SPS agreement as some sort of contestation of precaution as a value and see the Cartagena Protocol as a reaction, which in the end did not succeed. In this way, it is fair to doubt whether the value of precaution as initially established by the Rio Conference still stands. The unresolved disparities between the WTO SPS and the Cartagena Protocol norms and the state of ongoing fragmentation may fit into the picture if we consider, that the coherence of international law also plays a role and that incoherences occurring might also imply a norm change.

# PART IV
# CONCLUSION

# 18
# Conclusion
## Turbulence, Robustness, and Value Change

*Heike Krieger and Andrea Liese*

### 1. Introduction

'In shaping the new world order, controversies over sovereignty and non-interference, human rights, international criminal justice, climate change, and environmental protection, in the final analysis, are questions of values.'[1] This observation by Hanqin Xue, judge at the International Court of Justice (ICJ), exemplifies both the centrality of international law's value orientation and its inherent contestedness. New transnational problems such as the Covid-19 pandemic and the loss of biological diversity in the oceans call for global solutions that require states to (re)negotiate the priority of certain values within the international legal order. Plans for a global treaty on plastic pollution[2] and the draft agreement on marine biological diversity of areas beyond national jurisdiction[3] reflect the continuing demand to expand and deepen international law. These and other global challenges will likely only be tackled when the international community comes to agreement on foundational values.

However, legal change is not a one-way street. It does not always lead to more legal rules or to normative improvements, but it may also lead in the opposite direction: the legal effects of a treaty or a legal rule, such as the material, personal, or geographical scope of application, may be reduced, and the legal protection of values may even be removed. Over the past several years, challenges to international law have multiplied. States have withdrawn from or terminated treaties such as those on disarmament, thereby limiting the reach of legal obligations. Discursive attacks and obvious, sometimes blatant, violations of international legal norms, most notably in the 2022 Russian war against Ukraine, have put international law under stress.

Possible trajectories for international law point in various directions. Many tensions put the current international legal order under strain, and it remains unclear which direction it will take. We were therefore interested in exploring whether we are currently observing protracted turbulences, norm change, or a metamorphosis—that

[1] Hanqin Xue, 'Meaningful Dialogue Through a Common Discourse: Law and Values in a Multi-Polar World' (2011) 1 Asian Journal of International Law 13, 17.

[2] United Nations (UN) Environmental Assembly, Draft Resolution, 'End Plastic Pollution: Towards an International Legally Binding Instrument' (2 March 2022) UN Doc UNEP/EA.5/L.23/Rev.1.

[3] UN General Assembly (UNGA), 'Draft agreement under the United Nations Convention on the Law of the Sea on the conservation and sustainable use of marine biological diversity of areas beyond national jurisdiction' (4 March 2023) <https://www.un.org/bbnj/sites/www.un.org.bbnj/files/draft_agreement_advanced_unedited_for_posting_v1.pdf> accessed 8 March 2023.

Heike Krieger and Andrea Liese, *Conclusion* In: *Tracing Value Change in the International Legal Order*.
Edited by: Heike Krieger and Andrea Liese, Oxford University Press. © Heike Krieger and Andrea Liese 2023.
DOI: 10.1093/oso/9780192855831.003.0018

is, a more fundamental transformation—of international law, or whether this can be better characterized as a period of robustness.

For this purpose, the contributions in this book have systematically explored value change regarding specific international norms from the perspectives of international law and international relations (IR). As a yardstick and starting point for comparison, we used international law's function of protecting specific values and its value orientation during the 1990s, which is considered a historical high point of international law. We have argued that value change is a key indicator of metamorphosis: Since law serves to lock-in values, ie protect them from future policy choices, international law's value orientation constitutes one of its foundational features. Below, we present the book's main findings, identify and discuss drivers of change as well as hurdles to change, and consider the implications.

## 2. A Mixed Picture: Metamorphosis, Norm Change, Turbulences, but also Robustness

The central question of this book has been whether we are observing a period of fundamental transformation or metamorphosis (*Verwandlung*) of international law with potentially irreversible effects, whether this is a period of norm change *within* international law (*Wandel*), or whether it is a period of turbulence and ambivalence that will ultimately leave the value orientation of international law unaffected. A metamorphosis would require that more is changing than a single legal norm or a specific international institution. Accordingly, the case studies in this book focused on changes in political and legal discourse and social and legal practices and assessed whether these changes affect the underlying values and/or the social and legal validity of the respective norms. By examining these findings together, we are now able to better understand the types of change that are currently taking place.

In the introduction to this book, we proposed several ways to conceive of a genuine metamorphosis of international law. In addition, we explained why we suggest focusing on foundational paradigm shifts that occur when the values protected by international law change either in substance or in legal or social validity. This would include shifts in the prioritization of these values, and the extreme case in which the idea of legally protecting such values itself is dismissed. We argue that to understand value change, three elements must be examined: the value protected by a legal norm, its legal validity, and its social validity. Metamorphosis may be set in motion when a change occurs in more than one of the foundational values of international law:

> First, the value protected by a legal norm may change (*substantial value change*). Second, the institutionalization of a value, that is, the degree to which it is legally protected, may change (*change in the legal status of a value*). Third, even if legally protected values do not change in the formal sense, they may lose their social validity and, thus, lose their power to structure actors' behaviour (*social validity decline*).

The widely discussed end of the liberal international order seems to imply that we are indeed witnessing a more fundamental transformation of international law and the values it protects. After all, the ideational entanglement of liberal thinking, mainstream human rights conceptions, and the idea of the rule of law suggests that they share the same fate.[4] However, the chapters in this book draw a much more differentiated picture of an ambivalent situation that is oscillating between metamorphosis, norm change, turbulence, and robustness. While certain norms and the values they protect have changed either in substance or legal or social validity, in other cases, legal norms seem to be more robust than many observers may have anticipated.

The case studies in this book (Chapters 6 to 17) examined value change in the foundational norms of the post-1945 order and in norms representing the rise of the international legal order post-1990. The norms that were the focus of the case studies include:

- the prohibition of torture and the protection of women's rights as two core human rights norms protecting fundamental values such as physical integrity and gender equality;
- the prohibition of the use of force as well as the non-proliferation of nuclear weapons as two core norms related to international peace and security;
- sustainability norms and accountability for core international crimes as two norms that were institutionalized mainly after the Cold War. The latter norm's protection by the International Criminal Court (ICC) represents 'the golden age of international courts'.

The case studies provide evidence of several ongoing value changes. They identify a *decline in the social validity* of values prohibiting the use of force and promoting gender equality,[5] but disagree on whether the value change has been substantial in both cases. The studies agree that sustainability norms are undergoing either *substantial value change* or a *change in legal status*. The evidence shows that more than one of international law's foundational values and that more than one element of these values has been affected, but the authors disagree about the extent of the observable value change. In sum, while the case studies show that a metamorphosis is underway, the exact state of that metamorphosis remains controversial.

At the same time, not all of the cases analysed in this book show evidence of value change. The values underlying the prohibition of torture, for instance, have proven quite robust, and other norms have also not changed considerably over time. In the case of non-impunity norms and accountability, a protected value in international criminal justice and one advanced by the ICC, it might still be too early to say whether the values are changing or robust. Furthermore, the values underlying the nuclear non-proliferation treaty (NPT) have not changed either in social validity or in legal status. However, there are indications that the priority accorded to specific values is shifting in case of the ICC and the NPT.

[4] Kleinlein, Chapter 4 in this book.

[5] See, however, Kuhlmann, Chapter 15 in this book, who stresses that contestations of women's rights are ongoing with uncertain outcome.

In Section 2.1 below, we discuss several instances of identifiable value change, and in Section 2.2, we summarize the findings on one instance of clear robustness and several ambiguous instances of change.

## 2.1 Instances of Value Change

Several contributions to this book identify value change in one of the three dimensions outlined above. The *prohibition of the use of force* is a case where the authors agree on the value's unchanged legal status despite a decline in its social validity. The authors do not agree, however, on the question of substantial value change. Reinold argues that the established narrow reading of the right to self-defence was given up after the 9/11 attacks and subsequent shift in attitudes and interventionist state practice. While she acknowledges that many voices in the international legal literature hold otherwise, she points to 'the lack of efforts at justification and the absence of demands for such justifications [that] could be another indicator that the defensive use of force on the soil of states harbouring terrorists is increasingly seen as non-controversial'.[6] Thus, Reinold describes a social validity decline accompanied by substantial value change where the scope of a prohibition—the non-use of force—is reduced by an expansive reading of an exception. Applying the three dimensions of value change outlined above to the law of self-defence, she finds that 'indeed profound changes are taking place. As the restrictive, sovereignty-friendly interpretation of Article 51 had lost its social validity . . ., the right to self-defence subsequently underwent a broadening that Krieger and Liese would describe as substantive value change'.[7] While Burra agrees that 'there are indications that the law on the right of self-defence has either undergone or is undergoing change', he argues that there is 'no unambiguous change in the law accommodating the right of self-defence against non-state actors'[8] and that only few actors contribute to a limited practice. While 'proponents of this change continue to sway the discourse,'[9] he points to the Third World perspective and formulates a textual and doctrinal critique emphasizing that 'the treaty law position on the use of force and self-defence has remained static in the form of United Nations (UN) Charter and still does not expressly provide for this right'.[10] Contrasting both chapters reveals that, in itself, the assessment of a substantial value change is a matter of ongoing contestation.

In the case of *women's rights*, Roggeband finds indications of a loss of social validity of the legally protected value of gender equality, while Kuhlmann sees this value as more robust and argues that women's rights, especially reproductive rights, have been contested since they were first placed on the international agenda. Whereas Kuhlmann focuses on observable outcomes, particularly in the legal status of values, Roggeband focuses on process. She points our attention to a transnational coalition of conservative and religious actors that have contested women's rights and mobilized

[6] Reinold, Chapter 8 in this book, p. 141.
[7] ibid., p. 151.
[8] Burra, Chapter 9 in this book, p. 168.
[9] ibid, p. 168.
[10] ibid., p. 168.

against them at the transnational and national level since the mid-1990s. This coalition rejects gender equality as a foundational value in human rights law and promotes alternative values instead. While this is an ongoing process, it means that those actors who promote women's rights need to shift the focus of their efforts from expanding the implementation of the Beijing Declaration to safeguarding its legal status and protecting the underlying values.[11]

The authors of the case studies on women's rights disagree about the effects of these developments. Kuhlmann argues that discursive and behavioural contestations have long been part of the move to protect the value of gender equality. In this respect, she discusses the high number of reservations to pertinent treaties, particularly regarding women's reproductive rights, and points to the persistent strategies of those contesting women's rights. Consequently, she finds it 'difficult to attest to a change regarding women's rights and gender equality. Rather, they remain suspended between advances and regresses, a constant back and forth'.[12]

Roggeband invites us to look closely at differences in legal and social validity. In her analysis, the development of women's rights cannot be understood as a process of alternating expansion and retraction. Instead, she paints a more ambiguous picture of policies masquerading as reforms and cases of symbolic compliance. An emphasis on the legal validity of norms and their underlying values may give the impression that norms are resilient and will foster a transformative process that will ultimately enshrine and protect the underlying value. However, in light of democratic backsliding and a diminishing civic space for women's rights defenders, Roggeband warns of 'an erosion of women's rights at the national level'[13] that may spill over to the international level.

*Sustainability norms* are encountering substantial value change or a decline in legal validity as they are being played off against other norms or interpreted restrictively. Schwindenhammer analyses the effects of contestation over the risk-benefit assessment of genetically modified (GM) insect technology. She stresses the dangerous potential of contestations: they can hinder agreement on the content of legal rules and regulatory capacities in cases where new technological developments trigger further norm development because the existing rules and principles no longer fit and must be adapted. This adaptation may increase uncertainties about the content of norms, and these uncertainties are further aggravated by the complexities of the respective legal regimes. When mandates differ, the international organizations (IOs) that are involved may take different approaches that are difficult to reconcile because international law does not provide formal mechanisms for alignment. Moreover, the public and private actors involved may differ widely in their capacities and access to contestations that favour private companies from the Global North over local stakeholders. As Schwindenhammer stresses, 'unequal levels of knowledge and knowledge gaps inhibit norm contestation on an equal footing and involve the risk of excluding local and traditional perspectives in norm dynamics'.[14] All this may prompt a restrictive reading

[11] Roggeband, Chapter 14 in this book.
[12] Kuhlmann, Chapter 15 in this book, p. 285.
[13] Roggeband, Chapter 14 in this book, p. 268.
[14] Schwindenhammer, Chapter 16 in this book, p. 300.

of the precautionary principle and undermine the value of sustainable development that was established at the Rio Conference in 1990.

Stoll shares the findings on the ambivalent effects of regime complexity or fragmentation in protecting the value of sustainable development through the precautionary principle. Focusing on trade in genetically modified organisms, Stoll observes an erosion of the precautionary principle and its underlying value of sustainable development due to a process of fragmentation. The principle is included, mutatis mutandis, in both the World Trade Organization (WTO) Agreement on Sanitary and Phytosanitary Measures, and the Cartagena Protocol. In the *EC-Biotech* case, despite a formal and institutionalized procedure, the WTO panel could not limit the fragmentation effects, since it refused to rely on the Cartagena Protocol for interpreting the pertinent WTO rules. The decision may indicate a shift in the prioritization of values and thus contribute to an erosion in the legal validity or legal status of the precautionary principle: 'We could understand the WTO contracting parties' version of the precautionary principle in the SPS agreement as some sort of contestation of precaution as a value and see the Cartagena Protocol as a reaction, which in the end did not succeed. In this way, it is fair to doubt whether the value of precaution as initially established by the Rio Conference still stands.'[15]

## 2.2 Norms at the Intersection Between Robustness and Ambiguous Modification

A few contributions to this book show that legal and non-legal norms have remained robust despite contestation and crisis and thus continue to protect an underlying value. The only clear cut case concerns the *prohibition of torture. Lesch and Zimmermann* find that the international torture prohibition has not been weakened, despite the use and justification of torture by the United States after the 9/11 attacks and the challenges made by other states such as Israel. They analyse potential norm and value change in four dimensions of practice and discourse. They find that, first, the presence of torture has remained surprisingly constant between 1990 and 2010. Second, the prohibition of torture has been integrated to an increasing degree into domestic law. Third, states have increasingly ratified treaties prohibiting torture and, in the 2000s, criticized other states for their reservations. In addition, states have affirmed this norm in their statements in the UN General Assembly, particularly after 2001, when the United States began explicitly challenging the prohibition's applicability. Fourth, states have responded by condemning norm violations, both in general and in the specific cases of the United States and Israel. Lesch and Zimmermann conclude that 'the strength of the international torture prohibition did not change—at least not for the worse'.[16] Steiger also finds no evidence of legal or social validity decline and writes that 'the prohibition of torture is highly robust'.[17] First, the United States, as a norm challenger, has not declared the prohibition obsolete, nor has it been able to change the

[15] Stoll, Chapter 17 in this book, p. 316.
[16] Lesch and Zimmermann, Chapter 6 in this book, p. 102.
[17] Steiger, Chapter 7 in this book, p. 119.

definition of torture, nor has it questioned the duties of investigating and prosecuting torture. Second, the chapter finds no change in interpretation or in *opinio iuris*. Third, there have been various attempts by third states to reaffirm the torture prohibition, for example, by states opening public inquiries into US torture cases. Taken together, there are no signs of substantial value change, change in legal status, or social validity decline. Overall, the 'prohibition is alive and well and remains unchanged' and 'cannot serve as an example for value change and the metamorphosis of international law'.[18]

While this norm has remained robust, others have been modified slightly but still preserve the underlying value, at least in principle. An example of a norm whose fate remains in flux is the *anti-impunity norm* advanced by the ICC. Both Bower and Jorgensen identify a gradual narrowing in the value of accountability that may be seen as a minor change in the legal status of the norm. According to Bower, the exemption of acting heads of state from this norm has gained acceptance, but without destroying the legally protected value of accountability. Like the norm of women's rights, the anti-impunity norm has been contested since its inception, but the number of states contesting it, the nature of the contestation, and the degree of transnational opposition differ. In the case of women's rights, the value of gender equality was rejected almost as soon as it was enshrined in law, and those opposed to this norm formed strong alliances. In the case of the anti-impunity norm, however, there was wide-ranging agreement over the establishment of the ICC, with only a few actors voicing opposing views. Even when one sees some of the contestations as implying a foundational rejection, the relevant actors have failed to create an overarching coalition outside the African Union. Moreover, 'even the contesting states themselves continue to officially reaffirm their commitment to ending impunity—albeit under revised conditions'.[19] According to Bower, until 2018, the analysed ICC contestations had rather led to a 'gradual and informal narrowing of the anti-impunity norm to recognise some exceptions'.[20] Bower concludes by reminding critics that the non-impunity norm 'retains aspirational appeal in the contemporary international system'.[21]

Jorgensen identifies stronger signs that value change is already underway with regard to the ICC and the value of accountability. He focuses on another incident of a gradual narrowing, with 'shifting assertions of ICC jurisdiction over US personnel in the Afghanistan investigation'.[22] The concern here lies in the unequal enforcement of accountability towards US citizens. Again, the dispute over the court's authority to adjudicate US citizens goes back to the time of the ICC's establishment. It has been ongoing ever since and seems to now have been decided in favour of the US position—fostering yet again the perception of double standards being applied in international law. Overall, his impression is that a 'more complex, potentially subversive process' is underway, 'in which Court personnel are guided by particularistic yet sincerely held conceptions of accountability'.[23] As Jorgensen predicts, if 'the turn to ICC pragmatism

18 ibid., pp. 135 and 135.
19 Bower, Chapter 10 in this book, p. 189.
20 ibid., p. 190.
21 ibid., p. 190.
22 Jorgensen, Chapter 11 in this book, p. 192.
23 ibid., p. 209.

stabilizes as a trend . . ., that may ultimately signal a change in the substantive meaning of "accountability" as a protected value in international criminal justice'.[24]

Another case in which recurrent contestations have not yet led to value change is the NPT regime. Tokhi acknowledges that non-compliance does not automatically translate into norm or value change, but questions whether this holds for security treaties in general and the NPT in particular: 'Running a secret nuclear weapons program or ignoring NPT safeguards is a major threat to the NPT's stability'.[25] Non-compliance 'has the potential to weaken the NPT's normative fabric and its underlying values'[26] and undermine the norm against the possession of nuclear weapons. Analysing varying compliance behaviour of authoritarian states and norm defenders' responses, he finds that 'the central NPT norms are not eroding in the sense of losing their social or legal validity'.[27]

Sossai stresses that, with its review conferences, the NPT regime provides a forum specifically designed to allow member states to voice their criticism. The proposals put forward by most of the non-nuclear-weapon states (NNWS) do not contest either specific treaty rules or the underlying values but aim to push for compliance, particularly with the obligation of nuclear weapon states (NWS) under Article VI of the NPT to pursue negotiations on disarmament in good faith. Yet the lack of any meaningful effort to negotiate nuclear weapons disarmament has pushed the NNWS, except for the North Atlantic Treaty Organization allies, to pursue the goal of disarmament through other channels, notably through the Treaty on the Prohibition of Nuclear Weapons (TPNW). While the TPNW reemphasizes the legal protection of disarmament norms and underlying values of peace and security, it also shifts the emphasis to core humanitarian values. The question of whether this implies a weakening of the NPT is contested. On the one hand, by referring to the NPT in its preamble, the TPNW aims to reconcile both treaties. On the other hand, creating a stronger legal taboo against the use of nuclear weapons may exceed the objectives of the NPT and weaken the safeguards regime, as member states claim.[28] Sossai concludes that, ultimately, 'changes in the priority of values within the international community might have an impact in determining a new balance of general principles, with a further prevalence those of humanitarian nature'.[29]

## 3. Drivers for Change

How and why do the values of the international legal order change? Our framework[30] suggested several challenges to the international legal order. Which of these challenges have indeed been drivers of change affecting the international legal order?

[24] Jorgensen, Chapter 11 in this book, p. 209.
[25] Tokhi, Chapter 12 in this book, p. 222.
[26] ibid p. 212.
[27] ibid., p. 232.
[28] Sossai, Chapter 13 in this book, p. 243.
[29] ibid., p. 251.
[30] Krieger and Liese, Chapter 1 in this book, Section 4.4.

## 3.1 Exceptionalism, Populism, Autocratization, and the Increasing Contestation of Norms and Underlying Values

The chapters in our book demonstrate that states are engaging to an increasing degree in norm contestation, non-compliance, norm antipreneurship, and even norm sabotage, in which state actors resist or even obstruct international law.[31] When and how do states engage in these actions? In the following, we will first summarize the findings on factors such as national interests during the war on terror, changing long-term foreign policy beliefs, and the rise in populism and autocracy before discussing the most common strategies the actors involved use.

What unites the relevant cases is that international norms and their underlying values are challenged, if not attacked, because they conflict with domestic policies, national or local values, self-perceptions and identities.

The post-9/11 interests, policies, and practices that comprise the so-called war on terror have jeopardized significant parts of the international legal order.[32] Several chapters in this volume show how a single powerful state, the United States, has attacked the same international legal norms it helped to shape and that it now deems to contravene its own national interests in the fight against terrorism. The United States advances what Sandholtz has called 'anti-norm arguments' and engages in what others have called norm antipreneurship, that is, resistance to the implementation of norms.[33] In the so-called war on terror, the United States has challenged norms such as the prohibition of torture and the general prohibition of the use of force and has done so both discursively and through non-compliant behaviour.[34] While the United States contestation did not change the prohibition against torture, its efforts to widen exceptions to the prohibition of the use of force and non-intervention have had a stronger impact.

Beyond national security interests, domestic values 'at the level of the foreign policy beliefs of the states and policymakers'[35] also threaten legal norms. The dispute about the ICC's jurisdiction over US soldiers is a particularly pertinent case in point. Here, the United States does not directly contest the value of non-impunity and justice but instead insists that it should be exempted from the pertinent international legal rules. The United States argues, first, that its national legal system already ensures accountability and, second, that other states abuse international legal fora to propagate anti-American sentiment. US exceptionalism—the belief that it is unique in the international legal system—strongly determines its strategic approach to international law.[36]

[31] For a distinction between norm antipreneurs as actors 'who seek to prevent a new norm from being accepted and/or implemented' and norm saboteurs as 'those who oppose an already accepted norm and seek to obstruct other actors' collective efforts to adhere to this norm and thereby seek to undo the normative status quo', see Andrea Schneiker, 'Norm Sabotage: Conceptual Reflection on a Phenomenon That Challenges Well-Established Norms' (2021) 22 International Studies Perspectives 106, 107.

[32] Helen Duffy, *The 'War on Terror' and the Framework of International Law* (2nd edn, CUP 2015).

[33] Alan Bloomfield, 'Norm Antipreneurs and Theorising Resistance to Normative Change' (2016) 42 Review of International Studies 310; Alan Bloomfield and Shirley Scott (eds), *Norm Antipreneurs and the Politics of Resistance to Global Normative Change* (Routledge 2018).

[34] See Chapter 6 by Lesch and Zimmermann; Chapter 8 by Reinold, and Chapter 9 by Burra, in this book.

[35] Jorgensen, Chapter 11 in this book, p. 207.

[36] ibid., p. 196.

The authors in this volume find evidence that less powerful states also contest legal norms or the authority of the very institution that safeguards the norm, as the example of contestation by several African states and the African Union against the ICC shows. These states have opposed cooperation with ICC investigations and have accused the ICC of Western bias and unfair treatment of states from the Global South. Thus, exceptionalism and exemptionalism of hegemonic powers may, in turn, encourage contestations from less powerful states.

The persistence of (traditional) domestic value conceptions in the face of international norms that 'require deep regime change'—for instance, the norm of gender equality—offers another explanation for why states may act as norm antipreneurs or norm saboteurs. Domestic value conceptions 'are embedded in social systems that link and structure ideas and practices and tend to reproduce themselves'.[37] The profound societal change that international legal norms require is bound to face resistance, to affect internal power relations, and to depend on far-reaching alteration of established processes.

The rise of populism and the growth of autocratic regimes also affect how states position themselves in relation to the international legal order. In the case of populism, identity mobilization and proclaimed national value conceptions operate as drivers of norm and value change. Populist governments use holistic exclusionary identity politics to foster anti-elitist and anti-pluralist attitudes.[38] Claiming that they are championing the people's interests, they discredit and weaken important values and institutions of the international legal order, including civil liberties, minority rights, and the European Union.[39] In their contestations, populist governments refer to and promote international legal rules that centre around state sovereignty and the *domaine réservé*.[40] In the case of women's rights, democratic backsliding has been accompanied by a shrinking space for civil society: policy changes, reallocations of funds, and other legislative measures promote heteronormative values.[41] The effect of these contestations is an increase in strategically formed alliances.

The war against Ukraine has renewed scholarly and public awareness that regime type has a significant impact on states' attitudes toward international law and their intentions to either preserve, instrumentalize, or erode it.[42] The recent trend toward democratic decline poses a particularly severe challenge to the international (legal) order. In 2021, after a decade of autocratization, a record number of 33 countries were autocratizing and 70 per cent of the world's population was living in an autocracy, reverting the level of democracy enjoyed by the average citizen back to 1989 levels.[43]

[37] Roggeband, Chapter 14 in this book, p. 254.

[38] Jan-Werner Müller, *What Is Populism?* (University of Pennsylvania Press, 2016) 3.

[39] Georg Löfflmann, 'Introduction to Special Issue: The Study of Populism in International Relations' (2022) 24 The British Journal of Politics and International Relations 403.

[40] Heike Krieger, 'Populist Governments and International Law' (2019) 30 European Journal of International Law 971, 984.

[41] Roggeband, Chapter 14 in this book.

[42] Tom Ginsburg, 'Authoritarian International Law?' (2020) 114 American Journal of International Law 221; Maria J Debre, 'The Dark Side of Regionalism: How Regional Organizations Help Authoritarian Regimes to Boost Survival' (2021) 28 Democratization 394.

[43] Vanessa A Boese and others 'State of the world 2021: autocratization changing its nature?' (published online 23 May 2022) Democratization 2.

However, as Tokhi argues, not all autocracies share the same attitudes. In the case of the NPT, the distribution of power between the autocratic leader and the ruling elite is decisive: a balanced and stable power distribution serves as a domestic barrier to unlimited discretion and, thereby, creates a more compliance-friendly environment. In the case of the NPT, 'dictatorships with few internal decision-making constraints are more likely to proliferate than other regime types'.[44]

Although populist, autocratic, and exceptionalist actors differ in many ways, they use many of the same strategies. One strategy combines a rejection of a particular norm interpretation with a rejection of the jurisdiction or authority of the norm-interpreting or norm-protecting institution, that is, a court or a treaty body. Our contributions show how the US government, populist Eastern European governments, and several autocracies employ behavioural and discursive forms of contestation when interacting with the ICC or with the treaty bodies responsible for the antitorture norm or women's rights. In some cases, they still do so after previously expressing disagreement with a treaty or some of its provisions. This contestation or resistance comes in the form of valid or invalid reservations to specific norms in a treaty, non-ratification after signature, non-accession where certain political expectations about accession exist, or withdrawal or announcements of a pending withdrawal. In cases of reservations, room for value change is created by legal ambiguities about who has the authority to decide on the validity of a reservation. Whereas non-accession or withdrawal are legally permissible and can therefore be deemed legitimate, these practices nonetheless contribute to diminishing the applicability of treaty norms and may exert negative political effects. But even after ratification, commitment may be symbolic and norm diffusion may be hampered. As Jorgensen explains with regard to the ICC's jurisdiction over US soldiers, 'competing conceptions of underlying values' continue to erode the overall objectives of the fight against impunity.[45] Correspondingly, the case of women's rights and the case of precaution and sustainable development both indicate that processes of contestation that do not end in agreement may at some point drive delegalization.

Another strategy is to mobilize counter-norms and competing values. Since international law protects diverging values, this strategy can be used within the legal system. Sovereignty, sovereign equality, state consent, and non-interference can be used to justify a restrictive reading of a prohibition or an expansive reading of its exceptions and to thereby contest certain values of the international community. Actors may employ such strategies to shift the prioritization of values within the international legal order and thus to mask the resulting erosion of norms. This has been done, for instance, to contest the ICC and to promote exceptions for acting heads of state. In the case that other conflicting values are not explicitly covered by international law, actors need to claim that these values should be part of the body of law or that the existing laws contain the basis for a new interpretation of these values. The counter-framing strategy of conservative alliances, which pit traditional values against women's rights, is a case in point.

[44] Tokhi, Chapter 12 in this book, pp. 224 and 213.
[45] Jorgensen, Chapter 11 in this book, p. 201.

A further strategy to change international legal norms and their underlying values is overt non-compliance. When non-compliance directly undermines the very objective of a legal regime and impacts the stability of the international order, non-compliance becomes a relevant driver of norm erosion and value change. This is particularly evident in the case of the NPT, where non-compliance 'can directly threaten international peace and security'.[46] Because of the interdependencies between the rules enshrined in the NPT and the importance of trust to legitimate the regime, non-compliance with one rule impacts the entire treaty.[47]

### 3.2 Changes in the Political Environment: Shocks and Power Shifts

Some of the contributions to this book have identified shocks as a central driver of value change. A severe crisis or shock may upset the previously existing balance between legal norms and the values they protect. The dissonances it creates may also open up new political space and offer opportunities for action.[48] Several of the contributions identify the 9/11 attacks as such a shock.[49]

The fact that shocks and crises play such an important role as drivers of norm change may be seen as one of the weaknesses of the international (legal) order. Given that shocks tend to be rare and actors may miss the opportunity to spur change, the window of opportunity for change remains small.[50] Judge Hilary Charlesworth's criticism of international lawyers for focusing on crises as 'the engine of progressive development' is well known. She fears that due to the selectivity of a narrowly crisis-focused approach, it provides only a limited understanding of what is unfolding, misses broader structural challenges, and ignores 'the politics of everyday life'.[51] Moreover, where norm change only occurs as a result of a crisis or a severe shock, the legal responses may come too late to address the new challenges effectively, as the example of climate change appears to show. It will remain a question for further research whether the seeming crescendo of crises over the last two decades—including the financial crisis, the Mediterranean refugee crisis, the climate crisis, the Covid-19 pandemic, and the Russian aggression against Ukraine—reflects the inappropriateness of earlier efforts to reform and adapt the pertinent legal regimes, or whether it is indicative of efforts to redefine events in crisis language to push for legal reforms.

Technological innovation may also be seen as a form of an external shock to a system, but it works through a different pathway. As Schwindenhammer argues in her Chapter 16, synthetic biotechnology innovation challenges previous rules, sometimes rendering them obsolete. The introduction of GM insect technology, for instance, was hailed by some as a welcome alternative to (environmentally harmful) chemical

46 Tokhi, Chapter 12 in this book, p. 212.

47 Tokhi, Chapter 12 in this book; Sossai, Chapter 13 in this book.

48 Reinold, Chapter 8 in this book; see also Paul Diehl and Charlotte Ku, *The Dynamics of International Law* (CUP 2010) 155.

49 See the Chapter 6 by Lesch and Zimmermann; Chapter 7 by Steiger; Chapter 8 by Reinold, in this book.

50 Diehl and Ku (n 48) 157.

51 Hilary Charlesworth, 'International Law: A Discipline of Crisis' (2002) 65 The Modern Law Review 377, 382, 389, and 391.

insecticides, but politicians and scientists warned of unintended environmental and health risks and of a potential monopoly of ownership rights. In this case, norm entrepreneurs and antipreneurs demanded a rebalancing of older and newer regulations, which means contesting established norms. The non-simultaneity of technological developments and social and legal responses to them further intensifies the pressure on legal values. Typically, technical innovation occurs faster than legal change.

Power shifts, that is, changes in the political environment, also affect legal norms. Previous research in the fields of international law and IR has focused primarily on the changes in the distribution of political power that occurred with the end of the Cold War or the rise of China. However, none of the legal norms analysed by the contributors to this book seems to have been directly affected by China's changing role in international relations or the corresponding geopolitical shifts. The impression of China's lacking impact is likely the consequence of our case selection. Observers have argued that China acts as a norm entrepreneur or norm antipreneur only in those areas of international law where its national interests are directly affected, particularly the Law of the Sea.[52]

Moreover, the diffusion of power and agency among diverse non-state actors proves to be a major driver of change. In addition to states, non-state actors frequently act as norm entrepeneurs, antipreneurs, or even as norm saboteurs. Chapter 8 by Roggeband demonstrates to what extent the space for progressive NGOs acting as norm entrepreneurs is shrinking. At the same time, numerous NGOs that have only recently arrived on the scene are forming conservative strategic alliances aiming to erode previously agreed rules that protect legal values. In addition, the rise in the authority of private actors also affects international norm dynamics. For example, the private company Oxitec is a dominant norm entrepreneur in GM insect technology. While state action remains decisive for the creation of legal norms, the latter case demonstrates that in the process of changing legal norms, private actors can exert substantial influence, for instance, when there is an asymmetry in the distribution of knowledge, access to knowledge, and the means of spreading it.[53]

### 3.3 The Ambiguous Role of Fragmentation and Regime Interplay

The increasing proliferation of norms and rules at the global and regional level and the expansion of mandates of international and regional organizations[54] have led to a fragmentation of rule systems and international law and an overlap of previously separated spheres of authority and related norms and values.[55] While institutional

[52] Robert D Williams, 'International Law with Chinese Characteristics: Beijing and the "Rules-Based" Global Order' (October 2020) <https://www.brookings.edu/wp-content/uploads/2020/10/FP_20201012_international_law_china_williams.pdf> accessed 15 July 2022.

[53] Schwindenhammer, Chapter 16 in this book.

[54] See, for example, Nina Hall, *Displacement, Development, and Climate Change: International Organizations Moving Beyond Their Mandates* (Routledge 2016).

[55] Karen J Alter and Kal Raustiala, 'The Rise of International Regime Complexity' (2018) 14 Annual Review of Law and Social Science 329; Christian Kreuder-Sonnen and Michael Zürn, 'After Fragmentation: Norm Collisions, Interface Conflicts, and Conflict Management' (2020) 9 Global Constitutionalism 241.

complexity results from 'a calculated strategy by powerful states to create a legal order that . . . closely reflects their interests',[56] it is believed to hinder the effectiveness of individual rules, if not governance in general.[57]

The literature conceptualizes this phenomenon as a regime complex, defined as 'nested, partially overlapping and parallel international regimes that are not hierarchically ordered'[58] and 'that continuously affect each other's operations'.[59] A core argument advanced in the regime complexity literature is that, in the absence of a central authority, increasing institutional density heightens the potential for collisions between rules, norms, and underlying values in a given issue area. States may exploit this fragmentation by choosing the forum that best furthers their interests by engaging in practices such as forum shopping[60] or regime shifting.[61]

The adoption of the TPNW is an example of forum shopping and demonstrates the ambiguity of regime interplay. In view of the non-compliance of NWS with Article VI of the NPT and their unwillingness to enter into serious negotiations about disarmament, NNWS used other fora, in particular the UN General Assembly and the International Committee of the Red Cross (ICRC), to increase political pressure on NWS to comply with their obligations by establishing a countervailing obligation not only to disarm but to abolish nuclear weapons entirely. Forum-shifting also made it possible to bring alternative values to the fore: with the ICRC as a key actor, there were new grounds for the humanitarian objective of prohibiting nuclear weapons that were not expressly included in the NPT, which mainly protected values of international peace and security.[62] Whether this development represents an erosion of the NPT and endangers the regime, as claimed by NWS, whether it is a push toward a normatively more desirable legal evolution, or whether it will simply continue in a stalemate remains to be seen.

Different forums emphasize different norms and may advocate for different norm interpretations, leading to conflicts between states or to norm collisions, that is, instances where more than one norm is applicable but the behavioural prescriptions of these norms are mutually incompatible.[63] Many international norms are vague; others are contradictory.[64] The human rights regime may serve as an example of within-regime tensions; tensions between norms on trade and sustainable development exemplify tensions between different norm clusters. This ambiguity, as Roggeband argues, not only 'facilitates the spread of international norms to different places and arenas

[56] Eyal Benvenisti and George W Downs, 'The Empire's New Clothes: Political Economy and the Fragmentation of International Law' (2007) 60 Standford Law Review 595, 597–98.

[57] Daniel W Drezner, 'The Power and Peril of International Regime Complexity' (2009) 7 Perspectives on Politics 65.

[58] Karen J Alter and Sophie Meunier, 'The Politics of International Regime Complexity' (2009) 7 Perspectives on Politics 13, 14.

[59] Thomas Gehring and Benjamin Faude, 'The Dynamics of Regime Complexes: Microfoundations and Systemic Effects' (2013) 19 Global Governance 119, 121.

[60] Drezner (n 57).

[61] Laurence R Helfer, 'Regime Shifting: The TRIPs Agreement and New Dynamics of International Intellectual Property Lawmaking' (2004) 29 The Yale Journal of International Law 2.

[62] Sossai, Chapter 13 in this book.

[63] Sassan Gholiagha, Anna Holzscheiter, and Andrea Liese, 'Activating Norm Collisions: Interface Conflicts in International Drug Control' (2020) 9 Global Constitutionalism 290.

[64] Roggeband, Chapter 14 in this book; see also Schwindenhammer, Chapter 16 in this book.

because it allows different actors to inscribe them with their own interpretations' but also 'makes norms open to continuous amendments and (re)interpretations'.[65] Moreover, some norms, such as reproductive rights, are protected in different treaties. This leads to a diffusion of the authority to interpret them.[66] As Schwindenhammer observes, the WTO and the environmental regime interpret sustainability differently and 'pursue distinct or even mutually exclusive norm understandings'.[67]

On rare occasions, a court or an adjudicatory body has the competence to resolve conflicts between norms and their underlying values and to restore a coherent legal order. Inconsistencies between norms that originate from separate rule systems may, whether formally adjudicated by a court or informally managed by states or IOs, lead to rebalancing of norms, that is, to a reprioritization. Ultimately, this may contribute to a loss in one of these norms' legal or social validity. Chapter 16 by Schwindenhammer and Chapter 17 by Stoll use the precautionary principle as an illustrative example.

## 4. The Robustness of Legal Norms

During what many have claimed is the 'end of the liberal order', most of the norms examined in this book have remained stable and robust. Even in the cases of the right to self-defence and women's rights, it is far from clear that the observed processes of social and legal validity decline and value change are irreversible. This observation invites us to look more closely at the factors that make legal norms robust. The framework of this book and Chapter 3 by Sandholtz proposed several scope conditions for establishing the robustness of international law. The empirical chapters 6–17 provided an in-depth discussion of the conditions affecting the robustness of the norm under investigation. As each contribution in this book focused on a single norm only, a systematic comparative assessment still awaits future research. However, when comparing the findings of the different chapters, overarching patterns appear, revealing the vital role of norm defenders and legal and institutional structures as stabilizing elements.

### 4.1 The Vital Role of Norm Defenders

Opposition to and contestation of legal norms and their underlying values is nothing new. For decades, the United States has held dissenting opinions on the right to self-defence, and both the Vatican and several Muslim countries have opposed certain women's rights. Several contributions to this book argue that opposition has become fiercer and more widespread over time given the rise of populism and autocratic regimes, the fragmentation of international law, and global power shifts. While the type and intensity of reactive contestation do matter for the robustness of international legal norms and their underlying values, what seems equally important is whether

[65] Roggeband, Chapter 14 in this book, p. 255.
[66] Kuhlmann, Chapter 15 in this book.
[67] Schwindenhammer, Chapter 16 in this book, p. 290.

the actors involved 'achieve renewed consensus or compromise on a norm's meaning and application'[68] or whether they are able to defend the norm against attacks and obstruction. The actors involved play a decisive role not only in norm change, but also in stabilizing international legal norms. It is critical how judicial, state, and non-state actors react to norm violation and discursive contestation. Their motivation to react stems from the belief or experience that norms serve their interests and reflect their values and that they benefit from the international order.[69] Several contributions to this book illustrate how norm defenders actively protect international law. Lesch and Zimmermann and Steiger describe how international legal bodies, state parties to international treaties, coalitions of non-state actors, and eminent scholars respond to violations of the norm against torture by condemning them. Bower also finds that 'the campaign by (some) African states and the African Union to discredit the [International Criminal] Court' has prompted counter- mobilization in support of the ICC within the region.[70]

In particular, international courts, treaty bodies, and independent experts have an essential function in monitoring compliance. Since they are in a position to advance interpretations that can spur progress in developing norms, they can also act to shelter norms against a decline in social or legal validity. The role of state parties and NGOs is more ambiguous. As shown above, they may act as norm saboteurs, but they can also act as norm entrepreneurs, stabilizing legal opinions, furthering progressive interpretations, countering discursive attacks, and condemning non-compliance. State parties may consequently try to hinder the work of NGOs that pursue policies that are not in line with a state's official position. Legislative measures may restrict NGOs from promoting and defending international human rights standards,[71] and repressive policies may go hand in hand with support for NGOs that advocate government strategies.[72]

It is not only democracies that act as norm defenders: in certain contexts and constellations, autocracies—or, more precisely, factions within autocratic regimes—also act as norm defenders. As Tokhi highlights in Chapter 12, many states view compliance with the NPT as central to their national security. For international efforts to succeed in strengthening the NPT regime, it is, therefore, crucial to identify factions within autocratic regimes that favour compliance with non-proliferation norms and support international cooperation.[73]

## 4.2 Institutional and Legal Structures as a Stabilizing Element

Norm defenders' agency and their impact on the robustness of legal norms also depend on structural features. Institutional and legal structures legitimize actors' claims, provide them with the opportunity to act, but also limit their strategies. A core

[68] Nicole Deitelhoff and Lisbeth Zimmermann, 'Things we Lost in the Fire: How Different Types of Contestation Affect the Robustness of International Norms' (2020) 22 International Studies Review 51, 58.

[69] See Sandholtz, Chapter 3 in this book, Section 5.

[70] Bower, Chapter 10 in this book, p. 189.

[71] Krieger, 'Populist Governments' (n 40) 989 et seq.

[72] Roggeband, Chapter 14 in this book.

[73] Tokhi, Chapter 12 in this book, p. 231.

function of institutions is to stabilize norms. Therefore, we expect a norm's degree of institutional embeddedness to matter for its robustness. Highly institutionalized norms seem less prone to change than less institutionalized norms, all else being equal (Section 4.2.1).[74] Moreover, the systematic character of law is another decisive element supporting the robustness of legally protected values (4.2.2).

### 4.2.1 Institutional and Legal Embeddedness

When a norm is being challenged, its institutional context is often regarded as decisive for its fate. First, membership in or access to a formal institution that defends a norm enables more actors to engage in a dialogue with actors that contest it. Antje Wiener has argued that balanced access to reactive and proactive contestation and access to formal, social, and cultural norm validation achieves 'the highest legitimacy, therewith sustaining the legality of a norm'.[75] A core argument of Wiener's theory of contestation is that norm validation hinges on affected stakeholders' 'opportunity, if not the right, to partake in this interaction'. She points out that 'in most cases of conflict about extant fundamental norms in IR, access to norm validation and contestation remains clearly restricted (ie favouring state representatives operating through international organizations)'.[76] This deprives other actors of the opportunity to contest and validate a norm and its underlying value proactively. In addition, potential norm-defenders may be sidelined: in her analysis of the precautionary principle's fate, Schwindenhammer confirms that access is unevenly distributed among non-state actors: 'Norm dynamics privilege scientific expert knowledge over local knowledge and foster unequal access to norm contestation.'[77] Actors who cannot take part in institutional deliberations are more likely to sabotage a norm or rely on behavioural contestation. They may even do so when they endorse the protected value and merely question the institution's legitimacy.

Second, the institutional context offers political and discursive resources to those who advance 'pro-norm arguments'. In this vein, norms may be cushioned by higher levels of institutionalization—the embeddedness of individual norms in norm clusters or regimes and their incorporation into state practices and law[78]—or legalization, for instance, the degree of obligation: 'These qualities can help to buoy norms against possible weakening effects of contestation and insulate core norms from validity challenges.'[79] Or, as Sandholtz has put it, 'when a norm is part of a broader regime, it both supports other regime norms and is reinforced by them'.[80] First, a norm's linkage to other norms protect it against attacks. Second, institutionalized monitoring and adjudication mobilize norm defenders.

[74] See also Monica Hakimi, 'The Work of International Law' (2017) 58 Harvard International Law Journal 1; Gráinne de Burca, 'Human Rights Experimentalism' (2017) 111 American Journal of International Law 277.

[75] Wiener, Chapter 2 in this book, p. 42.

[76] ibid., p. 43.

[77] Schwindenhammer, Chapter 16 in this book, p. 298.

[78] See Sandholtz, Chapter 3 in this book, Section 4.

[79] Jeffrey Lantis and Carmen Wunderlich, 'Resiliency Dynamics of Norm Clusters: Norm Contestation and International Cooperation' (2018) 44 Review of International Studies 570, 572.

[80] Sandholtz, Chapter 3 in this book, p. 58.

Many human rights treaty norms, notably the prohibition of torture, are protected by an institutionalized supervisory system of independent experts. Despite concerns of politicization, many states see these individuals as possessing independent expertise.[81] State parties have delegated authority to them to interpret treaty obligations, monitor compliance, and engage in dialogue with state parties. The Committee Against Torture is even permitted to visit national detention centres, so the degree of supervision over the prohibition against torture is uniquely high. In addition, the norm is part of domestic legislation, which empowers domestic actors—state and non-state—to mobilize against norm regress and to initiate litigation. Thus, as Steiger and also Lesch and Zimmermann argue, multiple fora and pathways are available for norm defenders—that is, states, non-state actors, and legal bodies—to discuss and initiate but also prevent changes in legal norms.

Third, legal structures provide a frame for assessing the legitimacy of arguments and thus set limits on what can be accepted as valid argument. They also distribute, increase, and specify argumentative burdens for 'anti-norm arguments'. Legal norms, as 'intersubjectively accepted practices and linguistic structures', constrain actors' choices.[82] Even in instances where norm violation and norm contestation, if not norm sabotage, are omnipresent, these may not affect an international norm, when legitimate 'pro-norm arguments' can counter 'anti-norm arguments'.[83] The legitimacy of 'pro-norm arguments' benefits from the specific structures of international law.

According to Roggeband, 'scholars that work in the field of gender and politics have argued that soft law on gender equality tends to be more transformative, yet hard law may result to be more resilient',[84] but the degree of legalization—including the dimension of obligation or bindingness—is not sufficient to stabilize a norm and shield it from erosion. If a legal rule is considered a *ius cogens* norm and non-derogable, this can ensure its robustness. This has been true of the prohibition of torture, but less true of the prohibition of the use of force. Why are some *ius cogens* norms, then, more robust than others?

We find that the fate of *ius cogens* norms depends on the intensity of contestation, norm saboteurs' power, and norm defenders' strength and decisiveness. Compared to the prohibition of torture, norm defenders were less united and active in the case of the prohibition on the use of force. As outlined in Section 4.1, norm sabotage needs to be condemned and argumentatively countered to mitigate the weakening effect of norm contestation.

As Kleinlein argues, a norm's quality as *ius cogens* does not per se guarantee its stability.[85] In her Chapter 5, de Wet illustrates the reasons behind this observation: In particular, a prohibition with a *ius cogens* character that leaves room for exceptions may be subject to processes of legal or social validity decline if the exceptions are continuously expanded and if the scope of application of the prohibition is thereby

[81] Valentina Carraro, 'Electing the Experts: Expertise and Independence in the UN Human Rights Treaty Bodies' (2019) 25 European Journal of International Relations 826.

[82] Bower, Chapter 10 in this book, p. 175.

[83] Sandholtz, Chapter 3 in this book.

[84] Roggeband, Chapter 14 in this book, p. 268.

[85] Kleinlein, Chapter 4 in this book, p. 72.

reduced. Despite the ICJ's restrictive interpretation of the right to self-defence in the 1986 Nicaragua judgment, attempts to lower the threshold for the right to operate have persisted.[86] Furthermore, as Burra argues in line with Kleinlein,[87] *ius cogens* rules are not shielded against legal change through informal means of interpretation. While even a hegemonic actor like the United States would face hurdles that are hard to overcome if it wanted to change the explicit text of a treaty, a hegemonic actor's powerful position may facilitate interpretative change. In her Chapter 8, Reinold argues that the group of actors objecting to the US harbouring doctrine, which initially applied to most states and the ICJ, diminished in size over time.[88]

Still, *ius cogens* norms possess three key qualities or built-in mechanisms of robustness that work against norm erosion. First, *ius cogens* norms raise the argumentative burden for those who want to deviate from the norm or reduce its scope of application.[89] Second, *ius cogens* norms entail a 'moral appeal of the (underpinning values of the) obligations in question' thereby increasing political and moral pressure on policymakers.[90] Third, *ius cogens* norms are accompanied by further obligations that strengthen the rules and their underlying values. According to Article 53 VCLT, treaties conflicting with a *ius cogens* norm are void. The same applies to unilateral acts.[91] Articles 40 and 41 of the Articles on State Responsibility stipulate a duty to cooperate to bring to an end through lawful means any serious breach of a peremptory norm, a duty of non-recognition, and a duty not to render aid and assistance.

Finally, the chapters in this book provide indications that less precise norms are also less resilient. In global sustainability governance, many norms are only vaguely defined and, therefore, open to conflicting interpretations. Schwindenhammer and Stoll use the precautionary principle as an illustrative example: WTO agreements and the Rio Regulations define and understand this principle differently. Similarly, Erika de Wet highlights the indeterminacy of *ius cogens* rules to explain why these norms may not be as stable as one might assume. There is still a certain indeterminacy to the scope of the prohibition since the definition of torture itself requires an act of interpretation and may be altered by competent actors, including states or courts. As a consequence of this indeterminacy, she argues that the idea of *ius cogens* norms as 'core values of the international community aspires to more unity than the highly diverse international legal order can accommodate'.[92]

[86] de Wet, Chapter 5 in this book, p. 97.

[87] Burra, Chapter 9 in this book; Kleinlein, Chapter 4 in this book.

[88] Reinold, Chapter 8 in this book.

[89] de Wet, Chapter 5 in this book, p. 97; Paulina Starski, 'Silence within the Process of Normative Change and Evolution of the Prohibition on the Use of Force: Normative Volatility and Legislative Responsibility' (2017) 4 Journal on the Use of Force and International Law 14, 43.

[90] de Wet, Chapter 5 in this book, p. 97; on moral principles as a relevant driver for legal change: Mary Ellen O'Connell, *The Art of Law in the International Community* (CUP 2019) 12.

[91] Víctor Rodríguez Cedeño, María Isabel, and Torres Cazorla 'Unilateral Acts of States in International Law' in Rüdiger Wolfrum (ed), *Max Planck Encyclopedia of Public International Law* (online edn, OUP 2008) para 29 <https://opil.ouplaw.com/view/10.1093/law:epil/9780199231690/law-9780199231690-e1496?rskey=tv5HQz&result=2&prd=MPIL> accessed 5 June 2022.

[92] de Wet, Chapter 5 in this book, p. 98.

### 4.2.2 Law as a System

A further decisive element supporting the robustness of legally protected values lies in law's characteristic as a system. An international legal norm does not come in a normative vacuum but is related to other legal and non-legal norms.[93] As Reinold argues in her contribution, attempts to change the law, even those by the most powerful states, have to be consistent with existing legal (and non-legal) norms.[94] Indeed, the notion of coherence serves as a shield against value change.[95] If changed practices cannot be integrated into the existing system, they face higher hurdles to being accepted as law. To guarantee coherence, any change to or erosion of legal norms needs to be brought into line with the existing structures. This can be done through systematic and teleological interpretations, for instance, which are often put forward to guarantee that a rule or its interpretation fits with the broader legal context.

The systemic character of law also contributes to its robustness, in that law regulates for itself how and by whom it can be changed.[96] A critical threshold for the stability of legal norms derives from the requirement that any statement or practice is only taken into account if it amounts to a legally relevant practice. To be recognized as such, a practice must fulfil certain requirements. Not all types of contestations are equally important: either because the actors do not have the competence to transform social practices into legally relevant ones, or because the practices do not fulfil the requirements to be recognized and thus transformed into legally relevant practices. A discernible act is required to signal that a practice should be recognized as law. States and the authorities to which they have delegated the competence to perform such acts, such as international courts and tribunals, therefore remain the gatekeepers for international lawmaking. At the same time, the threshold for transforming social practices into legally relevant ones is high. Take the traditional threshold for customary international law (CIL) as formulated by the ICJ in the *North Sea Continental Shelf* case: 'State practice ... should have been both extensive and virtually uniform in the sense of the provision invoked;— and should moreover have occurred in a way as to show a general recognition of that rule of law or legal obligation is involved'.[97]

While there has been much debate as to whether these criteria are still appropriate,[98] the International Law Commission (ILC) stressed in 2018 that for the identification of a rule of CIL, the two elements remain constitutive, practice and *opinio iuris*, and that 'each of the two constituent elements is to be separately ascertained'.[99] What might be seen from one perspective as a hindrance for desired forms of progressive change

[93] See on the 'system-related function' of law Dana Burchardt, 'The Functions of Law and their Challenges: The Differentiated Functionality of International Law' (2019) 20 German Law Journal 409, 413 and for its limits in international law: at 421–24.

[94] Reinold, Chapter 8 in this book, pp. 136 and 147.

[95] See also Bower, Chapter 10 in this book.

[96] Reinold, Chapter 8 in this book, p. 143.

[97] *North Sea Continental Shelf (Germany v Denmark and Netherlands)* (Judgement) [1969] ICJ Rep 3, 43, para 74.

[98] BS Chimni, 'Customary International Law: A Third World Perspective' (2018) 112 American Journal of International Law 1; Andrew T Guzman, 'Saving Customary International Law' (2005) 27 Michigan Journal of International Law 116, 123–28.

[99] ILC, 'Draft conclusions on identification of customary international law, with commentaries' Yearbook of the International Law Commission, 2018, vol. II, Part Two, conclusion 2 and 3.

works as an essential barrier for the erosion of legal norms given regressive forms of change.

Moreover, due to the decentralized structure of international law, with only a few voices having the authority to settle interpretative disputes, international legal norms may face opposition and even show indications of a decline in legal or social validity without actually changing over time. For example, the question of whether the restrictive reading of the right to self-defence that the ICJ authoritatively established in the *Nicaragua* case[100] has changed remains an open question as long as there is no change in jurisprudence. Admittedly, the limited number of opportunities for the ICJ to make a ruling on such questions and the role of states as lawmakers in international law weaken the claim that only the ICJ can authoritatively settle interpretative disputes. Still, without an ICJ pronouncement, a change in the meaning of the right to self-defence will remain uncertain over time and may still be reversed. Changes in international law often remain in limbo over protracted periods.

Such uncertainties are aggravated where a claim of change rests on assumptions built around the silence of third states. The effects of silence in general international law, and specifically in the context of norm change within treaty interpretation or CIL, are disputed in the academic literature.[101] In Chapter 8, Teresa Reinold explored the legal controversy regarding the role of silence in establishing an expansive reading of the right to self-defence. She concluded that 'the lack of efforts at justification and the absence of demands for such justifications could be another indicator that the defensive use of force on the soil of states harbouring terrorists is increasingly seen as non-controversial'.[102] Others reject this view. For example, the United States has expressed a critical view of the legal relevance of state silence in the creation of CIL rules, claiming that 'a State's failure to act rarely evidences its views on international law' because 'States frequently choose for political (international or domestic) or other reasons, such as limited government resources, to refrain from engaging in legally permissible acts'.[103] The ILC Draft Conclusions are not entirely clear on the case at hand. Conclusion 10, paragraph 3, states that 'failure to react over time to a practice may serve as evidence as acceptance as a law (*opinio iuris*), provided that States were in a position to react and the circumstances called for some reaction'.[104] At the same time, according to the ILC's commentary, for silence to be legally relevant, the inaction may not 'derive from causes unrelated to the legality of the practice in question' and 'a State may also provide other explanations for its inaction'.[105]

In addition, a reaction is expected where the 'interests or rights of the State failing or refusing to [re]act' are at stake.[106] Applying this prerequisite to cases of *erga omnes*

[100] *Military and Paramilitary Activities in and against Nicaragua (Nicaragua v USA)* (Judgement) [1986] ICJ Rep 14.

[101] For an overview see Dustin A Lewis, Naz K Modirzadeh, and Gabriella Blum, 'Quantum of Silence: Inaction and *Jus ad Bellum*' Harvard Law School Program on International Law and Armed Conflict, 2019; see also the project by Danae Azaria: The Silence of States in International Law at <https://www.statesilence.org> accessed 15 July 2022.

[102] Reinold, Chapter 8 in this book, p. 141.

[103] UNGA, 'Identification of Customary International Law' (14 February 2018) UN Doc A/CN.4/716, p. 42.

[104] ILC, 'Draft conclusions on identification of customary international law' (n 99) 140.

[105] ibid 142.

[106] ibid; for a detailed analysis of pertinent criteria see Starski (n 89) 26 et seq.

obligations, such as the prohibition of the use of force, would lead to the nonsensical consequence that it would become easier to change a rule of this kind when states are silent than other international legal rules.[107] Thus, a narrow reading of the role of silence, particularly regarding rules with a peremptory character, is at least one element of the legal system's barriers against legal validity decline.

## 5. Implications

In our book, we have identified several challenges to the international legal order, some of which have indeed driven value change. Some are not new: in particular, US exceptionalism has long impacted the international legal order.[108] Others, such as the rise of populism and autocracy, have gained further momentum. As noted in the introduction to this book, we assume that the diffusion of power and agency among states and diverse non-state actors in the context of changing power constellations has multiplied the challenges to the international legal order.

Still, this multiplication has not yet led to a clear-cut metamorphosis. The case studies identify a *social validity decline* regarding the prohibition on the use of force and gender equality. There is disagreement on whether a change in legal status or even a substantial value change has taken place in both. The case studies agree that sustainability norms seem to have undergone *substantial value change* and a *change in legal status*. Thus, we found that more than one of international law's foundational values, and more than one element thereof, has been affected. The chapters have shown that despite continuing reactive contestations and instances of what may be called norm sabotage, some norms remained surprisingly robust. In particular, the values underlying the prohibition of torture have proven quite robust. For other norms it might still be too early to declare them as declining. However, there are indications that the priority given to several values is shifting.

These findings have important implications for current debates on the state of the international legal order. First, our findings do not confirm previous research concluding that 'international law is a system that is characterized by stability, but punctuated by rapid and dramatic change' and indeed call this conclusion into question.[109] Second, they lend no support to the often implicit assumption of international law's progress narrative according to which the scope of international law is constantly being expanded. The findings in our book, in contrast, suggest that due to the decentralized nature of international law, norm change, either in the form of progressive evolution or norm erosion against an established standard, often remains in limbo for protracted periods of time. The accumulation, aggravation, and persistence of challenges and drivers over time and the ambiguous nature of change in international law seem to be mutually reenforcing.

[107] Starski (n 89) 40.

[108] Shirley Scott, 'Is There Room for International Law in Realpolitik?: Accounting for the US "Attitude" Towards International Law' (2004) 30 Review of International Studies 71.

[109] Diehl and Ku (n 48) 156.

Critics may claim that such a finding is not surprising. One might object that backlash politics and the signs of erosion of the (liberal) international order blur the picture and create an impression of metamorphosis that is not reflected by an analysis of pertinent norms. International law as a system with relative autonomy from politics may remain robust even though the international order is undergoing profound changes.[110] While we also find that a few norms and underlying values have remained intact, this is only part of the picture. We still argue that the processes analysed in this book also point to additional challenges for the international legal order.

Processes of value change seem to create further turbulence and ambivalence within the international legal order itself. The fact that change remains in limbo in the decentralized international legal order affects legal certainty and the ordering function of law if the standard against which a specific behaviour is to be assessed remains unsettled and unclear. Law's capacity to provide orientation or even constraints for policy decisions shrinks, and the room for acceptable arguments against the current legal order grows. Such an enlargement of the argumentative space, that is, of what is accepted as a valid legal argument, brings further effects in its wake. For example, in such a context, non-compliance can be understood as a plea for legal change or as a justified application of a changed legal norm. Thus, validity contestations can be framed as applicatory contestations. However, for those states that do not agree with the proposed change, such efforts may undermine trust in other actors' behaviour or, even worse, trust in the coherence of the legal system. These processes may also explain why there is an increasing scholarly focus on state silence, and a call for states to take their 'legislative responsibilities' more seriously.[111] Where uncertainty about legal norms increases and centralized actors, such as the ICJ, are only infrequently able to affirm the validity and content of norms, it is left to states as the primary actors in international law to (re)establish legal certainty and trust. The more values come under attack, the more states (and other actors) that perceive themselves as norm defenders need to respond and defend the substance, legal status, or social validity of a value.

Persistent insecurities about the content of legal rules may eventually create dissonances. As Reinold has explained in her Chapter 8, non-compliance may work as a driver of legal change if it aims to reduce dissonances between an existing rule and other important values and if the claim for change is accepted by the international community through the diverse channels of lawmaking as the creation of a new agreement.[112] However, such an explanation underestimates the often long periods of time over which uncertainties about the state of the law may persist, combined with the frequent lack of clear majorities in favour of one or the other interpretation of the rule. Claims of change based on non-compliance therefore risk creating a third

[110] In relation to the global order see also Mette Eilstrup-Sangiovanni and Stephanie C Hofmann, 'Of the Contemporary Global Order, Crisis, and Change' (2020) 27 Journal of European Public Policy 1077, 1085–86 who observe 'an on-going transformation from within' not a 'major transformation of the order'.

[111] Danae Azaria, 'Not All State Silences Speak: A Theory of (Non-) Communicative State Silences', Lecture at Harvard Law School on 29 March 2022; Heike Krieger, 'Let's speak law – A call for a legally embedded multilateralism', Global Trends, Analysis 02/2021, sef: Development and Peace Foundation Bonn <https://www.sef-bonn.org/en/publications/global-trends-analysis/022021/>; Starski (n 89) 29–30.

[112] Reinold, Chapter 8 in this book.

type of dissonance: one between expectations about law's stabilizing function and ongoing ambivalences about the content of a rule. The specificities of the international lawmaking process thus entail a risk that norm change that remains in limbo over protracted periods of time will come to be seen as a form of legal and social validity decline, which will ultimately weaken international law.

Our book has shown how increasing crises and other trends, including a rise in populism and autocratization, put pressure on the international legal order. Other developments, unaddressed in this book, such as elite scepticism and information warfare, put further pressure on the system. The case studies have pointed to the vital role of norm defenders, which have shielded some norms from attacks. Is this good news for the future of foundational values in the international legal order? We would like to caution against the optimistic view that all attacks can and will be countered. First, there are indications that the magnitude and frequency of non-compliance and reactive contestation have grown significantly since the 1990s. Consequently, norms have to be defended more often, making the defence of the international legal order more time-consuming and costly. This may put additional pressure on international judicial bodies. The more resources are needed to engage with critics or saboteurs, the fewer resources are available for core tasks such as monitoring. Maintaining the status quo becomes a priority, and norm development takes a back seat. There are indications that the already overloaded judicial and quasi-judicial bodies cannot fulfil both roles simultaneously. Norm-defending states also have to strike back against numerous attacks in multiple settings. They may eventually face difficult choices regarding which norm to defend. Second, autocratization has led to a diminished civic space, significantly weakening the opportunities for civil society actors to engage in norm-defending activities. These developments create serious concerns. The capacity of norm defenders is finite, and attacks may ultimately exhaust those actors that have so far repelled norm saboteurs.

One may be tempted to interpret the international community's reaction to the Russian Federation's unlawful invasion of Ukraine in 2022 as a sign of the robustness of the international legal order. However, condemnation of the invasion has not been universal:[113] States such as China, India, and South Africa have not enacted any legal responses in line with the Articles on State Responsibility, and West European states are still struggling to assist Ukraine in its self-defence. Even in such an extreme and obvious case of norm violation, the foundational value of the non-use of force is not being upheld unequivocally – at least not on the level of social practices. The dynamics between norm defenders and norm saboteurs leave their mark on the underlying values of this and other norms. The ultimate outcome of this struggle is still unclear, and the authors of this book are unable to predict it. Based on the overall analysis, however, we can conclude: If the attacks on the international order continue at the current frequency and magnitude, a metamorphosis of international law will likely be unstoppable.

[113] UNGA Res ES-11/1 (2 March 2022) was approved 141:5:35; UNGA Res ES-11/2 (24 March 2022) with 140:5:38; UNGA Res ES-11/3 (7 April 2022) with 93:24:58.

# Index

*For the benefit of digital users, indexed terms that span two pages (e.g., 52–53) may, on occasion, appear on only one of those pages.*

Tables and figures are indicated by *t* and *f* following the page number